Course   Macroeconomics

Custom for

Rowan College at Burlington Co

http://create.mheducation.com

ISBN-10: 1308755953   ISBN-13: 9781308755953

Contents

Credits

CHAPTER **1**

Limits, Alternatives, and Choices

Learning Objectives

LO1.1 Define economics and the features of the economic perspective.

LO1.2 Describe the role of economic theory in economics.

LO1.3 Distinguish microeconomics from macroeconomics and positive economics from normative economics.

LO1.4 Explain the individual's economizing problem and how trade-offs, opportunity costs, and attainable combinations can be illustrated with budget lines.

LO1.5 List the categories of scarce resources and delineate the nature of society's economizing problem.

LO1.6 Apply production possibilities analysis, increasing opportunity costs, and economic growth.

LO1.7 Explain how economic growth and international trade increase consumption possibilities.

LO1.8 (Appendix) Understand graphs, curves, and slopes as they relate to economics.

(An appendix on understanding graphs follows this chapter. If you need a quick review of this mathematical tool, you might benefit by reading the appendix first.) People's wants are numerous and varied. Biologically, people need only air, water, food, clothing, and shelter. But in modern societies people also desire goods and services that provide a more comfortable or affluent standard of living. We want bottled water, soft drinks, and fruit juices, not just water from the creek. We want salads, burgers, and pizzas, not just berries and nuts. We want jeans, suits, and coats, not just woven reeds. We want apartments, condominiums, or houses, not just mud huts. And, as the saying goes, "That is not

the half of it." We also want flat-panel TVs, Internet service, education, national defense, cell phones, health care, and much more.

Fortunately, society possesses productive resources, such as labor and managerial talent, tools and machinery, and land and mineral deposits. These resources, employed in the economic system (or simply the economy), help us produce goods and services that satisfy many of our economic wants. But the blunt reality is that our economic wants far exceed the productive capacity of our scarce (limited) resources. We are forced to make choices. This unyielding truth underlies the definition of **economics,** which is the social science concerned with how individuals, institutions, and society make optimal (best) choices under conditions of scarcity.

The Economic Perspective

LO1.1 Define economics and the features of the economic perspective.

Economists view things from a unique perspective. This **economic perspective,** or economic way of thinking, has several critical and closely interrelated features.

Scarcity and Choice

The economic resources needed to make goods and services are in limited supply. This **scarcity** restricts options and demands choices. Because we "can't have it all," we must decide what we will have and what we must forgo.

At the core of economics is the idea that "there is no free lunch." You may be treated to lunch, making it "free" from your perspective, but someone bears a cost. Because all resources are either privately or collectively owned by members of society, ultimately society bears the cost. Scarce inputs of land, equipment, farm labor, the labor of cooks and waiters, and managerial talent are required. Because society could have used these resources to produce something else, it sacrifices those other goods and services in making the lunch available. Economists call such sacrifices **opportunity costs:** To obtain more of one thing, society forgoes the opportunity of getting the next best thing. That sacrifice is the opportunity cost of the choice.

Purposeful Behavior

Economics assumes that human behavior reflects "rational self-interest." Individuals look for and pursue opportunities to increase their **utility**—the pleasure, happiness, or satisfaction obtained from consuming a good or service. They allocate their time, energy, and money to maximize their

CONSIDER THIS ...

FREE ACCESSORY SET!
with the purchase of any of our pool tables*
$99.00 VALUE
Shipping & Handling $9.95

Set Includes:
♦ Two 2-piece Cue Sticks
♦ Bridge Stick
♦ Set of Balls
♦ Plastic Triangle
♦ Plastic 9-Ball Rack
♦ Rail Brush
♦ Dozen Chalk
♦ Two Chalk Holders
♦ Table Cover

* Excludes the Prestige pool table which comes with it's own accessory kit

Free for All?

Free products are seemingly everywhere. Sellers offer free apps, free cell phones, and free checking accounts. Dentists give out free toothbrushes. At state visitor centers, there are free brochures and maps.

Does the presence of so many free products contradict the economist's assertion that "There is no free lunch"? No! Resources are used to produce each of these products, and because those resources have alternative uses, society gives up something else to get the "free" good. Because alternatives must be forsaken, there is no such thing as a free lunch.

So why are these goods offered for free? In a word: marketing! Firms sometimes offer free products to entice people to try them, hoping they will then purchase those goods later. Getting to try out the free version of an app may eventually entice you to buy the pay version that has more features. In other cases, a product is free only in conjunction with a larger purchase. To get the free bottle of soda, you must buy the large pizza. To get the free cell phone, you need to sign up for a year's worth of cell phone service.

But while "free" products may come at no cost to the individuals receiving them, they are never free to society because their manufacture requires the use of resources that could have been put to alternative uses.

ORIGIN OF THE IDEA

O1.2
Utility

satisfaction. Because they weigh costs and benefits, their economic decisions are "purposeful" or "rational," not "random" or "chaotic."

Consumers are purposeful in deciding what goods and services to buy. Business firms are purposeful in deciding what products to produce and how to produce them. Government entities are purposeful in deciding what public services to provide and how to finance them.

"Purposeful behavior" does not assume that people and institutions are immune from faulty logic and therefore are perfect decision makers. They sometimes make mistakes. Nor does it mean that people's decisions are unaffected by emotion or the decisions of those around them. Indeed, economists acknowledge that people are sometimes impulsive or emulative. "Purposeful behavior" simply means that people make decisions with some desired outcome in mind.

Rational self-interest is not the same as selfishness. In the economy, increasing one's own wage, rent, interest, or profit normally requires identifying and satisfying *somebody else's* wants! Also, people make personal sacrifices for others. They contribute time and money to charities because they derive pleasure from doing so. Parents help pay for their children's education for the same reason. These self-interested, but unselfish, acts help maximize the givers' satisfaction as much as any personal purchase of goods or services. Self-interested behavior is simply behavior designed to increase personal satisfaction, however it may be derived.

Marginal Analysis: Comparing Benefits and Costs

The economic perspective focuses largely on **marginal analysis**—comparisons of marginal benefits and marginal costs, usually for decision making. To economists, "marginal" means "extra," "additional," or "a change in." Most choices or decisions involve changes in the status quo, meaning the existing state of affairs.

Should you attend school for another year? Should you study an extra hour for an exam? Should you supersize your fries? Similarly, should a business expand or reduce its output? Should government increase or decrease its funding for a missile defense system?

Each option involves marginal benefits and, because of scarce resources, marginal costs. In making choices rationally, the decision maker must compare those two amounts. Example:

ORIGIN OF THE IDEA

O1.3
Marginal analysis

CONSIDER THIS . . .

Fast-Food Lines

The economic perspective is useful in analyzing all sorts of behaviors. Consider an everyday example: the behavior of fast-food customers. When customers enter the restaurant, they go to the shortest line, believing that line will minimize their time cost of obtaining food. They are acting purposefully; time is limited, and people prefer using it in some way other than standing in line.

If one fast-food line is temporarily shorter than other lines, some people will move to that line. These movers apparently view the time saving from the shorter line (marginal benefit) as exceeding the cost of moving from their present line (marginal cost). The line switching tends to equalize line lengths. No further movement of customers between lines occurs once all lines are about equal.

Fast-food customers face another cost-benefit decision when a clerk opens a new station at the counter. Should they move to the new station or stay put? Those who shift to the new line decide that the time saving from the move exceeds the extra cost of physically moving. In so deciding, customers must also consider just how quickly they can get to the new station compared with others who may be contemplating the same move. (Those who hesitate in this situation are lost!)

Customers at the fast-food establishment do not have perfect information when they select lines. Thus, not all decisions turn out as expected. For example, you might enter a short line only to find that someone in front of you is ordering hamburgers and fries for 40 people in the Greyhound bus parked out back (and also that the guy taking orders in your new line is a trainee)! Nevertheless, at the time you made your decision, you thought it was optimal.

Finally, customers must decide what food to order when they arrive at the counter. In making their choices, they again compare marginal costs and marginal benefits in attempting to obtain the greatest personal satisfaction for their expenditure.

Economists believe that what is true for the behavior of customers at fast-food restaurants is true for economic behavior in general. Faced with an array of choices, consumers, workers, and businesses rationally compare marginal costs and marginal benefits when making decisions.

sion maker must compare those two amounts. Example: You and your fiancée are shopping for an engagement ring. Should you buy a $\frac{1}{2}$-carat diamond, a $\frac{3}{4}$-carat diamond, a 1-carat diamond, or something even larger? The marginal cost of a larger-size diamond is the added expense beyond the cost of the smaller-size diamond. The marginal benefit is the perceived lifetime pleasure (utility) from the larger-size stone. If the marginal benefit of the larger diamond exceeds its marginal cost (and you can afford it), buy the larger stone. But if the marginal cost is more than the marginal benefit, you should buy the smaller diamond instead—even if you can afford the larger stone!

In a world of scarcity, the decision to obtain the marginal benefit associated with some specific option always includes the marginal cost of forgoing something else. The money spent on the larger-size diamond means forgoing some other product. An opportunity cost—the value of the next best thing forgone—is always present whenever a choice is made.

Theories, Principles, and Models

LO1.2 Describe the role of economic theory in economics.
Like the physical and life sciences, as well as other social sciences, economics relies on the **scientific method.** That procedure consists of several elements:

- Observing real-world behavior and outcomes.
- Based on those observations, formulating a possible explanation of cause and effect (hypothesis).
- Testing this explanation by comparing the outcomes of specific events to the outcome predicted by the hypothesis.
- Accepting, rejecting, and modifying the hypothesis, based on these comparisons.
- Continuing to test the hypothesis against the facts. If favorable results accumulate, the hypothesis evolves into a theory. A very well-tested and widely accepted theory is referred to as an economic law or an **economic principle**—a statement about economic behavior or the economy that enables prediction of the probable effects of certain actions. Combinations of such laws or principles are incorporated into models, which are simplified representations of how something works, such as a market or segment of the economy.

Economists develop theories of the behavior of individuals (consumers, workers) and institutions (businesses, governments) engaged in the production, exchange, and consumption of goods and services. Theories, principles, and models are "purposeful simplifications." The full scope of economic reality itself is too complex and bewildering to be understood as a whole. In developing theories, principles, and models economists remove the clutter and simplify.

Economic principles and models are highly useful in analyzing economic behavior and understanding how the economy operates. They are the tools for ascertaining cause and effect (or action and outcome) within the economic system. Good theories do a good job of explaining and predicting. They are supported by facts concerning how individuals and institutions actually behave in producing, exchanging, and consuming goods and services.

There are some other things you should know about economic principles.

- *Generalizations* Economic principles are generalizations relating to economic behavior or to the economy itself. Economic principles are expressed as the tendencies of typical or average consumers, workers, or business firms. For example, economists say that consumers buy more of a particular product when its price falls. Economists recognize that some consumers may increase their purchases by a large amount, others by a small amount, and a few not at all. This "price-quantity" principle, however, holds for the typical consumer and for consumers as a group.

- *Other-things-equal assumption* In constructing their theories, economists use the *ceteris paribus* or **other-things-equal assumption**—the assumption that factors other than those being considered do not change. They assume that all variables except those under immediate consideration are held constant for a particular analysis. For example, consider the relationship between the price of Pepsi and the amount of it purchased. Assume that of all the factors that might influence the amount of Pepsi purchased (for example, the price of Pepsi, the price of Coca-Cola, and consumer incomes and preferences), only the price of Pepsi varies. This is helpful because the economist can then focus on the relationship between the price of Pepsi and purchases of Pepsi in isolation without being confused by changes in other variables.

ORIGIN OF THE IDEA

01.4
Ceteris paribus

- *Graphical expression* Many economic models are expressed graphically. Be sure to read the special appendix at the end of this chapter as a review of graphs.

Microeconomics and Macroeconomics

LO1.3 Distinguish microeconomics from macroeconomics and positive economics from normative economics.
Economists develop economic principles and models at two levels.

Microeconomics

Microeconomics is the part of economics concerned with decision making by individual customers, workers, households, and business firms. At this level of analysis, we observe the details of their behavior under a figurative microscope. We measure the price of a specific product, the number of workers employed by a single firm, the revenue or income of a particular firm or household, or the expenditures of a specific firm, government entity, or family. In microeconomics, we examine the sand, rocks, and shells, not the beach.

Macroeconomics

Macroeconomics examines the performance and behavior of the economy as a whole. It focuses its attention on economic growth, the business cycle, interest rates, inflation, and the behavior of major economic aggregates such as the government, household, and business sectors. An **aggregate** is a collection of specific economic units treated as if they were one unit. Therefore, we might lump together the millions of consumers in the U.S. economy and treat them as if they were one huge unit called "consumers."

In using aggregates, macroeconomics seeks to obtain an overview, or general outline, of the structure of the economy and the relationships of its major aggregates. Macroeconomics speaks of such economic measures as total output, total employment, total income, aggregate expenditures, and the general level of prices in analyzing various economic problems. Very little attention is given to the specific units making up the various aggregates.

Figuratively, macroeconomics looks at the beach, not the pieces of sand, the rocks, and the shells.

The micro–macro distinction does not mean that economics is so highly compartmentalized that every topic can be readily labeled as either micro or macro; many topics and subdivisions of economics are rooted in both. Example: While the problem of unemployment is usually treated as a macroeconomic topic (because unemployment relates to aggregate production), economists recognize that the decisions made by *individual* workers on how long to search for jobs and the way *specific* labor markets encourage or impede hiring are also critical in determining the unemployment rate.

Positive and Normative Economics

Both microeconomics and macroeconomics contain elements of positive economics and normative economics.

Positive economics focuses on facts and cause-and-effect relationships. It includes description, theory development, and theory testing. Positive economics avoids value judgments. It tries to establish scientific statements about economic behavior and deals with what the economy is actually like. Such scientific-based analysis is critical to good policy analysis.

Economic policy, on the other hand, involves **normative economics,** which incorporates value judgments about what the economy should be like or what particular policy actions should be recommended to achieve a desirable goal. Normative economics looks at the desirability of certain aspects of the economy. It underlies expressions of support for particular economic policies.

Positive economics concerns *what is,* whereas normative economics embodies subjective feelings about *what ought to be.* Examples: Positive statement: "The unemployment rate in France is higher than that in the United States." Normative statement: "France ought to undertake policies to make its labor market more flexible to reduce unemployment rates." Whenever words such as "ought" or "should" appear in a sentence, you are very likely encountering a normative statement.

Most of the disagreement among economists involves normative, value-based policy questions. Of course, economists sometime disagree about which theories or models best represent the economy and its parts, but they agree on a full range of economic principles. Most economic controversy thus reflects differing opinions or value judgments about what society should be like.

QUICK REVIEW 1.1

- Economics examines how individuals, institutions, and society make choices under conditions of scarcity.
- The economic perspective stresses (a) resource scarcity and the necessity of making choices, (b) the assumption of purposeful (or rational) behavior, and (c) comparisons of marginal benefit and marginal cost.
- In choosing the best option, people incur an opportunity cost—the value of the next-best option.
- Economists use the scientific method to establish economic theories—cause-effect generalizations about the economic behavior of individuals and institutions.
- Microeconomics focuses on specific decision-making units within the economy. Macroeconomics examines the economy as a whole.
- Positive economics deals with factual statements ("what is"); normative economics involves value judgments ("what ought to be").

Individual's Economizing Problem

LO1.4 Explain the individual's economizing problem and how trade-offs, opportunity costs, and attainable combinations can be illustrated with budget lines.

A close examination of the **economizing problem**—the need to make choices because economic wants exceed economic means—will enhance your understanding of economic models and the difference between microeconomic and macroeconomic analysis. Let's first build a microeconomic model of the economizing problem faced by an individual.

Limited Income

We all have a finite amount of income, even the wealthiest among us. Even Donald Trump must decide how to spend his money! And the majority of us have much more limited means. Our income comes to us in the form of wages, interest, rent, and profit, although we may also receive money from government programs or family members. As Global Perspective 1.1 shows, the average income of Americans in 2011 was $48,450. In the poorest nations, it was less than $500.

Unlimited Wants

For better or worse, most people have virtually unlimited wants. We desire various goods and services that provide utility. Our wants extend over a wide range of products, from *necessities* (for example, food, shelter, and clothing) to *luxuries* (for example, perfumes, yachts, and sports cars). Some wants such as basic food, clothing, and shelter have biological roots. Other wants, for example, specific kinds of food, clothing, and shelter, arise from the conventions and customs of society.

Over time, as new and improved products are introduced, economic wants tend to change and multiply. Only recently have people wanted iPods, Internet service, or camera phones because those products did not exist a few decades ago. Also, the satisfaction of certain wants may trigger others: the acquisition of a Ford Focus or a Honda Civic has been known to whet the appetite for a Lexus or a Mercedes.

Services, as well as goods, satisfy our wants. Car repair work, the removal of an inflamed appendix, legal and accounting advice, and haircuts all satisfy human wants. Actually, we buy many goods, such as automobiles and washing machines, for the services they render. The differences between goods and services are often smaller than they appear to be.

For most people, the desires for goods and services cannot be fully satisfied. Bill Gates may have all that he

GLOBAL PERSPECTIVE 1.1

Average Income, Selected Nations

Average income (total income/population) and therefore typical individual budget constraints vary greatly among nations.

Country	Per Capita Income, 2011 (U.S. dollars, based on exchange rates)
Norway	$88,890
Switzerland	76,380
United States	48,450
Singapore	42,930
France	42,420
South Korea	20,870
Mexico	9240
China	4940
Iraq	2640
India	1410
Madagascar	430
Congo	190

Source: World Bank, **www.worldbank.org**.

wants for himself, but his massive charitable giving suggests that he keenly wants better health care for the world's poor. Our desires for a particular good or service can be satisfied; over a short period of time we can surely get enough toothpaste or pasta. And one appendectomy is plenty. But our broader desire for more goods and services and higher-quality goods and services seems to be another story.

Because we have only limited income (usually through our work) but seemingly insatiable wants, it is in our self-interest to economize: to pick and choose goods and services that maximize our satisfaction given the limitations we face.

A Budget Line

We can clarify the economizing problem facing consumers by visualizing a **budget line** (or, more technically, a *budget constraint*). It is a schedule or curve that shows various combinations of two products a consumer can purchase with a specific money income. Although we assume two products, the analysis generalizes to the full range of products available to consumers.

FIGURE 1.1 A consumer's budget line. The budget line (or budget constraint) shows all the combinations of any two products that can be purchased, given the prices of the products and the consumer's money income.

The Budget Line: Whole-Unit Combinations of DVDs and Paperback Books Attainable with an Income of $120		
Units of DVDs (Price = $20)	**Units of Books (Price = $10)**	**Total Expenditure**
6	0	$120 (= $120 + $0)
5	2	$120 (= $100 + $20)
4	4	$120 (= $80 + $40)
3	6	$120 (= $60 + $60)
2	8	$120 (= $40 + $80)
1	10	$120 (= $20 + $100)
0	12	$120 (= $0 + $120)

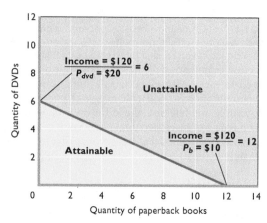

To understand the idea of a budget line, suppose that you received a Barnes & Noble gift card as a birthday present. The $120 card is soon to expire. You take the card to the store and confine your purchase decisions to two alternatives: DVDs and paperback books. DVDs are $20 each and paperback books are $10 each. Your purchase options are shown in the table in Figure 1.1.

At one extreme, you might spend all of your $120 "income" on 6 DVDs at $20 each and have nothing left to spend on books. Or, by giving up 2 DVDs and thereby gaining $40, you can have 4 DVDs at $20 each and 4 books at $10 each. And so on to the other extreme, at which you could buy 12 books at $10 each, spending your entire gift card on books with nothing left to spend on DVDs.

The graph in Figure 1.1 shows the budget line. Note that the graph is not restricted to whole units of DVDs and books as is the table. Every point on the graph represents a possible combination of DVDs and books, including fractional quantities. The slope of the graphed budget line measures the ratio of the price of books (P_b) to the price of DVDs (P_{dvd}); more precisely, the slope is $P_b/P_{dvd} = \$-10/\$+20 = -\frac{1}{2}$. So you must forgo 1 DVD (measured on the vertical axis) to buy 2 books (measured on the horizontal axis). This yields a slope of $-\frac{1}{2}$ or $-.5$.

The budget line illustrates several ideas.

Attainable and Unattainable Combinations All the combinations of DVDs and books on or inside the budget line are *attainable* from the $120 of money income. You can afford to buy, for example, 3 DVDs at $20 each and 6 books at $10 each. You also can obviously afford to buy 2 DVDs and 5 books, thereby using up only $90 of the $120 available on your gift card. But to achieve maximum

utility you will want to spend the full $120. The budget line shows all combinations that cost exactly the full $120.

In contrast, all combinations beyond the budget line are *unattainable*. The $120 limit simply does not allow you to purchase, for example, 5 DVDs at $20 each and 5 books at $10 each. That $150 expenditure would clearly exceed the $120 limit. In Figure 1.1 the attainable combinations are on and within the budget line; the unattainable combinations are beyond the budget line.

Trade-Offs and Opportunity Costs The budget line in Figure 1.1 illustrates the idea of trade-offs arising from limited income. To obtain more DVDs, you have to give up some books. For example, to obtain the first DVD, you trade off 2 books. So the opportunity cost of the first DVD is 2 books. To obtain the second DVD the opportunity cost is also 2 books. The straight-line budget constraint, with its constant slope, indicates constant opportunity cost. That is, the opportunity cost of 1 extra DVD remains the same (= 2 books) as more DVDs are purchased. And, in reverse, the opportunity cost of 1 extra book does not change (= $\frac{1}{2}$ DVD) as more books are bought.

ORIGIN OF THE IDEA

01.5

Opportunity costs

Choice Limited income forces people to choose what to buy and what to forgo to fulfill wants. You will select the combination of DVDs and paperback books that you think is "best." That is, you will evaluate your marginal benefits and marginal costs (here, product price) to make choices that maximize your satisfaction. Other people, with the same $120 gift card, would undoubtedly make different choices.

Income Changes The location of the budget line varies with money income. An increase in money income shifts the budget line to the right; a decrease in money income shifts it to the left. To verify this, recalculate the table in Figure 1.1, assuming the card value (income) is (a) $240 and (b) $60, and plot the new budget lines in the graph. No wonder people like to have more income: That shifts their budget lines outward and enables them to buy more goods and services. But even with more income, people will still face spending trade-offs, choices, and opportunity costs.

WORKED PROBLEMS

W1.1
Budget lines

CONSIDER THIS . . .

Did Zuckerberg, Winfrey, and James Make Bad Choices?

Opportunity costs come into play in decisions well beyond simple buying decisions. Consider the different choices people make with respect to college. The average salaries earned by college graduates are nearly twice as high as those earned by persons with just high school diplomas. For most capable students, "Go to college, stay in college, and earn a degree" is very sound advice.

Yet Facebook founder Mark Zuckerberg and talk show host Oprah Winfrey* both dropped out of college, and basketball star LeBron James never even bothered to start classes. What were they thinking? Unlike most students, Zukerberg faced enormous opportunity costs for staying in college. He had a vision for his company, and dropping out helped to ensure Facebook's success. Similarly, Winfrey landed a spot in local television news when she was a teenager, eventually producing and starring in the Oprah Winfrey Show when she was 32 years old. Getting a degree in her twenties might have interrupted the string of successes that made her famous talk show possible. And James knew that professional athletes have short careers. Therefore, going to college directly after high school would have taken away four years of his peak earning potential.

So Zuckerberg, Winfrey, and James understood opportunity costs and made their choices accordingly. The size of opportunity costs matters greatly in making individual decisions.

*Winfrey eventually went back to school and earned a degree from Tennessee State University when she was in her thirties.

QUICK REVIEW 1.2

- Because wants exceed incomes, individuals face an economizing problem; they must decide what to buy and what to forgo.
- A budget line (budget constraint) shows the various combinations of two goods that a consumer can purchase with a specific money income.
- Straight-line budget constraints imply constant opportunity costs for both goods.

Society's Economizing Problem

LO1.5 List the categories of scarce resources and delineate the nature of society's economizing problem.

Society must also make choices under conditions of scarcity. It, too, faces an economizing problem. Should it devote more of its limited resources to the criminal justice system (police, courts, and prisons) or to education (teachers, books, and schools)? If it decides to devote more resources to both, what other goods and services does it forgo? Health care? Energy development?

Scarce Resources

Society has limited or scarce **economic resources,** meaning all natural, human, and manufactured resources that go into the production of goods and services. This includes the entire set of factory and farm buildings and all the equipment, tools, and machinery used to produce manufactured goods and agricultural products; all transportation and communication facilities; all types of labor; and land and mineral resources.

Resource Categories

Economists classify economic resources into four general categories.

Land Land means much more to the economist than it does to most people. To the economist **land** includes all natural resources ("gifts of nature") used in the production process. These include forests, mineral and oil deposits, water resources, wind power, sunlight, and arable land.

Labor The resource **labor** consists of the physical actions and mental activities that people contribute to the production of goods and services. The work-related activities of a logger, retail clerk, machinist, teacher, professional football player, and nuclear physicist all fall under the general heading "labor."

Capital For economists, **capital** (or capital goods) includes all manufactured aids used in producing consumer goods and services. Included are all factory, storage, transportation, and distribution facilities, as well as tools and machinery. Economists use the term **investment** to describe spending that pays for the production and accumulation of capital goods.

Capital goods differ from consumer goods because consumer goods satisfy wants directly, whereas capital goods do so indirectly by aiding the production of consumer goods. For example, large commercial baking ovens (capital goods) help make loaves of bread (consumer goods). Note that the term "capital" as used by economists refers not to money but to tools, machinery, and other productive equipment. Because money produces nothing, economists do not include it as an economic resource. Money (or money capital or financial capital) is simply a means for purchasing goods and services, including capital goods.

Entrepreneurial Ability   Finally, there is the special human resource, distinct from labor, called **entrepreneurial ability**. It is supplied by **entrepreneurs**, who perform several critically important economic functions:

- The entrepreneur takes the initiative in combining the resources of land, labor, and capital to produce a good or a service. Both a sparkplug and a catalyst, the entrepreneur is the driving force behind production and the agent who combines the other resources in what is hoped will be a successful business venture.

- The entrepreneur makes the strategic business decisions that set the course of an enterprise.

- The entrepreneur innovates. He or she commercializes new products, new production techniques, or even new forms of business organization.

- The entrepreneur bears risk. Innovation is risky, as nearly all new products and ideas are subject to the possibility of failure as well as success. Progress would cease without entrepreneurs who are willing to take on risk by devoting their time, effort, and ability—as well as their own money and the money of others—to commercializing new products and ideas that may enhance society's standard of living.

Because land, labor, capital, and entrepreneurial ability are combined to produce goods and services, they are called the **factors of production,** or simply "inputs."

Production Possibilities Model

LO1.6 Apply production possibilities analysis, increasing opportunity costs, and economic growth.

Society uses its scarce resources to produce goods and services. The alternatives and choices it faces can best be understood through a macroeconomic model of production possibilities. To keep things simple, let's initially assume

- *Full employment*   The economy is employing all of its available resources.

- *Fixed resources*   The quantity and quality of the factors of production are fixed.

- *Fixed technology*   The state of technology (the methods used to produce output) is constant.

- *Two goods*   The economy is producing only two goods: pizzas and industrial robots. Pizzas symbolize **consumer goods,** products that satisfy our wants directly; industrial robots (for example, the kind used to weld automobile frames) symbolize **capital goods,** products that satisfy our wants indirectly by making possible more efficient production of consumer goods.

Production Possibilities Table

A production possibilities table lists the different combinations of two products that can be produced with a specific set of resources, assuming full employment. Table 1.1 presents a simple, hypothetical economy that is producing pizzas and industrial robots; the data are, of course, hypothetical. At alternative A, this economy would be devoting all its available resources to the production of industrial robots (capital goods); at alternative E, all resources would go to pizza production (consumer goods). Those alternatives are unrealistic extremes; an economy typically produces both capital goods and consumer goods, as in B, C, and D. As we move from alternative A to E, we increase the production of pizzas at the expense of the production of industrial robots.

Because consumer goods satisfy our wants directly, any movement toward E looks tempting. In producing more pizzas, society increases the satisfaction of its current wants. But there is a cost: More pizzas mean fewer industrial robots. This shift of resources to consumer goods catches up with society over time because the stock of capital goods expands more slowly, thereby reducing potential future production. By moving toward alternative E, society chooses "more now" at the expense of "much more later."

By moving toward A, society chooses to forgo current consumption, thereby freeing up resources that can be used to increase the production of capital goods. By building up

TABLE 1.1 Production Possibilities of Pizzas and Industrial Robots

Type of Product	Production Alternatives				
	A	**B**	**C**	**D**	**E**
Pizzas (in hundred thousands)	0	1	2	3	4
Robots (in thousands)	10	9	7	4	0

KEY GRAPH

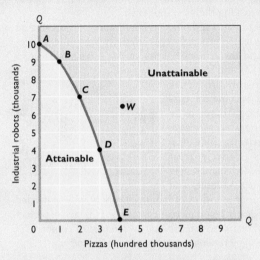

FIGURE 1.2 The production possibilities curve. Each point on the production possibilities curve represents some maximum combination of two products that can be produced if resources are fully employed. When an economy is operating on the curve, more industrial robots means fewer pizzas, and vice versa. Limited resources and a fixed technology make any combination of industrial robots and pizzas lying outside the curve (such as at *W*) unattainable. Points inside the curve are attainable, but they indicate that full employment is not being realized.

QUICK QUIZ FOR FIGURE 1.2

1. Production possibilities curve *ABCDE* is bowed out from the origin because:
   a. the marginal benefit of pizzas declines as more pizzas are consumed.
   b. the curve gets steeper as we move from *E* to *A*.
   c. it reflects the law of increasing opportunity costs.
   d. resources are scarce.

2. The marginal opportunity cost of the second unit of pizza is:
   a. 2 units of robots.
   b. 3 units of robots.
   c. 7 units of robots.
   d. 9 units of robots.

3. The total opportunity cost of 7 units of robots is:
   a. 1 unit of pizza.
   b. 2 units of pizza.
   c. 3 units of pizza.
   d. 4 units of pizza.

4. All points on this production possibilities curve necessarily represent:
   a. society's optimal choice.
   b. less than full use of resources.
   c. unattainable levels of output.
   d. full employment.

Answers: 1. c; 2. a; 3. b; 4. d

its stock of capital this way, society will have greater future production and, therefore, greater future consumption. By moving toward A, society is choosing "more later" at the cost of "less now."

Generalization: At any point in time, a fully employed economy must sacrifice some of one good to obtain more of another good. Scarce resources prohibit a fully employed economy from having more of both goods. Society must choose among alternatives. There is no such thing as a free pizza, or a free industrial robot. Having more of one thing means having less of something else.

Production Possibilities Curve

The data presented in a production possibilities table are shown graphically as a **production possibilities curve.** Such a curve displays the different combinations of goods and services that society can produce in a fully employed economy, assuming a fixed availability of supplies of resources and fixed technology. We arbitrarily represent the economy's output of capital goods (here, industrial robots) on the vertical axis and the output of consumer goods (here, pizzas) on the horizontal axis, as shown in **Figure 1.2 (Key Graph).**

Each point on the production possibilities curve represents some maximum output of the two products. The curve is a "constraint" because it shows the limit of attainable outputs. Points on the curve are attainable as long as the economy uses all its available resources. Points lying inside the curve are also attainable, but they reflect less total output and therefore are not as desirable as points on the curve. Points inside the curve imply that the economy could have more of both industrial robots and pizzas if it achieved full employment of its resources. Points lying beyond the production possibilities curve, like *W*, would represent a greater output than the output at any point on the curve. Such points, however, are unattainable with the current availability of resources and technology.

Law of Increasing Opportunity Costs

Figure 1.2 clearly shows that more pizzas mean fewer industrial robots. The number of units of industrial robots that must be given up to obtain another unit of pizzas, of course, is the opportunity cost of that unit of pizzas.

In moving from alternative A to alternative B in Table 1.1, the cost of 1 additional unit of pizzas is 1 fewer unit of industrial robots. But when additional units are considered—B to C, C to D, and D to E—an important economic principle is revealed: For society, the opportunity cost of each additional unit of pizzas is greater than the opportunity cost of the preceding one. When we move from A to B, just 1 unit of industrial robots is sacrificed for 1 more unit of pizzas; but in going from B to C we sacrifice 2 additional units of industrial robots for 1 more unit of pizzas; then 3 more of industrial robots for 1 more of pizzas; and finally 4 for 1. Conversely, confirm that as we move from E to A, the cost of an additional unit of industrial robots (on average) is $\frac{1}{4}$, $\frac{1}{3}$, $\frac{1}{2}$, and 1 unit of pizzas, respectively, for the four successive moves.

Our example illustrates the **law of increasing opportunity costs.** As the production of a particular good increases, the opportunity cost of producing an additional unit rises.

Shape of the Curve   The law of increasing opportunity costs is reflected in the shape of the production possibilities curve: The curve is bowed out from the origin of the graph. Figure 1.2 shows that when the economy moves from *A* to *E*, it must give up successively larger amounts of industrial robots (1, 2, 3, and 4) to acquire equal increments of pizzas (1, 1, 1, and 1). This is shown in the slope of the production possibilities curve, which becomes steeper as we move from *A* to *E*.

Economic Rationale   The law of increasing opportunity costs is driven by the fact that economic resources are not completely adaptable to alternative uses. Many resources are better at producing one type of good than at producing others. Consider land. Some land is highly suited to growing the ingredients necessary for pizza production. But as pizza production expands, society has to start using land that is less bountiful for farming. Other land is rich in mineral deposits and therefore well-suited to producing the materials needed to make industrial robots. That land will be the first land devoted to the production of industrial robots. But as society steps up the

production of robots, it must use land that is less and less suited to making their components.

If we start at *A* and move to *B* in Figure 1.2, we can shift resources whose productivity is relatively high in pizza production and low in industrial robots. But as we move from *B* to *C*, *C* to *D*, and so on, resources highly productive in pizzas become increasingly scarce. To get more pizzas, resources whose productivity in industrial robots is relatively great will be needed. Increasingly more of such resources, and hence greater sacrifices of industrial robots, will be needed to achieve each 1-unit increase in pizzas. This lack of perfect flexibility, or interchangeability, on the part of resources is the cause of increasing opportunity costs for society.

WORKED PROBLEMS

W1.2

Production possibilities

Optimal Allocation

Of all the attainable combinations of pizzas and industrial robots on the curve in Figure 1.2, which is optimal (best)? That is, what specific quantities of resources should be allocated to pizzas and what specific quantities should be allocated to industrial robots in order to maximize satisfaction?

Recall that economic decisions center on comparisons of marginal benefit (MB) and marginal cost (MC). Any economic activity should be expanded as long as marginal benefit exceeds marginal cost and should be reduced if marginal cost exceeds marginal benefit. The optimal amount of the activity occurs where MB = MC. Society needs to make a similar assessment about its production decision.

Consider pizzas. We already know from the law of increasing opportunity costs that the marginal cost of additional units of pizza will rise as more units are produced. At the same time, we need to recognize that the extra or marginal benefits that come from producing and consuming pizza decline with each successive unit of pizza. Consequently, each successive unit of pizza brings with it both increasing marginal costs and decreasing marginal benefits.

The optimal quantity of pizza production is indicated by point *e* at the intersection of the MB and MC curves: 200,000 units in Figure 1.3. Why is this amount the optimal quantity? If only 100,000 units of pizzas were produced, the marginal benefit of an extra unit of pizza (point *a*) would exceed its marginal cost (point *b*). In money terms, MB is $15, while MC is only $5. When society gains something worth $15 at a marginal cost of only $5, it is better off. In Figure 1.3, net gains can continue to be realized until pizza-product production has been increased to 200,000.

FIGURE 1.3 Optimal output: MB = MC. Achieving the optimal output requires the expansion of a good's output until its marginal benefit (MB) and marginal cost (MC) are equal. No resources beyond that point should be allocated to the product. Here, optimal output occurs at point *e*, where 200,000 units of pizzas are produced.

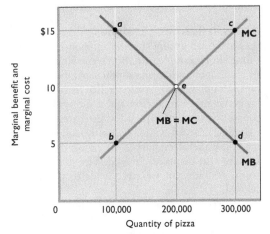

In contrast, the production of 300,000 units of pizzas is excessive. There the MC of an added unit is $15 (point *c*) and its MB is only $5 (point *d*). This means that 1 unit of pizza is worth only $5 to society but costs it $15 to obtain. This is a losing proposition for society!

So resources are being efficiently allocated to any product when the marginal benefit and marginal cost of its output are equal (MB = MC). Suppose that by applying the same analysis to industrial robots, we find that the optimal (MB = MC) quantity of robots is 7,000. This would mean that alternative *C* (200,000 units of pizzas and 7,000 units of industrial robots) on the production possibilities curve in Figure 1.2 would be optimal for this economy.

QUICK REVIEW 1.3

- Economists categorize economic resources as land, labor, capital, and entrepreneurial ability.
- The production possibilities curve illustrates several ideas: (a) scarcity of resources is implied by the area of unattainable combinations of output lying outside the production possibilities curve; (b) choice among outputs is reflected in the variety of attainable combinations of goods lying along the curve; (c) opportunity cost is illustrated by the downward slope of the curve; (d) the law of increasing opportunity costs is reflected in the bowed-outward shape of the curve.
- A comparison of marginal benefits and marginal costs is needed to determine the best or optimal output mix on a production possibilities curve.

CONSIDER THIS . . .

The Economics of War

Production possibilities analysis is helpful in assessing the costs and benefits of waging the broad war on terrorism, including the wars in Afghanistan and Iraq. At the end of 2011, the estimated cost of these efforts exceeded $1.4 trillion.

If we categorize all U.S. production as either "defense goods" or "civilian goods," we can measure them on the axes of a production possibilities diagram such as that shown in Figure 1.2. The opportunity cost of using more resources for defense goods is the civilian goods sacrificed. In a fully employed economy, more defense goods are achieved at the opportunity cost of fewer civilian goods—health care, education, pollution control, personal computers, houses, and so on. The cost of war and defense is the other goods forgone. The benefits of these activities are numerous and diverse but clearly include the gains from protecting against future loss of American lives, assets, income, and well-being.

Society must assess the marginal benefit (MB) and marginal cost (MC) of additional defense goods to determine their optimal amounts—where to locate on the defense goods–civilian goods production possibilities curve. Although estimating marginal benefits and marginal costs is an imprecise art, the MB-MC framework is a useful way of approaching choices. An optimal allocation of resources requires that society expand production of defense goods until MB = MC.

The events of September 11, 2001, and the future threats they foreshadowed increased the marginal benefits of defense goods, as perceived by Americans. If we label the horizontal axis in Figure 1.3 "defense goods" and draw in a rightward shift of the MB curve, you will see that the optimal quantity of defense goods rises. In view of the concerns relating to September 11, the United States allocated more of its resources to defense. But the MB-MC analysis also reminds us we can spend too much on defense, as well as too little. The United States should not expand defense goods beyond the point where MB = MC. If it does, it will be sacrificing civilian goods of greater value than the defense goods obtained.

Unemployment, Growth, and the Future

LO1.7 Explain how economic growth and international trade increase consumption possibilities.

In the depths of the Great Depression of the 1930s, one-quarter of U.S. workers were unemployed and one-third of

U.S. production capacity was idle. Subsequent downturns have been much less severe. During the deep 2007–2009 recession, for instance, production fell by a comparably smaller 3.7 percent and 1-in-10 workers was without a job.

Almost all nations have experienced widespread unemployment and unused production capacity from business downturns at one time or another. Since 2000, for example, many nations—including Argentina, Japan, Mexico, Germany, and South Korea—have had economic downturns and unemployment.

How do these realities relate to the production possibilities model? Our analysis and conclusions change if we relax the assumption that all available resources are fully employed. The five alternatives in Table 1.1 represent maximum outputs; they illustrate the combinations of pizzas and industrial robots that can be produced when the economy is operating at full employment. With unemployment, this economy would produce less than each alternative shown in the table.

Graphically, we represent situations of unemployment by points inside the original production possibilities curve (reproduced here in Figure 1.4). Point *U* is one such point. Here the economy is falling short of the various maximum combinations of pizzas and industrial robots represented by the points on the production possibilities curve. The arrows in Figure 1.4 indicate three possible paths back to full employment. A move toward full employment would yield a greater output of one or both products.

FIGURE 1.4 Unemployment and the production possibilities curve. Any point inside the production possibilities curve, such as *U*, represents unemployment or a failure to achieve full employment. The arrows indicate that by realizing full employment, the economy could operate on the curve. This means it could produce more of one or both products than it is producing at point *U*.

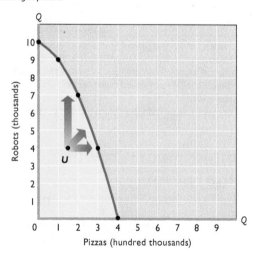

A Growing Economy

When we drop the assumptions that the quantity and quality of resources and technology are fixed, the production possibilities curve shifts positions and the potential maximum output of the economy changes.

Increases in Resource Supplies Although resource supplies are fixed at any specific moment, they change over time. For example, a nation's growing population brings about increases in the supplies of labor and entrepreneurial ability. Also, labor quality usually improves over time via more education and training. Historically, the economy's stock of capital has increased at a significant, though unsteady, rate. And although some of our energy and mineral resources are being depleted, new sources are also being discovered. The development of irrigation systems, for example, adds to the supply of arable land.

The net result of these increased supplies of the factors of production is the ability to produce more of both consumer goods and capital goods. Thus, 20 years from now, the production possibilities may supersede those shown in Table 1.1. The new production possibilities might look like those in the table in Figure 1.5. The greater abundance of resources will result in a greater potential output of one or both products at each alternative. The economy will have achieved economic growth in the form of expanded potential output. Thus, when an increase in the quantity or quality of resources occurs, the production possibilities curve shifts outward and to the right, as illustrated by the move from the inner curve to curve *A'B'C'D'E'* in Figure 1.5. This sort of shift represents growth of economic capacity, which, when used, means **economic growth:** a larger total output.

Advances in Technology An advancing technology brings both new and better goods and improved ways of producing them. For now, let's think of technological advance as being only improvements in the methods of production, for example, the introduction of computerized systems to manage inventories and schedule production. These advances alter our previous discussion of the economizing problem by allowing society to produce more goods with available resources. As with increases in resource supplies, technological advances make possible the production of more industrial robots *and* more pizzas.

A real-world example of improved technology is the recent surge of new technologies relating to computers, communications, and biotechnology. Technological advances have dropped the prices of computers and greatly

FIGURE 1.5 Economic growth and the production possibilities curve. The increase in supplies of resources, improvements in resource quality, and technological advances that occur in a dynamic economy move the production possibilities curve outward and to the right, allowing the economy to have larger quantities of both types of goods.

Type of Product	Production Alternatives				
	A′	B′	C′	D′	E′
Pizzas (in hundred thousands)	0	2	4	6	8
Robots (in thousands)	14	12	9	5	0

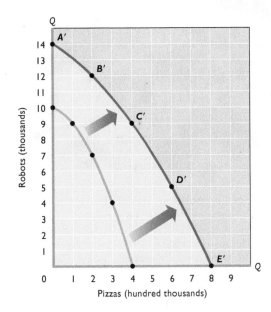

Present Choices and Future Possibilities

An economy's current choice of positions on its production possibilities curve helps determine the future location of that curve. Let's designate the two axes of the production possibilities curve as "goods for the future" and "goods for the present," as in Figure 1.6. Goods for the future are such

FIGURE 1.6 Present choices and future locations of production possibilities curves. (a) Presentville's current choice to produce more "present goods" and fewer "future goods," as represented by point *P,* will result in a modest outward shift of the production possibilities curve in the future. (b) Futureville's current choice of producing fewer "present goods" and more "future goods," as depicted by point *F,* will lead to a greater outward shift of the production possibilities curve in the future.

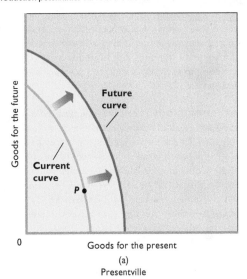

(a)
Presentville

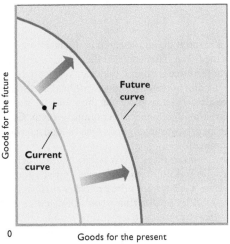

(b)
Futureville

increased their speed. Improved software has greatly increased the everyday usefulness of computers. Cellular phones and the Internet have increased communications capacity, enhancing production and improving the efficiency of markets. Advances in biotechnology have resulted in important agricultural and medical discoveries. These and other new and improved technologies have contributed to U.S. economic growth (outward shifts of the nation's production possibilities curve).

Conclusion: Economic growth is the result of (1) increases in supplies of resources, (2) improvements in resource quality, and (3) technological advances. The consequence of growth is that a full-employment economy can enjoy a greater output of both consumption goods and capital goods. Whereas static, no-growth economies must sacrifice some of one good to obtain more of another, dynamic, growing economies can have larger quantities of both goods.

LAST WORD

Pitfalls to Sound Economic Reasoning

Because They Affect Us So Personally, We Often Have Difficulty Thinking Accurately and Objectively About Economic Issues.

Here are some common pitfalls to avoid in successfully applying the economic perspective.

Biases Most people bring a bundle of biases and preconceptions to the field of economics. For example, some might think that corporate profits are excessive or that lending money is always superior to borrowing money. Others might believe that government is necessarily less efficient than businesses or that more government regulation is always better than less. Biases cloud thinking and interfere with objective analysis. All of us must be willing to shed biases and preconceptions that are not supported by facts.

Loaded Terminology The economic terminology used in newspapers and broadcast media is sometimes emotionally biased, or loaded. The writer or spokesperson may have a cause to promote or an ax to grind and may slant comments accordingly. High profits may be labeled "obscene," low wages may be called "exploitative," or self-interested behavior may be "greed." Government workers may be referred to as "mindless bureaucrats" and those favoring stronger government regulations may be called "socialists." To objectively analyze economic issues, you must be prepared to reject or discount such terminology.

Fallacy of Composition Another pitfall in economic thinking is the assumption that what is true for one individual or part of a whole is necessarily true for a group of individuals or the whole. This is a logical fallacy called the *fallacy of composition*; the assumption is not correct. A statement that is valid for an individual or part is not necessarily valid for the larger group or whole. Noneconomic example: You may see the action better if

things as capital goods, research and education, and preventive medicine. They increase the quantity and quality of property resources, enlarge the stock of technological information, and improve the quality of human resources. As we have already seen, goods for the future such as capital goods are the ingredients of economic growth. Goods for the present are consumer goods such as food, clothing, and entertainment.

Now suppose there are two hypothetical economies, Presentville and Futureville, that are initially identical in every respect except one: Presentville's current choice of positions on its production possibilities curve strongly favors present goods over future goods. Point *P* in Figure 1.6a indicates that choice. It is located quite far down the curve to the right, indicating a high priority

for goods for the present, at the expense of less goods for the future. Futureville, in contrast, makes a current choice that stresses larger amounts of future goods and smaller amounts of present goods, as shown by point *F* in Figure 1.6b.

Now, other things equal, we can expect Futureville's future production possibilities curve to be farther to the right than Presentville's future production possibilities curve. By currently choosing an output more favorable to technological advances and to increases in the quantity and quality of resources, Futureville will achieve greater economic growth than Presentville. In terms of capital goods, Futureville is choosing to make larger current additions to its "national factory" by devoting more of its current output to capital than does Presentville. The you leap to your feet to see an outstanding play at a football game. But if all the spectators leap to their feet at the same time, nobody—including you—will have a better view than when all remained seated.

Here are two economic examples: An individual stockholder can sell shares of, say, Google stock without affecting the price of the stock. The individual's sale will not noticeably reduce the share price because the sale is a negligible fraction of the total shares of Google being bought and sold. But if all the Google shareholders decide to sell their shares the same day, the market will be flooded with shares and the stock price will fall precipitously. Similarly, a single cattle ranch can increase its revenue by expanding the size of its livestock herd. The extra cattle will not affect the price of cattle when they are brought to market. But if all ranchers as a group expand their herds, the total output of cattle will increase so much that the price of cattle will decline when the cattle are sold. If the price reduction is relatively large, ranchers as a group might find that their income has fallen despite their having sold a greater number of cattle because the fall in price overwhelms the increase in quantity.

Post Hoc Fallacy You must think very carefully before concluding that because event A precedes event B, A is the cause of B. This kind of faulty reasoning is known as the *post hoc, ergo propter hoc*, or "after this, therefore because of this," fallacy. Noneconomic example: A professional football team hires a new coach and the team's record improves. Is the new coach the cause? Maybe. Perhaps the presence of more experienced and talented players or an easier schedule is the true cause. The rooster crows before dawn but does not cause the sunrise.

Economic example: Many people blamed the Great Depression of the 1930s on the stock market crash of 1929. But the crash did not cause the Great Depression. The same severe weaknesses in the economy that caused the crash caused the Great Depression. The depression would have occurred even without the preceding stock market crash.

Correlation but Not Causation Do not confuse correlation, or connection, with causation. Correlation between two events or two sets of data indicates only that they are associated in some systematic and dependable way. For example, we may find that when variable X increases, Y also increases. But this correlation does not necessarily mean that there is causation—that increases in X cause increases in Y. The relationship could be purely coincidental or dependent on some other factor, Z, not included in the analysis.

Here is an example: Economists have found a positive correlation between education and income. In general, people with more education earn higher incomes than those with less education. Common sense suggests education is the cause and higher incomes are the effect; more education implies a more knowledgeable and productive worker, and such workers receive larger salaries.

But might the relationship be explainable in other ways? Are education and income correlated because the characteristics required for succeeding in education—ability and motivation—are the same ones required to be a productive and highly paid worker? If so, then people with those traits will probably both obtain more education and earn higher incomes. But greater education will not be the sole cause of the higher income.

payoff from this choice for Futureville is greater future production capacity and economic growth. The opportunity cost is fewer consumer goods in the present for Futureville to enjoy.

Is Futureville's choice thus necessarily "better" than Presentville's? That, we cannot say. The different outcomes simply reflect different preferences and priorities in the two countries. But each country will have to live with the economic consequences of its choice.

A Qualification: International Trade

Production possibilities analysis implies that an individual nation is limited to the combinations of output indicated by its production possibilities curve. But we must modify this principle when international specialization and trade exist.

You will see in later chapters that an economy can circumvent, through international specialization and trade, the output limits imposed by its domestic production possibilities curve. Under international specialization and trade, each nation first specializes in the production of those items for which it has the lowest opportunity costs (due to an abundance of the necessary resources). Countries then engage in international trade, with each country exchanging the items that it can produce at the lowest opportunity costs for the items that other countries can produce at the lowest opportunity costs.

International specialization and trade allow a nation to get more of a desired good at less sacrifice of some other good. Rather than sacrifice three units of domestically produced robots to get a third unit of domestically produced pizza, as in Table 1.1, a nation that engages in international specialization and trade might be able to do much better. If it specializes in robots while another country specializes in pizza, then it may be able to obtain the third unit of pizza by trading only two units of domestically produced robots for one unit of foreign-produced pizza. Specialization and trade have the same effect as having more and better resources or discovering improved production techniques; both increase the quantities of capital and consumer goods available to society. Expansion of domestic production possibilities and international trade are two separate routes for obtaining greater output.

QUICK REVIEW 1.4

- Unemployment causes an economy to operate at a point inside its production possibilities curve.
- Increases in resource supplies, improvements in resource quality, and technological advance cause economic growth, which is depicted as an outward shift of the production possibilities curve.
- An economy's present choice of capital and consumer goods helps determine the future location of its production possibilities curve.
- International specialization and trade enable a nation to obtain more goods than its production possibilities curve indicates.

SUMMARY

LO1.1 Define economics and the features of the economic perspective.

Economics is the social science that examines how individuals, institutions, and society make optimal choices under conditions of scarcity. Central to economics is the idea of opportunity cost: the value of the next-best good or service forgone to obtain something.

The economic perspective includes three elements: scarcity and choice, purposeful behavior, and marginal analysis. It sees individuals and institutions making rational decisions based on comparisons of marginal costs and marginal benefits.

LO1.2 Describe the role of economic theory in economics.

Economists employ the scientific method, in which they form and test hypotheses of cause-and-effect relationships to generate theories, laws, and principles. Economists often combine theories into representations called models.

LO1.3 Distinguish microeconomics from macroeconomics and positive economics from normative economics.

Microeconomics examines the decision making of specific economic units or institutions. Macroeconomics looks at the economy as a whole or its major aggregates.

Positive economic analysis deals with facts; normative economics reflects value judgments.

LO1.4 Explain the individual's economizing problem and how trade-offs, opportunity costs, and attainable combinations can be illustrated with budget lines.

Individuals face an economizing problem. Because their wants exceed their incomes, they must decide what to purchase and what to forgo. Society also faces an economizing problem. Societal wants exceed the available resources necessary to fulfill them. Society therefore must decide what to produce and what to forgo.

Graphically, a budget line (or budget constraint) illustrates the economizing problem for individuals. The line shows the various combinations of two products that a consumer can purchase with a specific money income, given the prices of the two products.

LO1.5 List the categories of scarce resources and delineate the nature of society's economizing problem.

Economic resources are inputs into the production process and can be classified as land, labor, capital, or entrepreneurial ability. Economic resources are also known as factors of production or inputs.

Economists illustrate society's economizing problem through production possibilities analysis. Production possibilities tables and curves show the different combinations of goods and services that can be produced in a fully employed economy, assuming that resource quantity, resource quality, and technology are fixed.

LO1.6 Apply production possibilities analysis, increasing opportunity costs, and economic growth.

An economy that is fully employed and thus operating on its production possibilities curve must sacrifice the output of some types of goods and services to increase the production of others. The gain of one type of good or service is always accompanied by an opportunity cost in the form of the loss of some of the other type of good or service.

Because resources are not equally productive in all possible uses, shifting resources from one use to another creates increasing opportunity costs. The production of additional units of one product requires the sacrifice of increasing amounts of the other product.

The optimal (best) point on the production possibilities curve represents the most desirable mix of goods and is determined by expanding the production of each good until its marginal benefit (MB) equals its marginal cost (MC).

LO1.7 Explain how economic growth and international trade increase consumption possibilities.

Over time, technological advances and increases in the quantity and quality of resources enable the economy to produce more of all goods and services, that is, to experience economic growth. Society's choice as to the mix of consumer goods and capital goods in current output is a major determinant of the future location of the production possibilities curve and thus of the extent of economic growth.

International trade enables a nation to obtain more goods from its limited resources than its production possibilities curve indicates.

TERMS AND CONCEPTS

economics	macroeconomics	investment
economic perspective	aggregate	entrepreneurial ability
scarcity	positive economics	entrepreneurs
opportunity cost	normative economics	factors of production
utility	economizing problem	consumer goods
marginal analysis	budget line	capital goods
scientific method	economic resources	production possibilities curve
economic principle	land	law of increasing
other-things-equal assumption	labor	opportunity costs
microeconomics	capital	economic growth

The following and additional problems can be found in **connect** ECONOMICS

DISCUSSION QUESTIONS

1. What is an opportunity cost? How does the idea relate to the definition of economics? Which of the following decisions would entail the greater opportunity cost: Allocating a square block in the heart of New York City for a surface parking lot or allocating a square block at the edge of a typical suburb for such a lot? Explain. **LO1.1**

2. Cite three examples of recent decisions that you made in which you, at least implicitly, weighed marginal cost and marginal benefit. **LO1.1**

3. What is meant by the term "utility" and how does the idea relate to purposeful behavior? **LO1.1**

4. What are the key elements of the scientific method and how does this method relate to economic principles and laws? **LO1.2**

5. State (a) a positive economic statement of your choice, and then (b) a normative economic statement relating to your first statement. **LO1.3**

6. How does the slope of a budget line illustrate opportunity costs and trade-offs? How does a budget line illustrate scarcity and the effect of limited incomes? **LO1.4**

7. What are economic resources? What categories do economists use to classify them? Why are resources also called factors of production? Why are they called inputs? **LO1.5**

8. Why is money not considered to be a capital resource in economics? Why is entrepreneurial ability considered a category of economic resource, distinct from labor? What are the major functions of the entrepreneur? **LO1.5**

9. Specify and explain the typical shapes of marginal-benefit and marginal-cost curves. How are these curves used to determine the optimal allocation of resources to a particular product? If current output is such that marginal cost exceeds marginal benefit, should more or fewer resources be allocated to this product? Explain. **LO1.6**

10. Suppose that, on the basis of a nation's production possibilities curve, an economy must sacrifice 10,000 pizzas domestically to get the 1 additional industrial robot it desires but that it can get the robot from another country in exchange for 9,000 pizzas. Relate this information to the following statement: "Through international specialization and trade, a nation can reduce its opportunity cost of obtaining goods and thus 'move outside its production possibilities curve.'" **LO1.7**

11. **LAST WORD** Studies indicate that married men on average earn more income than unmarried men of the same age and education level. Why must we be cautious in concluding that marriage is the cause and higher income is the effect?

REVIEW QUESTIONS

1. Match each term with the correct definition. **LO1.1**
   economics
   opportunity cost
   marginal analysis
   utility
   a. The next-best thing that must be forgone in order to produce one more unit of a given product.
   b. The pleasure, happiness, or satisfaction obtained from consuming a good or service.
   c. The social science concerned with how individuals, institutions, and society make optimal (best) choices under conditions of scarcity.
   d. Making choices based on comparing marginal benefits with marginal costs.

2. Indicate whether each of the following statements applies to microeconomics or macroeconomics: **LO1.3**
   a. The unemployment rate in the United States was 8.1 percent in August 2012.
   b. A U.S. software firm discharged 15 workers last month and transferred the work to India.
   c. An unexpected freeze in central Florida reduced the citrus crop and caused the price of oranges to rise.
   d. U.S. output, adjusted for inflation, decreased by 2.4 percent in 2009.
   e. Last week Wells Fargo Bank lowered its interest rate on business loans by one-half of 1 percentage point.
   f. The consumer price index rose by 3.8 percent from August 2011 to August 2012.

3. Suppose that you initially have $100 to spend on books or movie tickets. The books start off costing $25 each and the movie tickets start off costing $10 each. For each of the following situations, would the attainable set of combinations that you can afford increase or decrease? **LO1.4**
   a. Your budget increases from $100 to $150 while the prices stay the same.

   b. Your budget remains $100, the price of books remains $25, but the price of movie tickets rises to $20.
   c. Your budget remains $100, the price of movie tickets remains $10, but the price of a book falls to $15.

4. Suppose that you are given a $100 budget at work that can be spent only on two items: staplers and pens. If staplers cost $10 each and pens cost $2.50 each, then the opportunity cost of purchasing one stapler is: **LO1.4**
   a. 10 pens.
   b. 5 pens.
   c. zero pens.
   d. 4 pens.

5. For each of the following situations involving marginal cost (MC) and marginal benefit (MB), indicate whether it would be best to produce more, fewer, or the current number of units. **LO1.4**
   a. 3,000 units at which MC = $10 and MB = $13.
   b. 11 units at which MC = $4 and MB = $3.
   c. 43,277 units at which MC = $99 and MB = $99.
   d. 82 units at which MC < MB.
   e. 5 units at which MB < MC.

6. Explain how (if at all) each of the following events affects the location of a country's production possibilities curve: **LO1.6**
   a. The quality of education increases.
   b. The number of unemployed workers increases.
   c. A new technique improves the efficiency of extracting copper from ore.
   d. A devastating earthquake destroys numerous production facilities.

7. What are the two major ways in which an economy can grow and push out its production possibilities curve? **LO1.7**
   a. Better weather and nicer cars.
   b. Higher taxes and lower spending.
   c. Increases in resource supplies and advances in technology.
   d. Decreases in scarcity and advances in auditing.

PROBLEMS

1. Potatoes cost Janice $1 per pound, and she has $5.00 that she could possibly spend on potatoes or other items. If she feels that the first pound of potatoes is worth $1.50, the second pound is worth $1.14, the third pound is worth $1.05, and all subsequent pounds are worth $0.30, how many pounds of potatoes will she purchase? What if she only had $2 to spend? **LO1.1**

2. Pham can work as many or as few hours as she wants at the college bookstore for $9 per hour. But due to her hectic schedule, she has just 15 hours per week that she can spend working at either the bookstore or other potential jobs. One potential job, at a café, will pay her $12 per hour for up to 6 hours per week. She has another job offer at a garage that will pay her $10 an hour for up to 5 hours per

week. And she has a potential job at a daycare center that will pay her $8.50 per hour for as many hours as she can work. If her goal is to maximize the amount of money she can make each week, how many hours will she work at the bookstore? **LO1.1**

3. Suppose you won $15 on a lotto ticket at the local 7-Eleven and decided to spend all the winnings on candy bars and bags of peanuts. Candy bars cost $0.75 each while bags of peanuts cost $1.50 each. **LO1.5**
   a. Construct a table showing the alternative combinations of the two products that are available.
   b. Plot the data in your table as a budget line in a graph. What is the slope of the budget line? What is the opportunity cost of one more candy bar? Of one more bag of

peanuts? Do these opportunity costs rise, fall, or remain constant as additional units are purchased?

   c. Does the budget line tell you which of the available combinations of candy bars and bags of peanuts to buy?

   d. Suppose that you had won $30 on your ticket, not $15. Show the $30 budget line in your diagram. Has the number of available combinations increased or decreased?

4. Suppose that you are on a desert island and possess exactly 20 coconuts. Your neighbor, Friday, is a fisherman, and he is willing to trade 2 fish for every 1 coconut that you are willing to give him. Another neighbor, Kwame, is also a fisherman, and he is willing to trade 3 fish for every 1 coconut. **LO1.5**

   a. On a single figure, draw budget lines for trading with Friday and for trading with Kwame. (Put coconuts on the vertical axis.)

   b. What is the slope of the budget line from trading with Friday?

   c. What is the slope of the budget line from trading with Kwame?

   d. Which budget line features a larger set of attainable combinations of coconuts and fish?

   e. If you are going to trade coconuts for fish, would you rather trade with Friday or Kwame?

5. To the right is a production possibilities table for consumer goods (automobiles) and capital goods (forklifts): **LO1.6**

   a. Show these data graphically. Upon what specific assumptions is this production possibilities curve based?

   b. If the economy is at point C, what is the cost of one more automobile? Of one more forklift? Which characteristic of the production possibilities curve reflects the law of increasing opportunity costs: its shape or its length?

   c. If the economy characterized by this production possibilities table and curve were producing 3 automobiles and 20 forklifts, what could you conclude about its use of its available resources?

   d. Is production at a point outside the production possibilities curve currently possible? Could a future advance in technology allow production beyond the current production possibilities curve? Could international trade allow a country to consume beyond its current production possibilities curve?

Type of Production	Production Alternatives				
	A	B	C	D	E
Automobiles	0	2	4	6	8
Forklifts	30	27	21	12	0

6. Look at Figure 1.3. Suppose that the cost of cheese falls, so that the marginal cost of producing pizza decreases. Will the MC curve shift up or down? Will the optimal amount of pizza increase or decrease? **LO1.6**

7. Referring to the table in problem 5, suppose improvement occurs in the technology of producing forklifts but not in the technology of producing automobiles. Draw the new production possibilities curve. Now assume that a technological advance occurs in producing automobiles but not in producing forklifts. Draw the new production possibilities curve. Now draw a production possibilities curve that reflects technological improvement in the production of both goods. **LO1.7**

8. Because investment and capital goods are paid for with savings, higher savings rates reflect a decision to consume fewer goods for the present in order to be able to invest in more goods for the future. Households in China save 40 percent of their annual incomes each year, whereas U.S. households save less than 5 percent. At the same time, production possibilities are growing at roughly 9 percent per year in China but only about 3.5 percent per year in the United States. Use graphical analysis of "present goods" versus "future goods" to explain the difference between China's growth rate and the U.S. growth rate. **LO1.7**

Graphs and Their Meaning

LO1.8 Understand graphs, curves, and slopes as they relate to economics.

If you glance quickly through this text, you will find many graphs. Some seem simple, while others seem more formidable. All are included to help you visualize and understand economic relationships. Physicists and chemists sometimes illustrate their theories by building arrangements of multicolored wooden balls, representing protons, neutrons, and electrons, that are held in proper relation to one another by wires or sticks. Economists most often use graphs to illustrate their models. By understanding these "pictures," you can more readily comprehend economic relationships.

Construction of a Graph

A *graph* is a visual representation of the relationship between two economic quantities, or variables. The table in Figure 1 is a hypothetical illustration showing the relationship between income and consumption for the economy as a whole. Without even studying economics, we would logically expect that people would buy more goods and services when their incomes go up. Thus, it is not surprising to find in the table that total consumption in the economy increases as total income increases.

The information in the table is expressed graphically in Figure 1. Here is how it is done: We want to show visually how consumption changes as income changes. We therefore represent income on the **horizontal axis** of the graph and consumption on the **vertical axis.**

Now we arrange the vertical and horizontal scales of the graph to reflect the ranges of values of consumption and income and mark the scales in convenient increments. As you can see, the values marked on the scales cover all the values in the table. The increments on both scales are $100.

Because the graph has two dimensions, each point within it represents an income value and its associated consumption value. To find a point that represents one of the five income-consumption combinations in the table in Figure 1, we draw straight lines from the appropriate values on the vertical and horizontal axes. For example, to plot point *c* (the $200 income–$150 consumption point), we draw straight lines up from the horizontal (income) axis at $200 and across from the vertical (consumption) axis at $150. These lines intersect at point *c*, which represents this particular income-consumption combination. You should verify that the other income-consumption combinations shown in the table are properly located in the graph in Figure 1. Finally, by assuming that the same general relationship between income and consumption prevails for all other incomes, we draw a line or smooth curve to connect these points. That line or curve represents the income-consumption relationship.

If the curve is a straight line, as in Figure 1, we say the relationship is *linear*. (It is permissible, and even customary, to refer to straight lines in graphs as "curves.")

Direct and Inverse Relationships

The line in Figure 1 slopes upward to the right, so it depicts a direct relationship between income and consumption. By a **direct relationship** (or positive relationship) we mean that two variables—in this case, consumption and

FIGURE 1 Graphing the direct relationship between consumption and income. Two sets of data that are positively or directly related, such as consumption and income, graph as an upsloping line.

Income per Week	Consumption per Week	Point
$ 0	$ 50	a
100	100	b
200	150	c
300	200	d
400	250	e

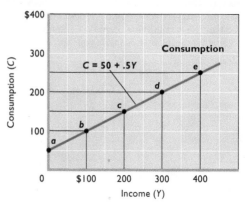

income—change in the *same* direction. An increase in consumption is associated with an increase in income; a decrease in consumption accompanies a decrease in income. When two sets of data are positively or directly related, they always graph as an *upsloping* line, as in Figure 1.

In contrast, two sets of data may be inversely related. Consider the table in Figure 2, which shows the relationship between the price of basketball tickets and game attendance at Gigantic State University (GSU). Here we have an **inverse relationship** (or negative relationship) because the two variables change in *opposite* directions. When ticket prices decrease, attendance increases. When ticket prices increase, attendance decreases. The six data points in the table in Figure 2 are plotted in the graph. Observe that an inverse relationship always graphs as a *downsloping* line.

Dependent and Independent Variables

Although it is not always easy, economists seek to determine which variable is the "cause" and which is the "effect." Or, more formally, they seek the independent variable and the dependent variable. The **independent variable** is the cause or source; it is the variable that changes first. The **dependent variable** is the effect or outcome; it is the variable that changes because of the change in the independent variable. As in our income-consumption example, income generally is the independent variable and consumption the dependent variable. Income causes consumption to be what it is rather than the other way around. Similarly, ticket prices (set in advance of the season and printed on the ticket) determine attendance at GSU basketball games; attendance at games does not determine the printed ticket prices for those games. Ticket price is the independent variable and the quantity of tickets purchased is the dependent variable.

You may recall from your high school courses that mathematicians put the independent variable (cause) on the horizontal axis and the dependent variable (effect) on the vertical axis. Economists are less tidy; their graphing of independent and dependent variables is more arbitrary. Their conventional graphing of the income-consumption relationship is consistent with mathematical convention, but economists put price and cost data on the vertical axis. Hence, economists' graphing of GSU's ticket price–attendance data differs from normal mathematical procedure. This does not present a problem, but we want you to be aware of this fact to avoid any possible confusion.

Other Things Equal

Our simple two-variable graphs purposely ignore many other factors that might affect the amount of consumption occurring at each income level or the number of people who attend GSU basketball games at each possible ticket price. When economists plot the relationship between any two variables, they employ the *ceteris paribus* (other-things-equal) assumption. Thus, in Figure 1 all factors other than income that might affect the amount of consumption are presumed to be constant or unchanged. Similarly, in Figure 2 all factors other than ticket price that might influence attendance at GSU basketball games are assumed constant. In reality, "other things" are not equal; they often change, and when they do, the relationship represented in our two tables and graphs will change. Specifically, the lines we have plotted would *shift* to new locations.

FIGURE 2 Graphing the inverse relationship between ticket prices and game attendance. Two sets of data that are negatively or inversely related, such as ticket price and the attendance at basketball games, graph as a downsloping line.

Ticket Price	Attendance, Thousands	Point
$50	0	a
40	4	b
30	8	c
20	12	d
10	16	e
0	20	f

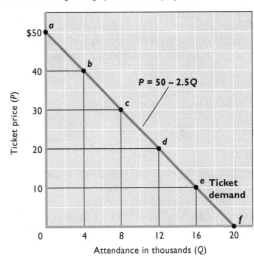

Consider a stock market "crash." The dramatic drop in the value of stocks might cause people to feel less wealthy and therefore less willing to consume at each level of income. The result might be a downward shift of the consumption line. To see this, you should plot a new consumption line in Figure 1, assuming that consumption is, say, $20 less at each income level. Note that the relationship remains direct; the line merely shifts downward to reflect less consumption spending at each income level.

Similarly, factors other than ticket prices might affect GSU game attendance. If GSU loses most of its games, attendance at GSU games might be less at each ticket price. To see this, redraw Figure 2 assuming that 2,000 fewer fans attend GSU games at each ticket price.

Slope of a Line

Lines can be described in terms of their slopes. The **slope of a straight line** is the ratio of the vertical change (the rise or drop) to the horizontal change (the run) between any two points of the line.

Positive Slope Between point *b* and point *c* in Figure 1, the rise or vertical change (the change in consumption) is +$50 and the run or horizontal change (the change in income) is +$100. Therefore:

$$\text{Slope} = \frac{\text{vertical change}}{\text{horizontal change}} = \frac{+50}{+100} = \frac{1}{2} = .5$$

Note that our slope of $\frac{1}{2}$ or .5 is positive because consumption and income change in the same direction; that is, consumption and income are directly or positively related.

The slope of .5 tells us there will be a $0.50 increase in consumption for every $1 increase in income. Similarly, there will be a $0.50 decrease in consumption for every $1 decrease in income.

Negative Slope Between any two of the identified points in Figure 2, say, point *c* and point *d*, the vertical change is −10 (the drop) and the horizontal change is +4 (the run). Therefore:

$$\text{Slope} = \frac{\text{vertical change}}{\text{horizontal change}} = \frac{-10}{+4}$$

$$= -2\frac{1}{2} = -2.5$$

This slope is negative because ticket price and attendance have an inverse relationship.

Note that on the horizontal axis attendance is stated in thousands of people. So the slope of −10/+4 or −2.5 means that lowering the price by $10 will increase attendance by

4,000 people. That ratio also implies that a $2.50 price reduction will increase attendance by 1,000 persons.

Slopes and Measurement Units The slope of a line will be affected by the choice of units for either variable. If, in our ticket price illustration, we had chosen to measure attendance in individual people, our horizontal change would have been 4,000 and the slope would have been

$$\text{Slope} = \frac{-10}{+4,000} = \frac{-1}{+400} = -.0025$$

The slope depends on the way the relevant variables are measured.

Slopes and Marginal Analysis Recall that economics is largely concerned with changes from the status quo. The concept of slope is important in economics because it reflects marginal changes—those involving 1 more (or 1 fewer) unit. For example, in Figure 1 the .5 slope shows that $0.50 of extra or marginal consumption is associated with each $1 change in income. In this example, people collectively will consume $0.50 of any $1 increase in their incomes and reduce their consumption by $0.50 for each $1 decline in income.

Infinite and Zero Slopes Many variables are unrelated or independent of one another. For example, the quantity of wristwatches purchased is not related to the price of bananas. In Figure 3a we represent the price of bananas on the vertical axis and the quantity of watches demanded on the horizontal axis. The graph of their relationship is the line parallel to the vertical axis. The line's vertical slope indicates that the same quantity of watches is purchased no matter what the price of bananas. The slope of vertical lines is *infinite*.

Similarly, aggregate consumption is completely unrelated to the nation's divorce rate. In Figure 3b we put consumption on the vertical axis and the divorce rate on the horizontal axis. The line parallel to the horizontal axis represents this lack of relatedness because the amount of consumption remains the same no matter what happens to the divorce rate. The slope of horizontal lines is *zero*.

Vertical Intercept

A line can be positioned on a graph (without plotting points) if we know just two things: its slope and its vertical intercept. We have already discussed slope. The **vertical intercept** of a line is the point where the line meets the vertical axis. In Figure 1 the intercept is $50. This intercept means that if current income were zero, consumers would still spend $50. They might do this through borrowing or by selling some of their assets. Similarly, the $50 vertical intercept in Figure 2 shows that at a $50 ticket price, GSU's basketball team would be playing in an empty arena.

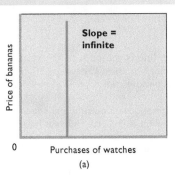 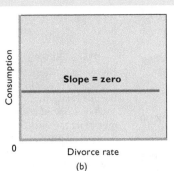

FIGURE 3 **Infinite and zero slopes.** (a) A line parallel to the vertical axis has an infinite slope. Here, purchases of watches remain the same no matter what happens to the price of bananas. (b) A line parallel to the horizontal axis has a slope of zero. In this case, consumption remains the same no matter what happens to the divorce rate. In both (a) and (b), the two variables are totally unrelated to one another.

Equation of a Linear Relationship

If we know the vertical intercept and slope, we can describe a line succinctly in equation form. In its general form, the equation of a straight line is

$$y = a + bx$$

where y = dependent variable
a = vertical intercept
b = slope of line
x = independent variable

For our income-consumption example, if C represents consumption (the dependent variable) and Y represents income (the independent variable), we can write $C = a + bY$. By substituting the known values of the intercept and the slope, we get

$$C = 50 + .5Y$$

This equation also allows us to determine the amount of consumption C at any specific level of income. You should use it to confirm that at the $250 income level, consumption is $175.

When economists reverse mathematical convention by putting the independent variable on the vertical axis and the dependent variable on the horizontal axis, then y stands for the independent variable, rather than the dependent variable in the general form. We noted previously that this case is relevant for our GSU ticket price–attendance data. If P represents the ticket price (independent variable) and Q represents attendance (dependent variable), their relationship is given by

$$P = 50 - 2.5Q$$

where the vertical intercept is 50 and the negative slope is $-2\frac{1}{2}$, or -2.5. Knowing the value of P lets us solve for Q, our dependent variable. You should use this equation to predict GSU ticket sales when the ticket price is $15.

Slope of a Nonlinear Curve

We now move from the simple world of linear relationships (straight lines) to the more complex world of nonlinear relationships (curvy lines). The slope of a straight line is the same at all its points. The slope of a line representing a non-linear relationship changes from one point to another. Such lines are always referred to as *curves*.

Consider the downsloping curve in Figure 4. Its slope is negative throughout, but the curve flattens as we move down along it. Thus, its slope constantly changes; the curve has a different slope at each point.

To measure the slope at a specific point, we draw a straight line tangent to the curve at that point. A straight line is *tangent* at a point if it touches, but does not intersect, the curve at that point. Thus line *aa* is tangent to the curve in Figure 4 at point A. The slope of the curve at that point is equal to the slope of the tangent line. Specifically, the total vertical change (drop) in the tangent line *aa* is -20 and the total horizontal change (run) is $+5$. Because the slope of the tangent line *aa* is $-20/+5$, or -4, the slope of the curve at point A is also -4.

Line *bb* in Figure 4 is tangent to the curve at point B. Following the same procedure, we find the slope at B to be $-5/+15$, or $-\frac{1}{3}$. Thus, in this flatter part of the curve, the slope is less negative.

FIGURE 4 **Determining the slopes of curves.** The slope of a nonlinear curve changes from point to point on the curve. The slope at any point (say, B) can be determined by drawing a straight line that is tangent to that point (line *bb*) and calculating the slope of that line.

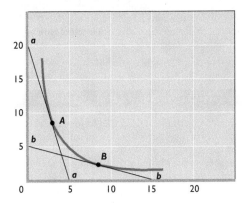

APPENDIX SUMMARY

LO1.8 Understand graphs, curves, and slopes as they relate to economics.

Graphs are a convenient and revealing way to represent economic relationships.

Two variables are positively or directly related when their values change in the same direction. The line (curve) representing two directly related variables slopes upward.

Two variables are negatively or inversely related when their values change in opposite directions. The line (curve) representing two inversely related variables slopes downward.

The value of the dependent variable (the "effect") is determined by the value of the independent variable (the "cause").

When the "other factors" that might affect a two-variable relationship are allowed to change, the graph of the relationship will likely shift to a new location.

The slope of a straight line is the ratio of the vertical change to the horizontal change between any two points. The slope of an upsloping line is positive; the slope of a downsloping line is negative.

The slope of a line or curve depends on the units used in measuring the variables. The slope is especially relevant for economics because it measures marginal changes.

The slope of a horizontal line is zero; the slope of a vertical line is infinite.

Together, the vertical intercept and slope of a line determine its location; they are used in expressing the line—and the relationship between the two variables—as an equation.

The slope of a curve at any point is determined by calculating the slope of a straight line tangent to the curve at that point.

APPENDIX TERMS AND CONCEPTS

horizontal axis

vertical axis

direct relationship

inverse relationship

independent variable

dependent variable

slope of a straight line

vertical intercept

The following and additional problems can be found in **connect** ECONOMICS

APPENDIX DISCUSSION QUESTIONS

1. Briefly explain the use of graphs as a way to represent economic relationships. What is an inverse relationship? How does it graph? What is a direct relationship? How does it graph? **LO1.8**

2. Describe the graphical relationship between ticket prices and the number of people choosing to visit amusement parks. Is that relationship consistent with the fact that, historically, park attendance and ticket prices have both risen? Explain. **LO1.8**

3. Look back at Figure 2, which shows the inverse relationship between ticket prices and game attendance at Gigantic State University. (a) Interpret the meaning of both the slope and the intercept. (b) If the slope of the line were steeper, what would that say about the amount by which ticket sales respond to increases in ticket prices? (c) If the slope of the line stayed the same but the intercept increased, what can you say about the amount by which ticket sales respond to increases in ticket prices? **LO1.8**

APPENDIX REVIEW QUESTIONS

1. Indicate whether each of the following relationships is usually a direct relationship or an inverse relationship. **LO1.8**
   a. A sports team's winning percentage and attendance at its home games.
   b. Higher temperatures and sweater sales.
   c. A person's income and how often he or she shops at discount stores.
   d. Higher gasoline prices and miles driven in automobiles.

2. Erin grows pecans. The number of bushels (*B*) that she can produce depends on the number of inches of rainfall (*R*) that her orchards get. The relationship is given algebraically as follows: $B = 3,000 + 800R$. Match each part of this equation with the correct term. **LO1.8**

B	slope
3,000	dependent variable
800	vertical intercept
R	independent variable

APPENDIX PROBLEMS

1. Graph and label as either direct or indirect the relationships you would expect to find between (a) the number of inches of rainfall per month and the sale of umbrellas, (b) the amount of tuition and the level of enrollment at a university, and (c) the popularity of an entertainer and the price of her concert tickets. **LO1.8**

2. Indicate how each of the following might affect the data shown in the table and graph in Figure 2 of this appendix: **LO1.8**
   a. GSU's athletic director schedules higher-quality opponents.
   b. An NBA team locates in the city where GSU plays.
   c. GSU contracts to have all its home games televised.

3. The following table contains data on the relationship between saving and income. Rearrange these data into a meaningful order and graph them on the accompanying grid. What is the slope of the line? The vertical intercept? Write the equation that represents this line. What would you predict saving to be at the $12,500 level of income? **LO1.8**

Income per Year	Saving per Year
$15,000	$1,000
0	−500
10,000	500
5,000	0
20,000	1,500

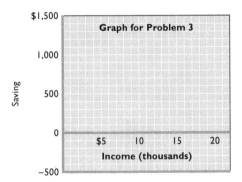

4. Construct a table from the data shown in the accompanying graph. Which is the dependent variable and which is the independent variable? Summarize the data in equation form. **LO1.8**

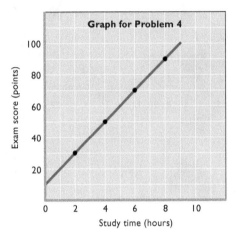

5. Suppose that when the interest rate on loans is 16 percent, businesses find it unprofitable to invest in machinery and equipment. However, when the interest rate is 14 percent, $5 billion worth of investment is profitable. At 12 percent interest, a total of $10 billion of investment is profitable. Similarly, total investment increases by $5 billion for each successive 2-percentage-point decline in the interest rate. Describe the relevant relationship between the interest rate and investment in a table, on a graph, and as an equation. Put the interest rate on the vertical axis and investment on the horizontal axis. In your equation use the form $i = a + bI$, where *i* is the interest rate, *a* is the vertical intercept, *b* is the slope of the line (which is negative), and *I* is the level of investment. **LO1.8**

6. Suppose that $C = a + bY$, where *C* = consumption, *a* = consumption at zero income, *b* = slope, and *Y* = income. **LO1.8**
   a. Are *C* and *Y* positively related or are they negatively related?
   b. If graphed, would the curve for this equation slope upward or slope downward?
   c. Are the variables *C* and *Y* inversely related or directly related?
   d. What is the value of *C* if $a = 10$, $b = 0.50$, and $Y = 200$?
   e. What is the value of *Y* if $C = 100$, $a = 10$, and $b = 0.25$?

7. The accompanying graph shows curve *XX′* and tangents at points *A*, *B*, and *C*. Calculate the slope of the curve at these three points. **LO1.8**

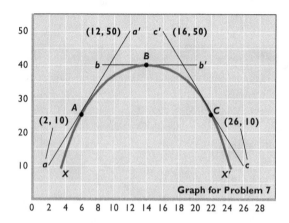

Graph for Problem 7

8. In the accompanying graph, is the slope of curve *AA′* positive or negative? Does the slope increase or decrease as we move along the curve from *A* to *A′*? Answer the same two questions for curve *BB′*. **LO1.8**

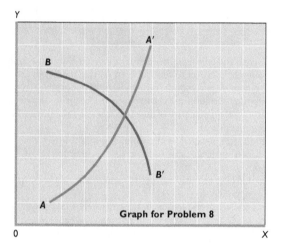

Graph for Problem 8

CHAPTER 2

The Market System and the Circular Flow

Learning Objectives

LO2.1 Differentiate between laissez-faire capitalism, the command system, and the market system.

LO2.2 List the main characteristics of the market system.

LO2.3 Explain how the market system answers the five fundamental questions of what to produce, how to produce, who obtains the output, how to adjust to change, and how to promote progress.

LO2.4 Explain the operation of the "invisible hand" and why market economies usually do a better job than command economies at efficiently transforming economic resources into desirable output.

LO2.5 Describe the mechanics of the circular flow model.

LO2.6 Explain how the market system deals with risk.

You are at the mall. Suppose you were assigned to compile a list of all the individual goods and services there, including the different brands and variations of each type of product. That task would be daunting and the list would be long! And even though a single shopping mall contains a remarkable quantity and variety of goods, it is only a tiny part of the national economy.

　　Who decided that the particular goods and services available at the mall and in the broader economy should be produced? How did the producers determine which technology and types of resources to use in producing these particular goods? Who will obtain these products? What accounts for the new and improved products among these goods? This chapter will answer these and related questions.

Economic Systems

LO2.1 Differentiate between laissez-faire capitalism, the command system, and the market system.

Every society needs to develop an **economic system**—a particular set of institutional arrangements and a coordinating mechanism—to respond to the economizing problem. The economic system has to determine what goods are produced, how they are produced, who gets them, how to accommodate change, and how to promote technological progress.

Economic systems differ as to (1) who owns the factors of production and (2) the method used to motivate, coordinate, and direct economic activity.

Economics systems can be classified by the degree to which they rely upon decentralized decision making based upon markets and prices or centralized government control based upon orders and mandates. At one extreme lies *laissez-faire capitalism*, in which government intervention is at a very minimum and markets and prices are allowed to direct nearly all economic activity. At the other extreme lie *command systems*, in which governments have total control over all economic activity. The vast majority of national economies lie somewhere in the middle, utilizing some mixture of centralized government regulation and decentralized markets and prices. These economies are said to have *market systems* or *mixed economies*.

Laissez-Faire Capitalism

In **laissez-faire capitalism**—or "pure capitalism"—the government's role would be limited to protecting private property from theft and aggression and establishing a legal environment in which contracts would be enforced and people could interact in markets to buy and sell goods, services, and resources.

The term "laissez-faire" is the French for "let it be," that is, keep the government from interfering with the economy. Proponents of laissez-faire believe that such interference reduces human welfare. They maintain that any government that intervenes widely in the economy will end up being corrupted by special interests that will use the government's economic influence to benefit themselves rather than society at large.

To prevent that from happening, the proponents of laissez-faire argue that government should restrict itself to preventing individuals and firms from coercing each other.

By doing so, it will ensure that only mutually beneficial economic transactions get negotiated and completed. That should lead to the highest possible level of human satisfaction because, after all, who knows better what people want than the people themselves?

It is important to note, however, that no society has ever employed a laissez-faire system. In fact, no government has *ever* limited its economic actions to the short list of functions that would be allowed under laissez-faire. Instead, every government known to history has undertaken a wider range of economic activities, many of which are widely popular and which include industrial safety regulations, various taxes and subsidies, occupational licensing requirements, and income redistribution.

ORIGIN OF THE IDEA

02.1
Laissez-faire

Thus, you should think of laissez-faire capitalism as a hypothetical system that is viewed by proponents as the ideal to which all economic systems should strive—but which is opposed by those who welcome greater government intervention in the economy.

The Command System

The polar opposite of laissez-faire capitalism is the **command system,** in which government owns most property resources and economic decision making is set by a central economic plan created and enforced by the government. The command system is also known as *socialism* or *communism*.

Under the command system, a central planning board appointed by the government makes all the major decisions concerning the use of resources, the composition and distribution of output, and the organization of production. The government owns most of the business firms, which produce according to government directives. The central planning board determines production goals for each enterprise and specifies the amount of resources to be allocated to each enterprise so that it can reach its production goals. The division of output between capital and consumer goods is centrally decided, and capital goods are allocated among industries on the basis of the central planning board's long-term priorities.

A pure command economy would rely exclusively on a central plan to allocate the government-owned property resources. But, in reality, even the preeminent command economy—the Soviet Union—tolerated some private ownership and incorporated some markets before its collapse in 1992. Recent reforms in Russia and most of the eastern European nations have, to one degree or another, transformed their command economies to capitalistic, market-oriented systems. China's reforms have not gone as far, but they have greatly reduced the reliance on central planning. Although government ownership of resources and capital in China is still extensive, the nation has increasingly relied on free markets to organize and coordinate its economy. North Korea and Cuba are the last prominent remaining examples of largely centrally planned economies. Other countries using mainly the command system include Turkmenistan, Laos, Belarus, Myanmar, and Iran. Later in this chapter, we will explore the main reasons for the general demise of command systems.

The Market System

The vast majority of the world's economies utilize the **market system,** which is also known as *capitalism* or the *mixed economy.*

The market system is characterized by a mixture of centralized government economic initiatives and decentralized actions taken by individuals and firms. The precise mixture varies from country to country, but in each case the system features the private ownership of resources and the use of markets and prices to coordinate and direct economic activity.

In the market system, individuals and businesses seek to achieve their economic goals through their own decisions regarding work, consumption, or production. The system allows for the private ownership of capital, communicates through prices, and coordinates economic activity through markets—places where buyers and sellers come together to buy and sell goods, services, and resources.

Participants act in their own self-interest and goods and services are produced and resources are supplied by whoever is willing and able to do so. The result is competition among independently acting buyers and sellers of each product and resource and an economic system in which decision making is widely dispersed.

The market system also offers high potential monetary rewards that create powerful incentives for existing firms to innovate and for entrepreneurs to pioneer new products and processes despite the financial risks involved and despite most innovations failing to catch on with consumers.

It is the case, however, that in the capitalism practiced in the United States and most other countries, the government plays a substantial role in the economy. It not only provides the rules for economic activity but also promotes economic stability and growth, provides certain goods and services that would otherwise be underproduced or not produced at all, and modifies the distribution of income. The government, however, is not the dominant economic force in deciding what to produce, how to produce it, and who will get it. That force is the market.

Characteristics of the Market System

LO2.2 List the main characteristics of the market system.
An examination of some of the key features of the market system in detail will be very instructive.

Private Property

In a market system, private individuals and firms, not the government, own most of the property resources (land and capital). It is this extensive private ownership of capital that gives capitalism its name. This right of **private property,** coupled with the freedom to negotiate binding legal contracts, enables individuals and businesses to obtain, use, and dispose of property resources as they see fit. The right of property owners to designate who will receive their property when they die helps sustain the institution of private property.

The most important consequence of property rights is that they encourage people to cooperate by helping to ensure that only *mutually agreeable* economic transactions take place. To consider why this is true, imagine a world without legally enforceable property rights. In such a world, the strong could simply take whatever they wanted from the weak without giving them any compensation. But in a world of legally enforceable property rights, any person wanting something from you has to get you to agree to give it to them. And you can say no. The result is that if they really want what you have, they must offer you something that you value more highly in return. That is, they must offer you a mutually agreeable economic transaction—one that benefits you as well as them.

Property rights also encourage investment, innovation, exchange, maintenance of property, and economic growth. Nobody would stock a store, build a factory, or clear land for farming if someone else, or the government itself, could take that property for his or her own benefit.

Property rights also extend to intellectual property through patents, copyrights, and trademarks. Such long-term protection encourages people to write books, music, and computer programs and to invent new products and production processes without fear that others will steal them and the rewards they may bring.

Moreover, property rights facilitate exchange. The title to an automobile or the deed to a cattle ranch assures the buyer that the seller is the legitimate owner. Also, property rights encourage owners to maintain or improve their property so as to preserve or increase its value. Finally, property rights enable people to use their time and resources to produce more goods and services, rather than using them to protect and retain the property they have already produced or acquired.

Freedom of Enterprise and Choice

Closely related to private ownership of property is freedom of enterprise and choice. The market system requires that various economic units make certain choices, which are expressed and implemented in the economy's markets:

- **Freedom of enterprise** ensures that entrepreneurs and private businesses are free to obtain and use economic resources to produce their choice of goods and services and to sell them in their chosen markets.

- **Freedom of choice** enables owners to employ or dispose of their property and money as they see fit. It also allows workers to try to enter any line of work for which they are qualified. Finally, it ensures that consumers are free to buy the goods and services that best satisfy their wants and that their budgets allow.

These choices are free only within broad legal limitations, of course. Illegal choices such as selling human organs or buying illicit drugs are punished through fines and imprisonment. (Global Perspective 2.1 reveals that the degree of economic freedom varies greatly from economy to economy.)

Self-Interest

In the market system, **self-interest** is the motivating force of the various economic units as they express their free choices. Self-interest simply means that each economic unit tries to achieve its own particular goal, which usually requires delivering something of value to others. Entrepreneurs try to maximize profit or minimize loss.

ORIGIN OF THE IDEA

02.2
Self-interest

Property owners try to get the highest price for the sale or rent of their resources. Workers try to maximize their utility (satisfaction) by finding jobs that offer the best combination of wages, hours,

GLOBAL PERSPECTIVE 2.1

Index of Economic Freedom, Selected Economies

The Index of Economic Freedom measures economic freedom using 10 major groupings such as trade policy, property rights, and government intervention, with each category containing more than 50 specific criteria. The index then ranks 179 economies according to their degree of economic freedom. A few selected rankings for 2012 are listed below.

FREE
1 Hong Kong
3 Australia
5 Switzerland

MOSTLY FREE
10 United States
18 Taiwan
26 Germany

MOSTLY UNFREE
99 Brazil
123 India
144 Russia

REPRESSED
158 Argentina
171 Iran
179 North Korea

Source: Used by permission of The Heritage Foundation, **www.heritage.org**.

fringe benefits, and working conditions. Consumers try to obtain the products they want at the lowest possible price and apportion their expenditures to maximize their utility. The motive of self-interest gives direction and consistency to what might otherwise be a chaotic economy.

Competition

The market system depends on **competition** among economic units. The basis of this competition is freedom of choice exercised in pursuit of a monetary return. Very broadly defined, competition requires

- Two or more buyers and two or more sellers acting independently in a particular product or resource market. (Usually there are many more than two buyers or sellers.)

- Freedom of sellers and buyers to enter or leave markets, on the basis of their economic self-interest.

Competition among buyers and sellers diffuses economic power within the businesses and households that make up the economy. When there are many buyers and sellers acting independently in a market, no single buyer or seller can dictate the price of the product or resource because others can undercut that price.

Competition also implies that producers can enter or leave an industry; no insurmountable barriers prevent an industry's expanding or contracting. This freedom of an industry to expand or contract provides the economy with the flexibility needed to remain efficient over time. Freedom of entry and exit enables the economy to adjust to changes in consumer tastes, technology, and resource availability.

The diffusion of economic power inherent in competition limits the potential abuse of that power. A producer that charges more than the competitive market price will lose sales to other producers. An employer who pays less than the competitive market wage rate will lose workers to other employers. A firm that fails to exploit new technology will lose profits to firms that do. A firm that produces shoddy products will be punished as customers switch to higher-quality items made by rival firms. Competition is the basic regulatory force in the market system.

Markets and Prices

We may wonder why an economy based on self-interest does not collapse in chaos. If consumers want breakfast cereal, but businesses choose to produce running shoes and resource suppliers decide to make computer software, production would seem to be deadlocked by the apparent inconsistencies of free choices.

In reality, the millions of decisions made by households and businesses are highly coordinated with one another by markets and prices, which are key components of the market system. They give the system its ability to coordinate millions of daily economic decisions. A **market** is an institution or mechanism that brings buyers ("demanders") and sellers ("suppliers") into contact. A market system conveys the decisions made by buyers and sellers of products and resources. The decisions made on each side of the market determine a set of product and resource prices that guide resource owners, entrepreneurs, and consumers as they make and revise their choices and pursue their self-interest.

Just as competition is the regulatory mechanism of the market system, the market system itself is the organizing and coordinating mechanism. It is an elaborate communication network through which innumerable individual free choices are recorded, summarized, and balanced.

Those who respond to market signals and heed market dictates are rewarded with greater profit and income; those who do not respond to those signals and choose to ignore market dictates are penalized. Through this mechanism society decides what the economy should produce, how production can be organized efficiently, and how the fruits of production are to be distributed among the various units that make up the economy.

QUICK REVIEW 2.1

- The market system rests on the private ownership of property and on freedom of enterprise and freedom of choice.
- Property rights encourage people to cooperate and make mutually agreeable economic transactions.
- The market system permits consumers, resource suppliers, and businesses to pursue and further their self-interest.
- Competition diffuses economic power and limits the actions of any single seller or buyer.
- The coordinating mechanism of capitalism is a system of markets and prices.

Technology and Capital Goods

In the market system, competition, freedom of choice, self-interest, and personal reward provide the opportunity and motivation for technological advance. The monetary rewards for new products or production techniques accrue directly to the innovator. The market system therefore encourages extensive use and rapid development of complex capital goods: tools, machinery, large-scale factories, and facilities for storage, communication, transportation, and marketing.

Advanced technology and capital goods are important because the most direct methods of production are often the least efficient. The only way to avoid that inefficiency is to rely on capital goods. It would be ridiculous for a farmer to go at production with bare hands. There are huge benefits to be derived from creating and using such capital equipment as plows, tractors, and storage bins. More efficient production means much more abundant output.

Specialization

The extent to which market economies rely on **specialization** is extraordinary. Specialization means using the resources of an individual, firm, region, or nation to produce one or a few goods or services rather than the entire range of goods and services. Those goods and services are then exchanged for a full range of desired products. The majority of consumers produce virtually none of the goods and services they consume, and they consume little or nothing of the items they produce. The person working nine to five installing windows in commercial aircraft may rarely fly. Many farmers sell their milk to the local dairy and then buy margarine at the local grocery store. Society learned long ago that self-sufficiency breeds inefficiency. The jack-of-all-trades may be a very colorful individual but is certainly not an efficient producer.

Division of Labor   Human specialization—called the **division of labor**—contributes to a society's output in several ways:

- *Specialization makes use of differences in ability.* Specialization enables individuals to take advantage of existing differences in their abilities and skills. If Peyton is strong, athletic, and good at throwing a football and Beyoncé is beautiful, is agile, and can sing, their distribution of talents can be most efficiently used if Peyton plays professional football and Beyoncé records songs and gives concerts.

ORIGIN OF THE IDEA

O2.3

Specialization: division of labor

- *Specialization fosters learning by doing.* Even if the abilities of two people are identical, specialization may still be advantageous. By devoting time to a single task, a person is more likely to develop the skills required and to improve techniques than by working at a number of different tasks. You learn to be a good lawyer by studying and practicing law.

- *Specialization saves time.* By devoting time to a single task, a person avoids the loss of time incurred in shifting from one job to another. Also, time is saved by not "fumbling around" with tasks that one is not trained to do.

For all these reasons, specialization increases the total output society derives from limited resources.

Geographic Specialization   Specialization also works on a regional and international basis. It is conceivable that oranges could be grown in Nebraska, but because of the unsuitability of the land, rainfall, and temperature, the costs would be very high. And it is conceivable that wheat could be grown in Florida, but such production would be costly for similar geographical reasons. So Nebraskans produce products—wheat in particular—for which their resources are best suited, and Floridians do the same,

producing oranges and other citrus fruits. By specializing, both economies produce more than is needed locally. Then, very sensibly, Nebraskans and Floridians swap some of their surpluses—wheat for oranges, oranges for wheat.

Similarly, on an international scale, the United States specializes in producing such items as commercial aircraft and software, which it sells abroad in exchange for video cameras from Japan, bananas from Honduras, and woven baskets from Thailand. Both human specialization and geographic specialization are needed to achieve efficiency in the use of limited resources.

Use of Money

A rather obvious characteristic of any economic system is the extensive use of money. Money performs several functions, but first and foremost it is a **medium of exchange.** It makes trade easier.

Specialization requires exchange. Exchange can, and sometimes does, occur through **barter**—swapping goods for goods, say, wheat for oranges. But barter poses serious problems because it requires a *coincidence of wants* between the buyer and the seller. In our example, we assumed that Nebraskans had excess wheat to trade and wanted oranges. And we assumed that Floridians had excess oranges to trade and wanted wheat. So an exchange occurred. But if such a coincidence of wants is missing, trade is stymied.

Suppose that Nebraska has no interest in Florida's oranges but wants potatoes from Idaho. And suppose that Idaho wants Florida's oranges but not Nebraska's wheat. And, to complicate matters, suppose that Florida wants some of Nebraska's wheat but none of Idaho's potatoes. We summarize the situation in Figure 2.1.

In none of the cases shown in the figure is there a coincidence of wants. Trade by barter clearly would be difficult. Instead, people in each state use **money,** which is simply a convenient social invention to facilitate exchanges of goods and services. Historically, people have used cattle, cigarettes, shells, stones, pieces of metal, and many other commodities, with varying degrees of success, as money. To serve as money, an item needs to pass only one test: It must be generally acceptable to sellers in exchange for their goods and services. Money is socially defined; whatever society accepts as a medium of exchange *is* money.

Today, most economies use pieces of paper as money. The use of paper dollars (currency) as a medium of exchange is what enables Nebraska, Florida, and Idaho to overcome their trade stalemate, as demonstrated in Figure 2.1.

On a global basis, specialization and exchange are complicated by the fact that different nations have different currencies. But markets in which currencies are bought

FIGURE 2.1 Money facilitates trade when wants do not coincide. The use of money as a medium of exchange permits trade to be accomplished despite a noncoincidence of wants. (1) Nebraska trades the wheat that Florida wants for money from Floridians; (2) Nebraska trades the money it receives from Florida for the potatoes it wants from Idaho; (3) Idaho trades the money it receives from Nebraska for the oranges it wants from Florida.

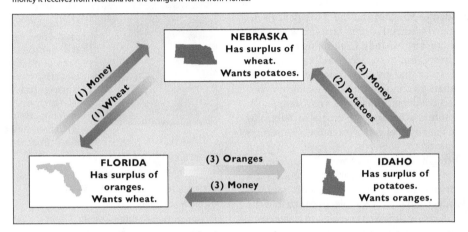

and sold make it possible for people living in different countries to exchange goods and services without resorting to barter.

Active, but Limited, Government

An active, but limited, government is the final characteristic of market systems in modern advanced industrial economies. Although a market system promotes a high degree of efficiency in the use of its resources, it has certain inherent shortcomings, called "market failures." We will discover in subsequent chapters that governments can often increase the overall effectiveness of a market system in several ways. That being said, governments have their own set of shortcomings that can themselves cause substantial misallocations of resources. Consequently, we will also investigate several types of "government failure."

QUICK REVIEW 2.2

- The market systems of modern industrial economies are characterized by extensive use of technologically advanced capital goods. Such goods help these economies achieve greater efficiency in production.
- Specialization is extensive in market systems; it enhances efficiency and output by enabling individuals, regions, and nations to produce the goods and services for which their resources are best suited.
- The use of money in market systems facilitates the exchange of goods and services that specialization requires.

Five Fundamental Questions

LO2.3 Explain how the market system answers the five fundamental questions of what to produce, how to produce, who obtains the output, how to adjust to change, and how to promote progress.

The key features of the market system help explain how market economies respond to five fundamental questions:

- What goods and services will be produced?
- How will the goods and services be produced?
- Who will get the goods and services?
- How will the system accommodate change?
- How will the system promote progress?

These five questions highlight the economic choices underlying the production possibilities curve discussed in Chapter 1. They reflect the reality of scarce resources in a world of unlimited wants. All economies, whether market or command, must address these five questions.

What Will Be Produced?

How will a market system decide on the specific types and quantities of goods to be produced? The simple answer is this: The goods and services that can be produced at a continuing profit will be produced, while those whose production generates a continuing loss will be discontinued. Profits and losses are the difference between the total revenue (TR) a firm receives from the sale of its products and the total cost (TC) of producing those products. (For economists, total costs include not only wage and salary payments to labor, and interest and rental payments for capital and land, but also payments to the entrepreneur for organizing and combining the other resources to produce a product.)

Continuing economic profit (TR > TC) in an industry results in expanded production and the movement of resources toward that industry. Existing firms grow and new firms enter. The industry expands. Continuing losses (TC > TR) in an industry lead to reduced production and the exit of resources from that industry. Some existing firms shrink in size; others go out of business. The industry contracts. In the market system, consumers are sovereign (in command). **Consumer sovereignty** is crucial in determining the types and quantities of goods produced. Consumers spend their income on the goods they are most willing and able to buy. Through these **"dollar votes"** they register their wants in the market. If the dollar votes for a certain product are great enough to create a profit, businesses will produce that product and offer it for sale. In contrast, if the dollar votes do not create sufficient revenues to cover costs, businesses will not produce the product. So the consumers are sovereign. They collectively direct resources to industries that are meeting consumer wants and away from industries that are not meeting consumer wants.

The dollar votes of consumers determine not only which industries will continue to exist but also which products will survive or fail. Only profitable industries, firms, and products survive. So firms are not as free to produce whatever products they wish as one might otherwise think. Consumers' buying decisions make the production of some products profitable and the production of other products unprofitable, thus restricting the choice of businesses in deciding what to produce. Businesses must match their production choices with consumer choices or else face losses and eventual bankruptcy.

The same holds true for resource suppliers. The employment of resources derives from the sale of the goods and services that the resources help produce. Autoworkers are employed because automobiles are sold. There are few remaining professors of early Latin because there are few people desiring to learn the Latin language. Resource suppliers, desiring to earn income, are not truly free to allocate their resources to the production of goods that consumers do not value highly. Consumers register their preferences in the market; producers and resource suppliers, prompted by their own self-interest, respond appropriately.

How Will the Goods and Services Be Produced?

What combinations of resources and technologies will be used to produce goods and services? How will the

CONSIDER THIS . . .

McHits and McMisses

McDonald's has introduced several new menu items over the decades. Some have been profitable "hits," while others have been "misses." In a market system, consumers ultimately decide whether a menu item is profitable and therefore whether it stays on the McDonald's menu.

- Hulaburger (1962)—McMiss
- Filet-O-Fish (1963)—McHit
- Strawberry shortcake (1966)—McMiss
- Big Mac (1968)—McHit
- Hot apple pie (1968)—McHit
- Egg McMuffin (1975)—McHit
- Drive-thru (1975)—McHit
- Chicken McNuggets (1983)—McHit
- Extra Value Meal (1991)—McHit
- McLean Deluxe (1991)—McMiss
- Arch Deluxe (1996)—McMiss
- 55-cent special (1997)—McMiss
- Big Xtra (1999)—McHit
- McSalad Shaker (2000)—McMiss
- McGriddle (2003)—McHit
- Snack Wrap (2006)—McHit

Source: "Polishing the Golden Arches," *Forbes,* June 15, 1998, pp. 42–43, updated. Reprinted by permission of Forbes Media LLC © 2010.

production be organized? The answer: In combinations and ways that minimize the cost per unit of output. This is true because inefficiency drives up costs and lowers profits. As a result, any firm wishing to maximize its profits will make great efforts to minimize production costs. These efforts will include using the right mix of labor and capital, given the prices and productivity of those resources. They also mean locating production facilities optimally to hold down production and transportation expenses.

Those efforts will be intensified if the firm faces competition, as consumers strongly prefer low prices and will shift their purchases over to the firms that can produce a quality product at the lowest possible price. Any firm foolish enough to use higher-cost production methods will go bankrupt as it is undersold by its more efficient competitors who can still make a profit when

TABLE 2.1 Three Techniques for Producing $15 Worth of Bar Soap

Resource	Price per Unit of Resource	Technique 1 Units	Technique 1 Cost	Technique 2 Units	Technique 2 Cost	Technique 3 Units	Technique 3 Cost
Labor	$2	4	$ 8	2	$ 4	1	$ 2
Land	1	1	1	3	3	4	4
Capital	3	1	3	1	3	2	6
Entrepreneurial ability	3	1	3	1	3	1	3
Total cost of $15 worth of bar soap			$15		$13		$15

selling at a lower price. Simply stated: Competition eliminates high-cost producers.

Least-cost production means that firms must employ the most economically efficient technique of production in producing their output. The most efficient production technique depends on

- The available technology, that is, the available body of knowledge and techniques that can be used to combine economic resources to produce the desired results.

- The prices of the needed resources.

A technique that requires just a few inputs of resources to produce a specific output may be highly inefficient economically if those resources are valued very highly in the market. Economic efficiency requires obtaining a particular output of product with the least input of scarce resources, when both output and resource inputs are measured in dollars and cents. The combination of resources that will produce, say, $15 worth of bathroom soap at the lowest possible cost is the most efficient.

Suppose there are three possible techniques for producing the desired $15 worth of bars of soap. Suppose also that the quantity of each resource required by each production technique and the prices of the required resources are as shown in Table 2.1. By multiplying the required quantities of each resource by its price in each of the three techniques, we can determine the total cost of producing $15 worth of soap by means of each technique.

Technique 2 is economically the most efficient because it is the least costly. It enables society to obtain $15 worth of output by using a smaller amount of resources—$13 worth—than the $15 worth required by the two other techniques. Competition will dictate that producers use technique 2. Thus, the question of how goods

WORKED PROBLEMS

W2.1
Least-cost production

will be produced is answered. They will be produced in a least-cost way.

A change in either technology or resource prices, however, may cause a firm to shift from the technology it is using. If the price of labor falls to $0.50, technique 1 becomes more desirable than technique 2. Firms will find they can lower their costs by shifting to a technology that uses more of the resource whose price has fallen. Exercise: Would a new technique involving 1 unit of labor, 4 of land, 1 of capital, and 1 of entrepreneurial ability be preferable to the techniques listed in Table 2.1, assuming the resource prices shown there?

Who Will Get the Output?

The market system enters the picture in two ways when determining the distribution of total output. Generally, any product will be distributed to consumers on the basis of their ability and willingness to pay its existing market price. If the price of some product, say, a small sailboat, is $3,000, then buyers who are willing and able to pay that price will "sail, sail away." Consumers who are unwilling or unable to pay the price will be "sitting on the dock of the bay."

The ability to pay the prices for sailboats and other products depends on the amount of income that consumers have, along with the prices of, and preferences for, various goods. If consumers have sufficient income and want to spend their money on a particular good, they can have it. The amount of income they have depends on (1) the quantities of the property and human resources they supply and (2) the prices those resources command in the resource market. Resource prices (wages, interest, rent, profit) are crucial in determining the size of each person's income and therefore each person's ability to buy part of the economy's output. If a lawyer earning $200 an hour and a janitor earning $10 an hour both work the same number of hours each year, then each year the lawyer will be able to purchase 20 times more of society's output than the janitor.

How Will the System Accommodate Change?

Market systems are dynamic: Consumer preferences, technologies, and resource supplies all change. This means that the particular allocation of resources that is now the most efficient for a specific pattern of consumer tastes, range of technological alternatives, and amount of available resources will become obsolete and inefficient as consumer preferences change, new techniques of production are discovered, and resource supplies change over time. Can the market economy adjust to such changes?

Suppose consumer tastes change. For instance, assume that consumers decide they want more fruit juice and less milk than the economy currently provides. Those changes in consumer tastes will be communicated to producers through an increase in spending on fruit and a decline in spending on milk. Other things equal, prices and profits in the fruit juice industry will rise and those in the milk industry will fall. Self-interest will induce existing competitors to expand output and entice new competitors to enter the prosperous fruit industry and will in time force firms to scale down—or even exit—the depressed milk industry.

The higher prices and greater economic profit in the fruit-juice industry will not only induce that industry to expand but will also give it the revenue needed to obtain the resources essential to its growth. Higher prices and profits will permit fruit producers to attract more resources from less urgent alternative uses. The reverse occurs in the milk industry, where fewer workers and other resources are employed. These adjustments in the economy are appropriate responses to the changes in consumer tastes. This is consumer sovereignty at work.

The market system is a gigantic communications system. Through changes in prices and profits, it communicates changes in such basic matters as consumer tastes and elicits appropriate responses from businesses and resource suppliers. By affecting price and profits, changes in consumer tastes direct the expansion of some industries and the contraction of others. Those adjustments are conveyed to the resource market. As expanding industries employ more resources and contracting industries employ fewer, the resulting changes in resource prices (wages and salaries, for example) and income flows guide resources from the contracting industries to the expanding industries.

This directing or guiding function of prices and profits is a core element of the market system. Without such a system, a government planning board or some other administrative agency would have to direct businesses and resources into the appropriate industries. A similar analysis shows that the system can and does adjust to other fundamental changes—for example, to changes in technology and in the prices of various resources.

How Will the System Promote Progress?

Society desires economic growth (greater output) and higher standards of living (greater output *per person*). How does the market system promote technological improvements and capital accumulation, both of which contribute to a higher standard of living for society?

Technological Advance The market system provides a strong incentive for technological advance and enables better products and processes to supplant inferior ones. An entrepreneur or firm that introduces a popular new product will gain revenue and economic profit at the expense of rivals. Firms that are highly profitable one year may find they are in financial trouble just a few years later. Technological advance also includes new and improved methods that reduce production or distribution costs. By passing part of its cost reduction on to the consumer through a lower product price, a firm can increase sales and obtain economic profit at the expense of rival firms.

Moreover, the market system promotes the *rapid spread* of technological advance throughout an industry. Rival firms must follow the lead of the most innovative firm or else suffer immediate losses and eventual failure. In some cases, the result is **creative destruction:** The creation of new products and production methods completely destroys the market positions of firms that are wedded to existing products and older ways of doing business. Example: The advent of compact discs largely demolished long-play vinyl records, and iPods and other digital technologies subsequently supplanted CDs.

Capital Accumulation Most technological advances require additional capital goods. The market system provides the resources necessary to produce additional capital goods through increased dollar votes for those goods. That is, the market system acknowledges dollar voting for capital goods as well as for consumer goods.

But who counts the dollar votes for capital goods? Answer: Entrepreneurs and business owners. As receivers of profit income, they often use part of that income to purchase capital goods. Doing so yields even greater profit income in the future if the technological innovation that required the additional capital goods is successful. Also, by paying interest or selling ownership shares, the entrepreneur and firm can attract some of the income of households as saving to increase their dollar votes for the production of more capital goods.

QUICK REVIEW 2.3

- The output mix of the market system is determined by profits, which in turn depend heavily on consumer preferences. Economic profits cause industries to expand; losses cause industries to contract.
- Competition forces industries to use the least costly production methods.
- Competitive markets reallocate resources in response to changes in consumer tastes, technological advances, and changes in availability of resources.
- In a market economy, consumer income and product prices determine how output will be distributed.
- Competitive markets create incentives for technological advance and capital accumulation, both of which contribute to increases in standards of living.

The "Invisible Hand"

LO2.4 Explain the operation of the "invisible hand" and why market economies usually do a better job than command economies at efficiently transforming economic resources into desirable output.

In his 1776 book *The Wealth of Nations*, Adam Smith first noted that the operation of a market system creates a curious unity between private interests and social interests. Firms and resource suppliers, seeking to further their own self-interest and operating within the framework of a highly competitive market system, will simultaneously, as though guided by an **"invisible hand,"** promote the public or social interest. For example, we have seen that in a competitive environment, businesses seek to build new and improved products to increase profits. Those enhanced products increase society's well-being. Businesses also use the least costly combination of resources to produce a specific output because doing so is in their self-interest. To act otherwise would be to forgo profit or even to risk business failure. But, at the same time, to use scarce resources in the least costly way is clearly in the social interest as well. It "frees up" resources to produce other things that society desires.

Self-interest, awakened and guided by the competitive market system, is what induces responses appropriate to the changes in society's wants. Businesses seeking to make higher profits and to avoid losses, and resource suppliers pursuing greater monetary rewards, negotiate changes in the allocation of resources and end up with the output that society wants. Competition controls or guides self-interest such that self-interest automatically and quite unintentionally furthers the best interest of society. The invisible hand ensures that when firms maximize their profits and resource suppliers maximize their incomes, these groups also help maximize society's output and income.

Of the various virtues of the market system, three merit reemphasis:

- *Efficiency* The market system promotes the efficient use of resources by guiding them into the production of the goods and services most wanted by society. It forces the use of the most efficient techniques in organizing resources for production, and it encourages the development and adoption of new and more efficient production techniques.
- *Incentives* The market system encourages skill acquisition, hard work, and innovation. Greater work skills and effort mean greater production and higher incomes, which usually translate into a higher standard of living. Similarly, the assuming of risks by entrepreneurs can result in substantial profit incomes. Successful innovations generate economic rewards.
- *Freedom* The major noneconomic argument for the market system is its emphasis on personal freedom. In contrast to central planning, the market system coordinates economic activity without coercion. The market system permits—indeed, it thrives on—freedom of enterprise and choice. Entrepreneurs and workers are free to further their own self-interest, subject to the rewards and penalties imposed by the market system itself.

Of course, no economic system, including the market system, is flawless. In Chapter 4 we will explain two well-known shortcomings of the market system and examine the government policies that try to remedy them.

The Demise of the Command Systems

Our discussion of how a market system answers the five fundamental questions provides insights on why the command systems of the Soviet Union, eastern Europe, and China (prior to its market reforms) failed. Those systems encountered two insurmountable problems.

The Coordination Problem The first difficulty was the coordination problem. The central planners had to coordinate the millions of individual decisions by consumers, resource suppliers, and businesses. Consider the setting up of a factory to produce tractors. The central planners had to establish a realistic annual production target, for example, 1,000 tractors. They then had to make available all the necessary inputs—labor, machinery, electric power, steel, tires, glass, paint, transportation—for the production and delivery of those 1,000 tractors.

Because the outputs of many industries serve as inputs to other industries, the failure of any single industry to achieve its output target caused a chain reaction of repercussions. For example, if iron mines, for want of machinery or labor or transportation, did not supply the steel industry with the required inputs of iron ore, the steel mills were unable to fulfill the input needs of the many industries that depended on steel. Those steel-using industries (such as tractor, automobile, and transportation) were unable to fulfill their planned production goals. Eventually the chain reaction spread to all firms that used steel as an input and from there to other input buyers or final consumers.

The coordination problem became more difficult as the economies expanded. Products and production processes grew more sophisticated and the number of industries requiring planning increased. Planning techniques that worked for the simpler economy proved highly inadequate and inefficient for the larger economy. Bottlenecks and production stoppages became the norm, not the exception. In trying to cope, planners further suppressed product variety, focusing on one or two products in each product category.

A lack of a reliable success indicator added to the coordination problem in the Soviet Union and China prior to its market reforms. We have seen that market economies rely on profit as a success indicator. Profit depends on consumer demand, production efficiency, and product quality. In contrast, the major success indicator for the command economies usually was a quantitative production target that the central planners assigned. Production costs, product quality, and product mix were secondary considerations. Managers and workers often sacrificed product quality and variety because they were being awarded bonuses for meeting quantitative, not qualitative, targets. If meeting production goals meant sloppy assembly work and little product variety, so be it.

It was difficult at best for planners to assign quantitative production targets without unintentionally producing distortions in output. If the plan specified a production target for producing nails in terms of *weight* (tons of nails), the enterprise made only large nails. But if it specified the target as a *quantity* (thousands of nails), the firm made all small nails, and lots of them! That is precisely what happened in the centrally planned economies.

The Incentive Problem

The command economies also faced an incentive problem. Central planners determined the output mix. When

CONSIDER THIS . . .

The Two Koreas

North Korea is one of the few command economies still standing. After the Second World War, the Korean peninsula was divided into North Korea and South Korea. North Korea, under the influence of the Soviet Union, established a command economy that emphasized government ownership and central government planning. South Korea, protected by the United States, established a market economy based upon private ownership and the profit motive. Today, the differences in the economic outcomes of the two systems are striking:

	North Korea	South Korea
GDP	$40 billion*	$1.6 trillion*
GDP per capita	$1,800*	$32,100*
Exports	$2.5 billion	$556.5 billion
Imports	$3.5 billion	$524.4 billion
Agrculture as % of GDP	23 percent	2.6 percent

*Based on purchasing power equivalencies to the U.S. dollar.

Source: *CIA World Fact Book*, 2011, **www.cia.gov**.

they misjudged how many automobiles, shoes, shirts, and chickens were wanted at the government-determined prices, persistent shortages and surpluses of those products arose. But as long as the managers who oversaw the production of those goods were rewarded for meeting their assigned production goals, they had no incentive to adjust production in response to the shortages and surpluses. And there were no fluctuations in prices and profitability to signal that more or less of certain products was desired. Thus, many products were unavailable or in short supply, while other products were overproduced and sat for months or years in warehouses.

The command systems of the former Soviet Union and China before its market reforms also lacked entrepreneurship. Central planning did not trigger the profit motive, nor did it reward innovation and enterprise. The route for getting ahead was through participation in the political hierarchy of the Communist Party. Moving up the hierarchy meant better housing, better

KEY GRAPH

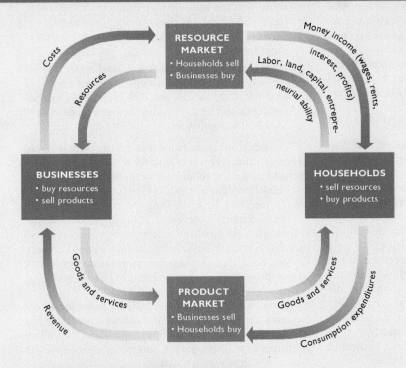

FIGURE 2.2   The circular flow diagram.
Resources flow from households to businesses through the resource market, and products flow from businesses to households through the product market. Opposite these real flows are monetary flows. Households receive income from businesses (their costs) through the resource market, and businesses receive revenue from households (their expenditures) through the product market.

QUICK QUIZ FOR FIGURE 2.2

1. The resource market is the place where:
   a. households sell products and businesses buy products.
   b. businesses sell resources and households sell products.
   c. households sell resources and businesses buy resources (or the services of resources).
   d. businesses sell resources and households buy resources (or the services of resources).

2. Which of the following would be determined in the product market?
   a. a manager's salary.
   b. the price of equipment used in a bottling plant.
   c. the price of 80 acres of farmland.
   d. the price of a new pair of athletic shoes.

3. In this circular flow diagram:
   a. money flows counterclockwise.
   b. resources flow counterclockwise.
   c. goods and services flow clockwise.
   d. households are on the selling side of the product market.

4. In this circular flow diagram:
   a. households spend income in the product market.
   b. firms sell resources to households.
   c. households receive income through the product market.
   d. households produce goods.

Answers: 1. c; 2. d; 3. b; 4. a

access to health care, and the right to shop in special stores. Meeting production targets and maneuvering through the minefields of party politics were measures of success in "business." But a definition of business success based solely on political savvy was not conducive to technological advance, which is often disruptive to existing products, production methods, and organizational structures.

The Circular Flow Model

LO2.5 Describe the mechanics of the circular flow model.
The dynamic market economy creates continuous, repetitive flows of goods and services, resources, and money. The **circular flow diagram,** shown in **Figure 2.2 (Key Graph),** illustrates those flows for a simplified economy in which there is no government. Observe that in the

ORIGIN OF THE IDEA

O2.4
Circular flow
diagram

diagram we group this economy's decision makers into *businesses* and *households*. Additionally, we divide this economy's markets into the *resource market* and the *product market*.

Households

The blue rectangle on the right side of the circular flow diagram in Figure 2.2 represents **households,** which are defined as one or more persons occupying a housing unit. There are currently about 118 million households in the U.S. economy. Households buy the goods and services that businesses make available in the product market. Households obtain the income needed to buy those products by selling resources in the resource market.

All the resources in our no-government economy are ultimately owned or provided by households. For instance, the members of one household or another directly provide all of the labor and entrepreneurial ability in the economy. Households also own all of the land and all of the capital in the economy either directly, as personal property, or indirectly, as a consequence of owning all of the businesses in the economy (and thereby controlling all of the land and capital owned by businesses). Thus, all of the income in the economy—all wages, rents, interest, and profits—flows to households because they provide the economy's labor, land, capital, and entrepreneurial ability.

Businesses

The blue rectangle on the left side of the circular flow diagram represents **businesses,** which are commercial establishments that attempt to earn profits for their owners by offering goods and services for sale. Businesses fall into three main categories.

- A **sole proprietorship** is a business owned and managed by a single person. The proprietor (the owner) may work alone or have employees. Examples include a woman who runs her own tree-cutting business and an independent accountant who, with two assistants, helps his clients with their taxes.

- The **partnership** form of business organization is a natural outgrowth of the sole proprietorship. In a partnership, two or more individuals (the partners) agree to own and operate a business together. They pool their financial resources and business skills to operate the business, and they share any profits or losses that the business may generate. Many law firms and dental practices are organized as partnerships, as are a wide variety of firms in many other industries.

- A **corporation** is an independent legal entity that can—on its own behalf—acquire resources, own assets, produce and sell products, incur debts, extend credit, sue and be sued, and otherwise engage in any legal business activity.

The fact that a corporation is an independent legal entity means that its owners bear no personal financial responsibility for the fulfillment of the corporation's debts and obligations. For instance, if a corporation has failed to repay a loan to a bank, the bank can sue the corporation but not its owners. Professional managers run most corporations. They are hired and supervised by a board of directors that is elected annually by the corporation's owners. Google, Ford, and American Airlines are examples of large corporations, but corporations come in all sizes and operate in every type of industry.

There currently are about 30 million businesses in the United States, ranging from enormous corporations like Walmart, with 2012 sales of $444 billion and 2.2 million employees, to single-person sole proprietorships with sales of less than $100 per day.

Businesses sell goods and services in the product market in order to obtain revenue, and they incur costs in the resource market when they purchase the labor, land, capital, and entrepreneurial ability that they need to produce their respective goods and services.

Product Market

The red rectangle at the bottom of the diagram represents the **product market,** the place where the goods and services produced by businesses are bought and sold. Households use the income they receive from the sale of resources to buy goods and services. The money that they spend on goods and services flows to businesses as revenue.

Resource Market

Finally, the red rectangle at the top of the circular flow diagram represents the **resource market** in which households sell resources to businesses. The households sell resources to generate income, and the businesses buy resources to produce goods and services. Productive resources flow from households to businesses, while money flows from businesses to households in the form of wages, rents, interest, and profits.

To summarize, the circular flow model depicts a complex web of economic activity in which businesses and households are both buyers and sellers. Businesses buy resources and sell products. Households buy products and sell resources. The counterclockwise flow of economic resources and finished products that is illustrated by the red arrows in Figure 2.2 is paid for by the clockwise flow of money income and consumption expenditures illustrated by the blue arrows.

QUICK REVIEW 2.4

- Competition directs individuals and firms to unwittingly promote the social interest, as if guided by a benevolent "invisible hand."
- The command systems of the Soviet Union and pre-reform China failed as a result of the coordination problem and the incentive problem.
- The circular flow model illustrates how resources flow from households to businesses and how payments for those resources flow from businesses to households.

How the Market System Deals with Risk

LO2.6 Explain how the market system deals with risk.
Producing goods and services is risky. Input shortages can suddenly arise. Consumer preferences can quickly change. Natural disasters can destroy factories and cripple supply chains.

For an economic system to maximize its potential, it must develop methods for assessing and managing risk. The market system does so by confronting business owners with the financial consequences of their decisions. If they manage risks well, they may prosper. If they manage risks poorly, they may lose everything.

The Profit System

As explained in Chapter 1, entrepreneurial ability is the economic resource that organizes and directs the other three resources of land, labor, and capital toward productive uses. The owners of a firm may attempt to supply the entrepreneurial ability themselves. Or they can hire professional managers to supply the necessary leadership and decision making. Either way, it falls to those acting as the firm's entrepreneurs to deal with risk.

They are guided toward sensible decisions by the so-called *profit system*. This system is actually a *profit and loss*

system because the entrepreneurs who must deal with risk and uncertainty gain profits if they choose wisely but suffer losses if they choose poorly. That provides them with a large financial incentive to avoid unnecessary risks and make prudent decisions.

By contrast, risk management tends to be done very poorly in command economies because the central planners who must allocate resources and deal with risk do not themselves face the possibility of losing money if they make bad decisions. As government employees, they tend to receive the same salaries whether things go well or poorly.

Shielding Employees and Suppliers from Business Risk

Under the market system, only a firm's owners are subject to business risk and the possibility of losing money. By contrast, the firm's employees and suppliers are shielded from business risk because they are legally entitled to receive their contracted wages and payments on time and in full regardless of whether the firm is earning a profit or generating a loss.

To see how this works, consider a pizza parlor that is being started in a small town. Its investors put up $50,000 to get it going. They rent a storefront, lease ovens, purchase computers, and leave some money set aside as a reserve.

The firm then has to attract employees. To do so, it will offer wage contracts that promise to pay employees every two weeks without regard to whether the firm is making a profit or generating a loss. This guarantee shields the firm's employees from the risks of owning and operating the business. They will get paid even if the pizza parlor is losing money.

In the same way, the contracts that the firm signs with its suppliers and with anyone who loans the firm money (for instance, the local bank) will also specify that they will be paid on time and in full no matter how the firm is doing in terms of profitability.

Dealing with Losses So what happens if the firm starts losing money? In that case, the owners will take the financial hit. To be concrete, suppose that the pizza parlor loses $1,500 during the month of October because it runs up $11,500 in costs but generates only $10,000 in revenue. In that situation, the investors' wealth will shrink by $1,500 as the firm is forced to dip into its reserve to cover the loss. If the firm continues to lose money in subsequent months and exhausts the reserve, the owners will then have to decide whether they want to close the shop or put in additional money in the hope that things will turn around.

Insurance

Insurance promotes economic growth and investment by transferring risk from those who have a low tolerance for risk to those who have a high tolerance for risk.

Consider fire insurance. Homeowners pay a monthly premium in exchange for which their insurance company guarantees to reimburse them if their house burns down. That guarantee transfers the risk of fire damage from the homeowners (who do not want to bear the risk) to the insurance company's owners (who are happy to bear the risk as a business proposition).

The insurance company will save the premiums that it receives from homeowners to help cover the rebuilding costs of any homes that do end up burning down. But it is quite possible that there will be so many fires that the insurance company will spend more money repairing fire damage than it received in premiums.

If that happens, the insurance company will suffer a loss that will fall upon the insurance company's owners. Their personal wealth will decline in order to make up for the unexpectedly high number of fires. Thus, the insurance company's owners ultimately bear the fire risk; it is to them that the insurance contract transfers risk.

But if the number of fires is unexpectedly small, the insurance company will turn a nice profit and the insurance company's owners will benefit from having been willing to bear the fire risk that the homeowners did not wish to bear.

More importantly, the economy's overall level of investment rises because the availability of insurance means that those who dislike risk are much more willing to invest their savings into the construction and purchase of capital goods like houses, cars, and factories.

But throughout all those months of losses, the suppliers and employees are safeguarded. Because they are paid on time and in full, they are shielded from the firm's business risks and whether it is generating a profit or a loss.

As a result, however, they are not legally entitled to share in the profits if the firm does end up being profitable. That privilege is reserved under the market system for the firm's owners as their reward for bearing business risk. In exchange for making sure that everyone else is shielded if things go badly, the owners are legally entitled to take all of the profits if things go well.

Benefits of Restricting Business Risk to Owners

There are two major benefits that arise from the market system's restriction of business risk to owners and investors.

Attracting Inputs Many people deeply dislike risk and would not be willing to participate in a business venture if they were exposed to the possibility of losing money. That is the case with many workers, who just want to do their jobs and get paid twice a month without having to worry about whether their employer is doing well or not. The same is true for most suppliers, who just want to get paid on time and in full for the inputs they supply to the firm.

For both groups, the concentration of business risk on owners and investors is very welcome because they can supply their resources to a firm without having to worry about the firm's profitability. That sense of security makes it much easier for firms to attract labor and other inputs, which in turn helps the economy innovate and grow.

Focusing Attention The profit system helps to achieve prudent risk management by focusing both the responsibility and the rewards for successfully managing risk onto a firm's owners. They can provide the risk-managing input of entrepreneurial ability themselves or hire it by paying a skilled manager. But either way, some individual's full-time job includes the specialized task of managing risk and making prudent decisions about the allocation of resources. By contrast, in a command system, the responsibility for managing risk tends to be spread out over several layers of government and many different committees so that nobody is personally responsible for bad outcomes.

QUICK REVIEW 2.5

- The market system incentivizes the prudent management of business risk by concentrating any profit or loss upon a firm's owners and investors.
- The market system shields employees, suppliers, and lenders from business risks, but in exchange for that protection, they are excluded from any profit that may be earned.
- By focusing risk on owners and investors, the market system (a) creates an incentive for owners and investors to hire managerial and entrepreneurial specialists to prudently manage business risks and (b) encourages the participation of workers, suppliers, and lenders who dislike risk.

LAST WORD

Shuffling the Deck

Economist Donald Boudreaux Marvels at the Way the Market System Systematically and Purposefully Arranges the World's Tens of Billions of Individual Resources.

In *The Future and Its Enemies*, Virginia Postrel notes the astonishing fact that if you thoroughly shuffle an ordinary deck of 52 playing cards, chances are practically 100 percent that the resulting arrangement of cards has never before existed. *Never.* Every time you shuffle a deck, you produce an arrangement of cards that exists for the first time in history.

The arithmetic works out that way. For a very small number of items, the number of possible arrangements is small. Three items, for example, can be arranged only six different ways. But the number of possible arrangements grows very large very quickly. The number of different ways to arrange five items is 120 . . . for ten items it's 3,628,800 . . . for fifteen items it's 1,307,674,368,000.

The number of different ways to arrange 52 items is 8.066×10^{67}. This is a *big* number. No human can comprehend its enormousness. By way of comparison, the number of possible ways to arrange a mere 20 items is 2,432,902,008,176,640,000—a number larger than the total number of seconds that have elapsed since the beginning of time ten billion years ago—and this number is Lilliputian compared to 8.066×10^{67}.

What's the significance of these facts about numbers? Consider the number of different resources available in the world—my labor, your labor, your land, oil, tungsten, cedar, coffee beans, chickens, rivers, the Empire State Building, [Microsoft] Windows, the wharves at Houston, the classrooms at Oxford, the airport at Miami, and on and on and on. No one can possibly count all of the different productive resources available for our use. But we can be sure that this number is at least in the tens of billions.

When you reflect on how incomprehensibly large is the number of ways to arrange a deck containing a mere 52 cards, the mind boggles at the number of different ways to arrange all the world's resources.

If our world were random—if resources combined together haphazardly, as if a giant took them all into his hands and tossed them down like so many [cards]—it's a virtual certainty that the resulting combination of resources would be useless. Unless this chance arrangement were quickly rearranged according to some productive logic, nothing worthwhile would be produced. We would all starve to death. Because only a tiny fraction of possible arrangements serves human ends, any arrangement will be useless if it is chosen randomly or with inadequate knowledge of how each and every resource might be productively combined with each other.

And yet, we witness all around us an arrangement of resources that's productive and serves human goals. Today's arrangement of resources might not be perfect, but it is vastly superior to most of the trillions upon trillions of other possible arrangements.

How have we managed to get one of the minuscule number of arrangements that works? The answer is private property—a social institution that encourages mutual accommodation.

Private property eliminates the possibility that resource arrangements will be random, for each resource owner chooses a course of action only if it promises rewards to the owner that exceed the rewards promised by all other available courses.

[The result] is a breathtakingly complex and productive arrangement of countless resources. This arrangement emerged over time (and is still emerging) as the result of billions upon billions of individual, daily, small decisions made by people seeking to better employ their resources and labor in ways that other people find helpful.

Source: Abridged from Donald J. Boudreaux, "Mutual Accommodation," *Ideas on Liberty*, May 2000, pp. 4–5. Used by permission of *The Freeman*.

SUMMARY

LO2.1 Differentiate between laissez-faire capitalism, the command system, and the market system.

Laissez-faire capitalism is a hypothetical economic system in which government's role would be restricted to protecting private property and enforcing contracts. All real-world economic systems have featured a more extensive role for government. Governments in command systems own nearly all property and resources and make nearly all decisions about what to produce, how to produce it, and who gets the output. Most countries today, including the United States, have market systems in which the government does play a large role, but in which most property and resources are privately owned and markets are the major force in determining what to produce, how to produce it, and who gets it.

LO2.2 List the main characteristics of the market system.

The market system is characterized by the private ownership of resources, including capital, and the freedom of individuals to engage in economic activities of their choice to advance their material well-being. Self-interest is the driving force of such an economy and competition functions as a regulatory or control mechanism.

In the market system, markets, prices, and profits organize and make effective the many millions of individual economic decisions that occur daily.

Specialization, use of advanced technology, and the extensive use of capital goods are common features of market systems. Functioning as a medium of exchange, money eliminates the problems of bartering and permits easy trade and greater specialization, both domestically and internationally.

LO2.3 Explain how the market system answers the five fundamental questions of what to produce, how to produce, who obtains the output, how to adjust to change, and how to promote progress.

Every economy faces five fundamental questions: (a) What goods and services will be produced? (b) How will the goods and services be produced? (c) Who will get the goods and services? (d) How will the system accommodate change? (e) How will the system promote progress?

The market system produces products whose production and sale yield total revenue sufficient to cover total cost. It does not produce products for which total revenue continuously falls short of total cost. Competition forces firms to use the lowest-cost production techniques.

Economic profit (total revenue minus total cost) indicates that an industry is prosperous and promotes its expansion. Losses signify that an industry is not prosperous and hasten its contraction.

Consumer sovereignty means that both businesses and resource suppliers are subject to the wants of consumers. Through their dollar votes, consumers decide on the composition of output.

The prices that a household receives for the resources it supplies to the economy determine that household's income. This income determines the household's claim on the economy's output. Those who have income to spend get the products produced in the market system.

By communicating changes in consumer tastes to entrepreneurs and resource suppliers, the market system prompts appropriate adjustments in the allocation of the economy's resources. The market system also encourages technological advance and capital accumulation, both of which raise a nation's standard of living.

LO2.4 Explain the operation of the "invisible hand" and why market economies usually do a better job than command economies at efficiently transforming economic resources into desirable output.

Competition, the primary mechanism of control in the market economy, promotes a unity of self-interest and social interests. As if directed by an invisible hand, competition harnesses the self-interested motives of businesses and resource suppliers to further the social interest.

The command systems of the Soviet Union and prereform China met their demise because of coordination difficulties caused by central planning and the lack of a profit incentive. The coordination problem resulted in bottlenecks, inefficiencies, and a focus on a limited number of products. The incentive problem discouraged product improvement, new product development, and entrepreneurship.

LO2.5 Describe the mechanics of the circular flow model.

The circular flow model illustrates the flows of resources and products from households to businesses and from businesses to households, along with the corresponding monetary flows. Businesses are on the buying side of the resource market and the selling side of the product market. Households are on the selling side of the resource market and the buying side of the product market.

LO2.6 Explain how the market system deals with risk.

By focusing business risks onto owners, the market system encourages the participation of workers and suppliers who dislike risk while at the same time creating a strong incentive for owners to manage business risks prudently.

TERMS AND CONCEPTS

economic system	market	"invisible hand"
laissez-faire capitalism	specialization	circular flow diagram
command system	division of labor	households
market system	medium of exchange	businesses
private property	barter	sole proprietorship
freedom of enterprise	money	partnership
freedom of choice	consumer sovereignty	corporation
self-interest	dollar votes	product market
competition	creative destruction	resource market

The following and additional problems can be found in **connect** ECONOMICS

DISCUSSION QUESTIONS

1. Contrast how a market system and a command economy try to cope with economic scarcity. **LO2.1**
2. How does self-interest help achieve society's economic goals? Why is there such a wide variety of desired goods and services in a market system? In what way are entrepreneurs and businesses at the helm of the economy but commanded by consumers? **LO2.2**
3. Why is private property, and the protection of property rights, so critical to the success of the market system? How do property rights encourage cooperation? **LO2.2**
4. What are the advantages of using capital in the production process? What is meant by the term "division of labor"? What are the advantages of specialization in the use of human and material resources? Explain why exchange is the necessary consequence of specialization. **LO2.2**
5. What problem does barter entail? Indicate the economic significance of money as a medium of exchange. What is meant by the statement "We want money only to part with it"? **LO2.2**
6. Evaluate and explain the following statements: **LO2.2**
   a. The market system is a profit-and-loss system.
   b. Competition is the disciplinarian of the market economy.
7. Some large hardware stores, such as Home Depot, boast of carrying as many as 20,000 different products in each store. What motivated the producers of those individual products

to make them and offer them for sale? How did the producers decide on the best combinations of resources to use? Who made those resources available, and why? Who decides whether these particular hardware products should continue to be produced and offered for sale? **LO2.3**
8. What is meant by the term "creative destruction"? How does the emergence of MP3 (or iPod) technology relate to this idea? **LO2.3**
9. In a sentence, describe the meaning of the phrase "invisible hand." **LO2.4**
10. In market economies, firms rarely worry about the availability of inputs to produce their products, whereas in command economies input availability is a constant concern. Why the difference? **LO2.4**
11. Distinguish between the resource market and the product market in the circular flow model. In what way are businesses and households both sellers and buyers in this model? What are the flows in the circular flow model? **LO2.5**
12. How does shielding employees and suppliers from business risk help to improve economic outcomes? Who is responsible for managing business risks in the market system? **LO2.6**
13. **LAST WORD** What explains why millions of economic resources tend to get arranged logically and productively rather than haphazardly and unproductively?

REVIEW QUESTIONS

1. Decide whether each of the following descriptions most closely corresponds to being part of a command system, a market system, or a laissez-faire system. **LO2.1**
   a. A woman who wants to start a flower shop finds she cannot do so unless the central government has already decided to allow a flower shop in her area.
   b. Shops stock and sell the goods their customers want but the government levies a sales tax on each transaction in

order to fund elementary schools, public libraries, and welfare programs for the poor.
   c. The only taxes levied by the government are to pay for national defense, law enforcement, and a legal system designed to enforce contracts between private citizens.

2. Match each term with the correct definition. **LO2.2**

private property
freedom of enterprise
mutually agreeable
freedom of choice
self-interest
competition
market

a. An institution that brings buyers and sellers together.

b. The right of private persons and firms to obtain, control, employ, dispose of, and bequeath land, capital, and other property.

c. The presence in a market of independent buyers and sellers who compete with one another and who are free to enter and exit the market as they each see fit.

d. The freedom of firms to obtain economic resources, decide what products to produce with those resources, and sell those products in markets of their choice.

e. What each individual or firm believes is best for itself and seeks to obtain.

f. Economic transactions willingly undertaken by both the buyer and the seller because each feels that the transaction will make him or her better off.

g. The freedom of resource owners to dispose of their resources as they think best; of workers to enter any line of work for which they are qualified; and of consumers to spend their incomes in whatever way they feel is most appropriate.

3. True or False: Money must be issued by a government for people to accept it. **LO2.2**

4. Assume that a business firm finds that its profit is greatest when it produces $40 worth of product A. Suppose also that each of the three techniques shown in the table to the right will produce the desired output. **LO2.3**

a. With the resource prices shown, which technique will the firm choose? Why? Will production using that technique entail profit or loss? What will be the amount of that profit or loss? Will the industry expand or contract? When will that expansion or contraction end?

b. Assume now that a new technique, technique 4, is developed. It combines 2 units of labor, 2 of land, 6 of capital, and 3 of entrepreneurial ability. In view of the resource prices in the table, will the firm adopt the new technique? Explain your answer.

c. Suppose that an increase in the labor supply causes the price of labor to fall to $1.50 per unit, all other resource prices remaining unchanged. Which technique will the producer now choose? Explain.

d. "The market system causes the economy to conserve most in the use of resources that are particularly scarce in supply. Resources that are scarcest relative to the demand for them have the highest prices. As a result, producers use these resources as sparingly as is possible." Evaluate this statement. Does your answer to part *c*, above, bear out this contention? Explain.

Resource	Price per Unit of Resource	Resource Units Required		
		Technique 1	Technique 2	Technique 3
Labor	$3	5	2	3
Land	4	2	4	2
Capital	2	2	4	5
Entrepreneurial ability	2	4	2	4

5. Identify each of the following quotes as being an example of either: the coordination problem, the invisible hand, creative destruction, or the incentive problem. **LO2.4**

a. "If you compare a list of today's most powerful and profitable companies with a similar list from 30 years ago, you will see lots of new entries."

b. "Managers in the old Soviet Union often sacrificed product quality and variety because they were being awarded bonuses for quantitative, not qualitative, targets."

c. "Each day, central planners in the old Soviet Union were tasked with setting 27 million prices—correctly."

d. "It is not from the benevolence of the butcher, the brewer, or the baker that we expect our dinner, but from their regard to their own interest."

6. True or False: Households sell finished products to businesses. **LO2.6**

7. Franklin, John, Henry, and Harry have decided to pool their financial resources and business skills in order to open up and run a coffee shop. They will share any profits or losses that the business generates and will be personally responsible for making good on any debt that their business undertakes. Their business should be classified as a: **LO2.6**

a. Corporation.

b. Sole proprietorship.

c. Partnership.

d. None of the above.

8. Ted and Fred are the owners of a gas station. They invested $150,000 each and pay an employee named Lawrence $35,000 per year. This year revenues are $900,000, while costs are $940,000. Who is legally responsible for bearing the $40,000 loss? **LO2.6**

a. Lawrence.

b. Ted.

c. Fred.

d. Ted and Fred.

e. Lawrence, Ted, and Fred.

PROBLEMS

1. Table 2.1 contains information on three techniques for producing $15 worth of bar soap. Assume that we said "$15 worth of bar soap" because soap cost $3 per bar and all three techniques produce 5 bars of soap ($15 = $3 per bar × 5 bars). So you know each technique produces 5 bars of soap. **LO2.3**
   a. What technique will you want to use if the price of a bar of soap falls to $2.75? What if the price of a bar of soap rises to $4? To $5?
   b. How many bars of soap will you want to produce if the price of a bar of soap falls to $2.00?
   c. Suppose that the price of soap is again $3 per bar but that the prices of all four resources are now $1 per unit. Which is now the least-profitable technique?
   d. If the resource prices return to their original levels (the ones shown in the table), but a new technique is invented that can produce 3 bars of soap (yes, 3 bars, not 5 bars!), using 1 unit of each of the four resources, will firms prefer the new technique?

2. Suppose Natasha currently makes $50,000 per year working as a manager at a cable TV company. She then develops two possible entrepreneurial business opportunities. In one, she will quit her job to start an organic soap company. In the other, she will try to develop an Internet-based competitor to the local cable company. For the soap-making opportunity, she anticipates annual revenue of $465,000 and costs for the necessary land, labor, and capital of $395,000 per year.

For the Internet opportunity, she anticipates costs for land, labor, and capital of $3,250,000 per year as compared to revenues of $3,275,000 per year. (a) Should she quit her current job to become an entrepreneur? (b) If she does quit her current job, which opportunity would she pursue? **LO2.3**

3. With current technology, suppose a firm is producing 400 loaves of banana bread daily. Also assume that the least-cost combination of resources in producing those loaves is 5 units of labor, 7 units of land, 2 units of capital, and 1 unit of entrepreneurial ability, selling at prices of $40, $60, $60, and $20, respectively. If the firm can sell these 400 loaves at $2 per unit, what is its total revenue? Its total cost? Its profit or loss? Will it continue to produce banana bread? If this firm's situation is typical for the other makers of banana bread, will resources flow toward or away from this bakery good? **LO2.3**

4. Let's put dollar amounts on the flows in the circular flow diagram of Figure 2.2. **LO2.5**
   a. Suppose that businesses buy a total of $100 billion of the four resources (labor, land, capital, and entrepreneurial ability) from households. If households receive $60 billion in wages, $10 billion in rent, and $20 billion in interest, how much are households paid for providing entrepreneurial ability?
   b. If households spend $55 billion on goods and $45 billion on services, how much in revenues do businesses receive in the product market?

FURTHER TEST YOUR KNOWLEDGE AT www.mcconnell20e.com

Practice quizzes, student PowerPoints, worked problems, Web-based questions, and additional materials are available at the text's Online Learning Center (OLC), **www.mcconnell20e.com**, or scan here. Need a barcode reader? Try ScanLife, available in your app store.

CHAPTER **3**

Demand, Supply, and Market Equilibrium

Learning Objectives

LO3.1 Characterize and give examples of markets.

LO3.2 Describe *demand* and explain how it can change.

LO3.3 Describe *supply* and explain how it can change.

LO3.4 Relate how supply and demand interact to determine market equilibrium.

LO3.5 Explain how changes in supply and demand affect equilibrium prices and quantities.

LO3.6 Identify what government-set prices are and how they can cause product surpluses and shortages.

LO3.7 (Appendix) Illustrate how supply and demand analysis can provide insights on actual-economy situations.

The model of supply and demand is the economics profession's greatest contribution to human understanding

ORIGIN OF THE IDEA

03.1
Demand and supply

because it explains the operation of the markets on which we depend for nearly everything that we eat, drink, or consume. The model is so powerful and so widely used that to many people it *is* economics.

This chapter explains how the model works and how it can explain both the *quantities* that are bought and sold in markets as well as the *prices* at which they trade.

Markets

LO3.1 Characterize and give examples of markets.

Markets bring together buyers ("demanders") and sellers ("suppliers"). The corner gas station, an e-commerce site, the local music store, a farmer's roadside stand—all are familiar markets. The New York Stock Exchange and the Chicago Board of Trade are markets in which buyers and sellers from all over the world communicate with one another to buy and sell bonds, stocks, and commodities. Auctioneers bring together potential buyers and sellers of art, livestock, used farm equipment, and, sometimes, real estate. In labor markets, new college graduates "sell" and employers "buy" specific labor services.

Some markets are local; others are national or international. Some are highly personal, involving face-to-face contact between demander and supplier; others are faceless, with buyer and seller never seeing or knowing each other.

To keep things simple, we will focus in this chapter on markets in which large numbers of independently acting buyers and sellers come together to buy and sell standardized products. Markets with these characteristics are the economy's most highly competitive. They include the wheat market, the stock market, and the market for foreign currencies. All such markets involve demand, supply, price, and quantity. As you will soon see, the price is "discovered" through the interacting decisions of buyers and sellers.

Demand

LO3.2 Describe *demand* and explain how it can change.

Demand is a schedule or a curve that shows the various amounts of a product that consumers are willing and able to purchase at each of a series of possible prices during a specified period of time.[1] Demand shows the quantities of a product that will be purchased at various possible prices, *other things equal*. Demand can easily be shown in table form. The table in Figure 3.1 is a hypothetical **demand schedule** for a *single consumer* purchasing bushels of corn.

The table reveals the relationship between the various prices of corn and the quantity of corn a particular consumer would be willing and able to purchase at each of these prices. We say "willing and able" because willingness alone is not effective in the market. You may be willing to buy a plasma television set, but if that willingness is not backed by the necessary dollars, it will not be effective and, therefore, will not be reflected in the market. In the table in Figure 3.1, if the price of corn were $5 per bushel, our consumer would be willing and able to buy 10 bushels per week; if it were $4, the consumer would be willing and able to buy 20 bushels per week; and so forth.

---

[1]This definition obviously is worded to apply to product markets. To adjust it to apply to resource markets, substitute the word "resource" for "product" and the word "businesses" for "consumers."

FIGURE 3.1 An individual buyer's demand for corn. Because price and quantity demanded are inversely related, an individual's demand schedule graphs as a downsloping curve such as D. Other things equal, consumers will buy more of a product as its price declines and less of the product as its price rises. (Here and in later figures, P stands for price and Q stands for quantity demanded or supplied.)

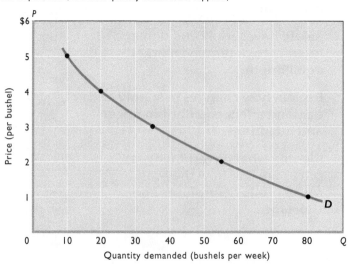

Demand for Corn	
Price per Bushel	Quantity Demanded per Week
$5	10
4	20
3	35
2	55
1	80

The table does not tell us which of the five possible prices will actually exist in the corn market. That depends on the interaction between demand and supply. Demand is simply a statement of a buyer's plans, or intentions, with respect to the purchase of a product.

To be meaningful, the quantities demanded at each price must relate to a specific period—a day, a week, a month. Saying "A consumer will buy 10 bushels of corn at $5 per bushel" is meaningless. Saying "A consumer will buy 10 bushels of corn *per week* at $5 per bushel" is meaningful. Unless a specific time period is stated, we do not know whether the demand for a product is large or small.

Law of Demand

A fundamental characteristic of demand is this: Other things equal, as price falls, the quantity demanded rises, and

ORIGIN OF THE IDEA

O3.2
Law of demand

as price rises, the quantity demanded falls. In short, there is a negative or *inverse* relationship between price and quantity demanded. Economists call this inverse relationship the **law of demand.**

The other-things-equal assumption is critical here. Many factors other than the price of the product being considered affect the amount purchased. For example, the quantity of Nikes purchased will depend not only on the price of Nikes but also on the prices of such substitutes as Reeboks, Adidas, and New Balances. The law of demand in this case says that fewer Nikes will be purchased if the price of Nikes rises and if the prices of Reeboks, Adidas, and New Balances all remain constant. In short, if the *relative price* of Nikes rises, fewer Nikes will be bought. However, if the price of Nikes and the prices of all other competing shoes increase by some amount—say, $5—consumers might buy more, fewer, or the same number of Nikes.

Why the inverse relationship between price and quantity demanded? Let's look at three explanations, beginning with the simplest one:

- The law of demand is consistent with common sense. People ordinarily *do* buy more of a product at a low price than at a high price. Price is an obstacle that deters consumers from buying. The higher that obstacle, the less of a product they will buy; the lower the price obstacle, the more they will buy. The fact that businesses have "sales" to clear out unsold items is evidence of their belief in the law of demand.

- In any specific time period, each buyer of a product will derive less satisfaction (or benefit, or utility) from

each successive unit of the product consumed. The second Big Mac will yield less satisfaction to the consumer than the first, and the third still less than the second.

ORIGIN OF THE IDEA

O3.3
Diminishing marginal utility

That is, consumption is subject to **diminishing marginal utility.** And because successive units of a particular product yield less and less marginal utility, consumers will buy additional units only if the price of those units is progressively reduced.

- We can also explain the law of demand in terms of income and substitution effects. The **income effect** indicates that a lower price increases the purchasing power of a buyer's money income, enabling the buyer to purchase more of the product than before. A higher price has the opposite effect. The **substitution effect** suggests that at a lower price buyers have the incentive to substitute what is now a less expensive product for other products that are now *relatively* more expensive. The product whose price has fallen is now "a better deal" relative to the other products.

For example, a decline in the price of chicken will increase the purchasing power of consumer incomes, enabling people to buy more chicken (the income effect). At a lower price, chicken is relatively more attractive and consumers tend to substitute it for pork, lamb, beef, and fish (the substitution effect). The income and substitution effects combine to make consumers able and willing to buy more of a product at a low price than at a high price.

ORIGIN OF THE IDEA

O3.4
Income and substitution effects

The Demand Curve

The inverse relationship between price and quantity demanded for any product can be represented on a simple graph, in which, by convention, we measure *quantity demanded* on the horizontal axis and *price* on the vertical axis. In the graph in Figure 3.1 we have plotted the five price-quantity data points listed in the accompanying table and connected the points with a smooth curve, labeled *D*. Such a curve is called a **demand curve.** Its downward slope reflects the law of demand—people buy more of a product, service, or resource as its price falls. The relationship between price and quantity demanded is inverse (or negative).

The table and graph in Figure 3.1 contain exactly the same data and reflect the same relationship between price and quantity demanded. But the graph shows that relationship much more simply and clearly than a table or a description in words.

Market Demand

So far, we have concentrated on just one consumer. But competition requires that more than one buyer be present in each market. By adding the quantities demanded by all consumers at each of the various possible prices, we can get from *individual* demand to *market* demand. If there are just three buyers in the market, as represented in the table in Figure 3.2, it is relatively easy to determine the total quantity demanded at each price. Figure 3.2 shows the graphical summing procedure: At each price we sum horizontally the quantities demanded by Joe, Jen, and Jay to obtain the total quantity demanded at that price; we then plot the price and the total quantity demanded as one point on the market demand curve. At the price of $3, for example, the three individual curves yield a total quantity demanded of 100 bushels (= 35 + 39 + 26).

Competition, of course, ordinarily entails many more than three buyers of a product. To avoid hundreds or thousands or millions of additions, we suppose that all the buyers in a market are willing and able to buy the same amounts at each of the possible prices. Then we just multiply those amounts by the number of buyers to obtain the market demand. That is how we arrived at the demand schedule and demand curve D_1 in Figure 3.3 for a market of 200 corn buyers, each with a demand as shown in the table in Figure 3.1.

In constructing a demand curve such as D_1 in Figure 3.3, economists assume that price is the most important influence on the amount of any product purchased. But economists know that other factors can and do affect purchases. These factors, called **determinants of demand,** are assumed to be constant when a demand curve like D_1 is drawn. They are the "other things equal" in the relationship between price and quantity demanded. When any of these determinants changes, the demand curve will shift to the right or left. For this reason, determinants of demand are sometimes referred to as *demand shifters*.

The basic determinants of demand are (1) consumers' tastes (preferences), (2) the number of buyers in the market, (3) consumers' incomes, (4) the prices of related goods, and (5) consumer expectations.

Changes in Demand

A change in one or more of the determinants of demand will change the demand data (the demand schedule) in the table accompanying Figure 3.3 and therefore the location of the demand curve there. A change in the

FIGURE 3.2 Market demand for corn, three buyers. The market demand curve *D* is the horizontal summation of the individual demand curves (D_1, D_2, and D_3) of all the consumers in the market. At the price of $3, for example, the three individual curves yield a total quantity demanded of 100 bushels (= 35 + 39 + 26).

	Market Demand for Corn, Three Buyers				
Price per Bushel	Quantity Demanded				Total Quantity Demanded per Week
	Joe		Jen	Jay	
$5	10	+	12 +	8 =	30
4	20	+	23 +	17 =	60
3	35	+	39 +	26 =	100
2	55	+	60 +	39 =	154
1	80	+	87 +	54 =	221

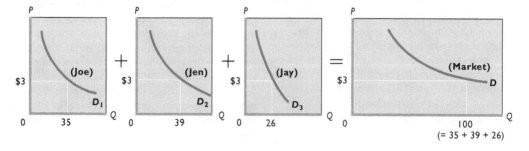

FIGURE 3.3   Changes in the demand for corn.   A change in one or more of the determinants of demand causes a change in demand. An increase in demand is shown as a shift of the demand curve to the right, as from D_1 to D_2. A decrease in demand is shown as a shift of the demand curve to the left, as from D_1 to D_3. These changes in demand are to be distinguished from a change in quantity demanded, which is caused by a change in the price of the product, as shown by a movement from, say, point *a* to point *b* on fixed demand curve D_1.

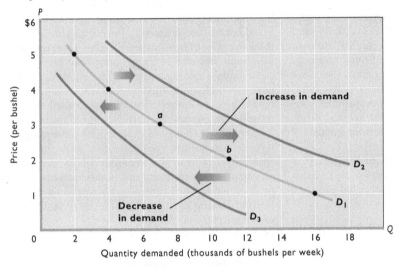

Market Demand for Corn, 200 Buyers, (D_1)	
(1) Price per Bushel	(2) Total Quantity Demanded per Week
$5	2,000
4	4,000
3	7,000
2	11,000
1	16,000

demand schedule or, graphically, a shift in the demand curve is called a *change in demand.*

If consumers desire to buy more corn at each possible price than is reflected in column 2 in the table in Figure 3.3, that *increase in demand* is shown as a shift of the demand curve to the right, say, from D_1 to D_2. Conversely, a *decrease in demand* occurs when consumers buy less corn at each possible price than is indicated in column 2. The leftward shift of the demand curve from D_1 to D_3 in Figure 3.3 shows that situation.

Now let's see how changes in each determinant affect demand.

Tastes   A favorable change in consumer tastes (preferences) for a product—a change that makes the product more desirable—means that more of it will be demanded at each price. Demand will increase; the demand curve will shift rightward. An unfavorable change in consumer preferences will decrease demand, shifting the demand curve to the left.

New products may affect consumer tastes; for example, the introduction of digital cameras greatly decreased the demand for film cameras. Consumers' concern over the health hazards of cholesterol and obesity have increased the demand for broccoli, low-calorie beverages, and fresh fruit while decreasing the demand for beef, veal, eggs, and whole milk. Over the past several years, the demand for coffee drinks and table wine has greatly increased, driven by a change in tastes. So, too, has the

demand for touch-screen mobile phones and fuel-efficient hybrid vehicles.

Number of Buyers   An increase in the number of buyers in a market is likely to increase demand; a decrease in the number of buyers will probably decrease demand. For example, the rising number of older persons in the United States in recent years has increased the demand for motor homes, medical care, and retirement communities. Large-scale immigration from Mexico has greatly increased the demand for a range of goods and services in the Southwest, including Mexican food products in local grocery stores. Improvements in communications have given financial markets international range and have thus increased the demand for stocks and bonds. International trade agreements have reduced foreign trade barriers to American farm commodities, increasing the number of buyers and therefore the demand for those products.

In contrast, emigration (out-migration) from many small rural communities has reduced the population and thus the demand for housing, home appliances, and auto repair in those towns.

Income   How changes in income affect demand is a more complex matter. For most products, a rise in income causes an increase in demand. Consumers typically buy more steaks, furniture, and electronic equipment as their incomes increase. Conversely, the demand for such products declines as their incomes fall. Products whose demand varies *directly* with money income are called *superior goods*, or **normal goods.**

Although most products are normal goods, there are some exceptions. As incomes increase beyond some point, the demand for used clothing, retread tires, and third-hand automobiles may decrease because the higher incomes enable consumers to buy new versions of those products. Rising incomes may also decrease the demand for soy-enhanced hamburger. Similarly, rising incomes may cause the demand for charcoal grills to decline as wealthier consumers switch to gas grills. Goods whose demand varies *inversely* with money income are called **inferior goods.**

Prices of Related Goods A change in the price of a related good may either increase or decrease the demand for a product, depending on whether the related good is a substitute or a complement:

- A **substitute good** is one that can be used in place of another good.

- A **complementary good** is one that is used together with another good.

Substitutes Häagen-Dazs ice cream and Ben & Jerry's ice cream are substitute goods or, simply, *substitutes*. When two products are substitutes, an increase in the price of one will increase the demand for the other. Conversely, a decrease in the price of one will decrease the demand for the other. For example, when the price of Häagen-Dazs ice cream rises, consumers will buy less of it and increase their demand for Ben & Jerry's ice cream. When the price of Colgate toothpaste declines, the demand for Crest decreases. So it is with other product pairs such as Nikes and Reeboks, Budweiser and Miller beer, or Chevrolets and Fords. They are *substitutes in consumption.*

Complements Because complementary goods (or, simply, *complements*) are used together, they are typically demanded jointly. Examples include computers and software, cell phones and cellular service, and snowboards and lift tickets. If the price of a complement (for example, lettuce) goes up, the demand for the related good (salad dressing) will decline. Conversely, if the price of a complement (for example, tuition) falls, the demand for a related good (textbooks) will increase.

Unrelated Goods The vast majority of goods are not related to one another and are called *independent goods*. Examples are butter and golf balls, potatoes and automobiles, and bananas and wristwatches. A change in the price of one has little or no effect on the demand for the other.

Consumer Expectations Changes in consumer expectations may shift demand. A newly formed expectation of higher future prices may cause consumers to buy now in order to "beat" the anticipated price rises, thus increasing current demand. That is often what happens in so-called hot real estate markets. Buyers rush in because they think the price of new homes will continue to escalate rapidly. Some buyers fear being "priced out of the market" and therefore not obtaining the home they desire. Other buyers—speculators—believe they will be able to sell the houses later at a higher price. Whichever their motivation, these buyers increase the current demand for houses.

Similarly, a change in expectations concerning future income may prompt consumers to change their current spending. For example, first-round NFL draft choices may splurge on new luxury cars in anticipation of lucrative professional football contracts. Or workers who become fearful of losing their jobs may reduce their demand for, say, vacation travel.

In summary, an *increase* in demand—the decision by consumers to buy larger quantities of a product at each possible price—may be caused by:

- A favorable change in consumer tastes.
- An increase in the number of buyers.
- Rising incomes if the product is a normal good.
- Falling incomes if the product is an inferior good.
- An increase in the price of a substitute good.
- A decrease in the price of a complementary good.
- A new consumer expectation that either prices or income will be higher in the future.

You should "reverse" these generalizations to explain a *decrease* in demand. Table 3.1 provides additional illustrations of the determinants of demand.

Changes in Quantity Demanded

A *change in demand* must not be confused with a *change in quantity demanded*. A **change in demand** is a shift of the demand curve to the right (an increase in demand) or to the left (a decrease in demand). It occurs because the consumer's state of mind about purchasing the product has been altered in response to a change in one or more of the determinants of demand. Recall that "demand" is a schedule or a curve; therefore, a "change in demand" means a change in the schedule and a shift of the curve.

In contrast, a **change in quantity demanded** is a movement from one point to another point—from one price-quantity combination to another—on a fixed demand curve. The cause of such a change is an increase or

TABLE 3.1 Determinants of Demand: Factors That Shift the Demand Curve

Determinant	Examples
Change in buyer tastes	Physical fitness rises in popularity, increasing the demand for jogging shoes and bicycles; cell phone popularity rises, reducing the demand for landline phones.
Change in number of buyers	A decline in the birthrate reduces the demand for children's toys.
Change in income	A rise in incomes increases the demand for normal goods such as restaurant meals, sports tickets, and necklaces while reducing the demand for inferior goods such as cabbage, turnips, and inexpensive wine.
Change in the prices of related goods	A reduction in airfares reduces the demand for bus transportation (substitute goods); a decline in the price of DVD players increases the demand for DVD movies (complementary goods).
Change in consumer expectations	Inclement weather in South America creates an expectation of higher future coffee bean prices, thereby increasing today's demand for coffee beans.

decrease in the price of the product under consideration. In the table in Figure 3.3, for example, a decline in the price of corn from \$5 to \$4 will increase the quantity demanded of corn from 2,000 to 4,000 bushels.

In Figure 3.3 the shift of the demand curve D_1 to either D_2 or D_3 is a change in demand. But the movement from point *a* to point *b* on curve D_1 represents a change in quantity demanded: Demand has not changed; it is the entire curve, and it remains fixed in place.

QUICK REVIEW 3.1

- Demand is a schedule or a curve showing the amount of a product that buyers are willing and able to purchase, in a particular time period, at each possible price in a series of prices.
- The law of demand states that, other things equal, the quantity of a good purchased varies inversely with its price.
- The demand curve shifts because of changes in (a) consumer tastes, (b) the number of buyers in the market, (c) consumer income, (d) the prices of substitute or complementary goods, and (e) consumer expectations.
- A change in demand is a shift of the demand curve; a change in quantity demanded is a movement from one point to another on a fixed demand curve.

Supply

LO3.3 Describe *supply* and explain how it can change.

Supply is a schedule or curve showing the various amounts of a product that producers are willing and able to make available for sale at each of a series of possible prices during a specific period.[2] The table in Figure 3.4 is a hypothetical **supply schedule** for a single producer of corn. It shows the quantities of corn that will be supplied at various prices, other things equal.

Law of Supply

The table in Figure 3.4 shows that a positive or direct relationship prevails between price and quantity supplied. As price rises, the quantity supplied rises; as price falls, the quantity supplied falls. This relationship is called the **law of supply.** A supply schedule tells us that, other things equal, firms will produce and offer for sale more of their product at a high price than at a low price. This, again, is basically common sense.

Price is an obstacle from the standpoint of the consumer, who is on the paying end. The higher the price, the less the consumer will buy. But the supplier is on the receiving end of the product's price. To a supplier, price represents *revenue*, which serves as an incentive to produce and sell a product. The higher the price, the greater this incentive and the greater the quantity supplied.

Consider a farmer who is deciding on how much corn to plant. As corn prices rise, as shown in the table in Figure 3.4, the farmer finds it profitable to plant more corn. And the higher corn prices enable the farmer to cover the increased costs associated with more intensive cultivation and the use of more seed, fertilizer, and pesticides. The overall result is more corn.

Now consider a manufacturer. Beyond some quantity of production, manufacturers usually encounter increases in *marginal cost*—the added cost of producing one more unit of output. Certain productive resources—in particular, the firm's plant and machinery—cannot be expanded quickly, so the firm uses more of other resources such as labor to produce more output. But as labor becomes more abundant relative to the fixed plant and equipment, the additional workers have relatively less space and access to equipment. For example, the added workers may have to wait to gain access to machines. As a result, each added worker produces less added output, and the marginal cost of successive units of output rises accordingly. The firm will not produce the

---

[2]This definition is worded to apply to product markets. To adjust it to apply to resource markets, substitute "resource" for "product" and "owners" for "producers."

FIGURE 3.4   An individual producer's supply of corn. Because price and quantity supplied are directly related, the supply curve for an individual producer graphs as an upsloping curve. Other things equal, producers will offer more of a product for sale as its price rises and less of the product for sale as its price falls.

Supply of Corn	
Price per Bushel	Quantity Supplied per Week
$5	60
4	50
3	35
2	20
1	5

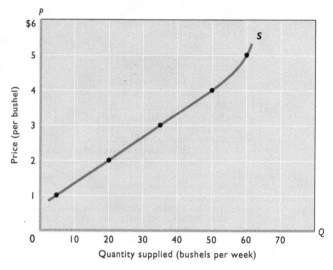

more costly units unless it receives a higher price for them. Again, price and quantity supplied are directly related.

The Supply Curve

As with demand, it is convenient to represent individual supply graphically. In Figure 3.4, curve S is the **supply curve** that corresponds with the price–quantity supplied data in the accompanying table. The upward slope of the curve reflects the law of supply—producers offer more of a good, service, or resource for sale as its price rises. The relationship between price and quantity supplied is positive, or direct.

Market Supply

Market supply is derived from individual supply in exactly the same way that market demand is derived from individual demand. We sum the quantities supplied by each producer at each price. That is, we obtain the market supply curve by "horizontally adding" the supply curves of the individual producers. The price–quantity supplied data in the table accompanying Figure 3.5 are for an assumed 200 identical producers in the market, each willing to supply corn according to the supply schedule shown in Figure 3.4. Curve S_1 in Figure 3.5 is a graph of the market supply data. Note that the values of the axes in Figure 3.5 are the same as those used in our graph of market demand (Figure 3.3). The only difference is that we change the label on the horizontal axis from "quantity demanded" to "quantity supplied."

Determinants of Supply

In constructing a supply curve, we assume that price is the most significant influence on the quantity supplied of any product. But other factors (the "other things equal") can and do affect supply. The supply curve is drawn on the assumption that these other things are fixed and do not change. If one of them does change, a *change in supply* will occur, meaning that the entire supply curve will shift.

The basic **determinants of supply** are (1) resource prices, (2) technology, (3) taxes and subsidies, (4) prices of other goods, (5) producer expectations, and (6) the number of sellers in the market. A change in any one or more of these determinants of supply, or *supply shifters*, will move the supply curve for a product either right or left. A shift to the *right*, as from S_1 to S_2 in Figure 3.5, signifies an *increase* in supply: Producers supply larger quantities of the product at each possible price. A shift to the *left*, as from S_1 to S_3, indicates a *decrease* in supply: Producers offer less output at each price.

Changes in Supply

Let's consider how changes in each of the determinants affect supply. The key idea is that costs are a major factor underlying supply curves; anything that affects costs (other than changes in output itself) usually shifts the supply curve.

Resource Prices The prices of the resources used in the production process help determine the costs of production incurred by firms. Higher *resource* prices raise

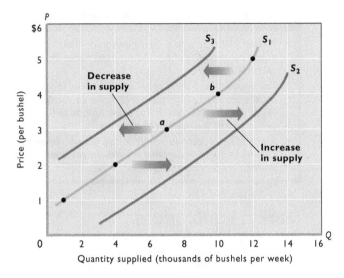

FIGURE 3.5 Changes in the supply of corn. A change in one or more of the determinants of supply causes a change in supply. An increase in supply is shown as a rightward shift of the supply curve, as from S_1 to S_2. A decrease in supply is depicted as a leftward shift of the curve, as from S_1 to S_3. In contrast, a change in the *quantity supplied* is caused by a change in the product's price and is shown by a movement from one point to another, as from *b* to *a* on fixed supply curve S_1.

Market Supply of Corn, 200 Producers, (S_1)	
(1) Price per Bushel	(2) Total Quantity Supplied per Week
$5	12,000
4	10,000
3	7,000
2	4,000
1	1,000

production costs and, assuming a particular *product* price, squeeze profits. That reduction in profits reduces the incentive for firms to supply output at each product price. For example, an increase in the price of sand, crushed rock, or Portland cement will increase the cost of producing concrete and reduce its supply.

In contrast, lower *resource* prices reduce production costs and increase profits. So when resource prices fall, firms supply greater output at each product price. For example, a decrease in the price of iron ore will decrease the price of steel.

Technology Improvements in technology (techniques of production) enable firms to produce units of output with fewer resources. Because resources are costly, using fewer of them lowers production costs and increases supply. Example: Technological advances in producing flat-panel computer monitors have greatly reduced their cost. Thus, manufacturers will now offer more such monitors than previously at the various prices; the supply of flat-panel monitors has increased.

Taxes and Subsidies Businesses treat most taxes as costs. An increase in sales or property taxes will increase production costs and reduce supply. In contrast, subsidies are "taxes in reverse." If the government subsidizes the production of a good, it in effect lowers the producers' costs and increases supply.

Prices of Other Goods Firms that produce a particular product, say, soccer balls, can sometimes use their plant and equipment to produce alternative goods, say, basketballs and volleyballs. The higher prices of these "other goods" may entice soccer ball producers to switch production to those other goods in order to increase profits. This *substitution in production* results in a decline in the supply of soccer balls. Alternatively, when the prices of basketballs and volleyballs decline relative to the price of soccer balls, producers of those goods may decide to produce more soccer balls instead, increasing their supply.

Producer Expectations Changes in expectations about the future price of a product may affect the producer's current willingness to supply that product. It is difficult, however, to generalize about how a new expectation of higher prices affects the present supply of a product. Farmers anticipating a higher wheat price in the future might withhold some of their current wheat harvest from the market, thereby causing a decrease in the current supply of wheat. In contrast, in many types of manufacturing industries, newly formed expectations that price will increase may induce firms to add another shift of workers or to expand their production facilities, causing current supply to increase.

Number of Sellers Other things equal, the larger the number of suppliers, the greater the market supply. As more firms enter an industry, the supply curve shifts to the right. Conversely, the smaller the number of firms in the industry, the less the market supply. This means that as firms leave an industry, the supply curve shifts to the left. Example: The United States and Canada have imposed restrictions on haddock fishing to replenish dwindling stocks. As part of that policy, the federal government has bought the boats of some of the haddock fishers as a way of putting

TABLE 3.2 Determinants of Supply: Factors That Shift the Supply Curve

Determinant	Examples
Change in resource prices	A decrease in the price of microchips increases the supply of computers; an increase in the price of crude oil reduces the supply of gasoline.
Change in technology	The development of more effective wireless technology increases the supply of cell phones.
Changes in taxes and subsidies	An increase in the excise tax on cigarettes reduces the supply of cigarettes; a decline in subsidies to state universities reduces the supply of higher education.
Change in prices of other goods	An increase in the price of cucumbers decreases the supply of watermelons.
Change in producer expectations	An expectation of a substantial rise in future log prices decreases the supply of logs today.
Change in number of suppliers	An increase in the number of tattoo parlors increases the supply of tattoos; the formation of women's professional basketball leagues increases the supply of women's professional basketball games.

them out of business and decreasing the catch. The result has been a decline in the market supply of haddock.

Table 3.2 is a checklist of the determinants of supply, along with further illustrations.

Changes in Quantity Supplied

The distinction between a *change in supply* and a *change in quantity supplied* parallels the distinction between a change in demand and a change in quantity demanded. Because supply is a schedule or curve, a **change in supply** means a change in the schedule and a shift of the curve. An increase in supply shifts the curve to the right; a decrease in supply shifts it to the left. The cause of a change in supply is a change in one or more of the determinants of supply.

In contrast, a **change in quantity supplied** is a movement from one point to another on a fixed supply curve. The cause of such a movement is a change in the price of the specific product being considered.

Consider supply curve S_1 in Figure 3.5. A decline in the price of corn from $4 to $3 decreases the quantity of corn supplied per week from 10,000 to 7,000 bushels. This movement from point *b* to point *a* along S_1 is a change in quantity supplied, not a change in supply. Supply is the full schedule of prices and quantities shown, and this schedule does not change when the price of corn changes.

Market Equilibrium

LO3.4 Relate how supply and demand interact to determine market equilibrium.

With our understanding of demand and supply, we can now show how the decisions of buyers of corn and sellers of corn interact to determine the equilibrium price and quantity of corn. In the table in Figure 3.6, columns 1 and 2 repeat the market supply of corn (from the table in Figure 3.5), and columns 2 and 3 repeat the market demand for corn (from the table in Figure 3.3). We assume this is a competitive market so that neither buyers nor sellers can set the price.

Equilibrium Price and Quantity

We are looking for the equilibrium price and equilibrium quantity. The **equilibrium price** (or *market-clearing price*) is the price where the intentions of buyers and sellers match. It is the price where quantity demanded equals quantity supplied. The table in Figure 3.6 reveals that at $3, *and only at that price*, the number of bushels of corn that sellers wish to sell (7,000) is identical to the number consumers want to buy (also 7,000). At $3 and 7,000 bushels of corn, there is neither a shortage nor a surplus of corn. So 7,000 bushels of corn is the **equilibrium quantity:** the quantity at which the intentions of buyers and sellers match, so that the quantity demanded and the quantity supplied are equal.

Graphically, the equilibrium price is indicated by the intersection of the supply curve and the demand curve in **Figure 3.6 (Key Graph).** (The horizontal axis now measures both quantity demanded and quantity supplied.) With neither a shortage nor a surplus at $3, the market is *in equilibrium*, meaning "in balance" or "at rest."

Competition among buyers and among sellers drives the price to the equilibrium price; once there, it will remain there unless it is subsequently disturbed by changes in demand or supply (shifts of the curves). To better understand the uniqueness of the equilibrium price, let's consider other

KEY GRAPH

FIGURE 3.6   Equilibrium price and quantity. The intersection of the downsloping demand curve *D* and the upsloping supply curve *S* indicates the equilibrium price and quantity, here $3 and 7,000 bushels of corn. The shortages of corn at below-equilibrium prices (for example, 7,000 bushels at $2) drive up price. The higher prices increase the quantity supplied and reduce the quantity demanded until equilibrium is achieved. The surpluses caused by above-equilibrium prices (for example, 6,000 bushels at $4) push price down. As price drops, the quantity demanded rises and the quantity supplied falls until equilibrium is established. At the equilibrium price and quantity, there are neither shortages nor surpluses of corn.

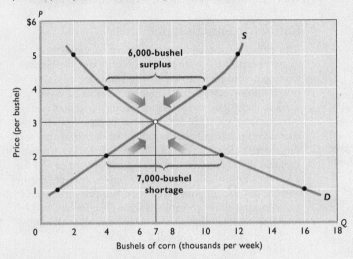

Market Supply of and Demand for Corn			
(1) Total Quantity Supplied per Week	(2) Price per Bushel	(3) Total Quantity Demanded per Week	(4) Surplus (+) or Shortage (−)*
12,000	$5	2,000	+10,000 ↓
10,000	4	4,000	+6,000 ↓
7,000	3	7,000	0
4,000	2	11,000	−7,000 ↑
1,000	1	16,000	−15,000 ↑

*Arrows indicate the effect on price.

QUICK QUIZ FOR FIGURE 3.6

1. Demand curve *D* is downsloping because:
   a. producers offer less of a product for sale as the price of the product falls.
   b. lower prices of a product create income and substitution effects that lead consumers to purchase more of it.
   c. the larger the number of buyers in a market, the lower the product price.
   d. price and quantity demanded are directly (positively) related.

2. Supply curve *S*:
   a. reflects an inverse (negative) relationship between price and quantity supplied.
   b. reflects a direct (positive) relationship between price and quantity supplied.
   c. depicts the collective behavior of buyers in this market.

   d. shows that producers will offer more of a product for sale at a low product price than at a high product price.

3. At the $3 price:
   a. quantity supplied exceeds quantity demanded.
   b. quantity demanded exceeds quantity supplied.
   c. the product is abundant and a surplus exists.
   d. there is no pressure on price to rise or fall.

4. At price $5 in this market:
   a. there will be a shortage of 10,000 units.
   b. there will be a surplus of 10,000 units.
   c. quantity demanded will be 12,000 units.
   d. quantity demanded will equal quantity supplied.

Answers: 1. b; 2. b; 3. d; 4. b.

prices. At any above-equilibrium price, quantity supplied exceeds quantity demanded. For example, at the $4 price, sellers will offer 10,000 bushels of corn, but buyers will purchase only 4,000. The $4 price encourages sellers to offer lots of corn but discourages many consumers from buying it. The result is a **surplus** (or *excess supply*) of 6,000 bushels. If corn sellers produced them all, they would find themselves with 6,000 unsold bushels of corn.

Surpluses drive prices down. Even if the $4 price existed temporarily, it could not persist. The large surplus would

prompt competing sellers to lower the price to encourage buyers to take the surplus off their hands. As the price fell, the incentive to produce corn would decline and the incentive for consumers to buy corn would increase. As shown in Figure 3.6, the market would move to its equilibrium at $3.

Any price below the $3 equilibrium price would create a shortage; quantity demanded would exceed quantity supplied. Consider a $2 price, for example. We see both from column 2 of the table and from the demand curve in Figure 3.6 that quantity demanded exceeds quantity supplied at

that price. The result is a **shortage** (or *excess demand*) of 7,000 bushels of corn. The $2 price discourages sellers from devoting resources to corn and encourages consumers to desire more bushels than are available. The $2 price cannot

CONSIDER THIS . . .

Ticket Scalping: A Bum Rap!

Ticket prices for athletic events and musical concerts are usually set far in advance of the events. Sometimes the original ticket price is too low to be the equilibrium price. Lines form at the ticket window and a severe shortage of tickets occurs at the printed price. What happens next? Buyers who are willing to pay more than the original price bid up the ticket price in resale ticket markets.

Tickets sometimes get resold for much greater amounts than the original price—market transactions known as "scalping." For example, an original buyer may resell a $75 ticket to a concert for $200. Reporters sometimes denounce scalpers for "ripping off" buyers by charging "exorbitant" prices.

But is scalping really a rip-off? We must first recognize that such ticket resales are voluntary transactions. If both buyer and seller did not expect to gain from the exchange, it would not occur! The seller must value the $200 more than seeing the event, and the buyer must value seeing the event at $200 or more. So there are no losers or victims here: Both buyer and seller benefit from the transaction. The scalping market simply redistributes assets (game or concert tickets) from those who would rather have the money (and the other things that the money can buy) to those who would rather have the tickets.

Does scalping impose losses or injury on the sponsors of the event? If the sponsors are injured, it is because they initially priced tickets below the equilibrium level. Perhaps they did this to create a long waiting line and the attendant news media publicity. Alternatively, they may have had a genuine desire to keep tickets affordable for lower-income, ardent fans. In either case, the event sponsors suffer an opportunity cost in the form of less ticket revenue than they might have otherwise received. But such losses are self-inflicted and separate and distinct from the fact that some tickets are later resold at a higher price.

So is ticket scalping undesirable? Not on economic grounds! It is an entirely voluntary activity that benefits both sellers and buyers.

persist as the equilibrium price. Many consumers who want to buy corn at this price will not obtain it. They will express a willingness to pay more than $2 to get corn. Competition among these buyers will drive up the price, eventually to the $3 equilibrium level. Unless disrupted by changes of supply or demand, this $3 price of corn will continue to prevail.

Rationing Function of Prices

The ability of the competitive forces of supply and demand to establish a price at which selling and buying decisions are consistent is called the rationing function of prices. In our case, the equilibrium price of $3 clears the market, leaving no burdensome surplus for sellers and no inconvenient shortage for potential buyers. And it is the combination of freely made individual decisions that sets this market-clearing price. In effect, the market outcome says that all buyers who are willing and able to pay $3 for a bushel of corn will obtain it; all buyers who cannot or will not pay $3 will go without corn. Similarly, all producers who are willing and able to offer corn for sale at $3 a bushel will sell it; all producers who cannot or will not sell for $3 per bushel will not sell their product.

Efficient Allocation

A competitive market such as that we have described not only rations goods to consumers but also allocates society's resources efficiently to the particular product. Competition among corn producers forces them to use the best technology and right mix of productive resources. If they didn't, their costs would be too high relative to the market price, and they would be unprofitable. The result is **productive efficiency:** the production of any particular good in the least costly way. When society produces corn at the lowest achievable per-unit cost, it is expending the least-valued combination of resources to produce that product and therefore is making available more-valued resources to produce other desired goods. Suppose society has only $100 worth of resources available. If it can produce a bushel of corn using $3 of those resources, then it will have available $97 of resources remaining to produce other goods. This is clearly better than producing the corn for $5 and having only $95 of resources available for the alternative uses.

Competitive markets also produce **allocative efficiency:** the *particular mix* of goods and services most highly valued by society (minimum-cost production assumed). For example, society wants land suitable for growing corn used for that purpose, not to grow dandelions. It wants diamonds to be used for jewelry, not crushed up and used as an additive to give concrete more sparkle. It wants iPods and MP4 players, not cassette players and tapes. Moreover, society does not want to devote all its resources to corn, diamonds, and portable digital media players. It wants to assign some resources to wheat, gasoline, and cell phones. Competitive markets make those allocatively efficient assignments.

The equilibrium price and quantity in competitive markets usually produce an assignment of resources that is "right" from an economic perspective. Demand essentially reflects the marginal benefit (MB) of the good, based on the utility received. Supply reflects the marginal cost (MC) of producing the good. The market ensures that firms produce all units of goods for which MB exceeds MC and no units for which MC exceeds MB. At the intersection of the demand and supply curves, MB equals MC and allocative efficiency results. As economists say, there is neither an "underallocaton of resources" nor an "overallocation of resources" to the product.

Changes in Supply, Demand, and Equilibrium

LO3.5 Explain how changes in supply and demand affect equilibrium prices and quantities.

We know that demand might change because of fluctuations in consumer tastes or incomes, changes in consumer expectations, or variations in the prices of related goods. Supply might change in response to changes in resource prices, technology, or taxes. What effects will such changes in supply and demand have on equilibrium price and quantity?

Changes in Demand

Suppose that the supply of some good (for example, health care) is constant and demand increases, as shown in Figure 3.7a. As a result, the new intersection of the supply and demand curves is at higher values on both the price and the quantity axes. Clearly, an increase in demand raises both equilibrium price and equilibrium quantity. Conversely, a decrease in demand such as that shown in Figure 3.7b reduces both equilibrium price and equilibrium quantity. (The value of graphical analysis is now apparent: We need not fumble with columns of figures to determine the outcomes; we need only compare the new and the old points of intersection on the graph.)

Changes in Supply

What happens if the demand for some good (for example, flash drives) is constant but supply increases, as in Figure 3.7c? The new intersection of supply and demand is located at a lower equilibrium price but at a higher equilibrium quantity. An increase in supply reduces equilibrium price but increases equilibrium quantity. In con-

trast, if supply decreases, as in Figure 3.7d, equilibrium price rises while equilibrium quantity declines.

Complex Cases

When both supply and demand change, the effect is a combination of the individual effects.

Supply Increase; Demand Decrease What effect will a supply increase and a demand decrease for some good (for example, apples) have on equilibrium price? Both changes decrease price, so the net result is a price drop greater than that resulting from either change alone.

What about equilibrium quantity? Here the effects of the changes in supply and demand are opposed: the increase

CONSIDER THIS . . .

Salsa and Coffee Beans

If you forget the other-things-equal assumption, you can encounter situations that *seem* to be in conflict with the laws of demand and supply. For example, suppose salsa manufacturers sell 1 million bottles of salsa at $4 a bottle in one year; 2 million bottles at $5 in the next year; and 3 million at $6 in the year thereafter. Price and quantity purchased vary directly, and these data seem to be at odds with the law of demand.

But there is no conflict here; the data do not refute the law of demand. The catch is that the law of demand's other-things-equal assumption has been violated over the three years in the example. Specifically, because of changing tastes and rising incomes, the demand for salsa has increased sharply, as in Figure 3.7a. The result is higher prices *and* larger quantities purchased.

Another example: The price of coffee beans occasionally shoots upward at the same time that the quantity of coffee beans harvested declines. These events seemingly contradict the direct relationship between price and quantity denoted by supply. The catch again is that the other-things-equal assumption underlying the upsloping supply curve is violated. Poor coffee harvests decrease supply, as in Figure 3.7d, increasing the equilibrium price of coffee and reducing the equilibrium quantity.

The laws of demand and supply are not refuted by observations of price and quantity made over periods of time in which either demand or supply curves shift.

FIGURE 3.7 Changes in demand and supply and the effects on price and quantity. The increase in demand from D_1 to D_2 in (a) increases both equilibrium price and equilibrium quantity. The decrease in demand from D_3 to D_4 in (b) decreases both equilibrium price and equilibrium quantity. The increase in supply from S_1 to S_2 in (c) decreases equilibrium price and increases equilibrium quantity. The decline in supply from S_3 to S_4 in (d) increases equilibrium price and decreases equilibrium quantity. The boxes in the top right corners summarize the respective changes and outcomes. The upward arrows in the boxes signify increases in equilibrium price (P) and equilibrium quantity (Q); the downward arrows signify decreases in these items.

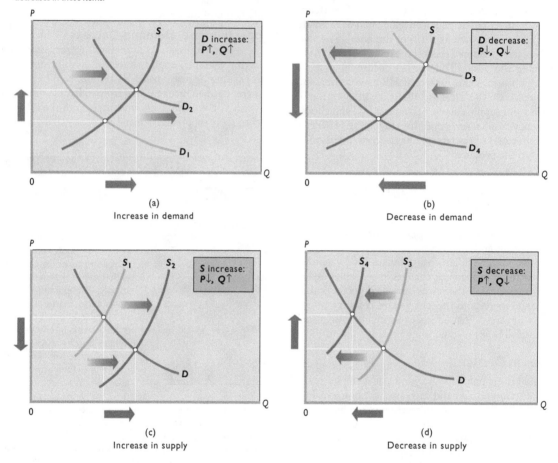

(a) Increase in demand

(b) Decrease in demand

(c) Increase in supply

(d) Decrease in supply

in supply increases equilibrium quantity, but the decrease in demand reduces it. The direction of the change in equilibrium quantity depends on the relative sizes of the changes in supply and demand. If the increase in supply is larger than the decrease in demand, the equilibrium quantity will increase. But if the decrease in demand is greater than the increase in supply, the equilibrium quantity will decrease.

Supply Decrease; Demand Increase A decrease in supply and an increase in demand for some good (for example, gasoline) both increase price. Their combined effect is an increase in equilibrium price greater than that caused by either change separately. But their effect on the equilibrium quantity is again indeterminate, depending on

the relative sizes of the changes in supply and demand. If the decrease in supply is larger than the increase in demand, the equilibrium quantity will decrease. In contrast, if the increase in demand is greater than the decrease in supply, the equilibrium quantity will increase.

Supply Increase; Demand Increase What if supply and demand both increase for some good (for example, cell phones)? A supply increase drops equilibrium price, while a demand increase boosts it. If the increase in supply is greater than the increase in demand, the equilibrium price will fall. If the opposite holds, the equilibrium price will rise.

The effect on equilibrium quantity is certain: The increases in supply and demand both raise the equilibrium

TABLE 3.3 Effects of Changes in Both Supply and Demand

Change in Supply	Change in Demand	Effect on Equilibrium Price	Effect on Equilibrium Quantity
1. Increase	Decrease	Decrease	Indeterminate
2. Decrease	Increase	Increase	Indeterminate
3. Increase	Increase	Indeterminate	Increase
4. Decrease	Decrease	Indeterminate	Decrease

FIGURE 3.8   A price ceiling. A price ceiling is a maximum legal price such as P_c. When the ceiling price is below the equilibrium price, a persistent product shortage results. Here that shortage is shown by the horizontal distance between Q_d and Q_s.

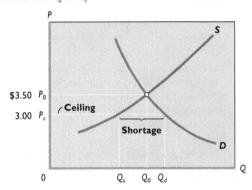

quantity. Therefore, the equilibrium quantity will increase by an amount greater than that caused by either change alone.

Supply Decrease; Demand Decrease What about decreases in both supply and demand for some good (for example, new homes)? If the decrease in supply is greater than the decrease in demand, equilibrium price will rise. If the reverse is true, equilibrium price will fall. Because the decreases in supply and demand each reduce equilibrium quantity, we can be sure that equilibrium quantity will fall.

Table 3.3 summarizes these four cases. To understand them fully, you should draw supply and demand diagrams for each case to confirm the effects listed in this table.

Special cases arise when a decrease in demand and a decrease in supply, or an increase in demand and an increase in supply, exactly cancel out. In both cases, the net effect on equilibrium price will be zero; price will not change.

The optional appendix accompanying this chapter provides additional examples of situations in which both supply and demand change at the same time.

Application: Government-Set Prices

LO3.6 Identify what government-set prices are and how they can cause product surpluses and shortages.

Prices in most markets are free to rise or fall to their equilibrium levels, no matter how high or low those levels might be. However, government sometimes concludes that supply and demand will produce prices that are unfairly high for buyers or unfairly low for sellers. So government may place legal limits on how high or low a price or prices may go. Is that a good idea?

Price Ceilings on Gasoline

A **price ceiling** sets the maximum legal price a seller may charge for a product or service. A price at or below the ceiling is legal; a price above it is not. The rationale for establishing price ceilings (or ceiling prices) on specific products is that they purportedly enable consumers to obtain some

"essential" good or service that they could not afford at the equilibrium price. Examples are rent controls and usury laws, which specify maximum "prices" in the forms of rent and interest that can be charged to borrowers.

Graphical Analysis We can easily show the effects of price ceilings graphically. Suppose that rapidly rising world income boosts the purchase of automobiles and shifts the demand for gasoline to the right so that the market equilibrium price reaches $3.50 per gallon, shown as P_0 in Figure 3.8. The rapidly rising price of gasoline greatly burdens low- and moderate-income households, which pressure government to "do something." To keep gasoline prices down, the government imposes a ceiling price P_c of $3 per gallon. To impact the market, a price ceiling must be below the equilibrium price. A ceiling price of $4, for example, would have had no effect on the price of gasoline in the current situation.

What are the effects of this $3 ceiling price? The rationing ability of the free market is rendered ineffective. Because the ceiling price P_c is below the market-clearing price P_0, there is a lasting shortage of gasoline. The quantity of gasoline demanded at P_c is Q_d and the quantity supplied is only Q_s; a persistent excess demand or shortage of amount $Q_d - Q_s$ occurs.

The price ceiling P_c prevents the usual market adjustment in which competition among buyers bids up price, inducing more production and rationing some buyers out of the market. That process would normally continue until the shortage disappeared at the equilibrium price and quantity, P_0 and Q_0.

By preventing these market adjustments from occurring, the price ceiling poses two related problems.

Rationing Problem How will the available supply Q_s be apportioned among buyers who want the greater

A Legal Market for Human Organs?

A Legal Market Might Eliminate the Present Shortage of Human Organs for Transplant. But There Are Many Serious Objections to "Turning Human Body Parts into Commodities" for Purchase and Sale.

It has become increasingly commonplace in medicine to transplant kidneys, lungs, livers, corneas, pancreases, and hearts from deceased individuals to those whose organs have failed or are failing. But surgeons and many of their patients face a growing problem: There are shortages of donated organs available for transplant. Not everyone who needs a transplant can get one. In 2012, there were 116,000 Americans on the waiting list for transplants. Indeed, an inadequate supply of donated organs causes an estimated 6,900 deaths in the United States each year.

Why Shortages? Seldom do we hear of shortages of desired goods in market economies. What is different about organs for transplant? One difference is that no legal market exists for human organs. To understand this situation, observe the demand curve D_1 and supply curve S_1 in the accompanying figure. The downward slope of the demand curve tells us that if there

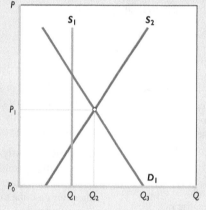

were a market for human organs, the quantity of organs demanded would be greater at lower prices than at higher prices. Vertical supply curve S_1 represents the fixed quantity of human organs now donated via consent before death. Because the price of these donated organs is in effect zero, quantity demanded Q_3 exceeds quantity supplied Q_1. The shortage of $Q_3 - Q_1$ is rationed through a waiting list of those in medical need of transplants. Many people die while still on the waiting list.

Use of a Market A market for human organs would increase the incentive to donate organs. Such a market might work like this: An individual might specify in a legal document that he or she is willing to sell one or more usable human organs upon death or near-death. The person could specify where the money from the sale would go, for example, to family, a church, an educational institution, or a charity. Firms would then emerge to purchase

amount Q_d? Should gasoline be distributed on a first-come, first-served basis, that is, to those willing and able to get in line the soonest or stay in line the longest? Or should gas stations distribute it on the basis of favoritism? Since an unregulated shortage does not lead to an equitable distribution of gasoline, the government must establish some formal system for rationing it to consumers. One option is to issue ration coupons, which authorize bearers to purchase a fixed amount of gasoline per month. The rationing system might entail first the printing of coupons for Q_s gallons of gasoline and then the equal distribution of the coupons among consumers so that the wealthy family of four and the poor family of four both receive the same number of coupons.

Black Markets But ration coupons would not prevent a second problem from arising. The demand curve in Figure 3.8 reveals that many buyers are willing to pay more than the ceiling price P_c. And, of course, it is more profit-

able for gasoline stations to sell at prices above the ceiling. Thus, despite a sizable enforcement bureaucracy that would have to accompany the price controls, *black markets* in which gasoline is illegally bought and sold at prices above the legal limits will flourish. Counterfeiting of ration coupons will also be a problem. And since the price of gasoline is now "set by government," government might face political pressure to set the price even lower.

Rent Controls

About 200 cities in the United States, including New York City, Boston, and San Francisco, have at one time or another enacted rent controls: maximum rents established by law (or, more recently, maximum rent increases for existing tenants). Such laws are well intended. Their goals are to protect low-income families from escalating rents caused by perceived housing shortages and to make housing more affordable to the poor.

organs and resell them where needed for profit. Under such a system, the supply curve of usable organs would take on the normal upward slope of typical supply curves. The higher the expected price of an organ, the greater the number of people who would be willing to have their organs sold at death. Suppose that the supply curve is S_2 in the figure. At the equilibrium price P_1, the number of organs made available for transplant (Q_2) would equal the number purchased for transplant (also Q_2). In this generalized case, the shortage of organs would be eliminated and, of particular importance, the number of organs available for transplanting would rise from Q_1 to Q_2. This means more lives would be saved and enhanced than under the present donor system.

Objections In view of this positive outcome, why is there no such market for human organs? Critics of market-based solutions have two main objections. The first is a moral objection: Critics feel that turning human organs into commodities commercializes human beings and diminishes the special nature of human life. They say there is something unseemly about selling and buying body organs as if they were bushels of wheat or ounces of gold. (There is, however, a market for blood!) Moreover, critics note that the market would ration the available organs (as represented by Q_2 in the figure) to people who either can afford them (at P_1) or have health insurance for transplants. The poor and uninsured would be left out.

Second, a health-cost objection suggests that a market for body organs would greatly increase the cost of health care. Rather than obtaining freely donated (although "too few") body organs, patients or their insurance companies would have to pay market prices for them, further increasing the cost of medical care.

Rebuttal Supporters of market-based solutions to organ shortages point out that the laws against selling organs are simply driving the market underground. Worldwide, an estimated $1 billion-per-year illegal market in human organs has emerged. As in other illegal markets, the unscrupulous tend to thrive. This fact is dramatized by the accompanying photo, in which four Pakistani villagers show off their scars after they each sold a kidney to pay off debts. Supporters say that legalization of the market for human organs would increase organ supply from legal sources, drive down the price of organs, and reduce the abuses such as those now taking place in illegal markets.

What have been the actual economic effects? On the demand side, the below-equilibrium rents attract a larger number of renters. Some are locals seeking to move into their own places after sharing housing with friends or family. Others are outsiders attracted into the area by the artificially lower rents. But a large problem occurs on the supply side. Price controls make it less attractive for landlords to offer housing on the rental market. In the short run, owners may sell their rental units or convert them to condominiums. In the long run, low rents make it unprofitable for owners to repair or renovate their rental units. (Rent controls are one cause of the many abandoned apartment buildings found in larger cities.) Also, insurance companies, pension funds, and other potential new investors in housing will find it more profitable to invest in office buildings, shopping malls, or motels, where rents are not controlled.

In brief, rent controls distort market signals and thus resources are misallocated: Too few resources are allocated to rental housing and too many to alternative uses. Ironically, although rent controls are often legislated to lessen the effects of perceived housing shortages, controls in fact are a primary cause of such shortages. For that reason, most American cities either have abandoned or are in the process of dismantling rent controls.

Price Floors on Wheat

A **price floor** is a minimum price fixed by the government. A price at or above the price floor is legal; a price below it is not. Price floors above equilibrium prices are usually invoked when society feels that the free functioning of the market system has not provided a sufficient income for certain groups of resource suppliers or producers. Supported prices for agricultural products and current minimum wages are two examples of price (or wage) floors. Let's look at the former.

Suppose that many farmers have extremely low incomes when the price of wheat is at its equilibrium value of $2 per bushel. The government decides to help out by establishing a legal price floor or price support of $3 per bushel.

What will be the effects? At any price above the equilibrium price, quantity supplied will exceed quantity demanded—that is, there will be a persistent excess supply or surplus of the product. Farmers will be willing to produce and offer for sale more than private buyers are willing to purchase at the price floor. As we saw with a price ceiling, an imposed legal price disrupts the rationing ability of the free market.

Graphical Analysis   Figure 3.9 illustrates the effect of a price floor graphically. Suppose that S and D are the supply and demand curves for wheat. Equilibrium price and quantity are P_0 and Q_0, respectively. If the government imposes a price floor of P_f, farmers will produce Q_s but private buyers will purchase only Q_d. The surplus is the excess of Q_s over Q_d.

The government may cope with the surplus resulting from a price floor in two ways:

- It can restrict supply (for example, by instituting acreage allotments by which farmers agree to take a certain amount of land out of production) or increase demand (for example, by researching new uses for the product involved). These actions may reduce the difference between the equilibrium price and the price floor and that way reduce the size of the resulting surplus.

- If these efforts are not wholly successful, then the government must purchase the surplus output at the $3 price (thereby subsidizing farmers) and store or otherwise dispose of it.

Additional Consequences   Price floors such as P_f in Figure 3.9 not only disrupt the rationing ability of prices

but distort resource allocation. Without the price floor, the $2 equilibrium price of wheat would cause financial losses and force high-cost wheat producers to plant other crops or abandon farming altogether. But the $3 price floor allows them to continue to grow wheat and remain farmers. So society devotes too many of its scarce resources to wheat production and too few to producing other, more valuable, goods and services. It fails to achieve allocative efficiency.

That's not all. Consumers of wheat-based products pay higher prices because of the price floor. Taxpayers pay higher taxes to finance the government's purchase of the surplus. Also, the price floor causes potential environmental damage by encouraging wheat farmers to bring hilly, erosion-prone "marginal land" into production. The higher price also prompts imports of wheat. But, since such imports would increase the quantity of wheat supplied and thus undermine the price floor, the government needs to erect tariffs (taxes on imports) to keep the foreign wheat out. Such tariffs usually prompt other countries to retaliate with their own tariffs against U.S. agricultural or manufacturing exports.

So it is easy to see why economists "sound the alarm" when politicians advocate imposing price ceilings or price floors such as price controls, rent controls, interest-rate lids, or agricultural price supports. In all these cases, good intentions lead to bad economic outcomes. Government-controlled prices cause shortages or surpluses, distort resource allocation, and produce negative side effects.

FIGURE 3.9   **A price floor.**   A price floor is a minimum legal price such as P_f. When the price floor is above the equilibrium price, a persistent product surplus results. Here that surplus is shown by the horizontal distance between Q_s and Q_d.

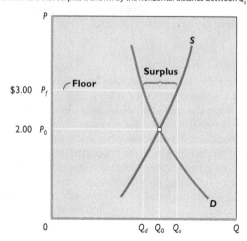

QUICK REVIEW 3.3

- In competitive markets, prices adjust to the equilibrium level at which quantity demanded equals quantity supplied.

- The equilibrium price and quantity are those indicated by the intersection of the supply and demand curves for any product or resource.

- An increase in demand increases equilibrium price and quantity; a decrease in demand decreases equilibrium price and quantity.

- An increase in supply reduces equilibrium price but increases equilibrium quantity; a decrease in supply increases equilibrium price but reduces equilibrium quantity.

- Over time, equilibrium price and quantity may change in directions that seem at odds with the laws of demand and supply because the other-things-equal assumption is violated.

- Government-controlled prices in the form of ceilings and floors stifle the rationing function of prices, distort resource allocations, and cause negative side effects.

SUMMARY

LO3.1 Characterize and give examples of markets.

Markets bring buyers and sellers together. Some markets are local, others international. Some have physical locations while others are online. For simplicity, this chapter focuses on highly competitive markets in which large numbers of buyers and sellers come together to buy and sell standardized products. All such markets involve demand, supply, price, and quantity, with price being "discovered" through the interacting decisions of buyers and sellers.

LO3.2 Describe *demand* and explain how it can change.

Demand is a schedule or curve representing the willingness of buyers in a specific period to purchase a particular product at each of various prices. The law of demand implies that consumers will buy more of a product at a low price than at a high price. So, other things equal, the relationship between price and quantity demanded is negative or inverse and is graphed as a downsloping curve.

Market demand curves are found by adding horizontally the demand curves of the many individual consumers in the market.

Changes in one or more of the determinants of demand (consumer tastes, the number of buyers in the market, the money incomes of consumers, the prices of related goods, and consumer expectations) shift the market demand curve. A shift to the right is an increase in demand; a shift to the left is a decrease in demand. A change in demand is different from a change in the quantity demanded, the latter being a movement from one point to another point on a fixed demand curve because of a change in the product's price.

LO3.3 Describe *supply* and explain how it can change.

Supply is a schedule or curve showing the amounts of a product that producers are willing to offer in the market at each possible price during a specific period. The law of supply states that, other things equal, producers will offer more of a product at a high price than at a low price. Thus, the relationship between price and quantity supplied is positive or direct, and supply is graphed as an upsloping curve.

The market supply curve is the horizontal summation of the supply curves of the individual producers of the product.

Changes in one or more of the determinants of supply (resource prices, production techniques, taxes or subsidies, the prices of other goods, producer expectations, or the number of sellers in the market) shift the supply curve of a product. A shift to the right is an increase in supply; a shift to the left is a decrease in supply. In contrast, a change in the price of the product being considered

causes a change in the quantity supplied, which is shown as a movement from one point to another point on a fixed supply curve.

LO3.4 Relate how supply and demand interact to determine market equilibrium.

The equilibrium price and quantity are established at the intersection of the supply and demand curves. The interaction of market demand and market supply adjusts the price to the point at which the quantities demanded and supplied are equal. This is the equilibrium price. The corresponding quantity is the equilibrium quantity.

The ability of market forces to synchronize selling and buying decisions to eliminate potential surpluses and shortages is known as the rationing function of prices. The equilibrium quantity in competitive markets reflects both productive efficiency (least-cost production) and allocative efficiency (producing the right amount of the product relative to other products).

LO3.5 Explain how changes in supply and demand affect equilibrium prices and quantities.

A change in either demand or supply changes the equilibrium price and quantity. Increases in demand raise both equilibrium price and equilibrium quantity; decreases in demand lower both equilibrium price and equilibrium quantity. Increases in supply lower equilibrium price and raise equilibrium quantity; decreases in supply raise equilibrium price and lower equilibrium quantity.

Simultaneous changes in demand and supply affect equilibrium price and quantity in various ways, depending on their direction and relative magnitudes (see Table 3.3).

LO3.6 Identify what government-set prices are and how they can cause product surpluses and shortages.

A price ceiling is a maximum price set by government and is designed to help consumers. Effective price ceilings produce persistent product shortages, and if an equitable distribution of the product is sought, government must ration the product to consumers.

A price floor is a minimum price set by government and is designed to aid producers. Effective price floors lead to persistent product surpluses; the government must either purchase the product or eliminate the surplus by imposing restrictions on production or increasing private demand.

Legally fixed prices stifle the rationing function of prices and distort the allocation of resources.

TERMS AND CONCEPTS

demand	income effect	normal goods
demand schedule	substitution effect	inferior goods
law of demand	demand curve	substitute good
diminishing marginal utility	determinants of demand	complementary good

change in demand	determinants of supply	shortage
change in quantity demanded	change in supply	productive efficiency
supply	change in quantity supplied	allocative efficiency
supply schedule	equilibrium price	price ceiling
law of supply	equilibrium quantity	price floor
supply curve	surplus	

The following and additional problems can be found in connect™

DISCUSSION QUESTIONS

1. Explain the law of demand. Why does a demand curve slope downward? How is a market demand curve derived from individual demand curves? **LO3.2**
2. What are the determinants of demand? What happens to the demand curve when any of these determinants change? Distinguish between a change in demand and a, movement along a fixed demand curve, noting the cause(s) of each. **LO3.2**
3. Explain the law of supply. Why does the supply curve slope upward? How is the market supply curve derived from the supply curves of individual producers? **LO3.3**
4. What are the determinants of supply? What happens to the supply curve when any of these determinants changes? Distinguish between a change in supply and a change in the quantity supplied, noting the cause(s) of each. **LO3.3**
5. In 2001 an outbreak of hoof-and-mouth disease in Europe led to the burning of millions of cattle carcasses. What impact do you think this had on the supply of cattle hides, hide prices, the supply of leather goods, and the price of leather goods? **LO3.5**
6. For each stock in the stock market, the number of shares sold daily equals the number of shares purchased. That is, the quantity of each firm's shares demanded equals the quantity supplied. So, if this equality always occurs, why do the prices of stock shares ever change? **LO3.5**
7. What do economists mean when they say "price floors and ceilings stifle the rationing function of prices and distort resource allocation"? **LO3.6**
8. **LAST WORD** In some countries, such as France, every corpse is available for doctors to "harvest" for organs unless the deceased, while still alive, signed a form forbidding the organs to be harvested. In the United States, it is the opposite: No harvesting is allowed unless the deceased had signed, while still alive, an organ donor form authorizing doctors to harvest any needed organs. Use supply and demand figures to show in which country organ shortages are likely to be less severe.

REVIEW QUESTIONS

1. What effect will each of the following have on the demand for small automobiles such as the Mini-Cooper and Fiat 500? **LO3.2**
   a. Small automobiles become more fashionable.
   b. The price of large automobiles rises (with the price of small autos remaining the same).
   c. Income declines and small autos are an inferior good.
   d. Consumers anticipate that the price of small autos will greatly come down in the near future.
   e. The price of gasoline substantially drops.
2. True or False: A "change in quantity demanded" is a shift of the entire demand curve to the right or to the left. **LO3.2**
3. What effect will each of the following have on the supply of auto tires? **LO3.3**
   a. A technological advance in the methods of producing tires.
   b. A decline in the number of firms in the tire industry.
   c. An increase in the prices of rubber used in the production of tires.
   d. The expectation that the equilibrium price of auto tires will be lower in the future than currently.
   e. A decline in the price of the large tires used for semi trucks and earth-hauling rigs (with no change in the price of auto tires).
   f. The levying of a per-unit tax on each auto tire sold.
   g. The granting of a 50-cent-per-unit subsidy for each auto tire produced.
4. "In the corn market, demand often exceeds supply and supply sometimes exceeds demand." "The price of corn rises and falls in response to changes in supply and demand." In which of these two statements are the terms "supply" and "demand" used correctly? Explain. **LO3.3**
5. Suppose that in the market for computer memory chips, the equilibrium price is $50 per chip. If the current price is $55 per chip, then there will be _____ of memory chips. **LO3.4**
   a. A shortage.
   b. A surplus.
   c. An equilibrium quantity.
   d None of the above.

6. Critically evaluate: "In comparing the two equilibrium positions in Figure 3.7b, I note that a smaller amount is actually demanded at a lower price. This refutes the law of demand." **LO3.5**

7. Label each of the following scenarios with the set of symbols that best indicates the price change and quantity change that occur in the scenario. In some scenarios, it may not be possible from the information given to determine the direction of a particular price change or a particular quantity change. We will symbolize those cases as, respectively, "P?" and "Q?" The four possible combinations of price and quantity changes are:. **LO3.5**

   $P \downarrow Q?$ $P? Q \downarrow$
   $P \uparrow Q?$ $P? Q \uparrow$

   a. On a hot day, both the demand for lemonade and the supply of lemonade increase.
   b. On a cold day, both the demand for ice cream and the supply of ice cream decrease.
   c. When Hawaii's Mt. Kilauea erupts violently, the demand on the part of tourists for sightseeing flights increases but the supply of pilots willing to provide these dangerous flights decreases.
   d. In a hot area of Arizona where they generate a lot of their electricity with wind turbines, the demand for electricity falls on windy days as people switch off their air conditioners and enjoy the breeze. But at the same time, the amount of electricity supplied increases as the wind turbines spin faster.

8. Suppose the total demand for wheat and the total supply of wheat per month in the Kansas City grain market are as shown in the table below. Suppose that the government establishes a price ceiling of $3.70 for wheat. What might prompt the government to establish this price ceiling? Explain carefully the main effects. Demonstrate your answer graphically. Next, suppose that the government establishes a price floor of $4.60 for wheat. What will be the main effects of this price floor? Demonstrate your answer graphically. **LO3.6**

Thousands of Bushels Demanded	Price per Bushel	Thousands of Bushels Supplied
85	$3.40	72
80	3.70	73
75	4.00	75
70	4.30	77
65	4.60	79
60	4.90	81

9. A price ceiling will result in a shortage only if the ceiling price is _____ the equilibrium price. **LO3.6**
   a. Less than.
   b. Equal to.
   c. Greater than.
   d. Louder than.

PROBLEMS

1. Suppose there are three buyers of candy in a market: Tex, Dex, and Rex. The market demand and the individual demands of Tex, Dex, and Rex are shown on the next page. **LO3.2**
   a. Fill in the table for the missing values.
   b. Which buyer demands the least at a price of $5? The most at a price of $7?
   c. Which buyer's quantity demanded increases the most when the price is lowered from $7 to $6?
   d. Which direction would the market demand curve shift if Tex withdrew from the market? What if Dex doubled his purchases at each possible price?
   e. Suppose that at a price of $6, the total quantity demanded increases from 19 to 38. Is this a "change in the quantity demanded" or a "change in demand"?

Price per Candy	Individual Quantities Demanded						Total Quantity Demanded
	Tex		Dex		Rex		
$8	3	+	1	+	0	=	___
7	8	+	2	+	___	=	12
6	___	+	3	+	4	=	19
5	17	+	___	+	6	=	27
4	23	+	5	+	8	=	___

2. The figure on the right shows the supply curve for tennis balls, S_1, for Drop Volley Tennis, a producer of tennis equipment.

Use the figure and the table below to give your answers to the following questions. **LO3.3**

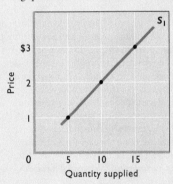

a. Use the figure to fill in the quantity supplied on supply curve S_1 for each price in the table below.

Price	S_1 Quantity Supplied	S_2 Quantity Supplied	Change in Quantity Supplied
$3	_____	4	_____
2	_____	2	_____
1	_____	0	_____

b. If production costs were to increase, the quantities supplied at each price would be as shown by the third column of the table ("S_2 Quantity Supplied"). Use those data to draw supply curve S_2 on the same graph as supply curve S_1.

c. In the fourth column of the table, enter the amount by which the quantity supplied at each price changes due to the increase in product costs. (Use positive numbers for increases and negative numbers for decreases.)

d. Did the increase in production costs cause a "decrease in supply" or a "decrease in quantity supplied"?

3. Refer to the expanded table below from review question 8. **LO3.4**

a. What is the equilibrium price? At what price is there neither a shortage nor a surplus? Fill in the surplus-shortage column and use it to confirm your answers.

b. Graph the demand for wheat and the supply of wheat. Be sure to label the axes of your graph correctly. Label equilibrium price P and equilibrium quantity Q.

c. How big is the surplus or shortage at $3.40? At $4.90? How big a surplus or shortage results if the price is 60 cents higher than the equilibrium price? 30 cents lower than the equilibrium price?

Thousands of Bushels Demanded	Price per Bushel	Thousands of Bushels Supplied	Surplus (+) or Shortage (−)
85	$3.40	72	_____
80	3.70	73	_____
75	4.00	75	_____
70	4.30	77	_____
65	4.60	79	_____
60	4.90	81	_____

4. How will each of the following changes in demand and/or supply affect equilibrium price and equilibrium quantity in a competitive market; that is, do price and quantity rise, fall, or remain unchanged, or are the answers indeterminate because they depend on the magnitudes of the shifts? Use supply and demand to verify your answers. **LO3.5**

a. Supply decreases and demand is constant.

b. Demand decreases and supply is constant.

c. Supply increases and demand is constant.

d. Demand increases and supply increases.

e. Demand increases and supply is constant.

f. Supply increases and demand decreases.

g. Demand increases and supply decreases.

h. Demand decreases and supply decreases.

5. Use two market diagrams to explain how an increase in state subsidies to public colleges might affect tuition and enrollments in both public and private colleges. **LO3.5**

6. **ADVANCED ANALYSIS** Assume that demand for a commodity is represented by the equation $P = 10 - .2Q_d$ and supply by the equation $P = 2 + .2Q_s$, where Q_d and Q_s are quantity demanded and quantity supplied, respectively, and P is price. Using the equilibrium condition $Q_s = Q_d$, solve the equations to determine equilibrium price. Now determine equilibrium quantity. **LO3.5**

7. Suppose that the demand and supply schedules for rental apartments in the city of Gotham are as given in the table below. **LO3.6**

Monthly Rent	Apartments Demanded	Apartments Supplied
$2,500	10,000	15,000
2,000	12,500	12,500
1,500	15,000	10,000
1,000	17,500	7,500
500	20,000	5,000

a. What is the market equilibrium rental price per month and the market equilibrium number of apartments demanded and supplied?

b. If the local government can enforce a rent-control law that sets the maximum monthly rent at $1,500, will there be a surplus or a shortage? Of how many units? And how many units will actually be rented each month?

c. Suppose that a new government is elected that wants to keep out the poor. It declares that the minimum rent that can be charged is $2,500 per month. If the government can enforce that price floor, will there be a surplus or a shortage? Of how many units? And how many units will actually be rented each month?

d. Suppose that the government wishes to decrease the market equilibrium monthly rent by increasing the supply of housing. Assuming that demand remains unchanged, by how many units of housing would the government have to increase the supply of housing in order to get the market equilibrium rental price to fall to $1,500 per month? To $1,000 per month? To $500 per month?

Additional Examples of Supply and Demand

LO3.7 Illustrate how supply and demand analysis can provide insights on actual-economy situations.

Our discussion has clearly demonstrated that supply and demand analysis is a powerful tool for understanding equilibrium prices and quantities. The information provided in the main body of this chapter is fully sufficient for moving forward in the book, but you may find that additional examples of supply and demand are helpful. This optional appendix provides several concrete illustrations of changes in supply and demand.

Your instructor may assign all, some, or none of this appendix, depending on time availability and personal preference.

Changes in Supply and Demand

As Figure 3.7 of this chapter demonstrates, changes in supply and demand cause changes in price, quantity, or both. The following applications illustrate this fact in several real-world markets. The simplest situations are those in which either supply changes while demand remains constant or demand changes while supply remains constant. Let's consider two such simple cases first, before looking at more complex applications.

Lettuce

Every now and then we hear on the news that extreme weather has severely reduced the size of some crop. Suppose, for example, that a severe freeze destroys a sizable portion of the lettuce crop. This unfortunate situation implies a significant decline in supply, which we represent as a leftward shift of the supply curve from S_1 to S_2 in Figure 1. At each price, consumers desire as much lettuce as before, so the freeze does not affect the demand for lettuce. That is, demand curve D_1 does not shift.

What are the consequences of the reduced supply of lettuce for equilibrium price and quantity? As shown in Figure 1, the leftward shift of the supply curve disrupts the previous equilibrium in the market for lettuce and drives the equilibrium price upward from P_1 to P_2. Consumers respond to that price hike by reducing the quantity of lettuce demanded from Q_1 to Q_2. Equilibrium is restored at P_2 and Q_2.

FIGURE 1 The market for lettuce. The decrease in the supply of lettuce, shown here by the shift from S_1 to S_2, increases the equilibrium price of lettuce from P_1 to P_2 and reduces the equilibrium quantity from Q_1 to Q_2.

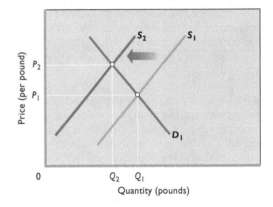

Consumers who are willing and able to pay price P_2 obtain lettuce; consumers unwilling or unable to pay that price do not. Some consumers continue to buy as much lettuce as before, even at the higher price. Others buy some lettuce but not as much as before, and still others opt out of the market completely. The latter two groups use the money they would have spent on lettuce to obtain other products, say, carrots. (Because of our other-things-equal assumption, the prices of other products have not changed.)

Exchange Rates

Exchange rates are the prices at which one currency can be traded (exchanged) for another. Exchange rates are normally determined in foreign exchange markets. One of the largest foreign exchange markets is the euro-dollar market in which the currency used in most of Europe, the *euro*, is exchanged for U.S. dollars. In the United States, this market is set up so that euros are priced in dollars—that is, the "product" being traded is euros and the "price" to buy that product is quoted in dollars. Thus, the market equilibrium price one day might be $1.25 to buy 1 euro, while on another day it might be $1.50 to buy 1 euro.

Foreign exchange markets are used by individuals and companies that need to make purchases or payments in a different currency. U.S. companies exporting goods to Germany, for instance, wish to be paid in U.S. dollars. Thus, their German customers will need to convert euros into dollars. The euros that they bring to the euro-dollar market will become part of the overall market supply of euros. Conversely, an American mutual fund may wish to purchase some French real estate outside of Paris. But to purchase that real estate, it will need to pay in euros because the current French owners will only accept payment in euros. Thus, the American mutual fund has a demand to purchase euros that will form part of the overall market demand for euros. The fund will bring dollars to the euro-dollar foreign exchange market in order to purchase the euros it desires.

Sometimes, the demand for euros increases. This might be because a European product surges in popularity in foreign countries. For example, if a new German-made automobile is a big hit in the United States, American car dealers will demand more euros with which to pay for more units of that new model. This will shift the demand curve for euros to the right, as from D_1 to D_2 in Figure 2. Given the fixed euro supply curve S_1, the increase in demand raises the equilibrium exchange rate (the equilibrium number of dollars needed to purchase 1 euro) from \$1.25 to \$1.50. The equilibrium quantity of euros purchased increases from Q_1 to Q_2. Because a higher dollar amount is now needed to purchase one euro, economists say that the dollar has *depreciated*—gone down in value—relative to the euro. Alternatively, the euro has *appreciated*—gone up in value—relative to the dollar, because one euro now buys \$1.50 rather than \$1.25.

Pink Salmon

Now let's see what happens when both supply and demand change at the same time. Several decades ago, people who caught salmon earned as much as \$1 for each pound of pink salmon—the type of salmon most commonly used for canning. In Figure 3 that price is represented as P_1, at the intersection of supply curve S_1 and demand curve D_1. The corresponding quantity of pink salmon is shown as Q_1 pounds.

As time passed, supply and demand changed in the market for pink salmon. On the supply side, improved technology in the form of larger, more efficient fishing boats greatly increased the catch and lowered the cost of obtaining it. Also, high profits at price P_1 encouraged many new fishers to enter the industry. As a result of these changes, the supply of pink salmon greatly increased and the supply curve shifted to the right, as from S_1 to S_2 in Figure 3.

Over the same years, the demand for pink salmon declined, as represented by the leftward shift from D_1 to D_2 in Figure 3. That decrease was caused by increases in consumer income and reductions of the price of substitute products. As buyers' incomes rose, consumers shifted demand away from canned fish and toward higher-quality fresh or frozen fish, including more-valued Atlantic, chinook, sockeye, and coho salmon. Moreover, the emergence of fish farming, in which salmon are raised in ocean

FIGURE 2 **The market for euros.** The increase in the demand for euros, shown here by the shift from D_1 to D_2, increases the equilibrium price of one euro from \$1.25 to \$1.50 and increases the equilibrium quantity of euros that are exchanged from Q_1 to Q_2. The dollar has depreciated.

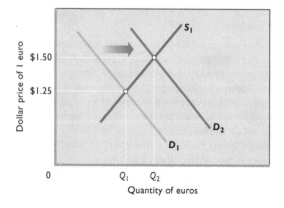

FIGURE 3 **The market for pink salmon.** In the last several decades, the supply of pink salmon has increased and the demand for pink salmon has decreased. As a result, the price of pink salmon has declined, as from P_1 to P_2. Because supply has increased by more than demand has decreased, the equilibrium quantity of pink salmon has increased, as from Q_1 to Q_2.

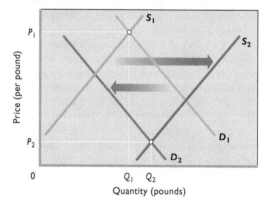

net pens, lowered the prices of these substitute species. That, too, reduced the demand for pink salmon.

The altered supply and demand reduced the price of pink salmon to as low as \$0.10 per pound, as represented by the drop in price from P_1 to P_2 in Figure 3. Both the supply increase and the demand decrease helped reduce the equilibrium price. However, in this particular case the equilibrium quantity of pink salmon increased, as represented by the move from Q_1 to Q_2. Both shifts reduced the equilibrium price, but equilibrium quantity increased because the increase in supply exceeded the decrease in demand.

Gasoline

The price of gasoline in the United States has increased rapidly several times during the past several years. For example, the average price of a gallon of gasoline rose from around \$2.60 in October 2010 to about \$3.90 in May 2011. What caused this 50 percent rise in the price of gasoline? How would we diagram this increase?

We begin in Figure 4 with the price of a gallon of gasoline at P_1, representing the \$2.60 price. Simultaneous supply and demand factors disturbed this equilibrium. Supply uncertainties relating to Middle East politics and warfare and expanded demand for oil by fast-growing countries such as China pushed up the price of a barrel of oil from under \$80 per barrel in October 2010 to well over \$100 per barrel in May 2011. Oil is the main input for producing gasoline, so any sustained rise in its price boosts the per-unit cost of producing gasoline. Such cost rises decrease the supply of gasoline, as represented by the leftward shift of the supply curve from S_1 to S_2 in Figure 4. At times refinery breakdowns in the United States also contributed to this reduced supply.

While the supply of gasoline declined between October 2010 and May 2011, the demand for gasoline increased, as depicted by the rightward shift of the demand curve from D_1 to D_2. Incomes in general were rising over this period because the U.S. economy was expanding. Rising incomes raise demand for all normal goods, including gasoline. An increased number of low-gas-mileage SUVs and light trucks on the road also contributed to growing gas demand.

The combined decline in gasoline supply and increase in gasoline demand boosted the price of gasoline from \$2.60 to \$3.90, as represented by the rise from P_1 to P_2 in Figure 4. Because the demand increase outweighed the supply decrease, the equilibrium quantity expanded, here from Q_1 to Q_2.

In other periods the price of gasoline has *declined* as the demand for gasoline has increased. Test your understanding of the analysis by explaining how such a price decrease could occur.

Sushi

Sushi bars are springing up like Starbucks in American cities (well, maybe not that fast!). Consumption of sushi, the raw-fish delicacy from Japan, has soared in the United States in recent years. Nevertheless, the price of sushi has remained relatively constant.

Supply and demand analysis helps explain this circumstance of increased quantity and constant price. A change in tastes has increased the U.S. demand for sushi. Many consumers of sushi find it highly tasty when they try it. And, as implied by the growing number of sushi bars in the United States, the supply of sushi has also expanded.

We represent these supply and demand changes in Figure 5 as the rightward shift of the demand curve from D_1 to D_2 and the rightward shift of the supply curve from S_1 to S_2. Observe that the equilibrium quantity of sushi increases from Q_1 to Q_2 and equilibrium price remains constant at P_1. The increase in supply, which taken alone would reduce price, has perfectly offset the increase in demand, which taken alone would raise price. The price of sushi does not change, but the equilibrium quantity greatly increases because both the increase in demand and the increase in supply expand purchases and sales.

Simultaneous increases in demand and supply can cause price to either rise, fall, or remain constant, depending on the relative magnitudes of the supply and demand increases. In this case, price remained constant.

FIGURE 4   The market for gasoline. An increase in the demand for gasoline, as shown by the shift from D_1 to D_2, coupled with a decrease in supply, as shown by the shift from S_1 to S_2, boosts equilibrium price (here from P_1 to P_2). In this case, equilibrium quantity increases from Q_1 to Q_2 because the increase in demand outweighs the decrease in supply.

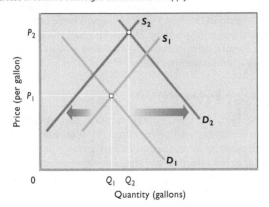

FIGURE 5 The market for sushi. Equal increases in the demand for sushi, as from D_1 to D_2, and in the supply of sushi, as from S_1 to S_2, expand the equilibrium quantity of sushi (here from Q_1 to Q_2) while leaving the price of sushi unchanged at P_1.

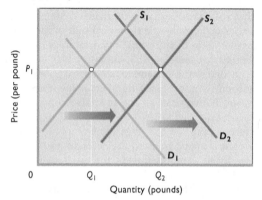

FIGURE 6 The market for land in San Francisco. Because the quantity of land in San Francisco is fixed at Q_0, the supply curve is vertical above Q_0 in order to indicate that the same quantity of land will be supplied no matter what the price is. As demand increases from D_1 to D_2, the equilibrium price rises from P_1 to P_2. Because the quantity of land is fixed at Q_0, the movement from equilibrium a to equilibrium b involves only a change in the equilibrium price; the equilibrium quantity remains at Q_0 due to land being in fixed supply.

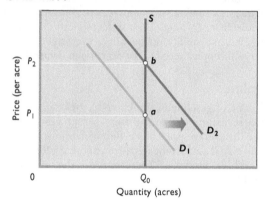

Upsloping versus Vertical Supply Curves

As you already know, the typical good or service possesses an upsloping supply curve because a higher market price will cause producers to increase the quantity supplied. There are, however, some goods and services whose quantities supplied are fixed and totally unresponsive to changes in price. Examples include the amount of land in a given area, the number of seats in a stadium, and the limited part of the electromagnetic spectrum that is reserved for cellular telephone transmissions. These sorts of goods and services have vertical supply curves because the same fixed amount is available no matter what price is offered to suppliers.

Reactions to Demand Shifts

Markets react very differently to a shift in demand depending upon whether they have upsloping or vertical supply curves.

Upsloping Supply Curves When a market has an upsloping supply curve, any shift in demand will cause both the equilibrium price *and* the equilibrium quantity to adjust. Consider Figure 2. When the demand for euros increases, the movement from the initial equilibrium to the final equilibrium involves the equilibrium price rising from $1.25 to $1.50 while the equilibrium quantity increases from Q_1 to Q_2. Price and quantity *both* change.

Vertical Supply Curves When a market has a vertical supply curve, any shift in demand will cause only the

equilibrium price to change; the equilibrium quantity remains the same because the quantity supplied is fixed and cannot adjust.

Consider Figure 6, in which the supply of land in San Francisco is fixed at quantity Q_0. If demand increases from D_1 to D_2, the movement from the initial equilibrium at point a to the final equilibrium at point b is accomplished solely by a rise in the equilibrium price from P_1 to P_2. Because the quantity of land is fixed, the increase in demand cannot cause any change in the equilibrium quantity supplied. The entire adjustment from the initial equilibrium to the final equilibrium has to come in the form of a higher equilibrium price.

This fact explains why real estate prices are so high in San Francisco and other major cities. Any increase in demand cannot be met by a combination of increases in price and increases in quantity. With the quantity of land in fixed supply, any increase in demand results solely in higher equilibrium land prices.

Preset Prices

In the body of this chapter, we saw that an effective government-imposed price ceiling (legal maximum price) causes quantity demanded to exceed quantity supplied—a shortage. An effective government-imposed price floor (legal minimum price) causes quantity supplied to exceed quantity demanded—a surplus. Put simply: Shortages result when prices are set below, and surpluses result when prices are set above, equilibrium prices.

We now want to establish that shortages and surpluses can occur in markets other than those in which government imposes price floors and ceilings. Such market imbalances happen when the seller or sellers set prices in advance of sales and the prices selected turn out to be below or above equilibrium prices. Consider the following two examples.

Olympic Figure Skating Finals

Tickets for the women's figure skating championship at the Olympics are among the world's "hottest tickets." The popularity of this event and the high incomes of buyers translate into tremendous ticket demand. The Olympic officials set the price for the tickets in advance. Invariably, the price, although high, is considerably below the equilibrium price that would equate quantity demanded and quantity supplied. A severe shortage of tickets therefore occurs in this *primary market*—the market involving the official ticket office.

The shortage, in turn, creates a *secondary market* in which buyers bid for tickets held by initial purchasers rather than the original seller. Scalping tickets—selling them above the original ticket price—may be legal or illegal, depending on local laws.

Figure 7 shows how the shortage in the primary ticket market looks in terms of supply and demand analysis. Demand curve D represents the strong demand for tickets

and supply curve S represents the supply of tickets. The supply curve is vertical because a fixed number of tickets are printed to match the capacity of the arena. At the printed ticket price of P_1, the quantity of tickets demanded, Q_2, exceeds the quantity supplied, Q_1. The result is a shortage of ab—the horizontal distance between Q_2 and Q_1 in the primary market.

If the printed ticket price had been the higher equilibrium price P_2, no shortage of tickets would have occurred. But at the lower price P_1, a shortage and secondary ticket market will emerge among those buyers willing to pay more than the printed ticket price and those sellers willing to sell their purchased tickets for more than the original price. Wherever there are shortages and secondary markets, it is safe to assume the original price was set below the equilibrium price.

Olympic Curling Preliminaries

Contrast the shortage of tickets for the women's figure skating finals at the Olympics to the surplus of tickets for one of the preliminary curling matches. For the uninitiated, curling is a sport in which participants slide a heavy round object called a "stone" down the ice toward a target while teammates called "sweepers" use brooms to alter the course of the stone when desired.

Curling is a popular spectator sport in a few nations such as Canada, but it does not draw many fans in most countries. So the demand for tickets to most of the preliminary curling events is not very strong. We demonstrate this weak demand as D in Figure 8. As in our previous

FIGURE 7 **The market for tickets to the Olympic women's figure skating finals.** The demand curve D and supply curve S for the Olympic women's figure skating finals produce an equilibrium price that is above the P_1 price printed on the ticket. At price P_1 the quantity of tickets demanded, Q_2, greatly exceeds the quantity of tickets available, Q_1. The resulting shortage of ab (= $Q_2 - Q_1$) gives rise to a legal or illegal secondary market.

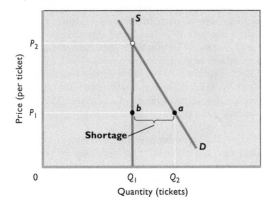

FIGURE 8 **The market for tickets to the Olympic curling preliminaries.** The demand curve D and supply curve S for the Olympic curling preliminaries produce an equilibrium price below the P_1 price printed on the ticket. At price P_1 the quantity of tickets demanded is less than the quantity of tickets available. The resulting surplus of ba (= $Q_1 - Q_2$) means the event is not sold out.

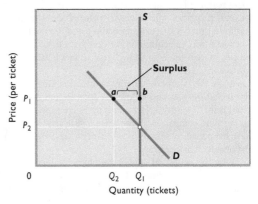

example, the supply of tickets is fixed by the size of the arena and is shown as vertical line S.

We represent the printed ticket price as P_1 in Figure 8. In this case the printed price is much higher than the equilibrium price of P_2. At the printed ticket price, quantity supplied is Q_1 and quantity demanded is Q_2. So a surplus of tickets of ba $(= Q_1 - Q_2)$ occurs. No ticket scalping occurs and there are numerous empty seats. Only if the

Olympic officials had priced the tickets at the lower price P_2, would the event have been a sellout. (Actually, the Olympic officials try to adjust to demand realities for curling contests by holding them in smaller arenas and by charging less for tickets. Nevertheless, the stands are rarely full for the preliminary contests, which compete against final events in other winter Olympic sports.)

APPENDIX SUMMARY

LO3.7 Illustrate how supply and demand analysis can provide insights on actual-economy situations.

A decrease in the supply of a product increases its equilibrium price and reduces its equilibrium quantity. In contrast, an increase in the demand for a product boosts both its equilibrium price and its equilibrium quantity.

Simultaneous changes in supply and demand affect equilibrium price and quantity in various ways, depending on the relative magnitudes of the changes in supply and demand. Equal increases in supply and demand, for example, leave equilibrium price unchanged.

Products (such as land) whose quantities supplied do not vary with price have vertical supply curves. For these products, any shift in demand will lead to a change in the equilibrium price but no change in the equilibrium quantity.

Sellers set prices of some items such as tickets in advance of the event. These items are sold in the primary market that involves the original sellers and buyers. If preset prices turn out to be below the equilibrium prices, shortages occur and scalping in legal or illegal secondary markets arises. The prices in the secondary market then rise above the preset prices. In contrast, surpluses occur when the preset prices happen to exceed the equilibrium prices.

The following and additional problems can be found in **connect**
ECONOMICS

APPENDIX DISCUSSION QUESTIONS

1. Why are shortages or surpluses more likely with preset prices, such as those on tickets, than flexible prices, such as those on gasoline? **LO3.7**

2. Most scalping laws make it illegal to sell—but not to buy—tickets at prices above those printed on the tickets. Assuming that is the case, use supply and demand analysis to explain why the equilibrium ticket price in an illegal secondary market tends to be higher than in a legal secondary market. **LO3.7**

3. Go to the Web site of the Energy Information Administration, **www.eia.doe.gov**, and follow the links to find the current retail price of gasoline. How does the current price of regular gasoline compare with the price a year ago? What must have happened to either supply, demand, or both to explain the observed price change? **LO3.7**

4. Suppose the supply of apples sharply increases because of perfect weather conditions throughout the growing season. Assuming no change in demand, explain the effect on the

equilibrium price and quantity of apples. Explain why quantity demanded increases even though demand does not change. **LO3.7**

5. Assume the demand for lumber suddenly rises because of a rapid growth of demand for new housing. Assume no change in supply. Why does the equilibrium price of lumber rise? What would happen if the price did not rise under the demand and supply circumstances described? **LO3.7**

6. Assume that both the supply of bottled water and the demand for bottled water rise during the summer but that supply increases more rapidly than demand. What can you conclude about the directions of the impacts on equilibrium price and equilibrium quantity? **LO3.7**

7. When asked for investment advice, humorist Will Rogers joked that people should "[b]uy land. They ain't making any more of the stuff." Explain his advice in terms of the supply and demand model. **LO3.7**

APPENDIX REVIEW QUESTIONS

1. Will the equilibrium price of orange juice increase or decrease in each of the following situations? **LO3.7**
   a. A medical study reporting that orange juice reduces cancer is released at the same time that a freak storm destroys half of the orange crop in Florida.
   b. The prices of all beverages except orange juice fall by half while unexpectedly perfect weather in Florida results in an orange crop that is 20 percent larger than normal.
2. Consider the market for coffee beans. Suppose that the prices of all other caffeinated beverages go up 30 percent while at the same time a new fertilizer boosts production at coffee plantations dramatically. Which of the following best describes what is likely to happen to the equilibrium price and quantity of coffee beans? **LO3.7**
   a. Both the equilibrium price and the quantity will rise.
   b. The equilibrium price will rise but the equilibrium quantity will fall.
   c. The equilibrium price may rise or fall but the equilibrium quantity will rise for certain.
   d. Neither the price change nor the quantity change can be determined for certain.
   e. None of the above.
3. A price ceiling will result in a shortage only if the ceiling price is _____ the equilibrium price. **LO3.7**
   a. Less than.
   b. Equal to.
   c. Greater than.
   d. Faster than.

4. Suppose that you are the economic advisor to a local government that has to deal with a politically embarrassing surplus that was caused by a price floor that the government recently imposed. Your first suggestion is to get rid of the price floor, but the politicians don't want to do that. Instead, they present you with the following list of options that they hope will get rid of the surplus while keeping the price floor. Identify each one as either *could work* or *can't work*. **LO3.7**
   a. Restricting supply.
   b. Decreasing demand.
   c. Purchasing the surplus at the floor price.
5. Suppose both the demand for olives and the supply of olives decline by equal amounts over some time period. Use graphical analysis to show the effect on equilibrium price and quantity. **LO3.7**
6. Governments can use subsidies to increase demand. For instance, a government can pay farmers to use organic fertilizers rather than traditional fertilizers. That subsidy increases the demand for organic fertilizer. Consider two industries, one in which supply is nearly vertical and the other in which supply is nearly horizontal. Assume that firms in both industries would prefer a higher market equilibrium price because a higher market equilibrium price would mean higher profits. Which industry would probably spend more resources lobbying the government to increase the demand for its output? (Assume that both industries have similarly sloped demand curves.) **LO3.7**
   a. The industry with a nearly flat supply curve.
   b. The industry with a nearly vertical supply curve.

APPENDIX PROBLEMS

1. Demand and supply often shift in the retail market for gasoline. Here are two demand curves and two supply curves for gallons of gasoline in the month of May in a small town in Maine. Some of the data are missing. **LO3.7**

Price	Quantities Demanded		Quantities Supplied	
	D_1	D_2	S_1	S_2
$4.00	5,000	7,500	9,000	9,500
____	6,000	8,000	8,000	9,000
2.00	____	8,500	____	8,500
____	____	9,000	5,000	____

   a. Use the following facts to fill in the missing data in the table. If demand is D_1 and supply is S_1, the equilibrium quantity is 7,000 gallons per month. When demand is D_2 and supply is S_1, the equilibrium price is $3.00 per gallon. When demand is D_2 and supply is S_1, there is an excess

demand of 4,000 gallons per month at a price of $1.00 per gallon. If demand is D_1 and supply is S_2, the equilibrium quantity is 8,000 gallons per month.
   b. Compare two equilibriums. In the first, demand is D_1 and supply is S_1. In the second, demand is D_1 and supply is S_2. By how much does the equilibrium quantity change? By how much does the equilibrium price change?
   c. If supply falls from S_2 to S_1 while demand declines from D_2 to D_1, does the equilibrium price rise, fall, or stay the same? What if only supply falls? What if only demand falls?
   d. Suppose that supply is fixed at S_1 and that demand starts at D_1. By how many gallons per month would demand have to increase at each price level such that the equilibrium price per gallon would be $3.00? $4.00?
2. The table at the top of the next page shows two demand schedules for a given style of men's shoe—that is, how many pairs per month will be demanded at various prices at a men's clothing store in Seattle called Stromnord.

Price	D_1 Quantity Demanded	D_2 Quantity Demanded
$75	53	13
70	60	15
65	68	18
60	77	22
55	87	27

Suppose that Stromnord has exactly 65 pairs of this style of shoe in inventory at the start of the month of July and will not receive any more pairs of this style until at least August 1. LO3.7

a. If demand is D_1, what is the lowest price that Stromnord can charge so that it will not run out of this model of shoe in the month of July? What if demand is D_2?

b. If the price of shoes is set at $75 for both July and August and demand will be D_2 in July and D_1 in August, how many pairs of shoes should Stromnord order if it wants to end the month of August with exactly zero pairs of shoes in its inventory? What if the price is set at $55 for both months?

3. Use the table below to answer the questions that follow: LO3.7

a. If this table reflects the supply of and demand for tickets to a particular World Cup soccer game, what is the stadium capacity?

b. If the preset ticket price is $45, would we expect to see a secondary market for tickets? Would the price of a ticket in the secondary market be higher than, the same as, or lower than the price in the primary (original) market?

c. Suppose for some other World Cup game the quantity of tickets demanded is 20,000 lower at each ticket price than shown in the table. If the ticket price remains $45, would the event be a sellout?

Quantity Demanded, Thousands	Price	Quantity Supplied, Thousands
80	$25	60
75	35	60
70	45	60
65	55	60
60	65	60
55	75	60
50	85	60

CHAPTER **4**

Market Failures: Public Goods and Externalities

Learning Objectives

LO4.1 Differentiate between demand-side market failures and supply-side market failures.

LO4.2 Explain the origin of both consumer surplus and producer surplus, and explain how properly functioning markets maximize their sum, total surplus, while optimally allocating resources.

LO4.3 Describe free riding and public goods, and illustrate why private firms cannot normally produce public goods.

LO4.4 Explain how positive and negative externalities cause under- and overallocations of resources.

LO4.5 Show why we normally won't want to pay what it would cost to

eliminate every last bit of a negative externality such as air pollution.

LO4.6 (Appendix) Describe how information failures may justify government intervention in some markets.

Competitive markets usually do a remarkably effective job of allocating society's scarce resources to their most highly valued uses. Thus, we begin this chapter by demonstrating how properly functioning markets efficiently allocate resources. We then explore what happens when markets don't function properly. In some circumstances, economically desirable goods are not produced at all. In other situations, they are either overproduced or underproduced. This chapter focuses on these situations, which economists refer to as **market failures**.

In such situations, an economic role for government may arise. We will examine that role as it relates to public goods and so-called externalities—situations where market failures lead to suboptimal outcomes that the government may be able to improve upon by using its powers to tax, spend, and regulate. The government may, for instance, pay for the production of goods that the private sector fails to produce. It may also act to reduce the production of those goods and services that the private sector overproduces. Implementing such policies can, however, be both costly and complicated. Thus, we conclude the chapter by noting the government inefficiencies that can hinder government efforts to improve economic outcomes.

Market Failures in Competitive Markets[1]

LO4.1 Differentiate between demand-side market failures and supply-side market failures.

In Chapter 3 we asserted that "competitive markets usually produce an assignment of resources that is 'right' from an economic perspective." We now want to focus on the word "usually" and discuss exceptions. We must do this because it is unfortunately the case that the presence of robust competition involving many buyers and many sellers may not, by itself, be enough to guarantee that a market will allocate resources correctly. Market failures sometimes happen in competitive markets. The focus of this chapter is to explain how and why such market failures can arise.

Fortunately, the broad picture is simple. Market failures in competitive markets fall into just two categories:

- **Demand-side market failures** happen when demand curves do not reflect consumers' full willingness to pay for a good or service.
- **Supply-side market failures** occur when supply curves do not reflect the full cost of producing a good or service.

Demand-Side Market Failures

Demand-side market failures arise because it is impossible in certain cases to charge consumers what they are willing to pay for a product. Consider outdoor fireworks displays. People enjoy fireworks and would therefore be *willing* to pay to see a fireworks display if the only way to see it was to have to pay for the right to do so. But because such displays are outdoors and in public, people don't actually *have* to pay to see the display because there is no way to exclude those who haven't paid from also enjoying the show. Private firms will therefore be unwilling to produce outdoor fireworks displays, as it will be nearly impossible for them to raise enough revenue to cover production costs.

Supply-Side Market Failures

Supply-side market failures arise in situations in which a firm does not have to pay the full cost of producing its output. Consider a coal-burning power plant. The firm running the plant will have to pay for all of the land, labor, capital, and entrepreneurship that it uses to generate electricity by burning coal. But if the firm is not charged for the smoke that it releases into the atmosphere, it will fail to pay another set of costs— the costs that its pollution imposes on other people. These include future harm from global warming, toxins that affect wildlife, and possible damage to agricultural crops downwind.

A market failure arises because it is not possible for the market to correctly weigh costs and benefits in a situation in which some of the costs are completely unaccounted for. The coal-burning power plant produces more electricity and generates more pollution than it would if it had to pay for each ton of smoke that it released into the atmosphere. The extra units that are produced are units of output for which the costs are *greater than* the benefits. Obviously, these units should not be produced.

---

[1] Other market failures arise when there are not enough buyers or sellers to ensure competition. In those situations, the lack of competition allows either buyers or sellers to restrict purchases or sales below optimal levels for their own benefit. As an example, a monopoly—a firm that is the only producer in its industry—can restrict the amount of output that it supplies in order to drive up the market price and thereby increase its own profit.

Efficiently Functioning Markets

LO4.2 Explain the origin of both consumer surplus and producer surplus, and explain how properly functioning markets maximize their sum, total surplus, while optimally allocating resources.

The best way to understand market failure is to first understand how properly functioning competitive markets achieve economic efficiency. We touched on this subject in Chapter 3, but we now want to expand and deepen that analysis, both for its own sake and to set up our discussion of public goods and externalities. Two conditions must hold if a competitive market is to produce efficient outcomes: The demand curve in the market must reflect consumers' full willingness to pay, and the supply curve in the market must reflect all the costs of production. If these conditions hold, then the market will produce only units for which benefits are at least equal to costs. It will also maximize the amount of "benefit surpluses" that are shared between consumers and producers.

Consumer Surplus

The benefit surplus received by a consumer or consumers in a market is called **consumer surplus.** It is defined as the difference between the maximum price a consumer is (or consumers are) willing to pay for a product and the actual price that they do pay.

The maximum price that a person is willing to pay for a unit of a product depends on the opportunity cost of that person's consumption alternatives. Suppose that Ted is offered the chance to purchase an apple. He would of course like to have it for free, but the maximum amount he would be willing to pay depends on the alternative uses to which he can put his money. If his maximum willingness to pay for that particular apple is $1.25, then we know that he is willing to forgo up to—but not more than—$1.25 of other goods and services. Paying even one cent more would entail having to give up too much of other goods and services.

It also means that if Ted is charged any market price less than $1.25, he will receive a consumer surplus equal to the difference between the $1.25 maximum price that he would have been willing to pay and the lower market price. For instance, if the market price is $0.50 per apple, Ted will receive a consumer surplus of $0.75 per apple (= $1.25 − $0.50). In nearly all markets, consumers individually and collectively gain greater total utility or satisfaction in dollar terms from their purchases than the amount of their expenditures (= product price × quantity). This utility surplus arises because each consumer who buys the product only has to pay the market equilibrium price

TABLE 4.1 Consumer Surplus

(1) Person	(2) Maximum Price Willing to Pay	(3) Actual Price (Equilibrium Price)	(4) Consumer Surplus
Bob	$13	$8	$5 (= $13 – $8)
Barb	12	8	4 (= $12 – $8)
Bill	11	8	3 (= $11 – $8)
Bart	10	8	2 (= $10 – $8)
Brent	9	8	1 (= $9 – $8)
Betty	8	8	0 (= $8 – $8)

even though many of them would have been willing to pay more than the equilibrium price to obtain the product.

The concept of maximum willingness to pay also gives us another way to understand demand curves. Consider Table 4.1, where the first two columns show the maximum amounts that six consumers would each be willing to pay for a bag of oranges. Bob, for instance, would be willing to pay a maximum of $13 for a bag of oranges. Betty, by contrast, would only be willing to pay a maximum of $8 for a bag of oranges.

Notice that the maximum prices that these individuals are willing to pay represent points on a demand curve because the lower the market price, the more bags of oranges will be demanded. At a price of $12.50, for instance, Bob will be the only person listed in the table who will purchase a bag. But at a price of $11.50, both Bob and Barb will want to purchase a bag. And at a price of $10.50, Bob, Barb, and Bill will each want to purchase a bag. The lower the price, the greater the total quantity demanded as the market price falls below the maximum prices of more and more consumers.

Lower prices also imply larger consumer surpluses. When the price is $12.50, Bob only gets $0.50 in consumer surplus because his maximum willingness to pay of $13 is only $0.50 higher than the market price of $12.50. But if the market price were to fall to $8, then his consumer surplus would be $5 (= $13 − $8). The third and fourth columns of Table 4.1 show how much consumer surplus each of our six consumers will receive if the market price of a bag of oranges is $8. Only Betty receives no consumer surplus because her maximum willingness to pay exactly matches the $8 equilibrium price.

It is easy to show on a graph both the individual consumer surplus received by each particular buyer in a market as well as the collective consumer surplus received by all buyers. Consider Figure 4.1, which shows the market equilibrium price P_1 = $8 as well as the downsloping

FIGURE 4.1 Consumer surplus. Consumer surplus—shown as the green triangle—is the difference between the maximum prices consumers are willing to pay for a product and the lower equilibrium price, here assumed to be $8. For quantity Q_1, consumers are willing to pay the sum of the amounts represented by the green triangle and the yellow rectangle. Because they need to pay only the amount shown as the yellow rectangle, the green triangle shows consumer surplus.

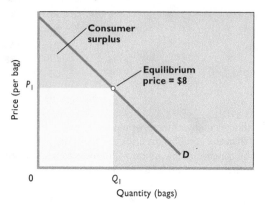

ORIGIN OF THE IDEA

04.1
Consumer surplus

consumer surplus. When price goes up, the gap narrows between the maximum willingness to pay and the actual price. Next, draw in an equilibrium price below $8 and see that consumer surplus increases. When price declines, the gap widens between maximum willingness to pay and actual price.

Producer Surplus

Like consumers, producers also receive a benefit surplus in markets. This **producer surplus** is the difference between the actual price a producer receives (or producers receive) and the minimum acceptable price that a consumer would have to pay the producer to make a particular unit of output available.

A producer's minimum acceptable price for a particular unit will equal the producer's marginal cost of producing that particular unit. That marginal cost will be the sum of the rent, wages, interest, and profit that the producer will need to pay in order to obtain the land, labor, capital, and entrepreneurship required to produce that particular unit. In this section, we are assuming that the marginal cost of producing a unit will include *all* of the costs of production. Unlike the coal-burning power plant mentioned previously, the producer must pay for all of its costs, including the cost of pollution. In later sections, we will explore the market failures that arise in situations where firms do not have to pay all their costs.

In addition to equaling marginal cost, a producer's minimum acceptable price can also be interpreted as the opportunity cost of bidding resources away from the production of other products. To see why this is true, suppose that Leah is an apple grower. The resources necessary for her to produce one apple could be used to produce other things. To get them directed toward producing an apple, it is necessary to pay Leah what it will cost her to bid the necessary resources away from other entrepreneurs who would like to use them to produce other products. Leah would, naturally, like to get paid as much as possible to produce the apple for you. But her minimum acceptable price is the lowest price you could pay her such that she can just break even after bidding away from other uses the land, labor, capital, and entrepreneurship necessary to produce the apple.

The size of the producer surplus earned on any particular unit will be the difference between the market price that the producer actually receives and the producer's

demand curve D for bags of oranges. Demand curve D includes not only the six consumers named in Table 4.1 but also every other consumer of oranges in the market. The individual consumer surplus of each particular person who is willing to buy at the $8 market price is simply the vertical distance from the horizontal line that marks the $8 market price up to that particular buyer's maximum willingness to pay. The collective consumer surplus obtained by all of our named and unnamed buyers is found by adding together each of their individual consumer surpluses. To obtain the Q_1 bags of oranges represented, consumers collectively are willing to pay the total amount shown by the sum of the green triangle and yellow rectangle under the demand curve and to the left of Q_1. But consumers need pay only the amount represented by the yellow rectangle ($= P_1 \times Q_1$). So the green triangle is the consumer surplus in this market. It is the sum of the vertical distances between the demand curve and the $8 equilibrium price at each quantity up to Q_1. Alternatively, it is the sum of the gaps between maximum willingness to pay and actual price, such as those we calculated in Table 4.1. Thus, consumer surplus can also be defined as the area that lies below the demand curve and above the price line that extends horizontally from P_1.

Consumer surplus and price are inversely (negatively) related. Given the demand curve, higher prices reduce consumer surplus; lower prices increase it. To test this generalization, draw in an equilibrium price above $8 in Figure 4.1 and observe the reduced size of the triangle representing

TABLE 4.2 Producer Surplus

(1) Person	(2) Minimum Acceptable Price	(3) Actual Price (Equilibrium Price)	(4) Producer Surplus
Carlos	$3	$8	$5 (= $8 − $3)
Courtney	4	8	4 (= $8 − $4)
Chuck	5	8	3 (= $8 − $5)
Cindy	6	8	2 (= $8 − $6)
Craig	7	8	1 (= $8 − $7)
Chad	8	8	0 (= $8 − $8)

FIGURE 4.2 Producer surplus. Producer surplus—shown as the blue triangle—is the difference between the actual price producers receive for a product (here $8) and the lower minimum payments they are willing to accept. For quantity Q_1, producers receive the sum of the amounts represented by the blue triangle plus the yellow area. Because they need to receive only the amount shown by the yellow area to produce Q_1, the blue triangle represents producer surplus.

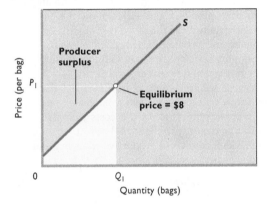

minimum acceptable price. Consider Table 4.2, which shows the minimum acceptable prices of six different orange growers. With a market price of $8, Carlos, for instance, has a producer surplus of $5, which is equal to the market price of $8 minus his minimum acceptable price of $3. Chad, by contrast, receives no producer surplus because his minimum acceptable price of $8 just equals the market equilibrium price of $8.

Carlos's minimum acceptable price is lower than Chad's minimum acceptable price because Carlos is a more efficient producer than Chad, by which we mean that Carlos produces oranges using a less-costly combination of resources than Chad uses. The differences in efficiency between Carlos and Chad are likely due to differences in the type and quality of resources available to them. Carlos, for instance, may own land perfectly suited to growing oranges, while Chad has land in the desert that requires costly irrigation if it is to be used to grow oranges. Thus, Chad has a higher marginal cost of producing oranges.

The minimum acceptable prices that producers are willing to accept form points on a supply curve because the higher the price, the more bags of oranges will be supplied. At a price of $3.50, for instance, only Carlos would be willing to supply a bag of oranges. But at a price of $5.50, Carlos, Courtney, and Chuck would all be willing to supply a bag of oranges. The higher the market price, the more oranges will be supplied, as the market price surpasses the marginal costs and minimum acceptable prices of more and more producers. Thus, supply curves shown in this competitive market are both marginal-cost curves and minimum-acceptable-price curves.

The supply curve in Figure 4.2 includes not only the six producers named in Table 4.2 but also every other producer of oranges in the market. At the market price of $8 per bag, Q_1 bags are produced because only those producers whose minimum acceptable prices are less than $8 per bag will choose to produce oranges with their

resources. Those lower acceptable prices for each of the units up to Q_1 are shown by the portion of the supply curve lying to the left of and below the assumed $8 market price.

The individual producer surplus of each of these sellers is thus the vertical distance from each seller's respective minimum acceptable price on the supply curve up to the $8 market price. Their collective producer surplus is shown by the blue triangle in Figure 4.2. In that figure, producers collect revenues of $P_1 \times Q_1$, which is the sum of the blue triangle and the yellow area. As shown by the supply curve, however, revenues of only those illustrated by the yellow area would be required to entice producers to offer Q_1 bags of oranges for sale. The sellers therefore receive a producer surplus shown by the blue triangle. That surplus is the sum of the vertical distances between the supply curve and the $8 equilibrium price at each of the quantities to the left of Q_1.

There is a direct (positive) relationship between equilibrium price and the amount of producer surplus. Given the supply curve, lower prices reduce producer surplus; higher prices increase it. If you pencil in a lower equilibrium price than $8, you will see that the producer surplus triangle gets smaller. The gaps between the minimum acceptable payments and the actual prices narrow when the price falls. If you pencil in an equilibrium price

WORKED PROBLEMS

W4.1

Consumer and producer surplus

above $8, the size of the producer surplus triangle increases. The gaps between minimum acceptable payments and actual prices widen when the price increases.

Efficiency Revisited

In Figure 4.3 we bring together the demand and supply curves of Figures 4.1 and 4.2 to show the equilibrium price and quantity and the previously described regions of consumer and producer surplus. All markets that have downsloping demand curves and upsloping supply curves yield consumer and producer surplus.

Because we are assuming in Figure 4.3 that the demand curve reflects buyers' full willingness to pay and the supply curve reflects all of the costs facing sellers, the equilibrium quantity in Figure 4.3 reflects economic efficiency, which consists of productive efficiency and allocative efficiency.

- *Productive efficiency* is achieved because competition forces orange growers to use the best technologies and combinations of resources available. Doing so minimizes the per-unit cost of the output produced.
- *Allocative efficiency* is achieved because the correct quantity of oranges—Q_1—is produced relative to other goods and services.

There are two ways to understand why Q_1 is the correct quantity of oranges. Both involve realizing that any resources directed toward the production of oranges are

resources that could have been used to produce other products. Thus, the only way to justify taking any amount of any resource (land, labor, capital, entrepreneurship) away from the production of other products is if it brings more utility or satisfaction when devoted to the production of oranges than it would if it were used to produce other products.

The first way to see why Q_1 is the allocatively efficient quantity of oranges is to note that demand and supply curves can be interpreted as measuring marginal benefit (MB) and marginal cost (MC). Recall from the discussion relating to Figure 1.3 that optimal allocation is achieved at the output level where MB = MC. We have already seen that supply curves are marginal cost curves. As it turns out, demand curves are marginal benefit curves. This is true because the maximum price that a consumer would be willing to pay for any particular unit is equal to the benefit that she would get if she were to consume that unit. Thus, each point on a demand curve represents both some consumer's maximum willingness to pay as well as the marginal benefit that he or she would get from consuming the particular unit in question.

Combining the fact that supply curves are MC curves with the fact that demand curves are MB curves, we see that points on the demand curve in Figure 4.3 measure the marginal benefit of oranges at each level of output, while points on the supply curve measure the marginal cost of oranges at each level of output. As a result, MB = MC where the demand and supply curves intersect—which means that the equilibrium quantity Q_1 must be allocatively efficient.

To gain a deeper understanding of why Q_1 is allocatively efficient, notice that for every unit up to Q_1 marginal benefit exceeds marginal cost (MB > MC). And because marginal cost includes the opportunity cost of not making other things with the resources needed to make these units, we know that people are made better off when the resources necessary to make these units are allocated to producing oranges rather than to producing anything else.

The second way to see why Q_1 is the correct quantity of oranges is based on our analysis of consumer and producer surplus and the fact that we can interpret demand and supply curves in terms of maximum willingness to pay and minimum acceptable price. In Figure 4.3, the maximum willingness to pay on the demand curve for each bag of oranges up to Q_1 exceeds the corresponding minimum acceptable price on the supply curve. Thus, each of these bags adds a positive amount (= maximum willingness to pay *minus* minimum acceptable price) to the *total* of consumer and producer surplus.

FIGURE 4.3 Efficiency: maximum combined consumer and producer surplus. At quantity Q_1 the combined amount of consumer surplus, shown as the green triangle, and producer surplus, shown as the blue triangle, is maximized. Efficiency occurs because, at Q_1, maximum willingness to pay, indicated by the points on the demand curve, equals minimum acceptable price, shown by the points on the supply curve.

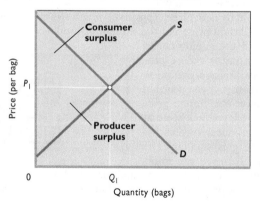

The fact that maximum willingness to pay exceeds minimum acceptable price for every unit up to Q_1 means that people gain more utility from producing and consuming those units than they would if they produced and consumed anything else that could be made with the resources that went into making those units. This is true because both the maximum willingness to pay and the minimum acceptable price take opportunity costs into account. As long as the maximum willingness to pay exceeds the minimum acceptable price, people are willing to pay more to consume a unit of the good in question (here, bags of oranges) than they would pay to consume anything else that could be made with the same resources. Only at the equilibrium quantity Q_1—where the maximum willingness to pay exactly equals the minimum acceptable price—does society exhaust all opportunities to produce units for which benefits exceed costs (including opportunity costs). Producing Q_1 units therefore achieves allocative efficiency because the market is producing and distributing only those units that make people happier with bags of oranges than they would be with anything else that could be produced with the same resources.

Geometrically, producing Q_1 units maximizes the combined area of consumer and producer surplus in Figure 4.3. In this context, the combined area is referred to as *total surplus*. Thus, when Q_1 units are produced, total surplus is equal to the large triangle formed by the green consumer-surplus triangle and the blue producer-surplus triangle.

When demand curves reflect buyers' full willingness to pay and when supply curves reflect all the costs facing sellers, competitive markets produce equilibrium quantities that maximize the sum of consumer and producer surplus. Allocative efficiency occurs at the market equilibrium quantity where three conditions exist simultaneously:

- MB = MC (Figure 1.3).
- Maximum willingness to pay = minimum acceptable price.
- Total surplus (= sum of consumer and producer surplus) is at a maximum.

Economists are enamored of markets because properly functioning markets automatically achieve allocative efficiency. Other methods of allocating resources—such as government central planning—do exist. But because other methods cannot do any better than properly functioning markets—and may, in many cases, do much worse—economists usually prefer that resources be allocated through markets whenever properly functioning markets are available.

Efficiency Losses (or Deadweight Losses)

Figures 4.4a and 4.4b demonstrate that **efficiency losses**—reductions of combined consumer and producer surplus—result from both underproduction and overproduction. First, consider Figure 4.4a, which analyzes the case of underproduction by considering what happens if output falls from the efficient level Q_1 to the smaller amount Q_2. When that happens, the sum of consumer and producer surplus, previously *abc*, falls to *adec*. So the combined consumer and producer surplus declines by the amount of the gray triangle to the left of Q_1. That triangle represents an efficiency loss to buyers and sellers. And because buyers

FIGURE 4.4 Efficiency losses (or deadweight losses). Quantity levels either less than or greater than the efficient quantity Q_1 create efficiency losses. (a) Triangle *dbe* shows the efficiency loss associated with underproduction at output Q_2. (b) Triangle *bfg* illustrates the efficiency loss associated with overproduction at output level Q_3.

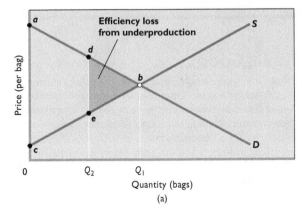

(a)

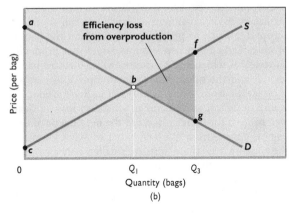

(b)

and sellers are members of society, it represents an efficiency loss (or a so-called **deadweight loss**) to society.

For output levels from Q_2 to Q_1, consumers' maximum willingness to pay (as reflected by points on the demand curve) exceeds producers' minimum acceptable price (as reflected by points on the supply curve). By failing to produce units of this product for which a consumer is willing to pay more than a producer is willing to accept, society suffers a loss of net benefits. As a concrete example, consider a particular unit for which a consumer is willing to pay $10 and a producer is willing to accept $6. The $4 difference between those values is a net benefit that will not be realized if this unit is not produced. In addition, the resources that should have gone to producing this unit will go instead to producing other products that will not generate as much utility as if those resources had been used here to produce this unit of this product. The triangle *dbe* in Figure 4.4a shows the total loss of net benefits that results from failing to produce the units from Q_2 to Q_1.

In contrast, consider the case of overproduction shown in Figure 4.4b, in which the number of oranges produced is Q_3 rather than the efficient level Q_1. In Figure 4.4b the combined consumer and producer surplus therefore declines by *bfg*—the gray triangle to the right of Q_1. This triangle subtracts from the total consumer and producer surplus of *abc* that would occur if the quantity had been Q_1. That is, for all units from 0 to Q_1, benefits exceed costs, so that those units generate the economic surplus shown by triangle *abc*. But the units from Q_1 to Q_3 are such that costs exceed benefits. Thus, they generate an economic loss shown by triangle *bfg*. The total economic surplus for all units from 0 to Q_3 is therefore the economic surplus given by *abc* for the units from 0 to Q_1 minus the economic loss given by *bfg* for the units from Q_1 to Q_3.

Producing any unit beyond Q_1 generates an economic loss because the willingness to pay for such units on the part of consumers is less than the minimum acceptable price to produce such units on the part of producers. As a concrete example, note that producing an item for which the maximum willingness to pay is, say, $7 and the minimum acceptable price is, say, $10 subtracts $3 from society's net benefits. Such production is uneconomical and creates an efficiency loss (or deadweight loss) for society. Because the net benefit of each bag of oranges from Q_1 to Q_3 is negative, we know that the benefits from these units are smaller than the opportunity costs of the other products that could have been produced with the resources that were used to produce these bags of oranges. The resources used to produce

the bags from Q_1 to Q_3 could have generated net benefits instead of net losses if they had been directed toward producing other products. The gray triangle *bfg* to the right of Q_1 in Figure 4.4b shows the total efficiency loss from overproduction at Q_3.

The magic of markets is that when demand reflects consumers' full willingness to pay and when supply reflects all costs, the market equilibrium quantity will automatically equal the allocatively efficient output level. Under these conditions, the market equilibrium quantity will ensure that there are neither efficiency losses from underproduction nor efficiency losses from overproduction. As we are about to see, however, such losses do happen when either demand does not reflect consumers' full willingness to pay or supply does not reflect all costs.

QUICK REVIEW 4.1

- Market failures in competitive markets have two possible causes: demand curves that do not reflect consumers' full willingness to pay and supply curves that do not reflect producers' full cost of production.

- Consumer surplus is the difference between the maximum price that a consumer is willing to pay for a product and the lower price actually paid.

- Producer surplus is the difference between the minimum price that a producer is willing to accept for a product and the higher price actually received.

- At the equilibrium price and quantity in competitive markets, marginal benefit equals marginal cost, maximum willingness to pay equals minimum acceptable price, and the total of consumer surplus and producer surplus is maximized. Each of these conditions defines allocative efficiency.

- Quantities less than or greater than the allocatively efficient level of output create efficiency losses, often called deadweight losses.

Public Goods

LO4.3 Describe free riding and public goods, and illustrate why private firms cannot normally produce public goods.

Demand-side market failures arise in competitive markets when demand curves fail to reflect consumers' full willingness to pay for a good or service. In such situations, markets fail to produce all of the units for which there are net benefits because demand curves underreport how much consumers are willing and able to pay. This underreporting problem reaches its most extreme form in the case of a public good: Markets may fail to produce *any* of the public good because its demand curve may reflect *none* of its consumers' willingness to pay.

To understand public goods, we first need to understand the characteristics that define private goods.

Private Goods Characteristics

We have seen that the market system produces a wide range of **private goods.** These are the goods offered for sale in stores, in shops, and on the Internet. Examples include automobiles, clothing, personal computers, household appliances, and sporting goods. Private goods are distinguished by rivalry and excludability.

- **Rivalry** (in consumption) means that when one person buys and consumes a product, it is not available for another person to buy and consume. When Adams purchases and drinks a bottle of mineral water, it is not available for Benson to purchase and consume.

- **Excludability** means that sellers can keep people who do not pay for a product from obtaining its benefits. Only people who are willing and able to pay the market price for bottles of water can obtain these drinks and the benefits they confer.

Consumers fully express their personal demands for private goods in the market. If Adams likes bottled mineral water, that fact will be known by her desire to purchase the product. Other things equal, the higher the price of bottled water, the fewer bottles she will buy. So Adams's demand for bottled water will reflect an inverse relationship between the price of bottled water and the quantity of it demanded. This is simply *individual* demand, as described in Chapter 3.

The *market* demand for a private good is the horizontal summation of the individual demand schedules (review Figure 3.2). Suppose just two consumers comprise the market for bottled water and the price is $1 per bottle. If Adams will purchase 3 bottles and Benson will buy 2, the market demand will reflect consumers' demand for 5 bottles at the $1 price. Similar summations of quantities demanded at other prices will generate the market demand schedule and curve.

Suppose the equilibrium price of bottled water is $1. Adams and Benson will buy a total of 5 bottles, and the sellers will obtain total revenue of $5 (= $1 × 5). If the sellers' cost per bottle is $0.80, their total cost will be $4 (= $0.80 × 5). So sellers charging $1 per bottle will obtain $5 of total revenue, incur $4 of total cost, and earn $1 of profit on the 5 bottles sold.

Because firms can profitably "tap market demand" for private goods, they will produce and offer them for sale. Consumers demand private goods, and profit-seeking suppliers produce goods that satisfy the demand. Consumers willing to pay the market price obtain the goods; nonpayers go without. A competitive market not only makes private goods available to consumers but also allocates society's resources efficiently to the particular product. There is neither underproduction nor overproduction of the product.

Public Goods Characteristics

Public goods have the opposite characteristics of private goods. Public goods are distinguished by nonrivalry and nonexcludability.

- **Nonrivalry** (in consumption) means that one person's consumption of a good does not preclude consumption of the good by others. Everyone can simultaneously obtain the benefit from a public good such as national defense, street lighting, a global positioning system, or environmental protection.

- **Nonexcludability** means there is no effective way of excluding individuals from the benefit of the good once it comes into existence. Once in place, you cannot exclude someone from benefiting from national defense, street lighting, a global positioning system, or environmental protection.

These two characteristics create a **free-rider problem.** Once a producer has provided a public good, everyone, including nonpayers, can obtain the benefit.

Because most people do not voluntarily pay for something that they can obtain for free, most people become free riders. These free riders like the public good and would be willing to pay for it if producers could somehow force them to pay—but nonexcludability means that there is no way for producers to withhold the good from the free riders without also denying it to the few who do pay. As a result, free riding means that the willingness to pay of the free riders is not expressed in the market. From the viewpoint of producers, free riding reduces demand. The more free riding, the less demand. And if all consumers free ride, demand will collapse all the way to zero.

The low or even zero demand caused by free riding makes it virtually impossible for private firms to profitably provide public goods. With little or no demand, firms cannot effectively "tap market demand" for revenues and profits. As a result, they will not produce public goods. Society will therefore suffer efficiency losses because

Street Entertainers

Street entertainers are often found in tourist areas of major cities. These entertainers illuminate the concepts of free riders and public goods.

Most street entertainers have a hard time earning a living from their activities (unless event organizers pay them) because they have no way of excluding nonpayers from the benefits of their entertainment. They essentially are providing public, not private, goods and must rely on voluntary payments.

The result is a significant free-rider problem. Only a few in the audience put money in the container or instrument case, and many who do so contribute only token amounts. The rest are free riders who obtain the benefits of the street entertainment and retain their money for purchases that they initiate.

Street entertainers are acutely aware of the free-rider problem, and some have found creative ways to lessen it. For example, some entertainers involve the audience directly in the act. This usually creates a greater sense of audience willingness (or obligation) to contribute money at the end of the performance.

"Pay for performance" is another creative approach to lessening the free-rider problem. A good example is the street entertainer painted up to look like a statue. When people drop coins into the container, the "statue" makes a slight movement. The greater the contributions, the greater the movement. But these human "statues" still face a free-rider problem: Nonpayers also get to enjoy the acts.

goods for which marginal benefits exceed marginal costs are not produced. Thus, if society wants a public good to be produced, it will have to direct government to provide it. Because the public good will still feature nonexcludability, the government won't have any better luck preventing free riding or charging people for it. But because the government can finance the provision of the public good through the taxation of other things, the government does not have to worry about profitability. It can therefore provide the public good even when private firms can't.

Examples of public goods include national defense, outdoor fireworks displays, the light beams thrown out by lighthouses, public art displays, public music concerts, MP3 music files posted to file-sharing Web sites, and ideas and inventions that are not protected by patents or copyrights. Each of these goods or services shows both nonrivalry and nonexcludability.

In a few special cases, private firms can provide public goods because the production costs of these public goods can be covered by the profits generated by closely related private goods. For instance, private companies can make a profit providing broadcast TV—which is a nonrival, nonexcludable public good—because they control who gets to air TV commercials, which are rival and excludable private goods. The money that broadcasters make from selling airtime for ads allows them to turn a profit despite having to give their main product, broadcast TV, away for free.

Unfortunately, only a few public goods can be subsidized in this way by closely related private goods. For the large majority of public goods, private provision is unprofitable. As a result, there are only two remaining ways for a public good to be provided: private philanthropy or government provision. For many less expensive or less important public goods like fireworks displays or public art, society may feel comfortable relying on private philanthropy. But when it comes to public goods like national defense, people normally look to the government.

This leads to an important question: Once a government decides to produce a particular public good, how can it determine the optimal amount that it should produce? How can it avoid either underallocating or overallocating society's scarce resources to the production of the public good?

Optimal Quantity of a Public Good

If consumers need not reveal their true demand for a public good in the marketplace, how can society determine the optimal amount of that good? The answer is that the government has to try to estimate the demand for a public good through surveys or public votes. It can then compare the marginal benefit (MB) of an added unit of the good against the government's marginal cost (MC) of providing it. Adhering to the MB = MC rule, government can provide the "right," meaning "efficient," amount of the public good.

Demand for Public Goods

The demand for a public good is somewhat unusual. Suppose Adams and Benson are the only two people in the society, and their marginal willingness to pay for a public good, national defense, is as shown in columns 1 and 2 and columns 1 and 3 in Table 4.3. Economists might have

TABLE 4.3 Demand for a Public Good, Two Individuals

(1) Quantity of Public Good	(2) Adams's Willingness to Pay (Price)		(3) Benson's Willingness to Pay (Price)		(4) Collective Willingness to Pay (Price)
1	$4	+	$5	=	$9
2	3	+	4	=	7
3	2	+	3	=	5
4	1	+	2	=	3
5	0	+	1	=	1

discovered these schedules through a survey asking hypothetical questions about how much each citizen was willing to pay for various types and amounts of public goods rather than go without them.

CONSIDER THIS ...

Responding to Digital Free Riding

Four teenage friends start a rock band. They practice hard, master their instruments, write their own songs, and do gig after gig for nearly nothing at local bars to gain experience and perfect their music.

After nearly five years of effort, they get signed to a major record label. But the year is 2005 and record sales are collapsing due to digital piracy. The rise of Internet file sharing has turned music into a public good and sales of recorded music have collapsed as hundreds of millions of music lovers have become digital free riders.

At first, the band struggles with the new reality. If they can't make a living selling music, they might have to quit music and get regular jobs. But then they realize that while recorded music is now free for anyone who wants it to be free, live music isn't. And neither are T-shirts or memorabilia.

So the band promotes itself online and allows free downloads to help propel its popularity. But then it charges steep prices at live concerts and makes sure that its T-shirts and memorabilia also generate substantial revenues. By doing so, the band adjusts to the new reality in which music has become a public good, but live concerts and T-shirts have not. They charge for the items that are still private goods.

Notice that the schedules in Table 4.3 are price-quantity schedules, implying that they are demand schedules. Rather than depicting demand in the usual way—the quantity of a product someone is willing to buy at each possible price—these schedules show the price someone is willing to pay for an extra unit at each possible quantity. That is, Adams is willing to pay $4 for the first unit of the public good, $3 for the second, $2 for the third, and so on.

Suppose the government produces 1 unit of this public good. Because of nonrivalry, Adams's consumption of the good does not preclude Benson from also consuming it, and vice versa. So both consume the good, and neither volunteers to pay for it. But from Table 4.3 we can find the amount these two people would be willing to pay, together, rather than do without this 1 unit of the good. Columns 1 and 2 show that Adams would be willing to pay $4 for the first unit of the public good; columns 1 and 3 show that Benson would be willing to pay $5 for it. So the two people are jointly willing to pay $9 (= $4 + $5) for this first unit.

For the second unit of the public good, the collective price they are willing to pay is $7 (= $3 from Adams + $4 from Benson); for the third unit they would pay $5 (= $2 + $3); and so on. By finding the collective willingness to pay for each additional unit (column 4), we can construct a collective demand schedule (a willingness-to-pay schedule) for the public good. Here we are *not* adding the quantities demanded at each possible price, as we do when we determine the market demand for a private good. Instead, we are adding the prices that people are willing to pay for the last unit of the public good at each possible quantity demanded.

Figure 4.5 shows the same adding procedure graphically, using the data from Table 4.3. Note that we sum Adams's and Benson's willingness-to-pay curves *vertically* to derive the collective willingness-to-pay curve (demand curve). The summing procedure is downward from the top graph to the middle graph to the bottom (total) graph. For example, the height of the collective demand curve D_c at 2 units of output in the bottom graph is $7, the sum of the amounts that Adams and Benson are each willing to pay for the second unit (= $3 + $4). Likewise, the height of the collective demand curve at 4 units of the public good is $3 (= $1 + $2).

What does it mean in Figure 4.5a that, for example, Adams is willing to pay $3 for the second unit of the public good? It means that Adams expects to receive $3 of extra benefit or utility from that unit. And we know from our discussion of diminishing marginal utility in Chapter 3 that successive units of any good yield less and less added

FIGURE 4.5 **The optimal amount of a public good.** Two people—Adams and Benson—are the only members of a hypothetical economy. (a) D_1 shows Adams's willingness to pay for various quantities of a particular public good. (b) D_2 shows Benson's willingness to pay for these same quantities of this public good. (c) The collective demand for this public good is shown by D_c and is found by summing vertically Adams's and Benson's individual willingness-to-pay curves. The supply (S) of the public good is upsloping, reflecting rising marginal costs. The optimal amount of the public good is 3 units, determined by the intersection of D_c and S. At that output, marginal benefit (reflected in the collective demand curve D_c) equals marginal cost (reflected in the supply curve S).

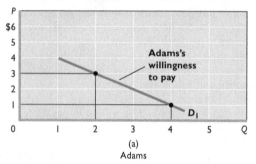

(a)
Adams

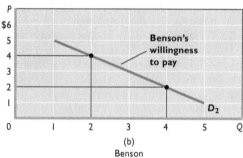

(b)
Benson

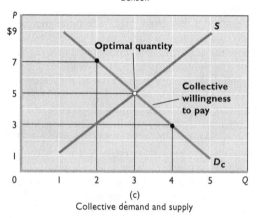

(c)
Collective demand and supply

benefit. This is also true for public goods, explaining the downward slope of the willingness-to-pay curves of Adams, Benson, and society. These curves, in essence, are marginal-benefit (MB) curves.

Comparing MB and MC

We can now determine the optimal quantity of the public good. The collective demand curve D_c in Figure 4.5c measures society's marginal benefit of each unit of this particular good. The supply curve S in that figure measures society's marginal cost of each unit. The optimal quantity of this public good occurs where marginal benefit equals marginal cost, or where the two curves intersect. In Figure 4.5c that point is 3 units of the public good, where the collective willingness to pay for the last (third) unit—the marginal benefit—just matches that unit's marginal cost ($\$5 = \$5$). As we saw in Chapter 1, equating marginal benefit and marginal cost efficiently allocates society's scarce resources.

WORKED PROBLEMS

W4.2

Optimal amount of a public good

Cost-Benefit Analysis

The above example suggests a practical means, called **cost-benefit analysis,** for deciding whether to provide a particular public good and how much of it to provide. Like our example, cost-benefit analysis (or marginal-benefit–marginal-cost analysis) involves a comparison of marginal costs and marginal benefits.

Concept   Suppose the federal government is contemplating a highway construction plan. Because the economy's resources are limited, any decision to use more resources in the public sector will mean fewer resources for the private sector. There will be an opportunity cost, as well as a benefit. The cost is the loss of satisfaction resulting from the accompanying decline in the production of private goods; the benefit is the extra satisfaction resulting from the output of more public goods. Should the needed resources be shifted from the private to the public sector? The answer is yes if the benefit from the extra public goods exceeds the cost that results from having fewer private goods. The answer is no if the cost of the forgone private goods is greater than the benefit associated with the extra public goods.

Cost-benefit analysis, however, can indicate more than whether a public program is worth doing. It can also help the government decide on the *extent* to which a project should be pursued. Real economic questions cannot usually be answered simply by "yes" or "no" but, rather, involve questions such as "how much" or "how little."

Illustration   Roads and highways can be run privately, as excludability is possible with toll gates. However, the federal highway system is almost entirely nonexclusive

TABLE 4.4 Cost-Benefit Analysis for a National Highway Construction Project (in Billions)

(1) Plan	(2) Total Cost of Project	(3) Marginal Cost	(4) Total Benefit	(5) Marginal Benefit	(6) Net Benefit (4) − (2)
No new construction	$ 0		$ 0		$ 0
		]————$ 4		]————$ 5	
A: Widen existing highways	4		5		1
		]———— 6		]———— 8	
B: New 2-lane highways	10		13		3
		]———— **8**		]———— **10**	
C: New 4-lane highways	**18**		**23**		**5**
		]———— 10		]———— 3	
D: New 6-lane highways	28		26		−2

because anyone with a car can get on and off most federal highways without restriction anytime they want. Federal highways therefore satisfy one characteristic of a public good, nonexcludability. The other characteristic, nonrivalry, is also satisfied by the fact that unless a highway is already extremely crowded, one person's driving on the highway does not preclude another person's driving on the highway. Thus, the federal highway system is effectively a public good. This leads us to ask: Should the federal government expand the federal highway system? If so, what is the proper size or scope for the overall project?

Table 4.4 lists a series of increasingly ambitious and increasingly costly highway projects: widening existing two-lane highways; building new two-lane highways; building new four-lane highways; building new six-lane highways. The extent to which government should undertake highway construction depends on the costs and benefits. The costs are largely the costs of constructing and maintaining the highways; the benefits are improved flows of people and goods throughout the country.[2]

The table shows that total annual benefit (column 4) exceeds total annual cost (column 2) for plans A, B, and C, indicating that some highway construction is economically justifiable. We see this directly in column 6, where total costs (column 2) are subtracted from total annual benefits (column 4). Net benefits are positive for plans A, B, and C. Plan D is not economically justifiable because net benefits are negative.

But the question of optimal size or scope for this project remains. Comparing the marginal cost (the change in total cost) and the marginal benefit (the change in total benefit) relating to each plan determines the answer. The guideline is well known to you from previous discussions: Increase an activity, project, or output as long as the marginal benefit (column 5) exceeds the marginal cost (column 3). Stop the

activity at, or as close as possible to, the point at which the marginal benefit equals the marginal cost. Do not undertake a project for which marginal cost exceeds marginal benefit.

In this case plan C (building new four-lane highways) is the best plan. Plans A and B are too modest; the marginal benefits exceed the marginal costs, and there is a better option. Plan D's marginal cost ($10 billion) exceeds the marginal benefit ($3 billion) and therefore cannot be justified; it overallocates resources to the project. Plan C is closest to the theoretical optimum because its marginal benefit ($10 billion) still exceeds marginal cost ($8 billion) but approaches the MB = MC (or MC = MB) ideal.

This **marginal-cost–marginal-benefit rule** actually tells us which plan provides the maximum excess of total benefits over total costs or, in other words, the plan that provides society with the maximum net benefit. You can confirm directly in column 6 that the maximum net benefit (= $5 billion) is associated with plan C.

Cost-benefit analysis shatters the myth that "economy in government" and "reduced government spending" are synonymous. "Economy" is concerned with using scarce resources efficiently. If the marginal cost of a proposed government program exceeds its marginal benefit, then the proposed public program should not be undertaken. But if the marginal benefit exceeds the marginal cost, then it would be uneconomical or "wasteful" not to spend on that government program. Economy in government does not mean minimization of public spending. It means allocating resources between the private and public sectors and among public goods to achieve maximum net benefit.

Quasi-Public Goods

Government provides many goods that fit the economist's definition of a public good. However, it also provides other goods and services that could be produced and delivered in such a way that exclusion would be possible. Such goods, called **quasi-public goods,** include education, streets and highways, police and fire protection, libraries and museums, preventive medicine, and sewage disposal. They could all be

_____
[2]Because the costs of public goods typically are immediate while the benefits often accrue over longer time periods, economists convert both costs and benefits to present values for comparison. Doing so properly accounts for the time-value of money, discussed at length in later chapters.

priced and provided by private firms through the market system. But, because the benefits of these goods flow well beyond the benefit to individual buyers, these goods would be underproduced by the market system. Therefore, government often provides them to avoid the underallocation of resources that would otherwise occur.

The Reallocation Process

How are resources reallocated from the production of private goods to the production of public and quasi-public goods? If the resources of the economy are fully employed, government must free up resources from the production of private goods and make them available for producing public and quasi-public goods. It does so by reducing private demand for them. And it does that by levying taxes on households and businesses, taking some of their income out of the circular flow. With lower incomes and hence less purchasing power, households and businesses must curtail their consumption and investment spending. As a result, the private demand for goods and services declines, as does the private demand for resources. So by diverting purchasing power from private spenders to government, taxes remove resources from private use.

Government then spends the tax proceeds to provide public and quasi-public goods and services. Taxation releases resources from the production of private consumer goods (food, clothing, television sets) and private investment goods (printing presses, boxcars, warehouses). Government shifts those resources to the production of public and quasi-public goods (post offices, submarines, parks), changing the composition of the economy's total output.

QUICK REVIEW 4.2

- Public goods are characterized by nonrivalry and nonexcludability.
- The demand (marginal-benefit) curve for a public good is found by vertically adding the prices that all the members of society are willing to pay for the last unit of output at various output levels.
- The socially optimal amount of a public good is the amount at which the marginal cost and marginal benefit of the good are equal.
- Cost-benefit analysis is the method of evaluating alternative projects or sizes of projects by comparing the marginal cost and marginal benefit and applying the MC = MB rule.
- The government uses taxes to reallocate resources from the production of private goods to the production of public and quasi-public goods.

Externalities

LO4.4 Explain how positive and negative externalities cause under- and overallocations of resources.

In addition to providing public goods, governments can also improve the allocation of resources in the economy by correcting for market failures caused by externalities. An **externality** occurs when some of the costs or the benefits of a good or service are passed onto or "spill over to" someone other than the immediate buyer or seller. Such spillovers are called externalities because they are benefits or costs that accrue to some third party that is external to the market transaction.

There are both positive and negative externalities. An example of a negative externality is the cost of breathing polluted air; an example of a positive externality is the benefit of having everyone else inoculated against some disease. When there are negative externalities, an overproduction of the related product occurs and there is an overallocation of resources to this product. Conversely, underproduction and underallocation of resources result when positive externalities are present.

Negative Externalities

Negative externalities cause supply-side market failures. These failures happen because producers do not take into account the costs that their negative externalities impose on others. This failure to account for all production costs causes firms' supply curves to shift to the right of (or below) where they would be if firms properly accounted for all costs. Consider the costs of breathing polluted air that are imposed on third parties living downwind of smoke-spewing factories. Because polluting firms do not take account of such costs, they oversupply the products they make, producing units for which total costs (including those that fall on third parties) exceed total benefits. The same is true when airlines fail to account for the costs that noisy jet engines impose on people living near airports and when biodiesel factories that convert dead animal parts into fuel release foul smelling gases that disgust those living nearby.

Figure 4.6a illustrates how negative externalities affect the allocation of resources. When producers shift some of their costs onto the community as external costs, producers' marginal costs are lower than they would be if they had to pay for those costs. So their supply curves do not include or "capture" all the costs legitimately associated with the production of their goods. A polluting producer's supply curve such as S in Figure 4.6a therefore understates the total cost of production. The firm's supply curve lies to the right of (or below) the total-cost supply curve S_t, which

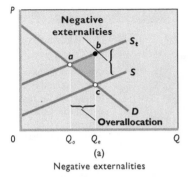

(a)

Negative externalities

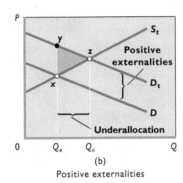

(b)

Positive externalities

FIGURE 4.6 Negative externalities and positive externalities. (a) With negative externalities borne by society, the producers' supply curve S is to the right of (below) the total-cost supply curve S_t. Consequently, the equilibrium output Q_e is greater than the optimal output Q_o, and the efficiency loss is abc. (b) When positive externalities accrue to society, the market demand curve D is to the left of (below) the total-benefit demand curve D_t. As a result, the equilibrium output Q_e is less than the optimal output Q_o, and the efficiency loss is xyz.

would include the spillover cost. Through polluting and thus transferring costs to society, the firm enjoys lower production costs and has the supply curve S.

The outcome is shown in Figure 4.6a, where equilibrium output Q_e is larger than the optimal output Q_o. This means that resources are overallocated to the production of this commodity; too many units of it are produced. In fact, there is a net loss to society for every unit from Q_o to Q_e because, for those units, the supply curve that accounts for all costs, S_t, lies above the demand curve. Therefore, MC exceeds MB for those units. The resources that went into producing those units should have been used elsewhere in the economy to produce other things.

In terms of our previous analysis, the negative externality results in an efficiency loss represented by triangle abc.

Positive Externalities

Positive externalities cause demand-side market failures. These failures happen because market demand curves in such cases fail to include the willingness to pay of the third parties who receive the external benefits caused by the positive externality. This failure to account for all benefits shifts market demand curves to the left of (or below) where they would be if they included all benefits and the willingness to pay of both the third parties as well as the primary beneficiaries. Because demand curves fail to take into account all benefits when there are positive externalities, markets in such cases fail to produce all units for which benefits (including those that are received by third parties) exceed costs. As a result, products featuring positive externalities are underproduced.

Vaccinations are a good example of how positive externalities reduce demand and shift demand curves down and to the left. When John gets vaccinated against a disease, he benefits not only himself (because he can no

longer contract the disease) but also everyone else around him (because they know that in the future he will never be able to infect them). These other people would presumably be willing to pay some positive amount of money for the benefits they receive when John is vaccinated. But because his vaccination is a public good, there is no way to make them pay.

To see why his vaccination is a public good, note that the vaccination benefits that John provides to others feature nonrivalry and nonexcludability. There is nonrivalry because the protection his vaccination provides to one person does not lessen the protection that it provides to other people. There is nonexcludability because once he is vaccinated, there is no way to exclude anyone in particular from benefiting from his vaccination. Thus, the market demand for vaccinations will only include John's personal willingness to pay for the benefits that he personally receives from the vaccination. The market demand will fail to include the benefits that others receive. As a result, demand will be too low and vaccinations will be underproduced.

ORIGIN OF THE IDEA

04.2
Externalities

Figure 4.6b shows the impact of positive externalities on resource allocation. When external benefits occur, the market demand curve D lies to the left of (or below) the total-benefits demand curve, D_t. That is, D does not include the external benefits of the product, whereas D_t does.

The outcome is that the equilibrium output Q_e is less than the optimal output Q_o. The market fails to produce enough vaccinations, and resources are underallocated to this product. The underproduction implies that society is missing out on a significant amount of potential net benefits. For every unit from Q_e to Q_o, the demand curve that accounts for all benefits, D_t, lies above the supply curve that accounts for all costs—including the opportunity cost of producing other items with the resources that would be needed to produce these units. Therefore, MB exceeds MC for each of these units, and we know that society should redeploy some of its resources away from the production of other things in order to produce these units that generate net benefits.

In terms of our previous analysis, the positive externality results in an efficiency loss represented by triangle xyz.

Government Intervention

Government intervention may be called upon to achieve economic efficiency when externalities affect large numbers of people or when community interests are at stake. Government can use direct controls and taxes to counter negative externalities; it may provide subsidies or public goods to deal with positive externalities.

Direct Controls   The direct way to reduce negative externalities from a certain activity is to pass legislation limiting that activity. Such direct controls force the offending firms to incur the actual costs of the offending activity. Historically, direct controls in the form of uniform emission standards—limits on allowable pollution—have dominated American air pollution policy. For example, the Clean Air Act of 1990 (1) forced factories and businesses to install "maximum achievable control technology" to reduce emissions of 189 toxic chemicals by 90 percent between 1990 and 2000; (2) required a 30 to 60 percent reduction in tailpipe emissions from automobiles by 2000; (3) mandated a 50 percent reduction in the use of chlorofluorocarbons (CFCs), which deplete the ozone layer (CFCs were used widely as a coolant in refrigeration, a blowing agent for foam, and a solvent in the electronics industry); and (4) forced coal-burning utilities to cut their emissions of sulfur dioxide by about 50 percent to reduce the acid-rain destruction of lakes and forests. Clean-water legislation limits the amount of heavy metals, detergents, and other pollutants firms can discharge into rivers and bays. Toxic-waste laws dictate special procedures and dump sites for disposing of contaminated soil and solvents. Violating these laws means fines and, in some cases, imprisonment.

Direct controls raise the marginal cost of production because the firms must operate and maintain pollution-control equipment. The supply curve S in Figure 4.7b, which does not reflect the external costs, shifts leftward to

CONSIDER THIS . . .

The Fable of the Bees

Economist Ronald Coase received the Nobel Prize for his so-called **Coase theorem**, which pointed out that under the right conditions, private individuals could often negotiate their own mutually agreeable solutions to externality problems through *private bargaining* without the need for government interventions like pollution taxes.

This is a very important insight because it means that we shouldn't automatically call for government intervention every time we see a potential externality problem. Consider the positive externalities that bees provide by pollinating farmers' crops. Should we assume that beekeeping will be underprovided unless the government intervenes with, for instance, subsidies to encourage more hives and hence more pollination?

As it turns out, no. Research has shown that farmers and beekeepers long ago used private bargaining to develop customs and payment systems that avoid free riding by farmers and encourage beekeepers to keep the optimal number of hives. Free riding is avoided by the custom that all farmers in an area simultaneously hire beekeepers to provide bees

ORIGIN OF THE IDEA

04.3
Coase theorem

to pollinate their crops. And farmers always pay the beekeepers for their pollination services because if they didn't, then no beekeeper would ever work with them in the future—a situation that would lead to massively reduced crop yields due to a lack of pollination.

The "Fable of the Bees" is a good reminder that it is a fallacy to assume that the government must always get involved to remedy externalities. In many cases, the private sector can solve both positive and negative externality problems on its own.

the total-cost supply curve, S_t. Product price increases, equilibrium output falls from Q_e to Q_o, and the initial overallocation of resources shown in Figure 4.7a is corrected. Observe that the efficiency loss shown by triangle *abc* in Figure 4.7a disappears after the overallocation is corrected in Figure 4.7b.

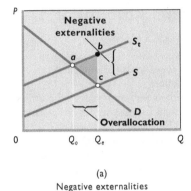

(a)

Negative externalities

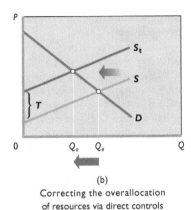

(b)

Correcting the overallocation
of resources via direct controls
or via a tax

FIGURE 4.7 Correcting for negative externalities. (a) Negative externalities result in an overallocation of resources. (b) Government can correct this overallocation in two ways: (1) using direct controls, which would shift the supply curve from S to S_t and reduce output from Q_e to Q_o, or (2) imposing a specific tax T, which would also shift the supply curve from S to S_t, eliminating the overallocation of resources and thus the efficiency loss.

Specific Taxes A second policy approach to negative externalities is for government to levy taxes or charges specifically on the related good. For example, the government has placed a manufacturing excise tax on CFCs, which deplete the stratospheric ozone layer protecting the earth from excessive solar ultraviolet radiation. Facing such an excise tax, manufacturers must decide whether to pay the tax or expend additional funds to purchase or develop substitute products. In either case, the tax raises the marginal cost of producing CFCs, shifting the private supply curve for this product leftward (or upward).

In Figure 4.7b, a tax equal to T per unit increases the firm's marginal cost, shifting the supply curve from S to S_t.

The equilibrium price rises, and the equilibrium output declines from Q_e to the economically efficient level Q_o. The tax thus eliminates the initial overallocation of resources and therefore the efficiency loss.

Subsidies and Government Provision Where spillover benefits are large and diffuse, as in our earlier example of inoculations, government has three options for correcting the underallocation of resources:

- **Subsidies to buyers** Figure 4.8a again shows the supply-demand situation for positive externalities. Government could correct the underallocation of

FIGURE 4.8 Correcting for positive externalities. (a) Positive externalities result in an underallocation of resources. (b) This underallocation can be corrected through a subsidy to consumers, which shifts market demand from D to D_t and increases output from Q_e to Q_o. (c) Alternatively, the underallocation can be eliminated by providing producers with a subsidy of U, which shifts their supply curve from S_t to S_t', increasing output from Q_e to Q_o and eliminating the underallocation, and thus the efficiency loss, shown in graph a.

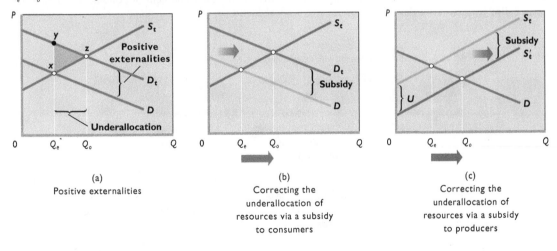

(a)

Positive externalities

(b)

Correcting the
underallocation of
resources via a subsidy
to consumers

(c)

Correcting the
underallocation of
resources via a subsidy
to producers

resources, for example, to inoculations, by subsidizing consumers of the product. It could give each new mother in the United States a discount coupon to be used to obtain a series of inoculations for her child. The coupon would reduce the "price" to the mother by, say, 50 percent. As shown in Figure 4.8b, this program would shift the demand curve for inoculations from too-low D to the appropriate D_t. The number of inoculations would rise from Q_e to the economically optimal Q_o, eliminating the under-allocation of resources and efficiency loss shown in Figure 4.8a.

- *Subsidies to producers* A subsidy to producers is a tax in reverse. Taxes are payments *to* the government that increase producers' costs. Subsidies are payments *from* the government that decrease producers' costs. As shown in Figure 4.8c, a subsidy of U per inoculation to physicians and medical clinics would reduce their marginal costs and shift their supply curve rightward from S_t to S_t'. The output of inoculations would increase from Q_e to the optimal level Q_o, correcting the underallocation of resources and efficiency loss shown in Figure 4.8a.

- *Government provision* Finally, where positive externalities are extremely large, the government may decide to provide the product for free to everyone. The U.S. government largely eradicated the crippling disease polio by administering free vaccines to all children. India ended smallpox by paying people in rural areas to come to public clinics to have their children vaccinated.

Table 4.5 lists several methods for correcting externalities, including those we have discussed thus far.

Society's Optimal Amount of Externality Reduction

LO4.5 Show why we normally won't want to pay what it would cost to eliminate every last bit of a negative externality such as air pollution.

Negative externalities such as pollution reduce the utility of those affected, rather than increase it. These spillovers are not economic goods but economic "bads." If something is bad, shouldn't society eliminate it? Why should society allow firms or municipalities to discharge *any* impure waste into public waterways or to emit *any* pollution into the air?

Economists answer these questions by pointing out that reducing pollution and negative externalities is not free. There are costs as well as benefits to reducing pollution. As a result, the correct question to ask when it comes to cleaning up negative externalities is not, "Do we pollute a lot or pollute zero?" That is an all-or-nothing question that ignores marginal costs and marginal benefits. Instead, the correct question is, "What is the optimal amount to clean up—the amount that equalizes the marginal cost of cleaning up with the marginal benefit of a cleaner environment?"

If we ask that question, we see that reducing a negative externality has a "price." Society must decide how much of a reduction it wants to "buy." High costs may mean that totally eliminating pollution might not be desirable, even if it is technologically feasible. Because of the law of diminishing returns, cleaning up the second 10 percent of pollutants from an industrial smokestack normally is more costly than cleaning up the first 10 percent. Eliminating the third 10 percent is more costly than cleaning up the second 10 percent, and so on. Therefore, cleaning up the last 10 percent of pollutants is the most costly reduction of all.

TABLE 4.5 Methods for Dealing with Externalities

Problem	Resource Allocation Outcome	Ways to Correct
Negative externalities (spillover costs)	Overproduction of output and therefore overallocation of resources	1. Private bargaining 2. Liability rules and lawsuits 3. Tax on producers 4. Direct controls 5. Market for externality rights
Positive externalities (spillover benefits)	Underproduction of output and therefore underallocation of resources	1. Private bargaining 2. Subsidy to consumers 3. Subsidy to producers 4. Government provision

The marginal cost (MC) to the firm and hence to society—the opportunity cost of the extra resources used—rises as pollution is reduced more and more. At some point MC may rise so high that it exceeds society's marginal benefit (MB) of further pollution abatement (reduction). Additional actions to reduce pollution will therefore lower society's well-being; total cost will rise more than total benefit.

MC, MB, and Equilibrium Quantity

Figure 4.9 shows both the rising marginal-cost curve, MC, for pollution reduction and the downsloping marginal-benefit curve, MB, for pollution reduction. MB slopes downward because of the law of diminishing marginal utility: The more pollution reduction society accomplishes, the lower the utility (and benefit) of the next unit of pollution reduction.

The **optimal reduction of an externality** occurs when society's marginal cost and marginal benefit of reducing that externality are equal (MC = MB). In Figure 4.9 this optimal amount of pollution abatement is Q_1 units. When MB exceeds MC, additional abatement moves society toward economic efficiency; the added benefit of cleaner air or water exceeds the benefit of any alternative use of the required resources. When MC exceeds MB, additional abatement reduces economic efficiency;

there would be greater benefits from using resources in some other way than to further reduce pollution.

In reality, it is difficult to measure the marginal costs and benefits of pollution control. Nevertheless, Figure 4.9 demonstrates that some pollution may be economically efficient. This is so not because pollution is desirable but because beyond some level of control, further abatement may reduce society's net well-being. As an example, it would cost the government billions of dollars to clean up every last piece of litter in America. Thus, it would be better to tolerate some trash blowing around if the money saved by picking up less trash would yield larger net benefits when spent on other things.

Shifts in Locations of the Curves

The locations of the marginal-cost and marginal-benefit curves in Figure 4.9 are not forever fixed. They can, and probably do, shift over time. For example, suppose that the technology of pollution-control equipment improved noticeably. We would expect the cost of pollution abatement to fall, society's MC curve to shift rightward, and the optimal level of abatement to rise. Or suppose that society were to decide that it wanted cleaner air and water because of new information about the adverse health effects of pollution. The MB curve in Figure 4.9 would shift rightward, and the optimal level of pollution control would increase beyond Q_1. Test your understanding of these statements by drawing the new MC and MB curves in Figure 4.9.

Government's Role in the Economy

Market failures can be used to justify government interventions in the economy. The inability of private-sector firms to break even when attempting to provide public goods and the over- and underproduction problems caused by positive and negative externalities mean that government can have an important role to play if society's resources are to be efficiently allocated to the goods and services that people most highly desire.

Correcting for market failures is not, however, an easy task. To begin with, government officials must correctly identify the existence and the cause of any given market failure. That by itself may be difficult, time-consuming, and costly. But even if a market failure is correctly identified and diagnosed, government may still fail to take appropriate corrective action due to the fact that government undertakes its economic role in the context of politics.

To serve the public, politicians need to get elected. To stay elected, officials (presidents, senators, representatives, mayors, council members, school board members) need to satisfy their particular constituencies. At best, the political

FIGURE 4.9 Society's optimal amount of pollution abatement. The optimal amount of externality reduction—in this case, pollution abatement—occurs at Q_1, where society's marginal cost MC and marginal benefit MB of reducing the spillover are equal.

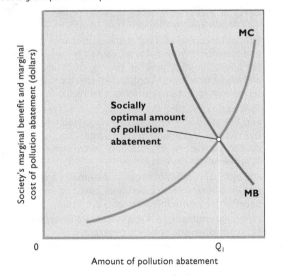

LAST WORD

Carbon Dioxide Emissions, Cap and Trade, and Carbon Taxes

Cap-and-trade systems and carbon taxes are two approaches to reducing carbon dioxide (CO_2) emissions.

Externality problems are property rights problems. Consider a landfill. Because the owner of the landfill has full rights to his land, people wishing to dump their trash into the landfill have to pay him. This payment implies that there is no externality: He happily accepts their trash in exchange for a dumping fee. By contrast, because nobody owns the atmosphere, all air pollution is an externality, since there is no way for those doing the polluting to work out a payment to compensate those affected by the pollution or for those threatened with pollution to simply refuse to be polluted on.

Conventional property rights therefore cannot fix the externalities associated with air pollution. But that does not mean property rights can't help fight pollution. The trick to making them work is to assign property rights not to the atmosphere itself, but to *polluting* the atmosphere. This is done in "cap-and-trade" systems, under which the government sets an annual limit, or cap, to the number of tons of a pollutant that firms can emit into the atmosphere.

Consider carbon dioxide, or CO_2. It is a colorless, odorless gas that many scientists consider to be a contributing cause of climate change, specifically global warming. To reduce CO_2 emissions, the U.S. government might set a cap of 5 billion tons of CO_2 emissions per year in the United States (which

would be about 25 percent below 2010 emissions levels for that molecule). The government then prints out emissions permits that sum to the limit set in the cap and distributes them to polluting firms. Once they are distributed, the only way a firm can legally emit a ton of CO_2 is if it owns a permit to do so.

Under this policy, the government can obviously adjust the total amount of air pollution by adjusting the cap. This by itself improves efficiency because the cap imposes scarcity. Because each firm has only a limited number of permits, each firm has a strong incentive to maximize the net benefit that it produces from every ton of pollution that it emits. But the *cap-and-trade* scheme leads to even greater improvements in efficiency because firms are free to trade (sell) them to each other in what are referred to as *markets for externality rights*.

For instance, suppose Smokestack Toys owns permits for 100 tons of CO_2 emissions and that it could use them to produce toy cars that would generate profits of $100,000. There is a power plant, however, that could make up to $1 million of profits by using those 100 tons of emissions permits to generate electricity. Because firms can trade their permits, Smokestack Toys will sell its permits to the power plant for more than the $100,000 in profits that it could make if it kept them and

realities complicate government's role in the economy; at worst, they produce undesirable economic outcomes.

In the political context, overregulation can occur in some cases; underregulation, in others. Some public goods and quasi-public goods can be produced not because their benefits exceed their costs but because their benefits accrue to firms located in states served by powerful elected officials. Inefficiency can easily creep into government activities because of the lack of a profit incentive to hold down costs. Policies to correct negative externalities can be politically blocked by the very parties that are producing the spillovers. In short, the economic role of government, although critical to a well-functioning economy, is not always perfectly carried out.

Economists use the term "government failure" to describe economically inefficient outcomes caused by shortcomings in the public sector.

QUICK REVIEW 4.3

- Policies for coping with the overallocation of resources, and therefore efficiency losses, caused by negative externalities are (a) private bargaining, (b) liability rules and lawsuits, (c) direct controls, (d) specific taxes, and (e) markets for externality rights (Last Word).

- Policies for correcting the underallocation of resources, and therefore efficiency losses, associated with positive externalities are (a) private bargaining, (b) subsidies to producers, (c) subsidies to consumers, and (d) government provision.

- The optimal amount of negative-externality reduction occurs where society's marginal cost and marginal benefit of reducing the externality are equal.

- Political pressures often lead government to respond inefficiently when attempting to correct for market failures.

produced toy cars. And the power plant will gladly pay more than $100,000 for those permits because it can turn around and use them to make up to $1 million of profits by using them to generate electricity.

Society will benefit hugely from this transaction because while 100 tons of CO_2 will be emitted no matter which firm uses the permits, society will receive much greater net benefits when they are used by the power plant, as indicated by the fact that the power plant can produce much larger profits than the toy company when using the same amount of this scarce resource.

Several words of caution, however! Cap-and-trade systems have proven very difficult to implement in cases where it is difficult for regulators to effectively check whether firms are obeying the system. This has been a major problem with the European Union's cap-and-trade system for CO_2 emissions. Because nearly every type of industrial activity releases CO_2 into the atmosphere, enforcement involves monitoring many thousands of factories of all sizes. That is very difficult and cheating has resulted. In addition, politically connected industries got politicians to give them exemptions or free permits.

By contrast, a cap-and-trade system on sulfur dioxide emissions from coal-burning public utilities has worked well in the United States since the 1980s. But in that case, there were only a few hundred polluting utilities, and they were already being monitored for emissions. So there was little ability to cheat. In addition, all of the firms were treated equally, with no firms allowed exemptions or free permits.

Due to the mixed results, many economists have concluded that a cap-and-trade system would not be the best way to curb CO_2 emissions in the United States. They believe that there are simply too many sources of pollution to make monitoring either possible or cost-effective. And it seems likely that politically connected industries will be granted exemptions. So, instead, many economists favor a carbon tax, which would involve taxing each ton of coal, each gallon of gasoline, and each barrel of oil on the basis of how much carbon it contains (and thus how much CO_2 will eventually be released into the atmosphere when it is used). By raising the cost of polluting, the tax would reduce consumption and lessen the externalities associated with CO_2 emissions. It would also be nearly impossible to evade, so that we would not have to worry about cheating.

SUMMARY

LO4.1 Differentiate between demand-side market failures and supply-side market failures.

A market failure happens in a particular market when the market produces an equilibrium level of output that either overallocates or underallocates resources to the product being traded in the market. In competitive markets that feature many buyers and many sellers, market failures can be divided into two types: Demand-side market failures occur when demand curves do not reflect consumers' full willingness to pay; supply-side market failures occur when supply curves do not reflect all production costs, including those that may be borne by third parties.

LO4.2 Explain the origin of both consumer surplus and producer surplus, and explain how properly functioning markets maximize their sum, total surplus, while optimally allocating resources.

Consumer surplus is the difference between the maximum price that a consumer is willing to pay for a product and the lower price actually paid; producer surplus is the difference between the minimum price that a producer is willing to accept for a product and the higher price actually received. Collectively, consumer surplus is represented by the triangle under the demand curve and above the actual price, whereas producer surplus is shown by the triangle above the supply curve and below the actual price.

Graphically, the combined amount of producer and consumer surplus is represented by the triangle to the left of the intersection of the supply and demand curves that is below the demand curve and above the supply curve. At the equilibrium price and quantity in competitive markets, marginal benefit equals marginal cost, maximum willingness to pay equals minimum acceptable price, and the combined amount of consumer surplus and producer surplus is maximized.

Output levels that are either less than or greater than the equilibrium output create efficiency losses, also called deadweight losses. These losses are reductions in the combined amount of consumer surplus and producer surplus. Underproduction creates efficiency losses because output is not being produced for which maximum willingness to pay exceeds minimum acceptable price. Overproduction creates efficiency losses because output is being produced for which minimum acceptable price exceeds maximum willingness to pay.

LO4.3 Describe free riding and public goods, and illustrate why private firms cannot normally produce public goods.

Public goods are distinguished from private goods. Private goods are characterized by rivalry (in consumption) and excludability. One person's purchase and consumption of a private good precludes others from also buying and consuming it. Producers can exclude nonpayers (free riders) from receiving the benefits. In contrast, public goods are characterized by nonrivalry (in consumption) and nonexcludability. Public goods are not profitable to private firms because nonpayers (free riders) can obtain and consume those goods without paying. Government can, however, provide desirable public goods, financing them through taxation.

The collective demand schedule for a particular public good is found by summing the prices that each individual is willing to pay for an additional unit. Graphically, that demand curve is found by summing vertically the individual demand curves for that good. The resulting total demand curve indicates the collective willingness to pay for (or marginal benefit of) any given amount of the public good.

The optimal quantity of a public good occurs where the society's willingness to pay for the last unit—the marginal benefit of the good—equals the marginal cost of the good.

LO4.4 Explain how positive and negative externalities cause under- and overallocations of resources.

Externalities, or spillovers, are costs or benefits that accrue to someone other than the immediate buyer or seller. Such costs or benefits are not captured in market demand or supply curves and therefore cause the output of certain goods to vary from society's optimal output. Negative externalities (or spillover costs or external costs) result in an overallocation of resources to a particular product. Positive externalities (or spillover benefits or external benefits) are accompanied by an underallocaton of resources to a particular product.

Direct controls and specific taxes can improve resource allocation in situations where negative externalities affect many people and community resources. Both direct controls (for example, smokestack emission standards) and specific taxes (for example, taxes on firms producing toxic chemicals) increase production costs and hence product price. As product price rises, the externality, overallocation of resources, and efficiency loss are reduced since less of the output is produced.

Government can correct the underallocation of resources and therefore the efficiency losses that result from positive externalities in a particular market either by subsidizing consumers (which increases market demand) or by subsidizing producers (which increases market supply). Such subsidies increase the equilibrium output, reducing or eliminating the positive externality and consequent underallocation of resources and efficiency loss.

The Coase theorem suggests that under the right circumstances private bargaining can solve externality problems. Thus, government intervention is not always needed to deal with externality problems.

LO4.5 Show why we normally won't want to pay what it would cost to eliminate every last bit of a negative externality such as air pollution.

The socially optimal amount of externality abatement occurs where society's marginal cost and marginal benefit of reducing the externality are equal. With pollution, for example, this optimal amount of pollution abatement is likely to be less than a 100 percent reduction. Changes in technology or changes in society's attitudes toward pollution can affect the optimal amount of pollution abatement.

Market failures present government with opportunities to improve the allocation of society's resources and thereby enhance society's total well-being. But even when government correctly identifies the existence and cause of a market failure, political pressures may make it difficult or impossible for government officials to implement a proper solution.

TERMS AND CONCEPTS

market failures	producer surplus	excludability
demand-side market failures	efficiency losses (or deadweight losses)	public goods
supply-side market failures	private goods	nonrivalry
consumer surplus	rivalry	nonexcludability

free-rider problem

cost-benefit analysis

marginal-cost–marginal-benefit rule

quasi-public goods

externality

Coase theorem

optimal reduction of an externality

The following and additional problems can be found in **connect** ECONOMICS

DISCUSSION QUESTIONS

1. Explain the two causes of market failures. Given their definitions, could a market be affected by both types of market failures simultaneously? **LO4.1**

2. Use the ideas of consumer surplus and producer surplus to explain why economists say competitive markets are efficient. Why are below- or above-equilibrium levels of output inefficient, according to these two sets of ideas? **LO4.2**

3. What are the two characteristics of public goods? Explain the significance of each for public provision as opposed to private provision. What is the free-rider problem as it relates to public goods? Is U.S. border patrol a public good or a private good? Why? How about satellite TV? Explain. **LO4.3**

4. What divergences arise between equilibrium output and efficient output when (a) negative externalities and (b) positive externalities are present? How might government correct these divergences? Cite an example (other than the text examples) of an external cost and an external benefit. **LO4.4**

5. Why are spillover costs and spillover benefits also called negative and positive externalities? Show graphically how a tax can correct for a negative externality and how a subsidy to producers can correct for a positive externality. How does a subsidy to consumers differ from a subsidy to producers in correcting for a positive externality? **LO4.4**

6. An apple grower's orchard provides nectar to a neighbor's bees, while the beekeeper's bees help the apple grower by pollinating his apple blossoms. Use Figure 4.6b to explain why this situation of dual positive externalities might lead to an underallocation of resources to both apple growing and beekeeping. How might this underallocation get resolved via the means suggested by the Coase theorem? **LO4.4**

7. The LoJack car recovery system allows the police to track stolen cars. As a result, they not only recover 90 percent of LoJack-equipped cars that are stolen but also arrest many auto thieves and shut down many "chop shops" that take apart stolen vehicles to get at their used parts. Thus, LoJack provides both private benefits and positive externalities. Should the government consider subsidizing LoJack purchases? **LO4.4**

8. Explain why zoning laws, which allow certain land uses only in specific locations, might be justified in dealing with a problem of negative externalities. Explain why in areas where buildings sit close together tax breaks to property owners for installing extra fire prevention equipment might be justified in view of positive externalities. Explain why excise taxes on beer might be justified in dealing with a problem of external costs. **LO4.5**

9. **LAST WORD** Distinguish between a carbon-tax and a cap-and-trade strategy for reducing carbon dioxide and other so-called greenhouse gases (that are believed by many scientists to be causing global warming). Which of the two strategies do you think would have the most political support in an election in your home state? Explain your thinking.

REVIEW QUESTIONS

1. Draw a supply and demand graph and identify the areas of consumer surplus and producer surplus. Given the demand curve, what impact will an increase in supply have on the amount of consumer surplus shown in your diagram? Explain why. **LO4.2**

2. Assume that candle wax is traded in a perfectly competitive market in which the demand curve captures buyers' full willingness to pay while the supply curve reflects all production costs. For each of the following situations, indicate whether the total output should be increased, decreased, or kept the same in order to achieve allocative and productive efficiency. **LO4.2**
   a. Maximum willingness to pay exceeds minimum acceptable price.
   b. MC > MB.

   c. Total surplus is at a maximum.
   d. The current quantity produced exceeds the market equilibrium quantity.

3. Efficiency losses _____. **LO4.2**
   a. Are not possible if suppliers are willing to produce and sell a product.
   b. Can only result from underproduction.
   c. Can only result from overproduction.
   d. None of the above.

4. Draw a production possibilities curve with public goods on the vertical axis and private goods on the horizontal axis. Assuming the economy is initially operating on the curve, indicate how the production of public goods might be increased. How might the output of public goods be increased

if the economy is initially operating at a point inside the curve? **LO4.3**

5. Use the distinction between the characteristics of private and public goods to determine whether the following should be produced through the market system or provided by government: (a) French fries, (b) airport screening, (c) court systems, (d) mail delivery, and (e) medical care. State why you answered as you did in each case. **LO4.3**

6. Match each of the following characteristics or scenarios with either the term *negative externality* or the term *positive externality*. **LO4.4**

   a. Overallocation of resources.

   b. Tammy installs a very nice front garden, raising the property values of all the other houses on her block.

c. Market demand curves are too far to the left (too low).

d. Underallocation of resources.

e. Water pollution from a factory forces neighbors to buy water purifiers.

7. Use marginal cost/marginal benefit analysis to determine if the following statement is true or false: "The optimal amount of pollution abatement for some substances, say, dirty water from storm drains, is very low; the optimal amount of abatement for other substances, say, cyanide poison, is close to 100 percent." **LO4.5**

PROBLEMS

1. Refer to Table 4.1. If the six people listed in the table are the only consumers in the market and the equilibrium price is $11 (not the $8 shown), how much consumer surplus will the market generate? **LO4.2**

2. Refer to Table 4.2. If the six people listed in the table are the only producers in the market and the equilibrium price is $6 (not the $8 shown), how much producer surplus will the market generate? **LO4.2**

3. Look at Tables 4.1 and 4.2 together. What is the total surplus if Bob buys a unit from Carlos? If Barb buys a unit from Courtney? If Bob buys a unit from Chad? If you match up pairs of buyers and sellers so as to maximize the total surplus of all transactions, what is the largest total surplus that can be achieved? **LO4.2**

4. **ADVANCED ANALYSIS**   Assume the following values for Figures 4.4a and 4.4b. Q_1 = 20 bags. Q_2 = 15 bags. Q_3 = 27 bags. The market equilibrium price is $45 per bag. The price at *a* is $85 per bag. The price at *c* is $5 per bag. The price at *f* is $59 per bag. The price at *g* is $31 per bag. Apply the formula for the area of a triangle (Area = ½ × Base × Height) to answer the following questions. **LO4.2**

   a. What is the dollar value of the total surplus (producer surplus plus consumer surplus) when the allocatively efficient output level is being produced? How large is the dollar value of the consumer surplus at that output level?

   b. What is the dollar value of the deadweight loss when output level Q_2 is being produced? What is the total surplus when output level Q_2 is being produced?

   c. What is the dollar value of the deadweight loss when output level Q_3 is produced? What is the dollar value of the total surplus when output level Q_3 is produced?

5. On the basis of the three individual demand schedules in the following table, and assuming these three people are the only ones in the society, determine (a) the market demand schedule on the assumption that the good is a private good

and (b) the collective demand schedule on the assumption that the good is a public good. **LO4.3**

P	Q_d (D₁)	Q_d(D₂)	Q_d(D₃)
$8	0	1	0
7	0	2	0
6	0	3	1
5	1	4	2
4	2	5	3
3	3	6	4
2	4	7	5
1	5	8	6

6. Use your demand schedule for a public good, determined in problem 5, and the following supply schedule to ascertain the optimal quantity of this public good. **LO4.3**

P	Q_s
$19	10
16	8
13	6
10	4
7	2
4	1

7. Look at Tables 4.1 and 4.2, which show, respectively, the willingness to pay and willingness to accept of buyers and sellers of bags of oranges. For the following questions, assume that the equilibrium price and quantity will depend on the indicated changes in supply and demand. Assume that the only market participants are those listed by name in the two tables. **LO4.4**

   a. What are the equilibrium price and quantity for the data displayed in the two tables?

b. What if, instead of bags of oranges, the data in the two tables dealt with a public good like fireworks displays? If all the buyers free ride, what will be the quantity supplied by private sellers?

c. Assume that we are back to talking about bags of oranges (a private good), but that the government has decided that tossed orange peels impose a negative externality on the public that must be rectified by imposing a $2-per-bag tax on sellers. What is the new equilibrium price and quantity? If the new equilibrium quantity is the optimal quantity, by how many bags were oranges being overproduced before?

Information Failures

LO4.6 Describe how information failures may justify government intervention in some markets.

This chapter discussed the two most common types of market failure, public goods and externalities. But there is also another, subtler, type of market failure. This one results when either buyers or sellers have incomplete or inaccurate information and their cost of obtaining better information is prohibitive. Technically stated, this market failure occurs because of **asymmetric information**—unequal knowledge possessed by the parties to a market transaction. Buyers and sellers do not have identical information about price, quality, or some other aspect of the good or service.

Sufficient market information is normally available to ensure that goods and services are produced and purchased efficiently. But in some cases inadequate information makes it difficult to distinguish trustworthy from untrustworthy sellers or trustworthy from untrustworthy buyers. In these markets, society's scarce resources may not be used efficiently, thus implying that the government should intervene by increasing the information available to the market participants. Under rare circumstances the government may itself supply a good for which information problems have prohibited efficient production.

ORIGIN OF THE IDEA

O4.4
Information failures

Inadequate Buyer Information about Sellers

Inadequate information among buyers about sellers and their products can cause market failure in the form of underallocation of resources. Two examples will help you understand this point.

Example: Gasoline Market

Assume an absurd situation: Suppose there is no system of weights and measures established by law, no government inspection of gasoline pumps, and no law against false advertising. Each gas station can use whatever measure it chooses; it can define a gallon of gas as it pleases. A station can advertise that its gas is 87 octane when in fact it is only

75. It can rig its pumps to indicate that it is providing more gas than the amount being delivered.

Obviously, the consumer's cost of obtaining reliable information under such chaotic conditions is exceptionally high, if not prohibitive. Customers or their representatives would have to buy samples of gas from various gas stations, have them tested for octane level, and test the accuracy of calibrations at the pump. And these activities would have to be repeated regularly, since a station owner could alter the product quality and the accuracy of the pump at will.

Because of the high cost of obtaining information about the seller, many consumers would opt out of this chaotic market. One tankful of a 50 percent mixture of gasoline and water would be enough to discourage most motorists from further driving. More realistically, the conditions in this market would encourage consumers to vote for political candidates who promise to provide a government solution. The oil companies and honest gasoline stations would most likely welcome government intervention. They would realize that accurate information, by enabling this market to work, would expand their total sales and profits.

The government has in fact intervened in the market for gasoline and other markets with similar potential information difficulties. It has established a system of weights and measures, employed inspectors to check the accuracy of gasoline pumps, and passed laws against fraudulent claims and misleading advertising. Clearly, these government activities have produced net benefits for society.

Example: Licensing of Surgeons

Suppose now that anyone could hang out a shingle and claim to be a surgeon, much as anyone can become a house painter. The market would eventually sort out the true surgeons from those who are "learning by doing" or are fly-by-night operators who move into and out of an area. As people died from unsuccessful surgeries, lawsuits for malpractice eventually would identify and eliminate most of the medical impostors. People needing surgery for themselves or their loved ones could obtain information from newspaper reports, Internet sites, or people who have undergone similar operations.

But this process of obtaining information for those needing surgery would take considerable time and would impose unacceptably high human and economic costs.

There is a fundamental difference between getting an amateurish paint job on one's house and being on the receiving end of heart surgery by a bogus physician. The marginal cost of obtaining information about sellers in the surgery market would be excessively high. The risk of proceeding without good information would result in much less surgery than desirable—an underallocation of resources to surgery.

The government has remedied this market failure through a system of qualifying tests and licensing. The licensing provides consumers with inexpensive information about a service they only infrequently buy. The government has taken a similar role in several other areas of the economy. For example, it approves new medicines, regulates the securities industry, and requires warnings on containers of potentially hazardous substances. It also requires warning labels on cigarette packages and disseminates information about communicable diseases. And it issues warnings about unsafe toys and inspects restaurants for health-related violations.

Inadequate Seller Information about Buyers

Just as inadequate information about sellers can keep markets from achieving economic efficiency, so can inadequate information about buyers. The buyers may be consumers who buy products or firms that buy resources.

Moral Hazard Problem

Private markets may underallocate resources to a particular good or service for which there is a severe **moral hazard problem.** The moral hazard problem is the tendency of one party to a contract or agreement to alter her or his behavior, after the contract is signed, in ways that could be costly to the other party.

Suppose a firm offers an insurance policy that pays a set amount of money per month to people who suffer divorces. The attractiveness of such insurance is that it would pool the economic risk of divorce among thousands of people and, in particular, would protect spouses and children from the economic hardship that divorce often brings. Unfortunately, the moral hazard problem reduces the likelihood that insurance companies can profitably provide this type of insurance.

After taking out such insurance, some people would alter their behavior in ways that impose heavy costs on the insurer. For example, married couples would have less of an incentive to get along and to iron out marital difficulties. At the extreme, some people might be motivated to

obtain a divorce, collect the insurance, and then continue to live together. Such insurance could even promote divorce, the very outcome that it is intended to protect against. The moral hazard problem would force the insurer to charge such high premiums for this insurance that few policies would be bought. If the insurer could identify in advance those people most prone to alter their behavior, the firm could exclude them from buying it. But the firm's marginal cost of getting such information is too high compared with the marginal benefit. Thus, this market would fail.

Although divorce insurance is not available in the marketplace, society recognizes the benefits of insuring against the hardships of divorce. It has corrected for this underallocation of "hardship insurance" through child-support laws that dictate payments to the spouse who retains the children, when the economic circumstances warrant them. Alimony laws also play a role.

The government also supplies "divorce insurance" of a sort through the Temporary Assistance for Needy Families (TANF) program. Though aimed at helping poor children in general rather than children of divorce specifically, parents with children can receive TANF payments if they are left destitute by divorce. Because government does not have to earn a profit when supplying services, it can offer this type of "divorce insurance" despite the fact that it, too, may be susceptible to the moral hazard problem.

The moral hazard problem is also illustrated in the following statements:

- Drivers may be less cautious because they have car insurance.
- Medical malpractice insurance may increase the amount of malpractice.
- Guaranteed contracts for professional athletes may reduce the quality of their performance.
- Unemployment compensation insurance may lead some workers to shirk.
- Government insurance on bank deposits may encourage banks to make risky loans.

Adverse Selection Problem

Another information problem resulting from inadequate information about buyers is the **adverse selection problem.** This problem arises when information known by the first party to a contract or agreement is not known by the second and, as a result, the second party incurs major costs. Unlike the moral hazard problem, which arises after a person signs a contract, the adverse selection problem arises at the time a person signs a contract.

In insurance, the adverse selection problem is that people who are most likely to need insurance payouts are those who buy insurance. For example, those in poorest health will seek to buy the most generous health insurance policies. Or, at the extreme, a person planning to hire an arsonist to "torch" his failing business has an incentive to buy fire insurance.

Our hypothetical divorce insurance sheds further light on the adverse selection problem. If the insurance firm sets the premiums on the basis of the average divorce rate, many married couples who are about to obtain a divorce will buy insurance. An insurance premium based on average probabilities will make a great buy for those about to get divorced. Meanwhile, those in highly stable marriages will not buy it.

The adverse selection problem thus tends to eliminate the pooling of low and high risks, which is the basis of profitable insurance. Insurance rates then must be so high that few people would want to (or be able to) buy such insurance.

Where private firms underprovide insurance because of information problems, the government often establishes some type of social insurance. It can require that everyone in a particular group take the insurance and thereby can overcome the adverse selection problem. Example: Although the Social Security system in the United States is partly insurance and partly an income transfer program, in its broadest sense it is insurance against poverty during old age. The Social Security program requires nearly universal participation: People who are most likely to need the minimum benefits that Social Security provides are automatically participants in the program. So, too, are those not likely to need the benefits. Consequently, no adverse selection problem emerges.

Qualification

Households and businesses have found many ingenious ways to overcome information difficulties without government intervention. For example, many firms offer product warranties to overcome the lack of information about themselves and their products. Franchising also helps overcome this problem. When you visit a Wendy's or a Marriott, you know what you are going to get, as opposed to stopping at Slim's Hamburger Shop or the Triple Six Motel.

Also, some private firms and organizations specialize in providing information to buyers and sellers. *Consumer Reports, Mobil Travel Guide,* and numerous Internet sites provide product information; labor unions collect and disseminate information about job safety; and credit bureaus provide information about credit histories and past bankruptcies to lending institutions and insurance companies. Brokers, bonding agencies, and intermediaries also provide information to clients.

Economists agree, however, that the private sector cannot remedy all information problems. In some situations, government intervention is desirable to promote an efficient allocation of society's scarce resources.

APPENDIX SUMMARY

LO4.6 Describe how information failures may justify government intervention in some markets.

Asymmetric information occurs when buyers and sellers do not have the same information about a product. It is a source of potential market failure, causing society's scarce resources to be allocated inefficiently.

Asymmetric information can cause a market to fail if the party that has less information decides to withdraw from the market because it fears that its lack of knowledge may be exploited by the party that has more information.

If the party that has less information reduces its participation in a market, the reduction in the size of the market may cause an underallocation of resources to the product produced for the market.

The moral hazard problem is the tendency of one party to a contract or agreement to alter its behavior in ways that are costly to the other party; for example, a person who buys insurance may willingly incur added risk.

The adverse selection problem arises when one party to a contract or agreement has less information than the other party and incurs a cost because of that asymmetrical information. For example, an insurance company offering "no medical-exam-required" life insurance policies may attract customers who have life-threatening diseases.

APPENDIX TERMS AND CONCEPTS

asymmetric information

moral hazard problem

adverse selection problem

The following and additional problems can be found in **connect** ECONOMICS

APPENDIX DISCUSSION QUESTIONS

1. Because medical records are private, an individual applying for health insurance will know more about his own health conditions than will the insurance companies to which he is applying for coverage. Is this likely to increase or decrease the insurance premium that he will be offered? Why? **LO4.6**
2. Why is it in the interest of new homebuyers and builders of new homes to have government building codes and building inspectors? **LO4.6**
3. Place an "M" beside the items in the following list that describe a moral hazard problem and an "A" beside those that describe an adverse selection problem. **LO4.6**

a. A person with a terminal illness buys several life insurance policies through the mail.
b. A person drives carelessly because she has automobile insurance.
c. A person who intends to torch his warehouse takes out a large fire insurance policy.
d. A professional athlete who has a guaranteed contract fails to stay in shape during the off season.
e. A woman who anticipates having a large family takes a job with a firm that offers exceptional childcare benefits.

APPENDIX REVIEW QUESTIONS

1. People drive faster when they have auto insurance. This is an example of: **LO4.6**
   a. Adverse selection.
   b. Asymmetric information.
   c. Moral hazard.
2. Government inspectors who check on the quality of services provided by retailers as well as government requirements

for licensing in various professions are both attempts to resolve: **LO4.6**
   a. The moral hazard problem.
   b. The asymmetric information problem.
3. True or False: A market may collapse and have relatively few transactions between buyers and sellers if buyers have more information than sellers. **LO4.6**

APPENDIX PROBLEMS

1. Consider a used car market with asymmetric information. The owners of used cars know what their vehicles are worth but have no way of credibly demonstrating those values to potential buyers. Thus, potential buyers must always worry that the used car they are being offered may be a low quality "lemon." **LO4.6**
   a. Suppose that there are equal numbers of good and bad used cars in the market and that good used cars are worth $13,000 while bad used cars are worth $5,000. What is the average value of a used car?
   b. By how much does the average value exceed the value of a bad used car? By how much does the value of a good used car exceed the average value?

   c. Would a potential seller of a good used car be willing to accept the average value as payment for her vehicle?
   d. If a buyer negotiates with a seller to purchase the seller's used car for a price equal to the average value, is the car more likely to be good or bad?
   e. Will the used-car market come to feature mostly—if not exclusively—lemons? How much will used cars end up costing if all the good cars are withdrawn?

CHAPTER **6**

An Introduction to Macroeconomics

Learning Objectives

LO6.1 Explain why economists focus on GDP, inflation, and unemployment when assessing the health of an entire economy.

LO6.2 Discuss why sustained increases in living standards are a historically recent phenomenon.

LO6.3 Identify why saving and investment are key factors in promoting rising living standards.

LO6.4 Describe why economists believe that "shocks" and "sticky prices" are responsible for short-run fluctuations in output and employment.

LO6.5 Characterize the degree to which various prices in the economy are sticky.

LO6.6 Explain why the greater flexibility of prices as time passes causes economists to utilize different macroeconomic models for different time horizons.

Macroeonomics focuses its attention on national economies while seeking answers to the largest of economic questions. For instance: Why are some countries really rich while others are really poor? Why do some countries enjoy sustained, long-run increases in living standards, while other countries simply stagnate? Why do all countries—even the richest—go through alternating boom and bust periods? And is there anything that governments can do to improve living standards or fight recessions?

This chapter provides an overview of the data that macroeconomists use to measure the status and growth of an entire economy as well as a preview of the models that they use to help explain both long-run growth and short-run fluctuations. Because it is an overview chapter, it raises many unanswered questions. Subsequent chapters will explain these topics in much greater detail.

Performance and Policy

LO6.1 Explain why economists focus on GDP, inflation, and unemployment when assessing the health of an entire economy.

As you know from Chapter 1, macroeconomics studies the behavior of the economy as a whole. It is primarily concerned with two topics: long-run economic growth and the short-run fluctuations in output and employment that are often referred to as the **business cycle.** These phenomena are closely related because they happen simultaneously. Economies show a distinct growth trend that leads to higher output and higher standards of living in the long run, but in the short run there is considerable variability. Sometimes growth proceeds more rapidly and sometimes it proceeds more slowly. It may even turn negative for a while so that output and living standards actually decline, a situation referred to as a **recession.** That is precisely what happened in late 2007 and continued through 2008 and into 2009. The economy experienced what has come to be called the Great Recession.

To understand how economies operate and how their performance might be improved, economists collect and analyze economic data. An almost infinite number of data items can be looked at, including the amount of new construction taking place each month, how many ships laden with cargo are arriving at our ports each year, and how many new inventions have been patented in the last few weeks. That being said, macroeconomists tend to focus on just a few statistics when trying to assess the health and development of an economy. Chief among these are real GDP, unemployment, and inflation.

- **Real GDP,** or **real gross domestic product,** measures the value of final goods and services produced within the borders of a country during a specific period of time, typically a year. This statistic is very useful because it can tell us whether an economy's output is growing. For instance, if U.S. real GDP in one year is larger than in the previous year, we know that U.S. output increased from the first year to the next. To determine real GDP, government statisticians first calculate **nominal GDP,** which totals the dollar value of all goods and services produced within the borders of a country using *their current prices during the year that they were produced.* But because nominal GDP uses the prices in place in the year the output was produced, it suffers from a major problem: It can increase from one year to the next even if there is no increase in output. To see how, consider a commercial blacksmith who produced 10 iron spiral staircases last year and 10 identical staircases this year. Clearly, the blacksmith's output did not change. But if the price of each staircase rose from $10,000 last year to $20,000 this year, nominal GDP increased from $100,000 (= 10 × $10,000) to $200,000 (= 10 × $20,000). Without knowing about the price increase, we might unwisely conclude that the output of staircases increased from 10 to 20. Real GDP statistically eliminates these kinds of price changes. As a result, we can compare real GDP numbers from one year to the next and really know if there is a change in output (rather than prices). Because more output means greater consumption possibilities—including not only the chance to consume more fun things such as movies, vacations, and video games, but also more serious things like better health care and safer roads—economists and policymakers are deeply committed to encouraging a large and growing real GDP.

- **Unemployment** is the state a person is in if he or she cannot get a job despite being willing to work and actively seeking work. High rates of unemployment are undesirable because they indicate that a nation is not using a large portion of its most important resource—the talents and skills of its people. Unemployment is a waste because we must count as a loss all the goods and services that unemployed workers could have produced if they had been working. Researchers have also drawn links between higher rates of unemployment and major social problems like higher crime rates and greater political unrest as well as higher rates of depression, heart disease, and other illnesses among unemployed individuals.

- **Inflation** is an increase in the overall level of prices. As an example, consider all the goods and services bought by a typical family over the course of one year. If the economy is experiencing inflation, it will cost the family more money to buy those goods and services this year than it cost to buy them last year. This can be troublesome for several reasons. First, if the family's income does not rise as fast as the prices of the goods and services that it consumes, it won't be able to purchase as much as it used to and its standard of living will fall. Along the same lines, a surprise jump in inflation reduces the purchasing power of people's savings. Savings that they believed would be able to buy them a specific amount of goods and services will turn out to buy them less than they expected due to the higher-than-expected prices.

Because these statistics are the standards by which economists keep track of long-run growth and short-run fluctuations, we will spend a substantial amount of time in the next few chapters examining how these statistics are computed, how well they are able to capture the well-being of actual people, and how they vary both across countries and over time. Once they are understood, we will build on them in subsequent chapters by developing macroeconomic models of both long-run growth and short-run fluctuations. These will help us understand how policymakers attempt to maximize growth while minimizing unemployment and inflation.

Macroeconomic models also clarify many important questions about the powers and limits of government economic policy. These include:

- Can governments promote long-run economic growth?

- Can they reduce the severity of recessions by smoothing out short-run fluctuations?

- Are certain government policy tools such as manipulating interest rates (monetary policy) more effective at mitigating short-run fluctuations than other government policy tools such as changes in tax rates or levels of government spending (fiscal policy)?

- Is there a trade-off between lower rates of unemployment and higher rates of inflation?

- Does government policy work best when it is announced in advance or when it is a surprise?

The answers to these questions are of crucial importance because of the vast differences in economic performance experienced by national economies at different times. For instance, the amount of output generated by the U.S. economy grew at an average rate of 2.7 percent per year between 1995 and the start of the recession of 2007–2009, while the amount of output generated by the Japanese economy grew at an average rate of only 1.0 percent per year over the same time period. In 2008 and 2009, however, the U.S. economy lost 8 million jobs, and the

unemployment rate rose from 4.6 percent to as high as 10.1 percent. A couple of years later, in 2011, the unemployment rate was 9.1 percent in the United States, 17.9 percent in Greece, 3.5 percent in South Korea, 9.3 percent in France, and 40.6 percent in Haiti. At the same time, the inflation rate was 3.0 percent in the United States, 1.3 percent in Norway, 14.0 percent in Kenya, 21.0 percent in Argentina, and 3.4 percent in Mexico.

Our models will help us understand why such large differences in rates of growth, unemployment, and inflation exist among countries and why those rates can change so substantially from one period to another. These models also will provide significant insights on how government policies can influence rates of growth, unemployment, and inflation.

QUICK REVIEW 6.1

- Macroeconomics studies long-run economic growth and short-run economic fluctuations.

- Macroeconomists focus their attention on three key economic statistics: real GDP, unemployment, and inflation.

- Macroeconomic models help to clarify many important questions about government economic policy.

The Miracle of Modern Economic Growth

LO6.2 Discuss why sustained increases in living standards are a historically recent phenomenon.

Rapid and sustained economic growth is a modern phenomenon. Before the Industrial Revolution began in the late 1700s in England, standards of living showed virtually no growth over hundreds or even thousands of years. For instance, the standard of living of the average Roman peasant was virtually the same at the start of the Roman Empire around the year 500 B.C. as it was at the end of the Roman Empire 1,000 years later. Similarly, historians and archaeologists have estimated that the standard of living enjoyed by the average Chinese peasant was essentially the same in the year A.D. 1800 as it was in the year A.D. 100.

That is not to say that the Roman and Chinese economies did not expand over time. They did. In fact, their total outputs of goods and services increased many times over. The problem was that as they did, their populations went up by similar proportions so that the amount of output *per person* remained virtually unchanged.

This historical pattern continued until the start of the Industrial Revolution, which ushered in not only factory production and automation but also massive increases in research and development so that new and better technologies were constantly being invented. The result was that output began to grow faster than the population. This meant that living standards began to rise as the amount of output *per person* increased.

Not all countries experienced this phenomenon, but those that did were said to be experiencing **modern economic growth** (in which output per person rises) as compared with earlier times in which output (but not output per person) increased. Under modern economic growth, the annual increase in output per person is often not large, perhaps 2 percent per year in countries such as England that were the first to industrialize. But when compounded over time, an annual growth rate of 2 percent adds up very rapidly. Indeed, it implies that the standard of living will double every 35 years. So if the average citizen of a country enjoying 2 percent growth begins this year with an income of $10,000, in 35 years that person will have an income of $20,000. And 35 years after that there will be another doubling so that her income in 70 years will be $40,000. And 35 years after that, the average citizen's income will double again to $80,000. Such high rates of growth are amazing when compared to the period before modern economic growth when standards of living remained unchanged century after century.

The vast differences in living standards seen today between rich and poor countries are almost entirely the result of the fact that only some countries have experienced modern economic growth. Indeed, before the start of the Industrial Revolution in the late 1700s, living standards around the world were very similar, so much so that the average standard of living in the richest parts of the world was at most only two or three times higher than the standard of living in the poorest parts of the world. By contrast, the citizens of the richest nations today have material standards of living that are on average more than 50 times higher than those experienced by citizens of the poorest nations, as can be seen by the GDP per person data for the year 2011 given in Global Perspective 6.1.

Global Perspective 6.1 facilitates international comparisons of living standards by making three adjustments to each country's GDP. First, it converts each country's GDP from its own currency into U.S. dollars so that there is no confusion about the values of different currencies. Second, it divides each country's GDP measured in dollars by the size of its population. The resulting number, *GDP per person*, is the average amount of output each person in each country could have if each country's total output were divided equally among its citizens. It is a measure of each country's average standard of living. Third, the table uses a method called *purchasing power*

GLOBAL PERSPECTIVE 6.1

GDP per Person, Selected Countries

Country	GDP per Person, 2011 (U.S. dollars based on purchasing power parity)
Canada	$50,496
United States	48,328
Japan	45,870
France	44,007
United Kingdom	38,811
South Korea	31,700
Saudi Arabia	21,196
Russia	12,993
Mexico	10,146
China	5,417
North Korea	1,800
India	1,514
Zimbabwe	752
Tanzania	566
Burundi	275

Source: International Monetary Fund, **www.imf.org**, for all countries except for North Korea, the estimate for which is from the *CIA World Factbook*, **www.cia.gov**.

parity to adjust for the fact that prices are much lower in some countries than others. By making this adjustment, we can trust that $1 of GDP per person in the United States represents about the same quantity of goods and services as $1 of GDP per person in any of the other countries. The resulting numbers—GDP per person adjusted for purchasing power parity—are presented in Global Perspective 6.1.

QUICK REVIEW 6.2

- Before the Industrial Revolution, living standards did not show any sustained increases over time because any increase in output tended to be offset by an equally large increase in population.
- Since the Industrial Revolution, many nations have experienced *modern economic growth* in which output grows faster than population—so that living standards rise over time.

Saving, Investment, and Choosing between Present and Future Consumption

LO6.3 Identify why saving and investment are key factors in promoting rising living standards.

At the heart of economic growth is the principle that to raise living standards over time, an economy must devote at least some fraction of its current output to increasing future output. As implied in Chapter 1, this process requires flows of both saving and investment, which we will define and discuss before returning to why they are so important for economic growth.

- **Saving** occurs when current consumption is less than current output (or when current spending is less than current income).

- **Investment** happens when resources are devoted to increasing future output—for instance by building a new research facility in which scientists invent the next generation of fuel-efficient automobiles or by constructing a modern, super-efficient factory. (A caution: In economics, the term "investment" differs from common usage. To understand why, be sure to read the Consider This box.)

When thinking about why saving and investment are so important for economic growth, the key point is that the amount of investment is ultimately limited by the amount of saving. The only way that more output can be directed at investment activities is if saving increases. But that, in turn, implies that individuals and society as a whole must make trade-offs between current and future consumption. This is true because the only way to pay for more investment—and the higher levels of future consumption that more investment can generate—is to increase present saving. But increased saving can only come at the price of reduced current consumption. Individuals and society as a whole must therefore wrestle with a choice between present consumption and future consumption. They must decide how to balance the reductions in current consumption required to fund current investment against the increases in future consumption that the added current investment will make possible.

Banks and Other Financial Institutions

Households are the principal source of savings. But businesses are the main economic investors. So how does the pool of savings generated by households when they spend less than they consume get transferred to businesses so that they can purchase newly created capital goods? The answer is through banks and other financial institutions

Economic versus Financial Investment

Economics students often are confused by how the word "investment" is used in economics. This is understandable, because economists draw a distinction between "financial investment" and "economic investment."

Financial investment captures what ordinary people mean when they say investment, namely, the purchase of assets like stocks, bonds, and real estate in the hope of reaping a financial gain. Anything of monetary value is an asset and, in everyday usage, people purchase—or "invest" in—assets hoping to receive a financial gain, either by eventually selling them at higher prices than they paid for them or by receiving a stream of payments from others who are allowed to use the asset. By contrast, when economists say "investment," they are referring to **economic investment,** which relates to the creation and expansion of business enterprises. Specifically, economic investment only includes spending on the production and accumulation of newly created capital goods such as machinery, tools, factories, and warehouses. For example, economic investment will occur when the airplane shown in the accompanying photo is purchased by a commercial airline.

For economists, purely financial transactions, such as swapping cash for a stock or a bond, are not "investment." Neither are the purchases of factories or apartment buildings built in previous years. These transactions simply transfer the ownership of financial assets or existing real assets from one party to another. They do not purchase newly created capital goods. As such, they are great examples of financial investment, but not of economic investment. So now that you know the difference, remember that purely financial transactions, like buying Google stock or a five-year-old factory, are indeed referred to as "investment"—except in economics!

such as mutual funds, pension plans, and insurance companies. These institutions collect the savings of households, rewarding savers with interest and dividends and sometimes capital gains (increases in asset values). The banks and other financial institutions then lend the funds to businesses, which invest in equipment, factories, and other capital goods.

Macroeconomics devotes considerable attention to money, banking, and financial institutions because a well-functioning financial system helps to promote economic growth and stability by encouraging saving and by properly directing that saving into the most productive possible investments. In contrast, a poorly functioning financial system can create serious problems for an economy.

QUICK REVIEW 6.3

- An economy can only grow if it invests, and it can only invest if it saves some of its current output. Thus, saving is crucial to increasing investment and, consequently, future output.
- Banks and other financial institutions channel household savings toward businesses, which invest in equipment, factories, and other capital goods.

Uncertainty, Expectations, and Shocks

LO6.4 Describe why economists believe that "shocks" and "sticky prices" are responsible for short-run fluctuations in output and employment.

Decisions about savings and investment are complicated by the fact that the future is uncertain. Investment projects sometimes produce disappointing results or even fail totally. As a result, firms spend considerable time trying to predict future trends so that they can, hopefully, invest only in projects that are likely to succeed. This implies that macroeconomics has to take into account **expectations** about the future.

The Importance of Expectations and Shocks

Expectations are hugely important for two reasons. The more obvious reason involves the effect that changing expectations have on current behavior. If firms grow more pessimistic about the future returns that are likely to come from current investments, they are going to invest less today than they would if they were more optimistic. Expectations therefore have a large effect on economic growth since increased pessimism will lead to less current investment and, subsequently, less future consumption.

The less-obvious reason that expectations are so important has to do with what happens when expectations are unmet. Firms are often forced to cope with **shocks**—situations in which they were expecting one thing to happen but then something else happened. For instance, consider a situation in which a firm decides to build a high-speed railroad that will shuttle passengers between Los Angeles and Las Vegas. The firm expects it to be very popular and make a handsome profit. But if it unexpectedly turns out to be unpopular and loses money, the railroad

must figure out how to respond. Should the railroad go out of business completely? Should it attempt to see if it can turn a profit by hauling cargo instead of passengers? Is there a possibility that the venture might succeed if the firm borrows $30 million from a bank to pay for a massive advertising campaign? These sorts of decisions are necessitated by the shock and surprise of having to deal with an unexpected situation.

Economies are exposed to both demand shocks and supply shocks. **Demand shocks** are unexpected changes in the demand for goods and services. **Supply shocks** are unexpected changes in the supply of goods and services. Note that the word *shock* only reveals that something unexpected has happened. It does not tell us whether what has happened is unexpectedly good or unexpectedly bad. To clarify this, economists use more specific terms. For instance, a *positive demand shock* refers to a situation in which demand turns out to be higher than expected, while a *negative demand shock* refers to a situation in which demand turns out to be lower than expected.

Demand Shocks and Sticky Prices

Economists believe that most short-run fluctuations in GDP and the business cycle are the result of demand shocks. Supply shocks do happen in some cases and are very important when they do occur. But we will focus most of our attention in this chapter and subsequent chapters on demand shocks, how they affect the economy, and how government policy may be able to help the economy adjust to them.

But why are demand shocks such a big problem? Why would we have to consider calling in the government to help deal with them? And why can't firms deal with demand shocks on their own?

The answer to these questions is that the prices of many goods and services are inflexible (slow to change, or "sticky") in the short run. As we will explain, this implies that price changes do not quickly equalize the quantities demanded of such goods and services with their respective quantities supplied. Instead, because prices are inflexible, the economy is forced to respond in the short run to demand shocks primarily through changes in output and employment rather than through changes in prices.

Example: A Single Firm Dealing with Demand Shocks and Sticky Prices

Although an economy as a whole is vastly more complex than a single firm, an analogy that uses a single car factory will be helpful in explaining why demand shocks and inflexible prices are so important to understanding most of the short-run fluctuations that affect the entire economy. Consider a car manufacturing company named Buzzer Auto. Like most companies, Buzzer Auto is in business to try to make a profit. Part of turning a profit involves trying to develop accurate expectations about future market conditions. Consequently, Buzzer constantly does market research to estimate future demand conditions so that it will, hopefully, only build cars that people are going to want to buy.

Setting Expectations

After extensive market research, Buzzer concludes that it could earn a modest profit if it builds and staffs an appropriately sized factory to build an environmentally friendly SUV, which it decides to call the Prion. Buzzer's marketing economists collaborate with Buzzer's engineers and conclude that expected profits will be maximized if the firm builds a factory that has an optimal output rate of 900 cars per week. If the factory operates at this rate, it can produce Prions for only $36,500 per vehicle. This is terrific because the firm's estimates for demand indicate that a supply of 900 vehicles per week can be sold at a price of $37,000 per vehicle—meaning that if everything goes according to plan, Buzzer Auto should make an accounting profit of $500 on each Prion that it produces and sells. Expecting these future conditions, Buzzer decides to build the factory, staff it with workers, and begin making the Prion.

Look at Figure 6.1a, which shows the market for Prions when the vertical supply curve for Prions is fixed at the factory's optimal output rate of 900 cars per week. Notice that we have drawn in three possible demand curves. D_L corresponds to low demand for the Prion; D_M corresponds to the medium level of demand that Buzzer's marketing economists are expecting to materialize; and D_H corresponds to high demand for the Prion. Figure 6.1a is consistent with the marketing economists' expectations: if all goes according to plan and the actual demand that materializes is D_M, the equilibrium price will in fact be $37,000 per Prion and the equilibrium quantity demanded will be 900 cars per week. Thus, if all goes according to expectations, the factory will have exactly the right capacity to meet the expected quantity demanded at the sales price of $37,000 per vehicle. In addition, the firm's books will show a profit of $500 per vehicle on each of the 900 vehicles that it builds and expects to sell each week at that price.

Full Employment If There Are No Shocks

Here is the key point. If expectations are always fulfilled, Buzzer Auto will never contribute to any of the short-run fluctuations in output and unemployment that affect real-world economies. First, if everything always goes according to plan and Buzzer Auto's expectations always come true, then the factory will always produce and sell at its optimal

FIGURE 6.1 **The effect of unexpected changes in demand under flexible and fixed prices.** (a) If prices are flexible, then no matter what demand turns out to be, Buzzer Auto can continue to sell its optimal output of 900 cars per week since the equilibrium price will adjust to equalize the quantity demanded with the quantity supplied. (b) By contrast, if Buzzer Auto sticks with a fixed-price policy, then the quantity demanded will vary with the level of demand. At the fixed price of $37,000 per vehicle, the quantity demanded will be 700 cars per week if demand is D_L, 900 cars per week if demand is D_M, and 1,150 cars per week if demand is D_H.

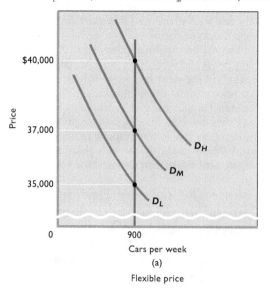

(a)

Flexible price

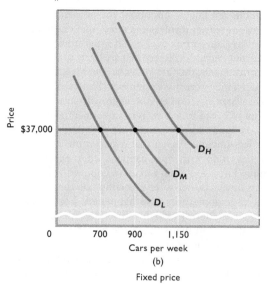

(b)

Fixed price

output rate of 900 cars per week. This would mean that it would never experience any fluctuations in output—either in the short run or in the long run. At the same time, since producing a constant output of 900 cars each week will always require the same number of workers, the factory's labor demand and employment should never vary. So if everything always goes according to plan, Buzzer Auto will never have any effect on unemployment because it will always hire a constant number of workers.

These facts imply that the short-run fluctuations in output and unemployment that we do see in the real world must be the result of shocks and things *not* going according to plan. In particular, business cycle fluctuations typically arise because the actual demand that materializes ends up being either lower or higher than what people were expecting. When this occurs, some adjustments will be necessary to bring quantity demanded and quantity supplied back into alignment. As we are about to explain, the nature of these adjustments varies hugely depending on whether prices are flexible or inflexible.

Price Changes If There Are Demand Shocks and Flexible Prices

Figure 6.1a illustrates the case of adjusting to unexpected changes in demand *when prices are flexible*. Here, if demand is unexpectedly low at D_L, the market price can adjust downward to $35,000 per vehicle so that the quantity demanded at that price will still be equal to the factory's optimal output rate of 900 cars per week. On the other hand, if demand is unexpectedly high at D_H, the market price can adjust upward to $40,000 per vehicle so that the quantity demanded will still be equal to the factory's optimal output rate of 900 cars per week. These adjustments imply that *if* the price of Prions is free to quickly adjust to new equilibrium levels in response to unexpected changes in demand, the factory could always operate at its optimal output rate of 900 cars per week. Only the amount of profit or loss will vary with demand.

Applying this logic to the economy as a whole, *if* the prices of goods and services could always adjust quickly to unexpected changes in demand, then the economy could always produce at its optimal capacity since prices would adjust to ensure that the quantity demanded of each good and service would always equal the quantity supplied. Simply put, if prices were fully flexible, there would be no short-run fluctuations in output. Production levels would remain constant and unemployment levels would not change because firms would always need the same number of workers to produce the same amount of output.

Output Changes If There Are Demand Shocks and Sticky Prices

In reality, many prices in the economy are inflexible and are not able to change rapidly when demand changes unexpectedly. Consider the extreme case shown in Figure 6.1b, in which the price of Prions is totally inflexible, fixed at $37,000 per Prion. Here, if demand unexpectedly falls from D_M to D_L, the quantity demanded at the fixed price of $37,000 will only be 700 cars per week, which is 200 cars fewer than the factory's optimal output of 900 cars per week. On the other hand, if demand is unexpectedly high at D_H, the quantity demanded at the fixed price of $37,000 will be 1,150 cars per week, which is 250 cars more than the factory's optimal output of 900 cars per week.

One way for companies to deal with these unexpected shifts in quantity demanded would be to try to adjust the factory's output to match them. That is, during weeks of low demand, Buzzer Auto could attempt to produce only 700 Prions, while during weeks of high demand it could try to produce 1,150 Prions. But this sort of flexible output strategy is very expensive because factories operate at their lowest costs when they are producing constantly at their optimal output levels; operating at either a higher or a lower production rate results in higher per-unit production costs.[1]

Knowing this, manufacturing firms typically attempt to deal with unexpected changes in demand by maintaining an inventory. An **inventory** is a store of output that has been produced but not yet sold. Inventories are useful because they can be allowed to grow or decline in periods when demand is unexpectedly low or high—thereby allowing production to proceed smoothly even when demand is variable. In our example, Buzzer Auto would maintain an inventory of unsold Prions. In weeks when demand is unexpectedly low, the inventory will increase by 200 Prions as the quantity demanded falls 200 vehicles short of the factory's optimal output. By contrast, during weeks when demand is unexpectedly high, the inventory will decrease as the quantity demanded exceeds the factory's optimal output by 250 cars. By allowing inventory levels to fluctuate with these unexpected shifts in demand, Buzzer Auto can respond by adjusting inventory levels rather than output levels. In addition, with any luck, the overall inventory level will stay roughly constant over time as unexpected increases and decreases in demand cancel each other out.

But consider what will happen if the firm experiences many successive weeks of unexpectedly low demand. For each such week, the firm's inventory of unsold Prions will increase by 200 cars. The firm's managers will not mind if

---

[1] If you have studied microeconomics, you will recognize that the firm's optimal output level of 900 cars per week is the level that minimizes the factory's average total cost (ATC) per vehicle of producing the Prion. Producing either more or fewer Prions will result in higher per-vehicle production costs.

this happens for a few weeks, but if it continues for many weeks, then the managers will be forced to cut production because, among other things, there will simply be no place to park so many unsold vehicles. More importantly, holding large numbers of unsold cars in inventory is unprofitable because while costs must be incurred to build an unsold car, an unsold car obviously brings in no revenue. Constantly rising inventories hurt firm profits and the management will want to reduce output if it sees inventories rising week after week due to unexpectedly low demand.

Generalizing from a Single Firm to the Entire Economy

This simplified story about a single car company explains why economists believe that a combination of unexpected changes in demand and inflexible prices are the key to understanding the short-run fluctuations that affect real-world economies. If prices were flexible, then the firm could always operate at the factory's optimal output level because prices would always adjust to ensure that it could sell its optimal output of 900 cars per week no matter what happens to demand. But if prices are inflexible, then an unexpected decline in demand that persists for any length of time will result in increasing inventories that will eventually force the firm's management to cut production to less than the optimal output level of 900 cars per week. When this happens, not only will output fall, but unemployment will also rise. The firm will lay off workers because fewer employees will be needed to produce fewer cars.

Generalizing this story to the economy as a whole, if demand falls off for many goods and services across the entire economy for an extended period of time, then the firms that make those goods and services will be forced to cut production. Manufacturing firms that maintain inventories will do so as they find inventories piling up due to sluggish sales. And services firms will do so as they encounter slow sales for their services. As both manufacturing and service output declines, the economy will recede, with GDP falling and unemployment rising.

On the other hand, if demand is unexpectedly high for a prolonged period of time, the economy will boom and unemployment will fall. In the case of our Prion example, for each week that demand is unexpectedly high, inventories will fall by 250 cars. If this keeps happening week after week, inventories will start to run out and the firm will have to react by increasing production to more than the optimal output rate of 900 cars per week so that orders do not go unfilled. When this happens, GDP will increase as more cars per week are produced and unemployment will fall because the factory will need to hire more workers to produce the larger number of cars.

CONSIDER THIS . . .

The Great Recession

In 2008 and 2009, the United States encountered its worst financial and economic crisis since the Great Depression of the 1930s.

The recession was so severe that it has been dubbed the Great Recession. The recession was triggered by a steep decline in housing prices and a crisis involving mortgage loans and the financial securities built on them. Several key U.S. financial institutions collapsed or nearly failed, and lending markets largely froze. Despite government bailout efforts, the financial crisis eventually spread to the broader economy. Employment fell by 8 million workers between 2007 and the end of 2009, and the unemployment rate rose from 4.6 percent to 10.1 percent over that same period. Economic growth slumped to 0.4 percent in 2008 and to a *negative* 2.4 percent in 2009, compared with the 2.7 percent annual increases occurring between 1995 and 2007.

And this is where Buzzer Auto comes into the picture. The situation in Figure 6.1b, where the price of Buzzer's autos is inflexible, is highly relevant to the Great Recession. Like Buzzer, actual auto producers such as GM, Ford, and Chrysler, as well as thousands of producers of other products across the economy, established their production capacity and set their expectations of product demand on the basis of normal times. But demand for their goods and services fell unexpectedly because of greater consumer difficulty in getting loans, declining consumer confidence, and eventually declining income. The economy's price level (essentially a weighted average of all prices) declined only slightly, and that was after the recession was well underway. Therefore, real output (not prices) took the major brunt of the decline of total demand in the economy. Output dropped, employment plummeted, and unemployment soared.

QUICK REVIEW 6.4

- Economic shocks occur when events unfold in ways that people were not expecting.
- Demand and supply shocks take place when demand or supply ends up being either higher or lower than expected.
- Real-world prices are often inflexible or "sticky" in the short run.
- When prices are sticky, the economy adjusts to demand shocks mostly through changes in output and employment (rather than through changes in prices).

LAST WORD

Debating the Great Recession

Economists Disagreed Vigorously about Both the Causes of the Great Recession and the Best Ways to Speed a Recovery.

The Great Recession of 2007–2009 was the worst economic downturn since the Great Depression of the 1930s. The government intervened massively to help promote recovery, but the recession was long-lasting and the subsequent recovery was the weakest since the Great Depression.

Explanations about what caused the Great Recession differ sharply among economists. Here are two of the more popular hypotheses.

The Minksy Explanation: Euphoric Bubbles Economist Hyman Minksy believed that severe recessions are often preceded by *asset-price bubbles*—periods during which euphoria and debt-fueled speculation cause the price of one or more financial assets to irrationally skyrocket before collapsing down to more realistic levels. Those who apply his ideas to the Great Recession note that easily obtained home-mortgage loans drove a massive bubble in housing prices.

When the bubble eventually collapsed, investors lost trillions of dollars in wealth. As a result, the demand for goods and services fell dramatically and unexpectedly. When combined with sticky prices, that leftward shift in demand forced many companies to reduce output and lay off workers (as in our Buzzer Auto

example in this chapter). The weakest firms went bankrupt and had to permanently fire all of their workers.

The Austrian Explanation: Excessively Low Interest Rates Economists of the so-called Austrian School also blame bubbles for severe recessions, but they put the blame for bubbles not on euphoria but on government actions that they say keep interest rates too low. Their contention is that excessively low interest rates induce firms and individuals to borrow excessively. Individuals borrow excessively to fund consumption. Firms borrow excessively for construction and investment. When the bubble pops, society has too many factories (as a result of the massive increase in construction and investment on the part of firms) combined with too little demand (as consumers struggle to repay all the money they borrowed to fund their consumption).

In terms of this chapter's Buzzer Auto example, it would be as though Buzzer borrowed lots of money to build several factories only to discover that demand was much lower than expected because consumers were cutting back on spending in order to repay debt. With demand shifting left and prices sticky, Buzzer and other companies are forced to reduce output and lay off workers. Thus begins the recession.

How Sticky Are Prices?

LO6.5 Characterize the degree to which various prices in the economy are sticky.

We have just shown that **inflexible prices**—or **"sticky prices"** as economists are fond of saying—help to explain how unexpected changes in demand lead to the fluctuations in GDP and employment that occur over the course of the business cycle. Of course, not all prices are sticky. Indeed, the markets for many commodities and raw materials such as corn, oil, and natural gas feature extremely **flexible prices** that react within seconds to changes in supply and demand. By contrast, the prices of most of the final goods and services that people consume are quite sticky, with the average good or service going 4.3 months between price changes. To get a better appreciation for the fact that price stickiness varies greatly by product or service, look at Table 6.1, which gives the average number of months between price

TABLE 6.1 Average Number of Months between Price Changes for Selected Goods and Services

Item	Months
Coin-operated laundry machines	46.4
Newspapers	29.9
Haircuts	25.5
Taxi fare	19.7
Veterinary services	14.9
Magazines	11.2
Computer software	5.5
Beer	4.3
Microwave ovens	3.0
Milk	2.4
Electricity	1.8
Airline tickets	1.0
Gasoline	0.6

Source: Mark Bils and Peter J. Klenow, "Some Evidence on the Importance of Sticky Prices." *Journal of Political Economy,* October 2004, pp. 947–985. Used with permission of The University of Chicago Press via Copyright Clearance Center.

Because economists did not have a consensus about what caused the Great Recession, it should not be surprising that they were also divided over the best policies for fighting the recession and improving upon the sluggish recovery that began in 2009. For simplicity, the wide variety of opinions can be grouped into two broad camps promoting two very different solutions.

The Stimulus Solution The majority of economists argued that the solution to the collapse in demand was to have the government take actions to shift demand curves rightward. For instance, the government could lower interest rates so that consumers and businesses would borrow and spend more. The government could also massively increase its purchases of goods and services so that a rightward shift in the government's demand for output could help to make up for the leftward shift in the private-sector demand for output.

This opinion in favor of *government stimulus* was the most commonly held view among economists and the government did in fact push interest rates very low while also massively increasing government spending.

The Structural Solution A vocal minority of economists rejected the stimulus policies. They argued that the economy required a *structural adjustment*. In their opinion, the bubble period before the recession had seen a major misallocation of resources toward inefficient firms that generated net losses for society (MB < MC). The only way to redirect the resources that those firms were using back toward productive activities would be to let the inefficient firms go bankrupt. The resources would then flow toward efficient firms whose output generated net benefits for society (MB > MC).

Under this way of thinking, government stimulus efforts delayed recovery by keeping many wasteful firms on life support. Those who took that opinion wanted the government to mostly hang back, let inefficient firms go bankrupt, and allow the invisible hand to reallocate resources.

This debate over government stimulus was ongoing and continual during the sluggish recovery from the Great Recession. Those in favor of stimulus argued that the sluggish recovery was the result of too little stimulus. Those against stimulus argued that the sluggish recovery was the result of too much stimulus.

One of your tasks as you work your way through the subsequent chapters will be to understand the nature of this debate and the arguments and evidence on both sides. But don't look for a definitive answer. The complexities of giant national economies are only partly understood and the best policy may turn out to be something unseen by either of the two camps.

changes for various common goods and services. The prices of some products like gasoline and airline tickets change very rapidly—about once a month or even less than once a month. By contrast, haircuts and newspapers average more than two years between price changes. And coin-operated laundry machines average nearly four years between price changes!

An important recent study has found that product prices are particularly sticky in response to widespread macroeconomic and monetary disturbances.[2] In later chapters, we will identify and discuss several factors that cause short-run price stickiness. But to keep the current discussion brief, let's focus on just two factors here. One factor is that companies selling final goods and services know that consumers prefer stable, predictable prices

that do not fluctuate rapidly with changes in demand. Consumers would be annoyed if the same bottle of soda or shampoo cost one price one day, a different price the next day, and yet another price a week later. Volatile prices make planning more difficult, and, in addition, consumers who come in to buy the product on a day when the price happens to be high will likely feel that they are being taken advantage of. To avoid this, most firms try to maintain stable prices that do not change very often. Firms do have occasional sales where they lower prices, but on the whole they tend to try to keep prices stable and predictable—the result being price inflexibility.

Another factor that causes sticky prices has to do with the fact that in certain situations, a firm may be afraid that cutting its price may be counterproductive because its rivals might simply match the price cut—a situation often referred to as a "price war." This possibility is common among firms that only have one or two

---

[2]Jean Boivin, Marc P. Giannoni, and Illian Mihov, "Sticky Prices and Monetary Policy: Evidence from Disaggregated US Data," *American Economic Review*, March 2009, pp. 350–384.

major rivals. Consider Coca-Cola and Pepsi. If Coca-Cola faces unexpectedly low demand for its product, it might be tempted to reduce its price in the hope that it can steal business away from Pepsi. But such a strategy would only work if Pepsi left its price alone when Coca-Cola cut its price. That, of course, is not likely. If Coca-Cola cuts its price, Pepsi will very likely cut its price in retaliation, doing its best to make sure that Coca-Cola doesn't steal away any of its customers. Thus, if Pepsi retaliates, Coca-Cola will only be made worse off by its decision to cut its price: It will not pick up much more business (because Pepsi also cut its price) and it will also be receiving less money for each bottle of Coke that it sells (because it lowered its own price.) Thus, firms that have to deal with the possibility of price wars often have sticky prices.

Categorizing Macroeconomic Models Using Price Stickiness

LO6.6 Explain why the greater flexibility of prices as time passes causes economists to utilize different macroeconomic models for different time horizons.

We have now demonstrated why price stickiness is believed to have such a large role in short-run economic fluctuations. It should be noted, however, that price stickiness moderates over time. This is true because firms that choose to use a fixed-price policy in the short run do not have to stick with that policy permanently. In particular, if unexpected changes in demand begin to look permanent, many firms will allow their prices to change so that price changes (in addition to quantity changes) can help to equalize quantities supplied with quantities demanded.

For this reason, economists speak of "sticky prices" rather than "stuck prices." Only in the very short run are prices totally inflexible. As time passes and prices are revised, the world looks much more like Figure 6.1a, in which prices are fully flexible, rather than Figure 6.1b, in which prices are totally inflexible. Indeed, the totally inflexible case shown in Figure 6.1b can be thought of as the extremely short-run response to an unexpected change in demand, while the fully flexible case shown in Figure 6.1a can be thought of as a longer-run response to an unexpected change in demand. In terms of time durations, the extreme short run can be thought of as the first few weeks and months after a demand shock, while the long run can be thought of as extending from many months to several years after a demand shock happens.

This realization is very useful in categorizing and understanding the differences between the various macroeconomic models that we will be presenting in subsequent chapters. For instance, the aggregate expenditures model presented in Chapter 11 assumes perfectly inflexible prices (and wages) and thus is a model in which prices are not just sticky but completely stuck. By contrast, the aggregate demand–aggregate supply model presented in Chapter 12 allows for flexible prices (with or without flexible wages) and is therefore useful for understanding how the economy behaves over longer periods of time.

As you study these various models, keep in mind that we need different models precisely because the economy behaves so differently depending on how much time has passed after a demand shock. The differences in behavior result from the fact that prices go from stuck in the extreme short run to fully flexible in the long run. Using different models for different stages in this process gives us much better insights into not only how economies actually behave but also how various government and central bank policies may have different effects in the short run when prices are fixed versus the long run when prices are flexible.

Where will we go from here? In the remainder of Part 3, we examine how economists measure GDP and why GDP has expanded over time. Then, we discuss the terminology of business cycles and explore the measurement and types of unemployment and inflation. At that point you will be well-prepared to examine the economic models, monetary considerations, and stabilization policies that lie at the heart of macroeconomics.

> ## QUICK REVIEW 6.5
>
> - Many commodity prices are extremely flexible and change constantly, but other prices in the economy change only very infrequently.
> - Some prices are inflexible in order to please retail customers, others because rival firms are afraid that price changes may trigger a price war.
> - Prices tend to become more flexible over time, so that as time passes, the economy can react to demand shocks with price changes as well as with output and employment changes.
> - Different macroeconomics models are required for the short run, during which prices are inflexible (so that demand shocks lead almost exclusively to output and employment changes), and for longer periods, during which prices become increasingly flexible (so that demand shocks lead more to price changes rather than output and employment changes).

SUMMARY

LO6.1 Explain why economists focus on GDP, inflation, and unemployment when assessing the health of an entire economy.

Macroeconomics studies long-run economic growth and short-run economic fluctuations.

Macroeconomists focus their attention on three key economic statistics: real GDP, unemployment, and inflation. Real GDP measures the value of all final goods and services produced in a country during a specific period of time. The unemployment rate measures the percentage of all workers who are not able to find paid employment despite being willing and able to work at currently available wages. The inflation rate measures the extent to which the overall level of prices is rising in the economy.

LO6.2 Discuss why sustained increases in living standards are a historically recent phenomenon.

Before the Industrial Revolution, living standards did not show any sustained increases over time. Economies grew, but any increase in output tended to be offset by an equally large increase in the population, so that the amount of output per person did not rise. By contrast, since the Industrial Revolution began in the late 1700s, many nations have experienced modern economic growth in which output grows faster than population—so that standards of living rise over time.

LO6.3 Identify why saving and investment are key factors in promoting rising living standards.

Macroeconomists believe that one of the keys to modern economic growth is the promotion of saving and investment (for economists, the purchase of capital goods). Investment activities increase the economy's future potential output level. But investment must be funded by saving, which is only possible if people are willing to reduce current consumption. Consequently, individuals and society face a trade-off between current consumption and future consumption since the only way to fund the investment necessary to increase future consumption is by reducing current consumption in order to gather the savings necessary to fund that investment. Banks and other financial institutions help to convert saving into investment by taking the savings generated by households and lending it to businesses that wish to make investments.

LO6.4 Describe why economists believe that "shocks" and "sticky prices" are responsible for short-run fluctuations in output and employment.

Expectations have an important effect on the economy for two reasons. First, if people and businesses are more positive about the future, they will save and invest more. Second, individuals and firms must make adjustments to shocks—situations in which expectations are unmet and the future does not turn out the way people were expecting. In particular, shocks often imply situations where the quantity supplied of a given good or service does not equal the quantity demanded of that good or service.

If prices were always flexible and capable of rapid adjustment, then dealing with situations in which quantities demanded did not equal quantities supplied would always be easy since prices could simply adjust to the market equilibrium price at which quantities demanded equal quantities supplied. Unfortunately, real-world prices are often inflexible (or "sticky") in the short run so that the only way for the economy to adjust to such situations is through changes in output levels.

Sticky prices combine with shocks to drive short-run fluctuations in output and employment. Consider a negative demand shock in which demand is unexpectedly low. Because prices are fixed, the lower-than-expected demand will result in unexpectedly slow sales. This will cause inventories to increase. If demand remains low for an extended period of time, inventory levels will become too high and firms will have to cut output and lay off workers. Thus, when prices are inflexible, the economy adjusts to unexpectedly low demand through changes in output and employment rather than through changes in prices (which are not possible when prices are inflexible).

LO6.5 Characterize the degree to which various prices in the economy are sticky.

Prices are inflexible in the short run for various reasons, two of which are discussed in this chapter. First, firms often attempt to set and maintain stable prices to please customers who like predictable prices because they make for easy planning (and who might become upset if prices were volatile). Second, a firm with just a few competitors may be reluctant to cut its price due to the fear of starting a price war, a situation in which its competitors retaliate by cutting their prices as well—thereby leaving the firm worse off than it was to begin with.

LO6.6 Explain why the greater flexibility of prices as time passes causes economists to utilize different macroeconomic models for different time horizons.

Price stickiness moderates over time. As a result, economists have found it sensible to build separate economic models for different time horizons. For instance, some models are designed to reflect the high degree of price inflexibility that occurs in the immediate short run, while other models reflect the high degree of price flexibility that occurs in the long run. The different models allow economists to have a better sense for how various government policies will affect the economy in the short run when prices are inflexible versus the long run when prices are flexible.

TERMS AND CONCEPTS

business cycle

recession

real GDP (gross domestic product)

nominal GDP

unemployment

inflation

modern economic growth

saving

investment

financial investment

economic investment

expectations

shocks

demand shocks

supply shocks

inventory

inflexible prices ("sticky prices")

flexible prices

The following and additional problems can be found in **connect**
ECONOMICS

DISCUSSION QUESTIONS

1. Why do you think macroeconomists focus on just a few key statistics when trying to understand the health and trajectory of an economy? Would it be better to try to examine all possible data? **LO6.1**

2. Consider a nation in which the volume of goods and services is growing by 5 percent per year. What is the likely impact of this high rate of growth on the power and influence of its government relative to other countries experiencing slower rates of growth? What about the effect of this 5 percent growth on the nation's living standards? Will these also necessarily grow by 5 percent per year, given population growth? Why or why not? **LO6.2**

3. Did economic output start growing faster than population from the beginning of the human inhabitation of the earth? When did modern economic growth begin? Have all of the world's nations experienced the same extent of modern economic growth? **LO6.2**

4. Why is there a trade-off between the amount of consumption that people can enjoy today and the amount of consumption that they can enjoy in the future? Why can't people enjoy more of both? How does saving relate to investment and thus to economic growth? What role do banks and other financial institutions play in aiding the growth process? **LO6.3**

5. How does investment as defined by economists differ from investment as defined by the general public? What would happen to the amount of economic investment made today if firms expected the future returns to such investment to be very low? What if firms expected future returns to be very high? **LO6.3**

6. Why, in general, do shocks force people to make changes? Give at least two examples from your own experience. **LO6.4**

7. Catalog companies are committed to selling at the prices printed in their catalogs. If a catalog company finds its inventory of sweaters rising, what does that tell you about the demand for sweaters? Was it unexpectedly high, unexpectedly low, or as expected? If the company could change the price of sweaters, would it raise the price, lower the price, or keep the price the same? Given that the company cannot change the price of sweaters, consider the number of sweaters it orders each month from the company that makes its sweaters. If inventories become very high, will the catalog company increase, decrease, or keep orders the same? Given what the catalog company does with its orders, what is likely to happen to employment and output at the sweater manufacturer? **LO6.4**

8. Are all prices in the economy equally inflexible? Which ones show large amounts of short-run flexibility? Which ones show a great deal of inflexibility even over months and years? **LO6.5**

9. Why do many firms strive to maintain stable prices? **LO6.5**

10. Do prices tend to become more or less flexible as time passes? If there is a trend, how does it affect macroeconomists' choice of models? **LO6.6**

11. **LAST WORD** How do the Minsky and Austrian explanations for the causes of the Great Recession differ? Explain how the proponents of government stimulus believe that it will affect aggregate demand and employment (be specific!). How might government stimulus possibly slow rather than accelerate a recovery?

REVIEW QUESTIONS

1. An increase in _____ GDP guarantees that more goods and services are being produced by an economy. **LO6.1**
   a. Nominal.
   b. Real.

2. True or False. The term *economic investment* includes purchasing stocks, bonds, and real estate. **LO6.3**

3. If an economy has sticky prices and demand unexpectedly increases, you would expect the economy's real GDP to: **LO6.4**
   a. Increase.
   b. Decrease.
   c. Remain the same.

4. If an economy has fully flexible prices and demand unexpectedly increases, you would expect that the economy's real GDP would tend to: **LO6.4**
   a. Increase.
   b. Decrease.
   c. Remain the same.
5. If the demand for a firm's output unexpectedly decreases, you would expect that its inventory would: **LO6.4**
   a. Increase.
   b. Decrease.

   c. Remain the same.
   d. Increase or remain the same, depending on whether prices are sticky.
6. True or False. Because price stickiness only matters in the short run, economists are comfortable using just one macroeconomic model for all situations. **LO6.6**

PROBLEMS

1. Suppose that the annual rates of growth of real GDP of Econoland over a five-year period were sequentially as follows: 3 percent, 1 percent, –2 percent, 4 percent, and 5 percent. What was the average of these growth rates in Econoland over these 5 years? What term would economists use to describe what happened in year 3? If the growth rate in year 3 had been a positive 2 percent rather than a negative 2 percent, what would have been the average growth rate? **LO6.1**

2. Suppose that Glitter Gulch, a gold mining firm, increased its sales revenues on newly mined gold from $100 million to $200 million between one year and the next. Assuming that the price of gold increased by 100 percent over the same period, by what numerical amount did Glitter Gulch's real output change? If the price of gold had not changed, what would have been the change in Glitter Gulch's real output? **LO6.1**

3. A mathematical approximation called the rule of 70 tells us that the number of years that it will take something that is growing to double in size is approximately equal to the number 70 divided by its percentage rate of growth. Thus, if Mexico's real GDP per person is growing at 7 percent per year, it will take about 10 years (= 70/7) to double. Apply the rule of 70 to solve the following problem. Real GDP per person in Mexico in 2005 was about $11,000 per person, while it was about $44,000 per person in the United States. If real GDP per person in Mexico grows at the rate of 5 percent per year, about how long will it take Mexico's real GDP per person to reach the level that the United States was at in 2005? (Hint: How many times would Mexico's 2005 real GDP per person have to double to reach the United States' 2005 real GDP per person?) **LO6.2**

4. Assume that a national restaurant firm called BBQ builds 10 new restaurants at a cost of $1 million per restaurant. It outfits each restaurant with an additional $200,000 of equipment and furnishings. To help partially defray the cost of this expansion, BBQ issues and sells 200,000 shares of stock at $30 per share. What is the amount of economic investment that has resulted from BBQ's actions? How much purely financial investment took place? **LO6.3**

5. Refer to Figure 6.1b and assume that price is fixed at $37,000 and that Buzzer Auto needs 5 workers for every 1 automobile produced. If demand is D_M and Buzzer wants to perfectly match its output and sales, how many cars will Buzzer produce and how many workers will it hire? If instead, demand unexpectedly falls from D_M to D_L, how many fewer cars will Buzzer sell? How many fewer workers will it need if it decides to match production to these lower sales? **LO6.4**

CHAPTER **7**

Measuring Domestic Output and National Income

Learning Objectives:

LO7.1 Explain how gross domestic product (GDP) is defined and measured.

LO7.2 Describe how expenditures on goods and services can be summed to determine GDP.

LO7.3 Explain how GDP can be determined by summing up all of the incomes that were derived from producing the economy's output of goods and services.

LO7.4 Describe the relationships among GDP, net domestic product, national income, personal income, and disposable income.

LO7.5 Discuss the nature and function of a GDP price index, and describe

the difference between nominal GDP and real GDP.

LO7.6 List and explain some limitations of the GDP measure.

"Disposable Income Flat." "Personal Consumption Surges." "Investment Spending Stagnates." "GDP Up 4 Percent." These headlines, typical of those found on Yahoo! Finance or in *The Wall Street Journal*, give knowledgeable readers valuable information on the state of the economy. This chapter will help you interpret such headlines and understand the stories reported under them. Specifically, it will help you become familiar with the vocabulary and methods of national income accounting. Such accounting enables economists to measure the long-run rate of economic growth and identify the recessions and expansions associated with the economic ups and downs known as the business cycle. In addition, the terms and ideas that you encounter in this chapter will provide a needed foundation for the macroeconomic models found in subsequent chapters.

Assessing the Economy's Performance

LO7.1 Explain how gross domestic product (GDP) is defined and measured.

National income accounting measures the economy's overall performance. It does for the economy as a whole what private accounting does for the individual firm or for the individual household.

A business firm measures its flows of income and expenditures regularly—usually every 3 months or once a year. With that information in hand, the firm can gauge its economic health. If things are going well and profits are good, the accounting data can be used to explain that success. Were costs down? Was output up? Have market prices risen? If things are going badly and profits are poor, the firm may be able to identify the reason by studying the record over several accounting periods. All this information helps the firm's managers plot their future strategy.

National income accounting operates in much the same way for the economy as a whole. The Bureau of Economic Analysis (BEA), an agency of the Commerce Department, compiles the National Income and Product Accounts (NIPA) for the U.S. economy. This accounting enables economists and policymakers to:

- Assess the health of the economy by comparing levels of production at regular intervals.
- Track the long-run course of the economy to see whether it has grown, been constant, or declined.
- Formulate policies that will safeguard and improve the economy's health.

Gross Domestic Product

The primary measure of the economy's performance is its annual total output of goods and services or, as it is called, its *aggregate output*. There are several ways to measure aggregate output depending upon how one wishes to define "an economy." For instance, should the value of the cars produced at a Toyota plant in Ohio count as part of the output of the U.S. economy because they are made within the United States or as part of the Japanese economy

TABLE 7.1 Comparing Heterogeneous Output by Using Money Prices

Year	Annual Output	Market Value
1	3 sofas and 2 computers	3 at $500 + 2 at $2,000 = $5,500
2	2 sofas and 3 computers	2 at $500 + 3 at $2,000 = $7,000

because Toyota is a Japanese company? As mentioned in Chapter 6, **gross domestic product (GDP)** defines aggregate output as the dollar value of all final goods and services produced within the borders of a country during a specific period of time, typically a year. Under this definition, the value of the cars produced at the Toyota factory in Ohio clearly count as part of U.S. aggregate output rather than Japanese aggregate output because the cars are made within the borders of the United States.[1]

A Monetary Measure

By necessity, GDP is a *monetary measure*. To see why, suppose that the economy produces three sofas and two computers in year 1 and two sofas and three computers in year 2. In which year is output greater? We can't answer that question until we attach a price tag to each of the two products to indicate how society evaluates their relative worth.

That's what GDP does. It measures the value of output in monetary terms. Without such a measure we would have no way of comparing the relative values of the vast number of goods and services produced in different years. In Table 7.1 the price of sofas is $500 and the price of computers is $2,000. GDP would gauge the output of year 2 ($7,000) as greater than the output of year 1 ($5,500) because society places a higher monetary value on the output of year 2. Society is willing to pay $1,500 more for the combination of goods produced in year 2 than for the combination of goods produced in year 1.

---

[1]In contrast to GDP, U.S. gross *national* product (GNP) consists of the total value of all the final goods and services produced by American-supplied resources, whether those goods and services are produced within the borders of the United States or abroad. The U.S. switched from GNP to GDP accounting in 1992 to match the type of accounting used by other countries worldwide.

Avoiding Multiple Counting

To measure aggregate output accurately, all goods and services produced in a particular year must be counted once and only once. Because most products go through a series of production stages before they reach the market, some of their components are bought and sold many times. To avoid counting those components each time, GDP includes only the market value of *final goods* and ignores *intermediate goods* altogether.

Intermediate goods are products that are purchased for resale or further processing or manufacturing. **Final goods** are products that are purchased by their end users. Crude oil is an intermediate good; gasoline used for personal transportation is a final good. Steel beams are intermediate goods; completed high-rise apartments are final goods. Lettuce, carrots, and vinegar in restaurant salads are intermediate goods; restaurant salads are final goods. Other examples of final goods are sunglasses bought by consumers, assembly machinery purchased by businesses, surveillance satellites bought by government, and smart phones purchased by foreign buyers.

Why is the value of final goods included in GDP but the value of intermediate goods excluded? Because the value of final goods already includes the value of all the intermediate goods that were used in producing them. Including the value of intermediate goods would amount to **multiple counting,** and that would distort the value of GDP.

To see why, suppose that five stages are needed to manufacture a wool coat and get it to the consumer— the final user. Table 7.2 shows that firm A, a sheep ranch, sells $120 worth of wool to firm B, a wool processor. Firm A pays out the $120 in wages, rent, interest, and profit. Firm B processes the wool and sells it to firm C, a coat manufacturer, for $180. What does firm B do with the $180 it receives? It pays $120 to firm A for the wool and uses the remaining $60 to pay wages, rent, interest, and profit for the resources used in processing the wool. Firm C, the manufacturer, sells the coat to firm D, a wholesaler, which sells it to firm E, a retailer. Then at last a consumer, the final user, comes in and buys the coat for $350.

How much of these amounts should we include in GDP to account for the production of the coat? Just $350, the value of the final product. The $350 includes all the intermediate transactions leading up to the product's final sale. Including the sum of all the intermediate sales, $1,140, in GDP would amount to multiple counting. The production and sale of the final coat generated just $350 of output, not $1,140.

Alternatively, we could avoid multiple counting by measuring and cumulating only the *value added* at each stage. **Value added** is the market value of a firm's output *less* the value of the inputs the firm has bought from others. At each stage, the difference between what a firm pays for inputs and what it receives from selling the product made from those inputs is paid out as wages, rent, interest, and profit. Column 3 of Table 7.2 shows that the value added by firm B is $60, the difference between the $180 value of its output and the $120 it paid for the input from firm A. We find the total value of the coat by adding together all the values added by the five firms. Similarly, by calculating and summing the values added to all the goods and services produced by all firms in the economy, we can find the market value of the economy's total output—its GDP.

GDP Excludes Nonproduction Transactions

Although many monetary transactions in the economy involve final goods and services, many others do not. These nonproduction transactions must be excluded from GDP because they have nothing to do with the generation of final goods. *Nonproduction transactions* are

TABLE 7.2   Value Added in a Five-Stage Production Process

(1) Stage of Production	(2) Sales Value of Materials or Product	(3) Value Added
	$ 0	$120 (= $120 − $ 0)
Firm A, sheep ranch	120	60 (= 180 − 120)
Firm B, wool processor	180	40 (= 220 − 180)
Firm C, coat manufacturer	220	50 (= 270 − 220)
Firm D, clothing wholesaler	270	80 (= 350 − 270)
Firm E, retail clothier	**350**	
Total sales values	$1,140	
Value added (total income)		**$350**

of two types: purely financial transactions and second-hand sales.

Financial Transactions Purely financial transactions include the following:

- *Public transfer payments* These are the social security payments, welfare payments, and veterans' payments that the government makes directly to households. Since the recipients contribute nothing to *current production* in return, to include such payments in GDP would be to overstate the year's output.

- *Private transfer payments* Such payments include, for example, the money that parents give children or the cash gifts given during the holidays. They produce no output. They simply transfer funds from one private individual to another and consequently do not enter into GDP.

- *Stock market transactions* The buying and selling of stocks (and bonds) is just a matter of swapping bits of paper. Stock market transactions create nothing in the way of current production and are not included in GDP. Payments for the services provided by a stockbroker *are* included, however, because their services are currently provided and are thus a part of the economy's current output of goods and services.

Secondhand Sales Secondhand sales contribute nothing to current production and for that reason are excluded from GDP. Suppose you sell your 2005 Ford Mustang to a friend; that transaction would be ignored in reckoning this year's GDP because it generates no current production. The same would be true if you sold a brand-new Mustang to a neighbor a week after you purchased it.

Two Ways of Looking at GDP: Spending and Income

Let's look again at how the market value of total output—or of any single unit of total output—is measured. Given the data listed in Table 7.2, how can we measure the market value of a coat?

One way is to see how much the final user paid for it. That will tell us the market value of the final product. Or we can add up the entire wage, rental, interest, and profit incomes that were created in producing the coat. The second approach is the value-added technique used in Table 7.2.

The final-product approach and the value-added approach are two ways of looking at the same thing. What is spent on making a product is income to those who helped make it. If $350 is spent on manufacturing a coat, then $350 is the total income derived from its production.

We can look at GDP in the same two ways. We can view GDP as the sum of all the money spent in buying it. That is the *output approach*, or **expenditures approach.** Or we can view GDP in terms of the income derived or created from producing it. That is the *earnings* or *allocations approach*, or the **income approach.**

As illustrated in Figure 7.1, we can determine GDP for a particular year either by adding up all that was spent to buy total output or by adding up all the money that was derived as income from its production. Buying (spending money) and selling (receiving income) are two aspects of the same transaction. On the expenditures side of GDP, all final goods produced by the economy are bought either by three domestic sectors (households, businesses, and government) or by foreign buyers. On the income side (once certain statistical adjustments are made), the

FIGURE 7.1 The expenditures and income approaches to GDP. There are two general approaches to measuring gross domestic product. We can determine GDP as the value of output by summing all expenditures on that output. Alternatively, with some modifications, we can determine GDP by adding up all the components of income arising from the production of that output.

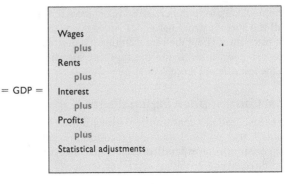

Expenditures, or output, approach

Income, or allocations, approach

TABLE 7.3 Accounting Statement for the U.S. Economy, 2012 (in Billions)*

Receipts: Expenditures Approach		Allocations: Income Approach	
Sum of:		Sum of:	
Personal consumption expenditures (C)	$11,150	Compensation of employees	$8,612
Gross private domestic investment (I_g)	2,475	Rents	541
Government purchases (G)	3,167	Interest	440
Net exports (X_n)	−547	Proprietors' income	1,225
		Corporate profits	2,031
		Taxes on production and imports	1,123
		Equals:	
		National income	**$13,972**
		National income	$13,972
		Less: Net foreign factor income	253
		Plus: Consumption of fixed capital	2,543
		Plus: Statistical discrepancy	−17
Equals:		*Equals:*	
Gross domestic product	**$16,245**	**Gross domestic product**	**$16,245**

*Some of the items in the Allocations column combine related categories that appear in the more detailed accounts. All data are subject to government revision.

Source: Bureau of Economic Analysis, **www.bea.gov**.

total receipts acquired from the sale of that total output are allocated to the suppliers of resources as wage, rent, interest, and profit.

Table 7.3 shows U.S. GDP for the year 2012 totaled up using both the expenditures approach (on the left side) and the income approach (on the right side). As you would expect, both methods reach the same conclusion: U.S. GDP in 2012 was $16,245 billion.

We will now go through both approaches in detail. Doing so will help you better understand both methods and, in particular, why the income side of Table 7.3 looks substantially more complicated than the income side of Figure 7.1.

The Expenditures Approach

LO7.2 Describe how expenditures on goods and services can be summed to determine GDP.

To determine GDP using the expenditures approach, we add up all the spending on final goods and services that has taken place throughout the year. National-income accountants use precise terms for the types of spending listed on the left side of Figure 7.1:

Personal Consumption Expenditures (C)

What we have called "consumption expenditures by households," the national income accountants call **personal consumption expenditures.** This term covers all expenditures by households on goods and services.

In a typical year, roughly 10 percent of these personal consumption expenditures are on **durable goods**—products that have expected lives of three years or more. Such goods include new automobiles, furniture, and refrigerators. Another 30 percent are on **nondurable goods**—products with less than three years of expected life. Included are goods like food, clothing, and gasoline. About 60 percent of personal consumption expenditures are on **services**—the work done by lawyers, hair stylists, doctors, mechanics, and other service providers. Because of this high percentage, economists sometimes refer to the U.S. economy as a *service economy*. National income accountants combine the household spending on durable goods, nondurable goods, and services and use the symbol C to designate the personal consumption expenditures component of GDP.

Gross Private Domestic Investment (I_g)

Under the heading **gross private domestic investment,** the accountants include the following items:

- All final purchases of machinery, equipment, and tools by business enterprises.

- All construction.

- Changes in inventories.

- Money spent on research and development (R&D) or for the creation of new works of art, music, writing, film, and so on.

Notice that this list, except for the first item, includes more than we have meant by "investment" so far. The second item includes residential construction as well as the construction of new factories, warehouses, and stores. Why do the accountants regard residential construction as investment rather than consumption? Because apartment buildings and houses, like factories and stores, earn income when they are rented or leased. Owner-occupied houses are treated as investment goods because they *could be* rented to bring in an income return. So the national income accountants treat all residential construction as investment.

Increases in inventories (unsold goods) are considered to be investment because they represent, in effect, "unconsumed output." For economists, all new output that is not consumed is, by definition, capital. An increase in inventories is an addition (although perhaps temporary) to the stock of capital goods, and such additions are precisely how we define investment.

Starting in 2013, the NIPA accountants who compile U.S. GDP statistics began to include expenditures on R&D as well as money spent to develop new works of writing, art, music, and software as a form of investment. They did so because a country's stock of "capital goods" useful in producing output can be thought of as including not only tangible pieces of physical capital like fiber optic networks and factories but also useful ideas that increase the economy's ability to produce goods and services.

Software is a great example, as it is merely sets of instructions for telling computers what to do. But without those instructions, computers would be useless. So spending on software as well as on R&D and other intellectual activities that improve the economy's stock of "know-how" are now counted as investment.

To make it possible to compare GDP numbers across time, the accountants have gone back and applied the new, more comprehensive definition of investment all the way back to 1929. The numbers for U.S. GDP for the year 2012 that are used in this chapter incorporate the revised definition of investment.

Positive and Negative Changes in Inventories

We need to look at changes in inventories more closely. Inventories can either increase or decrease over some period. Suppose they increased by $10 billion between December 31, 2012, and December 31, 2013. Therefore, in 2013 the economy produced $10 billion more output than people purchased. We need to count all output produced in 2013 as part of that year's GDP, even though some of it remained unsold at the end of the year. This is accomplished by including the $10 billion increase in

inventories as investment in 2013. That way the expenditures in 2013 will correctly measure the output produced that year.

Alternatively, suppose that inventories decreased by $10 billion in 2013. This "drawing down of inventories" means that the economy sold $10 billion more of output in 2013 than it produced that year. It did this by selling goods produced in prior years—goods already counted as GDP in those years. Unless corrected, expenditures in 2013 will overstate GDP for 2013. So in 2013 we consider the $10 billion decline in inventories as "negative investment" and subtract it from total investment that year. Thus, expenditures in 2013 will correctly measure the output produced in 2013.

Noninvestment Transactions So much for what investment *is*. You also need to know what it *isn't*. For economists and NIPA accountants, investment does *not* include noninvestment transactions such as the transfer of paper assets (stocks, bonds) or the resale of tangible assets (houses, jewelry, boats). Such financial transactions merely transfer the ownership of existing assets. The investment in the GDP accounts is economic investment—the creation of *new* capital assets. The mere transfer (sale) of claims to existing capital goods does not produce new capital goods. Therefore such transactions (so-called financial investments) are not included as investment in the GDP accounts.

Gross Investment versus Net Investment As we have seen, the category gross private domestic investment includes (1) all final purchases of machinery, equipment, and tools; (2) all construction; (3) changes in inventories; and (4) spending on R&D and other activities that expand the economy's stock of technology and know-how. The words "private" and "domestic" mean that we are speaking of spending by private businesses, not by government (public) agencies, and that the investment is taking place inside the country, not abroad.

The word "gross" means that we are referring to *all* investment goods—both those that replace machinery, equipment, and buildings that were used up (worn out or made obsolete) in producing the current year's output and any net additions to the economy's stock of capital. Gross investment includes investment in replacement capital *and* in added capital.

In contrast, **net private domestic investment** includes *only* investment in the form of added capital. The amount of capital that is used up over the course of a year is called *depreciation*. So

Net investment = gross investment − depreciation

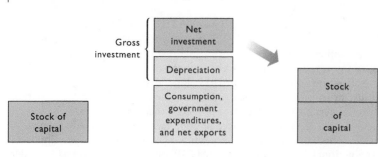

FIGURE 7.2 Gross investment, depreciation, net investment, and the stock of capital. When gross investment exceeds depreciation during a year, net investment occurs. This net investment expands the stock of private capital from the beginning of the year to the end of the year by the amount of the net investment. Other things equal, the economy's production capacity expands.

In typical years, gross investment exceeds depreciation. Thus net investment is positive and the nation's stock of capital rises by the amount of net investment. As illustrated in Figure 7.2, the stock of capital at the end of the year exceeds the stock of capital at the beginning of the year by the amount of net investment.

Gross investment need not always exceed depreciation, however. When gross investment and depreciation *are equal*, net investment is zero and there is no change in the size of the capital stock. When gross investment *is less than* depreciation, net investment is negative. The economy then is *disinvesting*—using up more capital than it is producing—and the nation's stock of capital shrinks. That happened in the Great Depression of the 1930s.

National income accountants use the symbol I for private domestic investment spending. To differentiate between gross investment and net investment, they add either the subscript g or the subscript n. But it is gross investment, I_g, that they use when tallying up GDP.

Government Purchases (G)

The third category of expenditures in the national income accounts is **government purchases,** officially labeled "government consumption expenditures and gross investment." These expenditures have three components: (1) expenditures for goods and services that government consumes in providing public services; (2) expenditures for *publicly owned capital* such as schools and highways, which have long lifetimes; and (3) government expenditures on R&D and other activities that increase the economy's stock of know-how. Government purchases (federal, state, and local) include all government expenditures on final goods and all direct purchases of resources, including labor. It does *not* include government transfer payments because, as we have seen, they merely transfer government receipts to certain households and generate no production of any sort. National income accountants use the symbol G to signify government purchases.

Net Exports (X_n)

International trade transactions are a significant item in national income accounting. But when calculating U.S. GDP, we must keep in mind that we want to total up only those expenditures that are used to purchase goods and services produced *within the borders of the United States*. Thus, we must add in the value of exports, X, since exports are by definition goods and services produced within the borders of the United States. Don't be confused by the fact that the expenditures made to buy our exports are made by foreigners. The definition of GDP does not care about *who* is making expenditures on U.S.-made goods and services—only that the goods and services that they buy are made within the borders of the United States. Thus, foreign spending on our exports *must* be included in GDP.

At this point, you might incorrectly think that GDP should be equal to the sum of $C + I_g + G + X$. But this sum overstates GDP. The problem is that, once again, we must consider only expenditures made on *domestically produced* goods and services. As it stands, C, I_g, and G count expenditures on consumption, investment, and government purchases *regardless* of where those goods and services are made. Crucially, not all of the C, I_g, or G expenditures are for domestically produced goods and services. Some of the expenditures are for imports—goods and services produced outside of the United States. Because we wish to count *only* the part of C, I_g, and G that goes to purchasing domestically produced goods and services, we must subtract the spending that goes to imports, M. That subtraction yields the correct formula for calculating gross domestic product: GDP = $C + I_g + G + X - M$.

Accountants simplify this formula for GDP by defining **net exports,** X_n, to be equal to exports minus imports:

$$\text{Net exports } (X_n) = \text{exports } (X) - \text{imports } (M)$$

CONSIDER THIS ...

Stocks versus Flows

An analogy of a reservoir is helpful in thinking about a nation's capital stock, investment, and depreciation. Picture a reservoir that has water flowing in from a river and flowing out from an outlet after it passes through turbines. The volume of water in the reservoir *at any particular point in time* is a "stock." In contrast, the inflow from the river and outflow from the outlet are "flows."

The volume or stock of water in the reservoir will rise if the weekly inflow exceeds the weekly outflow. It will fall if the inflow is less than the outflow. And it will remain constant if the two flows are equal.

Now let's apply this analogy to the stock of capital, gross investment, and depreciation. The stock of capital is the total capital in place at any point in time and is analogous to the level of water in the reservoir. Changes in this capital stock over some period, for example, one year, depend on *gross investment* and *depreciation*. Gross investment (analogous to the reservoir inflow) is an addition of capital goods and therefore adds to the stock of capital, while depreciation (analogous to the reservoir outflow) is the using up of capital and thus subtracts from the capital stock. The capital stock increases when gross investment exceeds depreciation, declines when gross investment is less than depreciation, and remains the same when gross investment and depreciation are equal.

Alternatively, the stock of capital increases when *net investment* (gross investment *minus* depreciation) is positive. When net investment is negative, the stock of capital declines, and when net investment is zero, the stock of capital remains constant.

Using this definition of net exports, the formula for gross domestic product simplifies to,

$$GDP = C + I_g + G + X_n$$

The left side of Table 7.3 shows that in 2012 Americans spent $560 billion more on imports than foreigners spent on U.S. exports. That is, net exports in 2012 were a *minus* $560 billion.

Putting It All Together: GDP = $C + I_g + G + X_n$

Taken together, the four categories of expenditures provide a measure of the market value of a specific year's total

GLOBAL PERSPECTIVE 7.1

Comparative GDPs in Trillions of U.S. Dollars, Selected Nations, 2011

The United States, China, and Japan have the world's highest GDPs. The GDP data charted below have been converted to U.S. dollars via international exchange rates.

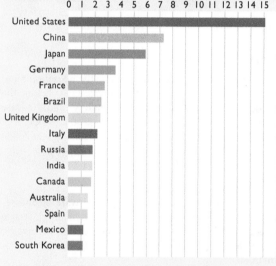

Source: International Monetary Fund, **www.imf.org**.

output—its GDP. For the United States in 2012, the left side of Table 7.3 indicates that

$$GDP = \$11{,}150 + \$2{,}475 + \$3{,}167 - 547 \text{ billion}$$

Global Perspective 7.1 lists the GDPs of several countries. The values of GDP are converted to dollars using international exchange rates.

The Income Approach

LO7.3 Explain how GDP can be determined by summing up all of the incomes that were derived from producing the economy's output of goods and services.

The right side of Table 7.3 shows how 2012's expenditures of $16,245 billion were allocated as income to those responsible for producing the output. It would be simple if we could say that the entire amount of expenditures flowed back to them in the form of wages, rent, interest, and profit. But some expenditures flow to other recipients (such as the government) or to other uses (such as paying to replace the capital goods that have worn out while producing this year's

GDP). These must be accounted for to balance the expenditures and income sides of the overall account. We will begin by looking at the items that make up *national income*.

Compensation of Employees

By far the largest share of national income—$8,612 billion in 2012—was paid as wages and salaries by business and government to their employees. That figure also includes wage and salary supplements, in particular, payments by employers into social insurance and into a variety of private pension, health, and welfare funds for workers.

Rents

Rents consist of the income received by the households and businesses that supply property resources. They include the monthly payments tenants make to landlords and the lease payments corporations pay for the use of office space. The figure used in the national accounts is *net* rent—gross rental income minus depreciation of the rental property.

Interest

Interest consists of the money paid by private businesses to the suppliers of loans used to purchase capital. It also includes such items as the interest households receive on savings deposits, certificates of deposit (CDs), and corporate bonds.

Proprietors' Income

What we have loosely termed "profits" is broken down by the national income accountants into two accounts: proprietors' income, which consists of the net income of sole proprietorships, partnerships, and other unincorporated businesses; and corporate profits. Proprietors' income flows to the proprietors.

Corporate Profits

Corporate profits are the earnings of corporations. National income accountants subdivide corporate profits into three categories:

- *Corporate income taxes* These taxes are levied on corporations' profits. They flow to the government.
- *Dividends* These are the part of after-tax profits that corporations choose to pay out, or distribute, to their stockholders. They thus flow to households—the ultimate owners of all corporations.
- *Undistributed corporate profits* Any after-tax profits that are not distributed to shareholders are saved, or

retained, by corporations to be invested later in new plants and equipment. Undistributed corporate profits are also called *retained earnings*.

Taxes on Production and Imports

The account called **taxes on production and imports** includes general sales taxes, excise taxes, business property taxes, license fees, and customs duties. Why do national income accountants add these indirect business taxes to wages, rent, interest, and profits in determining national income? The answer is, "to account for expenditures that are diverted to the government." Consider an item that would otherwise sell for $1 but costs $1.05 because the government has imposed a 5 percent sales tax. When this item is purchased, consumers will expend $1.05 to buy it. But only $1 will go to the seller (who will then distribute it as income in the form of wages, rent, interest, and profit in order to compensate resource providers). The remaining 5 cents will flow as revenue to the government. The GDP accountants handle the extra 5 cents by placing it into the category called "Taxes on Production and Imports" and loosely consider it to be "income" to government.

From National Income to GDP

We have just shown that expenditures on final goods and services flow either as income to private citizens or as "income" to government. As a result, **national income** is the total of all sources of private income (employee compensation, rents, interest, proprietors' income, and corporate profits) plus government revenue from taxes on production and imports. National income is all the income that flows to American-supplied resources, whether here or abroad, plus taxes on production and imports. But notice that the figure for national income shown in Table 7.3—$13,972 billion—is less than GDP as reckoned by the expenditures approach shown on the left side of the table. The two sides of the accounting statement are brought into balance by subtracting one item from national income and adding two others.

Net Foreign Factor Income First, we need to make a slight adjustment in "national" income versus "domestic" income. National income includes the total income of Americans, whether it was earned in the United States or abroad. But GDP is a measure of *domestic* output—total output produced within the United States regardless of the nationality of those who provide the resources. So in moving from national income to GDP, we must take out the income Americans gain from supplying resources abroad and add in the income that foreigners gain by supplying resources in the United States. That process provides *net foreign factor income*. In 2012, net foreign factor income was $253 billion, meaning that American-owned resources earned $253 billion more in other countries than foreign-owned resources earned in the United States. Because this $253 billion is earnings of Americans, it is included in U.S. national income. But this income is not part of U.S. domestic income because it reflects earnings from output produced in other nations. It is part of those nations' domestic income, derived from production of their domestic output. Thus, we subtract net foreign factor income from U.S. national income to stay on the correct path to use the income approach to determine the value of *U.S. domestic output* (output produced within U.S. borders).

Consumption of Fixed Capital Next, we must recognize that the useful lives of private capital equipment (such as bakery ovens or automobile assembly lines) extend far beyond the year in which they were produced. To avoid understating profit and income in the year of purchase and to avoid overstating profit and income in succeeding years, the cost of such capital must be allocated over its lifetime. The amount allocated is an estimate of how much of the capital is being used up each year. It is called *depreciation*. Accounting for depreciation results in a more accurate statement of profit and income for the economy each year. Publicly owned capital, such as courthouses and bridges, also requires a depreciation allowance in the national income accounts.

The huge depreciation charge made against private and publicly owned capital each year is called **consumption of fixed capital** because it is the allowance for capital that has been "consumed" in producing the year's GDP. It is the portion of GDP that is set aside to pay for the ultimate replacement of those capital goods.

The money allocated to consumption of fixed capital (the depreciation allowance) is a cost of production and thus included in the gross value of output. But this money is not available for other purposes, and, unlike other costs of production, it does not add to anyone's income. So it is not included in national income. We must therefore add it to national income to achieve balance with the economy's expenditures.

Statistical Discrepancy As you know, it should be possible to calculate GDP either by totaling up expenditures or by summing up incomes. Either method should give the same result.

In practice, however, it is not possible for NIPA accountants to measure every input into either set of calculations with total precision. Difficulties arise due to a wide range of factors including people misreporting their in-

comes on tax returns and the difficulty involved with accurately estimating depreciation. As a result, the GDP number produced by the income method always differs by a small percentage from the GDP number produced by the expenditures method.

To account for this difference, NIPA accountants add a statistical discrepancy to national income. The addition of that number equalizes the GDP totals produced by the two methods. In 2012 the discrepancy value was negative $17 billion, or less than one-half of one percent of GDP.

Table 7.3 summarizes both the expenditures approach and the income approach to GDP. The left side shows how much the U.S. economy produced in 2012 by showing how much was spent to purchase that year's output of goods and services. The right side shows how those expenditures were allocated either as income to individuals, as revenue to the government, or to other uses such as paying for the replacement of depreciated capital.

QUICK REVIEW 7.1

- Gross domestic product (GDP) is a measure of the total market value of all final goods and services produced by the economy in a specific year.
- The expenditures approach to GDP sums the total spending on final goods and services: GDP $= C + I_g + G + X_n$.
- The economy's stock of private capital expands when net investment is positive; stays constant when net investment is zero; and declines when net investment is negative.
- The income approach to GDP sums compensation to employees, rent, interest, proprietors' income, corporate profits, and taxes on production and imports to obtain national income, and then subtracts net foreign factor income and adds consumption of fixed capital and a statistical discrepancy to obtain GDP.

Other National Accounts

LO7.4 Describe the relationships among GDP, net domestic product, national income, personal income, and disposable income.

Several other national accounts provide additional useful information about the economy's performance. We can derive these accounts by making various adjustments to GDP.

Net Domestic Product

As a measure of total output, GDP does not make allowances for replacing the capital goods used up in each year's production. As a result, it does not tell us how much new output was available for consumption and for additions to the stock of capital. To determine that, we must subtract from GDP the capital that was consumed in producing the GDP and that had to be replaced. That is, we need to subtract consumption of fixed capital (depreciation) from GDP. The result is a measure of **net domestic product (NDP):**

$$NDP = GDP - \text{consumption of fixed capital} \\ \text{(depreciation)}$$

For the United States in 2012:

	Billions
Gross domestic product	$16,245
Less: Consumption of fixed capital	2,543
Equals: Net domestic product	$13,702

NDP is simply GDP adjusted for depreciation. It measures the total annual output that the entire economy—households, businesses, government, and foreigners—can consume without impairing its capacity to produce in ensuing years.

National Income

Sometimes it is useful to know how much Americans earned for their contributions of land, labor, capital, and entrepreneurial talent. Recall that U.S. national income (NI) includes all income earned through the use of American-owned resources, whether they are located at home or abroad. It also includes taxes on production and imports. To derive NI from NDP, we must subtract the aforementioned statistical discrepancy from NDP and add net foreign factor income, since the latter is income earned by Americans overseas minus income earned by foreigners in the United States.

For the United States in 2012:

	Billions
Net domestic product	$13,702
Less: Statistical discrepancy	−17
Plus: Net foreign factor income	253
Equals: National income	$13,972

We know, too, that we can calculate national income through the income approach by simply adding up employee compensation, rent, interest, proprietors' income, corporate profit, and taxes on production and imports.

Personal Income

Personal income (PI) includes all income received, whether earned or unearned. It is likely to differ from national income (income earned) because some income earned—taxes on production and imports, Social Security taxes (payroll taxes), corporate income taxes, and undistributed corporate profits—is not received by households. Conversely, some income received—such as Social Security payments, unemployment compensation payments, welfare payments, disability and education payments to veterans, and private pension payments—is not earned. These transfer payments must be added to obtain PI.

In moving from national income to personal income, we must subtract the income that is earned but not received and add the income that is received but not earned. For the United States in 2012:

	Billions
National income	$13,972
Less: Taxes on production and imports	1,066
Less: Social Security contributions	951
Less: Corporate income taxes	435
Less: Undistributed corporate profits	542
Plus: Transfer payments	2,766*
Equals: Personal income	$13,744

*Includes statistical discrepancy and rounding error.

Disposable Income

Disposable income (DI) is personal income less personal taxes. Personal taxes include personal income taxes, personal property taxes, and inheritance taxes. Disposable income is the amount of income that households have left over after paying their personal taxes. They are free to divide that income between consumption (C) and saving (S):

$$DI = C + S$$

For the United States in 2012:

	Billions
Personal income	$13,744
Less: Personal taxes	1,498
Equals: Disposable income	$12,246

Table 7.4 summarizes the relationships among GDP, NDP, NI, PI, and DI.

WORKED PROBLEMS

W7.1

Measuring output and income

TABLE 7.4 The Relationship between GDP, NDP, NI, PI, and DI in the United States, 2012*

	Billions
Gross domestic product (GDP)	$16,245
Less: Consumption of fixed capital	2,543
Equals: Net domestic product	$13,702
Net domestic product (NDP)	$13,702
Less: Statistical discrepancy	−17
Plus: Net foreign factor income	253
Equals: National income (NI)	$13,972
National income (NI)	$13,972
Less: Taxes on production and imports	1,066
Less: Social Security contributions	951
Less: Corporate income taxes	435
Less: Undistributed corporate profits	542
Plus: Transfer payments	2,766
Equals: Personal income (PI)	$13,744
Personal income (PI)	$13,744
Less: Personal taxes	1,498
Equals: Disposable income (DI)	$12,246

*Some of the items combine categories that appear in the more detailed accounts.
Source: Bureau of Economic Analysis, **www.bea.gov**.

The Circular Flow Revisited

Figure 7.3 is an elaborate flow diagram that shows the economy's four main sectors along with the flows of expenditures and allocations that determine GDP, NDP, NI, and PI. The orange arrows represent the spending flows—$C + I_g + G + X_n$—that together measure gross domestic product. To the right of the GDP rectangle are green arrows that show first the allocations of GDP and then the adjustments needed to derive NDP, NI, PI, and DI.

The diagram illustrates the adjustments necessary to determine each of the national income accounts. For example, net domestic product is smaller than GDP because consumption of fixed capital flows away from GDP in determining NDP. Also, disposable income is smaller than personal income because personal taxes flow away from PI (to government) in deriving DI.

Note the three domestic sectors of the economy: households, government, and businesses. The household sector has an inflow of disposable income and outflows of consumption spending and savings. The government sector has an inflow of revenue in the form of types of taxes and an outflow of government disbursements in the form of purchases and transfers. The business sector has inflows from three major sources of funds for business investment and an outflow of investment expenditures.

Also, take a look at the foreign sector (all other countries) in the flow diagram. Spending by foreigners on U.S. exports adds to U.S. GDP, but some of U.S. consumption, government, and investment expenditures buy imported products. The flow from foreign markets shows that we handle this complication by calculating net exports (U.S. exports minus U.S. imports). The net export flow may be a positive or negative amount, adding to or subtracting from U.S. GDP.

Finally, you need to be aware that the flows shown in Figure 7.3 are dynamic entities and generally expand in size over time as the economy grows. But not always! Case in point: The Great Recession of 2007–2009—first discussed in the Consider This box on page 143—produced a pronounced slowing of the main spending and income flows. Specifically, U.S. businesses greatly reduced investment expenditures and households initially reduced personal consumption expenditures. Consequently, GDP, NDP, NI, and PI all significantly declined.

> ### QUICK REVIEW 7.2
>
> - Net domestic product (NDP) is the market value of GDP minus consumption of fixed capital (depreciation).
> - National income (NI) is all income earned through the use of American-owned resources, whether located at home or abroad. NI also includes taxes on production and imports.
> - Personal income (PI) is all income received by households, whether earned or not.
> - Disposable income (DI) is all income received by households minus personal taxes.

Nominal GDP versus Real GDP

LO7.5 Discuss the nature and function of a GDP price index, and describe the difference between nominal GDP and real GDP.

Recall that GDP is a measure of the market or money value of all final goods and services produced by the economy in a given year. We use money or nominal values as a common denominator to sum that heterogeneous output into a meaningful total. But, as alluded to in Chapter 6, that creates a problem: How can we compare the market values of GDP from year to year if the value of money itself changes in response to inflation (rising prices) or deflation (falling prices)? After all, we determine the value of GDP by multiplying total output by market prices.

Whether there is a 5 percent increase in output with no change in prices or a 5 percent increase in prices with no change in output, the change in the value of GDP will

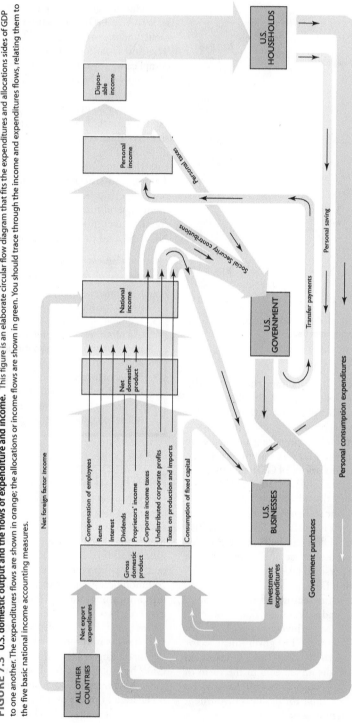

FIGURE 7.3 U.S. domestic output and the flows of expenditure and income. This figure is an elaborate circular flow diagram that fits the expenditures and allocations sides of GDP to one another. The expenditures flows are shown in orange; the allocations or income flows are shown in green. You should trace through the income and expenditures flows, relating them to the five basic national income accounting measures.

be the same. And yet it is the *quantity* of goods and services that get produced and distributed to households that affects our standard of living, not the price of those goods and services. For instance, the McDonald's hamburger that sold for 95 cents in 2013 yields the same satisfaction as a nearly identical McDonald's hamburger that sold for 18 cents in 1967.

The way around this problem is to *deflate* GDP when prices rise and to *inflate* GDP when prices fall. These adjustments give us a measure of GDP for various years as if the value of the dollar had always been the same as it was in some reference year. A GDP based on the prices that prevailed when the output was produced is called unadjusted GDP, or **nominal GDP.** A GDP that has been deflated or inflated to reflect changes in the price level is called adjusted GDP, or **real GDP.**

Adjustment Process in a One-Product Economy

There are two ways we can adjust nominal GDP to reflect price changes. For simplicity, let's assume that the economy produces only one good, pizza, in the amounts indicated in Table 7.5 for years 1, 2, and 3. Suppose that we gather revenue data directly from the financial reports of the economy's pizza businesses to measure nominal GDP in various years. After completing our effort, we will have determined nominal GDP for each year, as shown in column 4 of Table 7.5. We will have no way of knowing to what extent changes in price and/or changes in quantity of output have accounted for the increases or decreases in nominal GDP that we observe.

GDP Price Index   How can we determine real GDP in our pizza economy? One way is to assemble data on the price changes that occurred over various years (column 2) and use them to establish an overall price index for the entire period. Then we can use the index in each year to adjust nominal GDP to real GDP for that year.

In the actual economy, a **price index** is a measure of the price of a specified collection of goods and services, called a "market basket," in a given year as compared to the price of an identical (or highly similar) collection of goods and services in a reference year. That point of reference, or benchmark, is known as the base period, **base year,** or, simply, the reference year. More formally,

$$\begin{array}{c}\text{Price}\\\text{index}\\\text{in given}\\\text{year}\end{array} = \frac{\begin{array}{c}\text{price of market basket}\\\text{in specific year}\end{array}}{\begin{array}{c}\text{price of same market}\\\text{basket in base year}\end{array}} \times 100 \qquad (1)$$

By convention, the price ratio between a given year and the base year is multiplied by 100 to facilitate computation. For example, a price ratio of $2/1 (= 2)$ is expressed as a price index of 200. A price ratio of $1/3 (= 0.33)$ is expressed as a price index of 33.

In our pizza-only example, of course, our market basket consists of only one product. Column 2 of Table 7.5 reveals that the price of pizza was $10 in year 1, $20 in year 2, $25 in year 3, and so on. Let's select year 1 as our base year. Now we can express the successive prices of the contents of our market basket in, say, years 2 and 3 as compared to the price of the market basket in year 1:

$$\text{Price index, year 2} = \frac{\$20}{\$10} \times 100 = 200$$

$$\text{Price index, year 3} = \frac{\$25}{\$10} \times 100 = 250$$

For year 1 the index has to be 100, since that year and the base year are identical.

The index numbers tell us that the price of pizza rose from year 1 to year 2 by 100 percent $\{= [(200 - 100)/100] \times 100\}$ and from year 1 to year 3 by 150 percent $\{= [(250 - 100)/100] \times 100\}$.

Dividing Nominal GDP by the Price Index   We can now use the index numbers shown in column 3 to deflate

TABLE 7.5 Calculating Real GDP (Base Year = Year 1)

Year	(1) Units of Output	(2) Price of Pizza per Unit	(3) Price Index (Year 1 = 100)	(4) Unadjusted, or Nominal, GDP, (1) × (2)	(5) Adjusted, or Real, GDP
1	5	$10	100	$ 50	$50
2	7	20	200	140	70
3	8	25	250	200	80
4	10	30	—	—	—
5	11	28	—	—	—

the nominal GDP figures in column 4. The simplest and most direct method of deflating is to express the index numbers as hundredths—in decimal form—and then to divide them into corresponding nominal GDP. That gives us real GDP:

$$\text{Real GDP} = \frac{\text{nominal GDP}}{\text{price index (in hundredths)}} \quad (2)$$

WORKED PROBLEMS

W7.2

Real GDP and price indexes

Column 5 shows the results. These figures for real GDP measure the market value of the output of pizza in years 1, 2, and 3 as if the price of pizza had been a constant $10 throughout the 3-year period. In short, real GDP reveals the market value of each year's output measured in terms of dollars that have the same purchasing power as dollars had in the base year.

To test your understanding, extend Table 7.5 to years 4 and 5, using equations 1 and 2. Then run through the entire deflating procedure, using year 3 as the base period. This time you will have to inflate some of the nominal GDP data, using the same procedure as we used in the examples.

ORIGIN OF THE IDEA

07.1

GDP price index

An Alternative Method

Another way to calculate real GDP is to gather separate data on physical outputs (as in column 1) and their prices (as in column 2) of Table 7.5. We could then determine the market value of outputs in successive years *if the base-year price ($10) had prevailed*. In year 2, the 7 units of pizza would have a value of $70 (= 7 units × $10). As column 5 confirms, that $70 worth of output is year 2's real GDP. Similarly, we could determine the real GDP for year 3 by multiplying the 8 units of output that year by the $10 price in the base year.

Once we have determined real GDP through this method, we can identify the price index for a given year simply by dividing the nominal GDP by the real GDP for that year:

$$\frac{\text{Price index}}{\text{(in hundredths)}} = \frac{\text{nominal GDP}}{\text{real GDP}} \quad (3)$$

Example: In year 2 we get a price index of 200—or, in hundredths, 2.00—which equals the nominal GDP of

TABLE 7.6 Steps for Deriving Real GDP from Nominal GDP

Method 1

1. Find nominal GDP for each year.
2. Compute a GDP price index.
3. Divide each year's nominal GDP by that year's price index (in hundredths) to determine real GDP.

Method 2

1. Break down nominal GDP into physical quantities of output and prices for each year.
2. Find real GDP for each year by determining the dollar amount that each year's physical output would have sold for if base-year prices had prevailed. (The GDP price index can then be found by dividing nominal GDP by real GDP.)

$140 divided by the real GDP of $70. Note that equation 3 is simply a rearrangement of equation 2. Table 7.6 summarizes the two methods of determining real GDP in our single-good economy.

Real-World Considerations and Data

In the real world of many goods and services, of course, determining GDP and constructing a reliable price index are far more complex matters than in our pizza-only economy. The government accountants must assign a "weight" to each of several categories of goods and services based on the relative proportion of each category in total output. They update the weights annually as expenditure patterns change and roll the base year forward year by year using a moving average of expenditure patterns. The GDP price index used in the United States is called the *chain-type annual-weights price index*—which hints at its complexity. We spare you the details.

Table 7.7 shows some of the relationships between nominal GDP, real GDP, and the GDP price index for the

TABLE 7.7 Nominal GDP, Real GDP, and GDP Price Index for the United States, Selected Years

(1) Year	(2) Nominal GDP, Billions	(3) Real GDP, Billions	(4) GDP Price Index (2009 = 100)
1995	$ 7,664.0	$10,167.3	——
2000	10,289.7	——	81.9
2005	13,095.4	14,235.6	92.0
2009	14,417.9	——	100.0
2010	14,958.3	14,779.4	101.2
2012	16,244.6	15,547.0	104.5

Source: Bureau of Economic Analysis, **www.bea.gov**. All data are subject to government revision.

U.S. economy. Here the base year is 2009, where the value of the index is set at 100. Because the U.S. price level has been rising over the long run, the pre-2009 values of real GDP (column 3) are higher than the nominal values of GDP for those years (column 2). This upward adjustment acknowledges that prices were lower in the years before 2009, and thus nominal GDP understated the real output of those years in 2009 prices and must be inflated to show the correct relationship to other years.

Conversely, the rising price level of the post-2009 years caused nominal GDP figures for those years to over-state real output. So the statisticians deflate those figures to determine what real GDP would have been in other years if 2009 prices had prevailed. Doing so reveals that real GDP has been less than nominal GDP since 2009.

By inflating the nominal pre-2009 GDP data and de-flating the post-2009 data, government accountants determine annual real GDP, which can then be compared with the real GDP of any other year in the series of years. So the real GDP values in column 3 are directly comparable with one another.

Once we have determined nominal GDP and real GDP, we can compute the price index. And once we have determined nominal GDP and the price index, we can cal-culate real GDP. Example: Nominal GDP in 2012 was $16,244.6 billion and real GDP was $15,547.0 billion. So the price level in 2012 was 104.5 (= $16,244.6/$15,547.0 × 100), or 4.5 percent higher than in 2009. If we knew the nominal GDP and the price level only, we could find the real GDP for 2012 by dividing the nominal GDP of $15,684.8 by the 2012 price index, expressed in hun-dredths (1.045).

To test your understanding of the relationships be-tween nominal GDP, real GDP, and the price level, deter-mine the values of the price index for 1995 in Table 7.7 and determine real GDP for 2000 and 2009. We have left those figures out on purpose.

QUICK REVIEW 7.3

- Nominal GDP is output valued at current prices. Real GDP is output valued at constant base-year prices.
- The GDP price index compares the price (market value) of all the goods and services included in GDP in a given year to the price of the same market basket in a refer-ence year.
- Nominal GDP can be transformed into real GDP by dividing the nominal GDP by the GDP price index expressed in hundredths.

Shortcomings of GDP

LO7.6 List and explain some limitations of the GDP measure.

GDP is a reasonably accurate and highly useful measure of how well or how poorly the economy is performing. But it has several shortcomings as a measure of both total output and well-being (total utility).

Nonmarket Activities

Certain productive activities do not take place in any market—the services of stay-at-home parents, for exam-ple, and the labor of carpenters who repair their own homes. Such activities never show up in GDP because the accountants who tally up GDP only get data on economic transactions involving *market activities*—that is, transac-tions in which output or resources are traded for money. Consequently, GDP understates a nation's total output be-cause it does not count *unpaid work*. There is one excep-tion: The portion of farmers' output that farmers consume themselves *is* estimated and included in GDP.

Leisure

The average workweek (excluding overtime) in the United States has declined since the beginning of the 1900s—from about 53 hours to about 35 hours. Moreover, the greater frequency of paid vacations, holidays, and leave time has shortened the work year itself. This increase in leisure time has clearly had a positive effect on overall well-being. But our system of national income accounting understates well-being by ignoring leisure's value. Nor does the system accommodate the satisfaction—the "psy-chic income"—that many people derive from their work.

Improved Product Quality

Because GDP is a quantitative measure rather than a qual-itative measure, it fails to capture the full value of im-provements in product quality. A $200 cell phone purchased today is of very different quality than a cell phone that cost $200 just a decade ago. Today's cell phone is digital and has greater memory capacity, a viewing screen, and quite likely a camera and a music player.

Obviously quality improvement has a great effect on economic well-being, as does the quantity of goods pro-duced. Although the BEA adjusts GDP for quality im-provement for selected items, the vast majority of such improvement for the entire range of goods and services does not get reflected in GDP.

LAST WORD

Magical Mystery Tour

The Bureau of Economic Analysis (BEA), an Agency of the Department of Commerce, Compiles the NIPA Tables. Where Does It Get the Actual Data?

Discussions of national income accounting often leave the impression that the data for the National Income and Product Accounts magically appear from some mysterious place. Let's take a tour to see where economists get their data.

Consumption The BEA derives the data for the consumption component of the GDP accounts from four main sources:

- The Census Bureau's *Retail Trade Survey*, which gains sales information from a sample of 22,000 firms.
- The Census Bureau's *Survey of Manufacturers*, which gathers information on shipments of consumer goods from 50,000 establishments.
- The Census Bureau's *Service Survey*, which collects sales data from 30,000 service businesses.
- Industry trade sources. For example, data on auto sales and aircraft are collected directly from auto and aircraft manufacturers.

Investment The sources of the data for the investment component of GDP include:

- All the sources above used to determine consumption. Purchases of capital goods are separated from purchases of consumer goods. For example, estimates of investment in equipment and software are based on manufacturers' shipments reported in the *Survey of Manufacturers*, the *Service Survey*, and industry sources.
- Census construction surveys. The Census Bureau's *Housing Starts Survey* and *Housing Sales Survey* produce the data used to measure the amount of housing construction, and the *Construction Progress Reporting Survey* is the source of data on nonresidential construction. The BEA determines

changes in business inventories through the *Retail Trade Survey*, the *Wholesale Trade Survey* (of 7,100 wholesale firms), and the *Survey of Manufacturing*.

Government Purchases The data for government purchases (officially "government consumption and investment expenditures") are obtained through the following sources:

- The U.S. Office of Personnel Management, which collects data on wages and benefits, broken out by the private and public sector. Wages and benefits of government employees are the single largest "purchase" by federal, state, and local government.
- The previously mentioned Census Bureau's construction surveys, which break out private and public sector construction expenditures.
- The Census Bureau's *Survey of Government Finance*, which provides data on government consumption and investment expenditures.

Net Exports The BEA determines net exports through two main sources:

- The U.S. Customs Service, which collects data on exports and imports of goods.
- BEA surveys of potential domestic exporters and importers of services, which collect data on exports and imports of services.

So there you have it. Not so magical after all!

Source: Based on Joseph A. Ritter, "Feeding the National Accounts," *Federal Reserve Bank of St. Louis Review,* March–April 2000, pp. 11–20. For those interested, this article also provides information on the sources of data for the income side of the national accounts.

The Underground Economy

Embedded in our economy is a flourishing, productive underground sector. Some of the people who conduct business there are gamblers, smugglers, prostitutes, "fences" of stolen goods, drug growers, and drug dealers. They have good reason to conceal their incomes.

Most participants in the underground economy, however, engage in perfectly legal activities but choose illegally not to report their full incomes to the Internal Revenue Service (IRS). A barista at a coffee shop may report just a portion of the tips received from customers. Storekeepers may report only a portion of their sales receipts. Workers who want to hold on to their unemployment compensation benefits may take an "off-the-books" or "cash-only" job. A brick mason may agree to rebuild a neighbor's fireplace in exchange for the neighbor's repairing his boat engine. The value of none of these transactions shows up in GDP.

The value of underground transactions is estimated to be about 8 percent of the recorded GDP in the United States. That would mean that GDP in 2012 was understated by about $1.3 trillion. Global Perspective 7.2 shows estimates of the relative sizes of underground economies in selected nations.

GDP and the Environment

The growth of GDP is inevitably accompanied by "gross domestic by-products," including dirty air and polluted water, toxic waste, congestion, and noise. The social costs of the negative by-products reduce our economic well-being. And since those costs are not deducted from total output, GDP overstates our national well-being. Ironically, when money is spent to clean up pollution and reduce congestion, those expenses are added to GDP!

Composition and Distribution of Output

The composition of output is undoubtedly important for well-being. But GDP does not tell us whether the currently produced mix of goods and services is enriching or potentially detrimental to society. GDP assigns equal weight to an assault rifle and a set of encyclopedias, as long as both sell for the same price. Moreover, GDP reveals nothing about the way output is distributed. Does 90 percent of the output go to 10 percent of the households, for example, or is the output more evenly distributed? The distribution of output may make a big difference for society's overall well-being.

Noneconomic Sources of Well-Being

Finally, the connection between GDP and well-being is problematic for another reason. Just as a household's

GLOBAL PERSPECTIVE 7.2

The Underground Economy as a Percentage of GDP, Selected Nations

Underground economies vary in size worldwide. Three factors that help explain the variation are (1) the extent and complexity of regulation, (2) the type and degree of taxation, and (3) the effectiveness of law enforcement.

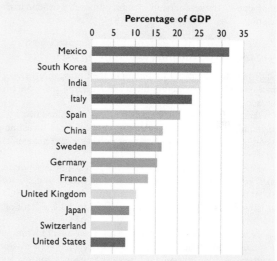

Source: Friedrich Schneider, "Shadow Economies and Corruption All Over the World: New Estimates for 145 Countries," *Economics: The Open-Access, Open-Assessment E-Journal*, vol. 1, no. 2007-9 (July 24, 2007). Used with permission of Friedrich Schneider.

income does not measure its total happiness, a nation's GDP does not measure its total well-being. Many things could make a society better off without necessarily raising GDP: a reduction of crime and violence, peaceful relations with other countries, people's greater civility toward one another, better understanding between parents and children, and a reduction of drug and alcohol abuse.

QUICK REVIEW 7.4

- GDP is a reasonably accurate and very useful indicator of a nation's economic performance but should not be interpreted as a comprehensive measure of well-being.
- The major limitations of GDP as an indicator of well-being are that it fails to account for nonmarket and illegal transactions, changes in leisure and in product quality, the composition and distribution of output, and the environmental effects of production.

SUMMARY

LO7.1 Explain how gross domestic product (GDP) is defined and measured.

Gross domestic product (GDP), a basic measure of an economy's economic performance, is the market value of all final goods and services produced within the borders of a nation in a year.

Final goods are those purchased by end users, whereas intermediate goods are those purchased for resale or for further processing or manufacturing. Intermediate goods, nonproduction transactions, and secondhand sales are purposely excluded in calculating GDP.

LO7.2 Describe how expenditures on goods and services can be summed to determine GDP.

GDP may be calculated by summing total expenditures on all final output or by summing the income derived from the production of that output.

By the expenditures approach, GDP is determined by adding consumer purchases of goods and services, gross investment spending by businesses, government purchases, and net exports: $GDP = C + I_g + G + X_n$.

Personal consumption expenditures consist of expenditures on goods (durable goods and nondurable goods) and services. About 60 percent of consumer expenditures in the United States are on services, leading economists to refer to the U.S. economy as a *service economy*.

Gross investment is divided into (*a*) replacement investment (required to maintain the nation's stock of capital at its existing level) and (*b*) net investment (the net increase in the stock of capital). In most years, net investment is positive and therefore the economy's stock of capital and production capacity increase.

LO7.3 Explain how GDP can be determined by summing up all of the incomes that were derived from producing the economy's output of goods and services.

By the income or allocations approach, GDP is calculated as the sum of compensation to employees, rents, interest, proprietors' income, corporate profits, taxes on production and imports *minus* net foreign factor income, *plus* consumption of fixed capital and a statistical discrepancy.

LO7.4 Describe the relationships among GDP, net domestic product, national income, personal income, and disposable income.

Other national accounts are derived from GDP. Net domestic product (NDP) is GDP less the consumption of fixed capital. National income (NI) is total income earned by a nation's resource suppliers plus taxes on production and imports; it is found by subtracting a statistical discrepancy from NDP and adding net foreign factor income to NDP. Personal income (PI) is the total income paid to households prior to any allowance for personal taxes. Disposable income (DI) is personal income after personal taxes have been paid. DI measures the amount of income available to households to consume or save.

LO7.5 Discuss the nature and function of a GDP price index, and describe the difference between nominal GDP and real GDP.

Price indexes are computed by dividing the price of a specific collection or market basket of output in a particular period by the price of the same market basket in a base period and multiplying the result (the quotient) by 100. The GDP price index is used to adjust nominal GDP for inflation or deflation and thereby obtain real GDP.

Nominal (current-dollar) GDP measures each year's output valued in terms of the prices prevailing in that year. Real (constant-dollar) GDP measures each year's output in terms of the prices that prevailed in a selected base year. Because real GDP is adjusted for price-level changes, differences in real GDP are due only to differences in production activity.

LO7.6 List and explain some limitations of the GDP measure.

GDP is a reasonably accurate and very useful indicator of a nation's economic performance, but it has its limitations. It fails to account for nonmarket and illegal transactions, changes in leisure and in product quality, the composition and distribution of output, and the environmental effects of production. GDP should not be interpreted as a complete measure of well-being.

TERMS AND CONCEPTS

national income accounting	durable goods	consumption of fixed capital
gross domestic product (GDP)	nondurable goods	net domestic product (NDP)
intermediate goods	services	personal income (PI)
final goods	gross private domestic investment (I_g)	disposable income (DI)
multiple counting	net private domestic investment	nominal GDP
value added	government purchases (G)	real GDP
expenditures approach	net exports (X_n)	price index
income approach	taxes on production and imports	base year
personal consumption expenditures (C)	national income	

The following and additional problems can be found in **connect**

DISCUSSION QUESTIONS

1. In what ways are national income statistics useful? **LO7.1**
2. Why do national income accountants compare the market value of the total outputs in various years rather than actual physical volumes of production? What problem is posed by any comparison over time of the market values of various total outputs? How is this problem resolved? **LO7.1**
3. Which of the following goods are usually intermediate goods and which are usually final goods: running shoes, cotton fibers, watches, textbooks, coal, sunscreen lotion, lumber? **LO7.1**
4. Why do economists include only final goods and services when measuring GDP for a particular year? Why don't they include the value of the stocks and bonds bought and sold? Why don't they include the value of the used furniture bought and sold? **LO7.1**
5. Explain why an economy's output, in essence, is also its income. **LO7.1**
6. Provide three examples of each: consumer durable goods, consumer nondurable goods, and services. **LO7.2**
7. Why are changes in inventories included as part of investment spending? Suppose inventories declined by $1 billion during 2014. How would this affect the size of gross private domestic investment and gross domestic product in 2014? Explain. **LO7.2**
8. What is the difference between gross private domestic investment and net private domestic investment? If you were to determine net domestic product (NDP) through the expenditures approach, which of these two measures of investment spending would be appropriate? Explain. **LO7.2**
9. Use the concepts of gross investment and net investment to distinguish between an economy that has a rising stock of capital and one that has a falling stock of capital. Explain: "Though net investment can be positive, negative, or zero, it is impossible for gross investment to be less than zero." **LO7.2**

10. Define net exports. Explain how U.S. exports and imports each affects domestic production. How are net exports determined? Explain how net exports might be a negative amount. **LO7.2**
11. Contrast the ideas of nominal GDP and real GDP. Why is one more reliable than the other for comparing changes in the standard of living over a series of years? What is the GDP price index and what is its role in differentiating nominal GDP and real GDP? **LO7.5**
12. Which of the following are included or excluded in this year's GDP? Explain your answer in each case. **LO7.6**
   a. Interest received on an AT&T corporate bond.
   b. Social Security payments received by a retired factory worker.
   c. Unpaid services of a family member in painting the family home.
   d. Income of a dentist from the dental services provided.
   e. A monthly allowance a college student receives from home.
   f. Money received by Josh when he resells his nearly brand-new Honda automobile to Kim.
   g. The publication and sale of a new college textbook.
   h. An increase in leisure resulting from a 2-hour decrease in the length of the workweek, with no reduction in pay.
   i. A $2 billion increase in business inventories.
   j. The purchase of 100 shares of Google stock.
13. **LAST WORD** What government agency compiles the U.S. NIPA tables? In what U.S. department is it located? Of the several specific sources of information, name one source for each of the four components of GDP: consumption, investment, government purchases, and net exports.

REVIEW QUESTIONS

1. Tina walks into Ted's sporting goods store and buys a punching bag for $100. That $100 payment counts as _____ for Tina and _____ for Ted. **LO7.1**
   a. Income; expenditure.
   b. Value added; multiple counting.
   c. Expenditure; income.
   d. Rents; profits.
2. Which of the following transactions would count in GDP? **LO7.1**
   *Select **one or more** answers from the choices shown.*
   a. Kerry buys a new sweater to wear this winter.
   b. Patricia receives a Social Security check.
   c. Roberto gives his daughter $50 for her birthday.
   d. Latika sells $1,000 of General Electric stock.
   e. Karen buys a new car.
   f. Amy buys a used car.

3. A small economy starts the year with $1 million in capital. During the course of the year, gross investment is $150,000 and depreciation is $50,000. How big is the economy's stock of capital at the end of the year? **LO7.2**
   a. $1,150,000.
   b. $1,100,000.
   c. $1,000,000.
   d. $850,000.
   e. $800,000.
4. Suppose that this year a small country has a GDP of $100 billion. Also assume that I_g = $30 billion, C = $60 billion, and X_n = − $10 billion. How big is G? **LO7.3**
   a. $0.
   b. $10 billion.
   c. $20 billion.
   d. $30 billion.

5. Suppose that California imposes a sales tax of 10 percent on all goods and services. A Californian named Ralph then goes into a home improvement store in the state capital of Sacramento and buys a leaf blower that is priced at $200. With the 10 percent sales tax, his total comes to $220. How much of the $220 paid by Ralph will be counted in the national income and product accounts as private income (employee compensation, rents, interest, proprietor's income, and corporate profits)? **LO7.3**
   a. $220.
   b. $200.
   c. $180.
   d. None of the above.

6. Suppose GDP is $16 trillion, with $10 trillion coming from consumption, $2 trillion coming from gross investment, $3.5 trillion coming from government expenditures, and $500 billion coming from net exports. Also suppose that across the whole economy, depreciation (consumption of fixed capital) totals $1 trillion. From these figures, we see that net domestic product equals: **LO7.4**
   a. $17.0 trillion.
   b. $16.0 trillion.
   c. $15.5 trillion.
   d. None of the above.

7. Suppose GDP is $15 trillion, with $8 trillion coming from consumption, $2.5 trillion coming from gross investment, $3.5 trillion coming from government expenditures, and $1 trillion coming from net exports. Also suppose that across the whole economy, personal income is $12 trillion. If the

government collects $1.5 trillion in personal taxes, then disposable income will be: **LO7.4**
   a. $13.5 trillion.
   b. $12.0 trillion.
   c. $10.5 trillion.
   d. None of the above.

8. Suppose that this year's nominal GDP is $16 trillion. To account for the effects of inflation, we construct a price-level index in which an index value of 100 represents the price level five years ago. Using that index, we find that this year's real GDP is $15 trillion. Given those numbers, we can conclude that the current value of the index is: **LO7.5**
   a. Higher than 100.
   b. Lower than 100.
   c. Still 100.

9. Which of the following items will be included in official U.S. GDP statistics? **LO7.6**
   *Select **one or more** answers from the choices shown.*
   a. Revenue generated by illegal marijuana growers in Oregon.
   b. Money spent to clean up a local toxic waste site in Ohio.
   c. Revenue generated by legal medical marijuana sales in California.
   d. The dollar value of the annoyance felt by local citizens living near a noisy airport in Georgia.
   e. Robert paying Ted for a haircut in Chicago.
   f. Emily and Rhonda trading an hour of dance lessons for a haircut in Dallas.

PROBLEMS

1. Suppose that annual output in year 1 in a 3-good economy is 3 quarts of ice cream, 1 bottle of shampoo, and 3 jars of peanut butter. In year 2, the output mix changes to 5 quarts of ice cream, 2 bottles of shampoo, and 2 jars of peanut butter. If the prices in both years are $4 per quart for ice cream, $3 per bottle of shampoo, and $2 per jar of peanut butter, what was the economy's GDP in year 1? What was its GDP in year 2? **LO7.1**

2. Assume that a grower of flower bulbs sells its annual output of bulbs to an Internet retailer for $70,000. The retailer, in turn, brings in $160,000 from selling the bulbs directly to final customers. What amount would these two transactions add to personal consumption expenditures and thus to GDP during the year? **LO7.1**

3. If in some country personal consumption expenditures in a specific year are $50 billion, purchases of stocks and bonds are $30 billion, net exports are −$10 billion, government purchases are $20 billion, sales of secondhand items are $8 billion, and gross investment is $25 billion, what is the country's GDP for the year? **LO7.2**

4. To the right is a list of domestic output and national income figures for a certain year. All figures are in billions. The questions that follow ask you to determine the major national

Personal consumption expenditures	$245
Net foreign factor income	4
Transfer payments	12
Rents	14
Consumption of fixed capital (depreciation)	27
Statistical discrepancy	8
Social Security contributions	20
Interest	13
Proprietors' income	33
Net exports	11
Dividends	16
Compensation of employees	223
Taxes on production and imports	18
Undistributed corporate profits	21
Personal taxes	26
Corporate income taxes	19
Corporate profits	56
Government purchases	72
Net private domestic investment	33
Personal saving	20

income measures by both the expenditures and the income approaches. The results you obtain with the different methods should be the same. **LO7.4**

a. Using the above data, determine GDP by both the expenditures and the income approaches. Then determine NDP.

b. Now determine NI in two ways: first, by making the required additions or subtractions from NDP; and second, by adding up the types of income and taxes that make up NI.

c. Adjust NI (from part *b*) as required to obtain PI.

d. Adjust PI (from part *c*) as required to obtain DI.

5. Using the following national income accounting data, compute (*a*) GDP, (*b*) NDP, and (*c*) NI. All figures are in billions. **LO7.4**

Compensation of employees	$194.2
U.S. exports of goods and services	17.8
Consumption of fixed capital	11.8
Government purchases	59.4
Taxes on production and imports	14.4
Net private domestic investment	52.1
Transfer payments	13.9
U.S. imports of goods and services	16.5
Personal taxes	40.5
Net foreign factor income	2.2
Personal consumption expenditures	219.1
Statistical discrepancy	0

6. Suppose that in 1984 the total output in a single-good economy was 7,000 buckets of chicken. Also suppose that in 1984 each bucket of chicken was priced at $10. Finally, assume that in 2005 the price per bucket of chicken was $16 and that 22,000 buckets were produced. Determine the GDP price index for 1984, using 2005 as the base year. By what percentage did the price level, as measured by this index, rise between 1984 and 2005? What were the amounts of real GDP in 1984 and 2005? **LO7.5**

7. The following table shows nominal GDP and an appropriate price index for a group of selected years. Compute real GDP. Indicate in each calculation whether you are inflating or deflating the nominal GDP data. **LO7.5**

Year	Nominal GDP, Billions	Price Index (2005 = 100)	Real GDP, Billions
1968	$ 909.8	22.01	$_____
1978	2,293.8	40.40	$_____
1988	5,100.4	66.98	$_____
1998	8,793.5	85.51	$_____
2008	14,441.4	108.48	$_____

8. Assume that the total value of the following items is $600 billion in a specific year for Upper Mongoose: net exports = $50 billion; value of new goods and services produced in the underground economy = $75 billion; personal consumption expenditures = $300 billion; value of the services of stay-at-home parents = $25 billion; gross domestic investment = $100 billion; government purchases = $50 billion. What is Upper Mongoose's GDP for the year? What is the size of the underground economy as a percentage of GDP? By what percentage would GDP be boosted if the value of the services of stay-at-home spouses were included in GDP? **LO7.6**

CHAPTER 8

Economic Growth

Learning Objectives

LO8.1 List two ways that economic growth is measured.

LO8.2 Define "modern economic growth" and explain the institutional structures needed for an economy to experience it.

LO8.3 Identify the general supply, demand, and efficiency forces that give rise to economic growth.

LO8.4 Describe "growth accounting" and the specific factors accounting for economic growth in the United States.

LO8.5 Explain why the trend rate of U.S. productivity growth has increased since the earlier 1973–1995 period.

LO8.6 Discuss differing perspectives as to whether growth is desirable and sustainable.

People living in rich countries tend to take economic growth and rising standards of living for granted. Recessions—periods during which output declines—are normally infrequent and temporary, usually lasting less than a year. Once they pass, modern capitalistic economies return to growing, and living standards continue their seemingly inexorable rise.

But a look back at history or a look around the world today quickly dispels any confidence that economic growth and rising standards of living are automatic or routine. Historically, continually rising living standards are a recent phenomenon, seen only during the last century or two. Before that time, living standards barely rose—if at all—from one generation to the next. And a look around the world today reveals huge differences in standards of living resulting from the disturbing fact that, although some countries have enjoyed decades or even centuries of steadily rising per capita income levels, other countries have experienced hardly any economic growth at all.

This chapter investigates the causes of economic growth, what institutional structures appear to promote economic growth, and the controversies surrounding the benefits and costs of economic growth. As you will see, economic growth has been perhaps the most revolutionary and powerful force in history. Consequently, no study of economics is complete without a thorough understanding of the causes and consequences of economic growth.

Economic Growth

LO8.1 List two ways that economic growth is measured. Economists define and measure **economic growth** as either:

- An increase in real GDP occurring over some time period.
- An increase in real GDP per capita occurring over some time period.

With either definition, economic growth is calculated as a percentage rate of growth per quarter (3-month period) or per year. For the first definition, for example, real GDP in the United States was $15,052.4 billion in 2011 and $15,470.0 in 2012. So the U.S. economic growth rate for 2012 was 2.8 percent {= [(15,470.0 billion − $15,052.4 billion)/$15,052.4 billion] × 100}. Growth rates normally are positive, but not always. In recession year 2009, for instance, the U.S. rate of economic growth was a *minus* 2.4 percent.

The second definition of economic growth in the bulleted list takes into consideration the size of the population. **Real GDP per capita** (or per capita output) is the amount of real output per person in a country. It is calculated, as follows.

$$\text{Real GDP per capita} = \frac{\text{Real GDP}}{\text{Population}}$$

For example, in 2011 the real GDP in the United States was $15,052.4 billion and population was 311.6 million. Therefore, real GDP per capita in that year was $48,307. In 2012 real GDP per capita increased to $49,283. So the growth rate of real GDP per capita in 2012 was 2.0 percent {= [($49,283 − $48,307)/$48,307] × 100}. In contrast, real GDP per capita fell by 3.3 percent in recession year 2009.

For measuring expansion of military potential or political preeminence, the growth of real GDP is more useful. Unless specified otherwise, growth rates reported in the news and by international agencies use this definition of economic growth. For comparing living standards, however, the second definition is superior. While China's GDP in 2012 was $12,380 billion compared with Denmark's $332 billion, Denmark's real GDP per capita was $37,700 compared with China's hugely lower $9,100. And in some cases growth of real GDP can be misleading. The African nation of Eritrea had real GDP growth of 1.3 percent per year from 2000–2008. But over the same period its annual growth of population was 3.8 percent, resulting in a decline in real GDP per capita of roughly 2.5 percent per year.

Growth as a Goal

Growth is a widely held economic goal. The expansion of total output relative to population results in rising real wages and incomes and thus higher standards of living. An economy that is experiencing economic growth is better able to meet people's wants and resolve socioeconomic problems. Rising real wages and income provide richer opportunities to individuals and families—a vacation trip, a personal computer, a higher education—without sacrificing other opportunities and pleasures. A growing economy can undertake new programs to alleviate poverty, embrace diversity, cultivate the arts, and protect the environment without impairing existing levels of consumption, investment, and public goods production.

In short, *growth lessens the burden of scarcity*. A growing economy, unlike a static economy, can consume more today while increasing its capacity to produce more in the future. By easing the burden of scarcity—by relaxing society's constraints on production—economic growth enables a nation to attain its economic goals more readily and to undertake new endeavors that require the use of goods and services to be accomplished.

Arithmetic of Growth

Why do economists pay so much attention to small changes in the rate of economic growth? Because those changes really matter! For the United States, with a current nominal GDP of about $16.2 trillion, the difference between a 3 percent and a 4 percent rate of growth is about $162 billion of output each year. For a poor country, a difference of one-half of a percentage point in the rate of growth may mean the difference between starvation and mere hunger.

The mathematical approximation called the **rule of 70** provides a quantitative grasp of the effect of economic growth. The rule of 70 tells us that we can find the number of years it will take for some measure to double, given its annual percentage increase, by dividing that percentage increase into the number 70. So

$$\begin{matrix} \text{Approximate} \\ \text{number of years} \\ \text{required to double} \\ \text{real GDP} \end{matrix} = \frac{70}{\begin{matrix}\text{annual percentage rate}\\\text{of growth}\end{matrix}}$$

Examples: A 3 percent annual rate of growth will double real GDP in about 23 (= 70 ÷ 3) years. Growth of 8 percent per year will double real GDP in about 9 (= 70 ÷ 8) years. The rule of 70 is applicable generally. For example, it works for estimating how long it will take the price level or a savings account to double at various percentage rates of inflation or interest.

WORKED PROBLEMS

W8.1
GDP growth

When compounded over many years, an apparently small difference in the rate of growth thus becomes highly significant. Suppose China and Italy start with identical GDPs, but then China grows at an 8 percent yearly rate, while Italy grows at 2 percent. China's GDP would double in about 9 years, while Italy's GDP would double in 35 years.

Growth in the United States

Table 8.1 gives an overview of economic growth in the United States since 1950. Column 2 reveals strong growth as measured by increases in real GDP. Note that between 1950 and 2012 real GDP increased more than sevenfold. But the U.S. population also increased. Nevertheless, in column 4 we find that real GDP per capita rose more than threefold over these years.

What has been the *rate* of U.S. growth? Real GDP grew at an annual rate of about 3.2 percent between 1950 and 2012. Real GDP per capita increased at roughly 2 percent per year over that time. But we must qualify these raw numbers in several ways:

- *Improved products and services* Since the numbers in Table 8.1 do not fully account for improvements

TABLE 8.1 Real GDP and Real GDP per Capita, Selected Years, 1950–2012

(1) Year	(2) Real GDP, Billions of 2009 $	(3) Population, Millions	(4) Real GDP Per Capita, 2009 $ (2) ÷ (3)
1950	$ 2,182	152	$14,355
1960	3,106	181	17,160
1970	4,718	205	23,015
1980	6,443	228	28,259
1990	8,945	250	35,780
2000	12,565	282	44,557
2012	15,471	313	49,428

Source: Data are from the Bureau of Economic Analysis, **www.bea.gov**, and the U.S. Census Bureau, **www.census.gov**. All data are subject to government revision.

in products and services, they understate the growth of economic well-being. Such purely quantitative data do not fully compare an era of vacuum tube computers and low-efficiency V8 hot rods with an era of digital cell phone networks and fuel-sipping, hybrid-drive vehicles.

- *Added leisure* The increases in real GDP and per capita GDP identified in Table 8.1 were accomplished despite increases in leisure. The average workweek, once 50 hours, is now about 35 hours (excluding overtime hours). Again the raw growth numbers understate the gain in economic well-being.

- *Other impacts* These measures of growth do not account for any effects growth may have had on the environment and the quality of life. If growth debases the physical environment, excessively warms the planet, and creates a stressful work environment, the bare growth numbers will overstate the gains in well-being that result from growth. On the other hand, if growth leads to stronger environmental protections or a more secure and stress-free lifestyle, these numbers will understate the gains in well-being.

In Chapter 6, we made two other key points about U.S. growth rates. First, they are not constant or smooth over time. Like those of other countries, U.S. growth rates vary quarterly and annually depending on a variety of factors such as the introduction of major new inventions and the economy's current position in the business cycle. Second, many countries share the U.S. experience of positive and ongoing economic growth. But sustained growth is both a historically new occurrence and also one that is not shared equally by all countries.

Modern Economic Growth

LO8.2 Define "modern economic growth" and explain the institutional structures needed for an economy to experience it.

We now live in an era of wireless high-speed Internet connections, genetic engineering, and space exploration. New inventions and new technologies drive continual economic growth and ongoing increases in living standards. But it wasn't always like this. Economic growth and sustained increases in living standards are a historically recent phenomenon that started with the Industrial Revolution of the late 1700s. Before the Industrial Revolution, living standards were basically flat over long periods of time so that, for instance, Greek peasants living in the year 300 B.C. had about the same material standard of living as Greek peasants living in the year A.D. 1500. By contrast, our current era of **modern economic growth** is characterized by sustained and ongoing increases in living standards that can cause dramatic increases in the standard of living within less than a single human lifetime.

Economic historians informally date the start of the Industrial Revolution to the year 1776, when the Scottish inventor James Watt perfected a powerful and efficient steam engine. This steam engine inaugurated the modern era since the device could be used to drive industrial factory equipment, steamships, and steam locomotives.

The new industrial factories mass-produced goods for the first time. This meant that nearly all manufacturing shifted from items produced by hand by local craftsmen to items mass-produced in distant factories. The new steamships and steam locomotives meant that resources could easily flow to factories and that the products of factories could be shipped to distant consumers at low cost. The result was a huge increase in long-distance trade and a major population shift as people left farms to go work in the towns and cities where the new industrial factories were concentrated.

Steam power would later be largely replaced by electric power, and many more inventions would follow the steam engine that started the Industrial Revolution. These included railroads, motorized vehicles, telephones, airplanes, container ships, computers, the Internet, and many more. But the key point is that the last 200 or so years of history have been fundamentally different from anything that went before.

The biggest change has been change itself. Whereas in earlier times material standards of living and the goods and services that people produced and consumed changed very little even over the course of an entire human life span, today people living in countries experiencing modern economic growth are constantly exposed to new technologies, new products, and new services.

What is more, modern economic growth has vastly affected cultural, social, and political arrangements.

- Culturally, the vast increases in wealth and living standards have allowed ordinary people for the first time in history to have significant time for leisure activities and the arts.
- Socially, countries experiencing modern economic growth have abolished feudalism, instituted universal public education, and largely eliminated ancient social norms and legal restrictions against women and minorities doing certain jobs or holding certain positions.
- Politically, countries experiencing modern economic growth have tended to move toward democracy, a form of government that was extremely rare before the start of the Industrial Revolution.

In addition, the average human lifespan has more than doubled, from an average of less than 30 years before modern economic growth began in the late 1700s to a worldwide average of over 67 years today. Thus, for the first time in world history, the average person can expect to live into old age. These and other changes speak to the truly revolutionary power of economic growth and naturally lead economists to consider the causes of economic growth and what policies could be pursued to sustain and promote it. Their desire is intensified by the reality that economic growth is distributed so unevenly around the world.

The Uneven Distribution of Growth

Modern economic growth has spread only slowly from its British birthplace. It first advanced to France, Germany, and other parts of western Europe in the early 1800s before spreading to the United States, Canada, and Australia by the mid 1800s. Japan began to industrialize in the 1870s, but the rest of Asia did not follow until the early to mid 1900s, at which time large parts of Central and South America as well

FIGURE 8.1 **The great divergence in standards of living.** Income levels around the world were very similar in 1820. But they are now very different because certain areas, including the United States and western Europe, began experiencing modern economic growth much earlier than other areas.

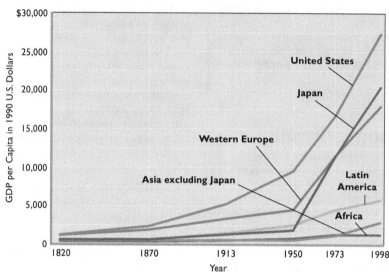

Source: Angus Maddison, *The World Economy: A Millennial Perspective* (Paris: OECD, 2001), p. 264.

as the Middle East also began to experience modern economic growth. Most recent has been Africa, which for the most part did not experience modern economic growth until the last few decades. Notably, some parts of the world have yet to experience modern economic growth at all.

The different starting dates for modern economic growth in various parts of the world are the main cause of the vast differences in per capita GDP levels seen today. The current huge gaps between rich countries like the United States and Japan and poor countries like North Korea and Burundi were shown previously in Global Perspective 6.1. But the huge divergence in living standards caused by the fact that different countries started modern economic growth at different times is best seen in Figure 8.1, which shows how GDP per capita has evolved since 1820 in the United States, western Europe, Latin America, Asia, and Africa.

To make the comparison of living standards easier, income levels in all places and at all times have been converted into 1990 U.S. dollars. Using this convention, it is clear that in 1820 per capita incomes in all areas were quite similar, with the richest area in the world in 1820, western Europe, having an average per capita income of $1,232, while the poorest area of the world at that time, Africa, had an average per capita income of $418. Thus, in 1820, average incomes in the richest area were only about three times larger than those in the poorest area.

But because western Europe and the United States started experiencing modern economic growth earlier than other areas, they have now ended up vastly richer than other areas, despite the fact that per capita incomes in nearly all places have increased at least a bit. For instance, per capita GDP in the United States in 1998 was $27,331 while it was only $1,368 in Africa. Thus, because modern economic growth has occurred for nearly two centuries in the United States compared to a few decades in Africa, average living standards in the United States in 1998 were nearly 20 times higher than those in Africa.

Catching Up Is Possible

Do not get the wrong impression looking at Figure 8.1. Countries that began modern economic growth more recently are *not* doomed to be permanently poorer than the countries that began modern economic growth at an earlier date. This is true because people can adopt technology more quickly than they can invent it. Broadly speaking, the richest countries today have achieved that status because they have the most advanced technology. But because they already have the most advanced technology, they must invent new technology to get even richer. Because inventing and implementing new technology is slow and costly, real GDP per capita in the richest **leader countries** typically grows by an average annual rate of just 2 or 3 percent per year.

By contrast, poorer **follower countries** can grow much faster because they can simply adopt existing technologies from rich leader countries. For instance, in many places in Africa today, the first telephones most people have ever been able to use are cell phones. That is, these countries have not even bothered to install the copper wires necessary for land-line telephones, which are basically a nineteenth-century technology. Instead, they have gone directly for Internet-capable mobile phone networks, a twenty-first-century technology. By doing so, they skip past many stages of technology and development that the United States and other currently rich countries had to pass through. In effect, they jump directly to the most modern, most highly productive technology. The result is that, under the right circumstances, it is possible for poorer countries to experience extremely rapid increases in living standards. This can continue until they have caught up with the leader countries and become leader countries themselves. Once that happens, their growth rates fall down to the 2 or 3 percent rate typical of leader countries. This happens because once they are also rich and using the latest technology, their growth rates are limited by the rate at which new technology can be invented and applied.

Table 8.2 shows both how the growth rates of leader countries are constrained by the rate of technological progress as well as how certain follower countries have been able to catch up by adopting more advanced technologies and growing rapidly. Table 8.2 shows real GDP per capita in 1960 and 2010 as well as the average annual growth rate of real GDP per capita between 1960 and 2010 for three countries—the United States, the United Kingdom, and France—that were already rich leader countries in 1960 as

well as for five other nations that were relatively poor follower countries at that time. To make comparisons easy, the GDPs and GDPs per capita for all countries are expressed in terms of 2005 U.S. dollars. The countries are ordered by their respective GDPs per capita in 1960, so that the richest country in the world at the time, the United States, is listed first while the poorest of the eight selected countries at the time, South Korea, is listed last.

First, notice that the average annual growth rates of the three leader countries—the United States, the United Kingdom, and France—have all been between 2.1 and 2.5 percent per year because their growth rates are limited by the rate at which new technologies can be invented and applied. By contrast, the five countries that were follower countries in 1960 have been able to grow much faster, between 3.3 percent per year and 5.4 percent per year. This has had remarkable effects on their standards of living relative to the leader countries. For instance, Ireland's

---

CONSIDER THIS . . .

Economic Growth Rates Matter!

When compounded over many decades, small absolute differences in rates of economic growth add up to substantial differences in real GDP and standards of living. Consider three hypothetical countries—Slogo, Sumgo, and Speedo. Suppose that in 2014 these countries have identical levels of real GDP ($6 trillion), population (200 million), and real GDP per capita ($30,000). Also, assume that annual real GDP growth is 2 percent in Slogo, 3 percent in Sumgo, and 4 percent in Speedo.

How will these alternative growth rates affect real GDP and real GDP per capita over a long period, say, a 70-year lifespan? By 2084 the 2, 3, and 4 percent growth rates would boost real GDP from $6 trillion to:

- $24 trillion in Slogo.
- $47 trillion in Sumgo.
- $93 trillion in Speedo.

For illustration, let's assume that each country experienced an average annual population growth of 1 percent over the 70 years. Then, in 2084 real GDP per capita would be about:

- $60,000 in Slogo.
- $118,000 in Sumgo.
- $233,000 in Speedo.

Even small differences in growth rates matter!

TABLE 8.2 Real GDP per Capita in 1960 and 2010 Plus Average Annual Growth Rates of Real GDP per Capita from 1960–2010 for Selected Countries. (Figures are in 2005 dollars.)

Country	Real GDP per Capita, 1960	Real GDP per Capita, 2010	Average Annual Growth Rate, 1960–2010
United States	$14,766	$41,365	2.1
United Kingdom	11,257	34,268	2.2
France	9,347	31,299	2.4
Ireland	6,666	34,877	3.3
Japan	5,472	31,477	3.5
Singapore	4,149	55,862	5.2
Hong Kong	3,849	38,865	4.6
South Korea	1,765	26,609	5.4

Note: GDP figures for all countries are measured in "international dollars" of equal value to U.S. dollars in 2005.

Source: Penn World Table version 6.3, **pwt.econ.upenn.edu**. Used by permission of the Center for International Comparisons at the University of Pennsylvania.

GDP per capita was only 60 percent that of its neighbor, the United Kingdom, in 1960. But because Ireland grew at a 3.3 percent rate for the next 50 years while the United Kingdom grew at only a 2.2 percent rate over that time period, by 2010 Ireland's GDP per capita was actually higher than the United Kingdom's GDP per capita. Ireland had become a leader country, too.

The growth experiences of the other four nations that were poor in 1960 have been even more dramatic. Hong Kong, for instance, moved from a GDP per capita that was less than one-third of that enjoyed by the United Kingdom in 1960 to a GDP per capita 13 percent higher than that of the United Kingdom in 2010. The Consider This box on the previous page emphasizes both how quickly small differences in growth rates can change the level of real GDP per capita and how countries stand in relation to each other in terms of real GDP per capita.

Finally, you may be puzzled as to why the GDP per capita of the United States in 2011 in Table 8.2 is so much higher than that of other rich leader countries. Why, for instance, is U.S. GDP per capita 32 percent higher than French GDP per capita? One important reason is that U.S. citizens put in substantially more labor time than do the citizens of most other leader countries. First, a much larger fraction of the U.S. population is employed than in other rich leader countries. Second, U.S. employees work many more hours per year than do employees in other rich leader countries. For example, 58 percent of the working-age population of the United States was employed in 2010 compared to 51 percent in France. That's a difference of about 14 percent. And American employees worked an average of 1,778 total hours during 2010, compared to an average of 1,478 total hours for French workers. That's a difference of about 20 percent. Added together, these two differences between U.S. and French labor supply imply about a 34 percent difference in the total number of hours worked in the French and American economies. Thus, differences in labor supply help explain differences between rich leader countries in terms of their differing levels of GDP per person.

Buy why do Americans supply so much more labor than workers in France and some of the other rich leader countries? Explanations put forth by economists include cultural differences regarding the proper balance between work and leisure, stronger unions in France and other rich leader countries, and more generous unemployment and welfare programs in France and other rich leader countries. France and other rich leader countries also tend to have higher tax rates than the United States—something that may significantly discourage employment. And, finally, the legal workweek is shorter in some countries than it is in the United States.

QUICK REVIEW 8.2

- Before the advent of modern economic growth starting in England in the late 1700s, living standards showed no sustained increases over time.
- Large differences in standards of living exist today because certain areas like the United States have experienced nearly 200 years of modern economic growth while other areas have had only a few decades of economic growth.
- Poor follower countries can catch up with and even surpass the living standards of rich leader countries by adopting the cutting-edge technologies and institutions already developed by rich leader countries.
- Substantial differences in GDP per capita among technologically advanced leader countries are often caused by differences in the amount of labor supplied.

Institutional Structures That Promote Modern Economic Growth

Table 8.2 demonstrates that poor follower countries can catch up and become rich leader countries by growing rapidly. But how does a country start that process and enter into modern economic growth? And once it has started modern economic growth, how does it keep the process going?

Economic historians have identified several institutional structures that promote and sustain modern economic growth. Some structures increase the savings and investment that are needed to fund the construction and maintenance of the huge amounts of infrastructure required to run modern economies. Other institutional structures promote the development of new technologies. And still others act to ensure that resources flow efficiently to their most productive uses. These growth-promoting institutional structures include:

- *Strong property rights* These appear to be absolutely necessary for rapid and sustained economic growth. People will not invest if they believe that thieves, bandits, or a rapacious and tyrannical government will steal their investments or their expected returns.

- *Patents and copyrights* Before patents and copyrights were first issued and enforced, inventors and authors usually saw their ideas stolen before they could profit from them. By giving inventors and authors the exclusive right to market and sell their creations, patents and copyrights give a strong financial incentive to invent and create.

- *Efficient financial institutions* These are needed to channel the savings generated by households toward the businesses, entrepreneurs, and inventors that do most of society's investing and inventing. Banks as well as stock and bond markets appear to be institutions crucial to modern economic growth.

- *Literacy and widespread education* Without highly educated inventors, new technologies do not get developed. And without a highly educated workforce, it is impossible to implement those technologies and put them to productive use.

- *Free trade* Free trade promotes economic growth by allowing countries to specialize so that different types of output can be produced in the countries where they can be made at the lowest opportunity cost. In addition, free trade promotes the rapid spread of new ideas so that innovations made in one country quickly spread to other countries.

- *A competitive market system* Under a market system, prices and profits serve as the signals that tell firms what to make and how much of it to make. Rich leader countries vary substantially in terms of how much government regulation they impose on markets, but in all cases, firms have substantial autonomy to follow market signals in deciding on current production and in making investments to produce what they believe consumers will demand in the future.

Several other difficult-to-measure factors also influence a nation's capacity for economic growth. The overall social-cultural-political environment of the United States, for example, has encouraged economic growth. Beyond the market system that has prevailed in the United States, the United States also has had a stable political system characterized by democratic principles, internal order, the right of property ownership, the legal status of enterprise, and the enforcement of contracts. Economic freedom and political freedom have been "growth-friendly."

In addition, and unlike some nations, there are virtually no social or moral taboos on production and material progress in the United States. The nation's social philosophy has embraced wealth creation as an attainable and desirable goal and the inventor, the innovator, and the businessperson are accorded high degrees of prestige and respect in American society. Finally, Americans have a positive attitude toward work and risk taking, resulting in an ample supply of willing workers and innovative entrepreneurs. A flow of energetic immigrants has greatly augmented that supply.

The nearby Consider This box deals with how fast-growing follower countries such as India sometimes alter their growth-related institutional structures as they grow richer. Web Chapter 21 looks at the special problems of economic growth in developing nations.

CONSIDER THIS . . .

Patents and Innovation

It costs U.S. and European drug companies about $1 billion to research, patent, and safety-test a new drug because literally thousands of candidate drugs fail for each drug that succeeds. The only way to cover these costs is by relying on patent protections that give a drug's developer the exclusive monopoly right to market and sell the new drug for 20 years following the patent application. The revenues over that time period will hopefully be enough to cover the drug's development costs and—if the drug is popular—generate a profit for the drug company.

Leader and follower countries have gotten into heated disputes over patented drugs, however, because the follower countries have often refused to recognize the patents granted to pharmaceutical companies in rich countries. India, for instance, has allowed local drug companies to copy and sell drugs that were developed by U.S. companies and are still under patent protection in the United States.

That policy benefits Indian consumers because competition among the local drug companies drives down the price to below the monopoly price that would be charged by the patent owner. But the weak patent protections in India have a side effect. They make it completely unprofitable for local drug producers to try to develop innovative new drugs. Local rivals would simply copy the new drugs and sell them at very low prices. So India has recently moved to strengthen its patent protections to try to provide financial incentives to transform its local drug companies from copycats into innovators. But note that the innovative new drugs that may result from the increased patent protections are not without a cost. As patent protections in India are improved, inexpensive local drugs copied from the leader countries will no longer be available to Indian consumers.

Determinants of Growth

LO8.3 Identify the general supply, demand, and efficiency forces that give rise to economic growth.

Our discussion of modern economic growth and the institutional structures that promote it has purposely been general. We now want to focus our discussion on six factors that directly affect the *rate* and quality of economic growth. These determinants of economic growth can be grouped into four supply factors, one demand factor, and one efficiency factor.

Supply Factors

The first four determinants of economic growth relate to the physical ability of the economy to expand. They are:

- Increases in the quantity and quality of natural resources.
- Increases in the quantity and quality of human resources.
- Increases in the supply (or stock) of capital goods.
- Improvements in technology.

Any increases or improvements in these **supply factors** will increase the *potential* size of an economy's GDP. The remaining two factors are necessary for that potential to be fulfilled not just in terms of the overall quantity of output but also in terms of the quality of that output and whether it is properly directed toward producing the items most highly valued by society.

Demand Factor

The fifth determinant of economic growth is the **demand factor:**

- To actually achieve the higher production potential created when the supply factors increase or improve, households, businesses, and the government must also expand their purchases of goods and services so as to provide a market for all the new output that can potentially be produced.

If that occurs, there will be no unplanned increases in inventories and resources will remain fully employed. The demand factor acknowledges that economic growth requires that increases in total spending must occur if we are to actually realize the output gains made available by increased production capacity.

Efficiency Factor

The sixth determinant of economic growth is the **efficiency factor:**

- To reach its full production potential, an economy must achieve economic efficiency as well as full employment.

The economy must use its resources in the least costly way (productive efficiency) to produce the specific mix of goods and services that maximizes people's well-being (allocative efficiency). The ability to expand production, together with the full use of available resources, is not

sufficient for achieving maximum possible growth. Also required is the efficient use of those resources.

The supply, demand, and efficiency factors in economic growth are related. Unemployment caused by insufficient total spending (the demand factor) may lower the rate of new capital accumulation (a supply factor) and delay expenditures on research (also a supply factor). Conversely, low spending on investment (a supply factor) may cause insufficient spending (the demand factor) and unemployment. Widespread inefficiency in the use of resources (the efficiency factor) may translate into higher costs of goods and services and thus lower profits, which in turn may slow innovation and reduce the accumulation of capital (supply factors). Economic growth is a dynamic process in which the supply, demand, and efficiency factors all interact.

ORIGIN OF THE IDEA

O8.1
Growth theory

Production Possibilities Analysis

To put the six factors affecting the rate of economic growth into better perspective, let's use the production possibilities analysis introduced in Chapter 1.

Growth and Production Possibilities Recall that a curve like *AB* in Figure 8.2 is a production possibilities

FIGURE 8.2 Economic growth and the production possibilities curve. Economic growth is made possible by the four supply factors that shift the production possibilities curve outward, as from *AB* to *CD*. Economic growth is realized when the demand factor and the efficiency factor move the economy from points such as *a* and *c* that are inside *CD* to the optimal output point, which is assumed to be point *b* in this figure.

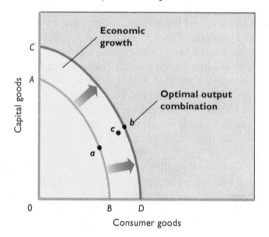

curve. It indicates the various *maximum* combinations of products an economy can produce with its fixed quantity and quality of natural, human, and capital resources and its stock of technological knowledge. An improvement in any of the supply factors will push the production possibilities curve outward, as from *AB* to *CD*.

But the demand factor reminds us that an increase in total spending is needed to move the economy from a point like *a* on curve *AB* to any of the points on the higher curve *CD*. And the efficiency factor reminds us that we need least-cost production and an optimal location on *CD* for the resources to make their maximum possible dollar contribution to total output. You will recall from Chapter 1 that this "best allocation" is determined by expanding the production of each good until its marginal benefit equals its marginal cost. Here, we assume that this optimal combination of capital and consumer goods occurs at point *b*. If the efficiency factor is in full effect, then the economy will produce at point *b* rather than at any other point along curve *CD*.

Example: The net increase in the size of the labor force in the United States in recent years has been 1.5 to 2 million workers per year. That increment raises the economy's production capacity. But obtaining the extra output that these added workers could produce depends on their success in finding jobs. It also depends on whether or not the jobs are in firms and industries where the workers' talents are fully and optimally used. Society does not want new labor-force entrants to be unemployed. Nor does it want pediatricians working as plumbers or pediatricians producing pediatric services for which marginal costs exceed marginal benefits.

Normally, increases in total spending match increases in production capacity, and the economy moves from a point on the previous production possibilities curve to a point on the expanded curve. Moreover, the competitive market system tends to drive the economy toward productive and allocative efficiency. Occasionally, however, the economy may end up at some point such as *c* in Figure 8.2. That kind of outcome occurred in the United States during the severe recession of 2007–2009. Real output fell far below the amount of output that the economy could have produced if it had achieved full employment and operated on its production possibilities curve.

Labor and Productivity Although the demand and efficiency factors are important, discussions of economic growth focus primarily on supply factors. Society can increase its real output and income in two fundamental ways: (1) by increasing its inputs of resources and (2) by raising the productivity of those inputs. Figure 8.3 concentrates

FIGURE 8.3 The supply determinants of real output. Real GDP is usefully viewed as the product of the quantity of labor inputs (hours of work) multiplied by labor productivity.

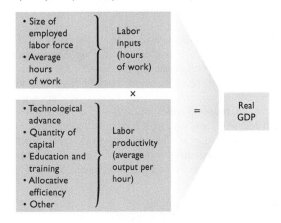

on the input of *labor* and provides a useful framework for discussing the role of supply factors in growth. A nation's real GDP in any year depends on the input of labor (measured in hours of work) multiplied by **labor productivity** (measured as real output per hour of work):

Real GDP = hours of work × labor productivity

Thought of this way, a nation's economic growth from one year to the next depends on its *increase* in labor inputs (if any) and its *increase* in labor productivity (if any).

Illustration: Assume that the hypothetical economy of Ziam has 10 workers in year 1, each working 2,000 hours per year (50 weeks at 40 hours per week). The total input of labor therefore is 20,000 hours. If productivity (average real output per hour of work) is $10, then real GDP in Ziam will be $200,000 (= 20,000 × $10). If work hours rise to 20,200 and labor productivity rises to $10.40, Ziam's real GDP will increase to $210,080 in year 2. Ziam's rate of economic growth will be about 5 percent [= ($210,080 − $200,000)/$200,000] for the year.

WORKED PROBLEMS

W8.2

Productivity and economic growth

Hours of Work What determines the number of hours worked each year? As shown in Figure 8.3, the hours of labor input depend on the size of the employed labor force and the length of the average workweek. Labor-force size depends on the size of the working-age population and the **labor-force participation rate**—the percentage of the working-age population actually in the labor force. The length of the average workweek is governed by legal and institutional considerations and by collective bargaining agreements negotiated between unions and employers.

Labor Productivity Figure 8.3 tells us that labor productivity is determined by technological progress, the quantity of capital goods available to workers, the quality of labor itself, and the efficiency with which inputs are allocated, combined, and managed. Productivity rises when the health, training, education, and motivation of workers improve; when workers have more and better machinery and natural resources with which to work; when production is better organized and managed; and when labor is reallocated from less-efficient industries to more-efficient industries.

Accounting for Growth

LO8.4 Describe "growth accounting" and the specific factors accounting for economic growth in the United States.

The president's Council of Economic Advisers uses a system called **growth accounting** to assess the relative importance of the supply-side elements that contribute to changes in real GDP. This system groups these elements into two main categories:

- Increases in hours of work.
- Increases in labor productivity.

Labor Inputs versus Labor Productivity

Table 8.3 provides the relevant data for the United States for five periods. The symbol "Q" in the table stands for "quarter" of the year. The beginning points for the first four periods are business-cycle peaks, and the last period includes future projections by the Council of Economic Advisers. It is clear from the table that both increases in the quantity of labor and increases in labor productivity are important sources of economic growth. Between 1953

and 2012, the labor force increased from 63 million to 155 million workers. Over that period the average length of the workweek remained relatively stable. Falling birthrates slowed the growth of the native population, but increased immigration partly offset that slowdown. As indicated in the Consider This box on the next page, of particular significance was a surge of women's participation in the labor force. Partly as a result, U.S. labor-force growth averaged 1.6 million workers per year over those 56 years.

The growth of labor productivity also has been important to economic growth. In fact, productivity growth has usually been the more significant factor, with the exception of 1973–1995 when productivity growth greatly slowed. For example, between 2001 and 2011, productivity growth was responsible for all of the 1.7 percent average annual economic rate because labor inputs were shrinking over that time period. The size of the labor force did increase over that decade, but fewer total hours were worked due to many workers shifting from full-time to part-time work and because of the high rates of unemployment experienced during and after that decade's two recessions (in 2001 and 2007–2009). As shown in the far right column of Table 8.3, productivity growth is projected to account for 92 percent of the growth of real GDP between 2011 and 2021.

Because increases in labor productivity are so important to economic growth, economists go to the trouble of investigating and assessing the relative importance of the factors that contribute to productivity growth. There are five factors that, together, appear to explain changes in productivity growth rates: technological advance, the amount of capital each worker has to work with, education and training, economies of scale, and resource allocation. We will examine each factor in turn, noting how much each factor contributes to productivity growth.

Technological Advance

The largest contributor to productivity growth is technological advance, which is thought to account for about

TABLE 8.3 Accounting for the Growth of U.S. Real GDP, 1953–2011 Plus Projection from 2011 to 2022 (Average Annual Percentage Changes)

Item	Actual				Projected
	1953 Q2 to 1973 Q4	1973 Q4 to 1995 Q2	1995 Q2 to 2001 Q1	2001 Q1 to 2011 Q1	2011 Q1 to 2021 Q4
Increase in real GDP	3.6	2.8	3.8	1.7	2.5
Increase in quantity of labor	1.1	1.3	1.4	−0.7	0.2
Increase in labor productivity	2.5	1.5	2.4	2.4	2.3

Source: Derived from *Economic Report of the President, 2008*, p. 45; *Economic Report of the President, 2010*, p. 76; *Economic Report of the President 2011*, p. 52; Bureau of Economic Analysis; and Bureau of Labor Statistics.

40 percent of productivity growth. As economist Paul Romer stated, "Human history teaches us that economic growth springs from better recipes, not just from more cooking."

Technological advance includes not only innovative production techniques but new managerial methods and new forms of business organization that improve the process of production. Generally, technological advance is generated by the discovery of new knowledge, which allows resources to be combined in improved ways that increase output. Once discovered and implemented, new knowledge soon becomes available to entrepreneurs and firms at relatively low cost. Technological advance therefore eventually spreads through the entire economy, boosting productivity and economic growth.

Technological advance and capital formation (investment) are closely related, since technological advance usually promotes investment in new machinery and equipment. In fact, technological advance is often *embodied* within new capital. For example, the purchase of new computers brings into industry speedier, more powerful computers that incorporate new technology.

Technological advance has been both rapid and profound. Gas and diesel engines, conveyor belts, and assembly lines are significant developments of the past. So, too, are fuel-efficient commercial aircraft, integrated microcircuits, personal computers, digital photography, and containerized shipping. More recently, technological advance has exploded, particularly in the areas of computers, photography, wireless communications, and the Internet. Other fertile areas of recent innovation are medicine and biotechnology.

Quantity of Capital

A second major contributor to productivity growth is increased capital, which explains roughly 30 percent of productivity growth. More and better plant and equipment make workers more productive. And a nation acquires more capital by saving some of its income and using that savings to invest in plant and equipment.

Although some capital substitutes for labor, most capital is complementary to labor—it makes labor more productive. A key determinant of labor productivity is the amount of capital goods available *per worker*. If both the aggregate stock of capital goods and the size of the labor force increase over a given period, the individual worker is not necessarily better equipped and productivity will not necessarily rise. But the quantity of capital equipment available per U.S. worker has increased greatly over time. (In 2011 it was about $126,062 per worker.)

CONSIDER THIS . . .

Women, the Labor Force, and Economic Growth

The substantial rise in the number of women working in the paid workforce in the United States has been one of the major labor market trends of the last 50 years. In 1960, about 40 percent of women worked full-time or part-time in paid jobs. Today, that number is about 60 percent.

Women have greatly increased their productivity in the workplace, mostly by becoming better educated and professionally trained. Rising productivity has increased women's wage rates. Those higher wages have raised the opportunity costs—the forgone wage earnings—of staying at home. Women have therefore substituted employment in the labor market for traditional home activities. This substitution has been particularly pronounced among married women. (Single women have always had high labor-force participation rates.)

Furthermore, changing lifestyles and the widespread availability of birth control have freed up time for greater labor-force participation by women. Women not only have fewer children, but those children are spaced closer together in age. Thus women who leave their jobs during their children's early years return to the labor force sooner.

Greater access to jobs by women also has raised the labor-force participation of women. Service industries—teaching, nursing, and office work, for instance—that traditionally have employed many women have expanded rapidly in the past several decades. Also, the population in general has shifted from farms and rural regions to urban areas, where jobs for women are more abundant and more geographically accessible. Additionally, occupational barriers to professions have greatly eroded, resulting in many more women becoming business managers, lawyers, professors, and physicians.

In summary, women in the United States are better educated, more productive, and more efficiently employed than ever before. Their greater presence in the labor force has contributed greatly to U.S. economic growth.

Public investment in the U.S. **infrastructure** (highways and bridges, public transit systems, wastewater treatment facilities, water systems, airports, educational facilities, and so on) has also grown over the years. This publicly owned capital complements private capital. Investments in new highways promote private investment in new factories and retail stores along their routes.

Industrial parks developed by local governments attract manufacturing and distribution firms.

Private investment in infrastructure also plays a large role in economic growth. One example is the tremendous growth of private capital relating to communications systems over the years.

Education and Training

Ben Franklin once said, "He that hath a trade hath an estate," meaning that education and training contribute to a worker's stock of **human capital**—the knowledge and skills that make a worker productive. Investment in human capital includes not only formal education but also on-the-job training. Like investment in physical capital, investment in human capital is an important means of increasing labor productivity and earnings. An estimated 15 percent of productivity growth derives from investments in people's education and skills.

One measure of a nation's quality of labor is its level of educational attainment. Figure 8.4 shows large gains in education attainment over the past several decades. In 1960 only 41 percent of the U.S. population age 25 or older had at least a high school education; and only 8 percent had a college or postcollege education. By 2012, those numbers had increased to 88 and 31 percent, respectively. Clearly, more people are receiving more education than ever before.

But all is not upbeat with education in the United States. Many observers think that the quality of education in the United States has declined. For example, U.S. students perform poorly on science and math tests relative to students in many other nations (see Global

FIGURE 8.4 Changes in the educational attainment of the U.S. adult population. The percentage of the U.S. adult population, age 25 or older, completing high school and college has been rising over recent decades.

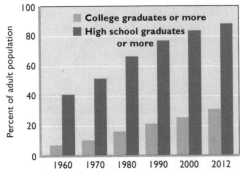

Source: U.S. Census Bureau, **www.census.gov**.

GLOBAL PERSPECTIVE 8.1

Average Test Scores of Eighth-Grade Students in Math and Science, Top 10 Test-Taking Countries

The test performance of U.S. eighth-grade students did not compare favorably with that of eighth-graders in several other nations in the Fifth International Math and Science Study (2011).

Mathematics

Rank		Score
1	South Korea	613
2	Singapore	611
3	Taiwan	609
4	Hong Kong	586
5	Japan	570
6	Russia	539
7	Israel	516
8	Finland	514
9	United States	509
10	Great Britain	507

Science

Rank		Score
1	Singapore	590
2	Taiwan	564
3	South Korea	560
4	Japan	558
5	Finland	552
6	Slovenia	543
7	Russia	542
8	Hong Kong	535
9	Great Britain	533
10	United States	525

Perspective 8.1). And the United States has been producing fewer engineers and scientists, a problem that may trace back to inadequate training in math and science in elementary and high schools. For these reasons, much recent public policy discussion and legislation have been directed toward improving the quality of the U.S. education and training system.

Economies of Scale and Resource Allocation

Economies of scale and improved resource allocation are a fourth and fifth source of productivity growth, and together they explain about 15 percent of productivity growth.

Economies of Scale Reductions in per-unit production costs that result from increases in output levels are called **economies of scale.** Markets have increased in size over time, allowing firms to increase output levels and thereby achieve production advantages associated with greater size. As firms expand their size and output, they are able to use larger, more productive equipment and employ methods of manufacturing and delivery that increase productivity. They also are better able to recoup substantial investments in developing new products and production methods. Examples: A large manufacturer of autos can use elaborate assembly lines with computerization and robotics, while smaller producers must settle for less-advanced technologies using more labor inputs. Large pharmaceutical firms greatly reduce the average amount of labor (researchers, production workers) needed to produce each pill as they increase the number of pills produced. Accordingly, economies of scale result in greater real GDP and thus contribute to economic growth.

Improved Resource Allocation Improved resource allocation means that workers over time have moved from low-productivity employment to high-productivity employment. Historically, many workers have shifted from agriculture, where labor productivity is low, to manufacturing, where it is quite high. More recently, labor has shifted away from some manufacturing industries to even higher-productivity industries such as computer software, business consulting, and pharmaceuticals. As a result of such shifts, the average productivity of U.S. workers has increased.

Also, discrimination in education and the labor market has historically deterred some women and minorities from entering high-productivity jobs. With the decline of such discrimination over time, many members of those groups have shifted from lower-productivity jobs to higher-productivity jobs. The result has been higher overall labor productivity and real GDP.

Finally, things such as tariffs, import quotas, and other barriers to international trade tend to relegate resources to relatively unproductive pursuits. The long-run movement toward liberalized international trade through international agreements has improved the allocation of resources, increased labor productivity, and expanded real output, both here and abroad.

QUICK REVIEW 8.3

- Institutional structures that promote growth include strong property rights, patents, efficient financial institutions, education, and a competitive market system.
- The determinants of economic growth include four supply factors (increases in the quantity and quality of natural resources, increases in the quantity and quality of human resources, increases in the stock of capital goods, and improvements in technology); one demand factor (increases in total spending); and one efficiency factor (achieving allocative and productive efficiency).
- Improvements in labor productivity accounted for about two-thirds of the increase in U.S. real GDP between 1990 and 2012; the use of more labor inputs accounted for the remainder.
- Improved technology, more capital, greater education and training, economies of scale, and better resource allocation have been the main contributors to U.S. productivity growth and thus to U.S. economic growth.

The Rise in the Average Rate of Productivity Growth

LO8.5 Explain why the trend rate of U.S. productivity growth has increased since the earlier 1973–1995 period.

Figure 8.5 shows the growth of labor productivity (as measured by changes in the index of labor productivity) in the United States from 1973 to 2012, along with separate trend lines for 1973–1995 and 1995–2012. Labor productivity in the business sector grew by an average of only 1.5 percent yearly over the 1973–1995 period. But productivity growth averaged 2.4 percent between 1995 and 2012. Many economists believe that this higher productivity growth resulted from a significant new wave of technological advance, coupled with global competition. Some economists think there is a good chance that the higher trend rates of productivity growth could continue for many years to come.

This increase in productivity growth is important because real output, real income, and real wages are linked to labor productivity. To see why, suppose you are alone on an uninhabited island. The number of fish you can catch or coconuts you can pick per hour—your productivity—is your real wage (or real income) per hour. By *increasing* your productivity, you can improve your standard of living because you can gather more fish and more coconuts (goods) for each hour of work.

So it is for the economy as a whole: Over long periods, the economy's labor productivity determines its average real hourly wage, which includes fringe benefits such as health

FIGURE 8.5 **Growth of labor productivity in the United States, 1973–2012.** U.S. labor productivity (here, for the business sector) increased at an average annual rate of only 1.5 percent from 1973 to 1995. But between 1995 and 2012, it rose at an annual rate of 2.4 percent.

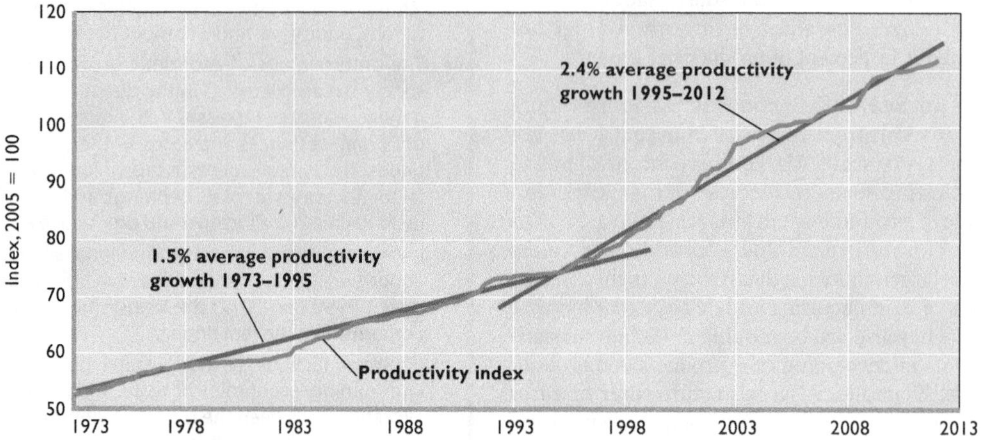

Source: U.S. Bureau of Labor Statistics, **www.bls.gov**.

care insurance and contributions to pensions. The economy's income per hour is equal to its output per hour. So productivity growth is the economy's main route for improving the living standards for its workers. It allows firms to pay higher wages without lowering their business profits.

Reasons for the Rise in the Average Rate of Productivity Growth

Why has productivity growth increased relative to earlier periods?

The Microchip and Information Technology The core element of the productivity speedup is an explosion of entrepreneurship and innovation based on the microprocessor, or *microchip*, which bundles transistors on a piece of silicon. Some observers liken the invention of the microchip to that of electricity, the automobile, air travel, the telephone, and television in importance and scope.

The microchip has found its way into thousands of applications. It has helped create a wide array of new products and services and new ways of doing business. Its immediate results were the pocket calculator, the bar-code scanner, the personal computer, the laptop computer, and more powerful business computers. But the miniaturization of electronic circuits also advanced the development of many other products such as cell phones and pagers, computer-guided lasers, global positioning equipment, energy conservation systems, Doppler radar, digital cameras, and machines to decipher the human genome.

Perhaps of greatest significance, the widespread availability of personal and laptop computers stimulated the

desire to tie them together. That desire promoted rapid development of the Internet and all its many manifestations, such as business-to-household and business-to-business electronic commerce (e-commerce). The combination of the computer, fiber-optic cable, wireless technology, and the Internet constitutes a spectacular advance in **information technology,** which has been used to connect all parts of the world.

New Firms and Increasing Returns Hundreds of new **start-up firms** advanced various aspects of the new information technology. Many of these firms created more "hype" than goods and services and quickly fell by the wayside. But a number of firms flourished, eventually to take their places among the nation's largest firms. Examples of those firms include Intel (microchips); Apple and Dell (personal computers); Microsoft and Oracle (computer software); Cisco Systems (Internet switching systems); America Online (Internet service provision); Yahoo and Google (Internet search engines); and eBay, PayPal, and Amazon.com (electronic commerce). There are scores more! Most of these firms were either "not on the radar" or "a small blip on the radar" 30 years ago. Today each of them has large annual revenue and employs thousands of workers.

Successful new firms often experience **increasing returns,** a situation in which a given percentage increase in the amount of inputs a firm uses leads to an even larger percentage increase in the amount of output the firm produces. For example, suppose that a company called Techco decides to double the size of its operations to meet the growing demand for its services. After doubling its plant and equipment and doubling its workforce, say, from

100 workers to 200 workers, it finds that its total output has tripled from 8,000 units to 24,000 units. Techco has experienced increasing returns; its output has increased by 200 percent, while its inputs have increased by only 100 percent. That is, its labor productivity has gone up from 80 units per worker (= 8,000 units/100 workers) to 120 units per worker (= 24,000 units/200 workers). Increasing returns boost labor productivity and reduce per-unit production costs. Since these cost reductions result from increases in output levels, they are examples of *economies of scale*.

Both emerging firms as well as established firms can exploit several different sources of increasing returns and economies of scale:

- *More specialized inputs* Firms can use more specialized and thus more productive capital and workers as they expand their operations. A growing new e-commerce business, for example, can purchase highly specialized inventory management systems and hire specialized personnel such as accountants, marketing managers, and system maintenance experts.

- *Spreading of development costs* Firms can spread high product development costs over greater output. For example, suppose that a new software product costs $100,000 to develop and only $2 per unit to manufacture and sell. If the firm sells 1,000 units of the software, its per-unit cost will be $102 [= ($100,000 + $2,000)/1,000], but if it sells 500,000 units, that cost will drop to only $2.20 [= ($100,000 + $1 million)/500,000].

- *Simultaneous consumption* Many recently developed products and services can satisfy large numbers of customers at the same time. Unlike a gallon of gas that needs to be produced for each buyer, a software program needs to be produced only once. It then becomes available at very low expense to thousands or even millions of buyers. The same is true of books delivered to electronic reading devices, movies distributed on DVDs, and information disseminated through the Internet.

- *Network effects* Software and Internet service become more beneficial to a buyer the greater the number of households and businesses that also buy them. When others have Internet service, you can send e-mail messages to them. And when they also have software that allows display of documents and photos, you can attach those items to your e-mail messages. These interconnectivity advantages are called **network effects,** which are increases in the value of a product to each user, including existing users, as the total number of users rises. The domestic and global expansion of the Internet in particular has produced network effects, as have cell phones, pagers, tablet computers, and other aspects of wireless communication. Network effects magnify the value of output well beyond the costs of inputs.

- *Learning by doing* Finally, firms that produce new products or pioneer new ways of doing business experience increasing returns through **learning by doing.** Tasks that initially may have taken firms hours may take them only minutes once the methods are perfected.

Whatever the particular source of increasing returns, the result is higher productivity, which tends to reduce the per-unit cost of producing and delivering products.

Global Competition The recent economy is characterized not only by information technology and increasing returns but also by heightened global competition. The collapse of the socialist economies in the late 1980s and early 1990s, together with the success of market systems, has led to a reawakening of capitalism throughout the world. The new information technologies have "shrunk the globe" and made it imperative for all firms to lower their costs and prices and to innovate in order to remain competitive. Free-trade zones such as NAFTA and the European Union (EU), along with trade liberalization through the World Trade Organization (WTO), have also heightened competition internationally by removing trade protection from domestic firms. The larger geographic markets, in turn, have enabled firms to expand beyond their national borders.

Implications for Economic Growth

Other things equal, stronger productivity growth and heightened global competition allow the economy to achieve a higher rate of economic growth. A glance back at Figure 8.2 will help make this point. Suppose that the shift of the production possibilities curve from *AB* to *CD* reflects annual changes in potential output levels before the recent increase in growth rates. Then the higher growth rates of the more recent period of accelerated productivity growth would be depicted by a *larger* outward shift of the economy's production possibilities from *AB* to a curve beyond *CD*. When coupled with economic efficiency and increased total spending, the economy's real GDP would rise by even more than what is shown.

Two cautions: Although the trend line of productivity growth seems to be steeper than in the past and bodes well for long-term economic growth, fluctuations of the rate of economic growth will still occur. Because of demand factors, real output periodically deviates below and above the growth trend—as it certainly did during the recession of 2007–2009. Also, you need to know that the growth of the U.S. labor force may be declining. That slowing may offset some or all of the extra potential for economic growth that would arise from greater productivity growth.

Skepticism about Longevity

Although most macroeconomists have revised their forecasts for long-term productivity growth upward, at least slightly, others are still skeptical and urge a "wait-and-see" approach. These macroeconomists acknowledge that the economy has experienced a rapid advance of new technology, some new firms have experienced increasing returns, and global competition has increased. But they wonder if these factors are sufficiently profound to produce a long-lasting new era of substantially higher rates of productivity growth and real GDP growth.

They also point out that productivity surged between 1975 and 1978 and between 1983 and 1986 but in each case soon reverted to its lower long-run trend. The higher trend line of productivity inferred from the short-run spurt of productivity could prove to be transient. Only by looking backward over long periods can economists distinguish the start of a new long-run trend from a shorter-term boost in productivity related to the business cycle and temporary factors.

What Can We Conclude?

Given the different views on the recent productivity acceleration, what should we conclude? Perhaps the safest conclusions are these:

- The prospects for a lasting increase in productivity growth are good (see Global Perspective 8.2). Studies indicate that productivity increases related to information technology have spread to a wide range of industries, including services. Even during the severe 2007–2009 recession, when real GDP fell by nearly 5 percent, productivity growth continued. Specifically, it ran at a 2.1 percent rate in 2007 just as the recession was starting, fell to 0.9 percent in 2008 when the recession was at its worst, and then jumped up to a very brisk 4.9 percent as the economy began to recover in 2009.

- Time will tell. After the rapid productivity growth of 2009, the growth rate fell to just 0.5 percent in 2010, 0.9 percent in 2011, and 1.0 percent in 2012. Consequently, the average growth rate over those four years is lower than the 2.4 percent rate shown by the trend line in Figure 8.5—but it is higher than the 1.5 percent rate for the 1973–1995 period. Clearly, many more years must elapse before economists will be ready to declare the post-1995 productivity acceleration a long-run, sustainable trend.

GLOBAL PERSPECTIVE 8.2

Global Competitiveness Index

The Global Competitiveness Index, published annually by the World Economic Forum, measures each country's potential for economic growth. The index uses various factors—such as innovativeness, the capability to transfer technology among sectors, the efficiency of the financial system, rates of investment, and the degree of integration with the rest of the world—to measure a country's ability to achieve economic growth over time. Here is the top 10 list for 2012–2013.

Country	Global Competitiveness Ranking, 2012–2013
Switzerland	1
Singapore	2
Finland	3
Sweden	4
Netherlands	5
Germany	6
United States	7
United Kingdom	8
Hong Kong	9
Japan	10

Source: Copyright World Economic Forum, **www.weforum.org.**

QUICK REVIEW 8.4

- Over long time periods, labor productivity growth determines an economy's growth of real wages and its standard of living.

- Many economists believe that the United States has entered a period of faster productivity growth and possibly higher rates of economic growth.

- The rise in the average rate of productivity growth is based on rapid technological change in the form of the microchip and information technology, increasing returns and lower per-unit costs, and heightened global competition that helps hold down prices.

- More-rapid U.S. productivity growth means that, other things equal, the U.S. economy can grow at higher annual rates than it could with less-rapid productivity growth. Nonetheless, many economists caution that it is still too early to determine whether the higher rates of productivity growth since 1995 are a lasting long-run trend or a fortunate short-lived occurrence.

Is Growth Desirable and Sustainable?

LO8.6 Discuss differing perspectives as to whether growth is desirable and sustainable.

Economists usually take for granted that economic growth is desirable and sustainable. But not everyone agrees.

The Antigrowth View

Critics of growth say industrialization and growth result in pollution, climate change, ozone depletion, and other environmental problems. These adverse negative externalities occur because inputs in the production process reenter the environment as some form of waste. The more rapid our growth and the higher our standard of living, the more waste the environment must absorb—or attempt to absorb. In an already wealthy society, further growth usually means satisfying increasingly trivial wants at the cost of mounting threats to the ecological system.

Critics of growth also argue that there is little compelling evidence that economic growth has solved sociological problems such as poverty, homelessness, and discrimination. Consider poverty: In the antigrowth view, American poverty is a problem of distribution, not production. The requisite for solving the problem is a firm commitment to redistribute wealth and income, not further increases in output.

Antigrowth sentiment also says that while growth may permit us to "make a better living," it does not give us "the good life." We may be producing more and enjoying it less. Growth means frantic paces on jobs, worker burnout, and alienated employees who have little or no control over decisions affecting their lives. The changing technology at the core of growth poses new anxieties and new sources of insecurity for workers. Both high-level and low-level workers face the prospect of having their hard-earned skills and experience rendered obsolete by onrushing technology. High-growth economies are high-stress economies, which may impair our physical and mental health.

Finally, critics of high rates of growth doubt that they are sustainable. The planet Earth has finite amounts of natural resources available, and they are being consumed at alarming rates. Higher rates of economic growth simply speed up the degradation and exhaustion of the earth's resources. In this view, slower economic growth that is environmentally sustainable is preferable to faster growth.

In Defense of Economic Growth

The primary defense of growth is that it is the path to the greater material abundance and higher living standards desired by the vast majority of people. Rising output and incomes allow people to buy

> more education, recreation, and travel, more medical care, closer communications, more skilled personal and professional services, and better-designed as well as more numerous products. It also means more art, music, and poetry, theater, and drama. It can even mean more time and resources devoted to spiritual growth and human development.[1]

Growth also enables society to improve the nation's infrastructure, enhance the care of the sick and elderly, provide greater access for the disabled, and provide more police and fire protection. Economic growth may be the only realistic way to reduce poverty, since there is only limited political support for greater redistribution of income. The way to improve the economic position of the poor is to increase household incomes through higher productivity and economic growth. Also, a no-growth policy among industrial nations might severely limit growth in poor nations. Foreign investment and development assistance in those nations would fall, keeping the world's poor in poverty longer.

Economic growth has not made labor more unpleasant or hazardous, as critics suggest. New machinery is usually less taxing and less dangerous than the machinery it replaces. Air-conditioned workplaces are more pleasant than steamy workshops. Furthermore, why would an end to economic growth reduce materialism or alienation? The loudest protests against materialism are heard in those nations and groups that now enjoy the highest levels of material abundance! The high standard of living that growth provides has increased our leisure and given us more time for reflection and self-fulfillment.

Does growth threaten the environment? The connection between growth and environment is tenuous, say growth proponents. Increases in economic growth need not mean increases in pollution. Pollution is not so much a by-product of growth as it is a "problem of the commons." Much of the environment—streams, lakes, oceans, and the air—is treated as common property, with insufficient or no restrictions on its use. The commons have become our dumping grounds; we have overused

---

[1] Alice M. Rivlin, *Reviving the American Dream* (Washington, D.C.: Brookings Institution, 1992), p. 36.

LAST WORD

Can Economic Growth Survive Population Decline?

The Demographic Transition Is Causing Greying Populations, Shrinking Labor Forces, and Overall Population Decreases in Many Nations. Can Economic Growth Survive?

As you know from this chapter, Real GDP = hours of work × labor productivity. The number of *hours of work* depends heavily, however, on the size of the working-age population. If it begins to shrink, the number of *hours of work* almost always falls. In such cases, the only way real GDP can rise is if *labor productivity* increases faster than *hours of work* decreases. The world is about to see if that can happen in countries that have populations that are greying and shrinking.

The historical background has to do with the fact that as nations industrialize, their economies shift from agriculture to industry. As that happens, fertility levels plummet because the shift to modern technology transforms children from being economically essential farm hands that can contribute to their families' incomes from a young age to expensive

investment goods that require many years of costly schooling before they can support themselves.

As people react to this change, birthrates tend to fall quite dramatically. The key statistic is the *total fertility rate* that keeps track of the average number of births that women have during their lifetimes. To keep the population stable in modern societies, the total fertility rate must be about 2.1 births per woman per lifetime (= 1 child to replace mom, 1 child to replace dad, and 0.1 child to compensate for those people who never end up reproducing as adults).

Every rich industrial nation has now seen its total fertility rate drop below the replacement level of 2.1 births per woman per lifetime. In Japan and many Eastern European countries, the number has been so low for so long that

and debased them. Environmental pollution is a case of negative externalities, and correcting this problem involves regulatory legislation, specific taxes ("effluent charges"), or market-based incentives to remedy misuse of the environment.

Those who support growth admit there are serious environmental problems. But they say that limiting growth is the wrong solution. Growth has allowed economies to reduce pollution, be more sensitive to environmental considerations, set aside wilderness, create national parks and monuments, and clean up hazardous waste, while still enabling rising household incomes.

Is growth sustainable? Yes, say the proponents of growth. If we were depleting natural resources faster than their discovery, we would see the prices of those resources rise. That has not been the case for most natural resources; in fact, the prices of most of them have declined. And if one natural resource becomes too expensive, another resource will be substituted for it. Moreover, say economists, economic growth has to do

with the expansion and application of human knowledge and information, not of extractable natural resources. In this view, economic growth is limited only by human imagination.

QUICK REVIEW 8.5

- Critics of growth argue that it adds to environmental degradation, increases human stress, and exhausts the earth's finite supply of natural resources.
- Defenders of growth say that it is the primary path to the rising living standards, that it need not debase the environment, and that there are no indications that we are running out of resources.
- Defenders of growth argue that it is sustainable because growth is based on the expansion and application of human knowledge, which is limited only by human imagination.

there are no longer enough children being born each year to replace the old folks who are dying. As a result, their overall populations are shrinking.

Economists only expect that pattern to become more common and more rapid, so that by the year 2050 the majority of nations will have decreasing populations. But decades before a nation's overall population begins to decrease, it faces a situation in which the labor force shrinks while the elderly population swells.

That pattern is the result of each generation being smaller than the one before. As an example, the Baby Boom generation born between 1946 and 1964 is much larger than the Baby Bust generation that followed it. So as the Boomers retire over the next two decades, there will be a lot of retirees as compared to working-age adults.

This trend can be quantified by the *inverse dependency ratio*, which is defined as the number of people of working age (ages 20 to 64) divided by the number of dependents (seniors over age 65 plus youths under age 20). In the United States, the inverse dependency ratio is set to fall from 1.5 people of working age per dependent in 2010 to just 1.16 people of working age per dependent in 2050. That is extremely problematic because it implies that worker productivity will have to rise dramatically just to make up for the relative decline in the number of workers as compared to dependents. If productivity doesn't keep up with the fall in the inverse dependency ratio, living standards will have to decline because there will simply be too many nonworking consumers relative to working-age producers.

The place where this problem is likely to show up first is Social Security. There are currently 2.9 workers paying into the Social Security system for each retiree receiving Social Security benefits. But that number is set to fall to just 2.0 workers per retiree in 2030. So worker productivity would have to increase by almost a third in under 20 years just to keep up with the decline in the number of workers relative to retirees.

Economists are uncertain about whether such large productivity increases will be forthcoming. The problem is that consumption competes with investment. A society with a larger fraction of dependents is a society that is likely to devote an increasingly high fraction of total output toward consumption rather than investment. If so, productivity growth may slow considerably.

Another possible problem is that, historically, most transformative new technologies and businesses have been created by energetic young people under the age of 40. With each generation getting smaller, there will be fewer people in that age range and thus, possibly, less innovation and slower productivity growth.

Other economists are more hopeful, however. They view old people as consumers and demanders. As their numbers swell, inventors may simply switch from inventing products for young people to inventing products for old people. If so, productivity growth and living standards could keep on rising at the rates we have come to expect.

SUMMARY

LO8.1 List two ways that economic growth is measured.

A nation's economic growth can be measured either as an increase in real GDP over time or as an increase in real GDP per capita over time. Real GDP in the United States has grown at an average annual rate of about 3.2 percent since 1950; real GDP per capita has grown at roughly a 2 percent annual rate over that same period.

LO8.2 Define "modern economic growth" and explain the institutional structures needed for an economy to experience it.

Sustained increases in real GDP per capita did not happen until the past two centuries, when England and then other countries began to experience modern economic growth, which is characterized by institutional structures that encourage savings, investment, and the development of new technologies. Institutional structures that promote growth include strong property rights, patents, efficient financial institutions, education, and a competitive market system.

Because some nations have experienced nearly two centuries of modern economic growth while others have only recently begun to experience modern economic growth, some countries today are much richer than other countries.

It is possible, however, for countries that are currently poor to grow faster than countries that are currently rich because the growth of real GDP per capita for rich countries is limited to about 2 percent per year. To continue growing, rich countries must invent and apply new technologies. By contrast, poor countries can grow much faster because they can simply adopt the institutions and cutting-edge technologies already developed by the rich countries.

LO8.3 Identify the general supply, demand, and efficiency forces that give rise to economic growth.

The determinants of economic growth to which we can attribute changes in growth rates include four supply factors (changes in the quantity and quality of natural resources, changes in the quantity and quality of human resources, changes in the stock of capital goods, and improvements in technology); one demand factor (changes in total spending); and one efficiency factor (changes in how well an economy achieves allocative and productive efficiency).

The growth of a nation's capacity to produce output can be illustrated graphically by an outward shift of its production possibilities curve.

LO8.4 Describe "growth accounting" and the specific factors accounting for economic growth in the United States.

Growth accounting attributes increases in real GDP either to increases in the amount of labor being employed or to increases in the productivity of the labor being employed. Increases in U.S. real GDP are mostly the result of increases in labor productivity. The increases in labor productivity can be attributed to technological progress, increases in the quantity of capital per worker, improvements in the education and training of workers, the exploitation of economies of scale, and improvements in the allocation of labor across different industries.

LO8.5 Explain why the trend rate of U.S. productivity growth has increased since the earlier 1973–1995 period.

Over long time periods, the growth of labor productivity underlies an economy's growth of real wages and its standard of living. U.S. productivity rose by 2.4 percent annually between 1995 and 2012, compared to 1.5 percent annually between 1973 and 1995.

This post-1995 increase in the average rate of productivity growth is based on (*a*) rapid technological change in the form of the microchip and information technology, (*b*) increasing returns and lower per-unit costs, and (*c*) heightened global competition that holds down prices.

The main sources of increasing returns in recent years are (*a*) the use of more specialized inputs as firms grow, (*b*) the spreading of development costs, (*c*) simultaneous consumption by consumers, (*d*) network effects, and (*e*) learning by doing. Increasing returns mean higher productivity and lower per-unit production costs.

LO8.6 Discuss differing perspectives as to whether growth is desirable and sustainable.

Skeptics wonder if the recent rise in the average rate of productivity growth is permanent, and suggest a wait-and-see approach. They point out that surges in productivity and real GDP growth have previously occurred but do not necessarily represent long-lived trends.

Critics of rapid growth say that it adds to environmental degradation, increases human stress, and exhausts the earth's finite supply of natural resources. Defenders of rapid growth say that it is the primary path to the rising living standards nearly universally desired by people, that it need not debase the environment, and that there are no indications that we are running out of resources. Growth is based on the expansion and application of human knowledge, which is limited only by human imagination.

TERMS AND CONCEPTS

economic growth	demand factor	economies of scale
real GDP per capita	efficiency factor	information technology
rule of 70	labor productivity	start-up firms
modern economic growth	labor-force participation rate	increasing returns
leader countries	growth accounting	network effects
follower countries	infrastructure	learning by doing
supply factors	human capital	

The following and additional problems can be found in **connect** ECONOMICS

DISCUSSION QUESTIONS

1. How is economic growth measured? Why is economic growth important? Why could the difference between a 2.5 percent and a 3 percent annual growth rate be of great significance over several decades? **LO8.1**

2. When and where did modern economic growth first happen? What are the major institutional factors that form the foundation for modern economic growth? What do they have in common? **LO8.2**

3. Why are some countries today much poorer than other countries? Are today's poor countries destined to always be poorer than today's rich countries? If so, explain why. If not, explain how today's poor countries can catch or even pass today's rich countries. **LO8.2**

4. What are the four supply factors of economic growth? What is the demand factor? What is the efficiency factor? Illustrate these factors in terms of the production possibilities curve. **LO8.3**

5. Suppose that Alpha and Omega have identically sized working-age populations but that total annual hours of work are much greater in Alpha than in Omega. Provide two possible reasons for this difference. **LO8.3**

6. What is growth accounting? To what extent have increases in U.S. real GDP resulted from more labor inputs? From greater labor productivity? Rearrange the following contributors to the growth of productivity in order of their quantitative importance: economies of scale, quantity of capital, improved resource allocation, education and training, and technological advance. **LO8.4**

7. True or False: If false, explain why. **LO8.4**
   a. Technological advance, which to date has played a relatively small role in U.S. economic growth, is destined to play a more important role in the future.

b. Many public capital goods are complementary to private capital goods.

c. Immigration has slowed economic growth in the United States.

8. Explain why there is such a close relationship between changes in a nation's rate of productivity growth and changes in its average real hourly wage. **LO8.5**

9. Relate each of the following to the recent increase in the trend rate of productivity growth: **LO8.5**
   a. Information technology.
   b. Increasing returns.
   c. Network effects.
   d. Global competition.

10. What, if any, are the benefits and costs of economic growth, particularly as measured by real GDP per capita? **LO8.6**

11. **LAST WORD** Would you expect a country with a total fertility rate of 2.7 to have a growing or a shrinking population over the long run? What about a country with a total fertility rate of 1.2? In 20 years, will America have more or fewer workers per retiree than it does today? Why does a falling inverse dependency ratio make it harder for real GDP to continue growing?

REVIEW QUESTIONS

1. If real GDP grows at 7 percent per year, then real GDP will double in approximately _____ years. **LO8.1**
   a. 70.
   b. 14.
   c. 10.
   d. 7.

2. In 1820 living standards in various places around the globe were _____ they are today. **LO8.2**
   a. More widely varying than.
   b. Just as widely varying as.
   c. Less widely varying than.

3. True or False: Countries that currently have low real GDPs per capita are destined to always have lower living standards than countries that currently have high real GDPs per capita. **LO8.2**

4. Identify each of the following situations as something that either promotes growth or retards growth. **LO8.2**
   a. Increasing corruption allows government officials to steal people's homes.
   b. A nation introduces patent laws for the first time.
   c. A court order shuts down all banks permanently.
   d. A poor country extends free public schooling from 8 years to 12 years.
   e. A nation adopts a free-trade policy.
   f. A formerly communist country adopts free markets.

5. Real GDP equals _____ times _____. **LO8.4**
   a. Average hours of work; quantity of capital.

b. Average hours of work; allocative efficiency.
   c. Labor input; labor productivity.
   d. Natural resources; improvements in technology.

6. Suppose that just by doubling the amount of output that it produces each year, a firm's per-unit production costs fall by 30 percent. This is an example of: **LO8.4**
   a. Economies of scale.
   b. Improved resource allocation.
   c. Technological advance.
   d. The demand factor.

7. True or False: Computers and increased global competition have retarded economic growth in recent decades. **LO8.5**

8. Identify following arguments about economic growth as being either anti-growth or pro-growth. **LO8.6**
   a. Growth means worker burnout and frantic schedules.
   b. Rising incomes allow people to buy more education, medical care, and recreation.
   c. The Earth has only finite amounts of natural resources.
   d. We still have poverty, homelessness, and discrimination even in the richest countries.
   e. Richer countries spend more money protecting the environment.
   f. Natural resource prices have fallen rather than increased over time.

PROBLEMS

1. Suppose an economy's real GDP is $30,000 in year 1 and $31,200 in year 2. What is the growth rate of its real GDP? Assume that population is 100 in year 1 and 102 in year 2. What is the growth rate of real GDP per capita? **LO8.1**

2. What annual growth rate is needed for a country to double its output in 7 years? In 35 years? In 70 years? In 140 years? **LO8.1**

3. Assume that a "leader country" has real GDP per capita of $40,000, whereas a "follower country" has real GDP per capita of $20,000. Next suppose that the growth of real GDP per capita falls to zero percent in the leader country and rises to 7 percent in the follower country. If these rates continue for long periods of time, how many years will it take for the follower country to catch up to the living standard of the leader country? **LO8.2**

4. Refer to Figure 8.2 and assume that the values for points a, b, and c are $10 billion, $20 billion, and $18 billion respec-

tively. If the economy moves from point a to point b over a 10-year period, what must have been its annual rate of economic growth? If, instead, the economy was at point c at the end of the 10-year period, by what percentage did it fall short of its production capacity? **LO8.3**

5. Suppose that work hours in New Zombie are 200 in year 1 and productivity is $8 per hour worked. What is New Zombie's real GDP? If work hours increase to 210 in year 2 and productivity rises to $10 per hour, what is New Zombie's rate of economic growth? **LO8.4**

6. The per-unit cost of an item is its average total cost (= total cost/quantity). Suppose that a new cell phone application costs $100,000 to develop and only $0.50 per unit to deliver to each cell phone customer. What will be the per-unit cost of the application if it sells 100 units? 1,000 units? 1 million units? **LO8.5**

CHAPTER **9**

Business Cycles, Unemployment, and Inflation

Learning Objectives

LO9.1 Describe the business cycle and its primary phases.

LO9.2 Illustrate how unemployment is measured and explain the different types of unemployment.

LO9.3 Explain how inflation is measured and distinguish between cost-push inflation and demand-pull inflation.

LO9.4 Relate how unanticipated inflation can redistribute real income.

LO9.5 Discuss how inflation may affect the economy's level of real output.

As indicated in Chapter 8, the United States has experienced remarkable economic growth over time. But this growth has not been smooth, steady, and predictable from year to year. At various times the United States has experienced recessions, high unemployment rates, or high inflation rates. For example, U.S. unemployment rose by 8 million workers and the unemployment rate increased from 4.7 percent to 10.1 percent during the 2007–2009 recession. Other nations have also suffered high unemployment rates at times. As just one example, Spain's unemployment rate exceeded 26 percent in 2012. Also, inflation has occasionally plagued the United States and other nations. For instance, the U.S. inflation rate in 1980 was 13.5 percent. Zimbabwe's inflation soared to 26,000 percent in 2007!

Our goal in this chapter is to examine the concepts, terminology, and facts relating to macroeconomic instability. Specifically, we want to discuss the business cycle, unemployment, and inflation. The concepts discussed are extremely important for understanding subsequent chapters on economic theory and economic policy.

The Business Cycle

LO9.1 Describe the business cycle and its primary phases.
The long-run trend of the U.S. economy is one of economic growth, as stylized by the upsloping line labeled "Growth Trend" in Figure 9.1. But growth has been interrupted by periods of economic instability usually associated with **business cycles.** Business cycles are alternating rises and declines in the level of economic activity, sometimes over several years. Individual cycles (one "up" followed by one "down") vary substantially in duration and intensity.

ORIGIN OF THE IDEA

O9.1
Business cycles

Phases of the Business Cycle

Figure 9.1 shows the four phases of a generalized business cycle:

- At a **peak,** such as the middle peak shown in Figure 9.1, business activity has reached a temporary maximum. Here the economy is near or at full employment and the level of real output is at or very close to the economy's capacity. The price level is likely to rise during this phase.

- A **recession** is a period of decline in total output, income, and employment. This downturn, which lasts 6 months or more, is marked by the widespread contraction of business activity in many sectors of the economy. Along with declines in real GDP, significant increases in unemployment occur. Table 9.1

FIGURE 9.1 The business cycle. Economists distinguish four phases of the business cycle; the duration and strength of each phase may vary.

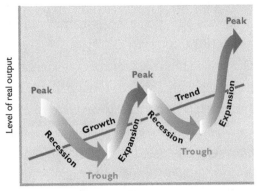

Time

TABLE 9.1 U.S. Recessions since 1950

Period	Duration, Months	Depth (Decline in Real Output)
1953–54	10	−2.6%
1957–58	8	−3.7
1960–61	10	−1.1
1969–70	11	−0.2
1973–75	16	−3.2
1980	6	−2.2
1981–82	16	−2.9
1990–91	8	−1.4
2001	8	−0.4
2007–09	18	−4.3

Source: National Bureau of Economic Research, **www.nber.org**, Bureau of Economic Analysis, **www.bea.gov**, and Minneapolis Federal Reserve Bank, "The Recession and Recovery in Perspective," **www.minneapolisfed.gov**. Output data are in 2000 dollars.

documents the 10 recessions in the United States since 1950.

- In the **trough** of the recession or depression, output and employment "bottom out" at their lowest levels. The trough phase may be either short-lived or quite long.

- A recession is usually followed by a recovery and **expansion,** a period in which real GDP, income, and employment rise. At some point, the economy again approaches full employment. If spending then expands more rapidly than does production capacity, prices of nearly all goods and services will rise. In other words, inflation will occur.

Although business cycles all pass through the same phases, they vary greatly in duration and intensity. Many economists prefer to talk of business "fluctuations" rather than cycles because cycles imply regularity while fluctuations do not. The Great Depression of the 1930s resulted in a 27 percent decline in real GDP over a 3-year period in the United States and seriously impaired business activity for a decade. By comparison, the U.S. recessions detailed in Table 9.1 were less severe in both intensity and duration.

The Business Cycle Dating Committee of the National Bureau of Economic Research (NBER), a nonprofit economic research organization, declares the start and end of recessions in the United States. Citing evidence of declining real output and falling employment, the NBER officially declared that the latest recession began in December 2007. The NBER subsequently declared that the Great Recession ended in June 2009, 18 months after it began. In making this announcement, the NBER pointed out that its declaration was not a forecast for the future path of the economy.

Recessions, of course, occur in other countries, too. For example, nearly all industrial nations and many developing nations have suffered recessions in the past several years.

Causation: A First Glance

The long-run trend of the U.S. economy is expansion and growth. That is why the business cycles in Figure 9.1 are drawn against a trend of economic growth. A key issue in macroeconomics is why the economy sees business cycle fluctuations rather than slow, smooth growth. In terms of Figure 9.1, why does output move up and down rather than just staying on the smooth growth trend line?

Economists have developed several possible explanations. But before turning to them, recall that in Chapter 6 we explained that these theories are founded on the idea that fluctuations are driven by shocks—unexpected events that individuals and firms may have trouble adjusting to. Also recall that short-run price stickiness is widely believed to be a major factor preventing the economy from rapidly adjusting to shocks. With prices sticky in the short run, price changes cannot quickly equalize the quantities demanded of goods and services with their respective quantities supplied after a shock has happened. Instead, the economy is forced to respond to shocks in the short run primarily through changes in output and employment rather than through changes in prices.

Economists cite several possible general sources of shocks that can cause business cycles.

- *Irregular innovation* Significant new products or production methods, such as those associated with the railroad, automobile, computer, and Internet, can rapidly spread through the economy, sparking sizable increases in investment, consumption, output, and employment. After the economy has largely absorbed the new innovation, the economy may for a time slow down or possibly decline. Because such innovations occur irregularly and unexpectedly, they may contribute to the variability of economic activity.

- *Productivity changes* When productivity—output per unit of input—unexpectedly increases, the economy booms; when productivity unexpectedly decreases, the economy recedes. Such changes in productivity can result from unexpected changes in resource availability (of, say, oil or agricultural

commodities) or from unexpected changes in the general rate of technological advance.

- *Monetary factors* Some economists see business cycles as purely monetary phenomena. When a nation's central bank shocks the economy by creating more money than people were expecting, an inflationary boom in output occurs. By contrast, printing less money than people were expecting triggers an output decline and, eventually, a price-level fall.

- *Political events* Unexpected political events, such as peace treaties, new wars, or the 9/11 terrorist attacks, can create economic opportunities or strains. In adjusting to these shocks, the economy may experience upswings or downswings.

- *Financial instability* Unexpected financial bubbles (rapid asset price increases) or bursts (abrupt asset price decreases) can spill over to the general economy by expanding or contracting lending, and boosting or eroding the confidence of consumers and businesses. Booms and busts in the rest of the economy may follow.

The severe recession of 2007–2009 was precipitated by a combination of excessive money and a financial frenzy that led to overvalued real estate and unsustainable mortgage debt. Institutions bundled this debt into new securities ("derivatives") that were sold to financial investors. Some of the investors, in turn, bought insurance against losses that might arise from the securities. As real estate prices plummeted and mortgage defaults unexpectedly rocketed, the securitization and insurance structure buckled and nearly collapsed. Credit markets froze, pessimism prevailed, and spending by businesses and households declined.

Whatever the source of economic shocks, most economists agree that the *immediate* cause of the large majority of cyclical changes in the levels of real output and employment is unexpected changes in the level of total spending. If total spending unexpectedly sinks and firms cannot lower prices, firms will find themselves selling fewer units of output (since with prices fixed, a decreased amount of spending implies fewer items purchased). Slower sales will cause firms to cut back on production. As they do, GDP will fall. And because fewer workers will be needed to produce less output, employment also will fall. The economy will contract and enter a recession.

By contrast, if the level of spending unexpectedly rises, output, employment, and incomes will rise. This is true because, with prices sticky, the increased spending will mean that consumers will be buying a larger volume of goods and services (since, with prices fixed, more spending means more items purchased). Firms will respond by increasing output. This will increase GDP. And because firms will need to hire more workers to produce the larger volume of output, employment also will increase. The economy will boom and enjoy an expansion. Eventually, as time passes and prices become more flexible, prices are also likely to rise as a result of the increased spending.

Cyclical Impact: Durables and Nondurables

Although the business cycle is felt everywhere in the economy, it affects different segments in different ways and to different degrees.

Firms and industries producing *capital goods* (for example, housing, commercial buildings, heavy equipment, and farm implements) and *consumer durables* (for example, automobiles, personal computers, and refrigerators) are affected most by the business cycle. Within limits, firms can postpone the purchase of capital goods. For instance, when the economy goes into recession, producers frequently delay the purchase of new equipment and the construction of new plants. The business outlook simply does not warrant increases in the stock of capital goods. In good times, capital goods are usually replaced before they depreciate completely. But when recession strikes, firms patch up their old equipment and make do. As a result, investment in capital goods declines sharply. Firms that have excess plant capacity may not even bother to replace all the capital that is depreciating. For them, net investment may be negative. The pattern is much the same for consumer durables such as automobiles and major appliances. When recession occurs and households must trim their budgets, purchases of these goods are often deferred. Families repair their old cars and appliances rather than buy new ones, and the firms producing these products suffer. (Of course, producers of capital goods and consumer durables also benefit most from expansions.)

In contrast, *service* industries and industries that produce *nondurable consumer goods* are somewhat insulated from the most severe effects of recession. People find it difficult to cut back on needed medical and legal services, for example. And a recession actually helps some service firms, such as pawnbrokers and law firms that specialize in bankruptcies. Nor are the purchases of many nondurable goods such as food and clothing easy to postpone. The quantity and quality of purchases of nondurables will decline, but not so much as will purchases of capital goods and consumer durables.

> **QUICK REVIEW 9.1**
>
> - The typical business cycle goes through four phases: peak, recession, trough, and expansion.
> - Fluctuations in output and employment are caused by economic shocks combining with sticky prices.
> - Sources of shocks that cause recessions include irregular innovation, productivity changes, monetary factors, political events, and financial instability.
> - During a recession, industries that produce capital goods and consumer durables normally suffer greater output and employment declines than do service and nondurable consumer goods industries.

Unemployment

LO9.2 Illustrate how unemployment is measured and explain the different types of unemployment.

Two problems that arise over the course of the business cycle are unemployment and inflation. Let's look at unemployment first.

Measurement of Unemployment

The U.S. Bureau of Labor Statistics (BLS) conducts a nationwide random survey of some 60,000 households each month to determine who is employed and who is not employed. In a series of questions, it asks which members of the household are working, unemployed and looking for work, not looking for work, and so on. From the answers, it determines an unemployment rate for the entire nation.

Figure 9.2 helps explain the mathematics. The BLS divides the total U.S. population into three groups. One group is made up of people under 16 years of age and people who are institutionalized, for example, in mental hospitals or correctional institutions. Such people are not considered potential members of the labor force.

A second group, labeled "Not in labor force," is composed of adults who are potential workers but are not employed and are not seeking work. For example, they are stay-at-home parents, full-time students, or retirees.

The third group is the **labor force,** which constituted slightly more than 50 percent of the total population in 2009. The labor force consists of people who are able and willing to work. Both those who are employed and those who are unemployed but actively seeking work are counted as being in the labor force. The **unemployment rate** is the percentage of the labor force unemployed:

$$\text{Unemployment rate} = \frac{\text{unemployed}}{\text{labor force}} \times 100$$

FIGURE 9.2 The U.S. labor force, employment, and unemployment, 2012.* The labor force consists of persons 16 years of age or older who are not in institutions and who are (1) employed or (2) unemployed but seeking employment.

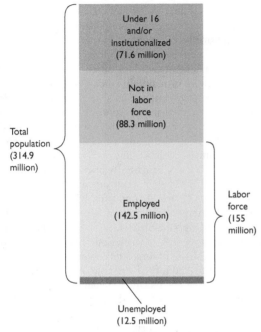

*Civilian labor-force data, which excludes military employment.

Source: Bureau of Labor Statistics, **www.bls.gov**.

The statistics underlying the rounded numbers in Figure 9.2 show that in 2012 the unemployment rate averaged

$$\frac{12,506,000}{154,975,000} \times 100 = 8.1\%$$

WORKED PROBLEMS

W9.1
Unemployment rate

Unemployment rates for selected years appear on the inside covers of this book.

Despite the use of scientific sampling and interviewing techniques, the data collected in this survey are subject to criticism:

- *Part-time employment* The BLS lists all part-time workers as fully employed. In 2012 about 26 million people worked part-time as a result of personal choice. But another 8 million part-time workers either wanted to work full-time and could not find suitable full-time work or worked fewer hours because of a temporary slack in consumer demand. These last two groups were, in effect, partially employed and partially unemployed. By counting them as fully employed, say critics, the official BLS data understate the unemployment rate.

- *Discouraged workers* You must be actively seeking work in order to be counted as unemployed. An unemployed individual who is not actively seeking employment is classified as "not in the labor force." The problem is that many workers, after unsuccessfully seeking employment for a time, become discouraged and drop out of the labor force. The number of such **discouraged workers** was roughly 909,000 in 2012, up from 396,000 in 2007. By not counting discouraged workers as unemployed, say critics, the official BLS data understate the unemployment problem.

Types of Unemployment

There are three *types* of unemployment: frictional, structural, and cyclical.

Frictional Unemployment At any given time some workers are "between jobs." Some of them will be moving voluntarily from one job to another. Others will have been fired and will be seeking reemployment. Still others will have been laid off temporarily because of seasonal demand. In addition to those between jobs, many young workers will be searching for their first jobs.

As these unemployed people find jobs or are called back from temporary layoffs, other job seekers and laid-off workers will replace them in the "unemployment pool." It is important to keep in mind that while the pool itself persists because there are always newly unemployed workers flowing into it, most workers do *not* stay in the unemployment pool for very long. Indeed, when the economy is strong, the majority of unemployed workers find new jobs within a couple of months. One should be careful not to make the mistake of confusing the permanence of the pool itself with the false idea that the pool's membership is permanent, too. On the other hand, there are workers who do remain unemployed and in the pool for very long periods of time—sometimes for many years. As we discuss the different types of unemployment below, notice that certain types tend to be transitory while others are associated with much longer spells of unemployment.

Economists use the term **frictional unemployment**—consisting of *search unemployment* and *wait unemployment*—for workers who are either searching for jobs or waiting to take jobs in the near future. The word "frictional" implies

CONSIDER THIS . . .

Downwardly Sticky Wages and Unemployment

Labor markets have an important quirk that helps to explain why unemployment goes up so much during a recession.

The quirk is that wages are flexible upward but sticky downward.

On the one hand, workers are perfectly happy to accept wage increases. So when the economy is booming and firms start bidding for the limited supply of labor, wages rise—often quite rapidly.

On the other hand, workers deeply resent pay cuts. So if the economy goes into a recession and firms need to reduce labor costs, managers almost never cut wages because doing so would only lead to disgruntled employees, low productivity, and—in extreme cases—workers stealing supplies or actively sabotaging their own firms.

Instead, managers usually opt for layoffs. The workers who are let go obviously don't like being unemployed. But those who remain get to keep their old wages and, consequently, keep on being as productive and cooperative as they were before.

This preference that firms show for layoffs over wage cuts results in downwardly sticky wages and an informal price floor that helps to explain why unemployment goes up so much during a recession. The problem is that when the demand for labor falls during a recession, the informal price floor prevents wages from falling. As a result, there is no way for falling wages to help entice at least some firms to hire a few more workers. Thus, when a recession hits, employment falls more precipitously than it would if wages were downwardly flexible and falling wages could help to increase hiring.

that the labor market does not operate perfectly and instantaneously (without friction) in matching workers and jobs.

Frictional unemployment is inevitable and, at least in part, desirable. Many workers who are voluntarily between jobs are moving from low-paying, low-productivity jobs to higher-paying, higher-productivity positions. That means greater income for the workers, a better allocation of labor resources, and a larger real GDP for the economy.

Structural Unemployment Frictional unemployment blurs into a category called **structural unemployment.** Here, economists use "structural" in the sense of "compositional." Changes over time in consumer demand and in technology alter the "structure" of the total demand for labor, both occupationally and geographically.

Occupationally, the demand for certain skills (for example, sewing clothes or working on farms) may decline or even vanish. The demand for other skills (for example, designing software or maintaining computer systems) will intensify. Unemployment results because the composition of the labor force does not respond immediately or completely to the new structure of job opportunities. Workers who find that their skills and experience have become obsolete or unneeded thus find that they have no marketable talents. They are structurally unemployed until they adapt or develop skills that employers want.

Geographically, the demand for labor also changes over time. An example: the migration of industry and thus of employment opportunities from the Snowbelt to the Sunbelt over the past few decades. Another example is the movement of jobs from inner-city factories to suburban industrial parks. And a final example is the so-called *offshoring* of jobs that occurs when the demand for a particular type of labor shifts from domestic firms to foreign firms. As job opportunities shift from one place to another, some workers become structurally unemployed.

The distinction between frictional and structural unemployment is hazy at best. The key difference is that *frictionally* unemployed workers have marketable skills and either live in areas where jobs exist or are able to move to areas where they do. *Structurally* unemployed workers find it hard to obtain new jobs without retraining, gaining additional education, or relocating. Frictional unemployment is short-term; structural unemployment is more likely to be long-term and consequently more serious.

Cyclical Unemployment Unemployment that is caused by a decline in total spending is called **cyclical unemployment** and typically begins in the recession phase of the business cycle. As the demand for goods and services decreases, employment falls and unemployment rises. Cyclical unemployment results from insufficient demand for goods and services. The 25 percent unemployment rate in the depth of the Great Depression in 1933 reflected mainly cyclical unemployment, as did significant parts of the 9.7 percent unemployment rate in 1982, the 7.5 percent rate in 1992, the 5.8 percent rate in 2002, and the 9.3 percent rate in 2009.

Cyclical unemployment is a very serious problem when it occurs. We will say more about its high costs later, but first we need to define "full employment."

Definition of Full Employment

Because frictional and structural unemployment are largely unavoidable in a dynamic economy, *full employment* is something less than 100 percent employment of the labor force. Economists say that the economy is "fully employed" when it is experiencing only frictional and structural unemployment. That is, full employment occurs when there is no cyclical unemployment.

Economists describe the unemployment rate that is consistent with full employment as the **full-employment rate of unemployment,** or the **natural rate of unemployment (NRU).** At the NRU, the economy is said to be producing its **potential output.** This is the real GDP that occurs when the economy is "fully employed."

Note that a fully employed economy does not mean zero unemployment. Even when the economy is fully employed, the NRU is some positive percentage because it takes time for frictionally unemployed job seekers to find open jobs they can fill. Also, it takes time for the structurally unemployed to achieve the skills and geographic relocation needed for reemployment.

"Natural" does not mean, however, that the economy will always operate at this rate and thus realize its potential output. When cyclical unemployment occurs, the economy has much more unemployment than that which would occur at the NRU. Moreover, the economy can operate for a while at an unemployment rate *below* the NRU. At times, the demand for labor may be so great that firms take a stronger initiative to hire and train the structurally unemployed. Also, some parents, teenagers, college students, and retirees who were casually looking for just the right part-time or full-time jobs may quickly find them. Thus the unemployment rate temporarily falls below the natural rate.

Also, the NRU can vary over time as demographic factors, job-search methods, and public policies change. In the 1980s, the NRU was about 6 percent. Today, it is 5 to 6 percent.

Economic Cost of Unemployment

Unemployment that is excessive involves great economic and social costs.

GDP Gap and Okun's Law The basic economic cost of unemployment is forgone output. When the economy fails to create enough jobs for all who are able and willing to work, potential production of goods and services is irretrievably lost. In terms of Chapter 1's analysis, unemployment above the natural rate means that society is operating at some point inside its production possibilities

curve. Economists call this sacrifice of output a **GDP gap**—the difference between actual and potential GDP. That is:

$$\text{GDP gap} = \text{actual GDP} - \text{potential GDP}$$

The GDP gap can be either negative (actual GDP < potential GDP) or positive (actual GDP > potential GDP). In the case of unemployment above the natural rate, it is negative because actual GDP falls short of potential GDP.

Potential GDP is determined by assuming that the natural rate of unemployment prevails. The growth of potential GDP is simply projected forward on the basis of the economy's "normal" growth rate of real GDP. Figure 9.3 shows the GDP gap for recent years in the United States. It also indicates the close correlation between the actual unemployment rate (Figure 9.3b) and the GDP gap (Figure 9.3a). The higher the unemployment rate, the larger is the GDP gap.

Macroeconomist Arthur Okun was the first to quantify the relationship between the unemployment rate and the GDP gap. **Okun's law** indicates that for every 1 percentage point by which the actual unemployment rate exceeds the natural rate, a negative GDP gap of about 2 percent occurs. With this information, we can calculate the absolute loss of output associated with any above-natural unemployment rate. For example, in 2009 the unemployment rate was 9.3 percent, or 4.3 percentage points above that period's 5.0 percent natural rate of unemployment. Multiplying this 4.3 percent by Okun's 2 indicates that 2009's GDP gap was 8.6 percent of potential GDP (in real terms). By applying this 8.6 percent loss to 2009's potential GDP of $13,894 billion, we find that the economy sacrificed $1,195 billion of real output because the natural rate of unemployment was not achieved.

WORKED PROBLEMS

W9.2
Okun's law

As you can see in Figure 9.3, sometimes the economy's actual output will exceed its potential or full-employment output. Figure 9.3 reveals that an economic expansion in 1999 and 2000, for example, caused actual GDP to exceed potential GDP in those years. There was a positive GDP gap in 1999 and 2000. Actual GDP for a time can exceed potential GDP, but positive GDP gaps create inflationary pressures and cannot be sustained indefinitely.

Unequal Burdens An increase in the unemployment rate from 5 to, say, 9 or 10 percent might be more tolerable to society if every worker's hours of work and wage

FIGURE 9.3 Actual and potential real GDP and the unemployment rate. (a) The difference between actual and potential GDP is the GDP gap. A negative GDP gap measures the output the economy sacrifices when actual GDP falls short of potential GDP. A positive GDP gap indicates that actual GDP is above potential GDP. (b) A high unemployment rate means a large GDP gap (negative), and a low unemployment rate means a small or even positive GDP gap.

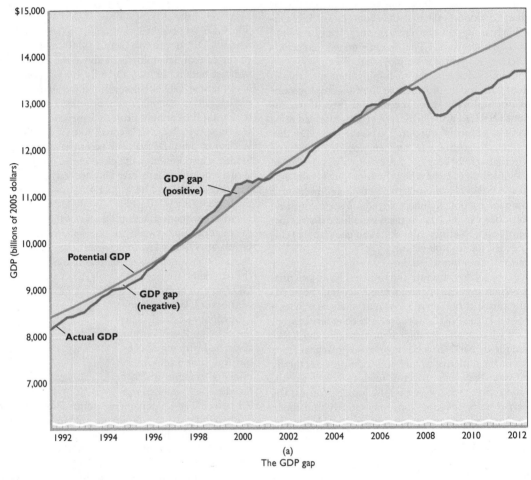

(a)
The GDP gap

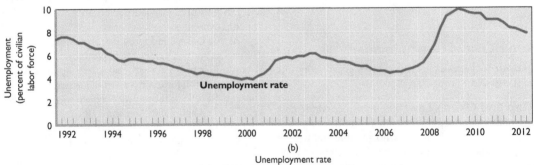

(b)
Unemployment rate

Source: Congressional Budget Office, **www.cbo.gov**; Bureau of Economic Analysis, **www.bea.gov**; and the Bureau of Labor Statistics, **www.bls.gov**. Note that the data for actual real GDP and potential real GDP above differ from the real GDP data in the previous two chapters. The data above are in 2005 dollars, not 2009 dollars, and do not reflect the 2013 redefinition of investment expenditures in the National Income and Product Accounts to include research and development spending.

TABLE 9.2 Unemployment Rates by Demographic Group: Full Employment Year (2007) and Recession Year (2009)*

Demographic Group	Unemployment Rate	
	2007	**2009**
Overall	4.6%	9.3%
Occupation:		
Managerial and professional	2.1	4.6
Construction and extraction	7.6	19.7
Age:		
16–19	15.7	24.3
African American, 16–19	29.4	39.5
White, 16–19	13.9	21.8
Male, 20+	4.1	9.6
Female, 20+	4.0	7.5
Race and ethnicity:		
African American	8.3	14.8
Hispanic	5.6	12.1
White	4.1	8.5
Gender:		
Women	4.5	8.1
Men	4.7	10.3
Education:†		
Less than high school diploma	7.1	14.6
High school diploma only	4.4	9.7
College degree or more	2.0	4.6
Duration:		
15 or more weeks	1.5	4.7

*Civilian labor-force data.

†People age 25 or over.

Source: Economic Report of the President; Bureau of Labor Statistics, **www.bls.gov**; Census Bureau, **www.census.gov**.

income were reduced proportionally. But this is not the case. Part of the burden of unemployment is that its cost is unequally distributed.

Table 9.2 examines unemployment rates for various labor market groups for 2 periods. In 2007, the economy achieved full employment, with a 4.6 percent unemployment rate. The economy receded in December 2007 and two years later was feeling the full unemployment impact of the Great Recession. By observing the large variance in unemployment rates for the different groups within each period and comparing the rates between the 2 periods, we can generalize as follows:

- *Occupation* Workers in lower-skilled occupations (for example, laborers) have higher unemployment rates than workers in higher-skilled occupations (for example, professionals). Lower-skilled workers have more and longer spells of structural unemployment than higher-skilled workers. They also are less likely to be

self-employed than are higher-skilled workers. Moreover, lower-skilled workers usually bear the brunt of recessions. Manufacturing, construction, and mining tend to be particularly hard-hit, and businesses generally retain most of their higher-skilled workers, in whom they have invested the expense of training.

- *Age* Teenagers have much higher unemployment rates than adults. Teenagers have lower skill levels, quit their jobs more frequently, are more frequently fired, and have less geographic mobility than adults. Many unemployed teenagers are new in the labor market, searching for their first jobs. Male African-American teenagers, in particular, have very high unemployment rates. The unemployment rate for all teenagers rises during recessions.

- *Race and ethnicity* The unemployment rates for African Americans and Hispanics are higher than that for whites. The causes of the higher rates include lower rates of educational attainment, greater concentration in lower-skilled occupations, and discrimination in the labor market. In general, the unemployment rate for African Americans is twice that of whites and rises by more percentage points than for whites during recessions.

- *Gender* The unemployment rates for men and women normally are very similar. But in the recent recession, the unemployment rate for men significantly exceeded that for women.

- *Education* Less-educated workers, on average, have higher unemployment rates than workers with more education. Less education is usually associated with lower-skilled, less-permanent jobs; more time between jobs; and jobs that are more vulnerable to cyclical layoff.

- *Duration* The number of persons unemployed for long periods—15 weeks or more—as a percentage of the labor force is much lower than the overall unemployment rate. But that percentage rises significantly during recessions. Notice from Table 9.2 that it rose from 1.5 percent of the labor force in 2007 to 4.7 percent in 2009.

Noneconomic Costs

Severe cyclical unemployment is more than an economic malady; it is a social catastrophe. Unemployment means idleness. And idleness means loss of skills, loss of self-respect, plummeting morale, family disintegration, and sociopolitical unrest. Widespread joblessness increases poverty, heightens racial and ethnic tensions, and reduces hope for material advancement.

History demonstrates that severe unemployment can lead to rapid and sometimes violent social and political change. Witness Hitler's ascent to power against a background of unemployment in Germany. Furthermore, relatively high unemployment among some racial and ethnic minorities has contributed to the unrest and violence that has periodically plagued some cities in the United States and abroad. At the individual level, research links increases in suicide, homicide, fatal heart attacks and strokes, and mental illness to high unemployment.

International Comparisons

Unemployment rates differ greatly among nations at any given time. One reason is that nations have different natural rates of unemployment. Another is that nations may be in different phases of their business cycles. Global Perspective 9.1 shows unemployment rates for five industrialized nations for the years 2002 through 2012. Between 2002 and 2008, the U.S. unemployment rate was considerably lower than the rates in Italy, France, and Germany. But during the Great Recession, U.S. unemployment spiked to the highest level among the five countries.

GLOBAL PERSPECTIVE 9.1

Unemployment Rates in Five Industrial Nations, 2002–2012

Compared with Italy, France, and Germany, the United States had a relatively low unemployment rate until the start of the 2007–2009 Great Recession, when the U.S. rate shot up to become the highest among the five nations.

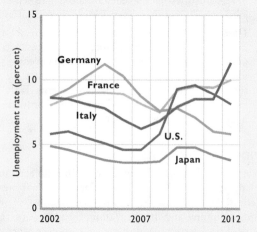

Source: Bureau of Labor Statistics, **www.bls.gov**. Based on U.S. unemployment concepts.

QUICK REVIEW 9.2

- Unemployment is of three general types: frictional, structural, and cyclical.
- The natural unemployment rate (frictional plus structural) is presently 5 to 6 percent in the United States.
- A positive GDP gap occurs when actual GDP exceeds potential GDP; a negative GDP gap occurs when actual GDP falls short of potential GDP.
- Society loses real GDP when cyclical unemployment occurs; according to Okun's law, for each 1 percentage point of unemployment above the natural rate, the U.S. economy suffers a 2 percent decline in real GDP below its potential GDP.
- Lower-skilled workers, teenagers, African Americans and Hispanics, and less-educated workers bear a disproportionate burden of unemployment.

Inflation

LO9.3 Explain how inflation is measured and distinguish between cost-push inflation and demand-pull inflation.

We now turn to inflation, another aspect of macroeconomic instability. The problems inflation poses are subtler than those posed by unemployment.

Meaning of Inflation

Inflation is a rise in the general level of prices. When inflation occurs, each dollar of income will buy fewer goods and services than before. Inflation reduces the "purchasing power" of money. But inflation does not mean that *all* prices are rising. Even during periods of rapid inflation, some prices may be relatively constant and others may even fall. For example, although the United States experienced high rates of inflation in the 1970s and early 1980s, the prices of video recorders, digital watches, and personal computers declined.

Measurement of Inflation

The main measure of inflation in the United States is the **Consumer Price Index (CPI),** compiled by the BLS. The government uses this index to report inflation rates each month and each year. It also uses the CPI to adjust Social Security benefits and income tax brackets for inflation. The CPI reports the price of a "market basket" of some 300 consumer goods and services that are purchased by a typical urban consumer. (The GDP price index of Chapter 7 is a much broader measure of inflation since it includes not only consumer goods and services but also capital goods, goods and services purchased by government, and goods and services that enter world trade.)

The composition of the market basket for the CPI is based on spending patterns of urban consumers in a specific period, presently 2009–2010. The BLS updates the composition of the market basket every 2 years so that it reflects the most recent patterns of consumer purchases and captures the inflation that consumers are currently experiencing. The BLS arbitrarily sets the CPI equal to 100 for 1982–1984. So the CPI for any particular year is found as follows:

$$\text{CPI} = \frac{\begin{array}{c}\text{price of the most recent market}\\ \text{basket in the particular year}\end{array}}{\begin{array}{c}\text{price estimate of the market}\\ \text{basket in 1982–1984}\end{array}} \times 100$$

The rate of inflation is equal to the percentage growth of CPI from one year to the next. For example, the CPI was 207.3 in 2007, up from 201.6 in 2006. So the rate of inflation for 2007 is calculated as follows:

$$\text{Rate of inflation} = \frac{207.3 - 201.6}{201.6} \times 100 = 2.8\%$$

In rare cases, the CPI declines from one year to the next. For example, the CPI fell from 215.3 in 2008 to 214.5 in 2009. The rate of inflation for 2009 therefore was −0.4 percent. Such price level declines are called **deflation.**

In Chapter 8, we discussed the mathematical approximation called *the rule of 70*, which tells us that we can find the number of years it will take for some measure to double, given its annual percentage increase, by dividing that percentage increase into the number 70. So a 3 percent annual rate of inflation will double the price level in about 23 (= 70 ÷ 3) years. Inflation of 8 percent per year will double the price level in about 9 (= 70 ÷ 8) years.

Facts of Inflation

Figure 9.4 shows December-to-December rates of annual inflation in the United States between 1960 and 2011. Observe that inflation reached double-digit rates in the 1970s and early 1980s but has since declined and has been relatively mild recently.

In recent years U.S. inflation has been neither unusually high nor low relative to inflation in several other industrial countries (see Global Perspective 9.2). Some nations (not shown) have had double-digit or even higher annual rates of inflation in recent years. In 2009, for example, the annual inflation rate in the Democratic Republic of Congo was 46 percent; Eritrea, 35 percent; Afghanistan, 31 percent; and Venezuela, 27 percent. Zimbabwe's inflation rate was 14.9 billion percent in 2008 before Zimbabwe did away with its existing currency.

Types of Inflation

Nearly all prices in the economy are set by supply and demand. Consequently, if the economy is experiencing inflation and the overall level of prices is rising, we need to look for an explanation in terms of supply and demand.

FIGURE 9.4 Annual inflation rates in the United States, 1960–2011 (December-to-December changes in the CPI). The major periods of inflation in the United States in the past 51 years were in the 1970s and 1980s.

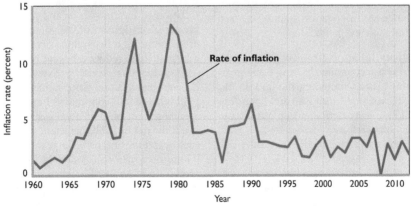

Source: Bureau of Labor Statistics, **www.bls.gov**.

GLOBAL PERSPECTIVE 9.2

Inflation Rates in Five Industrial Nations, 2002–2012

Inflation rates in the United States in recent years were neither extraordinarily high nor extraordinarily low relative to rates in other industrial nations.

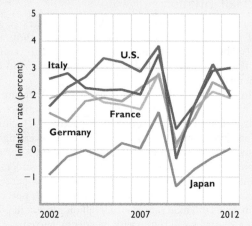

Source: World Economic Outlook Database, April 2013, International Monetary Fund, **www.imf.org.**

Demand-Pull Inflation Usually, increases in the price level are caused by an excess of total spending beyond the economy's capacity to produce. Where inflation is rapid and sustained, the cause invariably is an overissuance of money by the central bank (the Federal Reserve in the United States). When resources are already fully employed, the business sector cannot respond to excess demand by expanding output. So the excess demand bids up the prices of the limited output, producing **demand-pull inflation.** The essence of this type of inflation is "too much spending chasing too few goods."

Cost-Push Inflation Inflation also may arise on the supply, or cost, side of the economy. During some periods in U.S. economic history, including the mid-1970s, the price level increased even though total spending was not excessive. These were periods when output and employment were both *declining* (evidence that total spending was not excessive) while the general price level was *rising*.

The theory of **cost-push inflation** explains rising prices in terms of factors that raise **per-unit production costs** at each level of spending. A per-unit production cost is the average cost of a particular level of output. This average cost is found by dividing the total cost of all resource inputs by the amount of output produced. That is,

$$\text{Per-unit production cost} = \frac{\text{total input cost}}{\text{units of output}}$$

Rising per-unit production costs squeeze profits and reduce the amount of output firms are willing to supply at the existing price level. As a result, the economy's supply of goods and services declines and the price level rises. In this scenario, costs are *pushing* the price level upward, whereas in demand-pull inflation demand is *pulling* it upward.

The major source of cost-push inflation has been so-called *supply shocks*. Specifically, abrupt increases in the costs of raw materials or energy inputs have on occasion driven up per-unit production costs and thus product prices. The rocketing prices of imported oil in 1973–1974 and again in 1979–1980 are good illustrations. As energy prices surged upward during these periods, the costs of producing and transporting virtually every product in the economy rose. Cost-push inflation ensued.

Complexities

The real world is more complex than the distinction between demand-pull and cost-push inflation suggests. It is difficult to distinguish between demand-pull inflation and cost-push inflation unless the original source of inflation is known. For example, suppose a significant increase in total spending occurs in a fully employed economy, causing demand-pull inflation. But as the demand-pull stimulus works its way through various product and resource markets, individual firms find their wage costs, material costs, and fuel prices rising. From their perspective they must raise their prices because production costs (someone else's prices) have risen. Although this inflation is clearly demand-pull in origin, it may mistakenly appear to be cost-push inflation to business firms and to government. Without proper identification of the source of the inflation, government and the Federal Reserve may be slow to undertake policies to reduce excessive total spending.

Another complexity is that cost-push inflation and demand-pull inflation differ in their sustainability. Demand-pull inflation will continue as long as there is excess total spending. Cost-push inflation is automatically self-limiting; it will die out by itself. Increased per-unit costs will reduce supply, and this means lower real output and employment. Those decreases will constrain further per-unit cost increases. In other words, cost-push inflation generates a recession. And in a recession, households and businesses concentrate on keeping their resources employed, not on pushing up the prices of those resources.

Core Inflation

Another complication relating to inflation (regardless of type) is noteworthy. Some price-flexible items within the consumer price index—particularly, food and energy—experience rapid changes in supply and demand and therefore considerable price volatility from month to month and year to year. For example, the prices of grain, fruit, vegetables, and livestock sometimes move rapidly in one direction or the other, leading to sizable changes in the prices of food items such as bread, oranges, lettuce, and beef. Also, energy items such as gasoline and natural gas

can rise or fall rapidly from period to period. These ups and downs of food and energy prices usually are temporary and often cancel each other out over longer periods.

In tracking inflation, policymakers want to avoid being misled by rapid but temporary price changes that may distort the inflation picture. They mainly are interested in how rapidly the prices of the typically more stable components of the CPI are rising. By stripping volatile food and energy prices from the CPI, policymakers isolate so-called **core inflation,** the underlying increases in the CPI after volatile food and energy prices are removed.

If core inflation is low and stable, policymakers may be satisfied with current policy even though changes in the overall CPI index may be suggesting a rising rate of inflation. But policymakers become greatly concerned when core inflation is high and rising and take deliberate measures to try to halt it. We discuss these policies in later chapters.

Redistribution Effects of Inflation

LO9.4 Relate how unanticipated inflation can redistribute real income.

Inflation redistributes real income. This redistribution helps some people and hurts some others while leaving many people largely unaffected. Who gets hurt? Who benefits? Before we can answer, we need some terminology.

Nominal and Real Income There is a difference between money (or nominal) income and real income.

Nominal income is the number of dollars received as wages, rent, interest, or profit. **Real income** is a measure of the amount of goods and services nominal income can buy; it is the purchasing power of nominal income, or income adjusted for inflation. That is,

$$\text{Real income} = \frac{\text{nominal income}}{\text{price index (in hundredths)}}$$

Inflation need not alter an economy's overall real income—its total purchasing power. It is evident from the above equation that real income will remain the same when nominal income rises at the same percentage rate as does the price index.

But when inflation occurs, not everyone's nominal income rises at the same pace as the price level. Therein lies the potential for redistribution of real income from some to others. If the change in the price level differs from the change in a person's nominal income, his or her real income will be affected. The following approximation (shown by the ≅ sign) tells us roughly how much real income will change:

$$
\begin{array}{ccc}
\text{Percentage} & \text{percentage} & \text{percentage} \\
\text{change in} & \cong \text{change in} & - \text{change in} \\
\text{real income} & \text{nominal income} & \text{price level}
\end{array}
$$

For example, suppose that the price level rises by 6 percent in some period. If Bob's nominal income rises by 6 percent, his real income will *remain unchanged*. But if his nominal income instead rises by 10 percent, his real income will *increase* by about 4 percent. And if Bob's nominal income rises by only 2 percent, his real income will *decline* by about 4 percent.[1]

WORKED PROBLEMS

W9.3
Nominal and real income

Anticipations The redistribution effects of inflation depend upon whether or not it is expected. We will first discuss situations involving **unanticipated inflation.** As you will see, these cause real income and wealth to be

redistributed, harming some and benefiting others. We will then discuss situations involving **anticipated inflation.** These are situations in which people see an inflation coming in advance. With the ability to plan ahead, people are able to avoid or lessen the redistribution effects associated with inflation.

Who Is Hurt by Inflation?

Unanticipated inflation hurts fixed-income recipients, savers, and creditors. It redistributes real income away from them and toward others.

Fixed-Income Receivers People whose incomes are fixed see their real incomes fall when inflation occurs. The classic case is the elderly couple living on a private pension or annuity that provides a fixed amount of nominal income each month. They may have retired in, say, 1993 on what

CONSIDER THIS . . .

Could a Little Inflation Help Reduce Unemployment?

Economists have debated whether a little inflation—say two or three percent per year—might help to reduce the unemployment rate during recessions.

Proponents argue that a little inflation might have this beneficial effect by boosting firms' profits and their demand for labor. Their argument goes like this. If wages and other costs were to remained fixed while inflation increased the prices at which firms could sell their output, firms would see their profitability increase. That in turn would cause firms to want to hire more workers.

The economists who disagree argue that it is implausible to assume that wages and other costs would remain fixed while inflation drives up the price of output. They point out that wages and other costs may well rise as fast or possibly even faster than output prices rise. If so, firms would not see any increase in their profitability—and thus they would not see any reason to hire more workers.

In addition, the economists who disagree also point out that even if inflation did lower unemployment, it would do so at the cost of lowering real wages. That's because if wages stay fixed while output prices rise, workers' fixed paychecks would only be able to purchase a smaller amount of goods and services. So while more workers might have jobs, those with jobs would have a lower standard of living.

---

[1]A more precise calculation uses our equation for real income. In our first illustration above, if nominal income rises by 10 percent from $100 to $110 and the price level (index) rises by 6 percent from 100 to 106, then real income has increased as follows:

$$\frac{\$110}{1.06} = \$103.77$$

The 4 percent increase in real income shown by the simple formula in the text is a reasonable approximation of the 3.77 percent yielded by our more precise formula.

appeared to be an adequate pension. However, by 2009 they would have discovered that inflation had cut the annual purchasing power of that pension—their real income—by one-third.

Similarly, landlords who receive lease payments of fixed dollar amounts will be hurt by inflation as they receive dollars of declining value over time. Likewise, public sector workers whose incomes are dictated by fixed pay schedules may suffer from inflation. The fixed "steps" (the upward yearly increases) in their pay schedules may not keep up with inflation. Minimum-wage workers and families living on fixed welfare incomes also will be hurt by inflation.

Savers Unanticipated inflation hurts savers. As prices rise, the real value, or purchasing power, of an accumulation of savings deteriorates. Paper assets such as savings accounts, insurance policies, and annuities that were once adequate to meet rainy-day contingencies or provide for a comfortable retirement decline in real value during inflation. The simplest case is the person who hoards money as a cash balance. A $1,000 cash balance would have lost one-half its real value between 1985 and 2009. Of course, most forms of savings earn interest. But the value of savings will still decline if the rate of inflation exceeds the rate of interest.

Example: A household may save $1,000 in a certificate of deposit (CD) in a commercial bank or savings and loan association at 6 percent annual interest. But if inflation is 13 percent (as it was in 1980), the real value or purchasing power of that $1,000 will be cut to about $938 by the end of the year. Although the saver will receive $1,060 (equal to $1,000 plus $60 of interest), deflating that $1,060 for 13 percent inflation means that its real value is only about $938 (= $1,060 ÷ 1.13).

Creditors Unanticipated inflation harms creditors (lenders). Suppose Chase Bank lends Bob $1,000, to be repaid in 2 years. If in that time the price level doubles, the $1,000 that Bob repays will have only half the purchasing power of the $1,000 he borrowed. True, if we ignore interest charges, the same number of dollars will be repaid as was borrowed. But because of inflation, each of those dollars will buy only half as much as it did when the loan was negotiated. As prices go up, the purchasing power of the dollar goes down. So the borrower pays back less-valuable dollars than those received from the lender. The owners of Chase Bank suffer a loss of real income.

Who Is Unaffected or Helped by Inflation?

Some people are unaffected by inflation and others are actually helped by it. For the second group, inflation redistributes real income toward them and away from others.

Flexible-Income Receivers People who have flexible incomes may escape inflation's harm or even benefit from it. For example, individuals who derive their incomes solely from Social Security are largely unaffected by inflation because Social Security payments are *indexed* to the CPI. Benefits automatically increase when the CPI increases, preventing erosion of benefits from inflation. Some union workers also get automatic **cost-of-living adjustments (COLAs)** in their pay when the CPI rises, although such increases rarely equal the full percentage rise in inflation.

Some flexible-income receivers and all borrowers are helped by unanticipated inflation. The strong product demand and labor shortages implied by rapid demand-pull inflation may cause some nominal incomes to spurt ahead of the price level, thereby enhancing real incomes. For some, the 3 percent increase in nominal income that occurs when inflation is 2 percent may become a 7 percent increase when inflation is 5 percent. As an example, property owners faced with an inflation-induced real estate boom may be able to boost rents more rapidly than the rate of inflation. Also, some business owners may benefit from inflation. If product prices rise faster than resource prices, business revenues will increase more rapidly than costs. In those cases, the growth rate of profit incomes will outpace the rate of inflation.

Debtors Unanticipated inflation benefits debtors (borrowers). In our earlier example, Chase Bank's loss of real income from inflation is Bob's gain of real income. Debtor Bob borrows "dear" dollars but, because of inflation, pays back the principal and interest with "cheap" dollars whose purchasing power has been eroded by inflation. Real income is redistributed away from the owners of Chase Bank toward borrowers such as Bob.

The federal government, which had amassed $16.1 trillion of public debt through 2012, has also benefited from inflation. Historically, the federal government regularly paid off its loans by taking out new ones. Inflation permitted the Treasury to pay off its loans with dollars of less purchasing power than the dollars originally borrowed. Nominal national income and therefore tax collections rise with inflation; the amount of public debt owed does not. Thus, inflation reduces the real burden of the public debt to the federal government.

Anticipated Inflation

The redistribution effects of inflation are less severe or are eliminated altogether if people anticipate inflation and can adjust their nominal incomes to reflect the expected price-level rises. The prolonged inflation that began in the late 1960s prompted many labor unions in the 1970s to insist on labor contracts with cost-of-living adjustment clauses.

Similarly, if inflation is anticipated, the redistribution of income from lender to borrower may be altered. Suppose a lender (perhaps a commercial bank or a savings and loan institution) and a borrower (a household) both agree that 5 percent is a fair rate of interest on a 1-year loan provided the price level is stable. But assume that inflation has been occurring and is expected to be 6 percent over the next year. If the bank lends the household $100 at 5 percent interest, the bank will be paid back $105 at the end of the year. But if 6 percent inflation does occur during that year, the purchasing power of the $105 will have been reduced to about $99. The lender will, in effect, have paid the borrower $1 for the use of the lender's money for a year.

The lender can avoid this subsidy by charging an *inflation premium*—that is, by raising the interest rate by 6 percent, the amount of the anticipated inflation. By charging 11 percent, the lender will receive back $111 at the end of the year. Adjusted for the 6 percent inflation, that amount will have roughly the purchasing power of $105 worth of today's money. The result then will be a mutually agreeable transfer of purchasing power from borrower to lender of $5, or 5 percent, for the use of $100 for 1 year. Financial institutions have also developed variable-interest-rate mortgages to protect themselves from the adverse effects of inflation. (Incidentally, this example points out that, rather than being a *cause* of inflation, high nominal interest rates are a *consequence* of inflation.)

Our example reveals the difference between the real rate of interest and the nominal rate of interest. The **real interest rate** is the percentage increase in *purchasing power* that the borrower pays the lender. In our example the real interest rate is 5 percent. The **nominal interest rate** is the percentage increase in *money* that the borrower pays the lender, including that resulting from the built-in expectation of inflation, if any. In equation form:

Nominal interest rate = real interest rate +
inflation premium
(the expected rate of
inflation)

FIGURE 9.5 The inflation premium and nominal and real interest rates. The inflation premium—the expected rate of inflation—gets built into the nominal interest rate. Here, the nominal interest rate of 11 percent comprises the real interest rate of 5 percent plus the inflation premium of 6 percent.

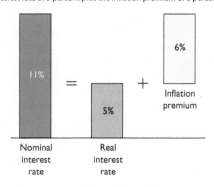

As illustrated in Figure 9.5, the nominal interest rate in our example is 11 percent.

Other Redistribution Issues

We end our discussion of the redistribution effects of inflation by making three final points:

- *Deflation* The effects of unanticipated deflation—declines in the price level—are the reverse of those of inflation. People with fixed nominal incomes will find their real incomes enhanced. Creditors will benefit at the expense of debtors. And savers will discover that the purchasing power of their savings has grown because of the falling prices.

- *Mixed effects* A person who is simultaneously an income earner, a holder of financial assets, and a debtor will probably find that the redistribution impact of unanticipated inflation is cushioned. If the person owns fixed-value monetary assets (savings accounts, bonds, and insurance policies), inflation will lessen their real value. But that same inflation may produce an increase in the person's nominal wage. Also, if the person holds a fixed-interest-rate mortgage, the real burden of that debt will decline. In short, many individuals are simultaneously hurt and helped by inflation. All these effects must be considered before we can conclude that any particular person's net position is better or worse because of inflation.

- *Arbitrariness* The redistribution effects of inflation occur regardless of society's goals and values. Inflation lacks a social conscience and takes from some and gives to others, whether they are rich, poor, young, old, healthy, or infirm.

Does Inflation Affect Output?

LO9.5 Discuss how inflation may affect the economy's level of real output.

Thus far, our discussion has focused on how inflation redistributes a specific level of total real income. But inflation also may affect an economy's level of real output (and thus its level of real income). The direction and significance of this effect on output depend on the type of inflation and its severity.

Cost-Push Inflation and Real Output

Recall that abrupt and unexpected rises in key resource prices such as oil can sufficiently drive up overall production costs to cause cost-push inflation. As prices rise, the quantity demanded of goods and services falls. So firms respond by producing less output, and unemployment goes up.

Economic events of the 1970s provide an example of how inflation can reduce real output. In late 1973 the Organization of Petroleum Exporting Countries (OPEC), by exerting its market power, managed to quadruple the price of oil. The cost-push inflationary effects generated rapid price-level increases in the 1973–1975 period. At the same time, the U.S. unemployment rate rose from slightly less than 5 percent in 1973 to 8.5 percent in 1975. Similar outcomes occurred in 1979–1980 in response to a second OPEC oil supply shock.

In short, cost-push inflation reduces real output. It redistributes a decreased level of real income.

Demand-Pull Inflation and Real Output

Economists do not fully agree on the effects of mild inflation (less than 3 percent) on real output. One perspective is that even low levels of inflation reduce real output because inflation diverts time and effort toward activities designed to hedge against inflation. Here are some examples of this:

- Businesses must incur the cost of changing thousands of prices on their shelves and in their computers simply to reflect inflation.
- Households and businesses must spend considerable time and effort obtaining the information they need to distinguish between real and nominal values such as prices, wages, and interest rates.
- To limit the loss of purchasing power from inflation, people try to limit the amount of money they hold in their billfolds and checking accounts at any one time and instead put more money into interest-bearing accounts and stock and bond funds. But cash and checks are needed in even greater amounts to buy the higher-priced goods and services. So more frequent trips, phone calls, or Internet visits to financial institutions are required to transfer funds to checking accounts and billfolds, when needed.

Without inflation, these uses of resources, time, and effort would not be needed, and they could be diverted toward producing more valuable goods and services. Proponents of "zero inflation" bolster their case by pointing to cross-country studies that indicate that lower rates of inflation are associated with higher rates of economic growth. Even mild inflation, say these economists, is detrimental to economic growth.

In contrast, other economists point out that full employment and economic growth depend on strong levels of total spending. Such spending creates high profits, strong demand for labor, and a powerful incentive for firms to expand their plants and equipment. In this view, the mild inflation that is a by-product of strong spending is a small price to pay for full employment and continued economic growth.

Moreover, a little inflation may have positive effects because it makes it easier for firms to adjust real wages downward when the demands for their products fall. With mild inflation, firms can reduce real wages by holding nominal wages steady. With zero inflation firms would need to cut nominal wages to reduce real wages. Such cuts in nominal wages are highly visible and may cause considerable worker resistance and labor strife.

Finally, defenders of mild inflation say that it is much better for an economy to err on the side of strong spending, full employment, economic growth, and mild inflation than on the side of weak spending, unemployment, recession, and deflation.

Unemployment after the Great Recession

Economists Have Been Vigorously Debating Why Employment Recovered So Slowly after the Great Recession of 2007–2009.

The Great Recession began in December 2007 and ended in June 2009. The downturn was the most severe since the Great Depression of the 1930s, with real GDP falling 4.3 percent from peak to trough. After growth returned in mid-2009, real GDP increased slowly, taking until July 2011 to pass its prerecession peak.

Employment showed a similar pattern of rapid decline followed by slow recovery: 8.7 million people lost their jobs after employment peaked in January 2008. Employment began to expand again in early 2010, but job growth was so slow that in December 2012—more than three years after the recession ended and more than a year after real GDP had passed its prerecession high—employment was still 3.4 million less than it had been at the start of the recession.

The recession also dramatically increased the average length of time that workers spent unemployed before finding a new job. The typical (median) spell of unemployment went from lasting 7.7 weeks in June 2007 to a peak of 24.8 weeks in June 2010. By way of comparison, the highest previous measurement for this statistic had been 12.3 weeks during the 1981–1982 recession. Thus, the Great Recession saw not only the loss of 8.7 million jobs, but unprecedentedly long wait times for unemployed workers to find new jobs.

When real GDP initially fell by 4.3 percent, it was easy to understand why employers might have shed 8.7 million jobs: Fewer workers were needed to produce less output. But after real GDP recovered fully and passed its prerecession peak, economists began to debate why employment was still millions of jobs lower than it had been before the recession began.

Here are a few of the possible culprits.

Hyperinflation

All economists agree that **hyperinflation,** which is extraordinarily rapid inflation, can have a devastating impact on real output and employment.

As prices shoot up sharply and unevenly during hyperinflation, people begin to anticipate even more rapid inflation and normal economic relationships are disrupted. Business owners do not know what to charge for their products. Consumers do not know what to pay. Resource suppliers want to be paid with actual output, rather than with rapidly depreciating money. Money eventually becomes almost worthless and ceases to do its job as a medium of exchange. Businesses, anticipating further price increases, may find that hoarding both materials and finished products is profitable. Individual savers may decide to buy nonproductive wealth—jewels,

gold and other precious metals, real estate, and so forth—rather than providing funds that can be borrowed to purchase capital equipment. The economy may be thrown into a state of barter, and production and exchange drop further. The net result is economic collapse and, often, political chaos.

Examples of hyperinflation are Germany after the First World War and Japan after the Second World War. In Germany, "prices increased so rapidly that waiters changed the prices on the menu several times during the course of a lunch. Sometimes customers had to pay double the price listed on the menu when they ordered."[2] In postwar Japan in 1947, "fisherman and farmers . . . used

---

[2]Theodore Morgan, *Income and Employment*, 2nd ed. (Englewood Cliffs, N.J.: Prentice Hall, 1952), p. 361.

Higher Federal Minimum Wage It is widely acknowledged that raising the minimum wage may increase unemployment by pricing low-productivity workers out of the labor market. Thus, one potential culprit for the slow recovery in employment was the July 2009 increase in the federal minimum wage from $6.55 to $7.25. But, at any given time, fewer than 3 percent of workers are employed at minimum-wage jobs. So it would be hard to blame the increase in the minimum wage for more than a very small fraction of the slow post-recession recovery in employment.

Longer Unemployment Benefits In November 2009, Congress decided to extend the maximum period of time that unemployed workers could draw unemployment benefits from 26 weeks to 99 weeks. That decision is believed by many economists to have affected a large enough fraction of unemployed workers to have contributed to the slow recovery in employment.

Congress had two intents when it extended the maximum draw period for unemployment benefits. The first was to help unemployed workers financially. The second was to help keep the economy moving by giving unemployed workers money to spend on goods and services.

One unintended consequence, however, was "inefficiently long search," meaning that many unemployed workers used the extended period during which they could survive on unemployment benefits to keep searching for perfect jobs even after they had been offered several so-so jobs. As a result, the unemployment rate stayed higher than it would have if benefits had continued to end after just 26 weeks and workers had felt financial pressure at an earlier date to accept so-so jobs rather than to keep on searching for perfect jobs.

Structural Adjustments Another explanation for the slow recovery in employment was that the economy required *structural adjustments*—changes in the basic structure of what was being produced and thus which industries needed workers. Consider the housing bubble that preceded the Great Recession. After the housing bubble collapsed, the economy needed to transition several million unemployed construction workers into other lines of work. Creating that many new jobs in other industries was going to take time. Thus, it was to be expected that employment was slow to recover after the recession ended.

Higher Labor Costs Other economists argued that worries about higher labor costs also contributed to the slow recovery in employment. In particular, they argued that several provisions of the 2010 health care reform law commonly known as Obamacare discouraged firms from hiring workers. One provision was an increase in the Medicare payroll tax. Another was the requirement that by 2014 any firm with more than 50 employees would have to provide health insurance coverage for all of its full-time workers.

That insurance provision was problematic because health insurance is very costly. In 2012, for example, the average cost for family coverage was $15,745 per worker. So, as the economy was making its way out of recession, it was the case that forward-looking employers may have reduced their hiring so as to have fewer full-time workers on the payroll when that provision of the law was scheduled to go into effect in 2014.

scales to weigh currency and change, rather than bothering to count it."[3]

There are also more recent examples: Between June 1986 and March 1991 the cumulative inflation in Nicaragua was 11,895,866,143 percent. From November 1993 to December 1994 the cumulative inflation rate in the Democratic Republic of Congo was 69,502 percent. From February 1993 to January 1994 the cumulative inflation rate in Serbia was 156,312,790 percent.[4]

Such dramatic hyperinflations are always the consequence of highly imprudent expansions of the money supply by government. The rocketing money supply produces frenzied total spending and severe demand-pull inflation. Zimbabwe's 14.9 billion percent inflation in 2008 is just the latest example.

> **QUICK REVIEW 9.5**
>
> - Cost-push inflation reduces real output and employment.
> - Economists argue about the effects of demand-pull inflation. Some argue that even mild demand-pull inflation (1 to 3 percent) reduces the economy's real output. Other say that mild inflation may be a necessary by-product of the high and growing spending that produces high levels of output, full employment, and economic growth.
> - Hyperinflation, caused by highly imprudent expansions of the money supply, may undermine the monetary system and cause severe declines in real output.

[3]Raburn M. Williams, *Inflation! Money, Jobs, and Politicians* (Arlington Heights, Ill.: AHM Publishing, 1980), p. 2.
[4]Stanley Fischer, Ratna Sahay, and Carlos Végh, "Modern Hyper- and High Inflations," *Journal of Economic Literature*, September 2002, p. 840.

SUMMARY

LO9.1 Describe the business cycle and its primary phases.

The United States and other industrial economies have gone through periods of fluctuations in real GDP, employment, and the price level. Although they have certain phases in common—peak, recession, trough, expansion—business cycles vary greatly in duration and intensity.

Although economists explain the business cycle in terms of underlying causal factors such as major innovations, productivity shocks, money creation, and financial crises, they generally agree that changes in the level of total spending are the immediate causes of fluctuating real output and employment.

The business cycle affects all sectors of the economy, though in varying ways and degrees. The cycle has greater effects on output and employment in the capital goods and durable consumer goods industries than in the services and nondurable goods industries.

LO9.2 Illustrate how unemployment is measured and explain the different types of unemployment.

Economists distinguish between frictional, structural, and cyclical unemployment. The full-employment or natural rate of unemployment, which is made up of frictional and structural unemployment, is currently between 5 and 6 percent. The presence of part-time and discouraged workers makes it difficult to measure unemployment accurately.

The GDP gap, which can be either a positive or a negative value, is found by subtracting potential GDP from actual GDP. The economic cost of unemployment, as measured by the GDP gap, consists of the goods and services forgone by society when its resources are involuntarily idle. Okun's law suggests that every 1-percentage-point increase in unemployment above the natural rate causes an additional 2 percent negative GDP gap.

LO9.3 Explain how inflation is measured and distinguish between cost-push inflation and demand-pull inflation.

Inflation is a rise in the general price level and is measured in the United States by the Consumer Price Index (CPI). When inflation occurs, each dollar of income will buy fewer goods and services than before. That is, inflation reduces the purchasing power of money. Deflation is a decline in the general price level.

Unemployment rates and inflation rates vary widely globally. Unemployment rates differ because nations have different natural rates of unemployment and often are in different phases of their business cycles. Inflation and unemployment rates in the United States recently have been in the middle to low range compared with rates in other industrial nations.

Economists discern both demand-pull and cost-push (supply-side) inflation. Demand-pull inflation results from an excess of total spending relative to the economy's capacity to produce. The main source of cost-push inflation is abrupt and rapid increases in the prices of key resources. These supply shocks push up per-unit production costs and ultimately raise the prices of consumer goods.

LO9.4 Relate how unanticipated inflation can redistribute real income.

Unanticipated inflation arbitrarily redistributes real income at the expense of fixed-income receivers, creditors, and savers. If inflation is anticipated, individuals and businesses may be able to take steps to lessen or eliminate adverse redistribution effects.

When inflation is anticipated, lenders add an inflation premium to the interest rate charged on loans. The nominal interest rate thus reflects the real interest rate plus the inflation premium (the expected rate of inflation).

LO9.5 Discuss how inflation may affect the economy's level of real output.

Cost-push inflation reduces real output and employment. Proponents of zero inflation argue that even mild demand-pull inflation (1 to 3 percent) reduces the economy's real output. Other economists say that mild inflation may be a necessary by-product of the high and growing spending that produces high levels of output, full employment, and economic growth.

Hyperinflation, caused by highly imprudent expansions of the money supply, may undermine the monetary system and cause severe declines in real output.

TERMS AND CONCEPTS

business cycles	frictional unemployment	inflation
peak	structural unemployment	Consumer Price Index (CPI)
recession	cyclical unemployment	deflation
trough	full-employment rate of unemployment	demand-pull inflation
expansion	natural rate of unemployment (NRU)	cost-push inflation
labor force	potential output	per-unit production costs
unemployment rate	GDP gap	core inflation
discouraged workers	Okun's law	nominal income

real income   cost-of-living adjustments (COLAs)   nominal interest rate

unanticipated inflation   real interest rate   hyperinflation

anticipated inflation

The following and additional problems can be found in connect

DISCUSSION QUESTIONS

1. What are the four phases of the business cycle? How long do business cycles last? Why does the business cycle affect output and employment in capital goods industries and consumer durable goods industries more severely than in industries producing consumer nondurables? **LO9.1**

2. How, in general, can a financial crisis lead to a recession? How, in general, can a major new invention lead to an expansion? **LO9.1**

3. How is the labor force defined and who measures it? How is the unemployment rate calculated? Does an increase in the unemployment rate necessarily mean a decline in the size of the labor force? Why is a positive unemployment rate—one more than zero percent—fully compatible with full employment? **LO9.2**

4. How, in general, do unemployment rates vary by race and ethnicity, gender, occupation, and education? Why does the average length of time people are unemployed rise during a recession? **LO9.2**

5. Why is it difficult to distinguish between frictional, structural, and cyclical unemployment? Why is unemployment an economic problem? What are the consequences of a negative GDP gap? What are the noneconomic effects of unemployment? **LO9.2**

6. Because the United States has an unemployment compensation program that provides income for those out of work, why should we worry about unemployment? **LO9.2**

7. What is the Consumer Price Index (CPI) and how is it determined each month? How does the Bureau of Labor Statistics calculate the rate of inflation from one year to the next? What effect does inflation have on the purchasing power of a dollar? How does it explain differences between nominal and real interest rates? How does deflation differ from inflation? **LO9.3**

8. Distinguish between demand-pull inflation and cost-push inflation. Which of the two types is most likely to be associated with a negative GDP gap? Which with a positive GDP gap, in which actual GDP exceeds potential GDP? What is core inflation? Why is it calculated? **LO9.3**

9. Explain how an increase in your nominal income and a decrease in your real income might occur simultaneously. Who loses from inflation? Who gains? **LO9.4**

10. Explain how hyperinflation might lead to a severe decline in total output. **LO9.5**

11. **LAST WORD** Why was the 2009 hike in the minimum wage probably not responsible for much of the slow growth in employment after the Great Recession? What is inefficiently long search and how is it affected by the duration of unemployment benefits? How might Obamacare have discouraged hiring?

REVIEW QUESTIONS

1. Place the phases of the business cycle in order. **LO9.1**
   Recession
   Trough
   Peak
   Expansion

2. Most economists agree that the immediate cause of the large majority of cyclical changes in the levels of real output and employment is unexpected changes in _____. **LO9.1**
   a. The level of total spending.
   b. The level of the stock market.
   c. The level of the trade deficit.
   d. The level of unemployment.

3. Suppose that an economy has 9 million people working full-time. It also has 1 million people who are actively seeking work but currently unemployed as well as 2 million discouraged workers who have given up looking for work and are currently unemployed. What is this economy's unemployment rate? **LO9.2**
   a. 10 percent.
   b. 15 percent.
   c. 20 percent.
   d. 25 percent.

4. Label each of the following scenarios as either frictional unemployment, structural unemployment, or cyclical unemployment. **LO9.2**
   a. Tim just graduated and is looking for a job.
   b. A recession causes a local factory to lay off 30 workers.
   c. Thousands of bus and truck drivers permanently lose their jobs when driverless, computer-driven vehicles make human drivers redundant.
   d. Hundreds of New York legal jobs permanently disappear when a lot of legal work gets outsourced to lawyers in India.

5. The unemployment rate that is consistent with full employment is known as _____. **LO9.2**
   a. The natural rate of unemployment.
   b. The unnatural rate of unemployment.
   c. The status quo rate of unemployment.
   d. Cyclical unemployment.
   e. Okun's rate of unemployment.

6. A country's current unemployment rate is 11 percent. Economists estimate that its natural rate of unemployment is 6 percent. About how large is this economy's negative GDP gap? **LO9.2**
   a. 1 percent.
   b. 3 percent.
   c. 6 percent.
   d. 10 percent.

7. Cost-push inflation occurs when there is _____. **LO9.3**
   a. Excess inventory.
   b. A trade deficit.
   c. Rising per-unit production costs.
   d. Excess demand for goods and services.

8. Jimmer's nominal income will go up by 10 percent next year. Inflation is expected to be −2 percent next year. By approximately how much will Jimmer's real income change next year? **LO9.3**
   a. −2 percent.
   b. 8 percent.
   c. 10 percent.
   d. 12 percent.

9. Kaitlin has $10,000 of savings that she may deposit with her local bank. Kaitlin wants to earn a real rate of return of at least 4 percent and she is expecting inflation to be exactly 3 percent. What is the lowest nominal interest rate that Kaitlin would be willing to accept from her local bank? **LO9.4**
   a. 4 percent.
   b. 5 percent.
   c. 6 percent.
   d. 7 percent.

10. True or False: Lenders are helped by unanticipated inflation. **LO9.4**

11. Economists agree that _____ inflation reduces real output. **LO9.5**
    a. Cost-push.
    b. Demand-pull.
    c. Push-pull.

PROBLEMS

1. Suppose that a country's annual growth rates were 5, 3, 4, −1, −2, 2, 3, 4, 6, and 3 in yearly sequence over a 10-year period. What was the country's trend rate of growth over this period? Which set of years most clearly demonstrates an expansionary phase of the business cycle? Which set of years best illustrates a recessionary phase of the business cycle? **LO9.1**

2. Assume the following data for a country: total population, 500; population under 16 years of age or institutionalized, 120; not in labor force, 150; unemployed, 23; part-time workers looking for full-time jobs, 10. What is the size of the labor force? What is the official unemployment rate? **LO9.2**

3. Suppose that the natural rate of unemployment in a particular year is 5 percent and the actual rate of unemployment is 9 percent. Use Okun's law to determine the size of the GDP gap in percentage-point terms. If the potential GDP is $500 billion in that year, how much output is being forgone because of cyclical unemployment? **LO9.2**

4. If the CPI was 110 last year and is 121 this year, what is this year's rate of inflation? In contrast, suppose that the CPI was 110 last year and is 108 this year. What is this year's rate of inflation? What term do economists use to describe this second outcome? **LO9.3**

5. How long would it take for the price level to double if inflation persisted at (*a*) 2 percent per year, (*b*) 5 percent per year, and (*c*) 10 percent per year? **LO9.3**

6. If your nominal income rose by 5.3 percent and the price level rose by 3.8 percent in some year, by what percentage would your real income (approximately) increase? If your nominal income rose by 2.8 percent and your real income rose by 1.1 percent in some year, what must have been the (approximate) rate of inflation? **LO9.4**

7. Suppose that the nominal rate of inflation is 4 percent and the inflation premium is 2 percent. What is the real interest rate? Alternatively, assume that the real interest rate is 1 percent and the nominal interest rate is 6 percent. What is the inflation premium? **LO9.4**

FURTHER TEST YOUR KNOWLEDGE AT www.mcconnell20e.com

CHAPTER **12**

Aggregate Demand and Aggregate Supply

Learning Objectives

LO12.1 Define aggregate demand (AD) and explain how its downward slope is the result of the real-balances effect, the interest-rate effect, and the foreign purchases effect.

LO12.2 Explain the factors that cause changes (shifts) in AD.

LO12.3 Define aggregate supply (AS) and explain how it differs in the immediate short run, the short run, and the long run.

LO12.4 Explain the factors that cause changes (shifts) in AS.

LO12.5 Discuss how AD and AS determine an economy's equilibrium price level and level of real GDP.

LO12.6 Describe how the AD-AS model explains periods of demand-pull inflation, cost-push inflation, and recession.

LO12.7 (Appendix) Identify how the aggregate demand curve relates to the aggregate expenditures model.

During the recession of 2007–2009, the economic terms *aggregate demand* and *aggregate supply* moved from the obscurity of economic journals and textbooks to the spotlight of national newspapers, Web sites, radio, and television.

The media and public asked: Why had *aggregate demand* declined, producing the deepest recession and highest rate of unemployment since 1982? Why hadn't the reductions in interest rates by the Federal Reserve boosted *aggregate demand*? Would the federal government's $787 billion stimulus package increase *aggregate demand* and reduce unemployment, as intended? Would a resurgence of oil prices and other energy prices reduce *aggregate supply,* choking off an economic expansion?

Aggregate demand and aggregate supply are the featured elements of the **aggregate demand–aggregate supply model (AD-AS model),** the focus of this chapter. The aggregate expenditures model of the previous chapter is an immediate-short-run model, in which prices are assumed to be fixed. In contrast, the AD-AS model in this chapter is a "variable price–variable output" model that allows both the price level and level of real GDP to change. It can also show longer time horizons, distinguishing between the immediate short run, the short run, and the long run. Further, in subsequent chapters, we will see that the AD-AS model easily depicts fiscal and monetary policies such as those used in 2008 and 2009 to try to halt the downward slide of the economy and promote its recovery.

Aggregate Demand

LO12.1 Define aggregate demand (AD) and explain how its downward slope is the result of the real-balances effect, the interest-rate effect, and the foreign purchases effect.

Aggregate demand is a schedule or curve that shows the amount of a nation's output (real GDP) that buyers collectively desire to purchase at each possible price level. These buyers include the nation's households, businesses, and government along with consumers located abroad (households, businesses, and governments in other nations). The relationship between the price level (as measured by the GDP price index) and the amount of real GDP demanded is inverse or negative: When the price level rises, the quantity of real GDP demanded decreases; when the price level falls, the quantity of real GDP demanded increases.

Aggregate Demand Curve

The inverse relationship between the price level and real GDP is shown in Figure 12.1, where the aggregate demand curve AD slopes downward, as does the demand curve for an individual product.

Why the downward slope? The explanation is *not* the same as that for why the demand for a single product slopes downward. That explanation centered on the income effect and the substitution effect. When the price of an *individual* product falls, the consumer's (constant) nominal income allows a larger purchase of the product (the income effect). And, as price falls, the consumer wants to buy more of the product because it becomes relatively less expensive than other goods (the substitution effect).

FIGURE 12.1 The aggregate demand curve. The downsloping aggregate demand curve AD indicates an inverse (or negative) relationship between the price level and the amount of real output purchased.

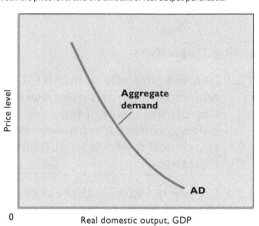

But these explanations do not work for aggregates. In Figure 12.1, when the economy moves down its aggregate demand curve, it moves to a lower general price level. But our circular flow model tells us that when consumers pay lower prices for goods and services, less nominal income flows to resource suppliers in the form of wages, rents, interest, and profits. As a result, a decline in the price level does not necessarily mean an increase in the nominal income of the economy as a whole. Thus, a decline in the price level need not produce an income effect, where more output is purchased because lower nominal prices leave buyers with greater real income.

Similarly, in Figure 12.1, prices in general are falling as we move down the aggregate demand curve, so the rationale for the substitution effect (where more of a specific product is purchased because it becomes cheaper relative to all other products) is not applicable. There is no *overall* substitution effect among domestically produced goods when the price level falls.

If the conventional substitution and income effects do not explain the downward slope of the aggregate demand curve, what does? The explanation rests on three effects of a price-level change.

Real-Balances Effect A change in the price level produces a **real-balances effect**. Here is how it works: A higher price level reduces the real value or purchasing power of the public's accumulated savings balances. In particular, the real value of assets with fixed money values,

such as savings accounts or bonds, diminishes. Because a higher price level erodes the purchasing power of such assets, the public is poorer in real terms and will reduce its spending. A household might buy a new car or a plasma TV if the purchasing power of its financial asset balances is, say, $50,000. But if inflation erodes the purchasing power of its asset balances to $30,000, the household may defer its purchase. So a higher price level means less consumption spending.

Interest-Rate Effect The aggregate demand curve also slopes downward because of the **interest-rate effect**. When we draw an aggregate demand curve, we assume that the supply of money in the economy is fixed. But when the price level rises, consumers need more money for purchases and businesses need more money to meet their payrolls and to buy other resources. A $10 bill will do when the price of an item is $10, but a $10 bill plus a $1 bill is needed when the item costs $11. In short, a higher price level increases the demand for money. So, given a fixed supply of money, an increase in money demand will drive up the price paid for its use. That price is the interest rate.

Higher interest rates curtail investment spending and interest-sensitive consumption spending. Firms that expect a 6 percent rate of return on a potential purchase of capital will find that investment potentially profitable when the interest rate is, say, 5 percent. But the investment will be unprofitable and will not be made when the interest rate has risen to 7 percent. Similarly, consumers may decide not

to purchase a new house or new automobile when the interest rate on loans goes up. So, by increasing the demand for money and consequently the interest rate, a higher price level reduces the amount of real output demanded.

Foreign Purchases Effect The final reason why the aggregate demand curve slopes downward is the **foreign purchases effect**. When the U.S. price level rises relative to foreign price levels (and exchange rates do not respond quickly or completely), foreigners buy fewer U.S. goods and Americans buy more foreign goods. Therefore, U.S. exports fall and U.S. imports rise. In short, the rise in the price level reduces the quantity of U.S. goods demanded as net exports.

These three effects, of course, work in the opposite direction for a decline in the price level. A decline in the price level increases consumption through the real-balances effect and interest-rate effect; increases investment through the interest-rate effect; and raises net exports by increasing exports and decreasing imports through the foreign purchases effect.

Changes in Aggregate Demand

LO12.2 Explain the factors that cause changes (shifts) in AD. Other things equal, a change in the price level will change the amount of aggregate spending and therefore change the amount of real GDP demanded by the economy. Movements along a fixed aggregate demand curve represent these changes in real GDP. However, if one or more of those "other things" change, the entire aggregate demand curve will shift. We call these other things **determinants of aggregate demand** or, less formally, *aggregate demand shifters*. They are listed in Figure 12.2.

Changes in aggregate demand involve two components:

- A change in one of the determinants of aggregate demand that directly changes the amount of real GDP demanded.

- A multiplier effect that produces a greater ultimate change in aggregate demand than the initiating change in spending.

In Figure 12.2, the full rightward shift of the curve from AD$_1$ to AD$_2$ shows an increase in aggregate demand, separated into these two components. The horizontal distance between AD$_1$ and the broken curve to its right illustrates an initial increase in spending, say, $5 billion of added investment. If the economy's MPC is 0.75, for example, then the simple multiplier is 4. So the aggregate demand curve shifts rightward from AD$_1$ to AD$_2$—four times the distance between AD$_1$ and the broken line. The multiplier process magnifies the initial change in spending into successive

FIGURE 12.2 Changes in aggregate demand. A change in one or more of the listed determinants of aggregate demand will shift the aggregate demand curve. The rightward shift from AD$_1$ to AD$_2$ represents an increase in aggregate demand; the leftward shift from AD$_1$ to AD$_3$ shows a decrease in aggregate demand. The vertical distances between AD$_1$ and the dashed lines represent the initial changes in spending. Through the multiplier effect, that spending produces the full shifts of the curves.

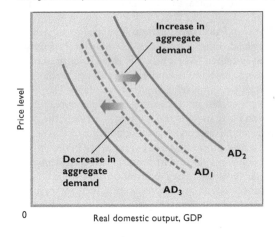

Determinants of Aggregate Demand: Factors That Shift the Aggregate Demand Curve

1. Change in consumer spending
   a. Consumer wealth
   b. Consumer expectations
   c. Household borrowing
   d. Taxes
2. Change in investment spending
   a. Interest rates
   b. Expected returns
      • Expected future business conditions
      • Technology
      • Degree of excess capacity
      • Business taxes
3. Change in government spending
4. Change in net export spending
   a. National income abroad
   b. Exchange rates

rounds of new consumption spending. After the shift, $20 billion (= $5 × 4) of additional real goods and services are demanded at each price level.

Similarly, the leftward shift of the curve from AD$_1$ to AD$_3$ shows a decrease in aggregate demand, the lesser amount of real GDP demanded at each price level. It also involves the initial decline in spending (shown as the horizontal distance between AD$_1$ and the dashed line to its left), followed by multiplied declines in consumption spending and the ultimate leftward shift to AD$_3$.

Let's examine each of the determinants of aggregate demand listed in Figure 12.2.

Consumer Spending

Even when the U.S. price level is constant, domestic consumers may alter their purchases of U.S.-produced real output. If those consumers decide to buy more output at each price level, the aggregate demand curve will shift to the right, as from AD$_1$ to AD$_2$ in Figure 12.2. If they decide to buy less output, the aggregate demand curve will shift to the left, as from AD$_1$ to AD$_3$.

Several factors other than a change in the price level may change consumer spending and therefore shift the aggregate demand curve. As Figure 12.2 shows, those factors are real consumer wealth, consumer expectations, household debt, and taxes. Because our discussion here parallels that of Chapter 10, we will be brief.

Consumer Wealth Consumer wealth is the total dollar value of all assets owned by consumers in the economy less the dollar value of their liabilities (debts). Assets include stocks, bonds, and real estate. Liabilities include mortgages, car loans, and credit card balances.

Consumer wealth sometimes changes suddenly and unexpectedly due to surprising changes in asset values. An unforeseen increase in the stock market is a good example. The increase in wealth prompts pleasantly surprised consumers to save less and buy more out of their current incomes than they had previously been planning. The resulting increase in consumer spending—the so-called *wealth effect*—shifts the aggregate demand curve to the right. In contrast, an unexpected decline in asset values will cause an unanticipated reduction in consumer wealth at each price level. As consumers tighten their belts in response to the bad news, a "reverse wealth effect" sets in. Unpleasantly surprised consumers increase savings and reduce consumption, thereby shifting the aggregate demand curve to the left.

Household Borrowing Consumers can increase their consumption spending by borrowing. Doing so shifts the aggregate demand curve to the right. By contrast, a decrease in borrowing for consumption purposes shifts the aggregate demand curve to the left. The aggregate demand curve will also shift to the left if consumers increase their savings rates to pay off their debts. With more money flowing to debt repayment, consumption expenditures decline and the AD curve shifts left.

Consumer Expectations Changes in expectations about the future may alter consumer spending. When people expect their future real incomes to rise, they tend to spend more of their current incomes. Thus, current consumption spending increases (current saving falls) and the aggregate demand curve shifts to the right. Similarly, a widely held expectation of surging inflation in the near future may increase aggregate demand today because consumers will want to buy products before their prices escalate. Conversely, expectations of lower future income or lower future prices may reduce current consumption and shift the aggregate demand curve to the left.

Personal Taxes A reduction in personal income tax rates raises take-home income and increases consumer purchases at each possible price level. Tax cuts shift the aggregate demand curve to the right. Tax increases reduce consumption spending and shift the curve to the left.

Investment Spending

Investment spending (the purchase of capital goods) is a second major determinant of aggregate demand. A decline in investment spending at each price level will shift the aggregate demand curve to the left. An increase in investment spending will shift it to the right. In Chapter 10 we saw that investment spending depends on the real interest rate and the expected return from investment.

Real Interest Rates Other things equal, an increase in real interest rates will raise borrowing costs, lower investment spending, and reduce aggregate demand. We are not referring here to the "interest-rate effect" that results from a change in the price level. Instead, we are identifying a change in the real interest rate resulting from, say, a change in a nation's money supply. An increase in the money supply lowers the interest rate, thereby increasing investment and aggregate demand. A decrease in the money supply raises the interest rate, reducing investment and decreasing aggregate demand.

Expected Returns Higher expected returns on investment projects will increase the demand for capital goods and shift the aggregate demand curve to the right. Alternatively, declines in expected returns will decrease investment and shift the curve to the left. Expected returns, in turn, are influenced by several factors:

- *Expectations about future business conditions* If firms are optimistic about future business conditions, they are more likely to forecast high rates of return

on current investment and therefore may invest more today. On the other hand, if they think the economy will deteriorate in the future, they will forecast low rates of return and perhaps will invest less today.

- *Technology* New and improved technologies enhance expected returns on investment and thus increase aggregate demand. For example, recent advances in microbiology have motivated pharmaceutical companies to establish new labs and production facilities.

- *Degree of excess capacity* A rise in excess capacity—unused capital—will reduce the expected return on new investment and hence decrease aggregate demand. Other things equal, firms operating factories at well below capacity have little incentive to build new factories. But when firms discover that their excess capacity is dwindling or has completely disappeared, their expected returns on new investment in factories and capital equipment rise. Thus, they increase their investment spending, and the aggregate demand curve shifts to the right.

- *Business taxes* An increase in business taxes will reduce after-tax profits from capital investment and lower expected returns. So investment and aggregate demand will decline. A decrease in business taxes will have the opposite effects.

The variability of interest rates and expected returns makes investment highly volatile. In contrast to consumption, investment spending rises and falls often, independent of changes in total income. Investment, in fact, is the least stable component of aggregate demand.

Government Spending

Government purchases are the third determinant of aggregate demand. An increase in government purchases (for example, more transportation projects) will shift the aggregate demand curve to the right, as long as tax collections and interest rates do not change as a result. In contrast, a reduction in government spending (for example, less military equipment) will shift the curve to the left.

Net Export Spending

The final determinant of aggregate demand is net export spending. Other things equal, higher U.S. *exports* mean an increased foreign demand for U.S. goods. So a rise in net exports (higher exports relative to imports) shifts the aggregate demand curve to the right. In contrast, a decrease in U.S. net exports shifts the aggregate demand curve leftward. (These changes in net exports are *not* those prompted by a change in the U.S. price level—those associated with the foreign purchases effect. The changes here are shifts of the AD curve, not movements along the AD curve.)

What might cause net exports to change, other than the price level? Two possibilities are changes in national income abroad and changes in exchange rates.

National Income Abroad Rising national income abroad encourages foreigners to buy more products, some of which are made in the United States. U.S. net exports thus rise, and the U.S. aggregate demand curve shifts to the right. Declines in national income abroad do the opposite: They reduce U.S. net exports and shift the U.S. aggregate demand curve to the left.

Exchange Rates Changes in the dollar's exchange rate—the price of foreign currencies in terms of the U.S. dollar—may affect U.S. exports and therefore aggregate demand. Suppose the dollar depreciates in terms of the euro (meaning the euro appreciates in terms of the dollar). The new, relatively lower value of dollars and higher value of euros enables European consumers to obtain more dollars with each euro. From their perspective, U.S. goods are now less expensive; it takes fewer euros to obtain them. So European consumers buy more U.S. goods, and U.S. exports rise. But American consumers can now obtain fewer euros for each dollar. Because they must pay more dollars to buy European goods, Americans reduce their imports. U.S. exports rise and U.S. imports fall. Conclusion: Dollar depreciation increases net exports (imports go down; exports go up) and therefore increases aggregate demand.

Dollar appreciation has the opposite effects: Net exports fall (imports go up; exports go down) and aggregate demand declines.

QUICK REVIEW 12.1

- Aggregate demand reflects an inverse relationship between the price level and the amount of real output demanded.

- Changes in the price level create real-balances, interest-rate, and foreign purchases effects that explain the downward slope of the aggregate demand curve.

- Changes in one or more of the determinants of aggregate demand (Figure 12.2) alter the amounts of real GDP demanded at each price level; they shift the aggregate demand curve. The multiplier effect magnifies initial changes in spending into larger changes in aggregate demand.

- An increase in aggregate demand is shown as a rightward shift of the aggregate demand curve; a decrease, as a leftward shift of the curve.

Aggregate Supply

LO12.3 Define aggregate supply (AS) and explain how it differs in the immediate short run, the short run, and the long run.

Aggregate supply is a schedule or curve showing the relationship between a nation's price level and the amount of real domestic output that firms in the economy produce. This relationship varies depending on the time horizon and how quickly output prices and input prices can change. We will define three time horizons:

- In the *immediate short run*, both input prices as well as output prices are fixed.
- In the *short run*, input prices are fixed, but output prices can vary.
- In the *long run*, input prices as well as output prices can vary.

In Chapter 6, we discussed both the immediate short run and the long run in terms of how an automobile maker named Buzzer Auto responds to changes in the demand for its new car, the Prion. Here we extend the logic of that chapter to the economy as a whole to discuss how total output varies with the price level in the immediate short run, the short run, and the long run. As you will see, the relationship between the price level and total output is different in each of the three time horizons because input prices are stickier than output prices. Although both sets of prices become more flexible as time passes, output prices usually adjust more rapidly.

Aggregate Supply in the Immediate Short Run

Depending on the type of firm, the immediate short run can last anywhere from a few days to a few months. It lasts as long as *both* input prices and output prices stay fixed. Input prices are fixed in both the immediate short run and the short run by contractual agreements. In particular, 75 percent of the average firm's costs are wages and salaries—and these are almost always fixed by labor contracts for months or years at a time. As a result, they are usually fixed for a much longer duration than output prices, which can begin to change within a few days or a few months depending on the type of firm.

That being said, output prices are also typically fixed in the immediate short run. This is most often caused by firms setting fixed prices for their customers and then agreeing to supply whatever quantity demanded results at those fixed prices. For instance, once an appliance manufacturer sets its annual list prices for refrigerators, stoves,

FIGURE 12.3 Aggregate supply in the immediate short run. In the immediate short run, the aggregate supply curve AS_{ISR} is horizontal at the economy's current price level, P_1. With output prices fixed, firms collectively supply the level of output that is demanded at those prices.

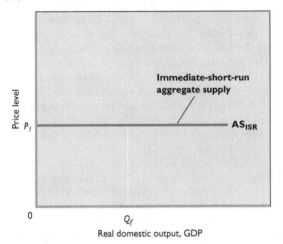

Aggregate Supply in the Short Run

The short run begins after the immediate short run ends. As it relates to macroeconomics, the short run is a period of time during which output prices are flexible, but input prices are either totally fixed or highly inflexible.

These assumptions about output prices and input prices are general—they relate to the economy in the aggregate. Naturally, some input prices are more flexible than others. Since gasoline prices are quite flexible, a package delivery firm like UPS that uses gasoline as an input will have at least one very flexible input price. On the other hand, wages at UPS are set by five-year labor contracts negotiated with its drivers' union, the Teamsters. Because wages are the firm's largest and most important input cost, UPS faces overall input prices that are inflexible for several years at a time. Thus, its "short run"—the period when it can change its shipping prices but not its substantially fixed input prices—is actually quite long. Keep this example in mind as we derive the short-run aggregate supply for the entire economy. Its applicability does not depend on some arbitrary definition of how long the "short run" should be. Instead, the short-run for which the model is relevant is any period of time during which output prices are flexible, but input prices are fixed or nearly fixed.

As illustrated in Figure 12.4, the **short-run aggregate supply curve** AS slopes upward because, with input prices

ovens, and microwaves, it is obligated to supply however many or few appliances customers want to buy at those prices. Similarly, a catalogue company is obliged to sell however much customers want to buy of its products at the prices listed in its current catalogue. And it is obligated to supply those quantities demanded until it sends out its next catalogue.

With output prices fixed and firms selling however much customers want to purchase at those fixed prices, the **immediate-short-run aggregate supply curve** AS_{ISR} is a horizontal line, as shown in Figure 12.3. The AS_{ISR} curve is horizontal at the overall price level P_1, which is calculated from all of the individual prices set by the various firms in the economy. Its horizontal shape implies that the total amount of output supplied in the economy depends directly on the volume of spending that results at price level P_1. If total spending is low at price level P_1, firms will supply a small amount of output to match the low level of spending. If total spending is high at price level P_1, they will supply a high level of output to match the high level of spending. The amount of output that results may be higher than or lower than the economy's full-employment output level Q_f.

Notice, however, that firms will respond in this manner to changes in total spending only as long as output prices remain fixed. As soon as firms are able to change their product prices, they can respond to changes in aggregate spending not only by increasing or decreasing output but also by raising or lowering prices. This is the situation that leads to the upsloping short-run aggregate supply curve that we discuss next.

FIGURE 12.4 The aggregate supply curve (short run). The upsloping aggregate supply curve AS indicates a direct (or positive) relationship between the price level and the amount of real output that firms will offer for sale. The AS curve is relatively flat below the full-employment output because unemployed resources and unused capacity allow firms to respond to price-level rises with large increases in real output. It is relatively steep beyond the full-employment output because resource shortages and capacity limitations make it difficult to expand real output as the price level rises.

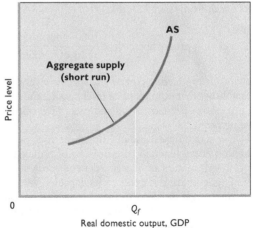

fixed, changes in the price level will raise or lower real firm profits. To see how this works, consider an economy that has only a single multiproduct firm called Mega Buzzer and in which the firm's owners must receive a real profit of $20 to produce the full-employment output of 100 units. Assume the owner's only input (aside from entrepreneurial talent) is 10 units of hired labor at $8 per worker, for a total wage cost of $80. Also, assume that the 100 units of output sell for $1 per unit, so total revenue is $100. Mega Buzzer's nominal profit is $20 (= $100 − $80), and using the $1 price to designate the base-price index of 100, its real profit is also $20 (= $20/1.00). Well and good; the full-employment output is produced.

Next consider what will happen if the price of Mega Buzzer's output doubles. The doubling of the price level will boost total revenue from $100 to $200, but since we are discussing the short run during which input prices are fixed, the $8 nominal wage for each of the 10 workers will remain unchanged so that total costs stay at $80. Nominal profit will rise from $20 (= $100 − $80) to $120 (= $200 − $80). Dividing that $120 profit by the new price index of 200 (= 2.0 in hundredths), we find that Mega Buzzer's real profit is now $60. The rise in the real reward from $20 to $60 prompts the firm (economy) to produce more output. Conversely, price-level declines reduce real profits and cause the firm (economy) to reduce its output. So, in the short run, there is a direct, or positive, relationship between the price level and real output. When the price level rises, real output rises and when the price level falls, real output falls. The result is an upsloping short-run aggregate supply curve.

Notice, however, that the upslope of the short-run aggregate supply curve is not constant. It is flatter at outputs below the full-employment output level Q_f and steeper at outputs above it. This has to do with the fact that per-unit production costs underlie the short-run aggregate supply curve. Recall from Chapter 9 that

$$\text{Per-unit production cost} = \frac{\text{total input cost}}{\text{units of output}}$$

The per-unit production cost of any specific level of output establishes that output's price level because the associated price level must cover all the costs of production, including profit "costs."

As the economy expands in the short run, per-unit production costs generally rise because of reduced efficiency. But the extent of that rise depends on where the economy is operating relative to its capacity. When the economy is operating below its full-employment output, it has large amounts of unused machinery and equipment and large numbers of unemployed workers. Firms can put these idle human and property resources back to work with little upward pressure on per-unit production costs. And as output expands, few if any shortages of inputs or production bottlenecks will arise to raise per-unit production costs. That is why the slope of the short-run aggregate supply curve increases only slowly at output levels below the full-employment output level Q_f.

On the other hand, when the economy is operating beyond Q_f, the vast majority of its available resources are already employed. Adding more workers to a relatively fixed number of highly used capital resources such as plant and equipment creates congestion in the workplace and reduces the efficiency (on average) of workers. Adding more capital, given the limited number of available workers, leaves equipment idle and reduces the efficiency of capital. Adding more land resources when capital and labor are highly constrained reduces the efficiency of land resources. Under these circumstances, total input costs rise more rapidly than total output. The result is rapidly rising per-unit production costs that give the short-run aggregate supply curve its rapidly increasing slope at output levels beyond Q_f.

Aggregate Supply in the Long Run

In macroeconomics, the long run is the time horizon over which both input prices as well as output prices are flexible. It begins after the short run ends. Depending on the type of firm and industry, this may be from a couple of weeks to several years in the future. But for the economy as a whole, it is the time horizon over which all output and input prices—including wage rates—are fully flexible.

The **long-run aggregate supply curve** AS_{LR} is vertical at the economy's full-employment output Q_f, as shown in Figure 12.5. The vertical curve means that in the long run the economy will produce the full-employment output level no matter what the price level is. How can this be? Shouldn't higher prices cause firms to increase output? The explanation lies in the fact that in the long run when both input prices as well as output prices are flexible, profit levels will always adjust to give firms exactly the right profit incentive to produce exactly the full-employment output level, Q_f.

To see why this is true, look back at the short-run aggregate supply curve AS shown in Figure 12.4. Suppose that the economy starts out producing at the full-employment output level Q_f and that the price level at that moment has an index value of $P = 100$. Now suppose that output prices double, so that the price index goes to $P = 200$. We previously demonstrated for our single-firm economy that this doubling of the price level would cause profits to rise in

FIGURE 12.5 **Aggregate supply in the long run.** The long-run aggregate supply curve AS$_{LR}$ is vertical at the full-employment level of real GDP (Q_f) because in the long run wages and other input prices rise and fall to match changes in the price level. So price-level changes do not affect firms' profits and thus they create no incentive for firms to alter their output.

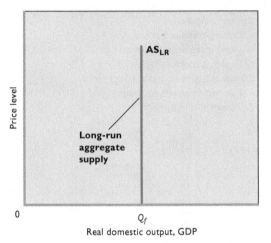

Real domestic output, GDP

or $P = 200$). That is why the long-run aggregate supply curve AS$_{LR}$ is vertical above the full-employment output level. Every possible price level on the vertical axis is associated with the economy producing at the full-employment output level in the long run once input prices adjust to exactly match changes in output prices.

Focusing on the Short Run

The immediate-short-run aggregate supply curve, the short-run aggregate supply curve, and the long-run aggregate supply curve are all important. Each curve is appropriate to situations that match their respective assumptions about the flexibility of input and output prices. In the remainder of the book, we will have several different opportunities to refer to each curve. But our focus in the rest of this chapter and the several chapters that immediately follow will be on short-run aggregate supply curves, such as the AS curve shown in Figure 12.4. Indeed, unless explicitly stated otherwise, all references to "aggregate supply" are to the AS curve and to aggregate supply in the short run.

Our emphasis on the short-run aggregate supply curve AS stems from out interest in understanding the business cycle in the simplest possible way. It is a fact that real-world economies typically manifest simultaneous changes in both their price levels and their levels of real output. The upsloping short-run AS curve is the only version of aggregate supply that can handle simultaneous movements in both of these variables. By contrast, the price level is assumed fixed in the immediate-short-run version of aggregate supply illustrated in Figure 12.3 and the economy's output is always equal to the full-employment output level in the long-run version of aggregate supply shown in Figure 12.5. This renders these versions of the aggregate supply curve less useful as part of a core model for analyzing business cycles and demonstrating the short-run government policies designed to deal with them. In our current discussion, we will reserve use of the immediate short run and the long run for specific, clearly identified situations. Later in the book we will explore how the short-run and long-run AS curves are linked, and how that linkage adds several additional insights about business cycles and policy.

the short run and that the higher profits would motivate the firm to increase output.

This outcome, however, is totally dependent on the fact that input prices are fixed in the short run. Consider what will happen in the long run when they are free to change. Firms can only produce beyond the full-employment output level by running factories and businesses at extremely high rates. This creates a great deal of demand for the economy's limited supply of productive resources. In particular, labor is in great demand because the only way to produce beyond full employment is if workers are working overtime.

As time passes and input prices are free to change, the high demand will start to raise input prices. In particular, overworked employees will demand and receive raises as employers scramble to deal with the labor shortages that arise when the economy is producing at above its full-employment output level. As input prices increase, firm profits will begin to fall. And as they decline, so does the motive firms have to produce more than the full-employment output level. This process of rising input prices and falling profits continues until the rise in input prices exactly matches the initial change in output prices (in our example, they both double). When that happens, firm profits in real terms return to their original level so that firms are once again motivated to produce at exactly the full-employment output level. This adjustment process means that in the long run the economy will produce at full employment regardless of the price level (in our example, at either $P = 100$

Changes in Aggregate Supply

LO12.4 Explain the factors that cause changes (shifts) in AS.

An existing aggregate supply curve identifies the relationship between the price level and real output, other things equal. But when one or more of these other things change, the curve itself shifts. The rightward shift of the curve

FIGURE 12.6 Changes in aggregate supply. A change in one or more of the listed determinants of aggregate supply will shift the aggregate supply curve. The rightward shift of the aggregate supply curve from AS₁ to AS₂ represents an increase in aggregate supply; the leftward shift of the curve from AS₁ to AS₃ shows a decrease in aggregate supply.

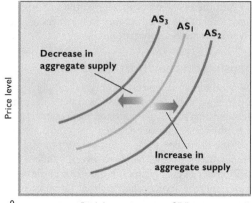

Determinants of Aggregate Supply: Factors That Shift the Aggregate Supply Curve

1. Change in input prices
   a. Domestic resource prices
   b. Prices of imported resources
2. Change in productivity
3. Change in legal-institutional environment
   a. Business taxes and subsidies
   b. Government regulations

from AS₁ to AS₂ in Figure 12.6 represents an increase in aggregate supply, indicating that firms are willing to produce and sell more real output at each price level. The leftward shift of the curve from AS₁ to AS₃ represents a decrease in aggregate supply. At each price level, firms produce less output than before.

Figure 12.6 lists the other things that cause a shift of the aggregate supply curve. Called the **determinants of aggregate supply** or *aggregate supply shifters*, they collectively position the aggregate supply curve and shift the curve when they change. Changes in these determinants raise or lower per-unit production costs *at each price level (or each level of output)*. These changes in per-unit production cost affect profits, thereby leading firms to alter the amount of output they are willing to produce *at each price level*. For example, firms may collectively offer $9 trillion of real output at a price level of 1.0 (100 in index value), rather than $8.8 trillion. Or they may offer $7.5 trillion rather than $8 trillion. The point is that when one of the determinants listed in Figure 12.6 changes, the aggregate supply curve shifts to the right or left. Changes that reduce per-unit production costs shift the aggregate supply curve to the right, as from AS₁ to AS₂; changes that increase per-unit production costs shift it to the left, as from AS₁ to AS₃. When per-unit production costs change for reasons other than changes in real output, the aggregate supply curve shifts.

The three aggregate supply determinants listed in Figure 12.6 require more discussion.

Input Prices

Input or resource prices—to be distinguished from the output prices that make up the price level—are a major

ingredient of per-unit production costs and therefore a key determinant of aggregate supply. These resources can be either domestic or imported.

Domestic Resource Prices As stated earlier, wages and salaries make up about 75 percent of all business costs. Other things equal, decreases in wages reduce per-unit production costs. So when wages fall, the aggregate supply curve shifts to the right. Increases in wages shift the curve to the left. Examples:

- Labor supply increases because of substantial immigration. Wages and per-unit production costs fall, shifting the AS curve to the right.

- Labor supply decreases because a rapid increase in pension income causes many older workers to opt for early retirement. Wage rates and per-unit production costs rise, shifting the AS curve to the left.

Similarly, the aggregate supply curve shifts when the prices of land and capital inputs change. Examples:

- The price of machinery and equipment falls because of declines in the prices of steel and electronic components. Per-unit production costs decline, and the AS curve shifts to the right.

- The supply of available land resources expands through discoveries of mineral deposits, irrigation of land, or technical innovations that transform "nonresources" (say, vast desert lands) into valuable resources (productive lands). The price of land declines, per-unit production costs fall, and the AS curve shifts to the right.

Prices of Imported Resources Just as foreign demand for U.S. goods contributes to U.S. aggregate demand, resources imported from abroad (such as oil, tin, and copper) add to U.S. aggregate supply. Added supplies of resources—whether domestic or imported—typically reduce per-unit production costs. A decrease in the price of imported resources increases U.S. aggregate supply, while an increase in their price reduces U.S. aggregate supply.

A good example of the major effect that changing resource prices can have on aggregate supply is the oil price hikes of the 1970s. At that time, a group of oil-producing nations called the Organization of Petroleum Exporting Countries (OPEC) worked in concert to decrease oil production in order to raise the price of oil. The 10-fold increase in the price of oil that OPEC achieved during the 1970s drove per-unit production costs up and jolted the U.S. aggregate supply curve leftward. By contrast, a sharp decline in oil prices in the mid-1980s resulted in a rightward shift of the U.S. aggregate supply curve. In 1999 OPEC again reasserted itself, raising oil prices and therefore per-unit production costs for some U.S. producers including airlines and shipping companies like FedEx and UPS. In 2007 the price of oil shot upward, but this increase was attributed to greater demand rather than to decreases in supply caused by OPEC. But keep in mind that no matter what their cause, increases in the price of oil and other resources raise production costs and decrease aggregate supply.

Exchange-rate fluctuations are another factor that may alter the price of imported resources. Suppose that the dollar appreciates, enabling U.S. firms to obtain more foreign currency with each dollar. This means that domestic producers face a lower *dollar* price of imported resources. U.S. firms will respond by increasing their imports of foreign resources, thereby lowering their per-unit production costs at each level of output. Falling per-unit production costs will shift the U.S. aggregate supply curve to the right.

A depreciation of the dollar will have the opposite set of effects and will shift the aggregate supply curve to the left.

Productivity

The second major determinant of aggregate supply is **productivity,** which is a measure of the relationship between a nation's level of real output and the amount of resources used to produce that output. Productivity is a measure of average real output, or of real output per unit of input:

$$\text{Productivity} = \frac{\text{total output}}{\text{total inputs}}$$

An increase in productivity enables the economy to obtain more real output from its limited resources. An increase in productivity affects aggregate supply by reducing the per-unit cost of output (per-unit production cost). Suppose, for example, that real output is 10 units, that 5 units of input are needed to produce that quantity, and that the price of each input unit is $2. Then

$$\text{Productivity} = \frac{\text{total output}}{\text{total inputs}} = \frac{10}{5} = 2$$

and

$$\text{Per-unit production cost} = \frac{\text{total input cost}}{\text{total output}}$$
$$= \frac{\$2 \times 5}{10} = \$1$$

Note that we obtain the total input cost by multiplying the unit input cost by the number of inputs used.

Now suppose productivity increases so that real output doubles to 20 units, while the price and quantity of the input remain constant at $2 and 5 units. Using the above equations, we see that productivity rises from 2 to 4 and that the per-unit production cost of the output falls from $1 to $0.50. The doubled productivity has reduced the per-unit production cost by half.

WORKED PROBLEMS

W12.1

Productivity and costs

By reducing the per-unit production cost, an increase in productivity shifts the aggregate supply curve to the right. The main source of productivity advance is improved production technology, often embodied within new plant and equipment that replaces old plant and equipment. Other sources of productivity increases are a better-educated and better-trained workforce, improved forms of business enterprises, and the reallocation of labor resources from lower-productivity to higher-productivity uses.

Much rarer, decreases in productivity increase per-unit production costs and therefore reduce aggregate supply (shift the curve to the left).

Legal-Institutional Environment

Changes in the legal-institutional setting in which businesses operate are the final determinant of aggregate supply. Such changes may alter the per-unit costs of output and, if so, shift the aggregate supply curve. Two changes of this type are (1) changes in taxes and subsidies and (2) changes in the extent of regulation.

Business Taxes and Subsidies Higher business taxes, such as sales, excise, and payroll taxes, increase per-unit costs and reduce short-run aggregate supply in much the same way as a wage increase does. An increase in such taxes paid by businesses will increase per-unit production costs and shift aggregate supply to the left.

Similarly, a business subsidy—a payment or tax break by government to producers—lowers production costs and increases short-run aggregate supply. For example, the federal government subsidizes firms that blend ethanol (derived from corn) with gasoline to increase the U.S. gasoline supply. This reduces the per-unit production cost of making blended gasoline. To the extent that this and other subsidies are successful, the aggregate supply curve shifts rightward.

Government Regulation It is usually costly for businesses to comply with government regulations. More regulation therefore tends to increase per-unit production costs and shift the aggregate supply curve to the left. "Supply-side" proponents of deregulation of the economy have argued forcefully that, by increasing efficiency and reducing the paperwork associated with complex regulations, deregulation will reduce per-unit costs and shift the aggregate supply curve to the right. Other economists are less certain. Deregulation that results in accounting manipulations, monopolization, and business failures is likely to shift the AS curve to the left rather than to the right.

QUICK REVIEW 12.2

- The immediate-short-run aggregate supply curve is horizontal; given fixed input and output prices, producers will supply whatever quantity of real output is demanded at the current price level.

- The short-run aggregate supply curve (or simply the "aggregate supply curve") is upsloping; given fixed resource prices, higher output prices raise firm profits and encourage them to increase their output levels.

- The long-run aggregate supply curve is vertical; given sufficient time, wages and other input prices rise or fall to match any change in the price level (that is, any change in the level of *output* prices).

- By altering per-unit production costs independent of changes in the level of output, changes in one or more of the determinants of aggregate supply (Figure 12.6) shift the aggregate supply curve.

- An increase in short-run aggregate supply is shown as a rightward shift of the aggregate supply curve; a decrease is shown as a leftward shift of the curve.

Equilibrium in the AD-AS Model

LO12.5 Discuss how AD and AS determine an economy's equilibrium price level and level of real GDP.

Of all the possible combinations of price levels and levels of real GDP, which combination will the economy gravitate toward, at least in the short run? **Figure 12.7 (Key Graph)** and its accompanying table provide the answer. Equilibrium occurs at the price level that equalizes the amounts of real output demanded and supplied. The intersection of the aggregate demand curve AD and the aggregate supply curve AS establishes the economy's **equilibrium price level** and **equilibrium real output.** So aggregate demand and aggregate supply *jointly* establish the price level and level of real GDP.

In Figure 12.7 the equilibrium price level and level of real output are 100 and $510 billion, respectively. To illustrate why, suppose the price level is 92 rather than 100. We see from the table that the lower price level will encourage businesses to produce real output of $502 billion. This is shown by point *a* on the AS curve in the graph. But, as revealed by the table and point *b* on the aggregate demand curve, buyers will want to purchase $514 billion of real output at price level 92. Competition among buyers to purchase the lesser available real output of $502 billion will eliminate the $12 billion (= $514 billion − $502 billion) shortage and pull up the price level to 100.

As the table and graph show, the rise in the price level from 92 to 100 encourages producers to increase their real output from $502 billion to $510 billion and causes buyers to scale back their purchases from $514 billion to $510 billion. When equality occurs between the amounts of real output produced and purchased, as it does at price level 100, the economy has achieved equilibrium (here, at $510 billion of real GDP).

A final note: Although the equilibrium price level happens to be 100 in our example, nothing special is implied by that. Any price level can be an equilibrium price level.

Changes in Equilibrium

LO12.6 Describe how the AD-AS model explains periods of demand-pull inflation, cost-push inflation, and recession.

Now let's apply the AD-AS model to various situations that can confront the economy. For simplicity we will use *P* and *Q* symbols, rather than actual numbers. Remember that these symbols represent, respectively, price index values and amounts of real GDP.

FIGURE 12.7 The equilibrium price level and equilibrium real GDP. The intersection of the aggregate demand curve and the aggregate supply curve determines the economy's equilibrium price level. At the equilibrium price level of 100 (in index-value terms), the $510 billion of real output demanded matches the $510 billion of real output supplied. So the equilibrium GDP is $510 billion.

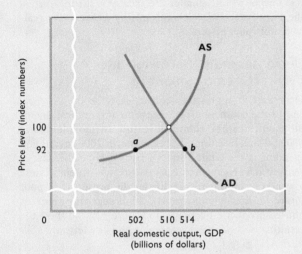

Real Output Demanded (Billions)	Price Level (Index Number)	Real Output Supplied (Billions)
$506	108	$513
508	104	512
510	**100**	**510**
512	96	507
514	92	502

QUICK QUIZ FOR FIGURE 12.7

1. The AD curve slopes downward because:
   a. per-unit production costs fall as real GDP increases.
   b. the income and substitution effects are at work.
   c. changes in the determinants of AD alter the amounts of real GDP demanded at each price level.
   d. decreases in the price level give rise to real-balances effects, interest-rate effects, and foreign purchases effects that increase the amount of real GDP demanded.

2. The AS curve slopes upward because:
   a. per-unit production costs rise as real GDP expands toward and beyond its full-employment level.
   b. the income and substitution effects are at work.
   c. changes in the determinants of AS alter the amounts of real GDP supplied at each price level.
   d. increases in the price level give rise to real-balances effects, interest-rate effects, and foreign purchases effects that increase the amounts of real GDP supplied.

3. At price level 92:
   a. a GDP surplus of $12 billion occurs that drives the price level up to 100.
   b. a GDP shortage of $12 billion occurs that drives the price level up to 100.
   c. the aggregate amount of real GDP demanded is less than the aggregate amount of real GDP supplied.
   d. the economy is operating beyond its capacity to produce.

4. Suppose real output demanded rises by $4 billion at each price level. The new equilibrium price level will be:
   a. 108.
   b. 104.
   c. 96.
   d. 92.

Answers: 1. d; 2. a; 3. b; 4. b

Increases in AD: Demand-Pull Inflation

Suppose the economy is operating at its full-employment output and businesses and government decide to increase their spending—actions that shift the aggregate demand curve to the right. Our list of determinants of aggregate demand (Figure 12.2) provides several reasons why this shift might occur. Perhaps firms boost their investment spending because they anticipate higher future profits from investments in new capital. Those profits are predicated on having new equipment and facilities that incorporate a number of new technologies. And perhaps government increases spending to expand national defense.

As shown by the rise in the price level from P_1 to P_2 in Figure 12.8, the increase in aggregate demand beyond the full-employment level of output causes inflation. This is

FIGURE 12.8   An increase in aggregate demand that causes demand-pull inflation. The increase of aggregate demand from AD_1 to AD_2 causes demand-pull inflation, shown as the rise in the price level from P_1 to P_2. It also causes an inflationary GDP gap of Q_1 minus Q_f. The rise of the price level reduces the size of the multiplier effect. If the price level had remained at P_1, the increase in aggregate demand from AD_1 to AD_2 would increase output from Q_f to Q_2 and the multiplier would have been at full strength. But because of the increase in the price level, real output increases only from Q_f to Q_1 and the multiplier effect is reduced.

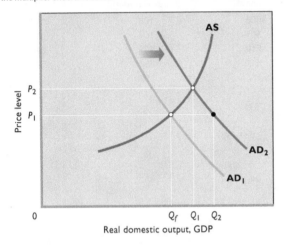

demand-pull inflation because the price level is being pulled up by the increase in aggregate demand. Also, observe that the increase in demand expands real output from the full-employment level Q_f to Q_1. The distance between Q_1 and Q_f is a positive, or "inflationary," GDP gap. Actual GDP exceeds potential GDP.

The classic American example of demand-pull inflation occurred in the late 1960s. The escalation of the war in Vietnam resulted in a 40 percent increase in defense spending between 1965 and 1967 and another 15 percent increase in 1968. The rise in government spending, imposed on an already growing economy, shifted the economy's aggregate demand curve to the right, producing the worst inflation in two decades. Actual GDP exceeded potential GDP, thereby creating an inflationary GDP gap. Inflation jumped from 1.6 percent in 1965 to 5.7 percent by 1970.

A careful examination of Figure 12.8 reveals an interesting point concerning the multiplier effect. The increase in aggregate demand from AD_1 to AD_2 increases real output only to Q_1, not to Q_2, because part of the increase in aggregate demand is absorbed as inflation as the price level rises from P_1 to P_2. Had the price level remained at P_1, the shift of aggregate demand from AD_1 to AD_2 would have increased real output to Q_2. The full-strength multiplier effect of Chapters 10

and 11 would have occurred. But in Figure 12.8 inflation reduced the increase in real output—and thus the multiplier effect—by about one-half. For any initial increase in aggregate demand, the resulting increase in real output will be smaller the greater is the increase in the price level. Price-level flexibility weakens the realized multiplier effect.

Decreases in AD: Recession and Cyclical Unemployment

Decreases in aggregate demand describe the opposite end of the business cycle: recession and cyclical unemployment (rather than above-full employment and demand-pull inflation). For example, in 2008 investment spending in the United States greatly declined because of sharply lower expected returns on investment. These lower expectations resulted from the prospects of poor future business conditions and high degrees of current unused production capacity. In Figure 12.9 we show the resulting decline in aggregate demand as a leftward shift from AD_1 to AD_2.

But we now add an important twist to the analysis: *Deflation*—a decline in the price level—is not the norm in the American economy. We discussed "sticky prices" in Chapter 6 and previously explained how fixed prices lead to horizontal immediate-short-run aggregate supply

FIGURE 12.9   A decrease in aggregate demand that causes a recession. If the price level is downwardly inflexible at P_1, a decline of aggregate demand from AD_1 to AD_2 will move the economy leftward from *a* to *b* along the horizontal broken-line segment and reduce real GDP from Q_f to Q_1. Idle production capacity, cyclical unemployment, and a recessionary GDP gap (of Q_1 minus Q_f) will result. If the price level were flexible downward, the decline in aggregate demand would move the economy depicted from *a* to *c* instead of from *a* to *b*.

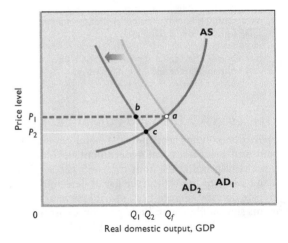

curves. For reasons we will examine soon, many important prices in the U.S. economy are downwardly inflexible such that the price level is sticky downward even when aggregate demand substantially declines. Consider Figure 12.9, where the aggregate demand declines from AD_1 to AD_2. If the price level is stuck at P_1, the economy moves from a to b along the broken horizontal line rather than from a to c along the short-run aggregate supply curve AS. The outcome is a decline of real output from Q_f to Q_1, with *no* change in the price level. In this case, it is as if the aggregate supply curve in Figure 12.9 is horizontal at P_1, to the left of Q_f, as indicated by the dashed line. This decline of real output from Q_f to Q_1 constitutes a *recession*, and since fewer workers are needed to produce the lower output, *cyclical unemployment* arises. The distance between Q_1 and Q_f is a negative, or "recessionary," GDP gap—the amount by which actual output falls short of potential output.

Close inspection of Figure 12.9 also reveals that without a fall in the price level, the multiplier is at full strength. With the price level stuck at P_1, real GDP decreases by $Q_f - Q_1$, which matches the full leftward shift of the AD curve. The multiplier of Chapters 10 and 11 is at full strength when changes in aggregate demand occur along what, in effect, is a horizontal segment of the AS curve. This full-strength multiplier would also exist for an increase in aggregate demand from AD_2 to AD_1 along this broken line, since none of the increase in output would be dissipated as inflation. We will say more about that in Chapter 13.

All recent recessions in the United States have generally mimicked the "GDP gap but no deflation" scenario shown in Figure 12.9. Consider the recession of 2007–2009, which resulted from chaos in the financial markets that quickly led to significant declines in spending by businesses and households. Because of the resulting decline in aggregate demand, real GDP fell short of potential real GDP by roughly $300 billion in 2008 and $1 trillion in 2009. The nation's unemployment rate rose from 4.7 percent in December 2007 to 10.1 percent in October 2009. The price level fell in some months and the rate of inflation declined—meaning that *disinflation* occurred. Considering the full period, however, *deflation* did not occur.

Real output takes the brunt of declines in aggregate demand in the U.S. economy because the price level tends to be downwardly rigid in the immediate short run. There are several reasons for this downward price stickiness.

- *Fear of price wars* Some large firms may be concerned that if they reduce their prices, rivals not

CONSIDER THIS . . .

Ratchet Effect

A *ratchet analogy* is a good way to think about the effects of changes in aggregate demand on the price level. A ratchet is a tool or mechanism such as a winch, car jack, or socket wrench that cranks a wheel forward but does not allow it to go backward. Properly set, each allows the operator to move an object (boat, car, or nut) in one direction while preventing it from moving in the opposite direction.

Product prices, wage rates, and per-unit production costs are highly flexible upward when aggregate demand increases along the aggregate supply curve. In the United States, the price level has increased in 60 of the 62 years since 1950.

But when aggregate demand decreases, product prices, wage rates, and per-unit production costs are inflexible downward. The U.S. price level has declined in only two years (1955 and 2009) since 1950, even though aggregate demand and real output have declined in a number of years.

In terms of our analogy, increases in aggregate demand ratchet the U.S. price level upward. Once in place, the higher price level remains until it is ratcheted up again. The higher price level tends to remain even with declines in aggregate demand.

only will match their price cuts but may retaliate by making even deeper cuts. An initial price cut may touch off an unwanted *price war:* successively deeper and deeper rounds of price cuts. In such a situation, each firm eventually ends up with far less profit or higher losses than would be the case if each had simply maintained its prices. For this reason, each firm may resist making the initial price cut, choosing instead to reduce production and lay off workers.

- *Menu costs* Firms that think a recession will be relatively short-lived may be reluctant to cut their prices. One reason is what economists metaphorically call **menu costs,** named after their most obvious example: the cost of printing new menus when a restaurant decides to reduce its prices. But lowering prices also creates other costs. Additional costs derive from (1) estimating the magnitude and duration of the shift in demand to determine whether prices should be lowered, (2) repricing items held in inventory, (3) printing and mailing new catalogs, and (4) communicating new prices to customers, perhaps through advertising. When menu costs are present, firms may choose to avoid them by retaining current prices. That is, they may wait to see if the decline in aggregate demand is permanent.

- *Wage contracts* Firms rarely profit from cutting their product prices if they cannot also cut their wage rates. Wages are usually inflexible downward because large parts of the labor force work under contracts prohibiting wage cuts for the duration of the contract. (Collective bargaining agreements in major industries frequently run for 3 years. Similarly, the wages and salaries of nonunion workers are usually adjusted once a year, rather than quarterly or monthly.)

- *Morale, effort, and productivity* Wage inflexibility downward is reinforced by the reluctance of many employers to reduce wage rates. Some current wages may be so-called **efficiency wages**—wages that elicit maximum work effort and thus minimize labor costs per unit of output. If worker productivity (output per hour of work) remains constant, lower wages *do* reduce labor costs per unit of output. But lower wages might impair worker morale and work effort, thereby reducing productivity. Considered alone, lower productivity raises labor costs per unit of output because less output is produced. If the higher labor costs resulting from reduced productivity exceed the cost savings from the lower wage, then wage cuts will increase rather than reduce labor costs per unit of output. In such situations, firms will resist lowering wages when they are faced with a decline in aggregate demand.

ORIGIN OF THE IDEA

O12.2
Efficiency wage

- *Minimum wage* The minimum wage imposes a legal floor under the wages of the least-skilled workers. Firms paying those wages cannot reduce that wage rate when aggregate demand declines.

Decreases in AS: Cost-Push Inflation

Suppose that a major terrorist attack on oil facilities severely disrupts world oil supplies and drives up oil prices

FIGURE 12.10   A decrease in aggregate supply that causes cost-push inflation. A leftward shift of aggregate supply from AS_1 to AS_2 raises the price level from P_1 to P_2 and produces cost-push inflation. Real output declines and a recessionary GDP gap (of Q_1 minus Q_f) occurs.

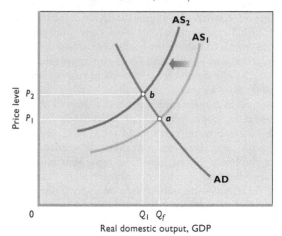

by, say, 300 percent. Higher energy prices would spread through the economy, driving up production and distribution costs on a wide variety of goods. The U.S. aggregate supply curve would shift to the left, say, from AS_1 to AS_2 in Figure 12.10. The resulting increase in the price level would be *cost-push inflation*.

The effects of a leftward shift in aggregate supply are doubly bad. When aggregate supply shifts from AS_1 to AS_2, the economy moves from *a* to *b*. The price level rises from P_1 to P_2 and real output declines from Q_f to Q_1. Along with the cost-push inflation, a recession (and negative GDP gap) occurs. That is exactly what happened in the United States in the mid-1970s when the price of oil rocketed upward. Then, oil expenditures were about 10 percent of U.S. GDP, compared to only 3 percent today. So the U.S. economy is now less vulnerable to cost-push inflation arising from such "aggregate supply shocks." That said, it is not *immune* from such shocks.

Increases in AS: Full Employment with Price-Level Stability

Between 1996 and 2000, the United States experienced a combination of full employment, strong economic growth, and very low inflation. Specifically, the unemployment rate fell to 4 percent and real GDP grew nearly 4 percent annually, *without igniting inflation*. At first thought, this "macroeconomic bliss" seems to be incompatible with the

FIGURE 12.11 Growth, full employment, and relative price stability. Normally, an increase in aggregate demand from AD_1 to AD_2 would move the economy from a to b along AS_1. Real output would expand to Q_2, and inflation would result (P_1 to P_3). But in the late 1990s, significant increases in productivity shifted the aggregate supply curve, as from AS_1 to AS_2. The economy moved from a to c rather than from a to b. It experienced strong economic growth (Q_1 to Q_3), full employment, and only very mild inflation (P_1 to P_2) before receding in March 2001.

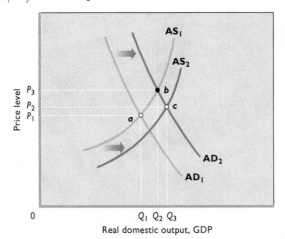

AD-AS model. The aggregate supply curve suggests that increases in aggregate demand that are sufficient for over-full employment will raise the price level (see Figure 12.8). Higher inflation, so it would seem, is the inevitable price paid for expanding output beyond the full-employment level.

But inflation remained very mild in the late 1990s. Figure 12.11 helps explain why. Let's first suppose that aggregate demand increased from AD_1 to AD_2 along aggregate supply curve AS_1. Taken alone, that increase in aggregate demand would move the economy from a to b. Real output would rise from full-employment output Q_1 to beyond-full-employment output Q_2. The economy would experience inflation, as shown by the increase in the price level from P_1 to P_3. Such inflation had occurred at the end of previous vigorous expansions of aggregate demand, including the expansion of the late 1980s.

Between 1990 and 2000, however, larger-than-usual increases in productivity occurred because of a burst of new technology relating to computers, the Internet, inventory management systems, electronic commerce, and so on. We represent this higher-than-usual productivity growth as the rightward shift from AS_1 to AS_2 in Figure 12.11. The relevant aggregate demand and aggregate supply curves thus became AD_2 and AS_2, not AD_2 and AS_1. Instead of moving

from a to b, the economy moved from a to c. Real output increased from Q_1 to Q_3, and the price level rose only modestly (from P_1 to P_2). The shift of the aggregate supply curve from AS_1 to AS_2 accommodated the rapid increase in aggregate demand and kept inflation mild. This remarkable combination of rapid productivity growth, rapid real GDP growth, full employment, and relative price-level stability led some observers to proclaim that the United States was experiencing a "new era" or a New Economy.

But in 2001 the New Economy came face-to-face with the old economic principles. Aggregate demand declined because of a substantial fall in investment spending, and in March 2001 the economy experienced a recession. The terrorist attacks of September 11, 2001, further dampened private spending and prolonged the recession throughout 2001. The unemployment rate rose from 4.2 percent in January 2001 to 6 percent in December 2002.

The economy rebounded between 2002 and 2007, eventually reachieving its earlier strong economic growth, low inflation, and low unemployment. Some economists began to refer to the period after 1982 as "The Great Moderation" because recessions were father apart and relatively mild. They drew the implication that businesses and government had smoothed out the business cycle. Wrong! The severity of the recession of 2007–2009 was a huge surprise to most economists. And so was the weakness of the subsequent recovery, as discussed in this chapter's Last Word.

QUICK REVIEW 12.3

- The equilibrium price level and amount of real output are determined at the intersection of the aggregate demand curve and the aggregate supply curve.

- Increases in aggregate demand beyond the full-employment level of real GDP cause demand-pull inflation.

- Decreases in aggregate demand cause recessions and cyclical unemployment, partly because the price level and wages tend to be inflexible in a downward direction.

- Decreases in aggregate supply cause cost-push inflation.

- Full employment, high economic growth, and price stability are compatible with one another if productivity-driven increases in aggregate supply are sufficient to balance growing aggregate demand.

LAST WORD

Stimulus and the Great Recession

Aggregate Demand Stimulus Helped to Prevent the 2007–2009 Downturn from Becoming Another Great Depression. But Why Was the Stimulus-Fueled Recovery Substantially Weaker Than Expected?

In retrospect, it is clear that the U.S. economy was in a precarious position in 2006. Trillions of dollars had been borrowed to buy housing on the expectation that home prices would keep on rising. That expectation made borrowing seem like a "no brainer" as a potential buyer could anticipate that if she borrowed $200,000 to buy a house in one year, she would be able to sell it the next year for, say, $215,000. Selling at a higher price would allow her to pay off the $200,000 loan and keep the rest as pure profit.

Unfortunately, home prices started to fall in 2006. When they did, many people who had borrowed to buy houses found themselves unable to pay off their loans. That in turn meant that many banks found themselves holding loans that would never be paid back. Soon, many banks teetered on bankruptcy, the financial markets began to freeze up, and it became clear by late 2007 that the overall economy would probably enter a recession as the result of the housing collapse.

When it was widely recognized in late 2008 that the downturn was going to be unusually severe, public officials took extraordinarily strong steps to stimulate aggregate demand. In terms of monetary policy, the Federal Reserve lowered short-term interest rates to nearly zero in order to shift AD to the right

by stimulating investment and consumption. In terms of fiscal policy, the federal government began the country's largest peacetime program of deficit-funded spending increases. Those spending increases also shifted AD to the right by increasing the total amount of government expenditures.

Those actions were widely credited with preventing a much worse downturn. Real GDP did fall by 4.7 percent and

SUMMARY

LO12.1 Define aggregate demand (AD) and explain how its downward slope is the result of the real-balances effect, the interest-rate effect, and the foreign purchases effect.

The aggregate demand–aggregate supply model (AD-AS model) is a flexible-price model that enables analysis of simultaneous changes of real GDP and the price level.

The aggregate demand curve shows the level of real output that the economy demands at each price level.

The aggregate demand curve is downsloping because of the real-balances effect, the interest-rate effect, and the foreign purchases effect. The real-balances effect indicates that inflation reduces the real value or purchasing power of fixed-value financial assets held by households, causing cutbacks in consumer spending. The interest-rate effect means that, with a specific supply of money,

a higher price level increases the demand for money, thereby raising the interest rate and reducing investment purchases. The foreign purchases effect suggests that an increase in one country's price level relative to the price levels in other countries reduces the net export component of that nation's aggregate demand.

LO12.2 Explain the factors that cause changes (shifts) in AD.

The determinants of aggregate demand consist of spending by domestic consumers, by businesses, by government, and by foreign buyers. Changes in the factors listed in Figure 12.2 alter the spending by these groups and shift the aggregate demand curve. The extent of the shift is determined by the size of the initial change in spending and the strength of the economy's multiplier.

the unemployment rate did rise from 4.6 to 10.1 percent. But those negative changes were much less severe than what had happened during the Great Depression of the 1930s, when real GDP fell by nearly 27 percent and the unemployment rate rose to nearly 25 percent.

As time passed, however, it became clear that the stimulus was having less of an effect than many economists had anticipated. White House economists, for instance, had predicted that the stimulus begun in 2009 would reduce the unemployment rate to 5.2 percent by 2012. But three years later the unemployment rate was still at 7.8 percent despite the Federal Reserve continuing to keep interest rates extremely low and despite the federal government continuing to run massive deficits to fund huge amounts of government expenditures.

GDP growth was also disappointing. Real GDP expanded by only 2.4 percent in 2010, 1.8 percent in 2011, and 1.6 percent in 2012. By contrast, the period after the early 1980s recession had seen annual growth rates as high as 7.2 percent per year.

One explanation for the disappointing unemployment and GDP numbers was that it was hard for the stimulus to be very effective given the high debt levels that were built up during the bubble years. The lower interest rates engineered by the Federal Reserve, for instance, were probably not much of an inducement for consumers to increase their borrowing when so many of them were already heavily in debt.

A related problem was that savings rates had risen. When the government attempted to use deficit spending and fiscal policy to stimulate the economy, policy makers were hoping that each dollar of government spending would induce many dollars of consumer spending. But debt-strapped consumers were devoting large parts of their income to making interest payments on debt or paying off loans. So, when stimulus dollars came their way, they often short-circuited the spending process by saving a lot rather than spending a lot.

Another issue was that the stimulus was diffuse while the sectors of the economy in greatest need of stimulus were focused. In particular, the government's stimulus efforts shifted *aggregate* demand to the right. But not all sectors had been hit equally hard by the recession. Thus, when AD shifted right, a lot of the effect was felt in business sectors that hadn't been hurt that badly during the recession. Meanwhile, many sectors that had been hit hard only received a small portion of the total amount of stimulus that they would have needed to see a full recovery.

A related problem is that in some sectors of the economy, the government's stimulus may have resulted mostly in price increases rather than output gains. That is because the supply curves for many industries are steep. Consider dentists and jewelers. It takes many years to train competent dentists or skilled jewelers. So even if the demand for their services shifts right, there is a nearly fixed supply of dental services and jewelry services in the short run—meaning that any increase in demand will mostly cause higher prices rather than higher output. So when the government shifted *aggregate* demand to the right, certain sectors probably saw mostly price increases rather than output gains.

LO12.3 Define aggregate supply (AS) and explain how it differs in the immediate short run, the short run, and the long run.

The aggregate supply curve shows the levels of real output that businesses will produce at various possible price levels. The slope of the aggregate supply curve depends upon the flexibility of input and output prices. Since these vary over time, aggregate supply curves are categorized into three time horizons, each having different underlying assumptions about the flexibility of input and output prices.

The *immediate-short-run aggregate supply curve* assumes that both input prices and output prices are fixed. With output prices fixed, the aggregate supply curve is a horizontal line at the current price level. The *short-run aggregate supply curve* assumes nominal wages and other input prices remain fixed while output prices vary. The aggregate supply curve is generally upsloping because per-unit production costs, and hence the prices that firms must receive, rise as real output expands. The aggregate

supply curve is relatively steep to the right of the full-employment output level and relatively flat to the left of it. The *long-run aggregate supply curve* assumes that nominal wages and other input prices fully match any change in the price level. The curve is vertical at the full-employment output level.

Because the short-run aggregate supply curve is the only version of aggregate supply that can handle simultaneous changes in the price level and real output, it serves well as the core aggregate supply curve for analyzing the business cycle and economic policy. Unless stated otherwise, all references to "aggregate supply" refer to short-run aggregate supply and the short-run aggregate supply curve.

LO12.4 Explain the factors that cause changes (shifts) in AS.

Figure 12.6 lists the determinants of aggregate supply: input prices, productivity, and the legal-institutional environment. A change in any one of these factors will change per-unit production costs at each level of output and therefore will shift the aggregate supply curve.

LO12.5 Discuss how AD and AS determine an economy's equilibrium price level and level of real GDP.

The intersection of the aggregate demand and aggregate supply curves determines an economy's equilibrium price level and real GDP. At the intersection, the quantity of real GDP demanded equals the quantity of real GDP supplied.

LO12.6 Describe how the AD-AS model explains periods of demand-pull inflation, cost-push inflation, and recession.

Increases in aggregate demand to the right of the full-employment output cause inflation and positive GDP gaps (actual GDP exceeds potential GDP). An upsloping aggregate supply curve weakens the multiplier effect of an increase in aggregate demand because a portion of the increase in aggregate demand is dissipated in inflation.

Shifts of the aggregate demand curve to the left of the full-employment output cause recession, negative GDP gaps, and cyclical unemployment. The price level may not fall during recessions because of downwardly inflexible prices and wages. This inflexibility results from fear of price wars, menu costs, wage contracts, efficiency wages, and minimum wages. When the price level is fixed, changes in aggregate demand produce full-strength multiplier effects.

Leftward shifts of the aggregate supply curve reflect increases in per-unit production costs and cause cost-push inflation, with accompanying negative GDP gaps.

Rightward shifts of the aggregate supply curve, caused by large improvements in productivity, help explain the simultaneous achievement of full employment, economic growth, and price stability that occurred in the United States between 1996 and 2000. The recession of 2001, however, ended the expansionary phase of the business cycle. Expansion resumed in the 2002–2007 period, before giving way to the severe recession of 2007–2009.

TERMS AND CONCEPTS

aggregate demand–aggregate supply (AD-AS) model

aggregate demand

real-balances effect

interest-rate effect

foreign purchases effect

determinants of aggregate demand

aggregate supply

immediate-short-run aggregate supply curve

short-run aggregate supply curve

long-run aggregate supply curve

determinants of aggregate supply

productivity

equilibrium price level

equilibrium real output

menu costs

efficiency wages

The following and additional problems can be found in **connect** ECONOMICS

DISCUSSION QUESTIONS

1. Why is the aggregate demand curve downsloping? Specify how your explanation differs from the explanation for the downsloping demand curve for a single product. What role does the multiplier play in shifts of the aggregate demand curve? **LO12.1**

2. Distinguish between "real-balances effect" and "wealth effect," as the terms are used in this chapter. How does each relate to the aggregate demand curve? **LO12.1**

3. What assumptions cause the immediate-short-run aggregate supply curve to be horizontal? Why is the long-run aggregate supply curve vertical? Explain the shape of the short-run aggregate supply curve. Why is the short-run aggregate supply curve relatively flat to the left of the full-employment output and relatively steep to the right? **LO12.3**

4. Explain how an upsloping aggregate supply curve weakens the realized multiplier effect from an initial change in investment spending. **LO12.6**

5. Why does a reduction in aggregate demand in the actual economy reduce real output, rather than the price level? Why might a full-strength multiplier apply to a decrease in aggregate demand? **LO12.6**

6. Explain: "Unemployment can be caused by a decrease of aggregate demand or a decrease of aggregate supply." In each case, specify the price-level outcomes. **LO12.6**

7. Use shifts of the AD and AS curves to explain (*a*) the U.S. experience of strong economic growth, full employment, and price stability in the late 1990s and early 2000s and (*b*) how a strong negative wealth effect from, say, a precipitous

drop in house prices could cause a recession even though productivity is surging. **LO12.6**

8. In early 2001 investment spending sharply declined in the United States. In the two months following the September 11, 2001, attacks on the United States, consumption also declined. Use AD-AS analysis to show the two impacts on real GDP. **LO12.6**

9. **LAST WORD** What were the monetary and fiscal policy responses to the Great Recession? What were some of the reasons suggested for why those policy responses didn't seem to have as large an effect as anticipated on unemployment and GDP growth?

REVIEW QUESTIONS

1. Which of the following help to explain why the aggregate demand curve slopes downward? **LO12.1**
   a. When the domestic price level rises, our goods and services become more expensive to foreigners.
   b. When government spending rises, the price level falls.
   c. There is an inverse relationship between consumer expectations and personal taxes.
   d. When the price level rises, the real value of financial assets (like stocks, bonds, and savings account balances) declines.

2. Which of the following will shift the aggregate demand curve to the left? **LO12.2**
   a. The government reduces personal income taxes.
   b. Interest rates rise.
   c. The government raises corporate profit taxes.
   d. There is an economic boom overseas that raises the incomes of foreign households.

3. Label each of the following descriptions as being either an immediate-short-run aggregate supply curve, a short-run aggregate supply curve, or a long-run aggregate supply curve. **LO12.3**
   a. A vertical line.
   b. The price level is fixed.
   c. Output prices are flexible, but input prices are fixed.
   d. A horizontal line.
   e. An upsloping curve.
   f. Output is fixed.

4. Which of the following will shift the aggregate supply curve to the right? **LO12.4**
   a. A new networking technology increases productivity all over the economy.
   b. The price of oil rises substantially.
   c. Business taxes fall.
   d. The government passes a law doubling all manufacturing wages.

5. At the current price level, producers supply $375 billion of final goods and services while consumers purchase $355 billion of final goods and services. The price level is: **LO12.5**
   a. Above equilibrium.
   b. At equilibrium.
   c. Below equilibrium.
   d. More information is needed.

6. What effects would each of the following have on aggregate demand or aggregate supply, other things equal? In each case, use a diagram to show the expected effects on the equilibrium price level and the level of real output, assuming that the price level is flexible both upward and downward. **LO12.5**
   a. A widespread fear by consumers of an impending economic depression.
   b. A new national tax on producers based on the value added between the costs of the inputs and the revenue received from their output.
   c. A reduction in interest rates at each price level.
   d. A major increase in spending for health care by the federal government.
   e. The general expectation of coming rapid inflation.
   f. The complete disintegration of OPEC, causing oil prices to fall by one-half.
   g. A 10 percent across-the-board reduction in personal income tax rates.
   h. A sizable increase in labor productivity (with no change in nominal wages).
   i. A 12 percent increase in nominal wages (with no change in productivity).
   j. An increase in exports that exceeds an increase in imports (not due to tariffs).

7. True or False: Decreases in AD normally lead to decreases in both output and the price level. **LO12.6**

8. Assume that (*a*) the price level is flexible upward but not downward and (*b*) the economy is currently operating at its full-employment output. Other things equal, how will each of the following affect the equilibrium price level and equilibrium level of real output in the short run? **LO12.6**
   a. An increase in aggregate demand.
   b. A decrease in aggregate supply, with no change in aggregate demand.
   c. Equal increases in aggregate demand and aggregate supply.
   d. A decrease in aggregate demand.
   e. An increase in aggregate demand that exceeds an increase in aggregate supply.

9. True or False: If the price of oil suddenly increases by a large amount, AS will shift left, but the price level will not rise thanks to price inflexibility. **LO12.6**

PROBLEMS

1. Suppose that consumer spending initially rises by $5 billion for every 1 percent rise in household wealth and that investment spending initially rises by $20 billion for every 1 percentage point fall in the real interest rate. Also assume that the economy's multiplier is 4. If household wealth falls by 5 percent because of declining house values, and the real interest rate falls by 2 percentage points, in what direction and by how much will the aggregate demand curve initially shift at each price level? In what direction and by how much will it eventually shift? **LO12.2**

2. Answer the following questions on the basis of the following three sets of data for the country of North Vaudeville: **LO12.4**

(A)		(B)		(C)	
Price Level	Real GDP	Price Level	Real GDP	Price Level	Real GDP
110	275	100	200	110	225
100	250	100	225	100	225
95	225	100	250	95	225
90	200	100	275	90	225

   a. Which set of data illustrates aggregate supply in the immediate short run in North Vaudeville? The short run? The long run?

   b. Assuming no change in hours of work, if real output per hour of work increases by 10 percent, what will be the new levels of real GDP in the right column of A? Do the new data reflect an increase in aggregate supply or do they indicate a decrease in aggregate supply?

3. Suppose that the aggregate demand and aggregate supply schedules for a hypothetical economy are as shown in the following table. **LO12.5**

Amount of Real GDP Demanded, Billions	Price Level (Price Index)	Amount of Real GDP Supplied, Billions
$100	300	$450
200	250	400
300	200	300
400	150	200
500	100	100

   a. Use the data above to graph the aggregate demand and aggregate supply curves. What are the equilibrium price level and the equilibrium level of real output in this hypothetical economy? Is the equilibrium real output also necessarily the full-employment real output?

   b. If the price level in this economy is 150, will quantity demanded equal, exceed, or fall short of quantity supplied? By what amount? If the price level is 250, will quantity demanded equal, exceed, or fall short of quantity supplied? By what amount?

   c. Suppose that buyers desire to purchase $200 billion of extra real output at each price level. Sketch in the new aggregate demand curve as AD_1. What are the new equilibrium price level and level of real output?

4. Suppose that the table presented below shows an economy's relationship between real output and the inputs needed to produce that output: **LO12.4**

Input Quantity	Real GDP
150.0	$400
112.5	300
75.0	200

   a. What is productivity in this economy?

   b. What is the per-unit cost of production if the price of each input unit is $2?

   c. Assume that the input price increases from $2 to $3 with no accompanying change in productivity. What is the new per-unit cost of production? In what direction would the $1 increase in input price push the economy's aggregate supply curve? What effect would this shift of aggregate supply have on the price level and the level of real output?

   d. Suppose that the increase in input price does not occur but, instead, that productivity increases by 100 percent. What would be the new per-unit cost of production? What effect would this change in per-unit production cost have on the economy's aggregate supply curve? What effect would this shift of aggregate supply have on the price level and the level of real output?

5. Refer to the data in the table that accompanies problem 2. Suppose that the present equilibrium price level and level of real GDP are 100 and $225, and that data set B represents the relevant aggregate supply schedule for the economy. **LO12.6**

   a. What must be the current amount of real output demanded at the 100 price level?

   b. If the amount of output demanded declined by $25 at the 100 price levels shown in B, what would be the new equilibrium real GDP? In business cycle terminology, what would economists call this change in real GDP?

FURTHER TEST YOUR KNOWLEDGE AT www.mcconnell20e.com

The Relationship of the Aggregate Demand Curve to the Aggregate Expenditures Model*

LO12.7 Identify how the aggregate demand curve relates to the aggregate expenditures model.

The aggregate demand curve of this chapter and the aggregate expenditures model of Chapter 11 are intricately related.

Derivation of the Aggregate Demand Curve from the Aggregate Expenditures Model

We can directly connect the downsloping aggregate demand curve to the aggregate expenditures model by relating various possible price levels to corresponding equilibrium GDPs. In Figure 1 we have stacked the aggregate expenditures model (Figure 1a) and the aggregate demand curve (Figure 1b) vertically. This is possible because the horizontal axes of both models measure real GDP. Now let's derive the AD curve in three distinct steps. (Throughout this discussion, keep in mind that price level P_1 is lower than price level P_2, which is lower than price level P_3.)

- First suppose that the economy's price level is P_1 and its aggregate expenditures schedule is AE_1, the top schedule in Figure 1a. The equilibrium GDP is then Q_1 at point 1. So in Figure 1b we can plot the equilibrium real output Q_1 and the corresponding price level P_1. This gives us point 1′ in Figure 1b.

- Now assume the price level rises from P_1 to P_2. Other things equal, this higher price level will (1) decrease the value of real balances (wealth), decreasing consumption expenditures; (2) increase the interest rate, reducing investment and interest-sensitive consumption expenditures; and (3) increase imports and decrease exports, reducing net export

*This appendix presumes knowledge of the aggregate expenditures model discussed in Chapter 11 and should be skipped if Chapter 11 was not assigned.

FIGURE 1 Deriving the aggregate demand curve from the aggregate expenditures model. (a) Rising price levels from P_1 to P_2 to P_3 shift the aggregate expenditures curve downward from AE_1 to AE_2 to AE_3 and reduce real GDP from Q_1 to Q_2 to Q_3. (b) The aggregate demand curve AD is derived by plotting the successively lower real GDPs from the upper graph against the P_1, P_2, and P_3 price levels.

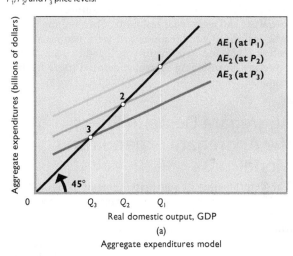

(a)

Aggregate expenditures model

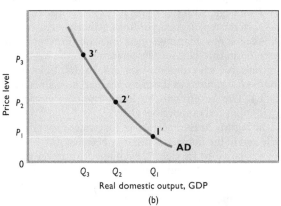

(b)

Aggregate demand–aggregate supply model

expenditures. The aggregate expenditures schedule will fall from AE_1 to, say, AE_2 in Figure 1a, giving us equilibrium Q_2 at point 2. In Figure 1b we plot this new price-level–real-output combination, P_2 and Q_2, as point $2'$.

- Finally, suppose the price level rises from P_2 to P_3. The value of real balances falls, the interest rate rises, exports fall, and imports rise. Consequently, the consumption, investment, and net export schedules fall, shifting the aggregate expenditures schedule downward from AE_2 to AE_3, which gives us equilibrium Q_3 at point 3. In Figure 1b, this enables us to locate point $3'$, where the price level is P_3 and real output is Q_3.

In summary, increases in the economy's price level will successively shift its aggregate expenditures schedule downward and will reduce real GDP. The resulting price-level–real-GDP combinations will yield various points such as $1'$, $2'$, and $3'$ in Figure 1b. Together, such points locate the downsloping aggregate demand curve for the economy.

Aggregate Demand Shifts and the Aggregate Expenditures Model

The determinants of aggregate demand listed in Figure 12.2 are the components of the aggregate expenditures model discussed in Chapter 11. When one of the determinants of aggregate demand changes, the aggregate expenditures schedule shifts upward or downward. We can easily link such shifts of the aggregate expenditures schedule to shifts of the aggregate demand curve.

Let's suppose that the price level is constant. In Figure 2 we begin with the aggregate expenditures schedule at AE_1 in the top diagram, yielding equilibrium real output Q_1. Assume now that investment increases in response to more optimistic business expectations, so the aggregate expenditures schedule rises from AE_1 to AE_2. (The notation "at P_1" reminds us that the price level is assumed constant.) The result will be a multiplied increase in equilibrium real output from Q_1 to Q_2.

In Figure 2b the increase in investment spending is reflected in the horizontal distance between AD_1 and the broken curve to its right. The immediate effect of the increase in investment is an increase in aggregate demand by the exact amount of the new spending. But then the multiplier process magnifies the initial increase in investment into successive rounds of consumption spending

FIGURE 2 Shifts of the aggregate expenditures schedule and of the aggregate demand curve. (a) A change in some determinant of consumption, investment, or net exports (other than the price level) shifts the aggregate expenditures schedule upward from AE_1 to AE_2. The multiplier increases real output from Q_1 to Q_2. (b) The counterpart of this change is an initial rightward shift of the aggregate demand curve by the amount of initial new spending (from AD_1 to the broken curve). This leads to a multiplied rightward shift of the curve to AD_2, which is just sufficient to show the same increase of real output as that in the aggregate expenditures model.

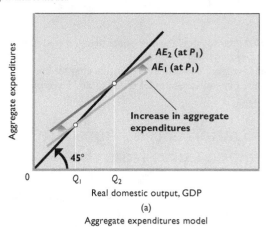

(a)
Aggregate expenditures model

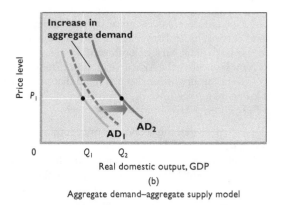

(b)
Aggregate demand–aggregate supply model

and an ultimate multiplied increase in aggregate demand from AD_1 to AD_2. Equilibrium real output rises from Q_1 to Q_2, the same multiplied increase in real GDP as that in the top graph. The initial increase in investment in the top graph has shifted the AD curve in the lower graph by a horizontal distance equal to the change in investment times the multiplier. This particular change in real GDP is still associated with the constant price level P_1. To generalize,

$$\text{Shift of AD curve} = \text{initial change in spending} \times \text{multiplier}$$

APPENDIX SUMMARY

LO12.7 Identify how the aggregate demand curve relates to the aggregate expenditures model.

A change in the price level alters the location of the aggregate expenditures schedule through the real-balances, interest-rate, and foreign purchases effects. The aggregate demand curve is derived from the aggregate expenditures model by allowing the price level to change and observing the effect on the aggregate expenditures schedule and thus on equilibrium GDP.

With the price level held constant, increases in consumption, investment, government, and net export expenditures shift the aggregate expenditures schedule upward and the aggregate demand curve to the right. Decreases in these spending components produce the opposite effects.

The following and additional problems can be found in connect ECONOMICS

APPENDIX DISCUSSION QUESTIONS

1. Explain carefully: "A change in the price level shifts the aggregate expenditures curve but not the aggregate demand curve." **LO12.7**
2. Suppose that the price level is constant and that investment decreases sharply. How would you show this decrease in the aggregate expenditures model? What would be the outcome for real GDP? How would you show this fall in investment in the aggregate demand–aggregate supply model, assuming the economy is operating in what, in effect, is a horizontal section of the aggregate supply curve? **LO12.7**

APPENDIX REVIEW QUESTIONS

1. True or False: A higher price level increases aggregate expenditures. **LO12.7**

2. If the government decreases expenditures, the AE curve will shift _____ and the AD curve will shift _____. **LO12.7**
   a. Down; left.
   b. Down; right.
   c. Up; left.
   d. Up; right.

APPENDIX PROBLEMS

1. Refer to Figures 1a and 1b in the Appendix. Assume that Q_1 is 300, Q_2 is 200, Q_3 is 100, P_3 is 120, P_2 is 100, and P_1 is 80. If the price level increases from P_1 to P_3 in graph 1b, in what direction and by how much will real GDP change? If the slopes of the AE lines in Figure 1a are 0.8 and equal to the MPC, in what direction will the aggregate expenditures schedule in Figure 1a need to shift to produce the previously determined change in real GDP? What is the size of the multiplier in this example? **LO12.7**

2. Refer to Figure 2 in the Appendix and assume that Q_1 is $400 and Q_2 is $500, the price level is stuck at P_1, and the slopes of the AE lines in Figure 2a are 0.75 and equal to the MPC. In what direction and by how much does the aggregate expenditures schedule in Figure 2a need to shift to move the aggregate demand curve in Figure 2b from AD_1 to AD_2? What is the multiplier in this example? Given the multiplier, what must be the distance between AD_1 and the broken line to its right at P_1? **LO12.7**

CHAPTER **13**

Fiscal Policy, Deficits, and Debt

Learning Objectives

LO13.1 Identify and explain the purposes, tools, and limitations of fiscal policy.

LO13.2 Explain the role of built-in stabilizers in moderating business cycles.

LO13.3 Describe how the cyclically adjusted budget reveals the status of U.S. fiscal policy.

LO13.4 Summarize recent U.S. fiscal policy and the projections for U.S. fiscal policy over the next few years.

LO13.5 Discuss the problems that governments may encounter in enacting and applying fiscal policy.

LO13.6 Discuss the size, composition, and consequences of the U.S. public debt.

In the previous chapter we saw that an excessive increase in aggregate demand can cause demand-pull inflation and that a significant decline in aggregate demand can cause recession and cyclical unemployment. For these reasons, the federal government sometimes uses budgetary actions to try to "stimulate the economy" or "rein in inflation." Such countercyclical **fiscal policy** consists of deliberate changes in government spending and tax collections designed to achieve full employment, control inflation, and encourage economic growth. (The adjective "fiscal" simply means "financial.")

ORIGIN OF THE IDEA

013.1
Fiscal policy

We begin this chapter by examining the logic behind fiscal policy, its current status, and its limitations. Then we examine a closely related topic: the U.S. public debt.

Our discussion of fiscal policy and public debt is very timely. In 2009, Congress and the Obama administration began a $787 billion stimulus program designed to help lift the U.S. economy out of deep recession. This fiscal policy contributed to a $1.4 trillion federal budget deficit in 2009, which increased the size of the U.S. public debt to $11.9 trillion. Large deficits continued in subsequent years, so that the U.S. public debt passed $17.0 trillion in 2013.

Fiscal Policy and the AD-AS Model

LO13.1 Identify and explain the purposes, tools, and limitations of fiscal policy.

The fiscal policy just defined is *discretionary* (or "active"). It is often initiated on the advice of the president's **Council of Economic Advisers (CEA),** a group of three economists appointed by the president to provide expertise and assistance on economic matters. Discretionary changes in government spending and taxes are *at the option* of the federal government. They do not occur automatically. Changes that occur without congressional action are *nondiscretionary* (or "passive" or "automatic"), and we will examine them later in this chapter.

Expansionary Fiscal Policy

When recession occurs, an **expansionary fiscal policy** may be in order. This policy consists of government spending increases, tax reductions, or both, designed to increase aggregate demand and therefore raise real GDP. Consider Figure 13.1, where we suppose that a sharp decline in investment spending has shifted the

economy's aggregate demand curve to the left from AD_1 to AD_2. (Disregard the arrows and dashed downsloping line for now.) The cause of the recession may be that profit expectations on investment projects have dimmed, curtailing investment spending and reducing aggregate demand.

Suppose the economy's potential or full-employment output is $510 billion in Figure 13.1. If the price level is inflexible downward at P_1, the broken horizontal line becomes relevant to the analysis. The aggregate demand curve moves leftward and reduces real GDP from $510 billion to $490 billion. A negative GDP gap of $20 billion (= $490 billion − $510 billion) arises. An increase in unemployment accompanies this negative GDP gap because fewer workers are needed to produce the reduced output. In short, the economy depicted is suffering both recession and cyclical unemployment.

What fiscal policy should the federal government adopt to try to stimulate the economy? It has three main options: (1) increase government spending, (2) reduce taxes, or (3) use some combination of the two. If the federal budget is balanced at the outset, expansionary fiscal policy will create a government **budget deficit**—government spending in excess of tax revenues.

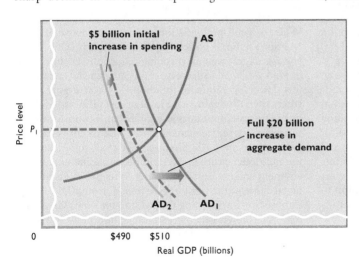

FIGURE 13.1 Expansionary fiscal policy. Expansionary fiscal policy uses increases in government spending or tax cuts to push the economy out of recession. In an economy with an MPC of 0.75, a $5 billion increase in government spending or a $6.67 billion decrease in personal taxes (producing a $5 billion initial increase in consumption) expands aggregate demand from AD_2 to the downsloping dashed curve. The multiplier then magnifies this initial increase in spending to AD_1. So real GDP rises along the broken horizontal line by $20 billion.

Increased Government Spending Other things equal, a sufficient increase in government spending will shift an economy's aggregate demand curve to the right, from AD_2 to AD_1 in Figure 13.1. To see why, suppose that the recession prompts the government to initiate $5 billion of new spending on highways, education, and health care. We represent this new $5 billion of government spending as the horizontal distance between AD_2 and the dashed downsloping line immediately to its right. At each price level, the amount of real output that is demanded is now $5 billion greater than that demanded before the expansion of government spending.

But the initial increase in aggregate demand is not the end of the story. Through the multiplier effect, the aggregate demand curve shifts to AD_1, a distance that exceeds that represented by the originating $5 billion increase in government purchases. This greater shift occurs because the multiplier process magnifies the initial change in spending into successive rounds of new consumption spending. If the economy's MPC is 0.75, then the simple multiplier is 4. So the aggregate demand curve shifts rightward by four times the distance between AD_2 and the broken downsloping line. Because this *particular* increase in aggregate demand occurs along the horizontal broken-line segment, real output rises by the full extent of the multiplier. Observe that real output rises to $510 billion, up $20 billion from its recessionary level of $490 billion. Concurrently, unemployment falls as firms increase their employment to the full-employment level that existed before the recession.

Tax Reductions Alternatively, the government could reduce taxes to shift the aggregate demand curve rightward, as from AD_2 to AD_1. Suppose the government cuts personal income taxes by $6.67 billion, which increases disposable income by the same amount. Consumption will rise by $5 billion (= MPC of 0.75 × $6.67 billion) and saving will go up by $1.67 billion (= MPS of 0.25 × $6.67 billion). In this case the horizontal distance between AD_2 and the dashed downsloping line in Figure 13.1 represents only the $5 billion initial increase in consumption spending. Again, we call it "initial" consumption spending because the multiplier process yields successive rounds of increased consumption spending. The aggregate demand curve eventually shifts rightward by four times the $5 billion initial increase in consumption produced by the tax cut. Real GDP rises by $20 billion, from $490 billion to $510 billion, implying a multiplier of 4. Employment increases accordingly.

You may have noted that a tax cut must be somewhat larger than the proposed increase in government spending if it is to achieve the same amount of rightward shift in the aggregate demand curve. This is because part of a tax reduction increases saving, rather than consumption. To increase initial consumption by a specific amount, the government must reduce taxes by more than that amount. With an MPC of 0.75, taxes must fall by $6.67 billion for $5 billion of new consumption to be forthcoming because $1.67 billion is saved (not consumed). If the MPC had instead been, say, 0.6, an $8.33 billion reduction in tax collections would have been necessary to increase initial consumption by $5 billion. The smaller the MPC, the greater the tax cut needed to accomplish a specific initial increase in consumption and a specific shift in the aggregate demand curve.

Combined Government Spending Increases and Tax Reductions The government may combine spending increases and tax cuts to produce the desired initial increase in spending and the eventual increase in aggregate demand and real GDP. In the economy depicted in Figure 13.1, the government might increase its spending by $1.25 billion while reducing taxes by $5 billion. As an exercise, you should explain why this combination will produce the targeted $5 billion initial increase in new spending.

If you were assigned Chapter 11, think through these three fiscal policy options in terms of the recessionary-expenditure-gap analysis associated with the aggregate expenditures model (Figure 11.7). And recall from the appendix to Chapter 12 that rightward shifts of the aggregate demand curve relate directly to upward shifts of the aggregate expenditures schedule.

Contractionary Fiscal Policy

When demand-pull inflation occurs, a restrictive or **contractionary fiscal policy** may help control it. This policy consists of government spending reductions, tax increases, or both, designed to decrease aggregate demand and therefore lower or eliminate inflation. Look at Figure 13.2, where the full-employment level of real GDP is $510 billion. The economy starts at equilibrium at point *a*, where the initial aggregate demand curve AD_3 intersects aggregate supply curve AS. Suppose that after going through the multiplier process, a $5 billion initial increase in investment and net export spending shifts the aggregate demand curve to the right by $20 billion, from AD_3 to AD_4. (Ignore the downsloping dashed line for now.) Given the upsloping AS curve, however, the equilibrium GDP does not rise by the full $20 billion. It only rises by $12 billion, to $522 billion, thereby creating an inflationary GDP gap

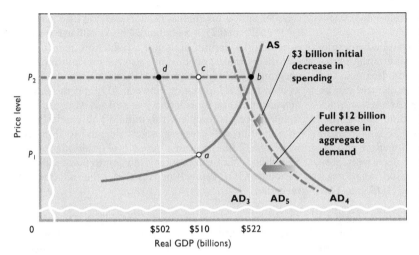

FIGURE 13.2 Contractionary fiscal policy. Contractionary fiscal policy uses decreases in government spending, increases in taxes, or both, to reduce demand-pull inflation. Here, an increase in aggregate demand from AD_3 to AD_4 has driven the economy to point *b* and ratcheted the price level up to P_2, where it becomes inflexible downward. If the economy's MPC is 0.75 and the multiplier therefore is 4, the government can either reduce its spending by $3 billion or increase its taxes by $4 billion (which will decrease consumption by $3 billion) to eliminate the inflationary GDP gap of $12 billion (= $522 billion − $510 billion). Aggregate demand will shift leftward, first from AD_4 to the dashed downsloping curve to its left, and then to AD_5. With the price level remaining at P_2, the economy will move from point *b* to point *c* and the inflationary GDP gap will disappear.

of $12 billion ($522 billion − $510 billion). The upslope of the AS curve means that some of the rightward movement of the AD curve ends up causing demand-pull inflation rather than increased output. As a result, the price level rises from P_1 to P_2 and the equilibrium moves to point *b*.

Without a government response, the inflationary GDP gap will cause further inflation (as input prices rise in the long run to meet the increase in output prices). If the government looks to fiscal policy to eliminate the inflationary GDP gap, its options are the opposite of those used to combat recession. It can (1) decrease government spending, (2) raise taxes, or (3) use some combination of those two policies. When the economy faces demand-pull inflation, fiscal policy should move toward a government **budget surplus**—tax revenues in excess of government spending.

But before discussing how the government can either decrease government spending or increase taxes to move toward a government budget surplus and control inflation, we have to keep in mind that the price level is like a ratchet. While increases in aggregate demand that expand real output beyond the full-employment level tend to ratchet the price level upward, declines in aggregate demand do not seem to push the price level downward. This means that stopping inflation is a matter of halting the rise of the price level, not trying to lower it to the previous level. It also means that the government must take the ratchet effect into account when deciding how big a cut in spending or an increase in taxes it should undertake.

Decreased Government Spending To control demand-pull inflation, the government can decrease

aggregate demand by reducing government spending. To see why the ratchet effect matters so much, look at Figure 13.2 and consider what would happen if the government ignored the ratchet effect and attempted to design a spending-reduction policy to eliminate the inflationary GDP gap. Since the $12 billion gap was caused by the $20 billion rightward movement of the aggregate demand curve from AD_3 to AD_4, the government might naively think that it could solve the problem by causing a $20 billion leftward shift of the aggregate demand curve to move it back to where it originally was. It could attempt to do so by reducing government spending by $5 billion and then allowing the multiplier effect to expand that initial decrease into a $20 billion decline in aggregate demand. That would shift the aggregate demand curve leftward by $20 billion, putting it back at AD_3.

This policy would work fine if there were no ratchet effect and if prices were flexible. The economy's equilibrium would move back from point *b* to point *a*, with equilibrium GDP returning to the full-employment level of $510 billion and the price level falling from P_2 back to P_1.

But because there *is* a ratchet effect, this scenario is not what will actually happen. Instead, the ratchet effect implies that the price level is stuck at P_2, so that the broken horizontal line at price level P_2 becomes important to the analysis. The fixed price level means that when the government reduces spending by $5 billion to shift the aggregate demand curve back to AD_3, it will actually cause a recession! The new equilibrium will not be at point *a*. It will be at point *d*, where aggregate demand curve AD_3 crosses the broken horizontal line. At point *d*, real GDP is only $502 billion, $8 billion below the full-employment level of $510 billion.

The problem is that, with the price level downwardly inflexible at P_2, the $20 billion leftward shift of the aggregate demand curve causes a full $20 billion decline in real GDP. None of the change in aggregate demand can be dissipated as a decline in the price level. As a result, equilibrium GDP declines by the full $20 billion, falling from $522 billion to $502 billion and putting it $8 billion below potential output. By not taking the ratchet effect into account, the government has overdone the decrease in government spending, replacing a $12 billion inflationary GDP gap with an $8 billion recessionary GDP gap. This is clearly not what it had in mind.

Here's how it can avoid this scenario. First, the government takes account of the size of the inflationary GDP gap. It is $12 billion. Second, it knows that with the price level fixed, the multiplier will be in full effect. Thus, it knows that any decline in government spending will be multiplied by a factor of 4. It then reasons that government spending will have to decline by only $3 billion rather than $5 billion. Why? Because the $3 billion initial decline in government spending will be multiplied by 4, creating a $12 billion decline in aggregate demand. Under the circumstances, a $3 billion decline in government spending is the correct amount to exactly offset the $12 billion GDP gap. This inflationary GDP gap is the problem that government wants to eliminate. To succeed, it need not undo the full increase in aggregate demand that caused the inflation in the first place.

Graphically, the horizontal distance between AD_4 and the dashed downsloping line to its left represents the $3 billion decrease in government spending. Once the multiplier process is complete, this spending cut will shift the aggregate demand curve leftward from AD_4 to AD_5. With the price level fixed at P_2, the economy will come to equilibrium at point c. The economy will operate at its potential output of $510 billion, and the inflationary GDP gap will be eliminated. Furthermore, because the government took the ratchet effect correctly into account, the government will not accidentally push the economy into a recession by making an overly large initial decrease in government spending.

Increased Taxes Just as government can use tax cuts to increase consumption spending, it can use tax *increases* to *reduce* consumption spending. If the economy in Figure 13.2 has an MPC of 0.75, the government must raise taxes by $4 billion to achieve its fiscal policy objective.

The $4 billion tax increase reduces saving by $1 billion (= the MPS of 0.25 × $4 billion). This $1 billion reduction in saving, by definition, is not a reduction in spending. But the $4 billion tax increase also reduces consumption spending by $3 billion (= the MPC of 0.75 × $4 billion), as shown by the distance between AD_4 and the dashed downsloping line to its left in Figure 13.2. After the multiplier process is complete, this initial $3 billion decline in consumption will cause aggregate demand to shift leftward by $12 billion at each price level (multiplier of 4 × $3 billion). With the economy moving to point c, the inflationary GDP gap will be closed and the inflation will be halted.

Combined Government Spending Decreases and Tax Increases The government may choose to combine spending decreases and tax increases in order to reduce aggregate demand and check inflation. To check your understanding, determine why a $1.5 billion decline in government spending combined with a $2 billion increase in taxes would shift the aggregate demand curve from AD_4 to AD_5. Also, if you were assigned Chapter 11, explain the three fiscal policy options for fighting inflation by referring to the inflationary-expenditure-gap concept developed with the aggregate expenditures model (Figure 11.7). And recall from the appendix to Chapter 12 that leftward shifts of the aggregate demand curve are associated with downshifts of the aggregate expenditures schedule.

Policy Options: *G* or *T*?

Which is preferable as a means of eliminating recession and inflation? The use of government spending or the use of taxes? The answer depends largely on one's view as to whether the government is too large or too small.

Economists who believe there are many unmet social and infrastructure needs usually recommend that government spending be increased during recessions. In times of demand-pull inflation, they usually recommend tax increases. Both actions either expand or preserve the size of government.

Economists who think that the government is too large and inefficient usually advocate tax cuts during recessions and cuts in government spending during times of demand-pull inflation. Both actions either restrain the growth of government or reduce its size.

The point is that discretionary fiscal policy designed to stabilize the economy can be associated with either an expanding government or a contracting government.

QUICK REVIEW 13.1

- Discretionary fiscal policy is the purposeful change of government expenditures and tax collections by government to promote full employment, price stability, and economic growth.
- Expansionary fiscal policy consists of increases in government spending, reductions in taxes, or both, and is designed to expand real GDP by increasing aggregate demand.
- Contractionary fiscal policy entails decreases in government spending, increases in taxes, or both, and is designed to reduce aggregate demand and slow or halt demand-pull inflation.
- To be implemented correctly, contractionary fiscal policy must properly account for the ratchet effect and the fact that the price level will not fall as the government shifts the aggregate demand curve leftward.

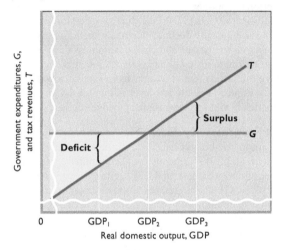

FIGURE 13.3 Built-in stability. Tax revenues, *T*, vary directly with GDP, and government spending, *G*, is assumed to be independent of GDP. As GDP falls in a recession, deficits occur automatically and help alleviate the recession. As GDP rises during expansion, surpluses occur automatically and help offset possible inflation.

Built-In Stability

LO13.2 Explain the role of built-in stabilizers in moderating business cycles.

To some degree, government tax revenues change automatically over the course of the business cycle and in ways that stabilize the economy. This automatic response, or built-in stability, constitutes nondiscretionary (or "passive" or "automatic") budgetary policy and results from the makeup of most tax systems. We did not include this built-in stability in our discussion of fiscal policy over the last few pages because we implicitly assumed that the same amount of tax revenue was being collected at each level of GDP. But the actual U.S. tax system is such that *net tax revenues* vary directly with GDP. (Net taxes are tax revenues less transfers and subsidies. From here on, we will use the simpler "taxes" to mean "net taxes.")

Virtually any tax will yield more tax revenue as GDP rises. In particular, personal income taxes have progressive rates and thus generate more-than-proportionate increases in tax revenues as GDP expands. Furthermore, as GDP rises and more goods and services are purchased, revenues from corporate income taxes and from sales taxes and excise taxes also increase. And, similarly, revenues from payroll taxes rise as economic expansion creates more jobs. Conversely, when GDP declines, tax receipts from all these sources also decline.

Transfer payments (or "negative taxes") behave in the opposite way from tax revenues. Unemployment compensation payments and welfare payments decrease during economic expansion and increase during economic contraction.

Automatic or Built-In Stabilizers

A **built-in stabilizer** is anything that increases the government's budget deficit (or reduces its budget surplus) during a recession and increases its budget surplus (or reduces its budget deficit) during an expansion without requiring explicit action by policymakers. As Figure 13.3 reveals, this is precisely what the U.S. tax system does. Government expenditures *G* are fixed and assumed to be independent of the level of GDP. Congress decides on a particular level of spending, but it does not determine the magnitude of tax revenues. Instead, it establishes tax rates, and the tax revenues then vary directly with the level of GDP that the economy achieves. Line *T* represents that direct relationship between tax revenues and GDP.

Economic Importance The economic importance of the direct relationship between tax receipts and GDP becomes apparent when we consider that:

- Taxes reduce spending and aggregate demand.
- Reductions in spending are desirable when the economy is moving toward inflation, whereas increases in spending are desirable when the economy is slumping.

As shown in Figure 13.3, tax revenues automatically increase as GDP rises during prosperity, and since taxes reduce household and business spending, they restrain the economic expansion. That is, as the economy moves toward a higher GDP, tax revenues automatically rise and move the budget from deficit toward surplus. In Figure 13.3, observe that the high and perhaps inflationary income level GDP$_3$ automatically generates a contractionary budget surplus.

Conversely, as GDP falls during recession, tax revenues automatically decline, increasing spending by households and businesses and thus cushioning the economic contraction. With a falling GDP, tax receipts decline and move the government's budget from surplus toward deficit. In Figure 13.3, the low level of income GDP$_1$ will automatically yield an expansionary budget deficit.

Tax Progressivity Figure 13.3 reveals that the size of the automatic budget deficits or surpluses—and therefore built-in stability—depends on the responsiveness of tax revenues to changes in GDP. If tax revenues change sharply as GDP changes, the slope of line T in the figure will be steep and the vertical distances between T and G (the deficits or surpluses) will be large. If tax revenues change very little when GDP changes, the slope will be gentle and built-in stability will be low.

The steepness of T in Figure 13.3 depends on the tax system itself. In a **progressive tax system,** the average tax rate (= tax revenue/GDP) rises with GDP. In a **proportional tax system,** the average tax rate remains constant as GDP rises. In a **regressive tax system,** the average tax rate falls as GDP rises. The progressive tax system has the steepest tax line T of the three. However, tax revenues will rise with GDP under both the progressive and the proportional tax systems, and they may rise, fall, or stay the same under a regressive tax system. The main point is this: The more progressive the tax system, the greater the economy's built-in stability.

The built-in stability provided by the U.S. tax system has reduced the severity of business fluctuations, perhaps by as much as 8 to 10 percent of the change in GDP that otherwise would have occurred.[1] In recession-year 2009, for example, revenues from the individual income tax fell by a staggering 22 percent. This decline helped keep household spending and real GDP from falling even more than they did. But built-in stabilizers can only dampen, not counteract, swings in real GDP. Discretionary fiscal policy (changes in tax rates and expenditures) or monetary policy (central bank–caused changes in interest rates) therefore may be needed to try to counter a recession or inflation of any appreciable magnitude.

[1]Alan J. Auerbach and Daniel Feenberg, "The Significance of Federal Taxes as Automatic Stabilizers," *Journal of Economic Perspectives,* Summer 2000, p. 54.

Evaluating How Expansionary or Contractionary Fiscal Policy Is Determined

LO13.3 Describe how the cyclically adjusted budget reveals the status of U.S. fiscal policy.

How can we determine whether a government's discretionary fiscal policy is expansionary, neutral, or contractionary? We cannot simply examine the actual budget deficits or surpluses that take place under the current policy because they will necessarily include the automatic changes in tax revenues that accompany every change in GDP. In addition, the expansionary or contractionary strength of any change in discretionary fiscal policy depends not on its absolute size but on how large it is relative to the size of the economy. So, in evaluating the status of fiscal policy, we must adjust deficits and surpluses to eliminate automatic changes in tax revenues and also compare the sizes of the adjusted budget deficits and surpluses to the level of potential GDP.

Cyclically Adjusted Budget

Economists use the **cyclically adjusted budget** (also called the *full-employment budget*) to adjust actual federal budget deficits and surpluses to account for the changes in tax revenues that happen automatically whenever GDP changes. The cyclically adjusted budget measures what the federal budget deficit or surplus would have been under existing tax rates and government spending levels if the economy had achieved its full-employment level of GDP (its potential output). The idea essentially is to compare *actual* government expenditures with the tax revenues *that would have occurred* if the economy had achieved full-employment GDP. That procedure removes budget deficits or surpluses that arise simply because of cyclical changes in GDP and thus tell us nothing about whether the government's current discretionary fiscal policy is fundamentally expansionary, contractionary, or neutral.

Consider Figure 13.4a, where line G represents government expenditures and line T represents tax revenues. In full-employment year 1, government expenditures of $500 billion equal tax revenues of $500 billion, as indicated by the intersection of lines G and T at point a. The cyclically adjusted budget deficit in year 1 is zero—government expenditures equal the tax revenues forthcoming at the full-employment output GDP$_1$. Obviously, the cyclically adjusted deficit *as a percentage of potential GDP* is also zero. The government's fiscal policy is neutral.

Now suppose that a recession occurs and GDP falls from GDP$_1$ to GDP$_2$, as shown in Figure 13.4a. Let's also

FIGURE 13.4 Cyclically adjusted deficits. (a) In the left-hand graph, the cyclically adjusted deficit is zero at the full-employment output GDP$_1$. But it is also zero at the recessionary output GDP$_2$ because the $500 billion of government expenditures at GDP$_2$ equals the $500 billion of tax revenues that would be forthcoming at the full-employment GDP$_1$. There has been no change in fiscal policy. (b) In the right-hand graph, discretionary fiscal policy, as reflected in the downward shift of the tax line from T_1 to T_2, has increased the cyclically adjusted budget deficit from zero in year 3 (before the tax cut) to $25 billion in year 4 (after the tax cut). This is found by comparing the $500 billion of government spending in year 4 with the $475 billion of taxes that would accrue at the full-employment GDP$_3$. Such a rise in the cyclically adjusted deficit (as a percentage of potential GDP) identifies an expansionary fiscal policy.

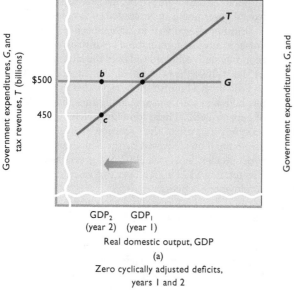

(a)
Zero cyclically adjusted deficits,
years 1 and 2

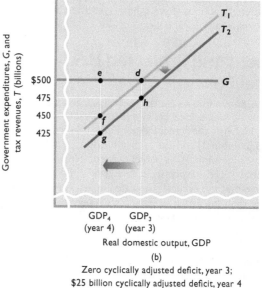

(b)
Zero cyclically adjusted deficit, year 3;
$25 billion cyclically adjusted deficit, year 4

assume that the government takes no discretionary action, so lines G and T remain as shown in the figure. Tax revenues automatically fall to $450 billion (point c) at GDP$_2$, while government spending remains unaltered at $500 billion (point b). A $50 billion budget deficit (represented by distance bc) arises. But this **cyclical deficit** is simply a by-product of the economy's slide into recession, not the result of discretionary fiscal actions by the government. We would be wrong to conclude from this deficit that the government is engaging in an expansionary fiscal policy. The government's fiscal policy has not changed. It is still neutral.

That fact is highlighted when we remove the cyclical part of the deficit and thus consider the cyclically adjusted budget deficit for year 2 in Figure 13.4a. The $500 billion of government expenditures in year 2 is shown by b on line G. And, as shown by a on line T, $500 billion of tax revenues would have occurred if the economy had achieved its full-employment GDP. Because both b and a represent $500 billion, the cyclically adjusted budget deficit in year 2 is zero, as is this deficit as a percentage of potential GDP. Since the cyclically adjusted deficits are zero in both years, we know that government did not change its discretionary

fiscal policy, even though a recession occurred and an actual deficit of $50 billion resulted.

Next, consider Figure 13.4b. Suppose that real output declined from full-employment GDP$_3$ in year 3 to GDP$_4$ in year 4. Also suppose that government responded to the recession by reducing tax rates in year 4, as represented by the downward shift of the tax line from T_1 to T_2. What has happened to the size of the cyclically adjusted deficit? Government expenditures in year 4 are $500 billion, as shown by e. Compare that amount with the $475 billion of tax revenues that would occur if the economy achieved its full-employment GDP. That is, compare position e on line G with position h on line T_2. The $25 billion of tax revenues by which e exceeds h is the cyclically adjusted budget deficit for year 4. As a percentage of potential GDP, the cyclically adjusted budget deficit has increased from zero in year 3 (before the tax-rate cut) to some positive percent [= ($25 billion/GDP$_3$) × 100] in year 4. This increase in the relative size of the full-employment deficit between the two years reveals that the new fiscal policy is *expansionary*.

In contrast, if we observed a cyclically adjusted deficit (as a percentage of potential GDP) of zero in one year, followed by a cyclically adjusted budget surplus in the next, we could conclude that fiscal policy has changed from being neutral to being contractionary. Because the cyclically adjusted budget adjusts for automatic changes in tax revenues, the increase in the cyclically adjusted budget surplus reveals that government either decreased its spending (G) or increased tax rates such that tax revenues (T) increased. These changes in G and T are precisely the discretionary actions that we have identified as elements of a *contractionary* fiscal policy.

Recent and Projected U.S. Fiscal Policy

LO13.4 Summarize recent U.S. fiscal policy and the projections for U.S. fiscal policy over the next few years.

Table 13.1 lists the actual federal budget deficits and surpluses (column 2) and the cyclically adjusted deficits and surpluses (column 3), as percentages of actual GDP and potential GDP, respectively, between 2000 and 2012. Observe that the cyclically adjusted deficits are generally smaller than the actual deficits. This is because the actual deficits include cyclical deficits, whereas the cyclically adjusted deficits eliminate them. Only cyclically adjusted surpluses and deficits as percentages of potential GDP (column 3) provide the information needed to assess discretionary fiscal policy and determine whether it is expansionary, contractionary, or neutral.

TABLE 13.1 Federal Deficits (−) and Surpluses (+) as Percentages of GDP, 2000–2012

(1) Year	(2) Actual Deficit − or Surplus +	(3) Cyclically adjusted Deficit − or Surplus +*
2000	+2.4	+1.2
2001	+1.3	+0.6
2002	−1.5	−1.2
2003	−3.4	−2.7
2004	−3.5	−3.2
2005	−2.6	−2.6
2006	−1.9	−2.2
2007	−1.2	−1.3
2008	−3.2	−2.9
2009	−10.1	−7.1
2010	−9.0	−5.7
2011	−8.7	−5.6
2012	−7.0	−4.3

*As a percentage of potential GDP.

Source: Congressional Budget Office, **www.cbo.gov**.

Fiscal Policy from 2000 to 2007

Take a look at the data for 2000, for example, which shows that fiscal policy was contractionary that year. Note that the actual budget surplus was 2.4 percent of GDP in 2000 and the cyclically adjusted budget surplus was 1.2 percent of potential GDP. Because the economy was fully employed and corporate profits were strong, tax revenues poured into the federal government and exceeded government expenditures.

But not all was well in 2000. Specifically, the so-called dot-com stock market bubble burst that year, and the U.S. economy noticeably slowed over the latter half of the year. In March 2001 the economy slid into a recession. Congress and the Bush administration responded by cutting taxes by $44 billion in 2001 and scheduling an additional $52 billion of cuts for 2002. These stimulus policies helped boost the economy and offset the recession as well as cushion the economic blow delivered by the September 11, 2001, terrorist attacks. In March 2002 Congress passed further tax cuts totaling $122 billion over two years and extended unemployment benefits.

As Table 13.1 reveals, the cyclically adjusted budget moved from a surplus of 1.2 percent of potential GDP in 2000 to a deficit of −1.2 percent two years later in 2002. Fiscal policy had definitely turned expansionary. Nevertheless, the economy remained sluggish through 2002 and into 2003. In June 2003 Congress again cut taxes, this time by a much larger $350 billion over several years. Specifically, the tax legislation accelerated the reduction of marginal tax rates already scheduled for future years and slashed tax rates on income from dividends and capital gains. It also increased tax breaks for families and small businesses. Note from the table that this tax package increased the cyclically adjusted budget deficit as a percentage of potential GDP to −2.7 percent in 2003. The economy strengthened and both real output and employment grew between 2003 and 2007. By 2007 full employment had been restored, although a −1.3 percent cyclically adjusted budget deficit still remained.

Fiscal Policy during and after the Great Recession

As pointed out in previous chapters, major economic trouble began in 2007. In the summer of 2007, a crisis in the market for mortgage loans flared up. Later in 2007 that crisis spread rapidly to other financial markets, threatened the survival of several major U.S. financial institutions, and severely disrupted the entire financial system. As credit markets began to freeze, general pessimism spread beyond the financial markets to the overall economy. Businesses and households retrenched on their borrowing and spending, and in December 2007 the economy entered a recession.

Over the following two years, it became known as the Great Recession—one of the steepest and longest economic downturns since the 1930s.

In 2008 Congress acted rapidly to pass an economic stimulus package. This law provided a total of $152 billion in stimulus, with some of it coming as tax breaks for businesses, but most of it delivered as checks of up to $600 each to taxpayers, veterans, and Social Security recipients.

As a percentage of GDP, the *actual* federal budget deficit jumped from −1.2 percent in 2007 to −3.2 percent in 2008. This increase resulted from an automatic drop-off of tax revenues during the recession, along with the tax rebates (fiscal stimulus checks) paid out in 2008. As shown in Table 13.1, the *cyclically adjusted* budget deficit rose from −1.3 percent of potential GDP in 2007 to −2.9 percent in 2008. This increase in the cyclically adjusted budget reveals that fiscal policy in 2008 was expansionary.

The government hoped that those receiving checks would spend the money and thus boost consumption and aggregate demand. But households instead saved substantial parts of the money from the checks or used some of the money to pay down credit card loans. Although this stimulus plan boosted output somewhat in mid-2008, it was neither as expansionary nor long-lasting as policymakers had hoped. The continuing forces of the Great Recession simply overwhelmed the policy.

With the economy continuing its precipitous slide, the Obama administration and Congress enacted the American Recovery and Reinvestment Act of 2009. This gigantic $787 billion program—coming on top of a $700 billion rescue package for financial institutions—consisted of low- and middle-income tax rebates, plus large increases in expenditures on infrastructure, education, and health care. The idea was to flood the economy with additional spending to try to boost aggregate demand and get people back to work.

The tax cuts in the package were aimed at lower- and middle-income individuals and households, who were thought to be more likely than high-income people to spend (rather than save) the extra income from the tax rebates. Rather than sending out lump-sum stimulus checks as in 2008, the new tax rebates showed up as small increases in workers' monthly payroll checks. With smaller amounts per month rather than a single large check, the government hoped that people would spend the bulk of their enhanced income—rather than save it as they had done with the one-time-only, lump-sum checks received in 2008. The second part of the fiscal policy (60 percent of the funding) consisted of increases in government expenditures on a wide assortment of programs, including transportation, education, and aid to state governments. The highly stimulative fiscal

policy for 2009 is fully reflected in column 3 of Table 13.1. The cyclically adjusted budget deficit rose dramatically from −2.9 percent of potential GDP in 2008 to a very high −7.1 percent of potential GDP in 2009.

The recession officially ended during the summer of 2009, but the economy did not rebound vigorously. Unemployment remained elevated and tax collections were low due to a stagnant economy. As a result, policymakers decided to continue with large amounts of fiscal stimulus. Annual actual (not cyclically adjusted) budget deficits amounted to −9.0, −8.7, and −7.0 percent of GDP, respectively, in years 2010, 2011, and 2012. The cyclically adjusted budget deficits for those years were, respectively, −5.7, −5.6, and −4.3 percent of potential GDP. Thus, while the intensity of fiscal stimulus was gradually diminishing, it remained very high by historical standards. The recession had been exceptionally strong, and so was the ongoing fiscal response.

Other nations also experienced recessions and also responded with expansionary fiscal policies. Global Perspective 13.1 shows the magnitudes of the cyclically

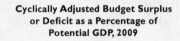

GLOBAL PERSPECTIVE 13.1

Cyclically Adjusted Budget Deficits or Surpluses as a Percentage of Potential GDP, Selected Nations

Because of the global recession, in 2009 all but a few of the world's major nations had cyclically adjusted budget deficits. These deficits varied as percentages of potential GDP, but they each reflected some degree of expansionary fiscal policy.

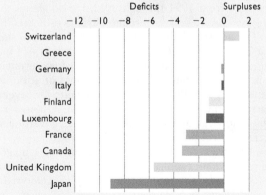

Source: OECD Economic Outlook, **http://www.oecd.org/eco/ economicoutlook.htm**.

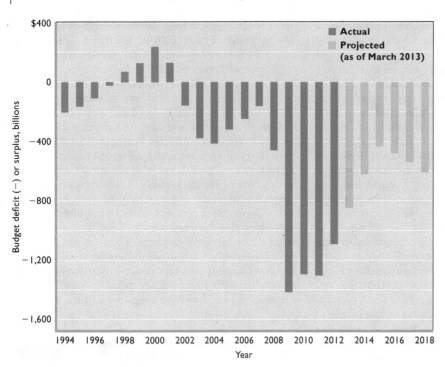

FIGURE 13.5 Federal budget deficits and surpluses, actual and projected, fiscal years 1994–2018 (in billions of nominal dollars). The annual budget deficits of 1994 through 1997 gave way to budget surpluses from 1998 through 2001. Deficits reappeared in 2002 and declined through 2007. They greatly ballooned in recessionary years 2008 and 2009 and are projected to remain high for many years to come.

Source: Congressional Budget Office, **www.cbo.gov**.

adjusted surpluses and deficits of a number of countries in 2009.

Past and Projected Budget Deficits and Surpluses

Figure 13.5 shows the absolute magnitudes of actual (not cyclically adjusted) U.S. budget surpluses and deficits, here from 1994 through 2012. It also shows the projected future deficits through 2018, as estimated by the Congressional Budget Office (CBO). In recession year 2009, the federal budget deficit reached $1,413 billion, mainly but not totally due to reduced tax revenues from lower income and record amounts of stimulus spending. The CBO projects high deficits for several years to come. But projected deficits and surpluses are subject to large and frequent changes, as government alters its fiscal policy and GDP growth accelerates or slows. So we suggest that you update this figure by going to the Congressional Budget Office Web site, **www.cbo.gov**, and find the document titled *The Budget and Economic Outlook*. Near the start of that document, you should find Summary Table 1. The numbers are in the row labeled "Deficit (−) or Surplus."

Problems, Criticisms, and Complications of Implementing Fiscal Policy

LO13.5 Discuss the problems that governments may encounter in enacting and applying fiscal policy.

Economists recognize that governments may encounter a number of significant problems in enacting and applying fiscal policy.

Problems of Timing

Several problems of timing may arise in connection with fiscal policy:

- ***Recognition lag*** The recognition lag is the time between the beginning of recession or inflation and the certain awareness that it is actually happening. This lag arises because the economy does not move smoothly through the business cycle. Even during good times, the economy has slow months interspersed with months of rapid growth and expansion. This makes recognizing a recession difficult since several slow months will have to happen in succession before people can conclude with any confidence that the good times are over and a recession has begun.

The same is true with inflation. Even periods of moderate inflation have months of high inflation—so that several high-inflation months must come in sequence before people can confidently conclude that inflation has moved to a higher level.

Attempts to reduce the length of the recognition lag by trying to predict the future course of the economy also have proven to be highly difficult, at best. As a result, the economy is often 4 to 6 months into a recession or inflation before the situation is clearly discernible in the relevant statistics. Due to this recognition lag, the economic downslide or the inflation may become more serious than it would have if the situation had been identified and acted on sooner.

- *Administrative lag* The wheels of democratic government turn slowly. There will typically be a significant lag between the time the need for fiscal action is recognized and the time action is taken. Following the terrorist attacks of September 11, 2001, the U.S. Congress was stalemated for 5 months before passing a compromise economic stimulus law in March 2002. (In contrast, the Federal Reserve began lowering interest rates the week after the attacks.)

- *Operational lag* A lag also occurs between the time fiscal action is taken and the time that action affects output, employment, or the price level. Although changes in tax rates can be put into effect relatively quickly once new laws are passed, government spending on public works—new dams, interstate highways, and so on—requires long planning periods and even longer periods of construction. Such spending is of questionable use in offsetting short (for example, 6- to 12-month) periods of recession. Consequently, discretionary fiscal policy has increasingly relied on tax changes rather than on changes in spending as its main tool.

Political Considerations

Fiscal policy is conducted in a political arena. That reality not only may slow the enactment of fiscal policy but also may create the potential for political considerations swamping economic considerations in its formulation. It is a human trait to rationalize actions and policies that are in one's self-interest. Politicians are very human—they want to get reelected. A strong economy at election time will certainly help them. So they may favor large tax cuts under the guise of expansionary fiscal policy even though

that policy is economically inappropriate. Similarly, they may rationalize increased government spending on popular items such as farm subsidies, health care, highways, education, and homeland security.

At the extreme, elected officials and political parties might collectively "hijack" fiscal policy for political purposes, cause inappropriate changes in aggregate demand, and thereby cause (rather than avert) economic fluctuations. For instance, before an election, they may try to stimulate the economy to improve their reelection hopes. And then after the election, they may try to use contractionary fiscal policy to dampen the excessive aggregate demand that they caused with their preelection stimulus. In short, elected officials may cause so-called **political business cycles**—swings in overall economic activity and real GDP resulting from election-motivated fiscal policy, rather than from inherent instability in the private sector. Political business cycles are difficult to document and prove, but there is little doubt that political considerations weigh heavily in the formulation of fiscal policy. The question is how often those political considerations run counter to "sound economics."

Future Policy Reversals

Fiscal policy may fail to achieve its intended objectives if households expect future reversals of policy. Consider a tax cut, for example. If taxpayers believe the tax reduction is temporary, they may save a large portion of their tax cut, reasoning that rates will return to their previous level in the future. They save more now so that they will be able to draw on this extra savings to maintain their future consumption levels if taxes do indeed rise again in the future. So a tax reduction thought to be temporary may not increase present consumption spending and aggregate demand by as much as our simple model (Figure 13.1) suggests.

The opposite may be true for a tax increase. If taxpayers think it is temporary, they may reduce their saving to pay the tax while maintaining their present consumption. They may reason they can restore their saving when the tax rate again falls. So the tax increase may not reduce current consumption and aggregate demand by as much as policymakers intended.

To the extent that this so-called *consumption smoothing* occurs over time, fiscal policy will lose some of its strength. The lesson is that tax-rate changes that households view as permanent are more likely to alter consumption and aggregate demand than tax changes they view as temporary.

Offsetting State and Local Finance

The fiscal policies of state and local governments are frequently *pro-cyclical*, meaning that they worsen rather than correct recession or inflation. Unlike the federal government, most state and local governments face constitutional or other legal requirements to balance their budgets. Like households and private businesses, state and local governments increase their expenditures during prosperity and cut them during recession.

During the Great Depression of the 1930s, most of the increase in federal spending was offset by decreases in state and local spending. During and immediately following the recession of 2001, many state and local governments had to offset lower tax revenues resulting from the reduced personal income and spending of their citizens. They offset the decline in revenues by raising tax rates, imposing new taxes, and reducing spending.

In view of these past experiences, the $787 billion fiscal package of 2009 made a special effort to reduce this problem by giving substantial aid dollars to state governments. Because of the sizable federal aid, the states did not have to increase taxes and reduce expenditure by as much as otherwise. So their collective fiscal actions did not fight as much against the increase in aggregate demand that the federal government wanted to achieve with its tax cuts and expenditure increases.

Crowding-Out Effect

Another potential flaw of fiscal policy is the so-called **crowding-out effect:** An expansionary fiscal policy (deficit spending) may increase the interest rate and reduce investment spending, thereby weakening or canceling the stimulus of the expansionary policy. The rising interest rate might also potentially crowd out interest-sensitive consumption spending (such as purchasing automobiles on credit). But since investment is the most volatile component of GDP, the crowding-out effect focuses its attention on investment and whether the stimulus provided by deficit spending may be partly or even fully neutralized by an offsetting reduction in investment spending.

To see the potential problem, realize that whenever the government borrows money (as it must if it is deficit spending), it increases the overall demand for money. If the monetary authorities are holding the money supply constant, this increase in demand will raise the price paid for borrowing money: the interest rate. Because investment spending varies inversely with the interest rate, some investment will be choked off or "crowded out."

ORIGIN OF THE IDEA

O13.2
Crowding out

Economists vary in their opinions about the strength of the crowding-out effect. An important thing to keep in mind is that crowding out is likely to be less of a problem when the economy is in recession because investment demand tends to be weak. Why? Because output purchases slow during recessions and therefore most businesses end up with substantial excess capacity. As a result, they do not have much incentive to add new machinery or build new factories. After all, why should they add capacity when some of the capacity they already have is lying idle?

With investment demand weak during a recession, the crowding-out effect is likely to be very small. Simply put, there is not much investment for the government to crowd out. Even if deficit spending does increase the interest rate, the effect on investment may be fully offset by the improved investment prospects that businesses expect from the fiscal stimulus.

By contrast, when the economy is operating at or near full capacity, investment demand is likely to be quite strong so that crowding out will probably be a much more serious problem. When the economy is booming, factories will be running at or near full capacity and firms will have high investment demand for two reasons. First, equipment running at full capacity wears out fast, so firms will be investing substantial amounts just to replace machinery and equipment that wears out and depreciates. Second, the economy is likely to be growing overall so that firms will be heavily investing to *add* to their production capacity to take advantage of the greater anticipated demand for their outputs.

Current Thinking on Fiscal Policy

Where do these complications leave us as to the advisability and effectiveness of discretionary fiscal policy? In view of the complications and uncertain outcomes of fiscal policy, some economists argue that it is better not to engage in it at all. Those holding that view point to the superiority of monetary policy (changes in interest rates engineered by the Federal Reserve) as a stabilizing device or believe that most economic fluctuations tend to be mild and self-correcting.

But most economists believe that fiscal policy remains an important, useful policy lever in the government's macroeconomic toolkit. The current popular view is that fiscal policy can help push the economy in a particular direction but cannot fine-tune it to a precise macroeconomic outcome. Mainstream economists generally agree that monetary policy is the best month-to-month stabilization tool for the U.S. economy. If monetary policy is doing its job, the government should maintain a relatively neutral fiscal policy, with a cyclically adjusted budget deficit or surplus of no more than 2 percent of potential GDP. It should hold major discretionary fiscal policy in reserve to help counter situations where recession threatens to be deep and long lasting, as in 2008 and 2009, or where a substantial reduction in aggregate demand might help the Federal Reserve to quell a major bout of inflation.

Finally, economists agree that any proposed fiscal policy should be evaluated for its potential positive and negative impacts on long-run productivity growth. The short-run policy tools used for conducting active fiscal policy often have long-run impacts. Countercyclical fiscal policy should be shaped to strengthen, or at least not impede, the growth of long-run aggregate supply (shown as a rightward shift of the long-run aggregate supply curve in Figure 12.5). For example, a tax cut might be structured to enhance work effort, strengthen investment, and encourage innovation. Alternatively, an increase in government spending might center on preplanned projects for public capital (highways, mass transit, ports, airports), which are complementary to private investment and thus support long-term economic growth.

QUICK REVIEW 13.2

- Automatic changes in net taxes (taxes minus transfers) add a degree of built-in stability to the economy.
- Cyclical deficits arise from declines in net tax revenues that automatically occur as the economy recedes and incomes and profits fall.
- The cyclically adjusted budget eliminates cyclical effects on net tax revenues; it compares actual levels of government spending to the projected levels of net taxes that would occur if the economy were achieving its full-employment output.
- Time lags, political problems, expectations, and state and local finances complicate fiscal policy.
- The crowding-out effect indicates that an expansionary fiscal policy may increase the interest rate and reduce investment spending.

The U.S. Public Debt

LO13.6 Discuss the size, composition, and consequences of the U.S. public debt.

The U.S. national debt, or **public debt,** is essentially the accumulation of all past federal deficits and surpluses. The deficits have greatly exceeded the surpluses and have emerged mainly from war financing, recessions, and fiscal policy. In 2012 the total public debt was $16.4 trillion—

$11.6 trillion held by the public, excluding the Federal Reserve; and $4.8 trillion held by federal agencies and the Federal Reserve. Between 2007 and 2009, the total public debt expanded by a huge $2.9 trillion. During the Great Recession, federal tax revenues plummeted because incomes and profit fell, and federal expenditures jumped because of huge spending to rescue failing financial institutions and to stimulate the shrinking economy.

Because large annual deficits continued over the next several years, the total public debt grew past $17.0 trillion in late 2013. It had doubled in just seven years, growing from $8.5 trillion in late 2006 to $17.0 trillion in late 2013. You can find the current size of the public debt at the Web site of the Department of Treasury, Bureau of the Public Debt, at **www.treasurydirect.gov/NP/BPDLogin?application=np**. At this site, you will see that the U.S. Treasury defines "the public" to include the Federal Reserve. But because the Federal Reserve is the nation's central bank, economists view it as essentially part of the federal government and not part of the public. Economists typically focus on the part of the debt that is not owned by the federal government and the Federal Reserve.

Ownership

The total public debt of $16.4 trillion represents the total amount of money owed by the federal government to the holders of **U.S. government securities:** financial instruments issued by the federal government to borrow money to finance expenditures that exceed tax revenues. U.S. government securities (loan instruments) are of four types: *Treasury bills* (short-term securities), *Treasury notes* (medium-term securities), *Treasury bonds* (long-term securities), and *U.S. savings bonds* (long-term, nonmarketable bonds).

Figure 13.6 shows that the public, sans the Federal Reserve, held 60 percent of the federal debt in 2012 and that federal government agencies and the Federal Reserve held the remaining 40 percent. The federal agencies hold U.S. government securities as risk-free assets that they can cash in as needed to make latter payments. The Federal Reserve holds these securities to facilitate the "open-market operations" that it uses to control the nation's money supply (Chapter 16). Observe that "the public" in the pie chart consists of individuals here and abroad, state and local governments, and U.S. financial institutions. Foreigners held about 33 percent of the total U.S. public debt in 2012, meaning that most of the U.S. public debt is held internally and not externally. Americans owed 67 percent of the public debt to Americans. Of the $5.3 trillion

FIGURE 13.6 Ownership of the total public debt, 2012. The $16.1 trillion public debt can be divided into the proportion held by the public, excluding the Federal Reserve (60 percent), and the proportion held by federal agencies and the Federal Reserve System (40 percent). Of the total debt, 33 percent is foreign-owned.

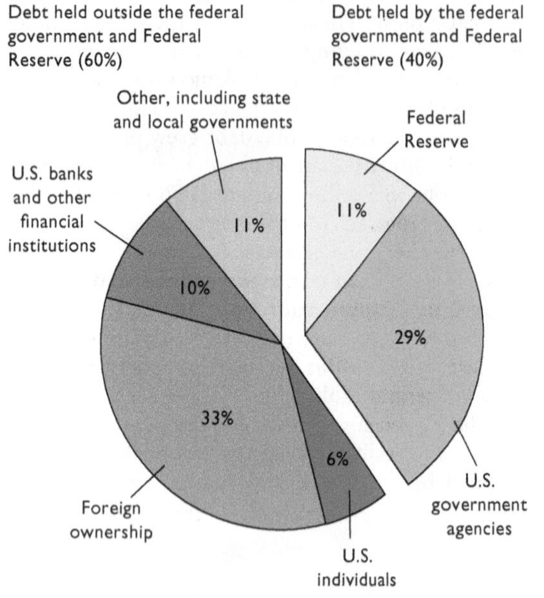

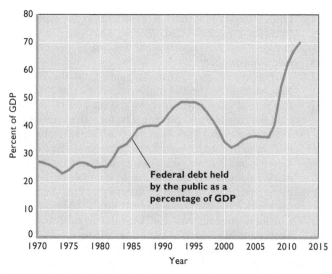

Debt held outside the federal government and Federal Reserve (60%)

Debt held by the federal government and Federal Reserve (40%)

Other, including state and local governments

Federal Reserve

U.S. banks and other financial institutions

11%

11%

10%

29%

33%

6%

Foreign ownership

U.S. government agencies

U.S. individuals

Total debt: $16.1 trillion

Source: Economic Report of the President, 2013, **www.gpo.gov/fdsys/browse/ collection.action?collectionCode=ERP**; authors' derivation from Table B-89, September 2012 data. Federal Reserve percentage is from the U.S. Treasury, **www.fms.treas.gov/bulletin**.

of debt held by foreigners, China held 22 percent, Japan held 20 percent, and oil-exporting nations held 5 percent.

Debt and GDP

A simple statement of the absolute size of the debt ignores the fact that the wealth and productive ability of the U.S. economy is also vast. A wealthy, highly productive nation can incur and carry a large public debt much more easily than a poor nation can. A more meaningful measure of the public debt relates it to an economy's GDP. Figure 13.7 shows the yearly relative sizes of the U.S. public debt held outside the Federal Reserve and federal agencies. In 2012 the percentage was 70 percent. Most noticeably, the percentage rose dramatically starting in 2008 because of massive annual budget deficits.

International Comparisons

It is not uncommon for countries to have sizable public debts. As shown in Global Perspective 13.2, the public debt as a percentage of real GDP in the United States is neither particularly high nor low relative to such debt percentages in other advanced industrial nations.

Interest Charges

Many economists conclude that the primary burden of the debt is the annual interest charge accruing on the bonds sold to finance the debt. In 2012 interest on the total public debt was $360 billion. Although this amount is sizable in absolute terms, it was only 2.3 percent of GDP for

FIGURE 13.7 Federal debt held by the public, excluding the Federal Reserve, as a percentage of GDP, 1970–2012. As a percentage of GDP, the federal debt held by the public (held outside the Federal Reserve and federal government agencies) increased sharply over the 1980–1995 period and declined significantly between 1995 and 2001. Since 2001, the percentage has gone up again, and jumped abruptly and sharply starting in 2008.

Source: FRED II database, St. Louis Federal Reserve Bank, **research.stlouisfed.org/fred2/**.

GLOBAL PERSPECTIVE 13.2

Publicly Held Debt: International Comparisons

Although the United States has the world's largest public debt, a number of other nations have larger debts as percentages of their GDPs.

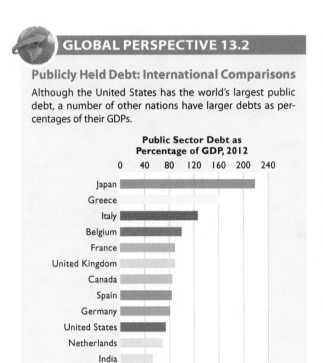

Public Sector Debt as Percentage of GDP, 2012

Source: CIA World Factbook, **www.cia.gov/library/publications/the-world-factbook/.** These debt calculations encompass federal, state, and local debt, including the debt of government-owned enterprises (not just federal debt as in Figure 13.7) and are 2012 estimates.

Refinancing   As long as the U.S. public debt is viewed by lenders as manageable and sustainable, the public debt is easily refinanced. As portions of the debt come due on maturing Treasury bills, notes, and bonds each month, the government does not cut expenditures or raise taxes to provide the funds required. Rather, it refinances the debt by selling new bonds and using the proceeds to pay holders of the maturing bonds. The new bonds are in strong demand because lenders can obtain a market-determined interest return with no risk of default by the federal government.

Of course, refinancing could become an issue with a high enough debt-to-GDP ratio. Some countries such as Greece have run into this problem. High and rising ratios in the United States might raise fears that the U.S. government might be unable to pay back loans as they come due. But, with the present U.S. debt-to-GDP ratio and the prospects of long-term economic growth, this is a false concern for the United States.

Taxation   The federal government has the constitutional authority to levy and collect taxes. A tax increase is a government option for gaining sufficient revenue to pay interest and principal on the public debt. Financially distressed private households and corporations cannot extract themselves from their financial difficulties by taxing the public. If their incomes or sales revenues fall short of their expenses, they can indeed go bankrupt. But the federal government does have the option to impose new taxes or increase existing tax rates if necessary to finance its debt. Such tax hikes may be politically unpopular and may weaken incentives to work and invest, but they *are* a means of raising funds to finance the debt.

Burdening Future Generations

In 2012 public debt per capita was $52,396. Was each child born in 2012 handed a $52,396 bill from the federal government? Not really. The public debt does not impose as much of a burden on future generations as commonly thought.

The United States owes a substantial portion of the public debt to itself. U.S. citizens and institutions (banks, businesses, insurance companies, governmental agencies, and trust funds) own about 67 percent of the U.S. government securities. Although that part of the public debt is a liability to Americans (as taxpayers), it is simultaneously an asset to Americans (as holders of Treasury bills, Treasury notes, Treasury bonds, and U.S. savings bonds).

To eliminate the American-owned part of the public debt would require a gigantic transfer payment from Americans to Americans. Taxpayers would pay higher taxes, and holders of the debt would receive an equal amount for their U.S. government securities. Purchasing power in the

2012. So, the federal government had to collect taxes equal to 2.3 percent of GDP to service the total public debt. This percentage was unchanged from 2000 despite the much higher total public debt. That was possible because interest rates were being kept extremely low by the Federal Reserve in order to help stimulate the economy in the wake of the Great Recession (Chapter 16).

False Concerns

You may wonder if the large public debt might bankrupt the United States or at least place a tremendous burden on your children and grandchildren. Fortunately, these are largely false concerns. People were wondering the same things 50 years ago!

Bankruptcy

The large U.S. public debt does not threaten to bankrupt the federal government, leaving it unable to meet its financial obligations. There are two main reasons: refinancing and taxation.

United States would not change. Only the repayment of the 33 percent of the public debt owned by foreigners would negatively impact U.S. purchasing power.

The public debt increased sharply during the Second World War. But the decision to finance military purchases through the sale of government bonds did not shift the economic burden of the war to future generations. The economic cost of the Second World War consisted of the civilian goods society had to forgo in shifting scarce resources to war goods production (recall production possibilities analysis). Regardless of whether society financed this reallocation through higher taxes or through borrowing, the real economic burden of the war would have been the same. That burden was borne almost entirely by those who lived during the war. They were the ones who did without a multitude of consumer goods to enable the United States to arm itself and its allies.

The next generation inherited the debt from the war but also an equal amount of government bonds that would pay them cash in future years. It also inherited the enormous benefits from the victory—namely, preserved political and economic systems at home and the "export" of those systems to Germany, Italy, and Japan. Those outcomes enhanced postwar U.S. economic growth and helped raise the standard of living of future generations of Americans.

Substantive Issues

Although the preceding issues relating to the public debt are false concerns, a number of substantive issues are not. Economists, however, attach varying degrees of importance to them.

Income Distribution

The distribution of ownership of government securities is highly uneven. Some people own much more than the $52,396-per-person portion of government securities; other people own less or none at all. In general, the ownership of the public debt is concentrated among wealthier groups, who own a large percentage of all stocks and bonds. Because the overall federal tax system is only slightly progressive, payment of interest on the public debt mildly increases income inequality. Income is transferred from people who, on average, have lower incomes to the higher-income bondholders. If greater income equality is one of society's goals, then this redistribution is undesirable.

Incentives

The current public debt necessitates annual interest payments of $360 billion. With no increase in the size of the

debt, that interest charge must be paid out of tax revenues. Higher taxes may dampen incentives to bear risk, to innovate, to invest, and to work. So, in this indirect way, a large public debt may impair economic growth and therefore impose a burden of reduced output (and income) on future generations.

Foreign-Owned Public Debt

The 33 percent of the U.S. debt held by citizens and institutions of foreign countries *is* an economic burden to Americans. Because we do not owe that portion of the debt "to ourselves," the payment of interest and principal on this **external public debt** enables foreigners to buy some of our output. In return for the benefits derived from the borrowed funds, the United States transfers goods and services to foreign lenders. Of course, Americans also own debt issued by foreign governments, so payment of principal and interest by those governments transfers some of their goods and services to Americans.

Crowding-Out Effect Revisited

A potentially more serious problem is the financing (and continual refinancing) of the large public debt, which can transfer a real economic burden to future generations by passing on to them a smaller stock of capital goods. This possibility involves the previously discussed crowding-out effect: the idea that public borrowing drives up real interest rates, which reduces private investment spending. If public borrowing only happened during recessions, crowding out would not likely be much of a problem. Because private investment demand tends to be weak during recessions, any increase in interest rates caused by public borrowing will at most cause a small reduction in investment spending.

In contrast, the need to continuously finance a large public debt may be more troublesome. At times, that financing requires borrowing large amounts of money when the economy is near or at its full-employment output. Because this usually is when private demand is strong, any increase in interest rates caused by the borrowing necessary to refinance the debt may result in a substantial decline in investment spending. If the amount of current investment crowded out is extensive, future generations will inherit an economy with a smaller production capacity and, other things equal, a lower standard of living.

A Graphical Look at Crowding Out We know from Chapter 10 that the amount of investment spending is

FIGURE 13.8 The investment demand curve and the crowding-out effect. If the investment demand curve (ID_1) is fixed, the increase in the interest rate from 6 percent to 10 percent caused by financing a large public debt will move the economy from *a* to *b*, crowding out $10 billion of private investment and decreasing the size of the capital stock inherited by future generations. However, if the public goods enabled by the debt improve the investment prospects of businesses, the private investment demand curve will shift rightward, as from ID_1 to ID_2. That shift may offset the crowding-out effect wholly or in part. In this case, it moves the economy from *a* to *c*.

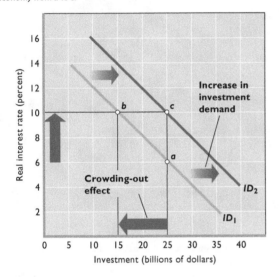

inversely related to the real interest rate. When graphed, that relationship is shown as a downsloping investment demand curve, such as either ID_1 or ID_2 in Figure 13.8. Let's first consider curve ID_1. (Ignore curve ID_2 for now.) Suppose that government borrowing increases the real interest rate from 6 percent to 10 percent. Investment spending will then fall from $25 billion to $15 billion, as shown by the economy's move from *a* to *b*. That is, the financing of the debt will compete with the financing of private investment projects and crowd out $10 billion of private investment. So the stock of private capital handed down to future generations will be $10 billion less than it would have been without the need to finance the public debt.

Public Investments and Public-Private Complementarities But even with crowding out, two factors could partly or fully offset the net economic burden shifted to future generations. First, just as private expenditures may involve either consumption or investment, so it is with public goods. Part of the government spending enabled by the public debt is for public investment outlays (for example, highways, mass transit systems, and electric

power facilities) and "human capital" (for example, investments in education, job training, and health). Like private expenditures on machinery and equipment, those **public investments** increase the economy's future production capacity. Because of the financing through debt, the stock of public capital passed on to future generations may be higher than otherwise. That greater stock of public capital may offset the diminished stock of private capital resulting from the crowding-out effect, leaving overall production capacity unimpaired.

So-called public-private complementarities are a second factor that could reduce the crowding-out effect. Some public and private investments are complementary. Thus, the public investment financed through debt could spur some private-sector investment by increasing its expected rate of return. For example, a federal building in a city may encourage private investment in the form of nearby office buildings, shops, and restaurants. Through its complementary effect, the spending on public capital may shift the private investment demand curve to the right, as from ID_1 to ID_2 in Figure 13.8. Even though the government borrowing boosts the interest rate from 6 percent to 10 percent, total private investment need not fall. In the case shown as the move from *a* to *c* in Figure 13.8, it remains at $25 billion. Of course, the increase in investment demand might be smaller than that shown. If it were smaller, the crowding-out effect would not be fully offset. But the point is that an increase in investment demand may counter the decline in investment that would otherwise result from the higher interest rate.

QUICK REVIEW 13.3

- The U.S. public debt—$16.4 trillion in 2012—is essentially the total accumulation of all past federal budget deficits and surpluses; about 33 percent of the U.S. public debt is held by foreigners.

- The U.S. public debt held by the public (excluding the Federal Reserve) was 70 percent of GDP in 2012, up from 30 percent in 2000.

- The federal government is in no danger of going bankrupt because it needs only to refinance (not retire) the public debt and it can raise revenues, if needed, through higher taxes.

- The borrowing and interest payments associated with the public debt may (a) increase income inequality; (b) require higher taxes, which may dampen incentives; and (c) impede the growth of the nation's stock of capital through crowding out of private investment.

LAST WORD

The Social Security and Medicare Shortfalls

Social Security and Medicare Face Gigantic Future Funding Shortfalls. Metaphorically Speaking, Some Economists See These Programs as Financial and Political Time Bombs.

The American population, on average, is getting decidedly older. The percentage of the population age 62 or older will rise substantially over the next several decades, with the greatest increases for people age 75 and above. In the future, more people will be receiving Social Security benefits (income during retirement) and Medicare (medical care during retirement) for longer periods. Each person's benefits will be paid for by fewer workers. The number of workers per Social Security and Medicare beneficiary was roughly 5:1 in 1960. Today it is 3:1, and by 2040 it will be only 2:1.

The combined cost of the Social Security and Medicare programs was 8.5 percent of GDP in 2011, and that percentage is projected to grow to 12 percent of GDP in 2035 and 13 percent of GDP in 2086.*

The Social Security Shortfall Social Security is the major public retirement program in the United States. The program costs $736 billion annually and is financed by a 12.4 percent tax on earnings up to a set level of earnings ($113,700 in 2013). Half the tax (6.2 percent) is paid by the worker; the other half by the employer. Social Security is largely an annual "pay-as-you-go" plan, meaning that most of the current revenues from the Social Security tax are paid to current Social Security retirees. Through the start of 2009, Social Security revenues exceeded Social Security payouts in anticipation of the large benefits promised to the baby boomers when they retire. That excess inflow was used

to buy U.S. Treasury securities that were credited to a government account called the Social Security Trust Fund. But the combined accumulation of money in the trust fund through 2009 plus the projected future revenues from the payroll tax in later years was expected to be greatly inadequate for paying the promised retirement benefits to all future retirees.

This underfunding of future retirement promises was brought into sharper focus in the latter half of 2009 when, for the first time, Social Security revenues fell below Social Security retirement payouts and the system started shifting money from the trust fund to make up the difference. The trust fund is expected to be exhausted in 2033. For each year thereafter, annual tax revenues will cover only 75 percent of the promised benefits.

---

*Social Security and Medicare Board of Trustees, "Status of the Social Security and Medicare Programs: A Summary of the 2012 Annual Reports," **www.ssa.gov**. This publication is also the source of most of the statistical information that follows.

SUMMARY

LO13.1 Identify and explain the purposes, tools, and limitations of fiscal policy.

Fiscal policy consists of deliberate changes in government spending, taxes, or some combination of both to promote full employment, price-level stability, and economic growth. Fiscal policy

requires increases in government spending, decreases in taxes, or both—a budget deficit—to increase aggregate demand and push an economy from a recession. Decreases in government spending, increases in taxes, or both—a budget surplus—are appropriate fiscal policy for decreasing aggregate demand to try to slow or halt demand-pull inflation.

The Medicare Shortfall The Medicare program is the U.S. health care program for people age 65 and older in the United States. The program costs $558 billion per year and has been growing at about 9 percent annually. Like Social Security, it also is a pay-as-you-go plan, meaning that current medical benefits for people age 65 or older are being funded by current tax revenues from the 2.9 percent Medicare tax on earnings and the 3.8 percent investment surtax on wealthier investors that was instituted in 2013 as part of Obamacare. Like the Social Security tax, half the Medicare earnings tax is paid by the employer (1.45 percent) and half the by the employee. But the 2.9 percent Medicare tax is applied to all earnings.

The financial status of Medicare is much worse than that of Social Security. To begin with, the Medicare Trust Fund will be depleted in 2024, 9 years before the Social Security Trust Fund is expected to be depleted. Then, in subsequent years, the percentage of scheduled Medicare benefits covered by the Medicare tax will decline from 97 percent in 2025 to 72 percent in 2035 and 69 percent in 2080.

The Unpleasant Options To restore long-run balance to Social Security and Medicare, the federal government must either reduce benefits or increase revenues. It's as simple—and as complicated—as that! The Social Security Administration concludes that bringing projected Social Security revenues and payments into balance over the next 75 years would require a 16 percent permanent reduction in Social Security benefits, a 13 percent permanent increase in tax revenues, or some combination of the two. To bring projected Medicare revenues and expenses into long-run balance would require an increase in the Medicare payroll tax by 122 percent, a 51 percent reduction of Medicare payments from their projected levels, or some combination of each.

All the general options for closing all or part of the Social Security and Medicare gaps involve difficult economic trade-offs and dangerous political risks because one group or another will strongly oppose them. Here are just a few examples:

- Increasing the retirement age for collecting Social Security or Medicare benefits will upset preretirement workers who have been paying into the system and will receive their benefits later than they expected.

- Subjecting a larger portion of total earnings to the Social Security tax would constitute a gigantic tax increase on the earnings of the country's highest trained and educated individuals. This might reduce the incentive of younger people to obtain education and advance in their careers.

- Disqualifying wealthy individuals from receiving Social Security and Medicare benefits would tilt the programs toward welfare and redistribution, rather than insurance programs. This would undermine the broad existing political support for the programs.

- Redirecting legal immigration toward high-skilled, high-earning entrants and away from low-skilled, low-earning immigrants to raise Social Security and Medicare revenues would also raise the ire of some native-born high-skilled workers and the proponents of immigration based on family reunification.

- Placing the payroll tax revenues into accounts that individuals, not the government, would own, maintain, and bequeath would transform the Social Security and Medicare programs from guaranteed "defined benefit plans" into much riskier "defined contribution plans." The extreme short-run volatility of the stock market might leave some unlucky people destitute in old age.

The problem is huge and will not go away. One recent attempt to add up the underfunding of all the promised Social Security and Medicare benefits finds that the total underfunding greatly exceeds the combined current wealth (net worth) of everyone in the United States today.[†] Even if this estimate is somewhat extreme, the fact remains: The federal government and American people eventually will have to face up to the over-promising-underfunding problem and find ways to resolve it.

[†]Bruce Bartlett, "The 81% Tax Increase," Forbes.com, August 8, 2009, **www.forbes.com**.

LO13.2 Explain the role of built-in stabilizers in moderating business cycles.

Built-in stability arises from net tax revenues, which vary directly with the level of GDP. During recession, the federal budget automatically moves toward a stabilizing deficit; during expansion, the budget automatically moves toward an anti-inflationary surplus. Built-in stability lessens, but does not fully correct, undesired changes in real GDP.

LO13.3 Describe how the cyclically adjusted budget reveals the status of U.S. fiscal policy.

Actual federal budget deficits can go up or down because of changes in GDP, changes in fiscal policy, or both. Deficits caused by changes in GDP are called cyclical deficits. The cyclically adjusted budget removes cyclical deficits from the budget and therefore measures the budget deficit or surplus that would occur if the economy operated at its full-employment output throughout the year. Changes in the cyclical-budget deficit or surplus provide meaningful information as to whether the government's fiscal policy is expansionary, neutral, or contractionary. Changes in the actual budget deficit or surplus do not, since such deficits or surpluses can include cyclical deficits or surpluses.

LO13.4 Summarize recent U.S. fiscal policy and the projections for U.S. fiscal policy over the next few years.

In 2001 the Bush administration and Congress chose to reduce marginal tax rates and phase out the federal estate tax. A recession occurred in 2001, and federal spending for the war on terrorism rocketed. The federal budget swung from a surplus of $128 billion in 2001 to a deficit of $158 billion in 2002. In 2003 the Bush administration and Congress accelerated the tax reductions scheduled under the 2001 tax law and cut tax rates on capital gains and dividends. The purposes were to stimulate a sluggish economy. By 2007 the economy had reached its full employment level of output.

The federal government responded to the deep recession of 2007–2009 by implementing highly expansionary fiscal policy. In 2008 the federal government passed a tax rebate program that sent $600 checks to qualified individuals. Later that year, it created a $700 billion emergency fund to keep key financial institutions from failing. These and other programs increased the cyclically adjusted budget deficit from -1.3 percent of potential GDP in 2007 to -2.9 percent in 2008. When the economy continued to plunge, the Obama administration and Congress enacted a massive $787 billion stimulus program to be implemented over 2½ years. The cyclically adjusted budget deficit shot up from -2.9 percent of potential GDP in 2008 to -7.1 percent in 2009.

LO13.5 Discuss the problems that governments may encounter in enacting and applying fiscal policy.

Certain problems complicate the enactment and implementation of fiscal policy. They include (a) timing problems associated with recognition, administrative, and operational lags; (b) the potential for misuse of fiscal policy for political rather than economic purposes; (c) the fact that state and local finances tend to be procyclical; (d) potential ineffectiveness if households expect future policy reversals; and (e) the possibility of fiscal policy crowding out private investment.

Most economists believe that fiscal policy can help move the economy in a desired direction but cannot reliably be used to fine-tune the economy to a position of price stability and full employment. Nevertheless, fiscal policy is a valuable backup tool for aiding monetary policy in fighting significant recession or inflation.

LO13.6 Discuss the size, composition, and consequences of the U.S. public debt.

The public debt is the total accumulation of all past federal government deficits and surpluses and consists of Treasury bills, Treasury notes, Treasury bonds, and U.S. savings bonds. In 2012 the U.S. public debt was $16.4 trillion, or $52,396 per person. The public (which here includes banks and state and local governments) holds 60 percent of that federal debt; the Federal Reserve and federal agencies hold the other 40 percent. Foreigners hold 33 percent of the federal debt. Interest payments as a percentage of GDP were about 2.3 percent in 2012. Because of large deficits during the Great Recession and in subsequent years, the total U.S. public debt passed $17.0 trillion in 2013. It had doubled in seven years.

The concern that a large public debt may bankrupt the U.S. government is generally a false worry because (a) the debt needs only to be refinanced rather than refunded and (b) the federal government has the power to increase taxes to make interest payments on the debt.

In general, the public debt is not a vehicle for shifting economic burdens to future generations. Americans inherit not only most of the public debt (a liability) but also most of the U.S. government securities (an asset) that finance the debt.

More substantive problems associated with public debt include the following: (a) Payment of interest on the debt may increase income inequality. (b) Interest payments on the debt require higher taxes, which may impair incentives. (c) Paying interest or principal on the portion of the debt held by foreigners means a transfer of real output abroad. (d) Government borrowing to refinance or pay interest on the debt may increase interest rates and crowd out private investment spending, leaving future generations with a smaller stock of capital than they would have had otherwise.

The increase in investment in public capital that may result from debt financing may partly or wholly offset the crowding-out effect of the public debt on private investment. Also, the added public investment may stimulate private investment, where the two are complements.

TERMS AND CONCEPTS

fiscal policy	built-in stabilizer	political business cycle
Council of Economic Advisers (CEA)	progressive tax system	crowding-out effect
expansionary fiscal policy	proportional tax system	public debt
budget deficit	regressive tax system	U.S. government securities
contractionary fiscal policy	cyclically adjusted budget	external public debt
budget surplus	cyclical deficit	public investments

The following and additional problems can be found in connect
ECONOMICS

DISCUSSION QUESTIONS

1. What is the role of the Council of Economic Advisers (CEA) as it relates to fiscal policy? Use an Internet search to find the names and university affiliations of the present members of the CEA. **LO13.1**

2. What are government's fiscal policy options for ending severe demand-pull inflation? Which of these fiscal options do you think might be favored by a person who wants to preserve the size of government? A person who thinks the public sector is too large? How does the "ratchet effect" affect anti-inflationary fiscal policy? **LO13.1**

3. (For students who were assigned Chapter 11) Use the aggregate expenditures model to show how government fiscal policy could eliminate either a recessionary expenditure gap or an inflationary expenditure gap (Figure 11.7). Explain how equal-size increases in G and T could eliminate a recessionary gap and how equal-size decreases in G and T could eliminate an inflationary gap. **LO13.1**

4. Some politicians have suggested that the United States enact a constitutional amendment requiring that the federal government balance its budget annually. Explain why such an amendment, if strictly enforced, would force the government to enact a contractionary fiscal policy whenever the economy experienced a severe recession. **LO13.1**

5. Explain how built-in (or automatic) stabilizers work. What are the differences between proportional, progressive, and regressive tax systems as they relate to an economy's built-in stability? **LO13.2**

6. Define the cyclically adjusted budget, explain its significance, and state why it may differ from the actual budget. Suppose the full-employment, noninflationary level of real output is GDP_3 (not GDP_2) in the economy depicted in Figure 13.3. If the economy is operating at GDP_2, instead of GDP_3, what is the status of its cyclically adjusted budget? The status of its current fiscal policy? What change in fiscal policy would you recommend? How would you accomplish that in terms of the G and T lines in the figure? **LO13.3**

7. Briefly state and evaluate the problem of time lags in enacting and applying fiscal policy. Explain the idea of a political business cycle. How might expectations of a near-term policy reversal weaken fiscal policy based on changes in tax rates? What is the crowding-out effect, and why might it be relevant to fiscal policy? In view of your answers, explain

the following statement: "Although fiscal policy clearly is useful in combating the extremes of severe recession and demand-pull inflation, it is impossible to use fiscal policy to fine-tune the economy to the full-employment, noninflationary level of real GDP and keep the economy there indefinitely." **LO13.5**

8. How do economists distinguish between the absolute and relative sizes of the public debt? Why is the distinction important? Distinguish between refinancing the debt and retiring the debt. How does an internally held public debt differ from an externally held public debt? Contrast the effects of retiring an internally held debt and retiring an externally held debt. **LO13.6**

9. True or false? If false, explain why. **LO13.6**
   a. The total public debt is more relevant to an economy than the public debt as a percentage of GDP.
   b. An internally held public debt is like a debt of the left hand owed to the right hand.
   c. The Federal Reserve and federal government agencies hold more than three-fourths of the public debt.
   d. The portion of the U.S. debt held by the public (and not by government entities) was larger as a percentage of GDP in 2012 than it was in 2000.
   e. As a percentage of GDP, the total U.S. public debt is the highest such debt among the world's advanced industrial nations.

10. Why might economists be quite concerned if the annual interest payments on the U.S. public debt sharply increased as a percentage of GDP? **LO13.6**

11. Trace the cause-and-effect chain through which financing and refinancing of the public debt might affect real interest rates, private investment, the stock of capital, and economic growth. How might investment in public capital and complementarities between public capital and private capital alter the outcome of the cause-effect chain? **LO13.6**

12. **LAST WORD** What do economists mean when they say Social Security and Medicare are "pay-as-you-go" plans? What are the Social Security and Medicare trust funds, and how long will they have money left in them? What is the key long-run problem of both Social Security and Medicare? Do you favor increasing taxes or do you prefer reducing benefits to fix the problem?

REVIEW QUESTIONS

1. Which of the following would help a government reduce an inflationary output gap? **LO13.1**
   a. Raising taxes.
   b. Lowering taxes.
   c. Increasing government spending.
   d. Decreasing government spending.

2. The economy is in a recession. A congresswoman suggests increasing spending to stimulate aggregate demand but also

at the same time raising taxes to pay for the increased spending. Her suggestion to combine higher government expenditures with higher taxes is: **LO13.1**
   a. The worst possible combination of tax and expenditure changes.
   b. The best possible combination of tax and expenditure changes.

c. A mediocre and contradictory combination of tax and expenditure changes.

d. None of the above.

3. During the recession of 2007–2009, the U.S. federal government's tax collections fell from about $2.6 trillion down to about $2.1 trillion while GDP declined by about 4 percent. Does the U.S. tax system appear to have built-in stabilizers? LO13.2

a. Yes.

b. No.

4. Last year, while an economy was in a recession, government spending was $595 billion and government revenue was $505 billion. Economists estimate that if the economy had been at its full-employment level of GDP last year, government spending would have been $555 billion and government revenue would have been $550 billion. Which of the following statements about this government's fiscal situation are true? LO13.3

a. The government has a non–cyclically adjusted budget deficit of $595 billion.

b. The government has a non–cyclically adjusted budget deficit of $90 billion.

c. The government has a non–cyclically adjusted budget surplus of $90 billion.

d. The government has a cyclically adjusted budget deficit of $555 billion.

e. The government has a cyclically adjusted budget deficit of $5 billion.

f. The government has a cyclically adjusted budget surplus of $5 billion.

5. Label each of the following scenarios in which there are problems enacting and applying fiscal policy as being an example of either recognition lag, administrative lag, or operational lag. LO13.5

a. To fight a recession, Congress has passed a bill to increase infrastructure spending—but the legally required environmental-impact statement for each new project will take at least two years to complete before any building can begin.

b. Distracted by a war that is going badly, inflation reaches 8 percent before politicians take notice.

c. A sudden recession is recognized by politicians, but it takes many months of political deal making before a stimulus bill is finally approved.

d. To fight a recession, the president orders federal agencies to get rid of petty regulations that burden private businesses—but the federal agencies begin by spending a year developing a set of regulations on how to remove petty regulations.

6. In January, the interest rate is 5 percent and firms borrow $50 billion per month for investment projects. In February, the federal government doubles its monthly borrowing from $25 billion to $50 billion. That drives the interest rate up to 7 percent. As a result, firms cut back their borrowing to only $30 billion per month. Which of the following is true? LO13.6

a. There is no crowding-out effect because the government's increase in borrowing exceeds firm's decrease in borrowing.

b. There is a crowding-out effect of $20 billion.

c. There is no crowding-out effect because both the government and firms are still borrowing a lot.

d. There is a crowding-out effect of $25 billion.

PROBLEMS

1. Assume that a hypothetical economy with an MPC of .8 is experiencing severe recession. By how much would government spending have to rise to shift the aggregate demand curve rightward by $25 billion? How large a tax cut would be needed to achieve the same increase in aggregate demand? Determine one possible combination of government spending increases and tax decreases that would accomplish the same goal. LO13.1

2. Refer back to the table in Figure 12.7 in the previous chapter. Suppose that aggregate demand increases such that the amount of real output demanded rises by $7 billion at each price level. By what percentage will the price level increase? Will this inflation be demand-pull inflation or will it be cost-push inflation? If potential real GDP (that is, full-employment GDP) is $510 billion, what will be the size of the positive GDP gap after the change in aggregate demand? If government wants to use fiscal policy to counter the resulting inflation without changing tax rates, would it increase government spending or decrease it? LO13.1

3. (For students who were assigned Chapter 11) Assume that, without taxes, the consumption schedule for an economy is as shown below: LO13.1

GDP, Billions	Consumption, Billions
$100	$120
200	200
300	280
400	360
500	440
600	520
700	600

a. Graph this consumption schedule. What is the size of the MPC?

b. Assume that a lump-sum (regressive) tax of $10 billion is imposed at all levels of GDP. Calculate the tax rate at each level of GDP. Graph the resulting consumption schedule and compare the MPC and the multiplier with those of the pretax consumption schedule.

c. Now suppose a proportional tax with a 10 percent tax rate is imposed instead of the regressive tax. Calculate and graph the new consumption schedule and note the MPC and the multiplier.

d. Finally, impose a progressive tax such that the tax rate is 0 percent when GDP is $100, 5 percent at $200, 10 percent at $300, 15 percent at $400, and so forth. Determine and graph the new consumption schedule, noting the effect of this tax system on the MPC and the multiplier.

e. Use a graph similar to Figure 13.3 to show why proportional and progressive taxes contribute to greater economic stability, while a regressive tax does not.

4. Refer to the following table for Waxwania: **LO13.2**

Government Expenditures, G	Tax Revenues, T	Real GDP
$160	$100	$500
160	120	600
160	140	700
160	160	800
160	180	900

What is the marginal tax rate in Waxwania? The average tax rate? Which of the following describes the tax system: proportional, progressive, regressive?

5. Refer to the table for Waxwania in problem 4. Suppose that Waxwania is producing $600 of real GDP, whereas the potential real GDP (or full-employment real GDP) is $700. How large is its budget deficit? Its cyclically adjusted budget deficit? Its cyclically adjusted budget deficit as a percentage of potential real GDP? Is Waxwania's fiscal policy expansionary or is it contractionary? **LO13.3**

6. Suppose that a country has no public debt in year 1 but experiences a budget deficit of $40 billion in year 2, a budget surplus of $10 billion in year 3, and a budget deficit of $2 billion in year 4. What is the absolute size of its public debt in year 4? If its real GDP in year 4 is $104 billion, what is this country's public debt as a percentage of real GDP in year 4? **LO13.6**

7. Suppose that the investment demand curve in a certain economy is such that investment declines by $100 billion for every 1 percentage point increase in the real interest rate. Also, suppose that the investment demand curve shifts rightward by $150 billion at each real interest rate for every 1 percentage point increase in the expected rate of return from investment. If stimulus spending (an expansionary fiscal policy) by government increases the real interest rate by 2 percentage points, but also raises the expected rate of return on investment by 1 percentage point, how much investment, if any, will be crowded out? **LO13.6**

CHAPTER **14**

Money, Banking, and Financial Institutions

Learning Objectives

LO14.1 Identify and explain the functions of money.

LO14.2 List and describe the components of the U.S. money supply.

LO14.3 Describe what "backs" the money supply, making us willing to accept it as payment.

LO14.4 Discuss the makeup of the Federal Reserve and its relationship to banks and thrifts.

LO14.5 Identify the functions and responsibilities of the Federal Reserve and explain why Fed independence is important.

LO14.6 Identify and explain the main factors that contributed to the financial crisis of 2007–2008.

LO14.7 Discuss the actions of the U.S. Treasury and the Federal Reserve that helped keep the banking and financial crisis of 2007–2008 from worsening.

LO14.8 Identify the main subsets of the financial services industry in the United States and provide examples of some firms in each category.

Money is a fascinating aspect of the economy:

> Money bewitches people. They fret for it, and they sweat for it. They devise most ingenious ways to get it, and most ingenuous ways to get rid of it. Money is the only commodity that is good for nothing but to be gotten rid of. It will not feed you, clothe you, shelter you, or amuse you unless you spend it or invest it. It

imparts value only in parting. People will do almost anything for money, and money will do almost anything for people. Money is a captivating, circulating, masquerading puzzle.[1]

In this chapter and the two chapters that follow, we want to unmask the critical role of money and

the monetary system in the economy. When the monetary system is working properly, it provides the lifeblood of the circular flows of income and expenditure. A well-operating monetary system helps the economy achieve both full employment and the efficient use of resources. A malfunctioning monetary system distorts the allocation of resources and creates severe fluctuations in the economy's levels of output, employment, and prices.

---

[1]"Creeping Inflation," *Business Review,* August 1957, p. 3. Federal Reserve Bank of Philadelphia. Used with permission.

The Functions of Money

LO14.1 Identify and explain the functions of money.

Just what is money? There is an old saying that "money *is* what money *does*." In a general sense, anything that performs the functions of money *is* money. Here are those functions:

- *Medium of exchange* First and foremost, money is a **medium of exchange** that is usable for buying and selling goods and services. A bakery worker does not want to be paid 200 bagels per week. Nor does the bakery owner want to receive, say, halibut in exchange for bagels. Money, however, is readily acceptable as payment. As we saw in Chapter 2, money is a social invention with which resource suppliers and producers can be paid and that can be used to buy any of the full range of items available in the marketplace. As a medium of exchange, money allows society to escape the complications of barter. And because it provides a convenient way of exchanging goods, money enables society to gain the advantages of geographic and human specialization.

- *Unit of account* Money is also a **unit of account.** Society uses monetary units—dollars, in the United States—as a yardstick for measuring the relative worth of a wide variety of goods, services, and resources. Just as we measure distance in miles or kilometers, we gauge the value of goods in dollars.

  With money as an acceptable unit of account, the price of each item need be stated only in terms of the monetary unit. We need not state the price of cows in terms of corn, crayons, and cranberries. Money aids rational decision making by enabling buyers and sellers to easily compare the prices of various goods, services, and resources. It also permits us to define

debt obligations, determine taxes owed, and calculate the nation's GDP.

- *Store of value* Money also serves as a **store of value** that enables people to transfer purchasing power from the present to the future. People normally do not spend all their incomes on the day they receive them. To buy things later, they store some of their wealth as money. The money you place in a safe or a checking account will still be available to you a few weeks or months from now. When inflation is nonexistent or mild, holding money is a relatively risk-free way to store your wealth for later use.

People can, of course, choose to hold some or all of their wealth in a wide variety of assets besides money. These include real estate, stocks, bonds, precious metals such as gold, and even collectible items like fine art or comic books. But a key advantage that money has over all other assets is that it has the most *liquidity*, or spendability.

An asset's **liquidity** is the ease with which it can be converted quickly into the most widely accepted and easily spent form of money, cash, with little or no loss of purchasing power. The more liquid an asset is, the more quickly it can be converted into cash and used for either purchases of goods and services or purchases of other assets.

Levels of liquidity vary radically. By definition, cash is perfectly liquid. By contrast, a house is highly illiquid for two reasons. First, it may take several months before a willing buyer can be found and a sale negotiated so that its value can be converted into cash. Second, there is a loss of purchasing power when the house is sold because numerous fees have to be paid to real estate agents and other individuals to complete the sale.

As we are about to discuss, our economy uses several different types of money including cash, coins, checking

FIGURE 14.1 Components of money supply *M*1 and money supply *M*2, in the United States. (a) *M*1 is a narrow definition of the money supply that includes currency (in circulation) and checkable deposits. (b) *M*2 is a broader definition that includes *M*1 along with several other relatively liquid account balances.

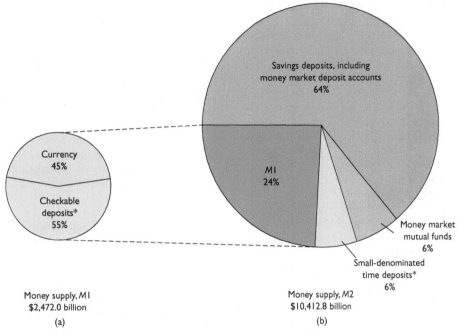

*These categories include other, quantitatively smaller components such as traveler's checks.

Source: Federal Reserve System, **www.federalreserve.gov**. Data are for February 2013.

account deposits, savings account deposits, and even more exotic things like deposits in money market mutual funds. As we describe the various forms of money in detail, take the time to compare their relative levels of liquidity—both with each other and as compared to other assets like stocks, bonds, and real estate. Cash is perfectly liquid. Other forms of money are highly liquid, but less liquid than cash.

The Components of the Money Supply

LO14.2 List and describe the components of the U.S. money supply.

Money is a "stock" of some item or group of items (unlike income, for example, which is a "flow"). Societies have used many items as money, including whales' teeth, circular stones, elephant-tail bristles, gold coins, furs, and pieces of paper. Anything that is widely accepted as a medium of exchange can serve as money. In the United States, currency is not the only form of money. As you will see, certain debts of government and financial institutions also are used as money.

Money Definition *M*1

The narrowest definition of the U.S. money supply is called ***M*1.** It consists of two components:

- Currency (coins and paper money) in the hands of the public.

- All checkable deposits (all deposits in commercial banks and "thrift" or savings institutions on which checks of any size can be drawn).[2]

Government and government agencies supply coins and paper money. Commercial banks ("banks") and savings institutions ("thrifts") provide checkable deposits. Figure 14.1a shows that *M*1 is about equally divided between the two components.

---

[2]In the ensuing discussion, we do not discuss several of the quantitatively less significant components of the definitions of money to avoid a maze of details. For example, traveler's checks are included in the *M*1 money supply. The statistical appendix of any recent *Federal Reserve Bulletin* provides more comprehensive definitions.

Currency: Coins + Paper Money The currency of the United States consists of metal coins and paper money. The coins are issued by the U.S. Treasury while the paper money consists of **Federal Reserve Notes** issued by the Federal Reserve System (the U.S. central bank). The coins are minted by the U.S. Mint while the paper money is printed by the Bureau of Engraving and Printing. Both the U.S. Mint and the Bureau of Engraving and Printing are part of the U.S. Department of the Treasury.

As with the currencies of other countries, the currency of the United States is **token money.** This means that the face value of any piece of currency is unrelated to its *intrinsic value*—the value of the physical material (metal or paper and ink) out of which that piece of currency is constructed. Governments make sure that face values exceed intrinsic values to discourage people from destroying coins and bills to resell the material that they are made out of. For instance, if 50-cent pieces each contained 75 cents' worth of metal, then it would be profitable to melt them down and sell the metal. Fifty-cent pieces would disappear from circulation very quickly!

Figure 14.1a shows that currency (coins and paper money) constitutes 45 percent of the $M1$ money supply in the United States.

Checkable Deposits The safety and convenience of checks has made **checkable deposits** a large component of the $M1$ money supply. You would not think of stuffing $4,896 in bills in an envelope and dropping it in a mailbox to pay a debt. But writing and mailing a check for a large sum is commonplace. The person cashing a check must endorse it (sign it on the reverse side); the writer of the check subsequently receives a record of the cashed check as a receipt attesting to the fulfillment of the obligation. Similarly, because the writing of a check requires endorsement, the theft or loss of your checkbook is not nearly as calamitous as losing an identical amount of currency. Finally, it is more convenient to write a check than to transport and count out a large sum of currency. For all these reasons, checkable deposits (checkbook money) are a large component of the stock of money in the United States. About 55 percent of $M1$ is in the form of checkable deposits, on which checks can be drawn.

It might seem strange that checking account balances are regarded as part of the money supply. But the reason is clear: Checks are nothing more than a way to transfer the ownership of deposits in banks and other financial institutions and are generally acceptable as a medium of exchange. Although checks are less generally accepted than currency for small purchases, for major purchases most sellers willingly accept checks as payment. Moreover, people can convert checkable deposits into paper money and coins on demand; checks drawn on those deposits are thus the equivalent of currency.

To summarize:

$$\text{Money, } M1 = \text{currency} + \text{checkable deposits}$$

Institutions That Offer Checkable Deposits In the United States, a variety of financial institutions allow customers to write checks in any amount on the funds they have deposited. **Commercial banks** are the primary depository institutions. They accept the deposits of households and businesses, keep the money safe until it is demanded via checks, and in the meantime use it to make available a wide variety of loans. Commercial bank loans provide short-term financial capital to businesses, and they finance consumer purchases of automobiles and other durable goods.

Savings and loan associations (S&Ls), mutual savings banks, and credit unions supplement the commercial banks and are known collectively as savings or **thrift institutions,** or simply "thrifts." *Savings and loan associations* and *mutual savings banks* accept the deposits of households and businesses and then use the funds to finance housing mortgages and to provide other loans. *Credit unions* accept deposits from and lend to "members," who usually are a group of people who work for the same company.

The checkable deposits of banks and thrifts are known variously as demand deposits, NOW (negotiable order of withdrawal) accounts, ATS (automatic transfer service) accounts, and share draft accounts. Their commonality is that depositors can write checks on them whenever, and in whatever amount, they choose.

Two Qualifications We must qualify our discussion in two important ways. First, currency held by the U.S. Treasury, the Federal Reserve banks, commercial banks, and thrift institutions is *excluded* from $M1$ and other measures of the money supply. A paper dollar or four quarters in the billfold of, say, Emma Buck obviously constitutes just $1 of the money supply. But if we counted currency held by banks as part of the money supply, the same $1 would count for $2 of money supply when Emma deposited the currency into her checkable deposit in her bank. It would count for $1 of checkable deposit owned by Buck and also $1 of currency in the bank's cash drawer or vault. By excluding currency held by banks when determining the total supply of money, we avoid this problem of double counting.

Also *excluded* from the money supply are any checkable deposits of the government (specifically, the U.S. Treasury) or the Federal Reserve that are held by commercial banks or thrift institutions. This exclusion is designed to enable a better assessment of the amount of money available *to the private sector* for potential spending. The amount of money available to households and businesses is of keen interest to the Federal Reserve in conducting its monetary policy (a topic we cover in detail in Chapter 16).

Money Definition *M*2

A second and broader definition of money includes *M*1 plus several near-monies. **Near-monies** are certain highly liquid financial assets that do not function directly or fully as a medium of exchange but can be readily converted into currency or checkable deposits. The ***M*2** definition of money includes three categories of near-monies.

- *Savings deposits, including money market deposit accounts* A depositor can easily withdraw funds from a **savings account** at a bank or thrift or simply request that the funds be transferred from a savings account to a checkable account. A person can also withdraw funds from a **money market deposit account (MMDA),** which is an interest-bearing account containing a variety of interest-bearing short-term securities. MMDAs, however, have a minimum-balance requirement and a limit on how often a person can withdraw funds.

- *Small-denominated (less than $100,000) time deposits* Funds from **time deposits** become available at their maturity. For example, a person can convert a 6-month time deposit ("certificate of deposit," or "CD") to currency without penalty 6 months or more after it has been deposited. In return for this withdrawal limitation, the financial institution pays a higher interest rate on such deposits than it does on its MMDAs. Also, a person can "cash in" a CD at any time but must pay a severe penalty.

- *Money market mutual funds held by individuals* By making a telephone call, using the Internet, or writing a check for $500 or more, a depositor can redeem shares in a **money market mutual fund (MMMF)** offered by a mutual fund company. Such companies use the combined funds of individual shareholders to buy interest-bearing short-term credit instruments such as certificates of deposit and U.S. government securities. Then they can offer interest on the MMMF accounts of the shareholders (depositors) who jointly own those financial assets. The MMMFs in *M*2 include only the MMMF accounts held by individuals; those held by businesses and other institutions are excluded.

All three categories of near-monies imply substantial liquidity. Thus, in equation form,

$$\text{Money, } M2 = \begin{array}{l} M1 + \text{savings deposits, including} \\ \text{MMDAs} + \text{small-denominated} \\ \text{(less than \$100,000) time deposits} \\ + \text{MMMFs held by individuals} \end{array}$$

In summary, *M*2 includes the immediate medium-of-exchange items (currency and checkable deposits) that constitute *M*1 plus certain near-monies that can be easily

CONSIDER THIS . . .

Are Credit Cards Money?

You may wonder why we have ignored credit cards such as Visa and MasterCard in our discussion of how the money supply is defined. After all, credit cards are a convenient way to buy things and account for about 25 percent of the dollar value of all transactions in the United States. The answer is that a credit card is not money. Rather, it is a convenient means of obtaining a short-term loan from the financial institution that issued the card.

What happens when you purchase an item with a credit card? The bank that issued the card will reimburse the seller by making a money payment and charging the establishment a transaction fee, and later you will reimburse the bank for its loan to you by also making a money payment. Rather than reduce your cash or checking account with each purchase, you bunch your payments once a month. You may have to pay an annual fee for the services provided, and if you pay the bank in installments, you will pay a sizable interest charge on the loan. Credit cards are merely a means of deferring or postponing payment for a short period. Your checking account balance that you use to pay your credit card bill *is* money; the credit card is *not* money.*

Although credit cards are not money, they allow individuals and businesses to "economize" in the use of money. Credit cards enable people to hold less currency in their billfolds and, prior to payment due dates, fewer checkable deposits in their bank accounts. Credit cards also help people coordinate the timing of their expenditures with their receipt of income.

---

*A bank debit card, however, is very similar to a check in your checkbook. Unlike a purchase with a credit card, a purchase with a debit card creates a direct "debit" (a subtraction) from your checking account balance. That checking account balance is money—it is part of *M*1.

converted into currency and checkable deposits. In Figure 14.1b we see that the addition of all these items yields an *M*2 money supply that is about five times larger than the narrower *M*1 money supply.

QUICK REVIEW 14.1

- Money serves as a medium of exchange, a unit of account, and a store of value.
- The narrow *M*1 definition of money includes currency held by the public plus checkable deposits in commercial banks and thrift institutions.
- Thrift institutions as well as commercial banks offer accounts on which checks can be written.
- The *M*2 definition of money includes *M*1 plus savings deposits, including money market deposit accounts, small-denominated (less than $100,000) time deposits, and money market mutual fund balances held by individuals.

What "Backs" the Money Supply?

LO14.3 Describe what "backs" the money supply, making us willing to accept it as payment.

The money supply in the United States essentially is "backed" (guaranteed) by the government's ability to keep the value of money relatively stable. Nothing more!

Money as Debt

The major components of the money supply—paper money and checkable deposits—are debts, or promises to pay. In the United States, paper money is the circulating debt of the Federal Reserve Banks. Checkable deposits are the debts of commercial banks and thrift institutions.

Paper currency and checkable deposits have no intrinsic value. A $5 bill is just an inscribed piece of paper. A checkable deposit is merely a bookkeeping entry. And coins, we know, have less intrinsic value than their face value. Nor will government redeem the paper money you hold for anything tangible, such as gold. To many people, the fact that the government does not back the currency with anything tangible seems implausible and insecure. But the decision not to back the currency with anything tangible was made for a very good reason. If the government backed the currency with something tangible like gold, then the supply of money would vary with how much gold was available. By not backing the currency, the government avoids this constraint and indeed receives a key freedom—the ability to provide as much or as little money as needed to maintain the value of money and to best suit

the economic needs of the country. In effect, by choosing not to back the currency, the government has chosen to give itself the ability to freely "manage" the nation's money supply. Its monetary authorities attempt to provide the amount of money needed for the particular volume of business activity that will promote full employment, price-level stability, and economic growth.

Nearly all today's economists agree that managing the money supply is more sensible than linking it to gold or to some other commodity whose supply might change arbitrarily and capriciously. For instance, if we used gold to back the money supply so that gold was redeemable for money and vice versa, then a large increase in the nation's gold stock as the result of a new gold discovery might increase the money supply too rapidly and thereby trigger rapid inflation. Or a long-lasting decline in gold production might reduce the money supply to the point where recession and unemployment resulted.

In short, people cannot convert paper money into a fixed amount of gold or any other precious commodity. Money is exchangeable only for paper money. If you ask the government to redeem $5 of your paper money, it will swap one paper $5 bill for another bearing a different serial number. That is all you can get. Similarly, checkable deposits can be redeemed not for gold but only for paper money, which, as we have just seen, the government will not redeem for anything tangible.

Value of Money

So why are currency and checkable deposits money, whereas, say, Monopoly (the game) money is not? What gives a $20 bill or a $100 checking account entry its value? The answer to these questions has three parts.

Acceptability Currency and checkable deposits are money because people accept them as money. By virtue of long-standing business practice, currency and checkable deposits perform the basic function of money: They are acceptable as a medium of exchange. We accept paper money in exchange because we are confident it will be exchangeable for real goods, services, and resources when we spend it.

Legal Tender Our confidence in the acceptability of paper money is strengthened because the government has designated currency as **legal tender**. Specifically, each bill contains the statement "This note is legal tender for all debts, public and private." That means paper money is a valid and legal means of payment of any debt that was contracted in dollars. (But private firms and government are not mandated to accept cash. It is not illegal for them to specify payment in noncash forms such as checks, cashier's checks, money orders, or credit cards.)

The general acceptance of paper currency in exchange is more important than the government's decree that money is legal tender, however. The government has never decreed checks to be legal tender, and yet they serve as such in many of the economy's exchanges of goods, services, and resources. But it is true that government agencies—the Federal Deposit Insurance Corporation (FDIC) and the National Credit Union Administration (NCUA)—insure individual deposits of up to $250,000 at commercial banks and thrifts. That fact enhances our willingness to use checkable deposits as a medium of exchange.

Relative Scarcity   The value of money, like the economic value of anything else, depends on its supply and demand. Money derives its value from its scarcity relative to its utility (its want-satisfying power). The utility of money lies in its capacity to be exchanged for goods and services, now or in the future. The economy's demand for money thus depends on the total dollar volume of transactions in any period plus the amount of money individuals and businesses want to hold for future transactions. With a reasonably constant demand for money, the supply of money provided by the monetary authorities will determine the domestic value or "purchasing power" of the monetary unit (dollar, yen, peso, or whatever).

Money and Prices

The purchasing power of money is the amount of goods and services a unit of money will buy. When money rapidly loses its purchasing power, it loses its role as money.

The Purchasing Power of the Dollar   The amount a dollar will buy varies inversely with the price level; that is, a reciprocal relationship exists between the general price level and the purchasing power of the dollar. When the consumer price index or "cost-of-living" index goes up, the value of the dollar goes down, and vice versa. Higher prices lower the value of the dollar because more dollars are needed to buy a particular amount of goods, services, or resources. For example, if the price level doubles, the value of the dollar declines by one-half, or 50 percent.

Conversely, lower prices increase the purchasing power of the dollar because fewer dollars are needed to obtain a specific quantity of goods and services. If the price level falls by, say, one-half, or 50 percent, the purchasing power of the dollar doubles.

In equation form, the relationship looks like this:

$$\$V = 1/P$$

To find the value of the dollar $\$V$, divide 1 by the price level P expressed as an index number (in hundredths). If the price level is 1, then the value of the dollar is 1. If the price level rises to, say, 1.20, $\$V$ falls to 0.833; a 20 percent increase in the price level reduces the value of the dollar by 16.67 percent. Check your understanding of this reciprocal relationship by determining the value of $\$V$ and its percentage rise when P falls by 20 percent from $1 to 0.80.

Inflation and Acceptability   In Chapter 9 we noted situations in which a nation's currency became worthless and unacceptable in exchange. These instances of runaway inflation, or *hyperinflation*, happened when the government issued so many pieces of paper currency that the purchasing power of each of those units of money was almost totally undermined. The infamous post–World War I hyperinflation in Germany is an example. In December 1919 there were about 50 billion marks in circulation. Four years later there were 496,585,345,900 billion marks in circulation! The result? The German mark in 1923 was worth an infinitesimal fraction of its 1919 value.[3]

Runaway inflation may significantly depreciate the value of money between the time it is received and the time it is spent. Rapid declines in the value of a currency may cause it to cease being used as a medium of exchange. Businesses and households may refuse to accept paper money in exchange because they do not want to bear the loss in its value that will occur while it is in their possession. (All this despite the fact that the government says that paper currency is legal tender!) Without an acceptable domestic medium of exchange, the economy may simply revert to barter. Alternatively, more stable currencies such as the U.S. dollar or European euro may come into widespread use. At the extreme, a country may adopt a foreign currency as its own official currency as a way to counter hyperinflation.

Similarly, people will use money as a store of value only as long as there is no sizable deterioration in the value of that money because of inflation. And an economy can effectively employ money as a unit of account only when its purchasing power is relatively stable. A monetary yardstick that no longer measures a yard (in terms of purchasing power) does not permit buyers and sellers to establish the terms of trade clearly. When the value of the dollar is declining rapidly, sellers do not know what to charge and buyers do not know what to pay.

---

[3]Frank G. Graham, *Exchange, Prices, and Production in Hyperinflation Germany, 1920–1923* (Princeton, N.J.: Princeton University Press, 1930), p. 13.

Stabilizing Money's Purchasing Power

Rapidly rising price levels (rapid inflation) and the consequent erosion of the purchasing power of money typically result from imprudent economic policies. Since the purchasing power of money and the price level vary inversely, stabilization of the purchasing power of a nation's money requires stabilization of the nation's price level. Such price-level stability (2 to 3 percent annual inflation) mainly necessitates intelligent management or regulation of the nation's money supply and interest rates *(monetary policy)*. It also requires appropriate *fiscal policy* supportive of the efforts of the nation's monetary authorities to hold down inflation. In the United States, a combination of legislation, government policy, and social practice inhibits imprudent expansion of the money supply that might jeopardize money's purchasing power. The critical role of the U.S. monetary authorities (the Federal Reserve) in maintaining the purchasing power of the dollar is the subject of Chapter 16. For now, simply note that they make available a particular quantity of money, such as *M2* in Figure 14.1, and can change that amount through their policy tools.

QUICK REVIEW 14.2

- In the United States, all money consists essentially of the debts of government, commercial banks, and thrift institutions.
- These debts efficiently perform the functions of money as long as their value, or purchasing power, is relatively stable.
- The value of money is rooted not in specified quantities of precious metals but in the amounts of goods, services, and resources that money will purchase.
- The value of the dollar (its domestic purchasing power) is inversely related to the price level.
- Government's responsibility in stabilizing the purchasing power of the monetary unit calls for (a) effective control over the supply of money by the monetary authorities and (b) the application of appropriate fiscal policies by the president and Congress.

The Federal Reserve and the Banking System

LO14.4 Discuss the makeup of the Federal Reserve and its relationship to banks and thrifts.

In the United States, the "monetary authorities" we have been referring to are the members of the Board of Governors of the **Federal Reserve System** (the "Fed"). As shown in Figure 14.2, the Board directs the activities of the 12 Federal Reserve Banks, which in turn control the lending activity of the nation's banks and thrift institutions. The Fed's major goal is to control the money supply. But since checkable deposits in banks are such a large part of the money supply, an important part of its duties involves assuring the stability of the banking system.

Historical Background

Early in the twentieth century, Congress decided that centralization and public control were essential for an efficient banking system. Decentralized, unregulated banking had fostered the inconvenience and confusion of numerous private bank notes being used as currency. It also had resulted in occasional episodes of monetary mismanagement such that the money supply was inappropriate to the needs of the economy. Sometimes "too much" money precipitated rapid inflation; other times "too little money" stunted the economy's growth by hindering the production and exchange of goods and services. No single entity was charged with creating and implementing nationally consistent banking policies.

Furthermore, acute problems in the banking system occasionally erupted when banks either closed down or insisted on immediate repayment of loans to prevent their own failure. At such times, a banking crisis could emerge, with individuals and businesses who had lost confidence in their banks attempting to simultaneously withdraw all of their money—thereby further crippling the already weakened banks.

An unusually acute banking crisis in 1907 motivated Congress to appoint the National Monetary Commission to study the monetary and banking problems of the economy and to outline a course of action for Congress. The result was the Federal Reserve Act of 1913.

Let's examine the various parts of the Federal Reserve System and their relationship to one another.

Board of Governors

The central authority of the U.S. money and banking system is the **Board of Governors** of the Federal Reserve System. The U.S. president, with the confirmation of the Senate, appoints the seven Board members. Terms are 14 years and staggered so that one member is replaced every 2 years. In addition, new members are appointed when resignations occur. The president selects the chairperson and vice chairperson of the Board from among the members. Those officers serve 4-year terms and can be reappointed to new 4-year terms by the president. The long-term appointments provide the Board with continuity, experienced membership, and independence from political pressures that could result in inflation.

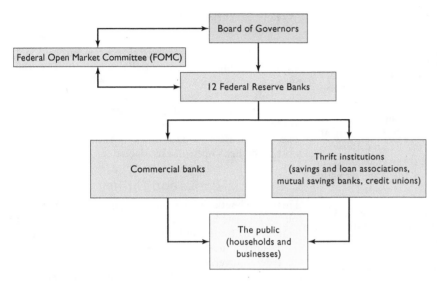

FIGURE 14.2 Framework of the Federal Reserve System and its relationship to the public. The Board of Governors makes the basic policy decisions that provide monetary control of the U.S. money and banking systems. The 12 Federal Reserve Banks implement these decisions. Both the Board of Governors and the 12 Federal Reserve Banks are aided by the Federal Open Market Committee (FOMC).

The 12 Federal Reserve Banks

The 12 **Federal Reserve Banks,** which blend private and public control, collectively serve as the nation's "central bank." These banks also serve as bankers' banks.

Central Bank Most nations have a single central bank—for example, Britain's Bank of England or Japan's Bank of Japan. The United States' central bank consists of 12 banks whose policies are coordinated by the Fed's Board of Governors. The 12 Federal Reserve Banks accommodate the geographic size and economic diversity of the United

States and the nation's large number of commercial banks and thrifts.

Figure 14.3 locates the 12 Federal Reserve Banks and indicates the district that each serves. These banks implement the basic policy of the Board of Governors.

Quasi-Public Banks The 12 Federal Reserve Banks are quasi-public banks, which blend private ownership and public control. Each Federal Reserve Bank is owned by the private commercial banks in its district. (Federally chartered banks are required to purchase shares of stock in

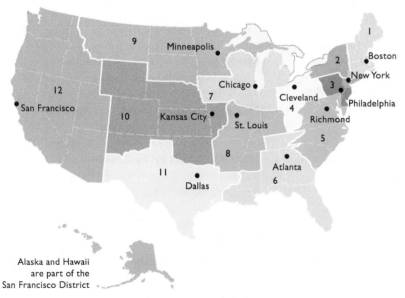

FIGURE 14.3 The 12 Federal Reserve Districts. The Federal Reserve System divides the United States into 12 districts, each having one central bank and in some instances one or more branches of the central bank.

Alaska and Hawaii are part of the San Francisco District

Source: Federal Reserve Bulletin, **www.federalreserve.gov/pubs/bulletin.**

the Federal Reserve Bank in their district.) But the Board of Governors, a government body, sets the basic policies that the Federal Reserve Banks pursue.

Despite their private ownership, the Federal Reserve Banks are in practice public institutions. Unlike private firms, they are not motivated by profit. The policies they follow are designed by the Board of Governors to promote the well-being of the economy as a whole. Thus, the activities of the Federal Reserve Banks are frequently at odds with the profit motive.[4] Also, the Federal Reserve Banks do not compete with commercial banks. In general, they do not deal with the public; rather, they interact with the government and commercial banks and thrifts.

Bankers' Banks   The Federal Reserve Banks are "bankers' banks." They perform essentially the same functions for banks and thrifts as those institutions perform for the public. Just as banks and thrifts accept the deposits of and make loans to the public, so the central banks accept the deposits of and make loans to banks and thrifts. Normally, these loans average only about $150 million a day. But in emergency circumstances the Federal Reserve Banks become the "lender of last resort" to the banking system and can lend out as much as needed to ensure that banks and thrifts can meet their cash obligations. On the day after terrorists attacked the United States on September 11, 2001, the Fed lent $45 *billion* to U.S. banks and thrifts. The Fed wanted to make sure that the destruction and disruption in New York City and the Washington, D.C., area did not precipitate a nationwide banking crisis.

The Fed assumed an even greater role as a lender of last resort during the financial crisis of 2007–2008. We discuss that crisis and the Fed's emergency response to the crisis later in this chapter.

But the Federal Reserve Banks have a third function, which banks and thrifts do not perform: They issue currency. Congress has authorized the Federal Reserve Banks to put into circulation Federal Reserve Notes, which constitute the economy's paper money supply.

FOMC

The **Federal Open Market Committee (FOMC)** aids the Board of Governors in conducting monetary policy. The FOMC is made up of 12 individuals:

- The seven members of the Board of Governors.
- The president of the New York Federal Reserve Bank.

---

[4]Although it is not their goal, the Federal Reserve Banks have actually operated profitably, largely as a result of the Treasury debts they hold. Part of the profit is used to pay 6 percent annual dividends to the commercial banks that hold stock in the Federal Reserve Banks; the remaining profit is usually turned over to the U.S. Treasury.

- Four of the remaining presidents of Federal Reserve Banks on a 1-year rotating basis.

The FOMC meets regularly to direct the purchase and sale of government securities (bills, notes, bonds) in the open market in which such securities are bought and sold on a daily basis. We will find in Chapter 16 that the purpose of these aptly named *open-market operations* is to control the nation's money supply and influence interest rates. The Federal Reserve Bank in New York City conducts most of the Fed's open-market operations.

Commercial Banks and Thrifts

There are about 6,000 commercial banks. Roughly three-fourths are state banks. These are private banks chartered (authorized) by the individual states to operate within those states. One-fourth are private banks chartered by the federal government to operate nationally; these are national banks. Some of the U.S. national banks are very large, ranking among the world's largest financial institutions (see Global Perspective 14.1).

The 8,500 thrift institutions—most of which are credit unions—are regulated by agencies in addition to the

GLOBAL PERSPECTIVE 14.1

The World's 12 Largest Financial Institutions

The world's 12 largest private sector financial institutions are headquartered in Europe, Japan, and the United States (2012 data).

Source: **www.forbes.com/global2000/list/**. Reprinted by Permission of Forbes Media LLC © 2012.

Board of Governors and the Federal Reserve Banks. For example, credit unions are regulated and monitored by the National Credit Union Administration (NCUA). But the thrifts *are* subject to monetary control by the Federal Reserve System. In particular, like the banks, thrifts are required to keep a certain percentage of their checkable deposits as "reserves." In Figure 14.2 we use arrows to indicate that the thrift institutions are subject to the control of the Board of Governors and the central banks. Decisions concerning monetary policy affect the thrifts along with the commercial banks.

Fed Functions, Responsibilities, and Independence

LO14.5 Identify the functions and responsibilities of the Federal Reserve and explain why Fed independence is important.

The Fed performs several functions, some of which we have already identified, but they are worth repeating:

- *Issuing currency* The Federal Reserve Banks issue Federal Reserve Notes, the paper currency used in the U.S. monetary system. (The Federal Reserve Bank that issued a particular bill is identified in black in the upper left of the front of the newly designed bills. "A1," for example, identifies the Boston bank, "B2" the New York bank, and so on.)

- *Setting reserve requirements and holding reserves* The Fed sets reserve requirements, which are the fractions of checking account balances that banks must maintain as currency reserves. The central banks accept as deposits from the banks and thrifts any portion of their mandated reserves not held as vault cash.

- *Lending to financial institutions and serving as an emergency lender of last resort* The Fed makes routine short-term loans to banks and thrifts and charges them an interest rate called the *discount rate*. It also occasionally auctions off loans to banks and thrifts through its *Term Auction Facility*, discussed in Chapter 16. In times of financial emergencies, the Fed serves as a lender of last resort to critical parts of the U.S. financial industry.

- *Providing for check collection* The Fed provides the banking system with a means for collecting on checks. If Sue writes a check on her Miami bank or thrift to Joe, who deposits it in his Dallas bank or thrift, how does the Dallas bank collect the money represented by the check drawn against the Miami bank? Answer: The Fed handles it by adjusting the reserves (deposits) of the two banks.

- *Acting as fiscal agent* The Fed acts as the fiscal agent (provider of financial services) for the federal government. The government collects huge sums through taxation, spends equally large amounts, and sells and redeems bonds. To carry out these activities, the government uses the Fed's facilities.

- *Supervising banks* The Fed supervises the operations of banks. It makes periodic examinations to assess bank profitability, to ascertain that banks perform in accordance with the many regulations to which they are subject, and to uncover questionable practices or fraud. Following the financial crisis of 2007–2008, Congress expanded the Fed's supervisory powers over banks.[5]

- *Controlling the money supply* Finally, the Fed has ultimate responsibility for regulating the supply of money, and this enables it to influence interest rates. The major task of the Fed under usual economic circumstances is to manage the money supply (and thus interest rates) according to the needs of the economy. This involves making an amount of money available that is consistent with high and rising levels of output and employment *and* a relatively stable price level. While most of the other functions of the Fed are routine activities or have a service nature, managing the nation's money supply requires making basic, but unique, policy decisions. (We discuss those decisions in detail in Chapter 16.)

Federal Reserve Independence

Congress purposely established the Fed as an independent agency of government. The objective was to protect the Fed from political pressures so that it could effectively control the money supply and maintain price stability. Political pressures on Congress and the executive branch may at times result in inflationary fiscal policies, including tax cuts and special-interest spending. If Congress and the executive branch also controlled the nation's monetary policy, citizens and lobbying groups undoubtedly would pressure elected officials to keep interest rates low even

---

[5] The Fed is not alone in this task of supervision. The individual states supervise the banks that they charter. The Office of the Comptroller of the Currency has separate supervisory authority over the banks and the thrifts. Also, the Federal Deposit Insurance Corporation supervises the banks and thrifts whose deposits it insures.

though at times high interest rates are necessary to reduce aggregate demand and thus control inflation. An independent monetary authority (the Fed) can take actions to increase interest rates when higher rates are needed to stem inflation. Studies show that countries that have independent central banks like the Fed have lower rates of inflation, on average, than countries that have little or no central bank independence.

QUICK REVIEW 14.3

- The U.S. banking system consists of (a) the Board of Governors of the Federal Reserve System, (b) the 12 Federal Reserve Banks, and (c) some 6,000 commercial banks and 8,500 thrift institutions (mainly credit unions).
- The 12 Federal Reserve Banks are simultaneously (a) central banks, (b) quasi-public banks, and (c) bankers' banks.
- The major functions of the Fed are to (a) issue Federal Reserve Notes, (b) set reserve requirements and hold reserves deposited by banks and thrifts, (c) lend money to financial institutions and serve as the lender of last resort in national financial emergencies, (d) provide for the rapid collection of checks, (e) act as the fiscal agent for the federal government, (f) supervise the operations of the banks, and (g) regulate the supply of money in the best interests of the economy.

The Financial Crisis of 2007 and 2008

LO14.6 Identify and explain the main factors that contributed to the financial crisis of 2007–2008.

As previously noted, a properly functioning monetary system supports the continuous circular flows of income and expenditures in the economy. In contrast, a malfunctioning monetary system causes major problems in credit markets and can cause severe fluctuations in the economy's levels of output, employment, and prices.

"Malfunctioning" is too gentle an adjective to describe the monetary system in late 2007 and 2008. In that period, the U.S. financial system faced its most serious crisis since the Great Depression of the 1930s. The financial crisis soon spread to the entire economy, culminating in the severe recession of 2007–2009. We discussed the recession in detail in previous chapters, and we now want to examine the financial crisis that led up to it. What was the nature of the financial crisis? What caused it? How has it changed the structure of the U.S. financial services industry?

The Mortgage Default Crisis

In 2007 a major wave of defaults on home mortgage loans threatened the health of not only the original mortgage lenders but of any financial institution that had made such loans or invested in such loans either directly or indirectly. A majority of these mortgage defaults were on **subprime mortgage loans**—high-interest-rate loans to home buyers with higher-than-average credit risk. Ironically, the federal government had encouraged banks to make these types of loans as part of an effort to broaden home ownership to more Americans. But more directly to the point, several of the biggest indirect investors in these subprime loans had been banks. The banks had lent money to investment companies that had purchased many of the mortgages from mortgage lenders. When the mortgages started to go bad, many investment funds "blew up" and could not repay the loans they had taken out from the banks. The banks thus had to "write off" (declare unrecoverable) the loans they had made to the investment companies, but doing that meant reducing their banks' reserves and limiting their ability to generate new loans. This greatly threatened the economy because both consumers and businesses rely on loans to finance consumption and investment expenditures.

A strange thing about the crisis was that before it happened, banks and government regulators had mistakenly believed that an innovation known as the "mortgage-backed security" had eliminated most of the bank exposure to mortgage defaults. **Mortgage-backed securities** are bonds backed by mortgage payments. To create them, banks and other mortgage lenders first made mortgage loans. But then instead of holding all of those loans as assets on their balance sheets and collecting the monthly mortgage payments, the banks and other mortgage lenders bundled hundreds or thousands of them together and sold them off as bonds—in essence selling the right to collect all the future mortgage payments. The banks obtained a single, up-front cash payment for the bond and the bond buyer started to collect the mortgage payments as the return on the investment.

From the banks' perspective, this seemed like a smart business decision because it transferred any future default risk on those mortgages to the buyer of the bond. The banks thought that they were off the hook for these mortgages. Unfortunately for them, however, they lent a substantial portion of the money they received from selling the bonds to investment funds that invested in mortgage-backed bonds. They also purchased large amounts of mortgage-backed securities as financial investments to help meet bank capital requirements set by bank regulators. So while the banks were no longer directly exposed to major portions of the mortgage default risk, they were still indirectly exposed to it. When many homebuyers started to default on their mortgages, the banks lost money on the mortgages they still held. The banks also lost money on the loans they had made to the investors who had purchased mortgage-backed securities, and also on the mortgage-backed securities the banks had purchased from investment firms.

But what had caused the skyrocketing mortgage default rates in the first place? There were many causes, including certain government programs that greatly encouraged and subsidized home ownership for former renters. Also contributing were declining real estate values that arrived at the end of a long housing boom during which house prices had greatly increased. But an equally important factor was the bad incentives provided by the previously discussed mortgage-backed bonds. Because the banks and other mortgage lenders thought that they were no longer exposed to large portions of their mortgage default risk, they became lax in their lending practices—so much so that people were granted subprime mortgage loans that they were unlikely to be able to repay. Some mortgage companies were so eager to sign up new homebuyers (in order to bundle their loans together to sell bonds) that they stopped running credit checks and even allowed applicants to claim higher incomes than they were actually earning in order to qualify them for big loans. The natural result was that many people took on "too much mortgage" and were soon failing to make their monthly payments.

Securitization

The problems just described relate to **securitization**—the process of slicing up and bundling groups of loans, mortgages, corporate bonds, or other financial debts into distinct new securities. This process was not new and was viewed favorably by government regulators, who thought securitization made the banking system safer by allowing banks to shed risk. As noted in our discussion of mortgages, these securities were sold to financial investors, who purchased them to obtain the interest payments and the eventual return of principal generated by the underlying securities. For example, the mortgage loans provided to the subprime borrowers were bundled together as mortgage-backed securities and sold to private investors, mutual fund firms, and pension funds. These securities were attractive to many private investors and financial institutions alike because they offered higher-interest returns than securities backed by less-risky mortgages or other safer investments.

Once created, loan-backed securities are bought and sold in financial markets just like other securities such as

stocks and bonds. These sorts of securities can therefore end up worldwide in the investment portfolios of banks, thrifts, insurance companies, and pensions, as well as in personal accounts.

To reduce the risk for holders of these securities, a few large insurance companies developed other securities that the holders of loan-backed securities could purchase to insure against losses from defaults. American International Group (AIG), in particular, issued billions of dollars of *collateralized default swaps*—essentially insurance policies—that were designed to compensate the holders of loan-backed securities if the loans underlying these investments went into default and did not pay off. Thus, collateralized default swaps became yet another category of investment security that was highly exposed to mortgage-loan risk.

Securitization is so widespread and so critical to the modern financial system that economists sometimes refer to it as the *shadow banking system*. All sorts of securities backed by loans or other securities are issued, bought, sold, and resold each day in a process that helps to keep credit flowing to the households and firms that rely on it for their personal and business needs. In general, securitization therefore is a positive financial innovation. But mortgage-backed securities, in particular, turned out to contain much more risk than most people thought.

Investors and government regulators failed to ask three related questions about mortgage-backed securities: What would happen if the value of one of the types of loans (say, mortgages) that underlies part of the securitization process unexpectedly plunged? And what then would happen if some of the largest holders of the securities based on these mortgages were major U.S. financial institutions that are vitally important to the day-to-day financing of the credit needed to keep the American economy running smoothly? And what would happen after that if the main insurer of these securities not only was the largest insurance company in the United States but in the world?

All three seemingly improbable "what ifs?" occurred! As previously explained, interest rates on adjustable-rate mortgages increased and house prices fell. Borrowers who had made relatively small down payments on home purchases or had previously cashed out home equity through refinancing discovered that they owed more on their mortgages than their properties were worth. Their loans were said to be "underwater." As interest rates adjusted upward and the economy slowed, borrowers began falling behind on their monthly mortgage payments. Lenders began to foreclose on many houses, while other borrowers literally handed in their house keys and walked away from their houses *and* their mortgages.

Failures and Near-Failures of Financial Firms

When the mortgage loan "card" underpinning mortgage-based securitization fell, the securitization layers above it collapsed like a house of cards. First, the big mortgage lenders faced demise because they still held large amounts of the bad debt. Three huge mortgage lenders collapsed or nearly collapsed. Countrywide, the second largest mortgage lender, was saved from bankruptcy by Bank of America. Regulators also seized Washington Mutual bank, the nation's largest mortgage lender, and arranged a quick takeover by JPMorgan Chase. Wachovia bank's heavy exposure to mortgages through its Golden West subsidiary resulted in near bankruptcy, and it was rescued through acquisition by Wells Fargo.

The exposure to the growing problem of loan defaults quickly jumped from direct mortgage lenders to other financial institutions. Securities firms and investment banks that held large amounts of loan-backed securities began to suffer huge losses. Merrill Lynch lost more in two years than it made in the prior decade and was acquired at a fire-sale price by Bank of America. Lehman Brothers, a major holder of mortgage-backed securities, declared bankruptcy. Goldman Sachs, Morgan Stanley, and other financial firms that had heavy exposures to mortgage-backed securities and collateralized default swaps rushed to become bank holding companies so they could qualify for the massive emergency loans that the Federal Reserve was making available to banks and bank holding companies. Citibank survived through infusions of federal government loans. Insurance company AIG suffered enormous losses because it had not set aside sufficient reserves to pay off the unexpectedly large losses that accrued on the insurance policies that it had sold to holders of mortgage-backed securities. The nightmarish thought of a total collapse of the U.S. financial system suddenly became a realistic possibility.

QUICK REVIEW 14.4

- The financial crisis of 2007–2008 consisted of an unprecedented rise in mortgage loan defaults, the collapse or near collapse of several major financial institutions, and the generalized freezing up of credit availability.
- The crisis resulted from bad mortgage loans together with declining real estate prices.
- The crisis exposed the underestimation of risk by holders of mortgage-backed securities as well as faulty insurance securities that had been designed to protect holders of mortgage-backed securities from the risk of default.

The Policy Response to the Financial Crisis

LO14.7 Discuss the actions of the U.S. Treasury and the Federal Reserve that helped keep the banking and financial crisis of 2007–2008 from worsening.

The U.S. government responded to the financial crisis with historically unprecedented fiscal policy actions while the Fed acted aggressively as a lender of last resort.

The Treasury Bailout: TARP

In late 2008 Congress passed the **Troubled Asset Relief Program (TARP),** which allocated $700 billion—yes, billion—to the U.S. Treasury to make emergency loans to critical financial and other U.S. firms. Most of this "bail-out" money eventually was lent out. In fact, as of March 2009, the federal government and Federal Reserve had spent $170 billion just keeping insurer AIG afloat. Other major recipients of TARP funds included Citibank, Bank of America, JPMorgan Chase, and Goldman Sachs. Later, nonfinancial firms such as General Motors and Chrysler also received several billion dollars of TARP loans.

TARP indeed saved several financial institutions whose bankruptcy would have caused a tsunami of secondary effects that probably would have brought down other financial firms and frozen credit throughout the economy. But this very fact demonstrates the problem of **moral hazard.** As it relates to financial investment, moral hazard is the tendency for financial investors and financial services firms to take on greater risks because they assume they are at least partially insured against losses. Without TARP, several firms would have gone bankrupt and their stockholders, bondholders, and executives all would have suffered large personal losses. With TARP, those outcomes were at least partially avoided. TARP and similar government bailouts were essentially government-provided insurance payouts to financial firms that never had to pay a single cent in insurance premiums for the massive bailouts that kept them afloat.

The correct assumption by large firms that they were simply too big for government to let them fail may have given them an incentive to make riskier investments than if no government bailouts were likely to be forthcoming.

The Fed's Lender-of-Last-Resort Activities

As noted in our previous list of Fed functions, one of the roles of the Federal Reserve is to serve as the lender of last resort to financial institutions in times of financial emergencies. The Fed performed this vital function well following the 9/11 terrorist attacks. The financial crisis of

2007–2008 presented another, broader-based financial emergency. Under Fed Chair Ben Bernanke, the Fed designed and implemented several highly creative new lender-of-last-resort facilities to pump liquidity into the financial system. These facilities, procedures, and capabilities were in addition to both the TARP efforts by the U.S. Treasury and the Fed's use of standard tools of monetary policy (the subject of Chapter 16) designed to reduce interest rates. All the new Fed facilities had the single purpose and desired outcome of keeping credit flowing.

Total Fed assets rose from $885 billion in February 2008 to $1,903 billion in March 2009. This increase reflected a huge rise in the amount of securities (U.S. securities, mortgage-backed securities, and others) owned by the Fed. In undertaking its lender-of-last-resort functions, the Fed bought these securities from financial institutions. The purpose was to increase liquidity in the financial system by exchanging illiquid bonds (that the firms could not easily sell during the crisis) for cash, the most liquid of all assets.

Many economists believe that TARP and the Fed's actions helped avert a second Great Depression. The following list of new Fed credit facilities underscores the extraordinary extent of the Fed's lender-of-last-resort response to the crisis.

- *Primary Dealer Credit Facility (PDCF)* Provided overnight loans to primary dealers who were willing to post loan-backed securities as collateral. (The Fed kept the collateral on any loan that was not repaid on time.) Primary dealers are the 21 major financial institutions that the Fed uses to buy and sell U.S. securities.

- *Term Securities Lending Facility (TSLF)* Lent U.S. securities to primary dealers for one-month terms to promote liquidity in the markets for these U.S. securities. The financial institutions obtained the securities from the Fed through participating in competitive single-bid auctions.

- *Asset-Backed Commercial Paper Money Market Mutual Fund Liquidity Facility* Provided loans to U.S. banks and thrifts to finance their purchases of *commercial paper* from money market mutual funds. Commercial paper consists of asset-backed, short-term IOUs that are mainly issued by corporations. These short-term loans are vital for financing the day-to-day operations of businesses.

- *Commercial Paper Funding Facility (CPFF)* Purchased commercial paper to support the commercial paper market and therefore the short-term credit needs of businesses.

- *Money Market Investor Funding Facility (MMIFF)* Provided funding support to a private-sector initiative designed to ensure the liquidity of U.S. money market mutual funds. Many Americans rely on money market mutual funds as low-risk investments.

- *Term Asset-Backed Securities Loan Facility (TALF)* Helped households and business with their credit needs by providing funding support for asset-backed securities collateralized by student loans, auto loans, credit card loans, and loans guaranteed by the Small Business Administration (SBA).

- *Interest Payments on Reserves* Bolstered the profitability of banks by paying interest on the reserves they hold in their vaults or in the Federal Reserve Banks.

These extraordinary efforts, like those of the Treasury, helped prevent total disarray in the credit markets. But like TARP, the Fed efforts intensified the moral hazard problem by greatly limiting the losses that otherwise would have resulted from bad financial assumptions and decisions.

QUICK REVIEW 14.5

- The Troubled Asset Relief Program (TARP) authorized the U.S. Treasury to spend up to $700 billion to make emergency loans and guarantees to failing financial firms.
- The Treasury rescue, or bailout, was aided by lender-of-last-resort loans provided by the Federal Reserve to financial institutions through a series of newly established Fed facilities.
- The TARP loans and the Fed's lender-of-last-resort actions intensified the moral hazard problem in which financial investors and financial firms take on greater risk because they assume that the government will bail them out if they lose money.

The Postcrisis U.S. Financial Services Industry

LO14.8 Identify the main subsets of the financial services industry in the United States and provide examples of some firms in each category.

Table 14.1 lists the major categories of firms within the U.S. financial services industry and gives examples of firms in each category. Note that the main categories of the **financial services industry** are commercial banks, thrifts,

LAST WORD

Too Big to Fail. Too Big to Jail?

In 2010, Congress Passed the Wall Street Reform and Consumer Protection Act in an Attempt to Better Regulate Big Financial Firms. But Their Enormous Size Has Now, Apparently, Placed Them Above the Law.

In early December 2012, Lanny Breuer, the Assistant U.S. Attorney General in charge of prosecuting financial crimes, explained at a press conference that he had decided to only fine HSBC bank $1.9 billion—or about five weeks' profits—as a punishment for nearly a decade of laundering money for the Sinaloa drug cartel, Al Qaeda, and Russian mobsters; helping Iran, the Sudan, and North Korea evade sanctions; and helping hundreds of individuals and businesses cheat on their taxes. Not a single HSBC official would face jail time or a personal fine.

Breuer explained that he chose not to criminally prosecute the bank and put any of its officers in jail because "HSBC would almost certainly have lost its banking license in the United States. The future of the institution would have been under threat and the entire banking system would have been destabilized." In other words, HSBC was not prosecuted because it was very large and very interconnected with other financial firms.

A week later Breuer was again in front of the press. This time it was to announce a set of minor penalties in the LIBOR interest-rate scandal, which involved major international banks illegally manipulating the London Interbank Offer Rate (LIBOR) for their own personal benefit. That manipulation affected trillions of dollars of financial contracts around the world, including millions of home mortgages in the United States. It was thus the most extensive financial crime in world history. But

Breuer worried aloud about global financial stability and stated, "Our goal here is: Not to destroy a major financial institution."

Breuer's decision to put financial stability ahead of prosecuting financial crimes was made even more clear in early January 2013 when on the TV show *Frontline* he was asked whether prosecutors should think about anything other than pursuing justice. He responded, "Well, I think I am pursuing justice. And I think the entire responsibility of the Department is to pursue justice. But in any given case, I think I and prosecutors around

insurance companies, mutual fund companies, pension funds, security firms, and investment banks. Even before the financial crisis of 2007–2008, the financial services industry was consolidating into fewer, larger firms, each offering a wider spectrum of services. In 1999 Congress ended the Depression-era prohibition against banks selling stocks, bonds, and mutual funds. Thus, the lines between the subsets of the financial industry began to blur. Many banks acquired stock brokerage firms and, in a few cases, insurance companies. For example, Citigroup, which was once only into banking, now owns Smith Barney, a large securities firm. Many large banks (for example, Wells Fargo) and pension funds (for example, TIAA-CREF) now provide mutual funds, including money market mutual funds that pay relatively high interest and on which checks of $500 or more can be written.

The upheaval in the financial markets caused by the financial crisis of 2007–2008 further consolidated the industry and further blurred the lines between its segments. Between September 2007 and September 2009, the FDIC shut down more than 200 U.S. banks and transferred their bank deposits to other, usually larger, banks. In 2009 the three largest U.S. banks (JPMorgan Chase, Bank of America, and Wells Fargo) held roughly $3 of every $10 on deposit in the United States.

Also, during the financial crisis of 2007–2008, major investment banks Goldman Sachs and Morgan Stanley opted to become commercial banks to gain access to emergency Federal Reserve loans. The nation's largest thrift—Washington Mutual—was absorbed by commercial bank JPMorgan Chase. But even with all this blending, the categories in Table 14.1 remain helpful. The

the country, being responsible, should speak to regulators, should speak to experts, because if I bring a case against institution A, and as a result of bringing that case, there's some huge economic effect—if it creates a ripple effect so that, suddenly, counterparties and other financial institutions or other companies that had nothing to do with this are affected badly—it's a factor we need to know and understand." It is perhaps not surprising that *Frontline* titled that episode "The Untouchables."

Many economists, however, sympathize with Breuer's position because legal changes made during the 1990s resulted in a financial system dominated by just a few large firms, each of which is now so large and so interconnected that if any were to collapse, the whole system would indeed be destabilized.

Before those legal changes were made, the structure of the U.S. financial system had been defined by the Glass-Steagall Act of 1933. That law required Wall Street to segregate high-risk and low-risk financial activities across different firms. In particular, Glass-Steagall had required commercial banks to only engage in low-risk lending activities like making home mortgages and small business loans. High-risk financial activities like stock picking, derivatives trading, and investment banking had to be handled by an entirely different set of firms. Thus, even if the firms that took high risks went bankrupt, they were not going to be able to affect the traditional banking system that the entire economy depended upon for making payments, providing cash, and issuing loans to individuals and small businesses.

The legal changes made during the 1990s were aimed at allowing financial firms to offer "one-stop shopping" for financial services. Instead of customers having to go to one firm for a checking account, another to buy life insurance, and yet another to invest in mutual funds, single companies were allowed to offer every imaginable financial service. Not only was this intended to

be more convenient, it was argued that it would actually increase financial stability because large firms that offered a full range of financial services would be diversified across different business activities. For example, if a firm's insurance division was losing money, some other division would probably be doing well enough to either partly or fully offset the loss.

By the time the financial crisis hit in 2007, however, things had turned out quite differently. The convenience factor was there, but the ability to go into other lines of business had caused a massive consolidation of banks, insurance companies, stock brokerages, and derivatives-trading companies. In particular, the major commercial banks were now engaged in massive amounts of speculative investing—much of it financed with the money deposited into checking accounts. Thus, when the crisis hit, it was impossible for any of the major financial firms to go bankrupt without severely affecting both the payments system and the financial viability of other financial firms. Each firm was now so large and so interconnected that it had to be treated as "too big to fail" by government regulators.

What Breuer's comments in 2012 and 2013 indicated, though, was that at least some of the firms had also become "too big to jail." There are, consequently, many economists calling for a return to a financial system in which the big financial firms are broken up into entities that are each small enough to fail without catastrophically affecting the entire financial system and in which Glass-Steagall-style separations once again divide high-risk and low-risk financial activities into separate firms.

An attempt to put that separation into practice was passed in 2010 as part of the Wall Street Reform and Consumer Protection Act. It was known as the Volker Rule after former Federal Reserve Chairman Paul Volker. But as of early 2013, it had yet to be implemented.

main lines of a firm's businesses often are in one category or another. For example, even though Goldman Sachs is licensed and regulated as a bank, it is first and foremost an investment company. And the insurance companies and pension funds do most of their business as such.

The financial crisis of 2007–2008 generated much introspection about what went wrong and how to prevent anything like it from happening again. Politicians and financial regulators tightened lending rules to offset the "pass the buck" incentives created by mortgage-backed securities and prevent loans from being issued to people who are unlikely to be able to make the required monthly payments. They also passed legislation to help homeowners who were "underwater" on mortgage loans remain in their homes.

In mid-2010 Congress passed and the president signed the **Wall Street Reform and Consumer Protection Act.** This sweeping law includes provisions that:

- Eliminate the Office of Thrift Supervision and give broader authority to the Federal Reserve to regulate all large financial institutions.

- Create a Financial Stability Oversight Council to be on the lookout for risks to the financial system.

- Establish a process for the federal government to liquidate (sell off) the assets of failing non-bank financial institutions, much like the FDIC does with failing banks.

- Provide federal regulatory oversight of mortgage-backed securities and other derivatives and require that they be traded on public exchanges.

TABLE 14.1 Major Categories of Financial Institutions within the U.S. Financial Services Industry

Institution	Description	Examples
Commercial banks	State and national banks that provide checking and savings accounts, sell certificates of deposit, and make loans. The Federal Deposit Insurance Corporation (FDIC) insures checking and savings accounts up to $250,000.	JPMorgan Chase, Bank of America, Citibank, Wells Fargo
Thrifts	Savings and loan associations (S&Ls), mutual saving banks, and credit unions that offer checking and savings accounts and make loans. Historically, S&Ls made mortgage loans for houses while mutual savings banks and credit unions made small personal loans, such as automobile loans. Today, major thrifts offer the same range of banking services as commercial banks. The Federal Deposit Insurance Corporation and the National Credit Union Administration insure checking and savings deposits up to $250,000.	Charter One, New York Community Bank, Pentagon Federal Credit Union, Boeing Employees Credit Union (BECU)
Insurance companies	Firms that offer policies (contracts) through which individuals pay premiums to insure against some loss, say, disability or death. In some life insurance policies and annuities, the funds are invested for the client in stocks and bonds and paid back after a specified number of years. Thus, insurance sometimes has a saving or financial-investment element.	Prudential, New York Life, Northwestern Mutual, Hartford, MetLife
Mutual fund companies	Firms that pool deposits by customers to purchase stocks or bonds (or both). Customers thus indirectly own a part of a particular set of stocks or bonds, say stocks in companies expected to grow rapidly (a growth fund) or bonds issued by state governments (a municipal bond fund).	Fidelity, Vanguard, Putnam, Janus, T. Rowe Price
Pension funds	For-profit or nonprofit institutions that collect savings from workers (or from employers on their behalf) throughout their working years and then buy stocks and bonds with the proceeds and make monthly retirement payments.	TIAA-CREF, Teamsters' Union, CalPERs
Securities firms	Firms that offer security advice and buy and sell stocks and bonds for clients. More generally known as *stock brokerage firms*.	Merrill Lynch, Smith Barney, Charles Schwab
Investment banks	Firms that help corporations and governments raise money by selling stocks and bonds. They also typically offer advisory services for corporate mergers and acquisitions as well as brokerage services and advice.	Goldman Sachs, Morgan Stanley, Deutsche Bank, Nomura Securities

- Require companies selling asset-backed securities to retain a portion of those securities so the sellers share part of the risk.

- Establish a stronger consumer financial protection role for the Fed through creation of the Bureau of Consumer Financial Protection.

Proponents of the new law say that it will help prevent many of the practices that led up to the financial crisis of 2007–2008. They also contend that the law will send a strong message to stockholders, bondholders, and executives of large financial firms that they will suffer unavoidable and extremely high personal financial losses if they allow their firms to ever again get into serious financial trouble.

Skeptics of the new law say that regulators already had all the tools they needed to prevent the financial crisis. They also point out that the government's own efforts to promote home ownership, via quasi-government institutions that purchased mortgage-backed securities, greatly contributed to the financial crisis. Critics of the new law

say that it will simply impose heavy new regulatory costs on the financial industry while doing little to prevent future government bailouts. This chapter's Last Word considers those suspicions.

QUICK REVIEW 14.6

- The main categories of the U.S. financial services industry are commercial banks, thrifts, insurance companies, mutual fund companies, pension funds, securities firms, and investment banks.

- The reassembly of the wreckage from the financial crisis of 2007–2008 has further consolidated the already-consolidating financial services industry and has further blurred some of the lines between the subsets of the industry.

- The Wall Street Reform and Consumer Financial Protection Act of 2010 responded to the financial crisis by consolidating financial regulation, providing federal oversight of mortgage-backed securities, and creating the Bureau of Consumer Financial Protection.

SUMMARY

LO14.1 Identify and explain the functions of money.

Anything that is accepted as (*a*) a medium of exchange, (*b*) a unit of monetary account, and (*c*) a store of value can be used as money.

LO14.2 List and describe the components of the U.S. money supply.

There are two major definitions of the money supply. *M*1 consists of currency and checkable deposits; *M*2 consists of *M*1 plus savings deposits, including money market deposit accounts, small-denominated (less than $100,000) time deposits, and money market mutual fund balances held by individuals.

LO14.3 Describe what "backs" the money supply, making us willing to accept it as payment.

Money represents the debts of government and institutions offering checkable deposits (commercial banks and thrift institutions) and has value because of the goods, services, and resources it will command in the market. Maintaining the purchasing power of money depends largely on the government's effectiveness in managing the money supply.

LO14.4 Discuss the makeup of the Federal Reserve and its relationship to banks and thrifts.

The U.S. banking system consists of (*a*) the Board of Governors of the Federal Reserve System, (*b*) the 12 Federal Reserve Banks, and (*c*) some 6,000 commercial banks and 8,500 thrift institutions (mainly credit unions). The Board of Governors is the basic policymaking body for the entire banking system. The directives of the Board and the Federal Open Market Committee (FOMC) are made effective through the 12 Federal Reserve Banks, which are simultaneously (*a*) central banks, (*b*) quasi-public banks, and (*c*) bankers' banks.

LO14.5 Identify the functions and responsibilities of the Federal Reserve and explain why Fed independence is important.

The major functions of the Fed are to (*a*) issue Federal Reserve Notes, (*b*) set reserve requirements and hold reserves deposited by banks and thrifts, (*c*) lend money to financial institutions and serve as the lender of last resort in national financial emergencies, (*d*) provide for the rapid collection of checks, (*e*) act as the fiscal agent for the federal government, (*f*) supervise the operations of the banks, and (*g*) regulate the supply of money in the best interests of the economy.

The Fed is essentially an independent institution, controlled neither by the president of the United States nor by Congress. This independence shields the Fed from political pressure and allows it to raise and lower interest rates (via changes in the money supply) as needed to promote full employment, price stability, and economic growth.

LO14.6 Identify and explain the main factors that contributed to the financial crisis of 2007–2008.

The financial crisis of 2007–2008 consisted of an unprecedented rise in mortgage loan defaults, the collapse or near-collapse of several major financial institutions, and the generalized freezing up of credit availability. The crisis resulted from bad mortgage loans together with declining real estate prices. It also resulted from underestimation of risk by holders of mortgage-backed securities and faulty insurance securities designed to protect holders of mortgage-backed securities from the risk of default.

LO14.7 Discuss the actions of the U.S. Treasury and the Federal Reserve that helped keep the banking and financial crisis of 2007–2008 from worsening.

In 2008 Congress passed the Troubled Asset Relief Program (TARP), which authorized the U.S. Treasury to spend up to $700 billion to make emergency loans and guarantees to failing financial firms. The Treasury rescue, or bailout, was aided by lender-of-last-resort loans provided by the Federal Reserve to financial institutions through a series of newly established Fed facilities.

The TARP loans and the Fed's lender-of-last-resort actions intensify the moral hazard problem. This is the tendency of financial investors and financial firms to take on greater risk when they assume they are at least partially insured against loss.

LO14.8 Identify the main subsets of the financial services industry in the United States and provide examples of some firms in each category.

The main categories of the U.S. financial services industry are commercial banks, thrifts, insurance companies, mutual fund companies, pension funds, securities firms, and investment banks. The reassembly of the wreckage from the financial crisis of 2007–2008 has further consolidated the already-consolidating financial services industry and has further blurred some of the lines between the subsets of the industry.

In response to the financial crisis, Congress passed the Wall Street Reform and Consumer Financial Protection Act of 2010.

TERMS AND CONCEPTS

medium of exchange	*M*1	commercial banks
unit of account	Federal Reserve Notes	thrift institutions
store of value	token money	near-monies
liquidity	checkable deposits	*M*2

savings account

money market deposit account (MMDA)

time deposits

money market mutual fund (MMMF)

legal tender

Federal Reserve System

Board of Governors

Federal Reserve Banks

Federal Open Market Committee (FOMC)

subprime mortgage loans

mortgage-backed securities

securitization

Troubled Asset Relief Program (TARP)

moral hazard

financial services industry

Wall Street Reform and Consumer Protection Act

The following and additional problems can be found in connect

DISCUSSION QUESTIONS

1. What are the three basic functions of money? Describe how rapid inflation can undermine money's ability to perform each of the three functions. **LO14.1**

2. Which two of the following financial institutions offer checkable deposits included within the $M1$ money supply: mutual fund companies; insurance companies; commercial banks; securities firms; thrift institutions? Which of the following items is not included in either $M1$ or $M2$: currency held by the public; checkable deposits; money market mutual fund balances; small-denominated (less than \$100,000) time deposits; currency held by banks; savings deposits? **LO14.2**

3. What are the components of the $M1$ money supply? What is the largest component? Which of the components of $M1$ is legal tender? Why is the face value of a coin greater than its intrinsic value? What near-monies are included in the $M2$ money supply? **LO14.2**

4. Explain and evaluate the following statements: **LO14.2**
   a. The invention of money is one of the great achievements of humankind, for without it the enrichment that comes from broadening trade would have been impossible.
   b. Money is whatever society says it is.
   c. In the United States, the debts of government and commercial banks are used as money.
   d. People often say they would like to have more money, but what they usually mean is that they would like to have more goods and services.
   e. When the price of everything goes up, it is not because everything is worth more but because the currency is worth less.
   f. Any central bank can create money; the trick is to create enough, but not too much, of it.

5. What "backs" the money supply in the United States? What determines the value (domestic purchasing power) of money? How does the purchasing power of money relate to the price level? Who in the United States is responsible for maintaining money's purchasing power? **LO14.3**

6. How is the chairperson of the Federal Reserve System selected? Describe the relationship between the Board of Governors of the Federal Reserve System and the 12 Federal Reserve Banks. What is the purpose of the Federal Open Market Committee (FOMC)? What is its makeup? **LO14.4**

7. The following are two hypothetical ways in which the Federal Reserve Board might be appointed. Would you favor either of these two methods over the present method? Why or why not? **LO14.4**
   a. Upon taking office, the U.S. president appoints seven people to the Federal Reserve Board, including a chair. Each appointee must be confirmed by a majority vote of the Senate, and each serves the same 4-year term as the president.
   b. Congress selects seven members from its ranks (four from the House of Representatives and three from the Senate) to serve at congressional pleasure as the Board of Governors of the Federal Reserve System.

8. What is meant when economists say that the Federal Reserve Banks are central banks, quasi-public banks, and bankers' banks? **LO14.4**

9. Why do economists nearly uniformly support an independent Fed rather than one beholden directly to either the president or Congress? **LO14.5**

10. Identify three functions of the Federal Reserve of your choice, other than its main role of controlling the supply of money. **LO14.5**

11. How does each of the following relate to the financial crisis of 2007–2008: declines in real estate values, subprime mortgage loans, mortgage-backed securities, AIG. **LO14.6**

12. What is TARP and how was it funded? What is meant by the term "lender of last resort" and how does it relate to the financial crisis of 2007–2008? How do government and Federal Reserve emergency loans relate to the concept of moral hazard? **LO14.7**

13. What are the major categories of firms that make up the U.S. financial services industry? Are there more or fewer banks today than before the start of the financial crisis of 2007–2008? Why are the lines between the categories of financial firms even more blurred than they were before the

crisis? How did the Wall Street Reform and Consumer Protection Act of 2010 try to address some of the problems that helped cause the crisis? **LO14.8**

14. **LAST WORD** Why are federal prosecutors reluctant to bring major charges against large financial firms? What was the main regulatory action of the Glass-Steagall law? Why might having many smaller financial firms be more stable than having fewer larger firms? What argument can be made for the possibility that larger financial firms might be more stable than smaller financial firms?

REVIEW QUESTIONS

1. The three functions of money are: **LO14.1**
   a. Liquidity, store of value, and gifting.
   b. Medium of exchange, unit of account, and liquidity.
   c. Liquidity, unit of account, and gifting.
   d. Medium of exchange, unit of account, and store of value.

2. Suppose that a small country currently has $4 million of currency in circulation, $6 million of checkable deposits, $200 million of savings deposits, $40 million of small-denominated time deposits, and $30 million of money market mutual fund deposits. From these numbers we see that this small country's $M1$ money supply is _____, while its $M2$ money supply is _____. **LO14.2**
   a. $10 million; $280 million.
   b. $10 million; $270 million.
   c. $210 million; $280 million.
   d. $250 million; $270 million.

3. Recall the formula that states that $V = 1/P$, where V is the value of the dollar and P is the price level. If the price level falls from 1 to 0.75, what will happen to the value of the dollar? **LO14.3**
   a. It will rise by a third (33.3 percent).
   b. It will rise by a quarter (25 percent).
   c. It will fall by a quarter (−25 percent).
   d. It will fall by a third (−33.3 percent).

4. Which group votes on the open-market operations that are used to control the U.S. money supply and interest rates? **LO14.4**
   a. The Federal Reserve System.
   b. The 12 Federal Reserve Banks.
   c. The Board of Governors of the Federal Reserve System.
   d. The Federal Open Market Committee (FOMC).

5. An important reason why members of the Federal Reserve's Board of Governors are each given extremely long, 14-year terms is to: **LO14.4**
   a. Insulate members from political pressures that could result in inflation.
   b. Help older members avoid job searches before retiring.

   c. Attract younger people with lots of time left in their careers.
   d. Avoid the trouble of constantly having to deal with new members.

6. Which of the following is *not* a function of the Fed? **LO14.5**
   a. Setting reserve requirements for banks.
   b. Advising Congress on fiscal policy.
   c. Regulating the supply of money.
   d. Serving as a lender of last resort.

7. James borrows $300,000 for a home from Bank A. Bank A resells the right to collect on that loan to Bank B. Bank B securitizes that loan with hundreds of others and sells the resulting security to a state pension plan, which at the same time purchases an insurance policy from AIG that will pay off if James and the other people whose mortgages are in the security can't pay off their mortgage loans. Suppose that James and all the other people can't pay off their mortgages. Which financial entity is legally obligated to suffer the loss? **LO14.6**
   a. Bank A.
   b. Bank B.
   c. The state pension plan.
   d. AIG.

8. City Bank is considering making a $50 million loan to a company named SheetOil that wants to commercialize a process for turning used blankets, pillowcases, and sheets into oil. This company's chances for success are dubious, but City Bank makes the loan anyway because it believes that the government will bail it out if SheetOil goes bankrupt and cannot repay the loan. City Bank's decision to make the loan has been affected by: **LO14.7**
   a. Liquidity.
   b. Moral hazard.
   c. Token money.
   d. Securitization.

9. True or False: The financial crisis hastened the ongoing process in which the financial services industry was transforming from having a few large firms to many small firms. **LO14.8**

PROBLEMS

1. Assume that the following asset values (in millions of dollars) exist in Ironmania: Federal Reserve Notes in circulation = $700; Money market mutual funds (MMMFs) held by individuals = $400; Corporate bonds = $300; Iron ore deposits = $50; Currency in commercial banks = $100; Savings deposits, including money market deposit accounts

(MMDAs) = $140; Checkable deposits = $1,500; Small-denominated (less than $100,000) time deposits = $100; Coins in circulation = $40. **LO14.1**

a. What is $M1$ in Ironmania?

b. What is $M2$ in Ironmania?

2. Assume that Jimmy Cash has $2,000 in his checking account at Folsom Bank and uses his checking account card to withdraw $200 of cash from the bank's ATM machine. By what dollar amount did the $M1$ money supply change as a result of this single, isolated transaction? **LO14.2**

3. Suppose the price level and value of the U.S. dollar in year 1 are 1 and $1, respectively. If the price level rises to 1.25 in year 2, what is the new value of the dollar? If, instead, the price level falls to 0.50, what is the value of the dollar? **LO14.3**

4. Assume that securitization combined with borrowing and irrational exuberance in Hyperville have driven up the value of existing financial securities at a geometric rate, specifically from $2 to $4 to $8 to $16 to $32 to $64 over a six-year time period. Over the same period, the value of the assets underlying the securities rose at an arithmetic rate from $2 to $3 to $4 to $5 to $6 to $7. If these patterns hold for decreases as well as for increases, by how much would the value of the financial securities decline if the value of the underlying asset suddenly and unexpectedly fell by $5? **LO14.6**

5. Suppose that Lady Gaga goes to Las Vegas to play poker and at the last minute her record company says it will reimburse her for 50 percent of any gambling losses that she incurs. Will Lady Gaga wager more or less as a result of the reimbursement offer? What economic concept does your answer illustrate? **LO14.7**

FURTHER TEST YOUR KNOWLEDGE AT www.mcconnell20e.com

Practice quizzes, student PowerPoints, worked problems, Web-based questions, and additional materials are available at the text's Online Learning Center (OLC), **www.mcconnell20e.com**, or scan here. Need a barcode reader? Try ScanLife, available in your app store.

CHAPTER **16**

Interest Rates and Monetary Policy

Learning Objectives

LO16.1 Discuss how the equilibrium interest rate is determined in the market for money.

LO16.2 Describe the balance sheet of the Federal Reserve and the meaning of its major items.

LO16.3 List and explain the goals and tools of monetary policy.

LO16.4 Describe the federal funds rate and how the Fed directly influences it.

LO16.5 Identify the mechanisms by which monetary policy affects GDP and the price level.

LO16.6 Explain the effectiveness of monetary policy and its shortcomings.

Some newspaper commentators have stated that the chairperson of the Federal Reserve Board (currently Ben Bernanke) is the second most powerful person in the United States, after the U.S. president. That is undoubtedly an exaggeration because the chair has only a single vote on the 7-person Federal Reserve Board and 12-person Federal Open Market Committee. But there can be no doubt about the chair's influence as well as the overall importance of the Federal Reserve and the **monetary policy** that it conducts. Such policy consists of deliberate changes in the money supply to influence interest rates and thus the total level of spending in the economy. The goal of monetary policy is to achieve and maintain price-level stability, full employment, and economic growth.

Interest Rates

LO16.1 Discuss how the equilibrium interest rate is determined in the market for money.

The Fed's primary influence on the economy in normal economic times is through its ability to change the money supply (M_1 and M_2) and therefore affect interest rates. Interest rates can be thought of in several ways. Most basically, **interest** is the price paid for the use of money. It is also the price that borrowers need to pay lenders for transferring purchasing power to the future. And it can be thought of as the amount of money that must be paid for the use of $1 for 1 year. Although there are many different interest rates that vary by purpose, size, risk, maturity, and taxability, we will simply speak of *the* interest rate unless stated otherwise.

Let's see how the interest rate is determined. Because it is a "price," we again turn to demand and supply analysis for the answer.

The Demand for Money

Why does the public want to hold some of its wealth as *money?* There are two main reasons: to make purchases with it and to hold it as an asset.

Transactions Demand, D_t People hold money because it is convenient for purchasing goods and services. Households usually are paid once a week, every 2 weeks, or monthly, whereas their expenditures are less predictable and typically more frequent. So households must have enough money on hand to buy groceries and pay mortgage and utility bills. Nor are business revenues and expenditures simultaneous. Businesses need to have money available to pay for labor, materials, power, and other inputs. The demand for money as a medium of exchange is called the **transactions demand for money.**

The level of nominal GDP is the main determinant of the amount of money demanded for transactions. The larger the total money value of all goods and services exchanged in the economy, the larger the amount of money needed to negotiate those transactions. The transactions demand for money varies directly with nominal GDP. We specify *nominal* GDP because households and firms will want more money for transactions if prices rise or if real output increases. In both instances a larger dollar volume will be needed to accomplish the desired transactions.

In **Figure 16.1a (Key Graph)** we graph the quantity of money demanded for transactions against the interest rate. For simplicity, let's assume that the amount demanded depends exclusively on the level of nominal GDP and is independent of the interest rate. (In reality, higher interest rates are associated with slightly lower volumes of money demanded for transactions.) Our simplifying assumption allows us to graph the transactions demand, D_t, as a vertical line. This demand curve is positioned at $100 billion, on the assumption that each dollar held for transactions purposes is spent an average of three times per year and that nominal GDP is $300 billion. Thus the public needs $100 billion (= $300 billion/3) to purchase that GDP.

Asset Demand, D_a The second reason for holding money derives from money's function as a store of value. People may hold their financial assets in many forms, including corporate stocks, corporate or government bonds, or money. To the extent they want to hold money as an asset, there is an **asset demand for money.**

People like to hold some of their financial assets as money (apart from using it to buy goods and services) because money is the most liquid of all financial assets; it is immediately usable for purchasing other assets when opportunities arise. Money is also an attractive asset to hold when the prices of other assets such as bonds are expected to decline. For example, when the price of a bond falls, the bondholder who sells the bond prior to the payback date of the full principal will suffer a loss (called a *capital loss*). That loss will partially or fully offset the interest received on the bond. Holding money presents no such risk of capital loss from changes in interest rates.

The disadvantage of holding money as an asset is that it earns no or very little interest. Checkable deposits pay either no interest or lower interest rates than bonds. Currency itself earns no interest at all.

Knowing these advantages and disadvantages, the public must decide how much of its financial assets to hold as money, rather than other assets such as bonds. The answer depends primarily on the rate of interest. A household or a business incurs an opportunity cost when it holds money; in both cases, interest income is forgone or sacrificed. If a bond pays 6 percent interest, for example, holding $100 as cash or in a noninterest checkable account costs $6 per year of forgone income.

The amount of money demanded as an asset therefore varies inversely with the rate of interest (which is the opportunity cost of holding money as an asset). When the interest rate rises, being liquid and avoiding

ORIGIN OF THE IDEA

O16.1
Liquidity preference

KEY GRAPH

FIGURE 16.1 The demand for money, the supply of money, and the equilibrium interest rate. The total demand for money D_m is determined by horizontally adding the asset demand for money D_a to the transactions demand D_t. The transactions demand is vertical because it is assumed to depend on nominal GDP rather than on the interest rate. The asset demand varies inversely with the interest rate because of the opportunity cost involved in holding currency and checkable deposits that pay no interest or very low interest. Combining the money supply (stock) S_m with the total money demand D_m portrays the market for money and determines the equilibrium interest rate i_e.

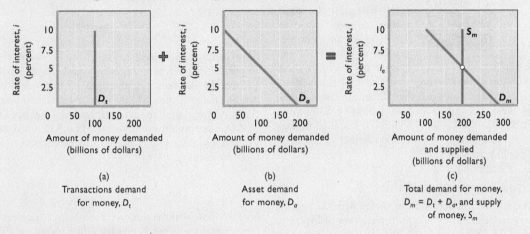

(a)
Transactions demand
for money, D_t

(b)
Asset demand
for money, D_a

(c)
Total demand for money,
$D_m = D_t + D_a$, and supply
of money, S_m

QUICK QUIZ FOR FIGURE 16.1

1. In this graph, at the interest rate i_e (5 percent):
   a. the amount of money demanded as an asset is $50 billion.
   b. the amount of money demanded for transactions is $200 billion.
   c. bond prices will decline.
   d. $100 billion is demanded for transactions, $100 billion is demanded as an asset, and the money supply is $200 billion.

2. In this graph, at an interest rate of 10 percent:
   a. no money will be demanded as an asset.
   b. total money demanded will be $200 billion.
   c. the Federal Reserve will supply $100 billion of money.
   d. there will be a $100 billion shortage of money.

3. Curve D_a slopes downward because:
   a. lower interest rates increase the opportunity cost of holding money.
   b. lower interest rates reduce the opportunity cost of holding money.

   c. the asset demand for money varies directly (positively) with the interest rate.
   d. the transactions-demand-for-money curve is perfectly vertical.

4. Suppose the supply of money declines to $100 billion. The equilibrium interest rate would:
   a. fall, the amount of money demanded for transactions would rise, and the amount of money demanded as an asset would decline.
   b. rise, and the amounts of money demanded both for transactions and as an asset would fall.
   c. fall, and the amounts of money demanded both for transactions and as an asset would increase.
   d. rise, the amount of money demanded for transactions would be unchanged, and the amount of money demanded as an asset would decline.

Answers: 1. d; 2. a; 3. b; 4. d

capital losses becomes more costly. The public reacts by reducing its holdings of money as an asset. When the interest rate falls, the cost of being liquid and avoiding capital losses also declines. The public therefore increases the amount of financial assets that it wants to hold as money. This inverse relationship just described is shown by D_a in Figure 16.1b.

Total Money Demand, D_m As shown in Figure 16.1, we find the **total demand for money, D_m**, by horizon-

tally adding the asset demand to the transactions demand. The resulting downsloping line in Figure 16.1c represents the total amount of money the public wants to hold, both for transactions and as an asset, at each possible interest rate.

Recall that the transactions demand for money depends on the nominal GDP. A change in the nominal GDP—working through the transactions demand for money—will shift the total money demand curve. Specifically, an increase in nominal GDP means that the public wants to hold a larger amount of money for transactions, and that

extra demand will shift the total money demand curve to the right. In contrast, a decline in the nominal GDP will shift the total money demand curve to the left. As an example, suppose nominal GDP increases from $300 billion to $450 billion and the average dollar held for transactions is still spent three times per year. Then the transactions demand curve will shift from $100 billion (= $300 billion/3) to $150 billion (= $450 billion/3). The total money demand curve will then lie $50 billion farther to the right at each possible interest rate.

The Equilibrium Interest Rate

We can combine the demand for money with the supply of money to determine the equilibrium rate of interest. In Figure 16.1c, the vertical line, S_m, represents the money supply. It is a vertical line because the monetary authorities and financial institutions have provided the economy with some particular stock of money. Here it is $200 billion.

Just as in a product market or a resource market, the intersection of demand and supply determines the equilibrium price in the market for money. In Figure 16.1, this equilibrium price is the equilibrium interest rate, i_e. At this interest rate, the quantity of money demanded (= $200 billion) equals the quantity of money supplied (= $200 billion). The equilibrium interest rate can be thought of as the market-determined price that borrowers must pay for using someone else's money over some period of time.

Changes in the demand for money, the supply of money, or both can change the equilibrium interest rate. For reasons that will soon become apparent, we are most interested in changes in the supply of money. The important generalization is this: An increase in the supply of money will lower the equilibrium interest rate; a decrease in the supply of money will raise the equilibrium interest rate.

Interest Rates and Bond Prices

Interest rates and bond prices are inversely related. When the interest rate increases, bond prices fall; when the interest rate falls, bond prices rise. Why so? First understand that bonds are bought and sold in financial markets and

that the price of bonds is determined by bond demand and bond supply.

Suppose that a bond with no expiration date pays a fixed $50 annual interest payment and is selling for its face value of $1,000. The interest yield on this bond is 5 percent:

$$\frac{\$50}{\$1,000} = 5\% \text{ interest yield}$$

Now suppose the interest rate in the economy rises to $7\frac{1}{2}$ percent from 5 percent. Newly issued bonds will pay $75 per $1,000 lent. Older bonds paying only $50 will not be salable at their $1,000 face value. To compete with the $7\frac{1}{2}$ percent bond, the price of this bond will need to fall to $667 to remain competitive. The $50 fixed annual interest payment will then yield $7\frac{1}{2}$ percent to whoever buys the bond:

$$\frac{\$50}{\$667} = 7\frac{1}{2}\%$$

Next suppose that the interest rate falls to $2\frac{1}{2}$ percent from the original 5 percent. Newly issued bonds will pay $25 on $1,000 loaned. A bond paying $50 will be highly attractive. Bond buyers will bid up its price to $2,000, where the yield will equal $2\frac{1}{2}$ percent:

$$\frac{\$50}{\$2,000} = 2\frac{1}{2}\%$$

The point is that bond prices fall when the interest rate rises and rise when the interest rate falls. There is an inverse relationship between the interest rate and bond prices.

The Consolidated Balance Sheet of the Federal Reserve Banks

LO16.2 Describe the balance sheet of the Federal Reserve and the meaning of its major items.

With this basic understanding of interest rates, we can turn to monetary policy, which relies on changes in interest rates to be effective. The 12 Federal Reserve Banks together constitute the U.S. "central bank," nicknamed the "Fed." (Global Perspective 16.1 also lists some of the other central banks in the world, along with their nicknames.)

The Fed's balance sheet helps us consider how the Fed conducts monetary policy. Table 16.1 consolidates the pertinent assets and liabilities of the 12 Federal Reserve Banks as of April 10, 2013. You will see that some of the Fed's assets and liabilities differ from those found on the balance sheet of a commercial bank.

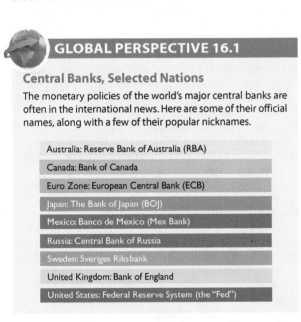

GLOBAL PERSPECTIVE 16.1

Central Banks, Selected Nations

The monetary policies of the world's major central banks are often in the international news. Here are some of their official names, along with a few of their popular nicknames.

Australia: Reserve Bank of Australia (RBA)

Canada: Bank of Canada

Euro Zone: European Central Bank (ECB)

Japan: The Bank of Japan (BOJ)

Mexico: Banco de Mexico (Mex Bank)

Russia: Central Bank of Russia

Sweden: Sveriges Riksbank

United Kingdom: Bank of England

United States: Federal Reserve System (the "Fed")

Assets

The two main assets of the Federal Reserve Banks are securities and loans to commercial banks. (Again, we will simplify by referring only to *commercial banks*, even though the analysis also applies to *thrifts*—savings and loans, mutual savings banks, and credit unions.)

Securities   The securities shown in Table 16.1 are government bonds that have been purchased by the Federal Reserve Banks. They consist largely of Treasury bills (short-term securities), Treasury notes (mid-term securities), and Treasury bonds (long-term securities) issued by the U.S. government to finance past budget deficits. These securities are part of the public debt—the money borrowed by the federal government. The Federal Reserve Banks bought these securities from commercial banks and the public through open-market operations. Although they are an important source of interest income to the Federal Reserve Banks, they are mainly bought and sold to influence the size of commercial bank reserves and, therefore, the ability of those banks to create money by lending.

Loans to Commercial Banks   For reasons that will soon become clear, commercial banks occasionally borrow from Federal Reserve Banks. The IOUs that commercial banks give these "bankers' banks" in return for loans are listed on the Federal Reserve balance sheet as "Loans to commercial banks." They are assets to the Fed because they are claims against the commercial banks. To commercial banks, of course, these loans are liabilities in that they must be repaid. Through borrowing in this way, commercial banks can increase their reserves.

Liabilities

On the "liabilities and net worth" side of the Fed's consolidated balance sheet, three entries are noteworthy: reserves, Treasury deposits, and Federal Reserve Notes.

Reserves of Commercial Banks   The Fed requires that the commercial banks hold reserves against their

TABLE 16.1   Consolidated Balance Sheet of the 12 Federal Reserve Banks, April 10, 2013 (in Millions)

Assets		Liabilities and Net Worth	
Securities	$2,957,619	Reserves of commercial banks	$1,851,361
Loans to commercial banks	439	Treasury deposits	52,478
All other assets	271,355	Federal Reserve Notes (outstanding)	1,137,087
		All other liabilities and net worth	188,487
Total	$3,229,413	Total	$3,229,413

Source: Federal Reserve Statistical Release, H.4.1, April 10, 2013, **www.federalreserve.gov.**

checkable deposits. The Fed pays interest on these required reserves and also on the excess reserves that banks choose to hold at the Fed. Banks held a huge amount of these excess reserves at the Fed during the severe recession of 2007–2009 and on through at least 2013 as the economy recovered only sluggishly after the Great Recession. Banks simply were highly concerned that loans to some private borrowers might not get paid back. When held in the Federal Reserve Banks, these reserves are listed as a liability on the Fed's balance sheet. They are assets on the books of the commercial banks, which still own them even though they are deposited at the Federal Reserve Banks.

Treasury Deposits   The U.S. Treasury keeps deposits in the Federal Reserve Banks and draws checks on them to pay its obligations. To the Treasury these deposits are assets; to the Federal Reserve Banks they are liabilities. The Treasury creates and replenishes these deposits by depositing tax receipts and money borrowed from the public or from the commercial banks through the sale of bonds.

Federal Reserve Notes Outstanding   As we have seen, the supply of paper money in the United States consists of Federal Reserve Notes issued by the Federal Reserve Banks. When this money is circulating outside the Federal Reserve Banks, it constitutes claims against the assets of the Federal Reserve Banks. The Fed thus treats these notes as a liability.

QUICK REVIEW 16.2

- The two main assets of the Federal Reserve Banks are securities and loans to commercial banks. Most of the securities are bills, notes, and bonds issued by the U.S. Treasury to finance past federal budget deficits.
- The three major liabilities of the Federal Reserve Banks are reserves of commercial banks, Treasury deposits, and outstanding Federal Reserve notes.

Tools of Monetary Policy

LO16.3 List and explain the goals and tools of monetary policy.

ORIGIN OF THE IDEA

O16.2

Tools of monetary policy

With this look at the Federal Reserve Banks' consolidated balance sheet, we can now explore how the Fed can influence the money-creating abilities of the commercial banking system. The Fed has four main tools of monetary control it can use to alter the reserves of commercial banks:

- Open-market operations
- The reserve ratio
- The discount rate
- Interest on reserves

Open-Market Operations

Bond markets are "open" to all buyers and sellers of corporate and government bonds (securities). The Federal Reserve is the largest single holder of U.S. government securities. The U.S. government, not the Fed, issued these Treasury bills, Treasury notes, and Treasury bonds to finance past budget deficits. Over the decades, the Fed has purchased these securities from major financial institutions that buy and sell government and corporate securities for themselves or their customers.

The Fed's **open-market operations** consist of buying government bonds (U.S. securities) from or selling government bonds to commercial banks and the general public. The conduit for the Fed's open-market operations is the New York Federal Reserve Bank and a group of 21 or so large financial firms called "primary dealers." These financial institutions, in turn, buy the bonds from and sell the bonds to commercial banks and the general public. Open-market operations are the Fed's most important day-to-day instrument for influencing the money supply.

Buying Securities   Suppose that the Fed decides to have the Federal Reserve Banks buy government bonds. They can purchase these bonds either from commercial banks or from the public. In both cases the reserves of the commercial banks will increase.

From Commercial Banks   When Federal Reserve Banks buy government bonds *from commercial banks,*

(*a*) The commercial banks give up part of their holdings of securities (the government bonds) to the Federal Reserve Banks.

(*b*) The Federal Reserve Banks, in paying for these securities, place newly created reserves in the accounts of the commercial banks at the Fed. (These reserves are created "out of thin air," so to speak!) The reserves of the commercial banks go up by the amount of the purchase of the securities.

We show these outcomes as (*a*) and (*b*) on the following consolidated balance sheets of the commercial banks and the Federal Reserve Banks:

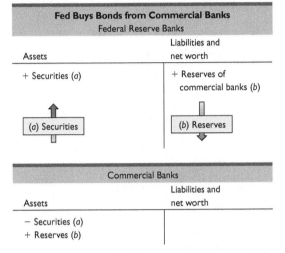

Fed Buys Bonds from Commercial Banks

The upward arrow shows that securities have moved from the commercial banks to the Federal Reserve Banks. So we enter "− Securities" (minus securities) in the asset column of the balance sheet of the commercial banks. For the same reason, we enter "+ Securities" in the asset column of the balance sheet of the Federal Reserve Banks.

The downward arrow indicates that the Federal Reserve Banks have provided reserves to the commercial banks. So we enter "+ Reserves" in the asset column of the balance sheet for the commercial banks. In the liability column of the balance sheet of the Federal Reserve Banks, the plus sign indicates that although commercial bank reserves have increased, they are a liability to the Federal Reserve Banks because the reserves are owned by the commercial banks.

What is most important about this transaction is that when Federal Reserve Banks purchase securities from commercial banks, they increase the reserves in the banking system, which then increases the lending ability of the commercial banks.

From the Public The effect on commercial bank reserves is much the same when Federal Reserve Banks purchase securities from the general public. Suppose the Gristly Meat Packing Company has government bonds that it sells in the open market to the Federal Reserve Banks. The transaction has several elements:

(*a*) Gristly gives up securities to the Federal Reserve Banks and gets in payment a check drawn by the Federal Reserve Banks on themselves.

(*b*) Gristly promptly deposits the check in its account with the Wahoo bank.

(*c*) The Wahoo bank sends this check against the Federal Reserve Banks to a Federal Reserve Bank for collection. As a result, the Wahoo bank enjoys an increase in its reserves.

To keep things simple, we will dispense with showing the balance sheet changes resulting from the Fed's sale or purchase of bonds from the public. But two aspects of this transaction are particularly important. First, as with Federal Reserve purchases of securities directly from commercial banks, the purchases of securities from the public increase the lending ability of the commercial banking system. Second, the supply of money is directly increased by the Federal Reserve Banks' purchase of government bonds (aside from any expansion of the money supply that may occur from the increase in commercial bank reserves). This direct increase in the money supply has taken the form of an increased amount of checkable deposits in the economy as a result of Gristly's deposit.

The Federal Reserve Banks' purchases of securities from the commercial banking system differ slightly from their purchases of securities from the public. If we assume that all commercial banks are loaned up initially, Federal Reserve bond purchases *from commercial banks* increase the actual reserves and excess reserves of commercial banks by the entire amount of the bond purchases. As shown in the left panel in Figure 16.2, a $1,000 bond purchase from a commercial bank increases both the actual and the excess reserves of the commercial bank by $1,000.

In contrast, Federal Reserve Bank purchases of bonds from the public increase actual reserves but also increase checkable deposits when the sellers place the Fed's check into their personal checking accounts. Thus, a $1,000 bond purchase from the public would increase checkable deposits by $1,000 and hence the actual reserves of the loaned-up banking system by the same amount. But with a 20 percent reserve ratio applied to the $1,000 checkable deposit, the excess reserves of the banking system would be only $800 since $200 of the $1,000 would have to be held as reserves.

However, in both transactions the end result is the same: When Federal Reserve Banks buy securities in the open market, commercial banks' reserves are increased. When the banks lend out an amount equal to their excess reserves, the nation's money supply will rise. Observe in Figure 16.2 that a $1,000 purchase of

FIGURE 16.2 The Federal Reserve's purchase of bonds and the expansion of the money supply. Assuming all banks are loaded up initially, a Federal Reserve purchase of a $1,000 bond from either a commercial bank or the public can increase the money supply by $5,000 when the reserve ratio is 20 percent. In the left panel of the diagram, the purchase of a $1,000 bond from a commercial bank creates $1,000 of excess reserves that support a $5,000 expansion of checkable deposits through loans. In the right panel, the purchase of a $1,000 bond from the public creates a $1,000 checkable deposit but only $800 of excess reserves because $200 of reserves is required to "back up" the $1,000 new checkable deposit. The commercial banks can therefore expand the money supply by only $4,000 by making loans. This $4,000 of checkable-deposit money plus the new checkable deposit of $1,000 equals $5,000 of new money.

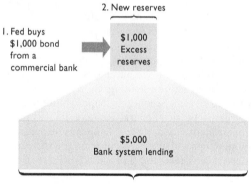

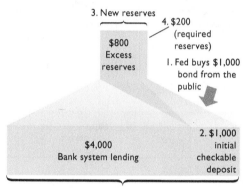

bonds by the Federal Reserve results in a potential of $5,000 of additional money, regardless of whether the purchase was made from commercial banks or from the general public.

Selling Securities As you may suspect, when the Federal Reserve Banks sell government bonds, commercial banks' reserves are reduced. Let's see why.

To Commercial Banks When the Federal Reserve Banks sell securities in the open market to commercial banks,

(*a*) The Federal Reserve Banks give up securities that the commercial banks acquire.

(*b*) The commercial banks pay for those securities by drawing checks against their deposits—that is, against their reserves—in Federal Reserve Banks. The Fed collects on those checks by reducing the commercial banks' reserves accordingly.

The balance-sheet changes—again identified by (*a*) and (*b*)—appear as shown in the following balance sheets. The reduction in commercial bank reserves is indicated by the minus signs before the appropriate entries.

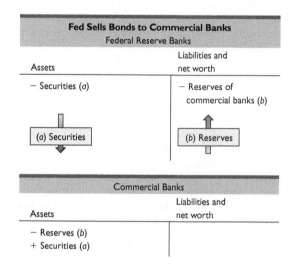

To the Public When the Federal Reserve Banks sell securities to the public, the outcome is much the same. Let's put the Gristly Company on the buying end of government bonds that the Federal Reserve Banks are selling:

(*a*) The Federal Reserve Banks sell government bonds to Gristly, which pays with a check drawn on the Wahoo bank.

(*b*) The Federal Reserve Banks clear this check against the Wahoo bank by reducing Wahoo's reserves.

TABLE 16.2 The Effects of Changes in the Reserve Ratio on the Lending Ability of Commercial Banks

(1) Reserve Ratio, %	(2) Checkable Deposits	(3) Actual Reserves	(4) Required Reserves	(5) Excess Reserves, (3) − (4)	(6) Money-Creating Potential of Single Bank, = (5)	(7) Money-Creating Potential of Banking System
(1) 10	$20,000	$5,000	$2,000	$ 3,000	$ 3,000	$ 30,000
(2) 20	20,000	5,000	4,000	1,000	1,000	5,000
(3) 25	20,000	5,000	5,000	0	0	0
(4) 30	20,000	5,000	6,000	−1,000	−1,000	−3,333

(*c*) The Wahoo bank returns the canceled check to Gristly, reducing Gristly's checkable deposit accordingly.

Federal Reserve bond sales of $1,000 to the commercial banking system reduce the system's actual and excess reserves by $1,000. But a $1,000 bond sale to the public reduces excess reserves by $800 because the public's checkable-deposit money is also reduced by $1,000 by the sale. Since the commercial banking system's outstanding checkable deposits are reduced by $1,000, banks need keep $200 less in reserves.

Whether the Fed sells bonds to the public or to commercial banks, the result is the same: When Federal Reserve Banks sell securities in the open market, commercial bank reserves are reduced. If all excess reserves are already lent out, this decline in commercial bank reserves produces a decline in the nation's money supply. In our example, a $1,000 sale of government securities results in a $5,000 decline in the money supply whether the sale is made to commercial banks or to the general public. You can verify this by reexamining Figure 16.2 and tracing the effects of a *sale* of a $1,000 bond by the Fed either to commercial banks or to the public.

What makes commercial banks and the public willing to sell government securities to, or buy them from, Federal Reserve Banks? The answer lies in the price of bonds and their interest yields. We know that bond prices and interest rates are inversely related. When the Fed buys government bonds, the demand for them increases. Government bond prices rise, and their interest yields decline. The higher bond prices and their lower interest yields prompt banks, securities firms, and individual holders of government bonds to sell them to the Federal Reserve Banks.

When the Fed sells government bonds, the additional supply of bonds in the bond market lowers bond prices and raises their interest yields, making government bonds attractive purchases for banks and the public.

The Reserve Ratio

The Fed also can manipulate the **reserve ratio** in order to influence the ability of commercial banks to lend. Suppose a commercial bank's balance sheet shows that reserves are $5,000 and checkable deposits are $20,000. If the legal reserve ratio is 20 percent (row 2, Table 16.2), the bank's required reserves are $4,000. Since actual reserves are $5,000, the excess reserves of this bank are $1,000. On the basis of $1,000 of excess reserves, this one bank can lend $1,000; however, the banking system as a whole can create a maximum of $5,000 of new checkable-deposit money by lending (column 7).

Raising the Reserve Ratio Now, what if the Fed raised the reserve ratio from 20 to 25 percent? (See row 3.) Required reserves would jump from $4,000 to $5,000, shrinking excess reserves from $1,000 to zero. Raising the reserve ratio increases the amount of required reserves banks must keep. As a consequence, either banks lose excess reserves, diminishing their ability to create money by lending, or they find their reserves deficient and are forced to contract checkable deposits and therefore the money supply. In the example in Table 16.2, excess reserves are transformed into required reserves, and the money-creating potential of our single bank is reduced from $1,000 to zero (column 6). Moreover, the banking system's money-creating capacity declines from $5,000 to zero (column 7).

What if the Fed increases the reserve requirement to 30 percent? (See row 4.) The commercial bank, to protect itself against the prospect of failing to meet this requirement, would be forced to lower its checkable deposits and at the same time increase its reserves. To reduce its checkable deposits, the bank could let outstanding loans mature and be repaid without extending new credit. To increase reserves, the bank might sell some of its bonds, adding the proceeds to its reserves. Both actions would reduce the supply of money.

Lowering the Reserve Ratio What would happen if the Fed lowered the reserve ratio from the original 20 percent to 10 percent? (See row 1.) In this case, required reserves would decline from $4,000 to $2,000, and excess reserves would jump from $1,000 to $3,000. The single bank's lending (money-creating) ability would increase from $1,000 to $3,000 (column 6), and the banking system's money-creating potential would expand from $5,000 to $30,000 (column 7). Lowering the reserve ratio transforms required reserves into excess reserves and enhances the ability of banks to create new money by lending.

The examples in Table 16.2 show that a change in the reserve ratio affects the money-creating ability of the *banking system* in two ways:

- It changes the amount of excess reserves.
- It changes the size of the monetary multiplier.

For example, when the legal reserve ratio is raised from 10 to 20 percent, excess reserves are reduced from $3,000 to $1,000 and the checkable-deposit multiplier is reduced from 10 to 5. The money-creating potential of the banking system declines from $30,000 (= $3,000 × 10) to $5,000 (= $1,000 × 5). Raising the reserve ratio forces banks to reduce the amount of checkable deposits they create through lending.

The Discount Rate

One of the functions of a central bank is to be a "lender of last resort." Occasionally, commercial banks have unexpected and immediate needs for additional funds. In such cases, each Federal Reserve Bank will make short-term loans to commercial banks in its district.

When a commercial bank borrows, it gives the Federal Reserve Bank a promissory note (IOU) drawn against itself and secured by acceptable collateral—typically U.S. government securities. Just as commercial banks charge interest on the loans they make to their clients, so too Federal Reserve Banks charge interest on loans they grant to commercial banks. The interest rate they charge is called the **discount rate.**

As a claim against the commercial bank, the borrowing bank's promissory note is an asset to the lending Federal Reserve Bank and appears on its balance sheet as "Loans to commercial banks." To the commercial bank the IOU is a liability, appearing as "Loans from the Federal Reserve Banks" on the commercial bank's balance sheet. [See the two (*a*) entries on the balance sheets that follow.]

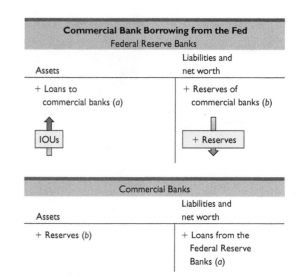

In providing the loan, the Federal Reserve Bank increases the reserves of the borrowing commercial bank. Since no required reserves need be kept against loans from Federal Reserve Banks, all new reserves acquired by borrowing from Federal Reserve Banks are excess reserves. [These changes are reflected in the two (*b*) entries on the balance sheets.]

In short, borrowing from the Federal Reserve Banks by commercial banks increases the reserves of the commercial banks and enhances their ability to extend credit.

The Fed has the power to set the discount rate at which commercial banks borrow from Federal Reserve Banks. From the commercial banks' point of view, the discount rate is a cost of acquiring reserves. A lowering of the discount rate encourages commercial banks to obtain additional reserves by borrowing from Federal Reserve Banks. When the commercial banks lend new reserves, the money supply increases.

An increase in the discount rate discourages commercial banks from obtaining additional reserves through borrowing from the Federal Reserve Banks. So the Fed may raise the discount rate when it wants to restrict the money supply.

Interest on Reserves

In 2008, federal law was changed so that the Federal Reserve could for the first time pay banks **interest on reserves** held at the Fed. Before that time, any reserves held on deposit at the Federal Reserve were paid zero interest. Thus, before 2008, banks had an incentive to keep their reserves as small as possible because any money kept on reserve at the Fed was money earning a zero percent rate of return for the banks.

The Fed's newfound ability to pay interest on reserves provided the Fed with a fourth policy tool by which it can implement monetary policy and either increase or decrease the amount of monetary stimulus in the economy. As an example, suppose that the Fed wishes to *reduce* the amount of bank lending and, consequently, the amount of money circulating in the economy. It can do so by increasing the rate of interest that it pays on reserves held at the Fed. The higher that interest rate, the more of an incentive banks will have to reduce their risky commercial lending for car, mortgage, and business loans in order to instead increase the reserves that they hold at the Fed and thereby earn the risk-free interest rate that the Fed is paying on reserves.

By contrast, if the Fed wishes to *increase* the amount of money that banks lend into the economy, the Fed can lower the interest rate that it pays on reserves. The lower rate will make it less attractive for banks to keep reserves, and, consequently, banks will be incentivized to increase consumer and commercial lending and thereby stimulate the economy.

In 2012, the rate of interest on reserves was 0.25 percent per year. Given that banks held about $1.7 trillion in reserves at the Fed that year, the Fed paid a total of about $4.25 billion (= 0.0025 times $1.7 trillion) in interest payments to banks for reserves held at the Fed in 2012.

Relative Importance

All four of the Fed's instruments of monetary control are useful in particular economic circumstances, but open-market operations are clearly the most important of the four tools over the course of the business cycle. The buying and selling of securities in the open market has the advantage of flexibility—government securities can be purchased or sold daily in large or small amounts—and the impact on bank reserves is prompt. And, compared with reserve-requirement changes, open-market operations work subtly and less directly. Furthermore, the ability of the Federal Reserve Banks to affect commercial bank reserves through the purchase and sale of bonds is virtually unquestionable. The Federal Reserve Banks have very large holdings of government securities ($2,958 billion in early 2013, for example). The sale of those securities could theoretically reduce commercial bank reserves to zero.

Changing the reserve requirement is a potentially powerful instrument of monetary control, but the Fed has used this technique only sparingly. Normally, it can accomplish its monetary goals more easily through open-market operations. The last change in the reserve requirement was in 1992, when the Fed reduced the requirement from 12 percent to 10 percent. The main purpose was to shore up the profitability of banks and thrifts in the aftermath of the 1990–1991 recession rather than to reduce interest rates by increasing reserves and expanding the money supply.

Until recently, the discount rate was mainly a passive tool of monetary control, with the Fed raising and lowering the rate simply to keep it in line with other interest rates. However, during the financial crisis of 2007–2008, the Fed aggressively lowered the discount rate independently of other interest rates to provide a cheap and plentiful source of reserves to banks whose reserves were being sharply reduced by unexpectedly high default rates on home mortgage loans. Banks borrowed billions at the lower discount rate. This allowed them to meet reserve ratio requirements and thereby preserved their ability to keep extending loans.

QUICK REVIEW 16.3

- The Fed has four main tools of monetary control, each of which works by changing the amount of reserves in the banking system: (a) conducting open-market operations (the Fed's buying and selling of government bonds to the banks and the public); (b) changing the reserve ratio (the percentage of commercial bank deposit liabilities required as reserves); (c) changing the discount rate (the interest rate the Federal Reserve Banks charge on loans to banks and thrifts); and (d) changing the interest rate that it pays on reserves held at the Fed.

- Open-market operations are the Fed's monetary control mechanism of choice for routine increases or decreases in bank reserves over the business cycle; in contrast, changes in reserve requirements and aggressive changes in discount rates or interest on reserves are used only in special situations.

Targeting the Federal Funds Rate

LO16.4 Describe the federal funds rate and how the Fed directly influences it.

The Federal Reserve focuses monetary policy on the interest rate that it can directly influence: the **federal funds rate**. From the previous chapter, you know that this is the rate of interest that banks charge one another on overnight loans made from temporary excess reserves. Recall that the Federal Reserve requires banks (and thrifts) to deposit in their regional Federal Reserve Bank a certain percentage of their checkable deposits as reserves. At the end of any business day, some banks temporarily have excess reserves (more actual reserves than required) and other banks have reserve deficiencies (fewer reserves than required). Because reserves held at the Federal Reserve Banks earn less interest than commercial banks can obtain from overnight loans to other banks, banks with excess reserves usually desire to make such loans to other banks that temporarily need them to meet their reserve requirements. The funds being lent and borrowed overnight are called "federal funds" because they are reserves (funds) that are required by the Federal Reserve to meet reserve requirements. An equilibrium interest rate—the federal funds rate—arises in this market for bank reserves.

The Federal Reserve targets the federal funds rate by manipulating the supply of reserves that are offered in the federal funds market. As previously explained, by buying and selling government bonds, the Fed can increase or decrease the reserves in the banking system. These changes in total reserves in turn affect the amount of *excess reserves* that are available for supply to the federal funds market by whichever banks end up with them on a given day. For instance, suppose that the level of loans and checkable deposits at Wahoo bank are constant on a certain day. If the Fed then engages in open-market operations such that Wahoo's total reserves increase, Wahoo will find that it has excess reserves. It will want to loan out these excess reserves to bank customers as soon as possible. But in the meanwhile it will supply these funds overnight in the federal funds market.

The Federal Open Market Committee (FOMC) meets regularly to choose a desired federal funds rate. It then directs the Federal Reserve Bank of New York to undertake whatever open-market operations may be necessary to achieve and maintain the targeted rate. We demonstrate how this works in Figure 16.3, where we initially assume the Fed desires a 4 percent interest rate. The demand curve for federal funds, D_f, is downsloping because lower interest rates give the banks with reserve deficiencies a greater incentive to borrow federal funds rather than reduce loans as a way to meet their reserve requirements. The supply curve for federal funds, S_{f1}, is somewhat unusual. Specifically, it is horizontal at the targeted federal funds rate, here 4 percent. (Disregard supply curves S_{f2} and S_{f3} for now.) It is horizontal because the Fed uses open-market operations to manipulate the supply of federal funds so that the quantity supplied of federal funds will exactly equal the quantity demanded of federal funds at the targeted interest rate.

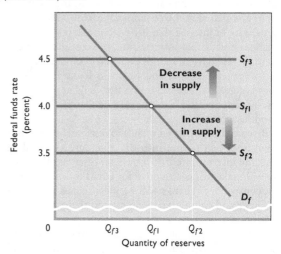

FIGURE 16.3 Targeting the federal funds rate. In implementing monetary policy, the Federal Reserve determines a desired federal funds rate and then uses open-market operations (buying and selling of U.S. securities) to add or subtract bank reserves to achieve and maintain that targeted rate. In an expansionary monetary policy, the Fed increases the supply of reserves, for example, from S_{f1} to S_{f2} in this case, to move the federal funds rate from 4 percent to 3.5 percent. In a restrictive monetary policy, it decreases the supply of reserves, say, from S_{f1} to S_{f3}. Here, the federal funds rate rises from 4 percent to 4.5 percent.

In this case, the Fed seeks to achieve an equilibrium federal funds rate of 4 percent. In Figure 16.3 it is successful. Note that at the 4 percent federal funds rate, the quantity of federal funds supplied (Q_{f1}) equals the quantity of funds demanded (also Q_{f1}). This 4 percent federal funds rate will remain, as long as the supply curve of federal funds is horizontal at 4 percent. If the demand for federal funds increases (D_f shifts to the right along S_{f1}), the Fed will use its open-market operations to increase the availability of reserves such that the 4 percent federal funds rate is retained. If the demand for federal funds declines (D_f shifts to the left along S_{f1}), the Fed will withdraw reserves to keep the federal funds rate at 4 percent. The Fed ensures that the supply curve is perfectly elastic at its targeted rate.

Expansionary Monetary Policy

Suppose that the economy faces recession and unemployment. How will the Fed respond? It will initiate an **expansionary monetary policy** (or "easy money policy"). This policy will lower the interest rate to bolster borrowing and spending, which will increase aggregate demand and expand real output. The Fed's immediate step will be to announce a lower target for the federal funds rate, say 3.5 percent instead of 4 percent. To achieve that lower

FIGURE 16.4 The prime interest rate and the federal funds rate in the United States, 1998–2013. The prime interest rate rises and falls with changes in the federal funds rate.

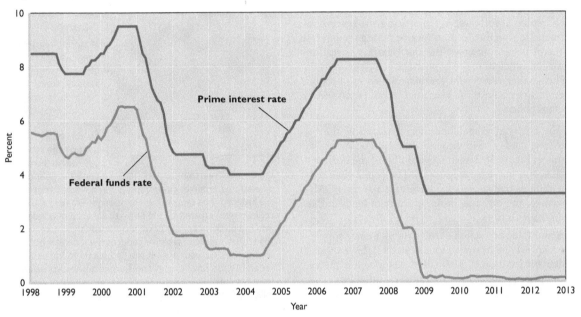

Source: Federal Reserve Statistical Release, Historical Data, H.15, **www.federalreserve.gov.**

rate, the Fed will use open-market operations to buy bonds from banks and the public. We know from previous discussion that the purchase of bonds increases the reserves in the banking system. Alternatively, the Fed could expand reserves by lowering the reserve requirement or lowering the discount rate, but these alternative tools are less frequently used than open-market operations. The Fed could also lower the interest rate that it pays on reserves so that banks will have more of an incentive to lend out reserves rather than keeping them on deposit at the Fed. But through 2013, the Fed had never changed the interest rate that it had paid on reserves after starting to pay interest on reserves in 2008. It remained at 0.25 percent.

The greater reserves in the banking system produce two critical results:

- The supply of federal funds increases, lowering the federal funds rate to the new targeted rate. We show this in Figure 16.3 as a downward shift to the horizontal supply curve from S_{f1} to S_{f2}. The equilibrium federal funds rate falls to 3.5 percent, just as the FOMC wanted. The equilibrium quantity of reserves in the overnight market for reserves rises from Q_{f1} to Q_{f2}.

- A multiple expansion of the nation's money supply occurs (as we demonstrated in Chapter 15). Given

the demand for money, the larger money supply places a downward pressure on other interest rates.

One such rate is the **prime interest rate**—the benchmark interest rate used by banks as a reference point for a wide range of interest rates charged on loans to businesses and individuals. The prime interest rate is higher than the federal funds rate because the prime rate involves longer, more risky loans than overnight loans between banks. But the federal funds rate and the prime interest rate closely track one another, as evident in Figure 16.4. Also evident are the changes in these rates over the period shown. We will address these changes later in our discussion of recent monetary policy.

Restrictive Monetary Policy

The opposite monetary policy is in order for periods of rising inflation. The Fed will then undertake a **restrictive monetary policy** (or "tight money policy"). This policy will increase the interest rate to reduce borrowing and spending, which will curtail the expansion of aggregate demand and hold down price-level increases. The Fed's immediate step will be to announce a higher target for the federal funds rate, say 4.5 percent instead of 4 percent.

Through open-market operations, the Fed will sell bonds to the banks and the public and the sale of those bonds will absorb reserves in the banking system. Alternatively, the Fed could absorb reserves by raising the reserve requirement, raising the discount rate, or raising the interest rate that it pays on reserves. But open-market operations are usually sufficient to accomplish the goal.

The smaller reserves in the banking system produce two results opposite those discussed for an expansionary monetary policy:

- The supply of federal funds decreases, raising the federal funds rate to the new targeted rate. We show this in Figure 16.3 as an upward shift of the horizontal supply curve from S_{f1} to S_{f3}. The equilibrium federal funds rate rises to 4.5 percent, just as the FOMC wanted, and the equilibrium quantity of funds in this market falls to Q_{f3}.

- A multiple contraction of the nation's money supply occurs (as demonstrated in Chapter 15). Given the demand for money, the smaller money supply places an upward pressure on other interest rates. For example, the prime interest rate rises.

The Taylor Rule

The proper federal funds rate for a certain period is a matter of policy discretion by the members of the FOMC. At each of their meetings, committee members assess whether the current target for the federal funds rate remains appropriate for achieving the twin goals of low inflation and full employment. If the majority of the FOMC members conclude that a change in the rate is needed, the FOMC sets a new targeted rate. This new target is established without adhering to any particular "inflationary target" or "monetary policy rule." Instead, the committee targets the federal funds rate at the level most appropriate for the current underlying economic conditions.

A rule of thumb suggested by economist John Taylor, however, roughly matches the actual policy of the Fed over many time periods. This rule of thumb builds on the belief held by many economists that central banks are willing to tolerate a small positive rate of inflation if doing so will help the economy to produce at potential output. The **Taylor rule** assumes that the Fed has a 2 percent "target rate of inflation" that it is willing to tolerate and that the FOMC follows three rules when setting its target for the federal funds rate:

- When real GDP equals potential GDP and inflation is at its target rate of 2 percent, the federal funds target rate should be 4 percent, implying a real

CONSIDER THIS . . .

The Fed as a Sponge

A good way to remember the role of the Fed in setting the federal funds rate might be to imagine a bowl of water, with the amount of water in the bowl representing the stock of reserves in the banking system. Then think of the FOMC as having a large sponge, labeled open-market operations. When it wants to decrease the federal funds rate, it uses the sponge—soaked with water (reserves) created by the Fed—to squeeze new reserves into the banking system bowl. It continues this process until the higher supply of reserves reduces the federal funds rate to the Fed's desired level. If the Fed wants to increase the federal funds rate, it uses the sponge to absorb reserves from the bowl (banking system). As the supply of reserves falls, the federal funds rate rises to the Fed's desired level.

federal funds rate of 2 percent (= 4 percent nominal federal funds rate *minus* 2 percent inflation rate).

- For each 1 percent increase of real GDP above potential GDP, the Fed should raise the *real* federal funds rate by $\frac{1}{2}$ percentage point.

- For each 1 percent increase in the inflation rate above its 2 percent target rate, the Fed should raise the *real* federal funds rate by $\frac{1}{2}$ percentage point. (Note, though, that in this case each $\frac{1}{2}$ percentage point increase in the real rate will require a 1.5 percentage point increase in the nominal rate to account for the underlying 1 percent increase in the inflation rate.)

The last two rules are applied independently of each other so that if real GDP is above potential output and at the same time inflation is above the 2 percent target rate, the Fed will apply both rules and raise real interest rates in response to both factors. For instance, if real GDP is 1 percent above potential output and inflation is simultaneously 1 percent above the 2 percent target rate, then the Fed will raise the *real* federal funds rate by 1 percentage point (= $\frac{1}{2}$ percentage point for

W16.4
Taylor rule

the excessive GDP $+ \frac{1}{2}$ percentage point for the excessive inflation).

Also notice that the last two rules are reversed for situations in which real GDP falls below potential GDP or inflation falls below 2 percent. Each 1 percent decline in real GDP below potential GDP or fall in inflation below 2 percent calls for a decline of the *real* federal funds rate by $\frac{1}{2}$ percentage point.

We reemphasize that the Fed has no official allegiance to the Taylor rule. It changes the federal funds rate to any level that it deems appropriate. During some periods, its policy has diverged significantly from the Taylor rule.

ORIGIN OF THE IDEA

O16.3
Taylor rule

QUICK REVIEW 16.4

- The Fed conducts its monetary policy by establishing a targeted federal funds interest rate—the rate that commercial banks charge one another for overnight loans of reserves.
- An expansionary monetary policy (loose money policy) lowers the federal funds rate, increases the money supply, and lowers other interest rates.
- A restrictive monetary policy (tight money policy) increases the federal funds rate, reduces the money supply, and increases other interest rates.
- The Fed uses it discretion in setting the federal funds target rate, but its decisions regarding monetary policy and the target rate appear to be broadly consistent with the Taylor rule over many time periods.

Monetary Policy, Real GDP, and the Price Level

LO16.5 Identify the mechanisms by which monetary policy affects GDP and the price level.

We have identified and explained the tools of expansionary and contractionary monetary policy. We now want to emphasize how monetary policy affects the economy's levels of investment, aggregate demand, real GDP, and prices.

Cause-Effect Chain

The four diagrams in **Figure 16.5 (Key Graph)** will help you understand how monetary policy works toward achieving its goals.

Market for Money   Figure 16.5a represents the market for money, in which the demand curve for money and the supply curve of money are brought together. Recall that the total demand for money is made up of the transactions and asset demands.

This figure also shows three potential money supply curves, S_{m1}, S_{m2}, and S_{m3}. In each case, the money supply is shown as a vertical line representing some fixed amount of money determined by the Fed.

The equilibrium interest rate is the rate at which the amount of money demanded and the amount supplied are equal. With money demand D_m in Figure 16.5a, if the supply of money is \$125 billion (S_{m1}), the equilibrium interest rate is 10 percent. With a money supply of \$150 billion (S_{m2}), the equilibrium interest rate is 8 percent; with a money supply of \$175 billion (S_{m3}), it is 6 percent.

You know from Chapter 10 that the real, not the nominal, rate of interest is critical for investment decisions. So here we assume that Figure 16.5a portrays real interest rates.

Investment   These 10, 8, and 6 percent real interest rates are carried rightward to the investment demand curve in Figure 16.5b. This curve shows the inverse relationship between the interest rate—the cost of borrowing to invest—and the amount of investment spending. At the 10 percent interest rate, it will be profitable for the nation's businesses to invest \$15 billion; at 8 percent, \$20 billion; at 6 percent, \$25 billion.

Changes in the interest rate mainly affect the investment component of total spending, although they also affect spending on durable consumer goods (such as autos) that are purchased on credit. The impact of changing interest rates on investment spending is great because of the large cost and long-term nature of capital purchases. Capital equipment, factory buildings, and warehouses are tremendously expensive. In absolute terms, interest charges on funds borrowed for these purchases are considerable.

Similarly, the interest cost on a house purchased on a long-term contract is very large: A $\frac{1}{2}$-percentage-point change in the interest rate could amount to thousands of dollars in the total cost of buying a home.

In brief, the impact of changing interest rates is mainly on investment (and, through that, on aggregate demand, output, employment, and the price level). Moreover, as Figure 16.5b shows, investment spending varies inversely with the real interest rate.

Equilibrium GDP   Figure 16.5c shows the impact of our three real interest rates and corresponding levels of

KEY GRAPH

FIGURE 16.5 Monetary policy and equilibrium GDP. An expansionary monetary policy that shifts the money supply curve rightward from S_{m1} to S_{m2} in (a) lowers the interest rate from 10 to 8 percent in (b). As a result, investment spending increases from $15 billion to $20 billion, shifting the aggregate demand curve rightward from AD_1 to AD_2 in (c) so that real output rises from the recessionary level of $880 billion to the full employment level Q_f = $900 billion along the horizontal dashed line. In (d), the economy at point *a* has an inflationary output gap of $10 billion because it is producing at $910 billion, $10 billion above potential output. A restrictive monetary policy that shifts the money supply curve leftward from S_{m3} = $175 billion to just $162.5 billion in (a) will increase the interest rate from 6 percent to 7 percent. Investment spending thus falls by $2.5 billion from $25 billion to $22.5 billion in (b). This initial decline is multiplied by 4 by the multiplier process so that the aggregate demand curve shifts leftward in (d) by $10 billion from AD_3 to AD_4, moving the economy along the horizontal dashed line to equilibrium *b*. This returns the economy to full employment output and eliminates the inflationary output gap.

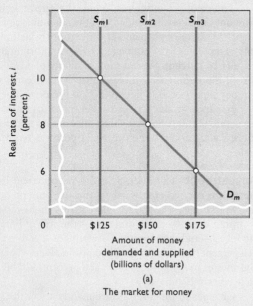

(a)
The market for money

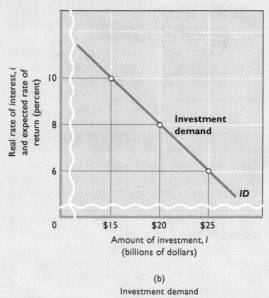

(b)
Investment demand

QUICK QUIZ FOR FIGURE 16.5

1. The ultimate objective of an expansionary monetary policy is depicted by:
   a. a decrease in the money supply from S_{m3} to S_{m2}.

   b. a reduction of the interest rate from 8 to 6 percent.
   c. an increase in investment from $20 billion to $25 billion.
   d. an increase in real GDP from Q_1 to Q_f.

investment spending on aggregate demand. (Ignore Figure 16.5d for the time being. We will return to it shortly.) As noted, aggregate demand curve AD_1 is associated with the $15 billion level of investment, AD_2 with investment of $20 billion, and AD_3 with investment of $25 billion. That is, investment spending is one of the determinants of aggregate demand. Other things equal, the greater the investment spending, the farther to the right lies the aggregate demand curve.

Suppose the money supply in Figure 16.5a is $150 billion ($S_{m2}$), producing an equilibrium interest rate of 8 percent. In Figure 16.5b we see that this 8 percent interest rate will bring forth $20 billion of investment spending. This $20 billion of investment spending joins with consumption spending, net exports, and government spending to yield aggregate demand curve AD_2 in Figure 16.5c. The equilibrium levels of real output and prices are Q_f = $900 billion and P_2, as determined by the intersection of AD_2 and the aggregate supply curve AS.

To test your understanding of these relationships, explain why each of the other two levels of money supply in Figure 16.5a results in a different interest rate, level of investment, aggregate demand curve, and equilibrium real output.

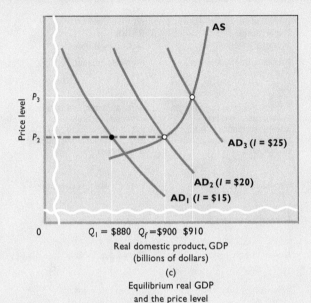

(c)
Equilibrium real GDP
and the price level

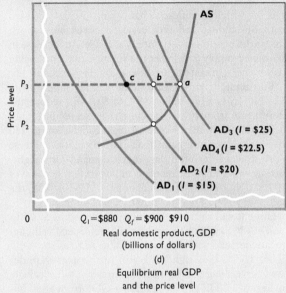

(d)
Equilibrium real GDP
and the price level

2. A successful restrictive monetary policy is evidenced by a shift in the money supply curve from:
   a. S_{m3} to a point halfway between S_{m2} and S_{m3}, a decrease in investment from $25 billion to $22.5 billion, and a decline in aggregate demand from AD_3 to AD_4.
   b. S_{m1} to S_{m2}, an increase in investment from $20 billion to $25 billion, and an increase in real GDP from Q_1 to Q_f.
   c. S_{m3} to S_{m2}, a decrease in investment from $25 billion to $20 billion, and a decline in the price level from P_3 to P_2.
   d. S_{m3} to S_{m2}, a decrease in investment from $25 billion to $20 billion, and an increase in aggregate demand from AD_2 to AD_3.

3. The Federal Reserve could increase the money supply from S_{m1} to S_{m2} by:
   a. increasing the discount rate.
   b. reducing taxes.
   c. buying government securities in the open market.
   d. increasing the reserve requirement.

4. If the spending-income multiplier is 4 in the economy depicted, an increase in the money supply from $125 billion to $150 billion will:
   a. shift the aggregate demand curve rightward by $20 billion.
   b. increase real GDP by $25 billion.
   c. increase real GDP by $100 billion.
   d. shift the aggregate demand curve leftward by $5 billion.

Answers: 1. d; 2. a; 3. c; 4. a

Effects of an Expansionary Monetary Policy

Recall that the inflationary ratchet effect discussed in Chapter 12 describes the fact that real-world price levels tend to be downwardly inflexible. Thus, with our economy starting from the initial equilibrium where AD_2 intersects AS, the price level will be downwardly inflexible at P_2 so that aggregate supply will be horizontal to the left of Q_f. This means that if aggregate demand decreases, the economy's equilibrium will move leftward along the dashed horizontal line shown in Figure 16.5c.

Just such a decline would happen if the money supply fell to $125 billion ($S_{m1}$), shifting the aggregate demand

curve leftward to AD_1 in Figure 16.5c. This results in a real output of $880 billion, $20 billion less than the economy's full-employment output level of $900 billion. The economy will be experiencing recession, a negative GDP gap, and substantial unemployment. The Fed therefore should institute an expansionary monetary policy.

To increase the money supply, the Fed will take some combination of the following actions: (1) buy government securities from banks and the public in the open market, (2) lower the legal reserve ratio, (3) lower the discount rate, and (4) reduce the interest rate that it pays on reserves. The intended outcome will be an increase in excess reserves in the commercial banking system and a decline in the federal funds rate. Because excess reserves are the basis on which commercial banks and thrifts can earn profit by lending and thus creating checkable-deposit money, the nation's money supply will rise. An increase in the money supply will lower the interest rate, increasing investment, aggregate demand, and equilibrium GDP.

For example, an increase in the money supply from $125 billion to $150 billion ($S_{m1}$ to S_{m2}) will reduce the interest rate from 10 to 8 percent, as indicated in Figure 16.5a, and will boost investment from $15 billion to $20 billion, as shown in Figure 16.5b. This $5 billion increase in investment will shift the aggregate demand curve rightward by more than the increase in investment because of the multiplier effect. If the economy's MPC is 0.75, the multiplier will be 4, meaning that the $5 billion increase in investment will shift the AD curve rightward by $20 billion (= 4 × $5 billion) at each price level. Specifically, aggregate demand will shift from AD_1 to AD_2, as shown in Figure 16.5c. This rightward shift in the aggregate demand curve along the dashed horizontal line will eliminate the negative GDP gap by increasing GDP from $880 billion to the full-employment GDP of $Q_f = $900 billion.[1]

Column 1 in Table 16.3 summarizes the chain of events associated with an expansionary monetary policy.

Effects of a Restrictive Monetary Policy

Next we consider restrictive monetary policy. To prevent overcrowding, we will use graphs *a*, *b*, and *d* (not *c*) in Figure 16.5 to demonstrate the effects of a restrictive monetary policy on the economy. Figure 16.5d represents exactly the same economy as Figure 16.5c but adds some extra curves that relate only to our explanation of restrictive monetary policy.

To see how restrictive monetary policy works, first consider a situation in which the economy moves from a full-employment equilibrium to operating at more than full employment so that inflation is a problem and restrictive monetary policy would be appropriate. Assume that the economy begins at the full-employment equilibrium where AD_2 and AS intersect. At this equilibrium, $Q_f = $900 billion and the price level is P_2.

Next, assume that the money supply expands from $150 billion to $175 billion ($S_{m3}$) in Figure 16.5a. This results in an interest rate of 6 percent, investment spending of $25 billion rather than $20 billion, and aggregate

TABLE 16.3 Monetary Policies for Recession and Inflation

(1) Expansionary Monetary Policy	(2) Restrictive Monetary Policy
Problem: unemployment and recession ↓	*Problem:* inflation ↓
Federal Reserve buys bonds, lowers reserve ratio, lowers the discount rate, or reduces the interest rate on reserves ↓	Federal Reserve sells bonds, increases reserve ratio, raises the discount rate, or increases the interest rate on reserves ↓
Excess reserves increase ↓	Excess reserves decrease ↓
Federal funds rate falls ↓	Federal funds rate rises ↓
Money supply rises ↓	Money supply falls ↓
Interest rate falls ↓	Interest rate rises ↓
Investment spending increases ↓	Investment spending decreases ↓
Aggregate demand increases ↓	Aggregate demand decreases ↓
Real GDP rises	Inflation declines

demand AD_3. As the AD curve shifts to the right from AD_2 to AD_3 in Figure 16.5d, the economy will move along the upsloping AS curve until it comes to an equilibrium at point *a*, where AD_3 intersects AS. At the new equilibrium, the price level has risen to P_3 and the equilibrium level of real GDP has risen to $910 billion, indicating an inflationary GDP gap of $10 billion (= $910 billion − $900 billion). Aggregate demand AD_3 is excessive relative to the economy's full-employment level of real output $Q_f = $900 billion. To rein in spending, the Fed will institute a restrictive monetary policy.

The Federal Reserve Board will direct Federal Reserve Banks to undertake some combination of the following actions: (1) sell government securities to banks and the public in the open market, (2) increase the legal reserve ratio, (3) increase the discount rate, and (4) increase the interest rate that it pays on reserves. Banks then will discover that their reserves are below those required and that the federal funds rate has increased. So they will need to reduce their checkable deposits by

---

[1] To keep things simple, we assume that the increase in real GDP does not increase the demand for money. In reality, the transactions demand for money would rise, slightly dampening the decline in the interest rate shown in Figure 16.5a.

refraining from issuing new loans as old loans are paid back. This will shrink the money supply and increase the interest rate. The higher interest rate will discourage investment, lowering aggregate demand and restraining demand-pull inflation.

But the Fed must be careful about just how much to decrease the money supply. The problem is that the inflation ratchet will take effect at the new equilibrium point a, such that prices will be inflexible at price level P_3. As a result, the dashed horizontal line to the left of point a in Figure 16.5d will become relevant. This means that the Fed cannot simply lower the money supply to S_{m2} in Figure 16.5a. If it were to do that, investment demand would fall to $20 billion in Figure 16.5b and the AD curve would shift to the left from AD_3 back to AD_2. But because of inflexible prices, the economy's equilibrium would move to point c, where AD_2 intersects the horizontal dashed line to the left of point a. This would put the economy into a recession, with equilibrium output below the full-employment output level of Q_f = $900 billion.

What the Fed needs to do to achieve full employment is to move the AD curve back only from AD_3 to AD_4, so that the economy will come to equilibrium at point b. This will require a $10 billion decrease in aggregate demand, so that equilibrium output falls from $910 billion at point a to Q_f = $900 billion at point b. The Fed can achieve this shift by setting the supply of money in Figure 16.5a at $162.5 billion. To see how this works, draw in a vertical money supply curve in Figure 16.5a at $162.5 billion and label it as S_{m4}. It will be exactly halfway between money supply curves S_{m2} and S_{m3}. Notice that the intersection of S_{m4} with the money demand curve D_m will result in an interest rate of 7 percent. In Figure 16.5b, this interest rate of 7 percent will result in investment spending of $22.5 billion (halfway between $20 billion and $25 billion). Thus, by setting the money supply at $162.5 billion, the Fed can reduce investment spending by $2.5 billion, lowering it from the $25 billion associated with AD_3 down to only $22.5 billion. This decline in investment spending will initially shift the AD curve only $2.5 billion to the left of AD_3. But then the multiplier process will work its magic. Since the multiplier is 4 in our model, the AD curve will end up moving by a full $10 billion (= $4 \times 2.5 billion) to the left, to AD_4. This shift will move the economy to equilibrium b, returning output to the full employment level and eliminating the inflationary GDP gap.[2]

Column 2 in Table 16.3 summarizes the cause-effect chain of a tight money policy.

> ### QUICK REVIEW 16.5
>
> - The Fed is engaging in an expansionary monetary policy when it increases the money supply to reduce interest rates and increase investment spending and real GDP.
> - The Fed is engaging in a restrictive monetary policy when it reduces the money supply to increase interest rates and reduce investment spending and inflation.

Monetary Policy: Evaluation and Issues

LO16.6 Explain the effectiveness of monetary policy and its shortcomings.

Monetary policy has become the dominant component of U.S. national stabilization policy. It has two key advantages over fiscal policy:

- Speed and flexibility.
- Isolation from political pressure.

Compared with fiscal policy, monetary policy can be quickly altered. Recall that congressional deliberations may delay the application of fiscal policy for months. In contrast, the Fed can buy or sell securities from day to day and thus affect the money supply and interest rates almost immediately.

Also, because members of the Fed's Board of Governors are appointed and serve 14-year terms, they are relatively isolated from lobbying and need not worry about retaining their popularity with voters. Thus, the Board, more readily than Congress, can engage in politically unpopular policies (higher interest rates) that may be necessary for the long-term health of the economy. Moreover, monetary policy is a subtler and more politically neutral measure than fiscal policy. Changes in government spending directly affect the allocation of resources, and changes in taxes can have extensive political ramifications. Because monetary policy works more subtly, it is more politically palatable.

Recent U.S. Monetary Policy

The Fed has been highly active in its use of monetary policy in recent decades.

The 2001 Recession In 2000, the economy abruptly slowed after a long period of full employment and strong economic growth. The Fed responded to the slowdown by

---

[2]Again, we assume for simplicity that the decrease in nominal GDP does not feed back to reduce the demand for money and thus the interest rate. In reality, this would occur, slightly dampening the increase in the interest rate shown in Figure 16.5a.

cutting the federal funds interest rate by a full percentage point in two increments in January 2001. Despite those rate cuts, the economy entered a recession in March 2001. Between March 20, 2001, and August 21, 2001, the Fed reduced the federal funds rate from 5 percent to 3.5 percent in a series of steps. In the 3 months following the terrorist attacks of September 11, 2001, it lowered the federal funds rate from 3.5 percent to 1.75 percent, and it left the rate there until it lowered it to 1.25 percent in November 2002. Partly because of the Fed's actions, the prime interest rate dropped from 9.5 percent at the end of 2000 to 4.25 percent in December 2002.

Economists generally give the Fed high marks for helping to keep the recession of 2001 relatively mild, particularly in view of the adverse economic impacts of the terrorist attacks of September 11, 2001, and the steep stock-market decline in 2001–2002.

The Fed left the federal funds rate at historic lows in 2003. But as the economy began to expand robustly in 2004, the Fed engineered a gradual series of rate hikes designed to boost the prime interest rate and other interest rates to make sure that aggregate demand continued to grow at a pace consistent with low inflation. By the summer of 2006, the target for the federal funds rate had risen to 5.25 percent and the prime rate was 8.25 percent. With the economy enjoying sustainable, noninflationary growth, the Fed left the federal funds rate at 5.25 percent for over a year.

The 2007–2009 Recession The mortgage default crisis (discussed in Chapter 14) began during the late summer of 2007 and posed a grave threat to the financial system and the economy. In response, the Fed took several actions. In August it lowered the discount rate by half a percentage point. Then, between September 2007 and April 2008, it lowered the target for the federal funds rate from 5.25 percent to 2 percent. And as discussed in Chapter 14, the Fed also took a series of extraordinary actions to prevent the failure of key financial firms.

In October 2008, the Fed first reduced the federal funds target rate to 1.5 percent and then later that same month to 1 percent. In December 2008, the Fed lowered it further to a targeted range of 0 percent to 0.25 percent. That near-zero targeted range was by far the lowest in history. Viewed through Figure 16.3, the Fed aggressively pushed the supply of federal funds curve downward (increased the supply of federal funds) to lower the actual federal funds rate to its target level. All these monetary actions and lender-of-last-resort functions helped to stabilize the banking sector and keep credit flowing—thereby offsetting at least some of the damage done by the financial crisis.

The decline in the federal funds rate to near zero during the financial and economic crisis dropped the prime interest rate (review Figure 16.4). In December 2007, the prime interest rate stood at 7.3 percent. By January 2009, it had declined to 3.25 percent, where it remained through 2013.

The Federal Reserve is lauded by most observers for its quick and innovative actions during the financial crisis and severe recession. Nevertheless, some economists contend that the Fed contributed to the financial crisis by holding the federal funds interest rate too low for too long during the recovery from the 2001 recession. These critics say that the artificially low interest rates made mortgage and other loans too inexpensive and therefore contributed to the borrowing frenzy by homeowners and other financial investors. Other economists counter that the low mortgage interest rates resulted from huge inflows of savings from abroad to a wide variety of U.S. financial markets.

After the Great Recession The U.S. economy recovered very slowly from the Great Recession, especially in terms of employment. After falling from a peak of 138.1 million in January 2008 to a trough of 129.9 million in September 2010, the total number of people with jobs rebounded to just 135.5 million by April 2013. Thus, nearly four years after the recession officially ended in the summer of 2009, 2.6 million fewer people were employed than before the recession. By contrast, after all other post–World War II recessions, employment had fully recovered within four years—and in most cases within two years.

The Federal Reserve understood the depth of the economy's problems early on and responded with a series of innovative monetary policy initiatives designed to stimulate GDP and employment growth.

Zero Interest Rate Policy   The Fed began by moving toward a **zero interest rate policy,** or ZIRP, in December 2008. Under ZIRP, the Fed aimed to keep short-term interest rates near zero to stimulate the economy. To that end, open-market operations were used to keep the federal funds rate between zero and 0.25 percent.

Zero Lower Bound Problem   After ZIRP was implemented and interest rates were pushed toward zero, the economic growth remained weak. That implied that the Fed would have to figure out a way to deal with the **zero lower bound problem,** under which a central bank is constrained in its ability to stimulate the economy through lower interest rates by the fact that nominal interest rates cannot be driven lower than zero.

Why can't nominal interest rates be driven lower than zero? Because if nominal interest rates were negative, people would not want to put their money into banks because doing so would mean that their balances would shrink over time (rather than grow over time, as they do when interest rates are positive). Thus, any central bank that attempted to impose negative nominal interest rates would see deposits withdrawn from banks. That could be economically catastrophic because if people withdrew deposits from banks, banks would have much less money to lend out to consumers and entrepreneurs. The monetary multiplier of Chapter 15 would work in reverse and the supply of lending and credit in the economy would decrease precipitously, thereby negatively affecting aggregate demand.

Quantitative Easing The Fed's response to the zero lower bound problem was **quantitative easing,** or QE. In terms of mechanics, quantitative easing looks exactly like open-market operations, with the Fed purchasing bonds in order increase the amount of reserves in the banking system. QE differs from ordinary open-market operations, however, in that it is not intended to lower interest rates. Under QE, the Fed buys bonds solely with the intention of increasing the quantity of reserves in the banking system. Interest rates remain at the same levels to avoid the zero lower bound problem. But with bank reserves increased, the economy will hopefully be stimulated through increased lending.

Another difference between QE and regular open-market operations is that QE can involve the purchase of not only U.S. government bonds but also debt issued by government agencies or government-backed corporations (which are known as government-sponsored entities, or GSEs).

The first round of quantitative easing began in March 2009 and involved the Fed purchasing $1.75 trillion worth of bonds. The bonds consisted of $300 billion worth of Treasury bonds and $1.45 trillion worth of bonds issued by either U.S. government agencies or the two government-backed mortgage lenders, Freddie Mac and Fannie Mae.

The second round of quantitative easing ("QE2") began in November 2010 and involved the Fed telling the public of its intention to purchase $600 billion of U.S. Treasury bonds at the rate of $75 billion per month over the following eight months.

Forward Commitment The innovative feature of QE2 was that the Fed engaged in **forward commitment,** preannouncing exactly how much it was going to buy during QE2 and how long the buying would last. This was a major change in monetary policy because up to that time the Fed had (along with most central banks) stuck to a policy of being vague about how long any particular policy initiative would last. For instance, if the Fed lowered or raised the federal funds target rate, it did not publicly announce for how long the change would last.

The rationale behind being vague was to preserve the Fed's flexibility to make changes if unexpected circumstances arose. However, that flexibility came at the cost of reduced credibility because the public might not react strongly to a policy change if it believed that the policy change might be reversed at any moment. By preannouncing the exact size and duration of QE, the Fed removed that worry. By making forward commitments, the public would know not only the content of a policy change but also that it wasn't going to be suddenly reversed.

With respect to the banking system, the announcement of both the size and duration of the Fed's open-market purchases of bonds meant that banks would know that the resulting increases in reserves would not suddenly be reversed. That would make the banks more likely to lend those new reserves because they wouldn't have any nagging doubts that the Fed might suddenly reverse policy, reduce reserves, and force the banks to suddenly and unexpectedly reduce their lending activities.

Operation Twist The Fed's use of forward commitment continued in September 2011, when it began the Maturity Extension Program, commonly known as Operation Twist. Under that program, the Fed preannounced that, by the end of 2012, it would purchase $677 billion in long-term government bonds while simultaneously selling an equivalent dollar amount of short-term government bonds. The Fed's motivation for doing so was to spur investment and consumption by reducing long-term interest rates, which were at that time several percentage points higher than short-term interest rates (which remained near zero thanks to ZIRP).

The intended reduction in long-term interest rates was accomplished by purchasing long-term bonds and driving up their prices. The money needed for those purchases was provided by selling an equivalent dollar amount of short-term bonds. Crucially, the amount of short-term bonds sold by the Fed was not nearly enough to alter short-term interest rates. Thus, they stayed near zero while longer-term rates fell.

QE3 When economic growth remained weak in 2012, the Fed decided that the lack of effectiveness of QE2 and

Operation Twist might have been due to the fact that both had featured limited time durations. Thus, banks might have been worried that the Fed might reverse policy as soon as the limited time durations of QE2 and Operation Twist came to an end.

To avoid that possibility going forward, the Fed's announcement of QE3 in September 2012 involved explicitly stating not only that the Fed would purchase $85 billion per month in bonds, but that those purchases had no specific end date and would in fact continue until the employment situation improved substantially. By making an open-ended commitment, the Fed hoped to enhance the credibility of its monetary stimulus policies.

In September 2012, the Fed also issued an open-ended policy commitment with respect to the federal funds rate. The Fed announced that the federal funds target rate would remain "exceptionally low" as long as the unemployment rate stayed above 6.5 percent and inflation remained muted, at 2 percent per year or less. Thus, the Fed committed itself to utilizing ZIRP until either the jobs situation dramatically improved or inflation started rising too high.

That forward commitment allowed businesses, banks, and consumers to have a much better sense of how long monetary stimulus would last and the circumstances under which it would be cut off. As the economy moved into 2013, the Fed hoped that its increasingly specific forward guidance would help to improve the effectiveness of its monetary stimulus efforts.

Problems and Complications

Despite its recent successes in the United States, monetary policy has certain limitations and faces actual-economy complications.

Lags Recall that fiscal policy is hindered by three delays, or lags—a recognition lag, an administrative lag, and an operational lag. Monetary policy also faces a recognition lag and an operational lag, but because the Fed can decide and implement policy changes within days, it avoids the long administrative lag that hinders fiscal policy.

A recognition lag affects monetary policy because normal monthly variations in economic activity and the price level mean that the Fed may not be able to quickly recognize when the economy is truly starting to recede or when inflation is really starting to rise. Once the Fed acts, an operation lag of 3 to 6 months affects monetary policy because that much time is typically required for interest-rate changes to have their full impacts on investment, aggregate demand, real GDP, and the price level. These two lags complicate the timing of monetary policy.

CONSIDER THIS ...

Up, Up, and Away

The consolidated balance sheet of the 12 Federal Reserve Banks changed markedly during the severe recession of 2007–2009. Total Fed assets increased from $885 billion in February 2008 to $2,317 billion in March 2010. This increase reflected an enormous rise in the number of U.S. securities, mortgage-backed securities, and other financial assets purchased by the Federal Reserve. In undertaking its monetary policy and its lender-of-last-resort functions, the Fed bought these securities from financial institutions—purposely increasing the liquidity of the financial system.

On the liability side, the reserves of commercial banks rose from $43 billion in February 2008 to $1,148 billion in March 2010. To make sure they were liquid and the funds were safe, banks placed much of the proceeds from selling securities to the Fed into their respective reserve accounts at the Fed. This flow was strengthened because the Fed began paying interest on the reserves that banks were holding at the Fed.

In March 2010 total bank reserves held at the Fed exceeded total checkable deposits held by the banks. The severe distress in the financial system had voluntarily turned the fractional reserve system into a 100-percent-plus reserve system! The banks had enormous excess reserves from which to increase lending once the banks became more certain of their own financial viability and the likelihood that newly issued loans would be paid back.

The Fed's use of quantitative easing caused the Fed's balance sheet to increase even further after the Great Recession ended. By May 2013, it had reached $3.3 trillion and was continuing to grow by $85 billion per month as QE3 continued. The Fed therefore faces the challenging task of using monetary policy to absorb large portions of this overstock of excess reserves as the economy recovers and picks up momentum. It does not want the banks to lend out the full amount of these excess reserves because that would flood the economy with bank-created money and excessively expand the money supply. During a vigorous economic expansion, the excessive money and resulting very low interest rates could produce such large expansions of aggregate demand that rapid inflation would occur.

Cyclical Asymmetry and the Liquidity Trap

Monetary policy may be highly effective in slowing expansions and controlling inflation but may be much less reliable in pushing the economy from a severe recession. Economists say that monetary policy may suffer from **cyclical asymmetry.** The metaphor of "pushing on a string" is often invoked to capture this problem. Imagine the Fed standing on the left-hand side of Figure 16.5d, holding one end of a "monetary-policy string." And imagine that the other end of the monetary-policy string is tied to the AD curve. Because the string would go taut if pulled on, monetary policy may be useful in *pulling* aggregate demand to the left. But because the string would go limp if pushed on, monetary policy will be rather ineffective at *pushing* aggregate demand to the right.

The reason for this asymmetry has to do with the asymmetric way in which people may act in response to changes in bank reserves. If pursued vigorously, a restrictive monetary policy can deplete commercial banking reserves to the point where banks are forced to reduce the volume of loans. That means a contraction of the money supply, higher interest rates, and reduced aggregate demand. The Fed can absorb sufficient reserves and eventually achieve its goal.

But the Fed cannot be certain of achieving its goal when it adds reserves to the banking system because of the so-called **liquidity trap,** in which adding more liquidity to banks has little or no additional positive effect on lending, borrowing, investment, or aggregate demand. For example, during the recent recession, the Fed created billions of dollars of excess reserves that drove down the federal funds rate to as low as 0.2 percent. The prime interest rate fell from 7.3 percent (December 2007) to 3.25 percent (March 2009). Nevertheless, lending by banks stalled throughout the first 15 months of the recession and remained weak even after the Fed implemented ZIRP, QE, Operation Twist, and forward commitments over the following four years. The banks were fearful that the loans they would make to households, businesses, and other financial institutions would not be paid back. Consequently, they were content to hold reserves at the Federal Reserve Banks.

To switch analogies, an expansionary monetary policy can suffer from a "you can lead a horse to water, but you can't make it drink" problem. The Fed can create excess reserves, but it cannot guarantee that the banks will actually make additional loans and thus promote spending. If commercial banks seek liquidity and are unwilling to lend, the efforts of the Fed will be of little avail. Similarly, households and businesses can frustrate the intentions of the Fed by not borrowing excess reserves being made available as loans. And when the Fed buys securities from the public, people may choose to pay off existing loans with the money received, rather than increasing their spending on goods and services.

Furthermore, a severe recession may so undermine business confidence that the investment demand curve shifts to the left and overwhelms the lower interest rates associated with an expansionary monetary policy. That is what happened in the most recent recession. Although the Fed drove the real interest rate down to zero percent, investment spending remained low and the economy remained mired in recession. The recent U.S. experience reminds us that active monetary policy certainly is not a cure-all for the business cycle. Under some circumstances, monetary policy may be like "pushing on a string."

The liquidity trap that occurred during the severe recession was a primary reason why public policy in the United States turned so significantly and forcefully toward fiscal policy in 2009. Recall our discussion of the American Recovery and Redevelopment Act of 2009, which authorized the infusion of $787 billion of new tax cuts and government spending in 2009 and 2010.

QUICK REVIEW 16.6

- The Fed aggressively lowered the federal funds interest rate following 9/11 and the 2001 recession and also during the severe recession of 2007–2009.
- To help stimulate the economy after the Great Recession, the Fed implemented the zero interest rate policy (ZIRP), quantitative easing (QE), Operation Twist, and forward commitment.
- The main strengths of monetary policy are (a) speed and flexibility and (b) political acceptability; its main weaknesses are (a) time lags and (b) potential ineffectiveness during severe recession.

The "Big Picture"

Figure 16.6 (Key Graph) on pages 374 and 375 brings together the analytical and policy aspects of macroeconomics discussed in this and the eight preceding chapters. This "big picture" shows how the many concepts and principles discussed relate to one another and how they constitute a coherent theory of the price level and real output in a market economy.

Study this diagram and you will see that the levels of output, employment, income, and prices all result from the interaction of aggregate supply and aggregate demand. The items shown in red relate to public policy.

KEY GRAPH

FIGURE 16.6 The AD-AS theory of the price level, real output, and stabilization policy. This figure integrates the various components of macroeconomic theory and stabilization policy. Determinants that either constitute public policy or are strongly influenced by public policy are shown in red.

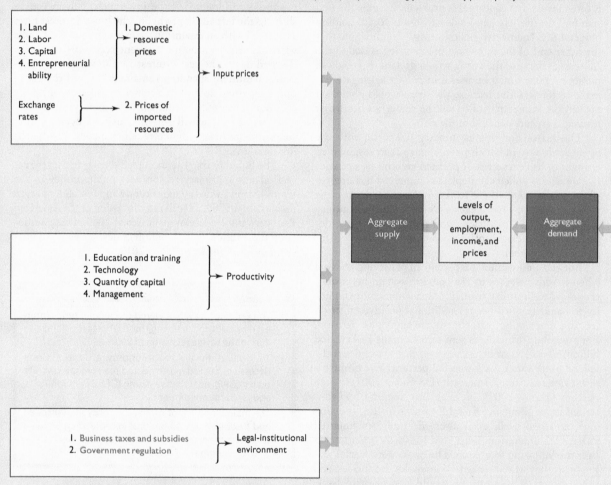

1. All else equal, an increase in domestic resource availability will:
   a. increase input prices, reduce aggregate supply, and increase real output.
   b. raise labor productivity, reduce interest rates, and lower the international value of the dollar.
   c. increase net exports, increase investment, and reduce aggregate demand.
   d. reduce input prices, increase aggregate supply, and increase real output.

2. All else equal, an expansionary monetary policy during a recession will:
   a. lower the interest rate, increase investment, and reduce net exports.
   b. lower the interest rate, increase investment, and increase aggregate demand.
   c. increase the interest rate, increase investment, and reduce net exports.
   d. reduce productivity, aggregate supply, and real output.

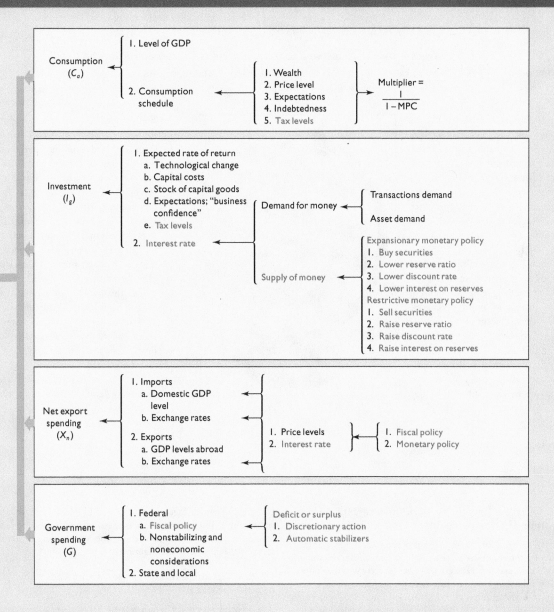

3. A personal income tax cut, combined with a reduction in corporate income and excise taxes, would:
   a. increase consumption, investment, aggregate demand, and aggregate supply.
   b. reduce productivity, raise input prices, and reduce aggregate supply.
   c. increase government spending, reduce net exports, and increase aggregate demand.
   d. increase the supply of money, reduce interest rates, increase investment, and expand real output.

4. An appreciation of the dollar would:
   a. reduce the price of imported resources, lower input prices, and increase aggregate supply.
   b. increase net exports and aggregate demand.
   c. increase aggregate supply and aggregate demand.
   d. reduce consumption, investment, net export spending, and government spending.

Answers: 1. d; 2. b; 3. a; 4.a

LAST WORD

Worries about ZIRP, QE, and Twist

ZIRP, QE, and Operation Twist Provided Massive Economic Stimulus During and After the Great Recession. But There Remain Many Worries About Unintended Consequences.

When the financial crisis reached its peak in 2008, the Fed acted aggressively to prevent bank runs and stabilize the financial system by acting as a lender of last resort. It also did its best to get the economy moving again by lowering short-term interest rates to nearly zero—a strategy that came to be known as the zero interest rate policy, or ZIRP.

When ZIRP by itself didn't seem to be causing enough stimulus, the Fed also began engaging in trillions of dollars' worth of bond purchases. Those purchases went by the name of quantitative easing, or QE, because the Fed printed up electronic money to pay for the purchases, thereby massively increasing (easing) the total quantity of money in circulation. The

Fed's hope was that the additional money would lead to additional spending and lending that would boost aggregate demand by increasing consumption and investment. Later, the policy known as Operation Twist lowered longer-term interest rates.

One important effect of ZIRP and Operation Twist was to help the U.S. federal government engage in aggressive deficit-financed fiscal stimulus. Thanks to ZIRP and Operation Twist, the federal government was able to fund large deficits by issuing 10-year bonds at nominal interest rates of about 2 percent—substantially lower than the historical average of about 6 percent.

But the Federal Reserve didn't just help the federal government with low

SUMMARY

LO16.1 Discuss how the equilibrium interest rate is determined in the market for money.

The total demand for money consists of the transactions demand for money plus the asset demand for money. The amount of money demanded for transactions varies directly with the nominal GDP; the amount of money demanded as an asset varies inversely with the interest rate. The market for money combines the total demand for money with the money supply to determine equilibrium interest rates.

Interest rates and bond prices are inversely related.

LO16.2 Describe the balance sheet of the Federal Reserve and the meaning of its major items.

The consolidated balance sheet of the Federal Reserve System lists the collective assets and liabilities of the 12 Federal Reserve banks. The assets consist largely of Treasury notes, Treasury bills, and Treasury bonds. The major liabilities are reserves of

commercial banks, Treasury deposits, and Federal Reserve notes outstanding. The balance sheet is useful in understanding monetary policy because open-market operations increase or decrease the Fed's assets and liabilities.

LO16.3 List and explain the goals and tools of monetary policy.

The goal of monetary policy is to help the economy achieve price stability, full employment, and economic growth.

The four main instruments of monetary policy are (a) open-market operations, (b) the reserve ratio, (c) the discount rate, and (d) interest on reserves.

LO16.4 Describe the federal funds rate and how the Fed directly influences it.

The federal funds rate is the interest rate that banks charge one another for overnight loans of reserves. The prime interest rate is the interest rates. It also served as the federal government's primary lender. In 2012, for instance, the Federal Reserve purchased over 70 percent of all U.S. government debt. Thus, 70 percent of the federal government's new borrowing came from the Federal Reserve in the form of newly printed money that the Fed created in order to fund its open-market purchases of government bonds.

The consensus among economists was that the Fed's aggressive use of ZIRP and QE were warranted by the severity of the financial crisis and the historically slow pace with which the economy recovered after the 2007–2009 recession. However, concerns were also raised about possible unintended consequences.

One worry had to do with the large annual budget deficits that the federal government was running. While many economists felt that the large deficits were appropriate given the sluggish economy, others believed that the federal government was overspending and taking resources away from the private sector. As a result, they felt that the Fed's use of ZIRP and QE was making it too easy for Congress to overspend and run large budget deficits because the Fed would always provide a ready buyer for the bonds that had to be issued to finance those large deficits.

A longer-term worry was that when ZIRP ended and interest rates began to rise again toward normal levels, the federal government would be suddenly confronted with huge interest costs. Consider the $16 trillion of debt that had accumulated by 2013: $16 trillion borrowed at 2 percent interest generates annual interest payments of $320 billion per year. But if the interest rate on government debt were to rise back to its historical average of 6 percent, the annual interest payments on $16 trillion would come to $960 billion per year. Such a huge increase in annual interest payments would likely require either massive budget cuts or even more borrowing, unless the economy began to grow so quickly that increased tax revenues were enough to compensate for the increased interest payments.

Another problem with extremely low interest rates is that they punish savers. A senior citizen who has saved for retirement will find that her investments yield very low rates of return when the Fed is keeping interest rates low. Instead of being able to live off of the interest generated by her investments, she may find herself spending down her accumulated savings because the interest payments amount to nearly nothing.

On a larger scale, pension plans and retirement funds are also hit hard by low interest rates. Those institutions take deposits from current workers, invest those funds, and promise to pay out certain amounts when workers retire. Prior to the financial crisis, most of those institutions had assumed that they would be able to earn 8 percent per year on the retirement funds that they were entrusted with. But with the Fed keeping interest rates so low, the pension plans and retirement funds were not earning anywhere near 8 percent per year on their investments. As a result, the low interest rates engineered by the Fed made it very unlikely that pension plans and retirement funds would be able to keep their promises to retirees and deliver enough money in 20 or 30 years to pay each individual retiree what he or she had been promised.

benchmark rate that banks use as a reference rate for a wide range of interest rates on short-term loans to businesses and individuals.

The Fed adjusts the federal funds rate to a level appropriate for economic conditions. Under an expansionary monetary policy, it purchases securities from commercial banks and the general public to inject reserves into the banking system. This lowers the federal funds rate to the targeted level and also reduces other interest rates (such as the prime rate). Under a restrictive monetary policy, the Fed sells securities to commercial banks and the general public via open-market operations. Consequently, reserves are removed from the banking system, and the federal funds rate and other interest rates rise.

LO16.5 Identify the mechanisms by which monetary policy affects GDP and the price level.

Monetary policy affects the economy through a complex cause-effect chain: (*a*) policy decisions affect commercial bank reserves; (*b*) changes in reserves affect the money supply; (*c*) changes in the money supply alter the interest rate; (*d*) changes in the interest rate affect investment; (*e*) changes in investment affect aggregate demand; (*f*) changes in aggregate demand affect the equilibrium real GDP and the price level. Table 16.3 draws together all the basic ideas relevant to the use of monetary policy.

LO16.6 Explain the effectiveness of monetary policy and its shortcomings.

The advantages of monetary policy include its flexibility and political acceptability. In recent years, the Fed has used monetary policy to keep inflation low while helping limit the depth of the recession of 2001, to boost the economy as it recovered from that recession, to help stabilize the banking sector in the wake of the mortgage debt crisis, and to promote recovery from the severe recession of 2007–2009. Today, nearly all economists view monetary policy as a significant stabilization tool.

Monetary policy has two major limitations and potential problems: (*a*) recognition and operation lags complicate the timing of monetary policy; (*b*) in a severe recession, the reluctance of banks to lend excess reserves and firms to borrow money to spend on capital goods may contribute to a liquidity trap that limits the effectiveness of an expansionary monetary policy.

TERMS AND CONCEPTS

monetary policy	discount rate	zero interest rate policy (ZIRP)
interest	interest on reserves	zero lower bound problem
transactions demand for money	federal funds rate	quantitative easing (QE)
asset demand for money	expansionary monetary policy	forward commitment
total demand for money	prime interest rate	cyclical asymmetry
open-market operations	restrictive monetary policy	liquidity trap
reserve ratio	Taylor rule	

The following and additional problems can be found in **connect** ECONOMICS

DISCUSSION QUESTIONS

1. What is the basic determinant of (*a*) the transactions demand and (*b*) the asset demand for money? Explain how these two demands can be combined graphically to determine total money demand. How is the equilibrium interest rate in the money market determined? Use a graph to show the effect of an increase in the total demand for money on the equilibrium interest rate (no change in money supply). Use your general knowledge of equilibrium prices to explain why the previous interest rate is no longer sustainable. **LO16.1**

2. What is the basic objective of monetary policy? What are the major strengths of monetary policy? Why is monetary policy easier to conduct than fiscal policy? **LO16.3**

3. Distinguish between the federal funds rate and the prime interest rate. Why is one higher than the other? Why do changes in the two rates closely track one another? **LO16.4**

4. Why is a decrease in the supply of federal funds shown as an upshift of the supply curve in Figure 16.3, whereas an increase in federal funds is shown as a downshift of the supply curve? **LO16.4**

5. Suppose that you are a member of the Board of Governors of the Federal Reserve System. The economy is experiencing a sharp rise in the inflation rate. What change in the federal funds rate would you recommend? How would your recommended change get accomplished? What impact would the actions have on the lending ability of the banking system, the real interest rate, investment spending, aggregate demand, and inflation? **LO16.5**

6. Explain the links between changes in the nation's money supply, the interest rate, investment spending, aggregate demand, real GDP, and the price level. **LO16.5**

7. What do economists mean when they say that monetary policy can exhibit cyclical asymmetry? How does the idea of a liquidity trap relate to cyclical asymmetry? Why is this possibility of a liquidity trap significant to policymakers? **LO16.6**

8. **LAST WORD** Did Operation Twist target long-term or short-term interest rates? How does ZIRP cause problems for savers and pension funds? How might low interest rates lead to problematic fiscal policy decisions?

REVIEW QUESTIONS

1. When bond prices go up, interest rates go _____. **LO16.1**
   a. Up.
   b. Down.
   c. Nowhere.

2. A commercial bank sells a Treasury bond to the Federal Reserve for $100,000. The money supply: **LO16.3**
   a. Increases by $100,000.
   b. Decreases by $100,000.
   c. Is unaffected by the transaction.

3. Use commercial bank and Federal Reserve Bank balance sheets to demonstrate the effect of each of the following transactions on commercial bank reserves: **LO16.3**
   a. Federal Reserve Banks purchase securities from banks.

   b. Commercial banks borrow from Federal Reserve Banks at the discount rate.
   c. The Fed reduces the reserve ratio.
   d. Commercial banks increase their reserves after the Fed increases the interest rate that it pays on reserves.

4. A bank currently has $100,000 in checkable deposits and $15,000 in actual reserves. If the reserve ratio is 20 percent, the bank has _____ in money-creating potential. If the reserve ratio is 14 percent, the bank has _____ in money-creating potential. **LO16.3**
   a. $20,000; $14,000.
   b. $3,000; $2,100.
   c. −$5,000; $1,000.
   d. $5,000; $1,000.

5. A bank borrows $100,000 from the Fed, leaving a $100,000 Treasury bond on deposit with the Fed to serve as collateral for the loan. The discount rate that applies to the loan is 4 percent and the Fed is currently mandating a reserve ratio of 10 percent. How much of the $100,000 borrowed by the bank must it keep as required reserves? **LO16.3**
   a. $0.
   b. $4,000.
   c. $10,000.
   d. $100,000.

6. Which of the following Fed actions will increase bank lending? **LO16.3**
   *Select **one or more** answers from the choices shown.*
   a. The Fed raises the discount rate from 5 percent to 6 percent.
   b. The Fed raises the reserve ratio from 10 percent to 11 percent.
   c. The Fed buys $400 million worth of Treasury bonds from commercial banks.
   d. The Fed lowers the discount rate from 4 percent to 2 percent.

7. If the Federal Reserve wants to increase the federal funds rate using open-market operations, it should _____ bonds. **LO16.4**
   a. Buy.
   b. Sell.

8. True or False: A liquidity trap occurs when expansionary monetary policy fails to work because an increase in bank reserves by the Fed does not lead to an increase in bank lending. **LO16.6**

9. True or False: In the United States, monetary policy has two key advantages over fiscal policy: (1) isolation from political pressure and (2) speed and flexibility. **LO16.6**

PROBLEMS

1. Assume that the following data characterize the hypothetical economy of Trance: money supply = $200 billion; quantity of money demanded for transactions = $150 billion; quantity of money demanded as an asset = $10 billion at 12 percent interest, increasing by $10 billion for each 2-percentage-point fall in the interest rate. **LO16.1**
   a. What is the equilibrium interest rate in Trance?
   b. At the equilibrium interest rate, what are the quantity of money supplied, the total quantity of money demanded, the amount of money demanded for transactions, and the amount of money demanded as an asset in Trance?

2. Suppose a bond with no expiration date has a face value of $10,000 and annually pays a fixed amount of interest of $800. In the table provided to the right, calculate and enter either the interest rate that the bond would yield to a bond buyer at each of the bond prices listed or the bond price at each of the interest yields shown. What generalization can be drawn from the completed table? **LO16.1**

Bond Price	Interest Yield, %
$ 8,000	_____
_____	8.9
$10,000	_____
$11,000	_____
_____	6.2

3. In the tables that follow you will find consolidated balance sheets for the commercial banking system and the 12 Federal Reserve Banks. Use columns 1 through 3 to indicate how the balance sheets would read after each of transactions *a* to *c* is completed. Do not cumulate your answers; that is, analyze each transaction separately, starting in each case from the numbers provided. All accounts are in billions of dollars. **LO16.3**
   a. A decline in the discount rate prompts commercial banks to borrow an additional $1 billion from the Federal Reserve Banks. Show the new balance-sheet numbers in column 1 of each table.

| | | Consolidated Balance Sheet: All Commercial Banks | | |
		(1)	(2)	(3)
Assets:				
Reserves	$33	_____	_____	_____
Securities	60	_____	_____	_____
Loans	60	_____	_____	_____
Liabilities and net worth:				
Checkable deposits	$150	_____	_____	_____
Loans from the Federal Reserve Banks	3	_____	_____	_____

		Consolidated Balance Sheet: The 12 Federal Reserve Banks		
		(1)	(2)	(3)
Assets:				
Securities....................	$60	_____	_____	_____
Loans to commercial banks.......	3	_____	_____	_____
Liabilities and net worth:				
Reserves of commercial banks....	$33	_____	_____	_____
Treasury deposits..............	3	_____	_____	_____
Federal Reserve Notes	27	_____	_____	_____

  b. The Federal Reserve Banks sell $3 billion in securities to members of the public, who pay for the bonds with checks. Show the new balance-sheet numbers in column 2 of each table.

  c. The Federal Reserve Banks buy $2 billion of securities from commercial banks. Show the new balance-sheet numbers in column 3 of each table.

  d. Now review each of the previous three transactions, asking yourself these three questions: (1) What change, if any, took place in the money supply as a direct and immediate result of each transaction? (2) What increase or decrease in the commercial banks' reserves took place in each transaction? (3) Assuming a reserve ratio of 20 percent, what change in the money-creating potential of the commercial banking system occurred as a result of each transaction?

4. Refer to Table 16.2 and assume that the Fed's reserve ratio is 10 percent and the economy is in a severe recession. Also suppose that the commercial banks are hoarding all excess reserves (not lending them out) because of their fear of loan defaults. Finally, suppose that the Fed is highly concerned that the banks will suddenly lend out these excess reserves and possibly contribute to inflation once the economy begins to recover and confidence is restored. By how many percentage points would the Fed need to increase the reserve ratio to eliminate one-third of the excess reserves? What would be the size of the monetary multiplier before and after the change in the reserve ratio? By how much would the lending potential of the banks decline as a result of the increase in the reserve ratio? **LO16.3**

5. Suppose that the demand for federal funds curve is such that the quantity of funds demanded changes by $120 billion for each 1 percent change in the federal funds interest rate. Also, assume that the current federal funds rate is at the 3 percent rate that is targeted by the Fed. Now suppose that the Fed retargets the rate to 3.5 percent. Assuming no change in demand, will the Fed need to increase or decrease the supply of federal funds? By how much will the quantity of federal funds have to change for the equilibrium to occur at the new target rate? **LO16.4**

6. Suppose that inflation is 2 percent, the federal funds rate is 4 percent, and real GDP falls 2 percent below potential GDP. According to the Taylor rule, in what direction and by how much should the Fed change the real federal funds rate? **LO16.4**

7. Refer to the table for Moola at the bottom of this page to answer the following questions. What is the equilibrium interest rate in Moola? What is the level of investment at the equilibrium interest rate? Is there either a recessionary output gap (negative GDP gap) or an inflationary output gap (positive GDP gap) at the equilibrium interest rate and, if either, what is the amount? Given money demand, by how much would the Moola central bank need to change the money supply to close the output gap? What is the expenditure multiplier in Moola? **LO16.5**

Money Supply	Money Demand	Interest Rate	Investment at Interest (Rate Shown)	Potential Real GDP	Actual Real GDP at Interest (Rate Shown)
$500	$800	2%	$50	$350	$390
500	700	3	40	350	370
500	600	4	30	350	350
500	500	5	20	350	330
500	400	6	10	350	310

FURTHER TEST YOUR KNOWLEDGE AT www.mcconnell20e.com

CHAPTER **18**

Extending the Analysis of Aggregate Supply

Learning Objectives

LO18.1 Explain the relationship between short-run aggregate supply and long-run aggregate supply.

LO18.2 Discuss how to apply the "extended" (short-run/long-run) AD-AS model to inflation, recessions, and economic growth.

LO18.3 Explain the short-run trade-off between inflation and unemployment (the Phillips Curve).

LO18.4 Discuss why there is no long-run trade-off between inflation and unemployment.

LO18.5 Explain the relationship between tax rates, tax revenues, and aggregate supply.

During the early years of the Great Depression, many economists suggested that the economy would correct itself in the *long run* without government intervention. To this line of thinking, economist John Maynard Keynes remarked, "In the long run we are all dead!"

For several decades following the Great Depression, macroeconomists understandably focused on refining fiscal policy and monetary policy to smooth business cycles and address the problems of unemployment and inflation. The main emphasis was on short-run problems and policies associated with the business cycle.

But over people's lifetimes, and from generation to generation, the long run is tremendously important for economic well-being. For that reason, macroeconomists have refocused attention on long-run macroeconomic adjustments, processes, and outcomes. The renewed emphasis on the long run has produced significant insights about aggregate supply, economic growth, and economic development. We will also see in the next chapter that it has renewed historical debates over the causes of macro instability and the effectiveness of stabilization policy.

Our goals in this chapter are to extend the analysis of aggregate supply to the long run, examine the inflation-unemployment relationship, and evaluate the effect of taxes on aggregate supply. The latter is a key concern of so-called *supply-side economics*.

From Short Run to Long Run

LO18.1 Explain the relationship between short-run aggregate supply and long-run aggregate supply.

In Chapter 12, we noted that in macroeconomics the difference between the **short run** and the **long run** has to do with the flexibility of input prices. Input prices are inflexible or even totally fixed in the short run but fully flexible in the long run. (By contrast, output prices are assumed under these definitions to be fully flexible in both the short run and the long run.)

The assumption that input prices are flexible only in the long run leads to large differences in the shape and position of the short-run aggregate supply curve and the long-run aggregate supply curve. As explained in Chapter 12, the short-run aggregate supply curve is an upsloping line, whereas the long-run aggregate supply curve is a vertical line situated directly above the economy's full-employment output level, Q_f.

We will begin this chapter by discussing how aggregate supply transitions *from* the short run *to* the long run. Once that is done, we will combine the long-run and short-run aggregate supply curves with the aggregate demand curve to form a single model that can provide insights into how the economy adjusts to economic shocks as well as changes in monetary and fiscal policy in both the short run and the long run. That will lead us to discuss how economic growth relates to long-run aggregate supply and how inflation and aggregate supply are related in the long run and the short run. We will conclude with a discussion of a particular set of economic policies that may help increase both short-run aggregate supply and long-run aggregate supply.

Short-Run Aggregate Supply

Our immediate objective is to demonstrate the relationship between short-run aggregate supply and long-run aggregate supply. We begin by briefly reviewing short-run aggregate supply.

Consider the short-run aggregate supply curve AS_1 in Figure 18.1a. This curve is based on three assumptions: (1) The initial price level is P_1, (2) firms and workers have established nominal wages on the expectation that this price level will persist, and (3) the price level is flexible both upward and downward. Observe from point a_1 that at price level P_1 the economy is operating at its full-employment output Q_f. This output is the real production forthcoming when the economy is operating at its natural rate of unemployment (or potential output).

Now let's review the short-run effects of changes in the price level, say, from P_1 to P_2 in Figure 18.1a. The higher prices associated with price level P_2 increase firms' revenues, and because their nominal wages and other input prices remain unchanged, their profits rise. Those higher profits lead firms to increase their output from Q_f to Q_2, and the economy moves from a_1 to a_2 on aggregate supply AS_1. At output Q_2 the economy is operating beyond its full-employment output. The firms make this possible by extending the work hours of part-time and full-time workers, enticing new workers such as homemakers and retirees into the labor force, and hiring and training the structurally unemployed. Thus, the nation's unemployment rate declines below its natural rate.

How will the firms respond when the price level *falls*, say, from P_1 to P_3 in Figure 18.1a? Because the prices they receive for their products are lower while the nominal wages they pay workers remain unchanged, firms discover that their revenues and profits have diminished or disappeared. So they reduce their production and employment, and, as shown by the movement from a_1 to a_3, real output falls to Q_3. Increased unemployment and a higher unemployment rate accompany the decline in real output. At output Q_3 the unemployment rate is greater than the natural rate of unemployment associated with output Q_f.

FIGURE 18.1   Short-run and long-run aggregate supply. (a) In the short run, nominal wages and other input prices do not respond to price-level changes and are based on the expectation that price level P_1 will continue. An increase in the price level from P_1 to P_2 increases profits and output, moving the economy from a_1 to a_2; a decrease in the price level from P_1 to P_3 reduces profits and real output, moving the economy from a_1 to a_3. The short-run aggregate supply curve therefore slopes upward. (b) In the long run, a rise in the price level results in higher nominal wages and other input prices and thus shifts the short-run aggregate supply curve to the left. Conversely, a decrease in the price level reduces nominal wages and shifts the short-run aggregate supply curve to the right. After such adjustments, the economy obtains equilibrium of points such as b_1 and c_1. Thus, the long-run aggregate supply curve is vertical at the full-employment output.

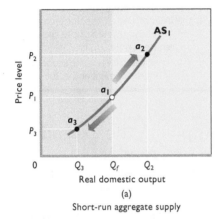

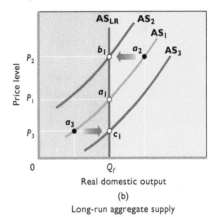

(a)
Short-run aggregate supply

(b)
Long-run aggregate supply

Long-Run Aggregate Supply

The outcomes are different in the long run. To see why, we need to extend the analysis of aggregate supply to account for changes in nominal wages that occur in response to changes in the price level. That will enable us to derive the economy's long-run aggregate supply curve.

We illustrate the implications for aggregate supply in Figure 18.1b. Again, suppose that the economy is initially at point a_1 (P_1 and Q_f). As we just demonstrated, an increase in the price level from P_1 to P_2 will move the economy from point a_1 to a_2 along the short-run aggregate supply curve AS_1. At a_2, the economy is producing at more than its potential output. This implies very high demand for productive inputs, so that input prices will begin to rise. In particular, the high demand for labor will drive up nominal wages, which will increase per unit production costs. As a result, the short-run supply curve shifts leftward from AS_1 to AS_2, which now reflects the higher price level P_2 and the new expectation that P_2, not P_1, will continue. The leftward shift in the short-run aggregate supply curve to AS_2 moves the economy from a_2 to b_1. Real output falls back to its full-employment level Q_f, and the unemployment rate rises to its natural rate.

What is the long-run outcome of a *decrease* in the price level? Assuming eventual downward wage flexibility, a

decline in the price level from P_1 to P_3 in Figure 18.1b works in the opposite way from a price-level increase. At first the economy moves from point a_1 to a_3 on AS_1. Profits are squeezed or eliminated because prices have fallen and nominal wages have not. But this movement along AS_1 is the short-run supply response that results only while input prices remain constant. As time passes, input prices will begin to fall because the economy is producing at below its full-employment output level. With so little output being produced, the demand for inputs will be low and their prices will begin to decline. In particular, the low demand for labor will drive down nominal wages and reduce per-unit production costs. Lower nominal wages therefore shift the short-run aggregate supply curve rightward from AS_1 to AS_3, and real output returns to its full-employment level of Q_f at point c_1.

By tracing a line between the long-run equilibrium points b_1, a_1, and c_1, we obtain a long-run aggregate supply curve. Observe that it is vertical at the full-employment level of real GDP. After long-run adjustments in nominal wages and other nominal input prices, real output is Q_f regardless of the specific price level.

Long-Run Equilibrium in the AD-AS Model

Figure 18.2 helps us understand the long-run equilibrium in the AD-AS model, now extended to include the

FIGURE 18.2 Equilibrium in the long-run AD-AS model.
The long-run equilibrium price level P_1 and level of real output Q_f occur at the intersection of the aggregate demand curve AD$_1$, the long-run aggregate supply curve AS$_{LR}$, and the short-run aggregate supply curve AS$_1$.

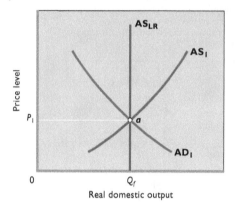

distinction between short-run and long-run aggregate supply. (Hereafter, we will refer to this model as the extended AD-AS model, with "extended" referring to the inclusion of both the short-run and the long-run aggregate supply curves.)

In the short run, equilibrium occurs wherever the downsloping aggregate demand curve and upsloping short-run aggregate supply curve intersect. This can be at any level of output, not simply the full-employment level. Either a negative GDP gap or a positive GDP gap is possible in the short run.

But in the long run, the short-run aggregate supply curve adjusts as we just described. After those adjustments, long-run equilibrium occurs where the aggregate demand curve, vertical long-run aggregate supply curve, and short-run aggregate supply curve all intersect. Figure 18.2 shows the long-run outcome. Equilibrium occurs at point a, where AD$_1$ intersects both AS$_{LR}$ and AS$_1$, and the economy achieves its full-employment (or potential) output, Q_f. At long-run equilibrium price level P_1 and output level Q_f, neither a negative GDP gap nor a positive GDP gap occurs. The economy's *natural rate of unemployment* prevails, meaning that the economy achieves full employment.

In the United States, output Q_f in Figure 18.2 implies a 4 to 5 percent unemployment rate. The natural rate of unemployment can vary from one time period to another and can differ between countries. But whatever the rate happens to be, it defines the level of potential output and establishes the location of the long-run AS curve.

QUICK REVIEW 18.1

- The short-run aggregate supply curve slopes upward because nominal wages and other input prices are fixed while output prices change.
- The long-run aggregate supply curve is vertical because input prices eventually rise in response to changes in output prices.
- The long-run equilibrium GDP and price level occur at the intersection of the aggregate demand curve, the long-run aggregate supply curve, and the short-run aggregate supply curve.
- In long-run equilibrium, the economy achieves its natural rate of unemployment and its full-potential real output.

Applying the Extended AD-AS Model

LO18.2 Explain how to apply the "extended" (short-run/long-run) AD-AS model to inflation, recessions, and economic growth.

The extended AD-AS model helps clarify the long-run aspects of demand-pull inflation, cost-push inflation, and recession.

Demand-Pull Inflation in the Extended AD-AS Model

Recall that demand-pull inflation occurs when an increase in aggregate demand pulls up the price level. Earlier, we depicted this inflation by shifting an aggregate demand curve rightward along a stable aggregate supply curve (see Figure 12.8).

In our more complex version of aggregate supply, an increase in the price level eventually leads to an increase in nominal wages and thus a leftward shift of the short-run aggregate supply curve. This is shown in Figure 18.3, where we initially suppose the price level is P_1 at the intersection of aggregate demand curve AD$_1$, short-run supply curve AS$_1$, and long-run aggregate supply curve AS$_{LR}$. Observe that the economy is achieving its full-employment real output Q_f at point a.

Now consider the effects of an increase in aggregate demand as represented by the rightward shift from AD$_1$ to AD$_2$. This shift might result from any one of a number of factors, including an increase in investment spending or a rise in net exports. Whatever its cause, the increase in aggregate demand boosts the price level from P_1 to P_2 and expands real output from Q_f to Q_2 at point b. There, a positive GDP gap of $Q_2 - Q_f$ occurs.

FIGURE 18.3 Demand-pull inflation in the extended AD-AS model.
An increase in aggregate demand from AD₁ to AD₂ drives up the price level and increases real output in the short run. But in the long run, nominal wages rise and the short-run aggregate supply curve shifts leftward, as from AS₁ to AS₂. Real output then returns to its prior level, and the price level rises even more. In this scenario, the economy moves from *a* to *b* and then eventually to *c*.

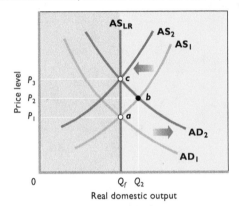

So far, none of this is new to you. But now the distinction between short-run aggregate supply and long-run aggregate supply becomes important. With the economy producing above potential output, inputs will be in high demand. Input prices including nominal wages will rise. As they do, the short-run aggregate supply curve will ultimately shift leftward such that it intersects long-run aggregate supply at point *c*.[1] There, the economy has reestablished long-run equilibrium, with the price level and real output now P_3 and Q_f, respectively. Only at point *c* does the new aggregate demand curve AD₂ intersect both the short-run aggregate supply curve AS₂ and the long-run aggregate supply curve AS$_{LR}$.

In the short run, demand-pull inflation drives up the price level and increases real output; in the long run, only the price level rises. In the long run, the initial increase in aggregate demand moves the economy along its vertical aggregate supply curve AS$_{LR}$. For a while, an economy can operate beyond its full-employment level of output. But the demand-pull inflation eventually causes adjustments of nominal wages that return the economy to its full-employment output Q_f.

---

[1] We say "ultimately" because the initial leftward shift in short-run aggregate supply will intersect the long-run aggregate supply curve AS$_{LR}$ at price level P_2 (review Figure 18.1b). But the intersection of AD₂ and this new short-run aggregate supply curve (that is not shown in Figure 18.3) will produce a price level above P_2. (You may want to pencil this in to make sure that you understand this point.) Again nominal wages will rise, shifting the short-run aggregate supply curve farther leftward. The process will continue until the economy moves to point *c*, where the short-run aggregate supply curve is AS₂, the price level is P_3, and real output is Q_f.

Cost-Push Inflation in the Extended AD-AS Model

Cost-push inflation arises from factors that increase the cost of production at each price level, shifting the aggregate supply curve leftward and raising the equilibrium price level. Previously (Figure 12.10), we considered cost-push inflation using only the short-run aggregate supply curve. Now we want to analyze that type of inflation in its long-run context.

Analysis Look at Figure 18.4, in which we again assume that the economy is initially operating at price level P_1 and output level Q_f (point *a*). Suppose that international oil producers agree to reduce the supply of oil to boost its price by, say, 100 percent. As a result, the per-unit production cost of producing and transporting goods and services rises substantially in the economy represented by Figure 18.4. This increase in per-unit production costs shifts the short-run aggregate supply curve to the left, as from AS₁ to AS₂, and the price level rises from P_1 to P_2 (as seen by comparing points *a* and *b*). In this case, the leftward shift of the aggregate supply curve is *not a response* to a price-level increase, as it was in our previous discussions of demand-pull inflation; it is the *initiating cause* of the price-level increase.

Policy Dilemma Cost-push inflation creates a dilemma for policymakers. Without some expansionary stabilization policy, aggregate demand in Figure 18.4 remains in

FIGURE 18.4 Cost-push inflation in the extended AD-AS model.
Cost-push inflation occurs when the short-run aggregate supply curve shifts leftward, as from AS₁ to AS₂. If government counters the decline in real output by increasing aggregate demand to the broken line, the price level rises even more. That is, the economy moves in steps from *a* to *b* to *c*. In contrast, if government allows a recession to occur, nominal wages eventually fall and the aggregate supply curve shifts back rightward to its original location. The economy moves from *a* to *b* and eventually back to *a*.

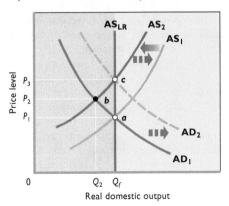

place at AD_1 and real output declines from Q_f to Q_2. Government can counter this recession, negative GDP gap, and attendant high unemployment by using fiscal policy and monetary policy to increase aggregate demand to AD_2. But there is a potential policy trap here: An increase in aggregate demand to AD_2 will further raise inflation by increasing the price level from P_2 to P_3 (a move from point b to point c).

Suppose the government recognizes this policy trap and decides not to increase aggregate demand from AD_1 to AD_2 (you can now disregard the dashed AD_2 curve) and instead decides to allow a cost-push-created recession to run its course. How will that happen? Widespread layoffs, plant shutdowns, and business failures eventually occur. At some point the demand for oil, labor, and other inputs will decline so much that oil prices and nominal wages will decline. When that happens, the initial leftward shift of the short-run aggregate supply curve will reverse itself. That is, the declining per-unit production costs caused by the recession will shift the short-run aggregate supply curve rightward from AS_2 to AS_1. The price level will return to P_1, and the full-employment level of output will be restored at Q_f (point a on the long-run aggregate supply curve AS_{LR}).

This analysis yields two generalizations:

- If the government attempts to maintain full employment when there is cost-push inflation, even more inflation will occur.

- If the government takes a hands-off approach to cost-push inflation, the recession will linger. Although falling input prices will eventually undo the initial rise in per-unit production costs, the economy in the meantime will experience high unemployment and a loss of real output.

Recession and the Extended AD-AS Model

By far the most controversial application of the extended AD-AS model is its application to recession (or depression) caused by decreases in aggregate demand. We will look at this controversy in detail in Chapter 19; here we simply identify the key point of contention.

Suppose in Figure 18.5 that aggregate demand initially is AD_1 and that the short-run and long-run aggregate supply curves are AS_1 and AS_{LR}, respectively. Therefore, as shown by point a, the price level is P_1 and output is Q_f. Now suppose that investment spending declines dramatically, reducing aggregate demand to AD_2. Observe that real output declines from Q_f to Q_1, indicating that a recession has occurred. But if we make the controversial assumption that prices and wages are flexible downward, the

FIGURE 18.5 Recession in the extended AD-AS model. A recession occurs when aggregate demand shifts leftward, as from AD_1 to AD_2. If prices and wages are downwardly flexible, the price level falls from P_1 to P_2 as the economy moves from point a to point b. With the economy in recession at point b, wages eventually fall, shifting the aggregate supply curve from AS_1 to AS_2. The price level declines to P_3, and real output returns to Q_f. The economy moves from a to b to c.

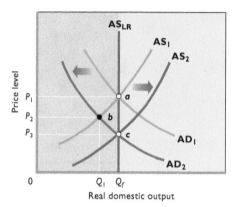

price level falls from P_1 to P_2. With the economy producing below potential output at point b, demand for inputs will be low. Eventually, nominal wages themselves fall to restore the previous real wage; when that happens, the short-run aggregate supply curve shifts rightward from AS_1 to AS_2. The negative GDP gap evaporates without the need for expansionary fiscal or monetary policy since real output expands from Q_1 (point b) back to Q_f (point c). The economy is again located on its long-run aggregate supply curve AS_{LR}, but now at lower price level P_3.

There is much disagreement about this hypothetical scenario. The key point of dispute revolves around the degree to which both input and output prices may be downwardly inflexible and how long it would take in the actual economy for the necessary downward price and wage adjustments to occur to regain the full-employment level of output. For now, suffice it to say that most economists believe that if such adjustments are forthcoming, they will occur only after the economy has experienced a relatively long-lasting recession with its accompanying high unemployment and large loss of output. The severity and length of the major recession of 2007–2009 has strengthened this view. Therefore, economists recommend active monetary policy, and perhaps fiscal policy, to counteract recessions.

Economic Growth with Ongoing Inflation

In our analysis so far, we have seen how demand and supply shocks can cause, respectively, demand-push inflation and cost-push inflation. But in these previous cases, the

FIGURE 18.6 **Production possibilities and long-run aggregate supply.** (a) Economic growth driven by supply factors (such as improved technologies or the use of more or better resources) shifts an economy's production possibilities curve outward, as from *AB* to *CD*. (b) The same factors shift the economy's long-run aggregate supply curve to the right, as from AS_{LR1} to AS_{LR2}.

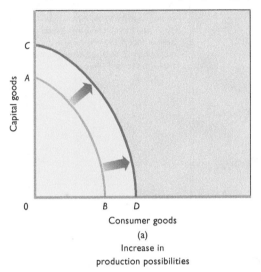
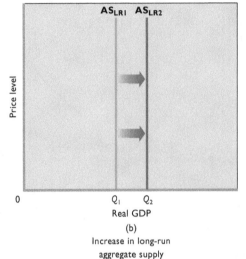

(a)

Increase in
production possibilities

(b)

Increase in long-run
aggregate supply

extent of the inflation was *finite* because the size of the initial movement in either the AD curve or the AS curve was *limited*. For instance, in Figure 18.3, the aggregate demand curve shifts right by a limited amount, from AD_1 to AD_2. As the economy's equilibrium moves from *a* to *b* to *c*, the price level rises from P_1 to P_2 to P_3. During this transition, inflation obviously occurs because the price level is rising. But once the economy reaches its new equilibrium at point *c*, the price level remains constant at P_3 and no further inflation takes place. That is, the limited movement in aggregate demand causes a limited amount of inflation that ends when the economy returns to full employment.

But the modern economy almost always experiences continuous, but usually mild, positive rates of inflation. That can only happen with ongoing shifts in either the aggregate demand or long-run aggregate supply curves because any single, finite shift will only cause inflation of limited duration. This insight is crucial to understanding why modern economies usually experience ongoing inflation while achieving economic growth. Both aggregate demand and long-run aggregate supply increase over time in the actual economy, and inflation occurs because the increases in aggregate demand generally exceed the increases in long-run aggregate supply. It will be helpful to examine this point graphically.

Increases in Long-Run Aggregate Supply As discussed in Chapter 8, economic growth is driven by supply

factors such as improved technologies and access to more or better resources. Economists illustrate economic growth as either an outward shift of an economy's production possibilities curve or as a rightward shift of its long-run aggregate supply curve. As shown in Figure 18.6, the outward shift of the production possibilities curve from *AB* to *CD* in graph *a* is equivalent to the rightward shift of the economy's long-run aggregate supply curve from AS_{LR1} to AS_{LR2} in graph *b*.

Let's simply transfer this rightward shift of the economy's long-run aggregate supply curve to Figure 18.7, which depicts economic growth in the United States in the context of the extended aggregate demand–aggregate supply model. Suppose the economy's long-run aggregate supply curve initially is AS_{LR1}, while its aggregate demand curve and short-run aggregate supply curve are AD_1 and AS_1, as shown. The equilibrium price level is P_1 and the equilibrium level of real output is Q_1.

Now let's assume that economic growth driven by changes in supply factors (quantity and quality of resources and technology) shifts the long-run aggregate supply curve rightward from AS_{LR1} to AS_{LR2} while the economy's aggregate demand curve remains at AD_1. Also, suppose that product and resource prices are flexible downward. The economy's potential output will expand, as reflected by the increase of available real output from Q_1 to Q_2. With aggregate demand constant at AD_1, the rightward shift of the long-run aggregate supply curve will lower the price level from P_1 to P_3. Taken alone,

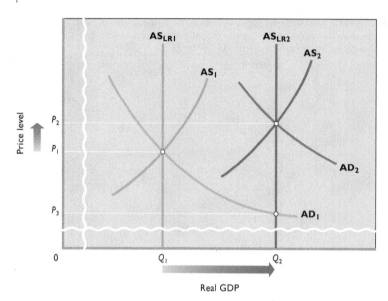

FIGURE 18.7 Depicting U.S. growth via the extended AD-AS model. Long-run aggregate supply and short-run aggregate supply have increased over time, as from AS_{LR1} to AS_{LR2} and AS_1 to AS_2. Simultaneously, aggregate demand has shifted rightward, as from AD_1 to AD_2. The actual outcome of these combined shifts has been economic growth, shown as the increase in real output from Q_1 to Q_2, accompanied by mild inflation, shown as the rise in the price level from P_1 to P_2.

expansions of long-run aggregate supply in the economy are deflationary.

Increases in Aggregate Demand and Inflation

But a decline in the price level, such as the one from P_1 to P_3 in Figure 18.7, is not part of the long-run U.S. growth experience. Why not? The answer is that the nation's central bank—the Federal Reserve—engineers ongoing increases in the nation's money supply to create rightward shifts of the aggregate demand curve. These increases in aggregate demand would be highly inflationary absent the increases in long-run aggregate supply. But because the Fed usually makes sure that the inflationary rightward shifts of the aggregate demand curve proceed only slightly faster than the deflationary rightward shifts of the aggregate supply curve, only mild inflation occurs along with economic growth.

We illustrate this outcome in Figure 18.7, where aggregate demand shifts to the right from AD_1 to AD_2 at the same time long-run aggregate supply shifts rightward from AS_{LR1} to AS_{LR2}. Real output expands from Q_1 to Q_2 and the price level increases from P_1 to P_2. At the higher price level P_2, the economy confronts a new short-run aggregate supply curve AS_2. The changes shown in Figure 18.7 describe the actual U.S. experience: economic growth, accompanied by mild inflation. Real output on average increases at about 3.4 percent annually and inflation averages 2 to 3 percent a year.

Of course, other long-term outcomes besides that depicted are entirely possible. Whether deflation, zero inflation, mild inflation, or rapid inflation accompanies economic growth depends on the extent to which aggregate demand increases relative to long-run aggregate supply. Over long periods, any inflation that accompanies economic growth is exclusively the result of aggregate demand increasing more rapidly than long-run aggregate supply. The expansion of long-run aggregate supply—of potential real GDP—is never the cause of inflation.

QUICK REVIEW 18.2

- In the short run, demand-pull inflation raises both the price level and real output; in the long run, nominal wages rise, the short-run aggregate supply curve shifts to the left, and only the price level increases.

- Cost-push inflation creates a policy dilemma for the government: If it engages in an expansionary policy to increase output, additional inflation will occur; if it does nothing, the recession will linger until input prices have fallen by enough to return the economy to producing at potential output.

- In the short run, a decline in aggregate demand reduces real output (creates a recession); in the long run, prices and nominal wages presumably fall, the short-run aggregate supply curve shifts to the right, and real output returns to its full-employment level.

- The economy has ongoing inflation because the Fed uses monetary policy to shift the AD curve to the right faster than the supply factors of economic growth shift the long-run AS curve to the right.

The Inflation-Unemployment Relationship

LO18.3 Explain the short-run trade-off between inflation and unemployment (the Phillips Curve).

We have just seen that the Fed can determine how much inflation occurs in the economy by how much it causes aggregate demand to shift relative to aggregate supply. Given that low inflation and low unemployment rates are the Fed's major economic goals, its ability to control inflation brings up at least two interesting policy questions: Are low unemployment and low inflation compatible goals or conflicting goals? What explains situations in which high unemployment and high inflation coexist?

The extended AD-AS model supports three significant generalizations relating to these questions:

- Under normal circumstances, there is a short-run trade-off between the rate of inflation and the rate of unemployment.

- Aggregate supply shocks can cause both higher rates of inflation and higher rates of unemployment.

- There is no significant trade-off between inflation and unemployment over long periods of time.

Let's examine each of these generalizations.

The Phillips Curve

We can demonstrate the short-run trade-off between the rate of inflation and the rate of unemployment through the **Phillips Curve,** named after A. W. Phillips, who developed the idea in Great Britain. This curve, generalized in Figure 18.8a, suggests an inverse relationship between the rate of inflation and the rate of unemployment. Lower unemployment rates (measured as leftward movements on the horizontal axis) are associated with higher rates of inflation (measured as upward movements on the vertical axis).

ORIGIN OF THE IDEA

O18.1
Phillips Curve

The underlying rationale of the Phillips Curve becomes apparent when we view the short-run aggregate supply curve in Figure 18.9 and perform a simple mental experiment. Suppose that in some short-run period aggregate demand expands from AD_0 to AD_2, either because firms decide to buy more capital goods or the government decides to increase its expenditures. Whatever the cause, in the short run the price level rises from P_0 to P_2 and real output rises from Q_0 to Q_2. As real output rises, the unemployment rate falls.

FIGURE 18.8 The Phillips Curve: concept and empirical data. (a) The Phillips Curve relates annual rates of inflation and annual rates of unemployment for a series of years. Because this is an inverse relationship, there presumably is a trade-off between unemployment and inflation. (b) Data points for the 1960s seemed to confirm the Phillips Curve concept. (Note: The unemployment rates are annual averages and the inflation rates are on a December-to-December basis.)

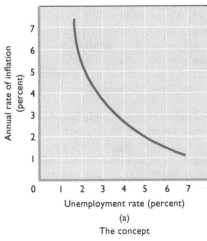

(a)
The concept

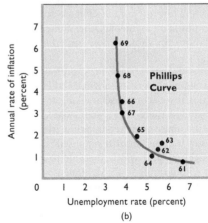

(b)
Data for the 1960s

Source: Bureau of Labor Statistics, **www.bls.gov**.

FIGURE 18.9 **The short-run effect of changes in aggregate demand on real output and the price level.** Comparing the effects of various possible increases in aggregate demand leads to the conclusion that the larger the increase in aggregate demand, the higher the rate of inflation and the greater the increase in real output. Because real output and the unemployment rate move in opposite directions, we can generalize that, given short-run aggregate supply, high rates of inflation should be accompanied by low rates of unemployment.

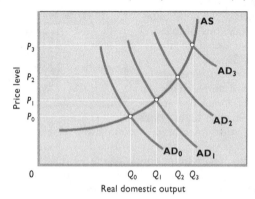

Now let's compare what would have happened if the increase in aggregate demand had been larger, say, from AD_0 to AD_3. The equilibrium at P_3 and Q_3 indicates that the amount of inflation and the growth of real output would both have been greater (and that the unemployment rate would have been lower). Similarly, suppose aggregate demand during the year had increased only modestly, from AD_0 to AD_1. Compared with our shift from AD_0 to AD_2, the amount of inflation and the growth of real output would have been smaller (and the unemployment rate higher).

The generalization we draw from this mental experiment is this: *Assuming a constant short-run aggregate supply curve,* high rates of inflation are accompanied by low rates of unemployment, and low rates of inflation are accompanied by high rates of unemployment. Other things equal, the expected relationship should look something like Figure 18.8a.

Figure 18.8b reveals that the facts for the 1960s nicely fit the theory. On the basis of that evidence and evidence from other countries, most economists working at the end of the 1960s concluded there was a stable, predictable trade-off between unemployment and inflation. Moreover, U.S. economic policy was built on that supposed trade-off. According to this thinking, it was impossible to achieve "full employment without inflation": Manipulation of aggregate demand through fiscal and monetary measures would simply move the economy along the Phillips Curve. An expansionary fiscal and monetary policy that boosted aggregate demand and lowered the unemployment rate would simultaneously increase inflation. A restrictive fiscal

and monetary policy could be used to reduce the rate of inflation but only at the cost of a higher unemployment rate and more forgone production. Society had to choose between the incompatible goals of price stability and full employment; it had to decide where to locate on its Phillips Curve.

For reasons we will soon see, today's economists reject the idea of a stable, predictable Phillips Curve. Nevertheless, they agree there is a short-run trade-off between unemployment and inflation. *Given short-run aggregate supply,* increases in aggregate demand increase real output and reduce the unemployment rate. As the unemployment rate falls and dips below the natural rate, the excessive spending produces demand-pull inflation. Conversely, when recession sets in and the unemployment rate increases, the weak aggregate demand that caused the recession also leads to lower inflation rates.

Periods of exceptionally low unemployment rates and inflation rates do occur, but only under special sets of economic circumstances. One such period was the late 1990s, when faster productivity growth increased aggregate supply and fully blunted the inflationary impact of rapidly rising aggregate demand (review Figure 12.11).

Aggregate Supply Shocks and the Phillips Curve

The unemployment-inflation experience of the 1970s and early 1980s demolished the idea of an always-stable Phillips Curve. In Figure 18.10 we show the Phillips Curve for the 1960s in blue and then add the data points for 1970 through 2012. Observe that in most of the years of the 1970s and early 1980s, the economy experienced both higher inflation rates and higher unemployment rates than it did in the 1960s. In fact, inflation and unemployment rose simultaneously in some of those years. This condition is called **stagflation**—a media term that combines the words "stagnation" and "inflation." If there still was any such thing as a Phillips Curve, it had clearly shifted outward, perhaps as shown.

Adverse Aggregate Supply Shocks The data points for the 1970s and early 1980s support our second generalization: Aggregate supply shocks can cause both higher rates of inflation and higher rates of unemployment. A series of adverse **aggregate supply shocks**—sudden, large increases in resource costs that jolt an economy's short-run aggregate supply curve leftward—hit the economy in the 1970s and early 1980s. The most significant of these shocks was a quadrupling of oil prices by the Organization of Petroleum Exporting Countries

FIGURE 18.10 Inflation rates and unemployment rates, 1960–2012. A series of aggregate supply shocks in the 1970s resulted in higher rates of inflation *and* higher rates of unemployment. So data points for the 1970s and 1980s tended to be above and to the right of the blue Phillips Curve for the 1960s. In the 1990s the inflation-unemployment data points slowly moved back toward the 1960s Phillips Curve. Points for the late 1990s and 2000s are similar to those from the 1960s. (Note: The unemployment rates are annual averages and the inflation rates are on a December-to-December basis.)

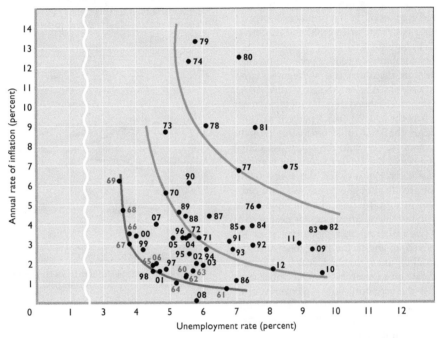

Source: Bureau of Labor Statistics, **www.bls.gov**.

(OPEC). Consequently, the cost of producing and distributing virtually every product and service rose rapidly. (Other factors working to increase U.S. costs during this period included major agricultural shortfalls, a greatly depreciated dollar, wage hikes previously held down by wage-price controls, and slower rates of productivity growth.)

These shocks shifted the aggregate supply curve to the left and distorted the usual inflation-unemployment relationship. Remember that we derived the inverse relationship between the rate of inflation and the unemployment rate shown in Figure 18.8a by shifting the aggregate demand curve along a stable short-run aggregate supply curve (Figure 18.9). But the cost-push inflation model shown in Figure 18.4 tells us that a *leftward shift* of the short-run aggregate supply curve increases the price level and reduces real output (and increases the unemployment rate). This, say most economists, is what happened in two periods in the 1970s. The U.S. unemployment rate shot up from 4.9 percent in 1973 to 8.5 percent in 1975, contributing to a significant decline in real GDP. In the same

period, the U.S. price level rose by 21 percent. The stagflation scenario recurred in 1978, when OPEC increased oil prices by more than 100 percent. The U.S. price level rose by 26 percent over the 1978–1980 period, while unemployment increased from 6.1 to 7.1 percent.

Stagflation's Demise Another look at Figure 18.10 reveals a generally inward movement of the inflation-unemployment points between 1982 and 1989. By 1989 the lingering effects of the earlier period had subsided. One precursor to this favorable trend was the deep recession of 1981–1982, largely caused by a restrictive monetary policy aimed at reducing double-digit inflation. The recession upped the unemployment rate to 9.5 percent in 1982. With so many workers unemployed, those who were working accepted smaller increases in their nominal wages—or, in some cases, wage reductions—in order to preserve their jobs. Firms, in turn, restrained their price increases to try to retain their relative shares of a greatly diminished market.

Other factors were at work. Foreign competition throughout this period held down wage and price hikes in several basic industries such as automobiles and steel. Deregulation of the airline and trucking industries also resulted in wage reductions or so-called wage givebacks. A significant decline in OPEC's monopoly power and a greatly reduced reliance on oil in the production process produced a stunning fall in the price of oil and its derivative products, such as gasoline.

All these factors combined to reduce per-unit production costs and to shift the short-run aggregate supply curve rightward (as from AS_2 to AS_1 in Figure 18.4). Employment and output expanded, and the unemployment rate fell from 9.6 percent in 1983 to 5.3 percent in 1989. Figure 18.10 reveals that the inflation-unemployment points for recent years are closer to the points associated with the Phillips Curve of the 1960s than to the points in the late 1970s and early 1980s. Even the recession of 2007–2009 did not greatly alter the recent inflation rate–unemployment rate pattern. In 2008, the unemployment rate was 5.8 percent, but the inflation rate was near zero at just 0.1 percent. The inflation-unemployment point for 2009, however, moved up and to the right relative to the point for 2008. In 2009 unemployment was 9.3 percent, while the inflation rate on a December-to-December basis was 2.7 percent. As the economy slowly recovered after the Great Recession, the points for 2010, 2011, and 2012 gradually moved leftward as the unemployment rate slowly declined from 9.6 percent to 8.1 percent and the inflation rate remained moderate at between 1.5 percent and 3.0 percent.

The media sometimes express the sum of the unemployment rate and the inflation rate as a rough gauge of the economic discomfort that inflation and unemployment jointly impose on an economy in a particular year. The sum of the two rates is used to compute the *misery index*. For example, a nation with a 5 percent unemployment rate and a 5 percent inflation rate has a misery index number of 10, as does a nation with an 8 percent unemployment rate and a 2 percent inflation rate.

Global Perspective 18.1 shows the misery index for several nations between 2001 and 2012. (It uses average annual inflation rates, not the December-to-December inflation rates used to construct Figure 18.10.) The U.S. misery index number has been neither exceptionally low nor exceptionally high relative to the misery index numbers for the other major economies shown. But bear in mind that economists do not put much stock in the misery index because they do not view the national discomfort associated with a 1 percent change in inflation and a 1 percent change in unemployment as

GLOBAL PERSPECTIVE 18.1

The Misery Index, Selected Nations, 2001–2012

The U.S. misery index number (the sum of its unemployment rate and inflation rate) has generally been in the mid-range of such numbers relative to other major economies in recent years.

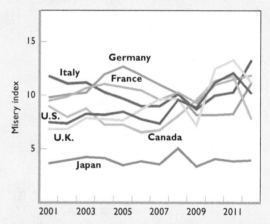

Source: Bureau of Labor Statistics, **stats.bls.gov**. Inflation rates and unemployment rates in this calculation are both on an average-annual basis.

necessarily equivalent. In particular, the misery index can greatly disguise the extent of hardship during a recession. The rise in the unemployment rate in these circumstances causes a huge loss of national output and income (and misery!), even if the higher unemployment rate is partially or fully offset with a decline in the rate of inflation.

The Long-Run Phillips Curve

LO18.4 Discuss why there is no long-run trade-off between inflation and unemployment.

The overall set of data points in Figure 18.10 supports our third generalization relating to the inflation-unemployment relationship: There is no apparent *long-run* trade-off between inflation and unemployment. Economists point out that when decades as opposed to a few years are considered, any rate of inflation is consistent with the natural rate of unemployment prevailing at that time. We know from Chapter 9 that the natural rate of unemployment is the unemployment rate that occurs when cyclical unemployment is zero; it is the full-employment rate of unemployment, or the rate of unemployment when the economy achieves its potential output.

FIGURE 18.11 **The long-run vertical Phillips Curve.** Increases in aggregate demand beyond those consistent with full-employment output may temporarily boost profits, output, and employment (as from a_1 to b_1). But nominal wages eventually will catch up so as to sustain real wages. When they do, profits will fall, negating the previous short-run stimulus to production and employment (the economy now moves from b_1 to a_2). Consequently, there is no trade-off between the rates of inflation and unemployment in the long run; that is, the long-run Phillips Curve is roughly a vertical line at the economy's natural rate of unemployment.

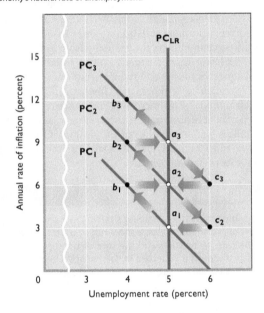

How can there be a short-run inflation-unemployment trade-off but not a long-run trade-off? Figure 18.11 provides the answer.

Short-Run Phillips Curve

Consider Phillips Curve PC_1 in Figure 18.11. Suppose the economy initially is experiencing a 3 percent rate of inflation and a 5 percent natural rate of unemployment. Such short-term curves as PC_1, PC_2, and PC_3 (drawn as straight lines for simplicity) exist because the actual rate of inflation is not always the same as the expected rate.

Establishing an additional point on Phillips Curve PC_1 will clarify this. We begin at a_1, where we assume nominal wages are set on the assumption that the 3 percent rate of inflation will continue. That is, because workers expect output prices to rise by 3 percent per year, they negotiate wage contracts that feature 3 percent per year increases in nominal wages so that these nominal wage increases will exactly offset the expected rise in prices and thereby keep their real wages the same.

But suppose that the rate of inflation rises to 6 percent, perhaps because the Fed has decided to move the AD curve to the right even faster than it had been before. With a nominal wage rate set on the expectation that the 3 percent rate of inflation will continue, the higher product prices raise business profits. Firms respond to the higher profits by hiring more workers and increasing output. In the short run, the economy moves to b_1, which, in contrast to a_1, involves a lower rate of unemployment (4 percent) and a higher rate of inflation (6 percent). The move from a_1 to b_1 is consistent both with an upsloping aggregate supply curve and with the inflation-unemployment trade-off implied by the Phillips Curve analysis. But this short-run Phillips Curve simply is a manifestation of the following principle: *When the actual rate of inflation is higher than expected, profits temporarily rise and the unemployment rate temporarily falls.*

Long-Run Vertical Phillips Curve

But point b_1 is not a stable equilibrium. Workers will recognize that their nominal wages have not increased as fast as inflation and will therefore renegotiate their labor contracts so that they feature faster increases in nominal wages. These faster increases in nominal wages make up for the higher rate of inflation and restore the workers' lost purchasing power. As these new labor contracts kick in, business profits will fall to their prior level. The reduction in profits means that the original motivation to employ more workers and increase output has disappeared.

Unemployment then returns to its natural level at point a_2. Note, however, that the economy now faces a higher actual and expected rate of inflation—6 percent rather than 3 percent. This happens because the new labor contracts feature 6 percent per year increases in wages to make up for the 6 percent per year inflation rate. Because wages are a production cost, this faster increase in wage rates will imply faster future increases in output prices as firms are forced to raise prices more rapidly to make up for the faster future rate of wage growth. Stated a bit differently, the initial increase in inflation will become *persistent* because it leads to renegotiated labor contracts that will perpetuate the higher rate of inflation. In addition, because the new labor contracts are public, it will also be the case that the higher rates of inflation that they will cause will be *expected* by everyone rather than being a surprise.

In view of the higher 6 percent expected rate of inflation, the short-run Phillips Curve shifts upward from PC_1 to PC_2 in Figure 18.11. An "along-the-Phillips-Curve" kind of move from a_1 to b_1 on PC_1 is merely a short-run or transient occurrence. In the long run, after nominal wage contracts catch up with increases in the inflation rate, unemployment returns to its natural rate at a_2, and there is a new short-run Phillips Curve PC_2 at the higher expected rate of inflation.

The scenario repeats if aggregate demand continues to increase. Prices rise momentarily ahead of nominal wages, profits expand, and employment and output increase (as implied by the move from a_2 to b_2). But, in time, nominal wages increase so as to restore real wages. Profits then fall to their original level, pushing employment back to the normal rate at a_3. The economy's "reward" for lowering the unemployment rate below the natural rate is a still higher (9 percent) rate of inflation.

Movements along the short-run Phillips Curve (a_1 to b_1 on PC_1) cause the curve to shift to a less favorable position (PC_2, then PC_3, and so on). A stable Phillips Curve with the dependable series of unemployment-rate–inflation-rate trade-offs simply does not exist in the long run. The economy is characterized by a **long-run vertical Phillips Curve.**

The vertical line through a_1, a_2, and a_3 shows the long-run relationship between unemployment and inflation. Any rate of inflation is consistent with the 5 percent natural rate of unemployment. So, in this view, society ought to choose a low rate of inflation rather than a high one.

ORIGIN OF THE IDEA

O18.2

Long-run vertical Phillips Curve

Disinflation

The distinction between the short-run Phillips Curve and the long-run Phillips Curve also helps explain **disinflation**—reductions in the inflation rate from year to year. Suppose that in Figure 18.11 the economy is at a_3, where the inflation rate is 9 percent. And suppose that a decline in the rate at which aggregate demand shifts to the right faster than aggregate supply (as happened during the 1981–1982 recession) reduces inflation below the 9 percent expected rate, say, to 6 percent. Business profits fall because prices are rising less rapidly than wages. The nominal wage increases, remember, were set on the assumption that the 9 percent rate of inflation would continue. In response to the decline in profits, firms reduce their employment and consequently the unemployment rate rises. The economy temporarily slides downward from point a_3 to c_3 along the short-run Phillips Curve PC_3. *When the actual rate of inflation is lower than the expected rate, profits temporarily fall and the unemployment rate temporarily rises.*

Firms and workers eventually adjust their expectations to the new 6 percent rate of inflation, and thus newly negotiated wage increases decline. Profits are restored, employment rises, and the unemployment rate falls back to its natural rate of 5 percent at a_2. Because the expected rate of inflation is now 6 percent, the short-run Phillips Curve PC_3 shifts leftward to PC_2.

If the rate at which aggregate demand shifts to the right faster than aggregate supply declines even more, the scenario will continue. Inflation declines from 6 percent to, say, 3 percent, moving the economy from a_2 to c_2 along PC_2. The lower-than-expected rate of inflation (lower prices) squeezes profits and reduces employment. But, in the long run, firms respond to the lower profits by reducing their nominal wage increases. Profits are restored and unemployment returns to its natural rate at a_1 as the short-run Phillips Curve moves from PC_2 to PC_1. Once again, the long-run Phillips Curve is vertical at the 5 percent natural rate of unemployment.

QUICK REVIEW 18.3

- As implied by the upsloping short-run aggregate supply curve, there may be a short-run trade-off between the rate of inflation and the rate of unemployment. This trade-off is reflected in the Phillips Curve, which shows that lower rates of inflation are associated with higher rates of unemployment.

- Aggregate supply shocks that produce severe cost-push inflation can cause stagflation—simultaneous increases in the inflation rate and the unemployment rate. Such stagflation occurred from 1973–1975 and recurred from 1978–1980, producing Phillips Curve data points above and to the right of the Phillips Curve for the 1960s.

- After all nominal wage adjustments to increases and decreases in the rate of inflation have occurred, the economy ends up back at its full-employment level of output and its natural rate of unemployment. The long-run Phillips Curve therefore is vertical at the natural rate of unemployment.

Taxation and Aggregate Supply

LO18.5 Explain the relationship between tax rates, tax revenues, and aggregate supply.

A final topic in our discussion of aggregate supply is taxation, a key aspect of **supply-side economics.** "Supply-side economists" or "supply-siders" stress that changes in aggregate supply are an active force in determining the levels of inflation, unemployment, and economic growth. Government policies can either impede or promote rightward shifts of the short-run and long-run aggregate supply curves shown in Figure 18.2. One such policy is taxation.

These economists say that the enlargement of the U.S. tax system has impaired incentives to work, save, and invest. In this view, high tax rates impede productivity growth and hence slow the expansion of long-run aggregate supply. By reducing the after-tax rewards of workers and producers, high tax rates reduce the financial attractiveness of working, saving, and investing.

Supply-siders focus their attention on *marginal tax rates*—the rates on extra dollars of income—because those rates affect the benefits from working, saving, or investing more. In 2013 marginal federal income tax rates varied from 10 to 39.6 percent in the United States.

Taxes and Incentives to Work

Supply-siders believe that how long and how hard people work depends on the amounts of additional after-tax earnings they derive from their efforts. They say that lower marginal tax rates on earned incomes induce more work, and therefore increase aggregate inputs of labor. Lower marginal tax rates increase the after-tax wage rate and make leisure more expensive and work more attractive. The higher opportunity cost of leisure encourages people to substitute work for leisure. This increase in productive effort is achieved in many ways: by increasing the number of hours worked per day or week, by encouraging workers to postpone retirement, by inducing more people to enter the labor force, by motivating people to work harder, and by avoiding long periods of unemployment.

Incentives to Save and Invest

High marginal tax rates also reduce the rewards for saving and investing. For example, suppose that Tony saves $10,000 at 8 percent interest, bringing him $800 of interest per year. If his marginal tax rate is 40 percent, his after-tax interest earnings will be $480, not $800, and his after-tax interest rate will fall to 4.8 percent. While Tony might be willing to save (forgo current consumption) for an 8 percent return on his saving, he might rather consume when the return is only 4.8 percent.

Saving, remember, is the prerequisite of investment. Thus, supply-side economists recommend lower marginal tax rates on interest earned from saving. They also call for lower taxes on income from capital to ensure that there are ready investment outlets for the economy's enhanced pool of saving. A critical determinant of

investment spending is the expected *after-tax* return on that spending.

To summarize: Lower marginal tax rates encourage saving and investing. Workers therefore find themselves equipped with more and technologically superior machinery and equipment. Labor productivity rises, and that expands long-run aggregate supply and economic growth, which in turn keeps unemployment rates and inflation low.

The Laffer Curve

In the supply-side view, reductions in marginal tax rates increase the nation's aggregate supply and can leave the nation's tax revenues unchanged or even enlarge them. Thus, supply-side tax cuts need not produce federal budget deficits.

This idea is based on the **Laffer Curve,** named after Arthur Laffer, who popularized it. As Figure 18.12 shows, the Laffer Curve depicts the relationship between tax rates and tax revenues. As tax rates increase from 0 to 100 percent, tax revenues increase from zero to some maximum level (at *m*) and then fall to zero. Tax revenues decline beyond some point because higher tax rates discourage economic activity, thereby shrinking the tax base (domestic output and income). This is easiest to see at the extreme, where the tax rate is 100 percent. Tax revenues here are, in theory, reduced to zero because the 100 percent confiscatory tax rate has halted production. A 100 percent tax rate applied to a tax base of zero yields no revenue.

In the early 1980s, Laffer suggested that the United States was at a point such as *n* on the curve in Figure 18.12.

FIGURE 18.12 The Laffer Curve. The Laffer Curve suggests that up to point *m* higher tax rates will result in larger tax revenues. But tax rates higher than *m* will adversely affect incentives to work and produce, reducing the size of the tax base (output and income) to the extent that tax revenues will decline. It follows that if tax rates are above *m*, reductions in tax rates will produce increases in tax revenues.

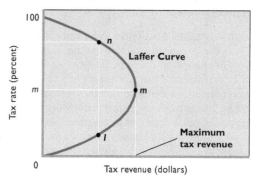

At *n*, tax rates are so high that production is discouraged to the extent that tax revenues are below the maximum at *m*. If the economy is at *n*, then lower tax rates can either increase tax revenues or leave them unchanged. For example, lowering the tax rate from point *n* to point *l* would bolster the economy such that the government would bring in the same total amount of tax revenue as before.

Laffer's reasoning was that lower tax rates stimulate incentives to work, save and invest, innovate, and accept business risks, thus triggering an expansion of real output and income. That enlarged tax base sustains tax revenues even though tax rates are lowered. Indeed, between *n* and *m* lower tax rates result in *increased* tax revenue.

Also, when taxes are lowered, tax avoidance (which is legal) and tax evasion (which is not) decline. High marginal tax rates prompt taxpayers to avoid taxes through various tax shelters, such as buying municipal bonds, on which the interest earned is tax-free. High rates also encourage some taxpayers to conceal income from the Internal Revenue Service. Lower tax rates reduce the inclination to engage in either tax avoidance or tax evasion.

The Laffer Curve also implies that for any particular amount of tax revenue that the government can possibly collect, there will be both a high tax rate at which that amount of revenue can be collected as well as a low tax rate at which that amount of revenue can be collected. As an example, compare points *n* an *l* in Figure 18.12. Point *n* has a high tax rate and point *l* has a low tax rate, but they both collect the same amount of tax revenue. So if the government's major goal when setting tax rates is simply to collect a particular total amount of tax revenue, Laffer argued that the government should always opt for the lower tax rate. By doing so, the government would collect the revenue it desired while impinging as little as possible on the private economy.

Criticisms of the Laffer Curve

The Laffer Curve and its supply-side implications have been subject to severe criticism.

Taxes, Incentives, and Time A fundamental criticism relates to the degree to which economic incentives are sensitive to changes in tax rates. Skeptics say ample empirical evidence shows that the impact of a tax cut on incentives is small, of uncertain direction, and relatively slow to emerge. For example, with respect to work incentives, studies indicate that decreases in tax rates lead some people to work more but lead others to work less. Those who work more are enticed by the higher after-tax pay; they substitute work for leisure because the opportunity cost of

CONSIDER THIS . . .

Sherwood Forest

The popularization of the idea that tax-rate reductions may increase tax revenues owes much to Arthur Laffer's ability to present his ideas simply. In explaining his thoughts to a *Wall Street Journal* editor over lunch, Laffer reportedly took out his pen and drew the curve on a napkin. The editor retained the napkin and later reproduced the curve in an editorial in *The Wall Street Journal*. The Laffer Curve was born. The idea it portrayed became the centerpiece of economic policy under the Reagan administration (1981–1989), which cut tax rates on personal income by 25 percent over a three-year period.

Laffer illustrated his supply-side views with a story relating to Robin Hood, who, you may recall, stole from the rich to give to the poor. Laffer likened people traveling through Sherwood Forest to taxpayers, whereas Robin Hood and his band of merry men were government. As taxpayers passed through the forest, Robin Hood and his men intercepted them and forced them to hand over their money. Laffer asked audiences, "Do you think that travelers continued to go through Sherwood Forest?"

The answer he sought and got, of course, was "no." Taxpayers will avoid Sherwood Forest to the greatest extent possible. They will lower their taxable income by reducing work hours, retiring earlier, saving less, and engaging in tax avoidance and tax evasion activities. Robin Hood and his men may end up with less revenue than if they collected a relatively small "tax" from each traveler for passage through the forest.

leisure has increased. But other people work less because the higher after-tax pay enables them to "buy more leisure." With the tax cut, they can earn the same level of after-tax income as before with fewer work hours.

Inflation or Higher Real Interest Rates Most economists think that the demand-side effects of a tax cut are more immediate and certain than longer-term supply-side effects. Thus, tax cuts undertaken when the economy is at or near full employment may produce increases in aggregate demand that overwhelm any increase in aggregate supply. The likely result is inflation or restrictive monetary policy to prevent it. If the latter, real interest rates will rise and investment will decline. This will defeat the purpose of the supply-side tax cuts.

Position on the Curve Skeptics say that the Laffer Curve is merely a logical proposition and assert that there must be some level of tax rates between 0 and 100 percent at which tax revenues will be at their maximum. Economists of all persuasions can agree with this. But the issue of where a particular economy is located on its Laffer Curve is an empirical question. If we assume that we are at point n in Figure 18.12, then tax cuts will increase tax revenues. But if the economy is at any point below m on the curve, tax-rate reductions will reduce tax revenues.

Rebuttal and Evaluation

Supply-side advocates respond to the skeptics by contending that the Reagan tax cuts in the 1980s worked as Laffer predicted. Although the top marginal income tax rates on earned income were cut from 50 to 28 percent in that decade, real GDP and tax revenues were substantially higher at the end of the 1990s than at the beginning.

But the general view among economists is that the Reagan tax cuts, coming at a time of severe recession, helped boost aggregate demand and return real GDP to its full-employment output and normal growth path. As the economy expanded, so did tax revenues despite the lower tax rates. The rise in tax revenues caused by economic growth swamped the declines in revenues from lower tax rates. In essence, the Laffer Curve shown in Figure 18.12 stretched rightward, increasing net tax revenues. But the tax-rate cuts did not produce extraordinary rightward shifts of the long-run aggregate supply curve. Indeed, saving fell as a percentage of personal income during the period and productivity growth was sluggish. Real GDP sprang back vigorously from recessionary levels, but the economic growth rate soon reverted back to its longer-term average.

Because government expenditures rose more rapidly than tax revenues in the 1980s, large budget deficits occurred. In 1993 the Clinton administration increased the top marginal tax rates from 31 to 39.6 percent to address these deficits. The economy boomed in the last half of the 1990s, and by the end of the decade tax revenues were so high relative to government expenditures that budget surpluses emerged. In 2001 the Bush administration reduced marginal tax rates over a series of years, partially "to return excess revenues to taxpayers." In 2003 the top marginal tax rate fell to 35 percent. Also, the income tax rates on capital gains and dividends were reduced to 15 percent. Economists generally agree that the Bush tax cuts, along with a highly expansionary monetary policy, helped revive and expand the economy following

the recession of 2001. Strong growth of output and income in 2004 and 2005 produced large increases in tax revenues, although large budget deficits remained because spending also increased rapidly. The 2004 deficit was $413 billion and the 2005 deficit was $318 billion. The deficit fell over the next two years, to $162 billion in 2007. But the previously discussed financial crisis plunged the economy into a severe recession beginning in December 2007 and lasting into 2009. That caused income to fall and tax revenues to plummet. Also, the government implemented highly expansionary fiscal policy. Budget deficits increased to $459 billion in 2008 and $1.4 trillion in 2009.

Today, there is general agreement that the U.S. economy is operating at a point below m—rather than above m—on the Laffer Curve in Figure 18.12. In this zone, the overall effect is that personal tax-rate increases raise tax revenues while personal tax-rate decreases reduce tax revenues. But at the same time, economists recognize that, other things being equal, cuts in tax rates reduce tax revenues in percentage terms by less than the tax-rate reductions. Similarly, tax-rate increases do not raise tax revenues by as much, in percentage terms as the tax-rate increases. This is true because changes in marginal tax rates alter taxpayer behavior and thus affect taxable income. Although these effects seem to be relatively modest, they need to be considered in designing tax policy—and, in fact, the federal government's Office of Tax Policy created a special division in 2007 devoted to estimating the magnitude of such effects when it comes to proposed changes in U.S. tax laws. Thus, supply-side economics has contributed to how economists and policymakers design and implement fiscal policy.

QUICK REVIEW 18.4

- Supply-side economists focus their attention on government policies, such as high taxation, that may impede the expansion of aggregate supply.

- The Laffer Curve relates tax rates to levels of tax revenue and suggests that, under some circumstances, cuts in tax rates will expand the tax base (output and income) and increase tax revenues.

- Most economists believe that the United States is currently operating in the range of the Laffer Curve where tax rates and tax revenues move in the same, not opposite, directions.

- Today's economists recognize the importance of considering supply-side effects in designing optimal fiscal policy.

LAST WORD

Do Tax Increases Reduce Real GDP?*

Determining the Relationship Between Changes in Taxes and Permanent Changes in Real GDP is Fraught with Complexities and Difficulties. University of California-Berkeley Economists Christina Romer and David Romer have Recently Devised a Novel Way to Approach the Topic. Their Findings Suggest That Tax Increases Reduce Real GDP.†

How do changes in the level of taxation affect the level of economic activity? The simple correlation between taxation and economic activity shows that, on average, when economic activity rises more rapidly, tax revenues also are rising more rapidly. But this correlation almost surely does not reflect a positive effect of tax increases on output. Rather, under our tax system, any positive shock to output raises tax revenues by increasing income.

In "The Macroeconomic Effects of Tax Changes: Estimates Based on a New Measure of Fiscal Shocks," authors Christina Romer and David Romer observe that this difficulty is just one of many manifestations of a more general problem. Changes in taxes occur for many reasons. And, because the factors that give rise to tax changes often are correlated with other developments in the economy, disentangling the effects of the tax changes from the other effects of these underlying factors is inherently difficult.

To address this problem, Romer and Romer use the narrative record—presidential speeches, executive branch documents, congressional reports, and so on—to identify the size, timing, and principal motivation for all major tax policy actions in the post–World War II United States. This narrative analysis allows them to separate revenue changes resulting from legislation from changes occurring for other reasons. It also allows them to classify legislated changes according to their primary motivation.

Romer and Romer find that despite the complexity of the legislative process, most significant tax changes have been motivated by one of four factors: counteracting other influences in the economy; paying for increases in government spending (or lowering taxes in conjunction with reductions in spending); addressing an inherited budget deficit; and promoting long-run growth. They observe that legislated tax changes taken to counteract other influences on the economy, or to pay for increases in government spending, are very likely to be correlated

with other factors affecting the economy. As a result these observations are likely to lead to unreliable estimates of the effect of tax changes.

Tax changes that are made to promote long-run growth, or to reduce an inherited budget deficit, in contrast, are undertaken for reasons essentially unrelated to other factors influencing output. Thus, examining the behavior of output following these tax changes is likely to provide more reliable estimates of the output effects of tax changes. *The results of this more reliable test indicate that tax changes have very large effects: a tax increase of 1 percent of GDP lowers real GDP by roughly 2 to 3 percent.*

These output effects are highly persistent. The behavior of inflation and unemployment suggests that this persistence reflects long-lasting departures of output from previous levels. Romer and Romer also find that output effects of tax changes are much more closely tied to the actual changes in taxes than news about future changes, and that investment falls sharply in response to tax changes. Indeed, the strong response of investment helps to explain why the output consequences of tax increases are so large.

Romer and Romer find suggestive evidence that tax increases to reduce an inherited budget deficit have much smaller output costs than other tax increases. This is consistent with the idea that deficit-driven tax increases may have important expansionary effects through [improved] expectations and [lower] long-term interest rates, or through [enhanced] confidence.

---

*Abridged from Les Picker, "Tax Increases Reduce GDP," *The NBER Digest*, February/March 2008. The *Digest* provides synopses of research papers in progress by economists affiliated with the National Bureau of Economic Research (NBER).

†Christina Romer and David Romer, "The Macroeconomic Effects of Tax Changes: Estimates Based on a New Measure of Fiscal Shocks," *American Economic Review*, June 2010, pp. 763–801.

SUMMARY

LO18.1 Explain the relationship between short-run aggregate supply and long-run aggregate supply.

In macroeconomics, the short run is a period in which nominal wages do not respond to changes in the price level. In contrast, the long run is a period in which nominal wages fully respond to changes in the price level.

The short-run aggregate supply curve is upsloping. Because nominal wages are unresponsive to price-level changes, increases in the price level (prices received by firms) increase profits and real output. Conversely, decreases in the price level reduce profits and real output. However, the long-run aggregate supply curve is vertical. With sufficient time for adjustment, nominal wages rise and fall with the price level, moving the economy along a vertical aggregate supply curve at the economy's full-employment output.

LO18.2 Discuss how to apply the "extended" (short-run/long-run) AD-AS model to inflation, recessions, and economic growth.

In the short run, demand-pull inflation raises the price level and real output. Once nominal wages rise to match the increase in the price level, the temporary increase in real output is reversed.

In the short run, cost-push inflation raises the price level and lowers real output. Unless the government expands aggregate demand, nominal wages will eventually decline under conditions of recession and the short-run aggregate supply curve will shift back to its initial location. Prices and real output will eventually return to their original levels.

If prices and wages are flexible downward, a decline in aggregate demand will lower output and the price level. The decline in the price level will eventually lower nominal wages and shift the short-run aggregate supply curve rightward. Full-employment output will thus be restored.

One-time changes in aggregate demand (AD) and aggregate supply (AS) can only cause limited bouts of inflation. Ongoing mild inflation occurs because the Fed purposely increases AD slightly faster than the expansion of long-run AS (driven by the supply factors of economic growth).

LO18.3 Explain the short-run trade-off between inflation and unemployment (the Phillips Curve).

Assuming a stable, upsloping short-run aggregate supply curve, rightward shifts of the aggregate demand curve of various sizes yield the generalization that high rates of inflation are associated with low rates of unemployment, and vice versa. This inverse relationship is known as the Phillips Curve, and empirical data for the 1960s seemed to be consistent with it.

In the 1970s and early 1980s the Phillips Curve apparently shifted rightward, reflecting stagflation—simultaneously rising inflation rates and unemployment rates. The higher unemployment rates and inflation rates resulted mainly from huge oil price increases that caused large leftward shifts in the short-run aggregate supply curve (so-called aggregate supply shocks). The Phillips Curve shifted inward toward its original position in the 1980s. By 1989 stagflation had subsided, and the data points for the late 1990s and first half of the first decade of the 2000s were similar to those of the 1960s. The new pattern continued until 2009, when the unemployment rate jumped to 9.3 percent and the inflation rate rose on a December-to-December basis to 2.7 percent.

LO18.4 Discuss why there is no long-run trade-off between inflation and unemployment.

Although there is a short-run trade-off between inflation and unemployment, there is no long-run trade-off. Workers will adapt their expectations to new inflation realities, and when they do, the unemployment rate will return to the natural rate. So the long-run Phillips Curve is vertical at the natural rate, meaning that higher rates of inflation do not permanently "buy" the economy less unemployment.

LO18.5 Explain the relationship between tax rates, tax revenues, and aggregate supply.

Supply-side economists focus attention on government policies, such as high taxation, that impede the expansion of aggregate supply. The Laffer Curve relates tax rates to levels of tax revenue and suggests that under some circumstances, cuts in tax rates will expand the tax base (output and income) and increase tax revenues. Most economists, however, believe that the United States is currently operating in the range of the Laffer Curve where tax rates and tax revenues move in the same, not opposite, direction.

Today's economists recognize the importance of considering supply-side effects in designing optimal fiscal policy.

TERMS AND CONCEPTS

short run

long run

Phillips Curve

stagflation

aggregate supply shocks

long-run vertical Phillips Curve

disinflation

supply-side economics

Laffer Curve

The following and additional problems can be found in **connect**

DISCUSSION QUESTIONS

1. Distinguish between the short run and the long run as they relate to macroeconomics. Why is the distinction important? **LO18.1**
2. Which of the following statements are true? Which are false? Explain why the false statements are untrue. **LO18.1**
   a. Short-run aggregate supply curves reflect an inverse relationship between the price level and the level of real output.
   b. The long-run aggregate supply curve assumes that nominal wages are fixed.
   c. In the long run, an increase in the price level will result in an increase in nominal wages.
3. Suppose the government misjudges the natural rate of unemployment to be much lower than it actually is, and thus undertakes expansionary fiscal and monetary policies to try to achieve the lower rate. Use the concept of the short-run Phillips Curve to explain why these policies might at first succeed. Use the concept of the long-run

Phillips Curve to explain the long-run outcome of these policies. **LO18.4**
4. What do the distinctions between short-run aggregate supply and long-run aggregate supply have in common with the distinction between the short-run Phillips Curve and the long-run Phillips Curve? Explain. **LO18.4**
5. What is the Laffer Curve, and how does it relate to supply-side economics? Why is determining the economy's location on the curve so important in assessing tax policy? **LO18.5**
6. Why might one person work more, earn more, and pay more income tax when his or her tax rate is cut, while another person will work less, earn less, and pay less income tax under the same circumstance? **LO18.5**
7. **LAST WORD** On average, does an increase in taxes raise or lower real GDP? If taxes as a percent of GDP go up 1 percent, by how much does real GDP change? Are the decreases in real GDP caused by tax increases temporary or permanent? Does the intention of a tax increase matter?

REVIEW QUESTIONS

1. Suppose the full-employment level of real output (Q) for a hypothetical economy is $250 and the price level (P) initially is 100. Use the short-run aggregate supply schedules below to answer the questions that follow: **LO18.1**

AS (P₁₀₀)		AS (P₁₂₅)		AS (P₇₅)	
P	Q	P	Q	P	Q
125	$280	125	$250	125	$310
100	250	100	220	100	280
75	220	75	190	75	250

   a. What will be the level of real output in the short run if the price level unexpectedly rises from 100 to 125 because of an increase in aggregate demand? What if the price level unexpectedly falls from 100 to 75 because of a decrease in aggregate demand? Explain each situation, using numbers from the table.
   b. What will be the level of real output in the long run when the price level rises from 100 to 125? When it falls from 100 to 75? Explain each situation.
   c. Show the circumstances described in parts a and b on graph paper, and derive the long-run aggregate supply curve.
2. Suppose that AD and AS intersect at an output level that is higher than the full-employment output level. After the economy adjusts back to equilibrium in the long run, the price level will be _____. **LO18.2**
   a. Higher than it is now.
   b. Lower than it is now.
   c. The same as it is now.

3. Suppose that an economy begins in long-run equilibrium before the price level and real GDP both decline simultaneously. If those changes were caused by only one curve shifting, then those changes are best explained as the result of: **LO18.2**
   a. The AD curve shifting right.
   b. The AS curve shifting right.
   c. The AD curve shifting left.
   d. The AS curve shifting left.
4. Identify the two descriptions below as being the result of either cost-push inflation or demand-pull inflation. **LO18.2**
   a. Real GDP is below the full-employment level and prices have risen recently.
   b. Real GDP is above the full-employment level and prices have risen recently.
5. Use graphical analysis to show how each of the following would affect the economy first in the short run and then in the long run. Assume that the United States is initially operating at its full-employment level of output, that prices and wages are eventually flexible both upward and downward, and that there is no counteracting fiscal or monetary policy. **LO18.2**
   a. Because of a war abroad, the oil supply to the United States is disrupted, sending oil prices rocketing upward.
   b. Construction spending on new homes rises dramatically, greatly increasing total U.S. investment spending.
   c. Economic recession occurs abroad, significantly reducing foreign purchases of U.S. exports.

6. Between 1990 and 2009, the U.S. price level rose by about 64 percent while real output increased by about 62 percent. Use the aggregate demand–aggregate supply model to illustrate these outcomes graphically. **LO18.2**

7. Assume there is a particular short-run aggregate supply curve for an economy and the curve is relevant for several years. Use the AD-AS analysis to show graphically why higher rates of inflation over this period would be associated with lower rates of unemployment, and vice versa. What is this inverse relationship called? **LO18.3**

8. Aggregate supply shocks can cause _____ rates of inflation that are accompanied by _____ rates of unemployment. **LO18.3**
   a. Higher; higher.
   b. Higher; lower.
   c. Lower; higher.
   d. Lower; lower.

9. Suppose that firms are expecting 6 percent inflation while workers are expecting 9 percent inflation. How much of a pay raise will workers demand if their goal is to maintain the purchasing power of their incomes? **LO18.4**
   a. 3 percent.
   b. 6 percent.
   c. 9 percent.
   d. 12 percent.

10. Suppose that firms were expecting inflation to be 3 percent, but then it actually turned out to be 7 percent. Other things equal, firm profits will be: **LO18.4**
    a. Smaller than expected.
    b. Larger than expected.

PROBLEMS

1. Use the figure below to answer the following questions. Assume that the economy initially is operating at price level 120 and real output level $870. This output level is the economy's potential (or full-employment) level of output. Next, suppose that the price level rises from 120 to 130. By how much will real output increase in the short run? In the long run? Instead, now assume that the price level dropped from 120 to 110. Assuming flexible product and resource prices, by how much will real output fall in the short run? In the long run? What is the long-run level of output at each of the three price levels shown? **LO18.1**

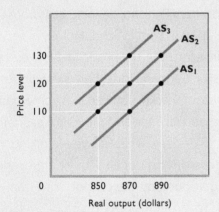

2. **ADVANCED ANALYSIS** Suppose that the equation for a particular short-run AS curve is $P = 20 + 0.5Q$, where P is the price level and Q is real output in dollar terms. What is Q if the price level is 120? Suppose that the Q in your answer is the full-employment level of output. By how much will Q increase *in the short run* if the price level unexpectedly rises from 120 to 132? By how much will Q increase *in the long run* due to the price level increase? **LO18.1**

3. Suppose that over a 30-year period Buskerville's price level increased from 72 to 138, while its real GDP rose from $1.2 trillion to $2.1 trillion. Did economic growth occur in Buskerville? If so, by what average yearly rate in percentage terms (rounded to one decimal place)? Did Buskerville experience inflation? If so, by what average yearly rate in percentage terms (rounded to one decimal place)? Which shifted rightward faster in Buskerville: its long-run aggregate supply curve (AS_{LR}) or its aggregate demand curve (AD)? **LO18.2**

4. Suppose that for years East Confetti's short-run Phillips Curve was such that each 1 percentage point increase in its unemployment rate was associated with a 2 percentage point decline in its inflation rate. Then, during several recent years, the short-run pattern changed such that its inflation rate rose by 3 percentage points for every 1 percentage point drop in its unemployment rate. Graphically, did East Confetti's Phillips Curve shift upward or did it shift downward? **LO18.3**

CHAPTER **20**

International Trade*

Learning Objective

LO20.1 List and discuss several key facts about international trade.

LO20.2 Define comparative advantage, and demonstrate how specialization and trade add to a nation's output.

LO20.3 Describe how differences between world prices and domestic prices prompt exports and imports.

LO20.4 Analyze the economic effects of tariffs and quotas.

LO20.5 Analyze the validity of the most frequently presented arguments for protectionism.

LO20.6 Identify and explain the objectives of GATT, WTO, EU, eurozone, and NAFTA, and discuss offshoring and trade adjustment assistance.

Backpackers in the wilderness like to think they are "leaving the world behind," but, like Atlas, they carry the world on their shoulders. Much of their equipment is imported—knives from Switzerland, rain gear from South Korea, cameras from Japan, aluminum pots from England, sleeping bags from China, and compasses from Finland. Moreover, they may have driven to the trailheads in Japanese-made Toyotas or German-made BMWs, sipping coffee from Brazil or snacking on bananas from Honduras.

International trade and the global economy affect all of us daily, whether we are hiking in the wilderness, driving our cars, buying groceries, or working at our jobs. We cannot "leave the world behind." We are enmeshed in a global web of economic relationships, such as trading goods and services, multinational corporations, cooperative

---

*Note to Instructors: If you prefer to cover international trade early in your course, you can assign this chapter at the end of either Part 1 or Part 2. This chapter builds on the introductory ideas of opportunity costs, supply and demand analysis, and economic efficiency but does not require an understanding of either market failures or government failures.

ventures among the world's firms, and ties among the world's financial markets.

The focus of this chapter is the trading of goods and services. Then in Chapter 21, we examine the U.S. balance of payments, exchange rates, and U.S. trade deficits. In Chapter 21W on our Web site, we look at the economics of developing nations.

Some Key Trade Facts

LO20.1 List and discuss several key facts about international trade.

The following are several important facts relating to international trade.

- U.S. exports and imports have more than doubled as percentages of GDP since 1980.

- A *trade deficit* occurs when imports exceed exports. The United States has a trade deficit in goods. In 2012 U.S. imports of goods exceeded U.S. exports of goods by $735 billion.

- A *trade surplus* occurs when exports exceed imports. The United States has a trade surplus in services (such as air transportation services and financial services). In 2012 U.S. exports of services exceeded U.S. imports of services by $196 billion.

- Principal U.S. exports include chemicals, agricultural products, consumer durables, semiconductors, and aircraft; principal imports include petroleum, automobiles, metals, household appliances, and computers.

- As with other advanced industrial nations, the United States imports many goods that are in some of the same categories as the goods that it exports. Examples: automobiles, computers, chemicals, semiconductors, and telecommunications equipment.

- Canada is the United States' most important trading partner quantitatively. In 2012 about 20 percent of U.S. exported goods were sold to Canadians, who in turn provided 15 percent of imported U.S. goods.

- The United States has a sizable trade deficit with China. In 2012 it was $315 billion.

- The U.S. dependence on foreign oil is reflected in its trade with members of OPEC. In 2012 the United States imported $181 billion of goods (mainly oil) from OPEC members, while exporting $82 billion of goods to those countries.

- The United States leads the world in the combined volume of exports and imports, as measured in

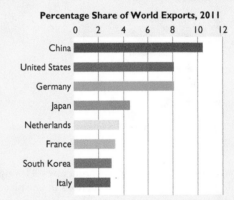

GLOBAL PERSPECTIVE 20.1

Shares of World Exports, Selected Nations

China has the largest share of world exports, followed by Germany and the United States. The eight largest export nations account for about 43.9 percent of world exports.

Percentage Share of World Exports, 2011

Source: International Trade Statistics, 2012, WTO Publications.

dollars. China, the United States, Germany, Japan, and the Netherlands were the top five exporters by dollar in 2012.

- Currently, the United States provides about 8.1 percent of the world's exports. (See Global Perspective 20.1.)

- Exports of goods and services (on a national income account basis) make up about 14 percent of total U.S. output. That percentage is much lower than the percentage in many other nations, including Canada, France, Germany, the Netherlands, and South Korea. (See Global Perspective 20.2.)

- China has become a major international trader, with an estimated $2.05 trillion of exports in 2012. Other Asian economies—including South Korea, Taiwan, and Singapore—are also active in international trade. Their combined exports exceed those of France, Britain, or Italy.

GLOBAL PERSPECTIVE 20.2

Exports of Goods and Services as a Percentage of GDP, Selected Countries

Although the United States is one of the world's largest exporters, as a percentage of GDP, its exports are quite low relative to many other countries.

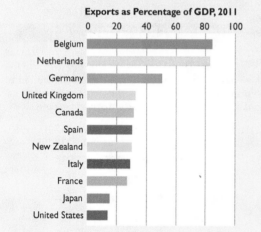

Exports as Percentage of GDP, 2011

Source: Derived by authors from *IMF International Financial Statistics,* 2012.

- International trade links world economies. Through trade, changes in economic conditions in one place on the globe can quickly affect other places.

- International trade is often at the center of debates over economic policy, both within the United States and internationally.

With this information in mind, let's turn to the economics of international trade.

The Economic Basis for Trade

LO20.2 Define comparative advantage, and demonstrate how specialization and trade add to a nation's output.

Sovereign nations, like individuals and the regions of a nation, can gain by specializing in the products they can produce with the greatest relative efficiency and by trading for the goods they cannot produce as efficiently. The simple answer to the question "Why do nations trade?" is "They trade because it is beneficial." The benefits that emerge relate to three underlying facts:

- The distribution of natural, human, and capital resources among nations is uneven; nations differ in their endowments of economic resources.

- Efficient production of various goods requires different technologies, and not all nations have the same level of technological expertise.

- Products are differentiated as to quality and other attributes, and some people may prefer certain goods imported from abroad rather than similar goods produced domestically.

To recognize the character and interaction of these three facts, think of China, which has abundant and inexpensive labor. As a result, China can produce efficiently (at low cost of other goods forgone) a variety of **labor-intensive goods,** such as textiles, electronics, apparel, toys, and sporting goods.

In contrast, Australia has vast amounts of land and can inexpensively produce such **land-intensive goods** as beef, wool, and meat. Mexico has the soil, tropical climate, rainfall, and ready supply of unskilled labor that allow for the efficient, low-cost production of vegetables. Industrially advanced economies such as the United States and Germany that have relatively large amounts of capital can inexpensively produce goods whose production requires much capital, including such **capital-intensive goods** as airplanes, automobiles, agricultural equipment, machinery, and chemicals.

Also, regardless of their resource intensities, nations can develop individual products that are in demand worldwide because of their special qualities. Examples: fashions from Italy, chocolates from Belgium, software from the United States, and watches from Switzerland.

The distribution of resources, technology, and product distinctiveness among nations is relatively stable in short time periods but certainly can change over time. When that distribution changes, the relative efficiency and success that nations have in producing and selling goods also change. For example, in the past several decades, South Korea has greatly expanded its stock of capital. Although South Korea was primarily an exporter of agricultural products and raw materials a half-century ago, it now exports large quantities of manufactured goods. Similarly, the new technologies that gave us synthetic fibers and synthetic rubber drastically altered the resource mix needed to produce fibers and rubber and changed the relative efficiency of nations in manufacturing them.

As national economies evolve, the size and quality of their labor forces may change, the volume and composition of their capital stocks may shift, new technologies may develop, and even the quality of land and the quantity of natural resources may be altered. As such changes take place, the relative efficiency with which a nation can produce specific goods will also change. As economists would say, comparative advantage can and does sometimes change.

Comparative Advantage

In an open economy (one with an international sector), a country produces more of certain goods (exports) and fewer of other goods (imports) than it would otherwise. Thus, the country shifts the use of labor and other productive resources toward export industries and away from import industries. For example, in the presence of international trade, the United States uses more resources to make commercial aircraft and to grow wheat and fewer resources to make television sets and sew clothes. So we ask: Do such shifts of resources make economic sense? Do they enhance U.S. total output and thus the U.S. standard of living?

The answers are affirmative. Specialization and international trade increase the productivity of U.S. resources and allow the United States to obtain greater total output than otherwise would be possible. These benefits are the result of exploiting both *absolute advantages* and *comparative advantages*. A country is said to have an *absolute advantage* over other producers of a product if it is the most efficient producer of that product (by which we mean that it can produce more output of that product from any given amount of resource inputs than can any other producer). A country is said to have a *comparative advantage* over other producers of a product if it can produce the product at a lower opportunity cost (by which we mean that it must forgo less output of alternative products when allocating productive resources to producing the product in question).

In 1776 Adam Smith used the concept of absolute advantage to argue for international specialization and trade. His point was that nations would be better off if each specialized in the production of those products in which it had an absolute advantage and was therefore the most efficient producer:

> It is the maxim of every prudent master of a family, never to attempt to make at home what it will cost him more to make than to buy. The taylor does not attempt to make his own shoes, but buys them of the shoemaker. The shoemaker does not attempt to make his own clothes, but employs a taylor. The farmer attempts to make neither the one nor the other, but employs those different artificers. . . .
>
> What is prudence in the conduct of every private family, can scarce be folly in that of a great kingdom. If a foreign country can supply us with a commodity cheaper than we can make it, better buy it of them with some part of the produce of our own industry, employed in a way in which we have some advantage.[1]

---

[1]Adam Smith, *The Wealth of Nations* (originally published, 1776; New York: Modern Library, 1937), p. 424.

CONSIDER THIS . . .

A CPA and a House Painter

Suppose that Madison, a certified public accountant (CPA), is a swifter painter than Mason, the professional painter she is thinking of hiring. Also assume that Madison can earn $50 per hour as an accountant but would have to pay Mason $15 per hour. And suppose that Madison would need 30 hours to paint her house but Mason would need 40 hours.

Should Madison take time from her accounting to paint her own house, or should she hire the painter? Madison's opportunity cost of painting her house is $1,500 (= 30 hours of sacrificed CPA time × $50 per CPA hour). The cost of hiring Mason is only $600 (= 40 hours of painting × $15 per hour of painting). Although Madison is better at both accounting and painting, she will get her house painted at lower cost by specializing in accounting and using some of her earnings from accounting to hire a house painter.

Similarly, Mason can reduce his cost of obtaining accounting services by specializing in painting and using some of his income to hire Madison to prepare his income tax forms. Suppose Mason would need 10 hours to prepare his tax return, while Madison could handle the task in 2 hours. Mason would sacrifice $150 of income (= 10 hours of painting time × $15 per hour) to do something he could hire Madison to do for $100 (= 2 hours of CPA time × $50 per CPA hour). By specializing in painting and hiring Madison to prepare his tax return, Mason lowers the cost of getting his tax return prepared.

We will see that what is true for our CPA and house painter is also true for nations. Specializing on the basis of comparative advantage enables nations to reduce the cost of obtaining the goods and services they desire.

In the early 1800s, David Ricardo extended Smith's idea by demonstrating that it is advantageous for a country to specialize and trade with another country even if it is more productive in all economic activities than that other country. Stated more formally, a nation does not need Smith's absolute advantage—total superiority in the efficiency with which it produces products—to benefit from specialization and trade. It needs only a comparative advantage.

The nearby Consider This box provides a simple, two-person illustration of Ricardo's principle of comparative advantage. Be sure to read it now because it will greatly help you understand the graphical analysis that follows.

Two Isolated Nations

Our goal is to place the idea of comparative advantage into the context of trading nations. Our method is to build a simple model that relies on the familiar concepts of production possibilities curves. Suppose the world consists of just two nations, the United States and Mexico. Also for simplicity, suppose that the labor forces in the United States and Mexico are of equal size. Each nation can produce both beef and raw (unprocessed) vegetables but at different levels of economic efficiency. Suppose the U.S. and Mexican domestic production possibilities curves for beef and vegetables are those shown in Figure 20.1a and Figure 20.1b. Note three realities relating to the production possibilities curves in the two graphs:

- *Constant costs* The curves derive from the data in Table 20.1 and are drawn as straight lines, in contrast

to the bowed-outward production possibilities frontiers we examined in Chapter 1. This means that we have replaced the law of increasing opportunity costs with the assumption of constant costs. This substitution simplifies our discussion but does not impair the validity of our analysis and conclusions. Later we will consider the effects of increasing opportunity costs.

- *Different costs* The production possibilities curves of the United States and Mexico reflect different resource mixes and differing levels of technology. Specifically, the differing slopes of the two curves reflect the numbers in the figures and reveal that the opportunity costs of producing beef and vegetables differ between the two nations.

- *U.S. absolute advantage in both* A producer (an individual, firm, or country) has an *absolute advantage* over another producer if it can produce more of a product than the other producer using the same amount of resources. Because of our convenient assumption that the U.S. and Mexican labor forces are the same size, the two production possibilities curves show that the United States has an absolute advantage in producing both products. If the United States and Mexico use their entire (equal-size) labor forces to produce either vegetables or beef, the United States can produce more of either than Mexico. The United States, using the same number of workers as Mexico, has greater production possibilities. So output per worker—labor productivity—in the United States exceeds that in Mexico in producing both products.

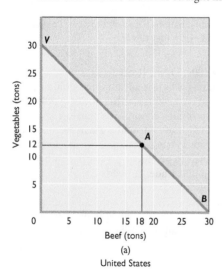

(a)
United States

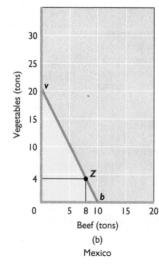

(b)
Mexico

FIGURE 20.1 Production possibilities for the United States and Mexico. The two production possibilities curves show the combinations of vegetables and beef that the United States and Mexico can produce domestically. The curves for both countries are straight lines because we are assuming constant opportunity costs. (a) As reflected by the slope of *VB* in the left graph, the opportunity-cost ratio in the United States is 1 vegetables ≡ 1 beef. (b) The production possibilities curve *vb* in the right graph has a steeper slope, reflecting the different opportunity-cost ratio in Mexico of 2 vegetables ≡ 1 beef. The difference in the opportunity-cost ratios between the two countries defines their comparative advantages and is the basis for specialization and international trade.

TABLE 20.1 International Specialization According to Comparative Advantage and the Gains from Trade

Country	(1) Outputs before Specialization	(2) Outputs after Specialization	(3) Amounts Exported (−) and Imported (+)	(4) Outputs Available after Trade	(5) Gains from Specialization and Trade (4) − (1)
United States	18 beef	30 beef	−10 beef	20 beef	2 beef
	12 vegetables	0 vegetables	+15 vegetables	15 vegetables	3 vegetables
Mexico	8 beef	0 beef	+10 beef	10 beef	2 beef
	4 vegetables	20 vegetables	−15 vegetables	5 vegetables	1 vegetables

Opportunity-Cost Ratio in the United States In Figure 20.1a, with full employment, the United States will operate at some point on its production possibilities curve. On that curve, it can increase its output of beef from 0 tons to 30 tons by forgoing 30 tons of vegetables output. So the slope of the production possibilities curve is 1 (= 30 vegetables/30 beef), meaning that 1 ton of vegetables must be sacrificed for each extra ton of beef. In the United States the **opportunity-cost ratio** (domestic exchange ratio) for the two products is 1 ton of vegetables (V) for 1 ton of beef (B), or

United States: $1V \equiv 1B$ (The "$\equiv$" sign simply means "equivalent to.")

Within its borders, the United States can "exchange" a ton of vegetables from itself for a ton of beef from itself. Our constant-cost assumption means that this exchange or opportunity-cost relationship prevails for all possible moves from one point to another along the U.S. production possibilities curve.

Opportunity-Cost Ratio in Mexico Mexico's production possibilities curve in Figure 20.1b represents a different full-employment opportunity-cost ratio. In Mexico, 20 tons of vegetables must be given up to obtain 10 tons of beef. The slope of the production possibilities curve is 2 (= 20 vegetables/10 beef). This means that in Mexico the opportunity-cost ratio for the two goods is 2 tons of vegetables for 1 ton of beef, or

Mexico: $2V \equiv 1B$

Self-Sufficiency Output Mix If the United States and Mexico are isolated and self-sufficient, then each country must choose some output mix on its production possibilities curve. It will select the mix that provides the greatest total utility or satisfaction. Let's assume that combination point A in Figure 20.1a is the optimal mix in the United States. That is, society deems the combination of 18 tons of beef and 12 tons of vegetables preferable to any other combination of the goods available along the production

possibilities curve. Suppose Mexico's optimal product mix is 8 tons of beef and 4 tons of vegetables, indicated by point Z in Figure 20.1b. These choices by the two countries are reflected in column 1 of Table 20.1.

Specializing Based on Comparative Advantage

A producer (an individual, firm, or nation) has a **comparative advantage** in producing a particular product if it can produce that product at a lower opportunity cost than other producers. Comparative advantage is the key determinant in whether or not nations can gain from specialization and trade. In fact, absolute advantage turns out to be irrelevant.

In our example, for instance, the United States has an absolute advantage over Mexico in producing both vegetables and beef. But it is still the case that the United States can gain from specialization and trade with Mexico. That is because what actually matters is whether the opportunity costs of producing the two products (beef and vegetables) differ in the two countries. If they do, then each nation will enjoy a comparative advantage in one of the products, meaning that it can produce that product at a lower opportunity cost than the other country. As a result, total output can increase if each country specializes in the production of the good in which it has the lower opportunity cost.

This idea is summarized in the **principle of comparative advantage,** which says that total output will be greatest when each good is produced by the nation that has the lowest domestic opportunity cost for producing that good. In our two-nation illustration, the United States has the lower domestic opportunity cost for beef; the United States must forgo only 1 ton of vegetables to produce 1 ton of beef, whereas Mexico must forgo 2 tons of vegetables for 1 ton of beef. The United States has a comparative (cost) advantage in beef and should specialize in beef production. The "world" (that is, the United States and Mexico) in our example would clearly not be economizing in the use of its resources if a high-cost producer (Mexico) produced a specific product (beef) when a low-cost producer (the United States) could have produced it. Having Mexico produce beef would mean that the world economy would have to give up more vegetables than is necessary to obtain a ton of beef.

Mexico has the lower domestic opportunity cost for vegetables. It must sacrifice only $\frac{1}{2}$ ton of beef to produce 1 ton of vegetables, while the United States must forgo 1 ton of beef to produce 1 ton of vegetables. Mexico has a comparative advantage in vegetables and should specialize in vegetable production. Again, the world would not be employing its resources economically if vegetables were produced by a high-cost producer (the United States) rather than by a low-cost producer (Mexico). If the United States produced vegetables, the world would be giving up more beef than necessary to obtain each ton of vegetables. Economizing requires that any particular good be produced by the nation having the lowest domestic opportunity cost or the nation having the comparative advantage for that good. The United States should produce beef, and Mexico should produce vegetables. The situation is summarized in Table 20.2.

A comparison of columns 1 and 2 in Table 20.1 verifies that specialized production enables the world to obtain more output from its fixed amount of resources. By specializing completely in beef, the United States can produce 30 tons of beef and no vegetables. Mexico, by specializing completely in vegetables, can produce 20 tons of vegetables and no beef. These figures exceed the yields generated without specialization: 26 tons of beef (= 18 in the United States + 8 in Mexico) and 16 tons of vegetables (= 12 in the United States + 4 in Mexico). As a result, the world ends up with 4 more tons of beef (= 30 tons − 26 tons) and 4 more tons of vegetables (= 20 tons − 16 tons) than it would if there were self-sufficiency and unspecialized production.

ORIGIN OF THE IDEA

O20.1

Absolute and comparative advantage

TABLE 20.2 Comparative-Advantage Example: A Summary

Beef	Vegetables
Mexico: Must give up 2 tons of vegetables to get 1 ton of beef.	***Mexico:*** Must give up $\frac{1}{2}$ ton of beef to get 1 ton of vegetables.
United States: Must give up 1 ton of vegetables to get 1 ton of beef.	***United States:*** Must give up 1 ton of beef to get 1 ton of vegetables.
Comparative advantage: United States	***Comparative advantage:*** Mexico

Terms of Trade

We have just seen that specialization in production will allow for the largest possible amounts of both beef and vegetables to be produced. But with each country specializing in the production of only one item, how will the vegetables that are all produced by Mexico and the beef that is all produced by the United States be divided between consumers in the two countries? The key turns out to be the **terms of trade,** the exchange ratio at which the United States and Mexico trade beef and vegetables.

Crucially, the terms of trade also establish whether each country will find it in its own better interest to bother specializing at all. This is because the terms of trade determine whether each country can "get a better deal" by specializing and trading than it could if it opted instead for self sufficiency. To see how this works, note that because $1B \equiv 1V (= 1V \equiv 1B)$ in the United States, it must get more than 1 ton of vegetables for each 1 ton of beef exported; otherwise, it will not benefit from exporting beef in exchange for Mexican vegetables. The United States must get a better "price" (more vegetables) for its beef through international trade than it can get domestically; otherwise, no gain from trade exists and such trade will not occur.

Similarly, because $1B \equiv 2V (= 2V \equiv 1B)$ in Mexico, Mexico must obtain 1 ton of beef by exporting less than 2 tons of vegetables to get it. Mexico must be able to pay a lower "price" for beef in the world market than it must pay domestically, or else it will not want to trade. The international exchange ratio or terms of trade must therefore lie somewhere between

$$1B \equiv 1V \text{ (United States' cost conditions)}$$

and

$$1B \equiv 2V \text{ (Mexico's cost conditions)}$$

Where between these limits will the world exchange ratio fall? The United States will prefer a rate close to $1B \equiv 2V$, say, $1B \equiv 1\frac{3}{4}V$. The United States wants to obtain as many vegetables as possible for each 1 ton of beef it exports. By contrast, Mexico wants a rate near $1B \equiv 1V$, say, $1B \equiv 1\frac{1}{4}V$. This is true because Mexico wants to export as few vegetables as possible for each 1 ton of beef it receives in exchange.

The actual exchange ratio depends on world supply and demand for the two products. If overall world demand for vegetables is weak relative to its supply and if the demand for beef is strong relative to its supply, the price of vegetables will be lower and the price of beef will be higher. The exchange ratio will settle nearer the $1B \equiv 2V$ figure the United States prefers. If overall world demand for vegetables is great relative to its supply and if the demand for beef is weak relative to its supply, the ratio will settle nearer the

KEY GRAPH

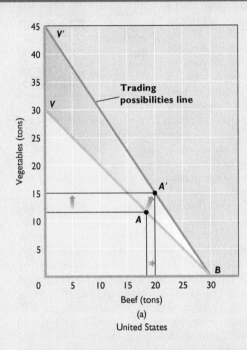

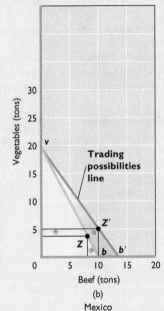

FIGURE 20.2 Trading possibilities lines and the gains from trade. As a result of specialization and trade, both the United States and Mexico can have higher levels of output than the levels attainable on their domestic production possibilities curves. (a) The United States can move from point *A* on its domestic production possibilities curve to, say, *A'* on its trading possibilities line. (b) Mexico can move from *Z* to *Z'*.

QUICK QUIZ FOR FIGURE 20.2

1. The production possibilities curves in graphs (a) and (b) imply:
   a. increasing domestic opportunity costs.
   b. decreasing domestic opportunity costs.
   c. constant domestic opportunity costs.
   d. first decreasing, then increasing, domestic opportunity costs.

2. Before specialization, the domestic opportunity cost of producing 1 unit of beef is:
   a. 1 unit of vegetables in both the United States and Mexico.
   b. 1 unit of vegetables in the United States and 2 units of vegetables in Mexico.
   c. 2 units of vegetables in the United States and 1 unit of vegetables in Mexico.
   d. 1 unit of vegetables in the United States and $\frac{1}{2}$ unit of vegetables in Mexico.

3. After specialization and international trade, the world output of beef and vegetables is:
   a. 20 tons of beef and 20 tons of vegetables.
   b. 45 tons of beef and 15 tons of vegetables.
   c. 30 tons of beef and 20 tons of vegetables.
   d. 10 tons of beef and 30 tons of vegetables.

4. After specialization and international trade:
   a. the United States can obtain units of vegetables at less cost than it could before trade.
   b. Mexico can obtain more than 20 tons of vegetables, if it so chooses.
   c. the United States no longer has a comparative advantage in producing beef.
   d. Mexico can benefit by prohibiting vegetables imports from the United States.

Answers: 1. c; 2. b; 3. c; 4. a

$1B \equiv 1V$ level favorable to Mexico. In this manner, the actual exchange ratio that is set by world supply and demand determines how the gains from international specialization and trade are divided between the two nations and, consequently, how the beef that is all produced in the United States and the vegetables that are all produced in Mexico get divided among consumers in the two countries. (We discuss equilibrium world prices later in this chapter.)

Gains from Trade

Suppose the international terms of trade are $1B \equiv 1\frac{1}{2}V$. The possibility of trading on these terms permits each nation to supplant its domestic production possibilities curve with a trading possibilities line (or curve), as shown in **Figure 20.2 (Key Graph)**. Just as a production possibilities curve shows the amounts of these products that a full-employment economy can obtain by shifting resources from one to the other, a **trading possibilities line** shows the amounts of the two products that a nation can obtain by specializing in one product and trading for the other. The trading possibilities lines in Figure 20.2 reflect the assumption that both nations specialize on the basis of comparative advantage: The United States specializes completely in beef (at point *B* in Figure 20.2a), and Mexico specializes completely in vegetables (at point *v* in Figure 20.2b).

Improved Alternatives With specialization and trade, the United States is no longer constrained by its domestic production possibilities line, which requires it to give up 1 ton of beef for every 1 ton of vegetables it wants as it moves up its domestic production possibilities line from, say, point *B*. Instead, the United States, through trade with Mexico, can get $1\frac{1}{2}$ tons of vegetables for every ton of beef that it exports to Mexico, as long as Mexico has vegetables to export. Trading possibilities line *BV'* thus represents the $1B \equiv 1\frac{1}{2}V$ trading ratio.

Similarly, Mexico, starting at, say, point *v*, no longer has to move down its domestic production possibilities curve, giving up 2 tons of vegetables for each ton of beef it wants. It can now export just $1\frac{1}{2}$ tons of vegetables for each 1 ton of beef that it wants by moving down its trading possibilities line *vb'*.

Specialization and trade create a new exchange ratio between beef and vegetables, and that ratio is reflected in each nation's trading possibilities line. For both nations, this exchange ratio is superior to the unspecialized exchange ratio embodied in their respective production possibilities curves. By specializing in beef and trading for Mexico's vegetables, the United States can obtain more than 1 ton of vegetables for 1 ton of beef. By specializing in vegetables and trading for U.S. beef, Mexico can obtain 1 ton of beef for less than 2 tons of vegetables. In both cases, self-sufficiency is inefficient and therefore undesirable.

Greater Output By specializing on the basis of comparative advantage and by trading for goods that are produced in the nation with greater domestic efficiency, the United States and Mexico can achieve combinations of beef and vegetables beyond their own individual production possibilities curves. Specialization according to comparative advantage results in a more efficient allocation of world resources, and larger outputs of both products are therefore available to both nations.

Suppose that at the $1B \equiv 1\frac{1}{2}V$ terms of trade, the United States exports 10 tons of beef to Mexico and in return Mexico exports 15 tons of vegetables to the United States. How do the new quantities of beef and vegetables available to the two nations compare with the optimal product mixes that existed before specialization and trade? Point *A* in

Figure 20.2a reminds us that the United States chose 18 tons of beef and 12 tons of vegetables originally. But by producing 30 tons of beef and no vegetables and by trading 10 tons of beef for 15 tons of vegetables, the United States can obtain 20 tons of beef and 15 tons of vegetables. This new, superior combination of beef and vegetables is indicated by point *A'* in Figure 20.2a. Compared with the no-trade amounts of 18 tons of beef and 12 tons of vegetables, the United States' **gains from trade** are 2 tons of beef and 3 tons of vegetables.

Similarly, recall that Mexico's optimal product mix was 4 tons of vegetables and 8 tons of beef (point *Z*) before specialization and trade. Now, after specializing in vegetables and trading for beef, Mexico can have 5 tons of vegetables and 10 tons of beef. It accomplishes that by producing 20 tons of vegetables and no beef and exporting 15 tons of its vegetables in exchange for 10 tons of American beef. This new position is indicated by point *Z'* in Figure 20.2b. Mexico's gains from trade are 1 ton of vegetables and 2 tons of beef.

Points *A'* and *Z'* in Figure 20.2 are superior economic positions to points *A* and *Z*. This fact is enormously important! We know that a nation can expand its production possibilities boundary by (1) expanding the quantity and improving the quality of its resources or (2) realizing technological progress. We have now established that international trade can enable a nation to circumvent the output constraint illustrated by its production possibilities curve. An economy can grow by expanding international trade. The outcome of international specialization and trade is equivalent to having more and better resources or discovering and implementing improved production techniques.

Table 20.1 summarizes the transactions and outcomes in our analysis. Please give it one final careful review.

QUICK REVIEW 20.2

- The principle of comparative advantage says that total world output will be greatest when each good is produced by the nation that has the lowest domestic opportunity cost.
- The rate at which countries can trade units of one product for units of another product is referred to as the terms of trade.
- A trading possibilities line shows the amounts of two products that a nation can obtain by specializing in the production of one product and then trading for the other.

CONSIDER THIS . . .

Misunderstanding the Gains from Trade

It is a common myth that the greatest benefit to be derived from international trade is greater domestic employment in the export sector. This suggests that exports are "good" because they increase domestic employment, whereas imports are "bad" because they deprive people of jobs at home. As we have demonstrated, the true benefit created by international trade is the overall increase in output available through specialization and exchange.

A nation does not need international trade to operate *on* its production possibilities curve. It can fully employ its resources, including labor, with or without international trade. International trade, however, enables a country to reach a point of consumption beyond its domestic production possibilities curve. The gain from trade to a nation is the extra output obtained from abroad—the imports obtained for less sacrifice of other goods than if they were produced at home.

Trade with Increasing Costs

To explain the basic principles underlying international trade, we simplified our analysis in several ways. For example, we limited discussion to two products and two nations. But multiproduct and multinational analysis yield the same conclusions. We also assumed constant opportunity costs (linear production possibilities curves), which is a more substantive simplification. Let's consider the effect of allowing increasing opportunity costs (concave-to-the-origin production possibilities curves) to enter the picture.

Suppose that the United States and Mexico initially are at positions on their concave production possibilities curves where their domestic cost ratios are $1B \equiv 1V$ and $1B \equiv 2V$, as they were in our constant-cost analysis. As before, comparative advantage indicates that the United States should specialize in beef and Mexico in vegetables. But now, as the United States begins to expand beef production, its cost of beef will rise; it will have to sacrifice more than 1 ton of vegetables to get 1 additional ton of beef. Resources are no longer perfectly substitutable between alternative uses, as the constant-cost assumption implied. Resources less and less suitable to beef production must be allocated to the U.S. beef industry in expanding beef output, and that means increasing costs—the

sacrifice of larger and larger amounts of vegetables for each additional ton of beef.

Similarly, suppose that Mexico expands vegetable production starting from its $1B \equiv 2V$ cost ratio position. As production increases, it will find that its $1B \equiv 2V$ cost ratio begins to rise. Sacrificing 1 ton of beef will free resources that are capable of producing only something less than 2 tons of vegetables because those transferred resources are less suitable to vegetable production.

As the U.S. cost ratio falls from $1B \equiv 1V$ and the Mexican ratio rises from $1B \equiv 2V$, a point will be reached where the cost ratios are equal in the two nations, perhaps at $1B \equiv 1\frac{3}{4}V$. At this point the underlying basis for further specialization and trade—differing cost ratios—has disappeared, and further specialization is therefore uneconomical. And, most important, this point of equal cost ratios may be reached while the United States is still producing some vegetables along with its beef and Mexico is producing some beef along with its vegetables. The primary effect of increasing opportunity costs is less-than-complete specialization. For this reason, we often find domestically produced products competing directly against identical or similar imported products within a particular economy.

The Case for Free Trade

The case for free trade reduces to one compelling argument: Through free trade based on the principle of comparative advantage, the world economy can achieve a more efficient allocation of resources and a higher level of material well-being than it can without free trade.

Since the resource mixes and technological knowledge of the world's nations are all somewhat different, each nation can produce particular commodities at different real costs. Each nation should produce goods for which its domestic opportunity costs are lower than the domestic opportunity costs of other nations and exchange those goods for products for which its domestic opportunity costs are high relative to those of other nations. If each nation does this, the world will realize the advantages of geographic and human specialization. The world and each free-trading nation can obtain a larger real income from the fixed supplies of resources available to it.

Government trade barriers lessen or eliminate gains from specialization. If nations cannot trade freely, they must shift resources from efficient (low-cost) to inefficient (high-cost) uses to satisfy their diverse wants. A recent study suggests that the elimination of trade barriers since the Second World War has increased the income of the average U.S. household by at least $7,000 and perhaps by as much as $13,000. These income gains are recurring; they happen year after year.[2]

One side benefit of free trade is that it promotes competition and deters monopoly. The increased competition from foreign firms forces domestic firms to find and use the lowest-cost production techniques. It also compels them to be innovative with respect to both product quality and production methods, thereby contributing to economic growth. And free trade gives consumers a wider range of product choices. The reasons to favor free trade are the same as the reasons to endorse competition.

A second side benefit of free trade is that it links national interests and breaks down national animosities. Confronted with political disagreements, trading partners tend to negotiate rather than make war.

QUICK REVIEW 20.3

- International trade enables nations to specialize, increase productivity, and increase output available for consumption.
- Comparative advantage means total world output will be greatest when each good is produced by the nation that has the lowest domestic opportunity cost.
- Specialization is less than complete among nations because opportunity costs normally rise as any specific nation produces more of a particular good.

Supply and Demand Analysis of Exports and Imports

LO20.3 Describe how differences between world prices and domestic prices prompt exports and imports.

Supply and demand analysis reveals how equilibrium prices and quantities of exports and imports are determined. The amount of a good or a service a nation will export or import depends on differences between the equilibrium world price and the equilibrium domestic price. The interaction of *world* supply and demand determines the equilibrium **world price**—the price that equates the quantities supplied and demanded globally. *Domestic* supply and demand determine the equilibrium **domestic price**—the price that would prevail in a closed economy that does not engage in international trade. The domestic price equates quantity supplied and quantity demanded domestically.

---

[2]Scott C. Bradford, Paul L. E. Grieco, and Gary C. Hufbauer, "The Payoff to America from Globalization," *The World Economy*, July 2006, pp. 893–916.

In the absence of trade, the domestic prices in a closed economy may or may not equal the world equilibrium prices. When economies are opened for international trade, differences between world and domestic prices encourage exports or imports. To see how, consider the international effects of such price differences in a simple two-nation world, consisting of the United States and Canada, that are both producing aluminum. We assume there are no trade barriers, such as tariffs and quotas, and no international transportation costs.

Supply and Demand in the United States

Figure 20.3a shows the domestic supply curve S_d and the domestic demand curve D_d for aluminum in the United States, which for now is a closed economy. The intersection of S_d and D_d determines the equilibrium domestic price of $1 per pound and the equilibrium domestic quantity of 100 million pounds. Domestic suppliers produce 100 million pounds and sell them all at $1 a pound. So there are no domestic surpluses or shortages of aluminum.

But what if the U.S. economy were opened to trade and the world price of aluminum were above or below this $1 domestic price?

U.S. Export Supply If the aluminum price in the rest of the world (that is, Canada) exceeds $1, U.S. firms will produce more than 100 million pounds and will export the excess domestic output. First, consider a world price of $1.25. We see from the supply curve S_d that U.S. aluminum firms will produce 125 million pounds of aluminum at that price. The demand curve D_d tells us that the United States will purchase only 75 million pounds at $1.25. The outcome is a domestic surplus of 50 million pounds of aluminum. U.S. producers will export those 50 million pounds at the $1.25 world price.

What if the world price were $1.50? The supply curve shows that U.S. firms will produce 150 million pounds of aluminum, while the demand curve tells us that U.S. consumers will buy only 50 million pounds. So U.S. producers will export the domestic surplus of 100 million pounds.

Toward the top of Figure 20.3b we plot the domestic surpluses—the U.S. exports—that occur at world prices above the $1 domestic equilibrium price. When the world and domestic prices are equal (= $1), the quantity of exports supplied is zero (point *a*). There is no surplus of domestic output to export. But when the world price is $1.25, U.S. firms export 50 million pounds of surplus aluminum (point *b*). At a $1.50 world price, the domestic surplus of 100 million pounds is exported (point *c*).

The U.S. **export supply curve,** found by connecting points *a*, *b*, and *c*, shows the amount of aluminum U.S.

FIGURE 20.3 U.S. export supply and import demand. (a) Domestic supply S_d and demand D_d set the domestic equilibrium price of aluminum at $1 per pound. At world prices above $1 there are domestic surpluses of aluminum. At prices below $1 there are domestic shortages. (b) Surpluses are exported (top curve), and shortages are met by importing aluminum (lower curve). The export supply curve shows the direct relationship between world prices and U.S. exports; the import demand curve portrays the inverse relationship between world prices and U.S. imports.

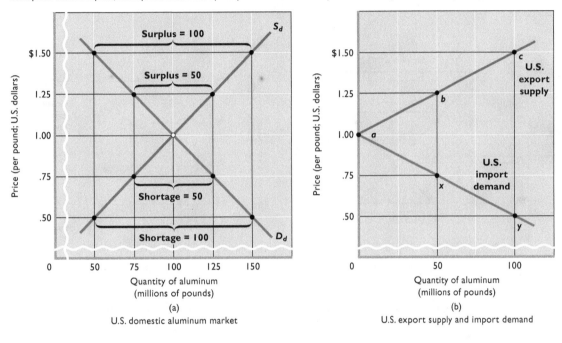

(a)
U.S. domestic aluminum market

(b)
U.S. export supply and import demand

producers will export at each world price above $1. This curve *slopes upward*, indicating a direct or positive relationship between the world price and the amount of U.S. exports. As world prices increase relative to domestic prices, U.S. exports rise.

U.S. Import Demand If the world price is below the domestic $1 price, the United States will import aluminum. Consider a $0.75 world price. The supply curve in Figure 20.3a reveals that at that price U.S. firms produce only 75 million pounds of aluminum. But the demand curve shows that the United States wants to buy 125 million pounds at that price. The result is a domestic shortage of 50 million pounds. To satisfy that shortage, the United States will import 50 million pounds of aluminum.

At an even lower world price, $0.50, U.S. producers will supply only 50 million pounds. Because U.S. consumers want to buy 150 million pounds at that price, there is a domestic shortage of 100 million pounds. Imports will flow to the United States to make up the difference. That is, at a $0.50 world price U.S. firms will supply 50 million pounds and 100 million pounds will be imported.

In Figure 20.3b we plot the U.S. **import demand curve** from these data. This *downsloping curve* shows the amounts of aluminum that will be imported at world prices below the $1 U.S. domestic price. The relationship between world prices and imported amounts is inverse or negative. At a world price of $1, domestic output will satisfy U.S. demand; imports will be zero (point *a*). But at $0.75 the United States will import 50 million pounds of aluminum (point *x*); at $0.50, the United States will import 100 million pounds (point *y*). Connecting points *a*, *x*, and *y* yields the *downsloping* U.S. import demand curve. It reveals that as world prices fall relative to U.S. domestic prices, U.S. imports increase.

Supply and Demand in Canada

We repeat our analysis in Figure 20.4, this time from the viewpoint of Canada. (We have converted Canadian dollar prices to U.S. dollar prices via the exchange rate.) Note that the domestic supply curve S_d and the domestic demand curve D_d for aluminum in Canada yield a domestic price of $0.75, which is $0.25 lower than the $1 U.S. domestic price.

FIGURE 20.4 Canadian export supply and import demand. (a) At world prices above the $0.75 domestic price, production in Canada exceeds domestic consumption. At world prices below $0.75, domestic shortages occur. (b) Surpluses result in exports, and shortages result in imports. The Canadian export supply curve and import demand curve depict the relationships between world prices and exports or imports.

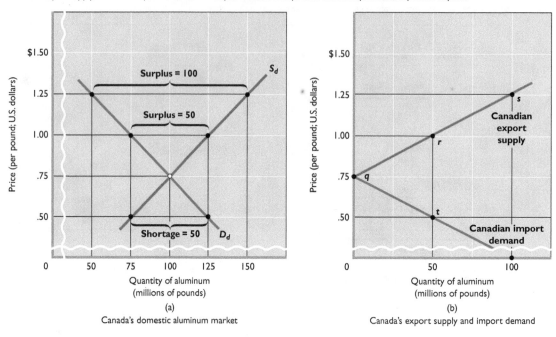

(a)
Canada's domestic aluminum market

(b)
Canada's export supply and import demand

The analysis proceeds exactly as above except that the domestic price is now the Canadian price. If the world price is $0.75, Canadians will neither export nor import aluminum (giving us point *q* in Figure 20.4b). At world prices above $0.75, Canadian firms will produce more aluminum than Canadian consumers will buy. Canadian firms will export the surplus. At a $1 world price, Figure 20.4b tells us that Canada will have and export a domestic surplus of 50 million pounds (yielding point *r*). At $1.25, it will have and will export a domestic surplus of 100 million pounds (point *s*). Connecting these points yields the upsloping Canadian export supply curve, which reflects the domestic surpluses (and hence the exports) that occur when the world price exceeds the $0.75 Canadian domestic price.

At world prices below $0.75, domestic shortages occur in Canada. At a $0.50 world price, Figure 20.4a shows that Canadian consumers want to buy 125 million pounds of aluminum but Canadian firms will produce only 75 million pounds. The shortage will bring 50 million pounds of imports to Canada (point *t* in Figure 20.4b). The Canadian import demand curve in that figure shows the Canadian imports that will occur at all world aluminum prices below the $0.75 Canadian domestic price.

Equilibrium World Price, Exports, and Imports

We now have the tools for determining the **equilibrium world price** of aluminum and the equilibrium world levels of exports and imports when the world is opened to trade. Figure 20.5 combines the U.S. export supply curve and import demand curve in Figure 20.3b and the Canadian export supply curve and import demand curve in Figure 20.4b. The two U.S. curves proceed rightward from the $1 U.S. domestic price; the two Canadian curves proceed rightward from the $0.75 Canadian domestic price.

International equilibrium occurs in this two-nation model where one nation's import demand curve intersects another nation's export supply curve. In this case the U.S. import demand curve intersects Canada's export supply curve at *e*. There, the world price of aluminum is $0.88. The Canadian export supply curve indicates that Canada will export 25 million pounds of aluminum at this price. Also at this price the United States will

WORKED PROBLEMS

W20.2

Equilibrium world price, exports, and imports

FIGURE 20.5 Equilibrium world price and quantity of exports and imports. In a two-nation world, the equilibrium world price (= $0.88) is determined by the intersection of one nation's export supply curve and the other nation's import demand curve. This intersection also decides the equilibrium volume of exports and imports. Here, Canada exports 25 million pounds of aluminum to the United States.

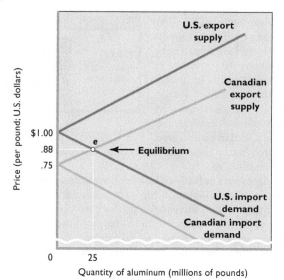

import 25 million pounds from Canada, indicated by the U.S. import demand curve. The $0.88 world price equates the quantity of imports demanded and the quantity of exports supplied (25 million pounds). Thus, there will be world trade of 25 million pounds of aluminum at $0.88 per pound.

Note that after trade, the single $0.88 world price will prevail in both Canada and the United States. Only one price for a standardized commodity can persist in a highly competitive world market. With trade, all consumers can buy a pound of aluminum for $0.88, and all producers can sell it for that price. This world price means that Canadians will pay more for aluminum with trade ($0.88) than without it ($0.75). The increased Canadian output caused by trade raises Canadian per-unit production costs and therefore raises the price of aluminum in Canada. The United States, however, pays less for aluminum with trade ($0.88) than without it ($1). The U.S. gain comes from Canada's comparative cost advantage in producing aluminum.

Why would Canada willingly send 25 million pounds of its aluminum output to the United States for U.S. consumption? After all, producing this output uses up scarce Canadian resources and drives up the price of aluminum for Canadians. Canadians are willing to export aluminum

to the United States because Canadians gain the means— the U.S. dollars—to import other goods, say, computer software, from the United States. Canadian exports enable Canadians to acquire imports that have greater value to Canadians than the exported aluminum. Canadian exports to the United States finance Canadian imports from the United States.

QUICK REVIEW 20.4

- A nation will export a particular product if the world price exceeds the domestic price; it will import the product if the world price is less than the domestic price.
- In a two-country world model, equilibrium world prices and equilibrium quantities of exports and imports occur where one nation's export supply curve intersects the other nation's import demand curve.

Trade Barriers and Export Subsidies

LO20.4 Analyze the economic effects of tariffs and quotas. While a nation as a whole gains from trade, trade may harm particular domestic industries and their workers. Those industries might seek to preserve their economic positions by persuading their respective governments to protect them from imports—perhaps through tariffs, import quotas, or other trade barriers.

Indeed, the public may be won over by the apparent plausibility ("Cut imports and prevent domestic unemployment") and the patriotic ring ("Buy American!") of the arguments. The alleged benefits of tariffs are immediate and clear-cut to the public, but the adverse effects cited by economists are obscure and dispersed over the entire economy. When political deal-making is added in—"You back tariffs for the apparel industry in my state, and I'll back tariffs for the auto industry in your state"—the outcome can be a politically robust network of trade barriers. These impediments to free international trade can take several forms.

Tariffs are excise taxes or "duties" on the dollar values or physical quantities of imported goods. They may be imposed to obtain revenue or to protect domestic firms. A **revenue tariff** is usually applied to a product that is not being produced domestically, for example, tin, coffee, or bananas in the case of the United States. Rates on revenue tariffs tend to be modest and are designed to provide the federal government with revenue. A **protective tariff** is

implemented to shield domestic producers from foreign competition. These tariffs impede free trade by increasing the prices of imported goods and therefore shifting sales toward domestic producers. Although protective tariffs are usually not high enough to stop the importation of foreign goods, they put foreign producers at a competitive disadvantage. A tariff on imported auto tires, for example, would make domestically produced tires more attractive to consumers.

An **import quota** is a limit on the quantities or total values of specific items that are imported in some period. Once a quota is filled, further imports of that product are choked off. Import quotas are more effective than tariffs in impeding international trade. With a tariff, a product can go on being imported in large quantities. But with an import quota, all imports are prohibited once the quota is filled.

A **nontariff barrier (NTB)** includes onerous licensing requirements, unreasonable standards pertaining to product quality, or simply bureaucratic hurdles and delays in customs procedures. Some nations require that importers of foreign goods obtain licenses and then restrict the number of licenses issued. Although many nations carefully inspect imported agricultural products to prevent the introduction of potentially harmful insects, some countries use lengthy inspections to impede imports. Japan and the European countries frequently require that their domestic importers of foreign goods obtain licenses. By restricting the issuance of licenses, governments can limit imports.

A **voluntary export restriction (VER)** is a trade barrier by which foreign firms "voluntarily" limit the amount of their exports to a particular country. VERs have the same effect as import quotas and are agreed to by exporters to avoid more stringent tariffs or quotas. In the late 1990s, for example, Canadian producers of softwood lumber (fir, spruce, cedar, pine) agreed to a VER on exports to the United States under the threat of a permanently higher U.S. tariff.

ORIGIN OF THE IDEA

O20.2
Trade protectionism

An **export subsidy** consists of a government payment to a domestic producer of export goods and is designed to aid that producer. By reducing production costs, the subsidies enable the domestic firm to charge a lower price and thus to sell more exports in world markets. Two examples: Some European governments have heavily subsidized Airbus Industries, a European firm that produces commercial aircraft. The subsidies help Airbus compete against the American firm Boeing. The United States and other nations have subsidized domestic farmers to boost the domestic food supply. Such subsidies have artificially lowered export prices on agricultural produce.

Later in this chapter we will discuss some of the specific arguments and appeals that are made to justify protection.

Economic Impact of Tariffs

We will confine our in-depth analysis of the effects of trade barriers to the two most common forms: tariffs and quotas. Once again, we turn to supply and demand analysis for help. Curves D_d and S_d in Figure 20.6 show domestic demand and supply for a product in which a nation, say, the United States, does *not* have a comparative advantage—for example, DVD players. (Disregard curve $S_d + Q$ for now.) Without world trade, the domestic price and output would be P_d and q, respectively.

Assume now that the domestic economy is opened to world trade and that Japan, which *does* have a comparative advantage in DVD players, begins to sell its players in the United States. We assume that with free trade the domestic price cannot differ from the world price, which here is P_w. At P_w domestic consumption is d and domestic production is a. The horizontal distance between the domestic supply and demand curves at P_w represents imports of ad.

FIGURE 20.6 The economic effects of a protective tariff or an import quota. A tariff that increases the price of a good from P_w to P_t will reduce domestic consumption from d to c. Domestic producers will be able to sell more output (b rather than a) at a higher price (P_t rather than P_w). Foreign exporters are injured because they sell less output (bc rather than ad). The yellow area indicates the amount of tariff paid by domestic consumers. An import quota of bc units has the same effect as the tariff, with one exception: The amount represented by the yellow area will go to foreign producers rather than to the domestic government.

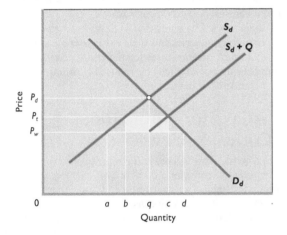

Thus far, our analysis is similar to the analysis of world prices in Figure 20.3.

Direct Effects Suppose now that the United States imposes a tariff on each imported DVD player. The tariff, which raises the price of imported players from P_w to P_t, has four effects:

- ***Decline in consumption*** Consumption of DVD players in the United States declines from d to c as the higher price moves buyers up and to the left along their demand curve. The tariff prompts consumers to buy fewer players, and reallocate a portion of their expenditures to less desired substitute products. U.S. consumers are clearly injured by the tariff, since they pay $P_t - P_w$ more for each of the c units they buy at price P_t.

- ***Increased domestic production*** U.S. producers—who are not subject to the tariff—receive the higher price P_t per unit. Because this new price is higher than the pretariff world price P_w, the domestic DVD-player industry moves up and to the right along its supply curve S_d, increasing domestic output from a to b. Domestic producers thus enjoy both a higher price and expanded sales; this explains why domestic producers lobby for protective tariffs. But from a social point of view, the increase in domestic production from a to b

means that the tariff permits domestic producers of players to bid resources away from other, more efficient, U.S. industries.

- ***Decline in imports*** Japanese producers are hurt. Although the sales price of each player is higher by $P_t - P_w$, that amount accrues to the U.S. government, not to Japanese producers. The after-tariff world price, or the per-unit revenue to Japanese producers, remains at P_w, but the volume of U.S. imports (Japanese exports) falls from ad to bc.

- ***Tariff revenue*** The yellow rectangle represents the amount of revenue the tariff yields. Total revenue from the tariff is determined by multiplying the tariff, $P_t - P_w$ per unit, by the number of players imported, bc. This tariff revenue is a transfer of income from consumers to government and does not represent any net change in the nation's economic well-being. The result is that government gains this portion of what consumers lose by paying more for DVD players.

Indirect Effect Tariffs have a subtle effect beyond what our supply and demand diagram can show. Because Japan sells fewer DVD players in the United States, it earns fewer dollars and so must buy fewer U.S. exports. U.S. export industries must then cut production and release resources. These are highly efficient industries, as we know from their comparative advantage and their ability to sell goods in world markets.

Tariffs directly promote the expansion of inefficient industries that do not have a comparative advantage; they also indirectly cause the contraction of relatively efficient industries that do have a comparative advantage. Put bluntly, tariffs cause resources to be shifted in the wrong direction—and that is not surprising. We know that specialization and world trade lead to more efficient use of world resources and greater world output. But protective tariffs reduce world trade. Therefore, tariffs also reduce efficiency and the world's real output.

Economic Impact of Quotas

We noted earlier that an import quota is a legal limit placed on the amount of some product that can be imported in a given year. Quotas have the same economic impact as a tariff, with one big difference: While tariffs generate revenue for the domestic government, a quota transfers that revenue to foreign producers.

Suppose in Figure 20.6 that, instead of imposing a tariff, the United States prohibits any imports of Japanese DVD players in excess of bc units. In other words, an import quota of bc players is imposed on Japan. We deliberately chose the size of this quota to be the same amount as imports would be under a $P_t - P_w$ tariff so that we can compare "equivalent" situations. As a consequence of the quota, the supply of players is $S_d + Q$ in the United States. This supply consists of the domestic supply plus the fixed amount bc $(= Q)$ that importers will provide at each domestic price. The supply curve $S_w + Q$ does not extend below price P_w because Japanese producers would not export players to the United States at any price below P_w; instead, they would sell them to other countries at the world market price of P_w.

Most of the economic results are the same as those with a tariff. Prices of DVD players are higher (P_t instead of P_w) because imports have been reduced from ad to bc. Domestic consumption of DVD players is down from d to c. U.S. producers enjoy both a higher price (P_t rather than P_w) and increased sales (b rather than a).

The difference is that the price increase of $P_t - P_w$ paid by U.S. consumers on imports of bc—the yellow area—no longer goes to the U.S. Treasury as tariff (tax) revenue but flows to the Japanese firms that have acquired the quota rights to sell DVD players in the United States. For consumers in the United States, a tariff produces a better economic outcome than a quota, other things being the same. A tariff generates government revenue that can be used to cut other taxes or to finance public goods and services that benefit the United States. In contrast, the higher price created by quotas results in additional revenue for foreign producers.

QUICK REVIEW 20.5

- A tariff on a product increases its price, reduces its consumption, increases its domestic production, reduces its imports, and generates tariff revenue for the government; an import quota does the same, except a quota generates revenue for foreign producers rather than for the government imposing the quota.

Net Costs of Tariffs and Quotas

Figure 20.6 shows that tariffs and quotas impose costs on domestic consumers but provide gains to domestic producers and, in the case of tariffs, revenue to the federal government. The consumer costs of trade restrictions are calculated by determining the effect the restrictions have on consumer prices. Protection raises the price of a product in three ways: (1) The price of the imported product goes up; (2) the higher price of imports causes some consumers to shift their purchases to higher-priced domestically produced goods; and (3) the prices of domestically produced goods rise because import competition has declined.

Study after study finds that the costs to consumers substantially exceed the gains to producers and government. A sizable net cost or efficiency loss to society arises from trade protection. Furthermore, industries employ large amounts of economic resources to influence Congress to pass and retain protectionist laws. Because these rent-seeking efforts divert resources away from more socially desirable purposes, trade restrictions impose these additional costs on society as well.

Conclusion: The gains that U.S. trade barriers create for protected industries and their workers come at the expense of much greater losses for the entire economy. The result is economic inefficiency, reduced consumption, and lower standards of living.

The Case for Protection: A Critical Review

LO20.5 Analyze the validity of the most frequently presented arguments for protectionism.

Despite the logic of specialization and trade, there are still protectionists in some union halls, corporate boardrooms, and congressional conference rooms. What arguments do protectionists make to justify trade barriers? How valid are those arguments?

Military Self-Sufficiency Argument

The argument here is not economic but political-military: Protective tariffs are needed to preserve or strengthen industries that produce the materials essential for national defense. In an uncertain world, the political-military objectives (self-sufficiency) sometimes must take precedence over economic goals (efficiency in the use of world resources).

Unfortunately, it is difficult to measure and compare the benefit of increased national security against the cost of economic inefficiency when protective tariffs are imposed. The economist can only point out that when a nation levies tariffs to increase military self-sufficiency, it incurs economic costs.

All people in the United States would agree that relying on hostile nations for necessary military equipment is not a good idea, yet the self-sufficiency argument is open to serious abuse. Nearly every industry can claim that it makes direct or indirect contributions to national security and hence deserves protection from imports.

Diversification-for-Stability Argument

Highly specialized economies such as Saudi Arabia (based on oil) and Cuba (based on sugar) are dependent on international markets for their income. In these economies, wars, international political developments, recessions abroad, and random fluctuations in world supply and demand for one or two particular goods can cause deep declines in export revenues and therefore in domestic income. Tariff and quota protection are allegedly needed in such nations to enable greater industrial diversification. That way, these economies will not be so dependent on exporting one or two products to obtain the other goods they need. Such goods will be available domestically, thereby providing greater domestic stability.

There is some truth in this diversification-for-stability argument. But the argument has little or no relevance to the United States and other advanced economies. Also, the economic costs of diversification may be great; for example, one-crop economies may be highly inefficient at manufacturing.

Infant Industry Argument

The infant industry argument contends that protective tariffs are needed to allow new domestic industries to establish themselves. Temporarily shielding young domestic firms from the severe competition of more mature and more efficient foreign firms will give infant industries a chance to develop and become efficient producers.

This argument for protection rests on an alleged exception to the case for free trade. The exception is that young industries have not had, and if they face mature foreign competition will never have, the chance to make the long-run adjustments needed for larger scale and greater efficiency in production. In this view, tariff protection for such infant industries will correct a misallocation of world resources perpetuated by historically different levels of economic development between domestic and foreign industries.

There are some logical problems with the infant industry argument. In the developing nations it is difficult to determine which industries are the infants that are capable of achieving economic maturity and therefore deserving protection. Also, protective tariffs may persist even after industrial maturity has been realized.

Most economists feel that if infant industries are to be subsidized, there are better means than tariffs for doing so. Direct subsidies, for example, have the advantage of making explicit which industries are being aided and to what degree.

Protection-against-Dumping Argument

The protection-against-dumping argument contends that tariffs are needed to protect domestic firms from "dumping" by foreign producers. **Dumping** is the sale of a product in a foreign country at prices either below cost or below the prices commonly charged at home.

Economists cite two plausible reasons for this behavior. First, with regard to below-cost dumping, firms in country A may dump goods at below cost into country B in an attempt to drive their competitors in country B out of business. If the firms in country A succeed in driving their competitors in country B out of business, they will enjoy monopoly power and monopoly prices and profits on the goods they subsequently sell in country B. Their hope is that the longer-term monopoly profits will more than offset the losses from below-cost sales that must take place while they are attempting to drive their competitors in country B out of business.

Second, dumping that involves selling abroad at a price that is below the price commonly charged in the home country (but that is still at or above production costs) may be a form of price discrimination, which is charging different prices to different customers. As an example, a foreign seller that has a monopoly in its home market may find that it can maximize its overall profit by charging a high price in its monopolized domestic market while charging a lower price in the United States, where it must compete with U.S. producers. Curiously, it may pursue this strategy even if it makes no profit at all from its sales in the United States, where it must charge the competitive price. So why bother selling in the United States? Because the increase in overall production that comes about by exporting to the United States may allow the firm to obtain the per-unit cost savings often associated with large-scale production. These cost savings imply even higher profits in the monopolized domestic market.

Because dumping is an "unfair trade practice," most nations prohibit it. For example, where dumping is shown to injure U.S. firms, the federal government imposes tariffs called *antidumping duties* on the goods in question. But relatively few documented cases of dumping occur each year, and specific instances of unfair trade do not justify widespread, permanent tariffs. Moreover, antidumping duties can be abused. Often, what appears to be dumping is simply comparative advantage at work.

Increased Domestic Employment Argument

Arguing for a tariff to "save U.S. jobs" becomes fashionable when the economy encounters a recession (such as the severe recession of 2007–2009 in the United States).

In an economy that engages in international trade, exports involve spending on domestic output and imports reflect spending to obtain part of another nation's output. So, in this argument, reducing imports will divert spending on another nation's output to spending on domestic output. Thus, domestic output and employment will rise. But this argument has several shortcomings.

While imports may eliminate some U.S. jobs, they create others. Imports may have eliminated the jobs of some U.S. steel and textile workers in recent years, but other workers have gained jobs unloading ships, flying imported aircraft, and selling imported electronic equipment. Import restrictions alter the composition of employment, but they may have little or no effect on the volume of employment.

The *fallacy of composition*—the false idea that what is true for the part is necessarily true for the whole—is also present in this rationale for tariffs. All nations cannot simultaneously succeed in restricting imports while maintaining their exports; what is true for one nation is not true for all nations. The exports of one nation must be the imports of another nation. To the extent that one country is able to expand its economy through an excess of exports over imports, the resulting excess of imports over exports worsens another economy's unemployment problem. It is no wonder that tariffs and import quotas meant to achieve domestic full employment are called "beggar my neighbor" policies: They achieve short-run domestic goals by making trading partners poorer.

Moreover, nations adversely affected by tariffs and quotas are likely to retaliate, causing a "trade war" (more precisely, a *trade barrier war*) that will choke off trade and make all nations worse off. The **Smoot-Hawley Tariff Act** of 1930 is a classic example. Although that act was meant to reduce imports and stimulate U.S. production, the high tariffs it authorized prompted adversely affected nations to retaliate with tariffs equally high. International trade fell, lowering the output and income of all nations. Economic historians generally agree that the Smoot-Hawley Tariff Act was a contributing cause of the Great Depression.

Finally, forcing an excess of exports over imports cannot succeed in raising domestic employment over the long run. It is through U.S. imports that foreign nations earn dollars for buying U.S. exports. In the long run, a nation must import in order to export. The long-run impact of tariffs is not an increase in domestic employment but, at best, a reallocation of workers away from export industries and to protected domestic industries. This shift implies a less efficient allocation of resources.

Cheap Foreign Labor Argument

The cheap foreign labor argument says that domestic firms and workers must be shielded from the ruinous competition of countries where wages are low. If protection is not provided, cheap imports will flood U.S. markets and the prices of U.S. goods—along with the wages of U.S. workers—will be pulled down. That is, domestic living standards in the United States will be reduced.

This argument can be rebutted at several levels. The logic of the argument suggests that it is not mutually beneficial for rich and poor persons to trade with one another. However, that is not the case. A low-income farmworker may pick lettuce or tomatoes for a rich landowner, and both may benefit from the transaction. And both U.S. consumers and Chinese workers gain when they "trade" a pair of athletic shoes priced at $30 as opposed to U.S. consumers being restricted to buying a similar shoe made in the United States for $60.

Also, recall that gains from trade are based on comparative advantage, not on absolute advantage. Look back at Figure 20.1, where we supposed that the United States and Mexico had labor forces of exactly the same size. Noting the positions of the production possibilities curves, observe that U.S. labor can produce more of either good. Thus, it is more productive. Because of this greater productivity, we can expect wages and living standards to be higher for U.S. labor. Mexico's less productive labor will receive lower wages.

The cheap foreign labor argument suggests that, to maintain its standard of living, the United States should not trade with low-wage Mexico. What if it does not trade with Mexico? Will wages and living standards rise in the United States as a result? No. To obtain vegetables, the United States will have to reallocate a portion of its labor from its relatively more-efficient beef industry to its relatively less-efficient vegetables industry. As a result, the average productivity of U.S. labor will fall, as will real wages and living standards. The labor forces of both countries will have diminished standards of living because without specialization and trade they will have less output available to them. Compare column 4 with column 1 in Table 20.1 or points A' and Z' with A and Z in Figure 20.2 to confirm this point.

Another problem with the cheap foreign labor argument is that its proponents incorrectly focus on labor costs per hour when what really matters is labor costs per unit of output. As an example, suppose that a U.S. factory pays its workers $20 per hour while a factory in a developing country pays its workers $4 per hour. The proponents of the cheap foreign labor argument look at these numbers and conclude—incorrectly—that it is impossible for the U.S. factory to compete with the factory in the developing country. But this conclusion fails to take into account two crucial facts:

- What actually matters is labor costs per *unit of output*, not labor costs per *hour of work*.

- Differences in productivity typically mean that labor costs per unit of output are often nearly identical despite huge differences in hourly labor costs.

To see why these points matter so much, let's take into account how productive the two factories are. Because the U.S. factory uses much more sophisticated technology, better trained workers, and a lot more capital per worker, one worker in one hour can produce 20 units of output. Since the U.S. workers get paid $20 per hour, this means the U.S. factory's labor cost *per unit of output* is $1. The factory in the developing country is much less productive since it uses less efficient technology and its relatively untrained workers have a lot less machinery and equipment to work with. A worker there produces only 4 units per hour. Given the foreign wage of $4 per hour, this means that the labor cost per unit of output at the factory in the developing country is also $1.

As you can see, the lower wage rate per hour at the factory in the developing country does not translate into lower labor costs per unit—meaning that it won't be able to undersell its U.S. competitor just because its workers get paid lower wages per hour.

Proponents of the cheap foreign labor argument tend to focus exclusively on the large international differences that exist in labor costs per hour. They typically fail to mention that these differences in labor costs per hour are mostly the result of tremendously large differences in productivity and that these large differences in productivity serve to equalize labor costs per unit of output. As a result, firms in developing countries only *sometimes* have an advantage in terms of labor costs per unit of output. Whether they do in any specific situation will vary by industry and firm and will depend on differences in productivity as well as differences in labor costs per hour. For many goods, labor productivity in high-wage countries like the United States is so much higher than labor productivity in low-wage countries that it is actually cheaper *per unit of output* to manufacture those goods in high-wage countries. That is why, for instance, Intel still makes microchips in the United States and why most automobiles are still produced in the United States, Japan, and Europe rather than in low-wage countries.

> **QUICK REVIEW 20.6**
>
> - Most rationales for trade protections are special-interest requests that, if followed, would create gains for protected industries and their workers at the expense of greater losses for the economy.

Multilateral Trade Agreements and Free-Trade Zones

LO20.6 Identify and explain the objectives of GATT, WTO, EU, eurozone, and NAFTA, and discuss offshoring and trade adjustment assistance.

Aware of the detrimental effects of trade wars and the general weaknesses of arguments for trade protections, nations have worked to lower tariffs worldwide. Their pursuit of freer trade has been aided by recently emerged special-interest groups that have offset the more-established special-interest groups that have traditionally supported tariffs and quotas. Specifically, lower tariffs are now supported by exporters of goods and services, importers of foreign components used in "domestic" products, and domestic sellers of imported products.

General Agreement on Tariffs and Trade

In 1947, 23 nations, including the United States, signed the **General Agreement on Tariffs and Trade (GATT).** GATT was based on three principles: (1) equal, nondiscriminatory trade treatment for all member nations; (2) the reduction of tariffs by multilateral negotiation; and (3) the elimination of import quotas. Basically, GATT provided a forum for the multilateral negotiation of reduced trade barriers.

Since the Second World War, member nations have completed eight "rounds" of GATT negotiations to reduce trade barriers. The eighth round of negotiations began in Uruguay in 1986. After seven years of complex discussions, in 1993 a new agreement was reached by the 128 nations that were by that time members of GATT. The Uruguay Round agreement took effect on January 1, 1995, and its provisions were phased in through 2005.

Under this agreement, tariffs on thousands of products were eliminated or reduced, with overall tariffs dropping by 33 percent. The agreement also liberalized government rules that in the past impeded the global market for such services as advertising, legal services, tourist services, and financial services. Quotas on imported textiles and apparel were phased out and replaced with tariffs. Other provisions reduced agricultural subsidies paid to farmers and protected intellectual property (patents, trademarks, and copyrights) against piracy.

World Trade Organization

The Uruguay Round agreement established the **World Trade Organization (WTO)** as GATT's successor. Some 159 nations belonged to the WTO in 2013. The WTO oversees trade agreements reached by the member nations, and rules on trade disputes among them. It also provides forums for further rounds of trade negotiations. The ninth and latest round of negotiations—the **Doha Development Agenda**—was launched in Doha, Qatar, in late 2001. (The trade rounds occur over several years in several venues but are named after the city or country of origination.) The negotiations are aimed at further reducing tariffs and quotas, as well as agricultural subsidies that distort trade. You can get an update on the status of the complex negotiations at **www.wto.org**.

GATT and the WTO have been positive forces in the trend toward liberalized world trade. The trade rules agreed upon by the member nations provide a strong and necessary bulwark against the protectionism called for by the special-interest groups in the various nations.

For that reason and others, the WTO is quite controversial. Critics are concerned that rules crafted to expand international trade and investment enable firms to circumvent national laws that protect workers and the environment. Critics ask: What good are minimum-wage laws, worker-safety laws, collective-bargaining rights, and environmental laws if firms can easily shift their production to nations that have weaker laws or if consumers can buy goods produced in those countries?

Proponents of the WTO respond that labor and environmental protections should be pursued directly in nations that have low standards and via international organizations other than the WTO. These issues should not be linked to the process of trade liberalization, which confers widespread economic benefits across nations. Moreover, say proponents of the WTO, many environmental and labor concerns are greatly overblown. Most world trade is among advanced industrial countries, not between them and countries that have lower environmental and labor standards. Moreover, the free flow of goods and resources raises output and income in the developing nations. Historically, such increases in living standards have eventually resulted in stronger, not weaker, protections for the environment and for workers.

The European Union

Countries have also sought to reduce tariffs by creating regional free-trade zones. The most dramatic example is the **European Union (EU)**. Initiated in 1958 as the Common Market, in 2003 the EU comprised 15 European nations—Austria, Belgium, Denmark, Finland, France, Germany, Greece, Ireland, Italy, Luxembourg, the Netherlands, Portugal, Spain, Sweden, and the United Kingdom. In 2004, the EU expanded by 10 additional European countries—Cyprus, the Czech Republic, Estonia, Hungary, Latvia, Lithuania, Malta, Poland, Slovakia, and Slovenia. The 2007 addition of Bulgaria and Romania plus the 2013 addition of Croatia expanded the EU to 28 nations.

The EU has abolished tariffs and import quotas on nearly all products traded among the participating nations and established a common system of tariffs applicable to all goods received from nations outside the EU. It has also liberalized the movement of capital and labor within the EU and has created common policies in other economic matters of joint concern, such as agriculture, transportation, and business practices.

EU integration has achieved for Europe what the U.S. constitutional prohibition on tariffs by individual states has achieved for the United States: increased regional specialization, greater productivity, greater output, and faster economic growth. The free flow of goods and services has created large markets for EU industries. The resulting economies of large-scale production have enabled these industries to achieve much lower costs than they could have achieved in their small, single-nation markets.

One of the most significant accomplishments of the EU was the establishment of the so-called **eurozone** or euro area in the early 2000s. As of 2013, 17 members of the EU (Austria, Belgium, Cyprus, Estonia, Finland, France, Germany, Greece, Ireland, Italy, Luxembourg, Malta, the Netherlands, Portugal, Slovenia, Slovakia, and Spain) use the euro as a common currency. Notably, the United Kingdom, Denmark, and Sweden have opted not to use the common currency, at least for now. But gone are French francs, German marks, Italian liras, and other national currencies that were once used by eurozone countries.

Economists expect the adoption of the euro to raise the standard of living in the eurozone nations over time. By ending the inconvenience and expense of exchanging currencies, the euro has enhanced the free flow of goods, services, and resources among the eurozone members. Companies that previously sold products in only one or two European nations have found it easier to price and sell their products in all 17 eurozone countries. The euro has also allowed consumers and businesses to comparison shop for outputs and inputs, and this capability has increased competition, reduced prices, and lowered costs.

North American Free Trade Agreement

In 1993 Canada, Mexico, and the United States created a major free-trade zone. The **North American Free Trade Agreement (NAFTA)** established a free-trade area that has about the same combined output as the EU but encompasses a much larger geographic area. NAFTA has eliminated tariffs and other trade barriers between Canada, Mexico, and the United States for most goods and services.

Critics of NAFTA feared that it would cause a massive loss of U.S. jobs as firms moved to Mexico to take advantage of lower wages and weaker regulations on pollution and workplace safety. Also, they were concerned that Japan and South Korea would build plants in Mexico and transport goods tariff-free to the United States, further hurting U.S. firms and workers.

In retrospect, critics were much too pessimistic. Since the passage of NAFTA in 1993, employment in the United States has increased by more than 20 million workers. NAFTA has increased trade among Canada, Mexico, and the United States and has enhanced the standard of living in all three countries.

QUICK REVIEW 20.7

- The General Agreement on Tariffs and Trade (GATT) of 1947 reduced tariffs and quotas and established a process for numerous subsequent rounds of multinational trade negotiations that have liberalized international trade.
- The World Trade Organization (WTO)—GATT's successor—rules on trade disputes and provides forums for negotiations on further rounds of trade liberalization. The current round of negotiations is called the Doha Development Agenda.
- The European Union (EU) and the North American Free Trade Agreement (NAFTA) have reduced internal trade barriers among their member nations by establishing multination free-trade zones.

Recognizing Those Hurt by Free Trade

Shifts in patterns of comparative advantage and removal of long-standing trade protection can hurt specific groups of workers. For example, the erosion of the United States' once strong comparative advantage in steel has caused production plant shutdowns and layoffs in the U.S. steel industry. The textile and apparel industries in the United States face similar difficulties. Clearly, not everyone wins from free trade (or freer trade). Some workers lose.

Trade Adjustment Assistance

The **Trade Adjustment Assistance Act** of 2002 introduced some innovative policies to help those hurt by shifts in international trade patterns. The law provides cash assistance (beyond unemployment insurance) for up to 78 weeks for workers displaced by imports or plant relocations abroad. To obtain the assistance, workers must participate in job searches, training programs, or remedial education. Also provided are relocation allowances to help displaced workers move geographically to new jobs within the United States. Refundable tax credits for health insurance serve as payments to help workers maintain their insurance coverage during the retraining and job-search period. Workers who are 50 years of age or older are eligible for "wage insurance," which replaces some of the difference in pay (if any) between their old and new jobs. Many economists support trade adjustment assistance because it not only helps workers hurt by international trade but also helps create the political support necessary to reduce trade barriers and export subsidies.

But not all economists favor trade adjustment assistance. Loss of jobs from imports, sending some work abroad, and plant relocations to other countries are only a small fraction (about 4 percent in recent years) of total job losses in the economy each year. Many workers also lose their jobs because of changing patterns of demand, changing technology, bad management, and other dynamic aspects of a market economy. Some critics ask, "What makes losing one's job to international trade worthy of such special treatment, compared to losing one's job to, say, technological change or domestic competition?" Economists can find no totally satisfying answer.

Offshoring of Jobs

Not only are some U.S. jobs lost because of international trade, but some are lost because of globalization of resource markets. In recent years U.S. firms have found the outsourcing of work abroad to be increasingly profitable. Economists call this business activity **offshoring**—shifting work previously done by American workers to workers located in other nations. Offshoring is not a new practice but traditionally has involved components for U.S. manufacturing goods. For example, Boeing has long offshored the production of major airplane parts for its "American" aircraft.

Recent advances in computer and communications technology have enabled U.S. firms to offshore service jobs such as data entry, book composition, software coding, call-center operations, medical transcription, and claims processing to countries such as India. Where offshoring

LAST WORD

Petition of the Candlemakers, 1845

French Economist Frédéric Bastiat (1801–1850) Devastated the Proponents of Protectionism by Satirically Extending Their Reasoning to Its Logical and Absurd Conclusions.

Petition of the Manufacturers of Candles, Waxlights, Lamps, Candlesticks, Street Lamps, Snuffers, Extinguishers, and of the Producers of Oil Tallow, Rosin, Alcohol, and, Generally, of Everything Connected with Lighting.

TO MESSIEURS THE MEMBERS OF THE CHAMBER OF DEPUTIES.

Gentlemen—You are on the right road. You reject abstract theories, and have little consideration for cheapness and plenty. Your chief care is the interest of the producer. You desire to emancipate him from external competition, and reserve the national market for national industry.

We are about to offer you an admirable opportunity of applying your—what shall we call it? your theory? No; nothing is more deceptive than theory; your doctrine? your system? your principle? but you dislike doctrines, you abhor systems, and as for principles, you deny that there are any in social economy: we shall say, then, your practice, your practice without theory and without principle.

We are suffering from the intolerable competition of a foreign rival, placed, it would seem, in a condition so far superior to ours for the production of light, that he absolutely inundates our national market with it at a price fabulously reduced. The moment he shows himself, our trade leaves us—all consumers apply to him; and a branch of native industry, having countless ramifications, is all at once rendered completely stagnant. This rival . . . is no other than the Sun.

What we pray for is, that it may please you to pass a law ordering the shutting up of all windows, skylights, dormer windows, outside and inside shutters, curtains, blinds, bull's-eyes; in a word, of all openings, holes, chinks, clefts, and fissures, by or through which the light of the sun has been in use to enter houses, to the prejudice of the meritorious manufacturers with which we flatter ourselves we have accommodated our country,—a country which, in gratitude, ought not to abandon us now to a strife so unequal.

If you shut up as much as possible all access to natural light, and create a demand for artificial light, which of our French manufacturers will not be encouraged by it? If more tallow is consumed, then there must be more oxen and sheep; and, consequently, we shall behold the multiplication of artificial meadows, meat, wool, hides, and, above all, manure, which is the basis and foundation of all agricultural wealth.

The same remark applies to navigation. Thousands of vessels will proceed to the whale fishery; and, in a short time, we shall possess a navy capable of maintaining the honor of France, and gratifying the patriotic aspirations of your petitioners, the undersigned candle-makers and others.

Only have the goodness to reflect, Gentlemen, and you will be convinced that there is, perhaps, no Frenchman, from the wealthy coalmaster to the humblest vender of lucifer matches, whose lot will not be ameliorated by the success of this our petition.

Source: Frédéric Bastiat, *Economic Sophisms* (Irvington-on-Hudson, NY: The Foundation for Economic Education, Inc., 1996), abridged. Used with permission of Foundation for Economic Education, **www.FEE.org**.

occurs, some of the value added in the production process accrues to foreign countries rather than the United States. So part of the income generated from the production of U.S. goods is paid to foreigners, not to American workers.

Offshoring is a wrenching experience for many Americans who lose their jobs, but it is not necessarily bad for the overall economy. Offshoring simply reflects growing specialization and international trade in services, or, more descriptively, "tasks." That growth has been made possible by recent trade agreements and new information and communication technologies. As with trade in goods, trade in services reflects comparative advantage and is beneficial to both trading parties. Moreover, the United States has a sizable trade surplus with other nations in services. The United States gains by specializing in high-valued services such as transportation services, accounting services, legal services, and advertising services, where it still has a comparative advantage. It then "trades" to obtain lower-valued services such as call-center and data-entry work, for which comparative advantage has gone abroad.

Offshoring also increases the demand for complementary jobs in the United States. Jobs that are close substitutes for existing U.S. jobs are lost, but complementary jobs in the United States are expanded. For example, the lower price of writing software code in India may mean a lower cost of software sold in the United States and abroad. That, in turn, may create more jobs for U.S.-based workers such as software designers, marketers, and distributors.

Moreover, offshoring may encourage domestic investment and the expansion of firms in the United States by reducing their production costs and keeping them competitive worldwide. In some instances, "offshoring jobs" may equate to "importing competitiveness." Entire firms that might otherwise disappear abroad may remain profitable in the United States only because they can offshore some of their work.

> **QUICK REVIEW 20.8**
>
> - Increased international trade and offshoring of jobs have harmed some specific U.S. workers and have led to policies such as trade adjustment assistance to try to help them with their transitions to new lines of work.

SUMMARY

LO20.1 List and discuss several key facts about international trade.

The United States leads the world in the combined volume of exports and imports. Other major trading nations are Germany, Japan, the western European nations, and the Asian economies of China, South Korea, Taiwan, and Singapore. The United States' principal exports include chemicals, agricultural products, consumer durables, semiconductors, and aircraft; principal imports include petroleum, automobiles, metals, household appliances, and computers.

LO20.2 Define comparative advantage, and demonstrate how specialization and trade add to a nation's output.

World trade is based on three considerations: the uneven distribution of economic resources among nations, the fact that efficient production of various goods requires particular techniques or combinations of resources, and the differentiated products produced among nations.

Mutually advantageous specialization and trade are possible between any two nations if they have different domestic opportunity-cost ratios for any two products. By specializing on the basis of comparative advantage, nations can obtain larger real incomes with fixed amounts of resources. The terms of trade determine how this increase in world output is shared by the trading nations. Increasing (rather than constant) opportunity costs limit specialization and trade.

LO20.3 Describe how differences between world prices and domestic prices prompt exports and imports.

A nation's export supply curve shows the quantities of a product the nation will export at world prices that exceed the domestic

price (the price in a closed, no-international-trade economy). A nation's import demand curve reveals the quantities of a product it will import at world prices below the domestic price.

In a two-nation model, the equilibrium world price and the equilibrium quantities of exports and imports occur where one nation's export supply curve intersects the other nation's import demand curve. A nation will export a particular product if the world price exceeds the domestic price; it will import the product if the world price is less than the domestic price. The country with the lower costs of production will be the exporter and the country with the higher costs of production will be the importer.

LO20.4 Analyze the economic effects of tariffs and quotas.

Trade barriers take the form of protective tariffs, quotas, nontariff barriers, and "voluntary" export restrictions. Export subsidies also distort international trade. Supply and demand analysis demonstrates that protective tariffs and quotas increase the prices and reduce the quantities demanded of the affected goods. Sales by foreign exporters diminish; domestic producers, however, gain higher prices and enlarged sales. Consumer losses from trade restrictions greatly exceed producer and government gains, creating an efficiency loss to society.

LO20.5 Analyze the validity of the most frequently presented arguments for protectionism.

The strongest arguments for protection are the infant industry and military self-sufficiency arguments. Most other arguments for protection are interest-group appeals or reasoning fallacies that emphasize producer interests over consumer interests or stress the immediate effects of trade barriers while ignoring long-run consequences.

The cheap foreign labor argument for protection fails because it focuses on labor costs per hour rather than on what really matters, labor costs per unit of output. Due to higher productivity, firms in high-wage countries like the United States can have lower wage costs per unit of output than competitors in low-wage countries. Whether they do will depend on how their particular wage and productivity levels compare with those of their competitors in low-wage countries.

LO20.6 Identify and explain the objectives of GATT, WTO, EU, eurozone, and NAFTA, and discuss offshoring and trade adjustment assistance.

In 1947 the General Agreement on Tariffs and Trade (GATT) was formed to encourage nondiscriminatory treatment for all member nations, to reduce tariffs, and to eliminate import quotas. The Uruguay Round of GATT negotiations (1993) reduced tariffs and quotas, liberalized trade in services, reduced agricultural subsidies, reduced pirating of intellectual property, and phased out quotas on textiles.

GATT's successor, the World Trade Organization (WTO), had 159 member nations in 2013. It implements WTO agreements, rules on trade disputes between members, and provides forums for continued discussions on trade liberalization. The latest round of trade negotiations—the Doha Development Agenda—began in late 2001 and as of 2013 was still in progress.

Free-trade zones liberalize trade within regions. Two examples of free-trade arrangements are the 28-member European Union (EU) and the North American Free Trade Agreement (NAFTA), comprising Canada, Mexico, and the United States. Seventeen EU nations have abandoned their national currencies for a common currency called the euro.

The Trade Adjustment Assistance Act of 2002 recognizes that trade liberalization and increased international trade can create job loss for many workers. The Act therefore provides cash assistance, education and training benefits, health care subsidies, and wage subsidies (for persons aged 50 or older) to qualified workers displaced by imports or relocations of plants from the United States to abroad.

Offshoring is the practice of shifting work previously done by Americans in the United States to workers located in other nations. Although offshoring reduces some U.S. jobs, it lowers production costs, expands sales, and therefore may create other U.S. jobs. Less than 4 percent of all job losses in the United States each year are caused by imports, offshoring, and plant relocation abroad.

TERMS AND CONCEPTS

labor-intensive goods

land-intensive goods

capital-intensive goods

opportunity-cost ratio

comparative advantage

principle of comparative advantage

terms of trade

trading possibilities line

gains from trade

world price

domestic price

export supply curve

import demand curve

equilibrium world price

tariffs

revenue tariff

protective tariff

import quota

nontariff barrier (NTB)

voluntary export restriction (VER)

export subsidy

dumping

Smoot-Hawley Tariff Act

General Agreement on Tariffs and Trade (GATT)

World Trade Organization (WTO)

Doha Development Agenda

European Union (EU)

eurozone

North American Free Trade Agreement (NAFTA)

Trade Adjustment Assistance Act

offshoring

The following and additional problems can be found in connect
ECONOMICS

DISCUSSION QUESTIONS

1. Quantitatively, how important is international trade to the United States relative to the importance of trade to other nations? What country is the United States' most important trading partner, quantitatively? With what country does the United States have the largest trade deficit? **LO20.1**

2. Distinguish among land-, labor-, and capital-intensive goods, citing an example of each without resorting to book examples. How do these distinctions relate to international trade? How do distinctive products, unrelated to resource intensity, relate to international trade? **LO20.1, LO20.2**

3. Explain: "The United States can make certain toys with greater productive efficiency than can China. Yet we import those toys from China." Relate your answer to the ideas of Adam Smith and David Ricardo. **LO20.2**

4. Suppose Big Country can produce 80 units of X by using all its resources to produce X or 60 units of Y by devoting all its resources to Y. Comparable figures for Small Nation are 60 units of X and 60 units of Y. Assuming constant costs, in which product should each nation specialize? Explain why. What are the limits of the terms of trade between these two countries? How would rising costs (rather than constant costs) affect the extent of specialization and trade between these two countries? **LO20.2**

5. What is an export supply curve? What is an import demand curve? How do such curves relate to the determination of the equilibrium world price of a tradable good? **LO20.3**

6. Why is a quota more detrimental to an economy than a tariff that results in the same level of imports as the quota? What is the net outcome of either tariffs or quotas for the world economy? **LO20.4**

7. "The potentially valid arguments for tariff protection—military self-sufficiency, infant industry protection, and diversification for stability—are also the most easily abused." Why are these arguments susceptible to abuse? **LO20.4**

8. Evaluate the effectiveness of artificial trade barriers, such as tariffs and import quotas, as a way to achieve and maintain full employment throughout the U.S. economy. How might such policies reduce unemployment in one U.S. industry but increase it in another U.S. industry? **LO20.4**

9. In 2012, manufacturing workers in the United States earned average compensation of $35.67 per hour. That same year, manufacturing workers in Mexico earned average compensation of $6.36 per hour. How can U.S. manufacturers possibly compete? Why isn't all manufacturing done in Mexico and other low-wage countries? **LO20.4**

10. How might protective tariffs reduce both the imports and the exports of the nation that levies tariffs? In what way do foreign firms that "dump" their products onto the U.S. market in effect provide bargains to American consumers? How might the import competition lead to quality improvements and cost reductions by American firms? **LO20.4**

11. Identify and state the significance of each of the following trade-related entities: (*a*) the WTO; (*b*) the EU; (*c*) the eurozone; and (*d*) NAFTA. **LO20.6**

12. What form does trade adjustment assistance take in the United States? How does such assistance promote political support for free-trade agreements? Do you think workers who lose their jobs because of changes in trade laws deserve special treatment relative to workers who lose their jobs because of other changes in the economy, say, changes in patterns of government spending? **LO20.6**

13. What is offshoring of white-collar service jobs and how does that practice relate to international trade? Why has offshoring increased over the past few decades? Give an example (other than that in the textbook) of how offshoring can eliminate some American jobs while creating other American jobs. **LO20.6**

14. **LAST WORD** What was the central point that Bastiat was trying to make in his imaginary petition of the candlemakers?

REVIEW QUESTIONS

1. In Country A, a worker can make 5 bicycles per hour. In Country B, a worker can make 7 bicycles per hour. Which country has an absolute advantage in making bicycles? **LO20.2**
   a. Country A.
   b. Country B.

2. In Country A, the production of 1 bicycle requires using resources that could otherwise be used to produce 11 lamps. In Country B, the production of 1 bicycle requires using resources that could otherwise be used to produce 15 lamps. Which country has a comparative advantage in making bicycles? **LO20.2**
   a. Country A.
   b. Country B.

3. True or False: If Country B has an absolute advantage over Country A in producing bicycles, it will also have a comparative advantage over Country A in producing bicycles. **LO20.2**

4. Suppose that the opportunity-cost ratio for sugar and almonds is $4S \equiv 1A$ in Hawaii but $1S \equiv 2A$ in California. Which state has the comparative advantage in producing almonds? **LO20.2**
   a. Hawaii.
   b. California.
   c. Neither.

5. Suppose that the opportunity-cost ratio for fish and lumber is $1F \equiv 1L$ in Canada but $2F \equiv 1L$ in Iceland. Then _____ should specialize in producing fish while _____ should specialize in producing lumber. **LO20.2**
   a. Canada; Iceland.
   b. Iceland; Canada.

6. Suppose that the opportunity-cost ratio for watches and cheese is $1C \equiv 1W$ in Switzerland but $1C \equiv 4W$ in Japan. At which of the following international exchange ratios (terms of trade) will Switzerland and Japan be willing to specialize and engage in trade with each other. **LO20.2**
   *Select **one or more** answers from the choices shown.*
   a. $1C \equiv 3W$.
   b. $1C \equiv \frac{1}{2}W$.
   c. $1C \equiv 5W$.
   d. $\frac{1}{2}C \equiv 1W$.
   e. $2C \equiv 1W$.

7. We see quite a bit of international trade in the real world. And trade is driven by specialization. So why don't we see full specialization—for instance, all cars in the world being made in South Korea, or all the mobile phones in the world

being made in China? Choose the best answer from among the following choices. LO20.2
a. High tariffs.
b. Extensive import quotas.
c. Increasing opportunity costs.
d. Increasing returns.

8. Which of the following are benefits of international trade? LO20.2
*Choose **one or more** answers from the choices shown.*
a. A more efficient allocation of resources.
b. A higher level of material well-being.
c. Gains from specialization.
d. Promoting competition.
e. Deterring monopoly.
f. Reducing the threat of war.

9. True or False: If a country is open to international trade, the domestic price can differ from the international price. LO20.3

10. Suppose that the current international price of wheat is $6 per bushel and that the United States is currently exporting 30 million bushels per year. If the United States suddenly became a closed economy with respect to wheat, would the domestic price of wheat in the United States end up higher or lower than $6? LO20.3
a. Higher.
b. Lower.
c. The same.

11. Suppose that if Iceland and Japan were both closed economies, the domestic price of fish would be $100 per ton in Iceland and $90 per ton in Japan. If the two countries decided to open up to international trade with each other, which of the following could be the equilibrium international price of fish once they begin trading? LO20.3
a. $75.
b. $85.
c. $95.
d. $105.

12. Draw a domestic supply-and-demand diagram for a product in which the United States does not have a comparative advantage. What impact do foreign imports have on domestic price and quantity? On your diagram show a protective tariff that eliminates approximately one-half of the assumed imports. What are the price-quantity effects of this tariff on (*a*) domestic consumers, (*b*) domestic producers, and (*c*) foreign exporters? How would the effects of a quota that creates the same amount of imports differ? LO20.4

13. American apparel makers complain to Congress about competition from China. Congress decides to impose either a tariff or a quota on apparel imports from China. Which policy would Chinese apparel manufacturers prefer? LO20.4
a. Tariff.
b. Quota.

PROBLEMS

1. Assume that the comparative-cost ratios of two products—baby formula and tuna fish—are as follows in the nations of Canswicki and Tunata:

   Canswicki: 1 can baby formula $\equiv$ 2 cans tuna fish
   Tunata: 1 can baby formula $\equiv$ 4 cans tuna fish

   In what product should each nation specialize? Which of the following terms of trade would be acceptable to both nations: (*a*) 1 can baby formula $\equiv 2\frac{1}{2}$ cans tuna fish; (*b*) 1 can baby formula $\equiv$ 1 can tuna fish; (*c*) 1 can baby formula $\equiv$ 5 cans tuna fish? LO20.2

2. The accompanying hypothetical production possibilities tables are for New Zealand and Spain. Each country can produce apples and plums. Plot the production possibilities data for each of the two countries separately. Referring to your graphs, answer the following: LO20.2

New Zealand's Production Possibilities Table (Millions of Bushels)

Product	Production Alternatives			
	A	B	C	D
Apples	0	20	40	60
Plums	15	10	5	0

Spain's Production Possibilities Table (Millions of Bushels)

Product	Production Alternatives			
	R	S	T	U
Apples	0	20	40	60
Plums	60	40	20	0

a. What is each country's cost ratio of producing plums and apples?
b. Which nation should specialize in which product?
c. Show the trading possibilities lines for each nation if the actual terms of trade are 1 plum for 2 apples. (Plot these lines on your graph.)
d. Suppose the optimum product mixes before specialization and trade were alternative B in New Zealand and alternative S in Spain. What would be the gains from specialization and trade?

3. The following hypothetical production possibilities tables are for China and the United States. Assume that before specialization and trade the optimal product mix for China is alternative B and for the United States is alternative U. LO20.2
a. Are comparative-cost conditions such that the two areas should specialize? If so, what product should each produce?

b. What is the total gain in apparel and chemical output that would result from such specialization?

c. What are the limits of the terms of trade? Suppose that the actual terms of trade are 1 unit of apparel for $1\frac{1}{2}$ units of chemicals and that 4 units of apparel are exchanged for 6 units of chemicals. What are the gains from specialization and trade for each nation?

Product	China Production Possibilities					
	A	B	C	D	E	F
Apparel (in thousands)	30	24	18	12	6	0
Chemicals (in tons)	0	6	12	18	24	30

Product	U.S. Production Possibilities					
	R	S	T	U	V	W
Apparel (in thousands)	10	8	6	4	2	0
Chemicals (in tons)	0	4	8	12	16	20

4. Refer to Figure 3.6, page 63. Assume that the graph depicts the U.S. domestic market for corn. How many bushels of corn, if any, will the United States export or import at a world price of $1, $2, $3, $4, and $5? Use this information to construct the U.S. export supply curve and import demand curve for corn. Suppose that the only other corn-producing nation is France, where the domestic price is $4. Which country will export corn; which county will import it? **LO20.3**

CHAPTER THIRTY-FOUR

College and University Education: Why Is It So Expensive?

Learning Objectives

After reading this chapter you should be able to:

LO1 Understand why a college education is so expensive and why those costs have been rising faster than inflation.

LO2 Explain the role of textbooks in those rising costs.

LO3 Apply the principle of present value so as to see why borrowing money to pay for a college education is a wise, if potentially risky, investment in future income potential.

LO4 Understand that the United States has a greater percentage of citizens with a college degree than other developed countries, though that advantage is rapidly evaporating.

Chapter Outline

Introduction

Why Are the Costs So High?

Why Are College Costs Rising So Fast?

Why Have Textbook Costs Risen So Rapidly?

What a College Degree Is Worth

How Do People Pay for College?

Summary

Introduction

In the preceding chapter, we raised questions about the costs and effectiveness of education through grade 12. Here we explore whether students in colleges and universities are receiving good value for their money. In 2010, a little more than $471 billion was spent educating 21 million college students, which works out to $22,429 per student, per year. Obviously it costs substantially more for higher education than it does for students in elementary or secondary schools. Moreover, tuition, room, and board have increased 629 percent over the last 31 years—a period when overall prices increased only 131 percent. Figure 34.1 shows that both college tuition and college textbook prices have increased much more rapidly than has inflation.

To find out why this is so, we examine some of the economic issues for higher education. We include a discussion of why it costs more and whether those costs are worth it to the college student consumer. We proceed to discuss how higher education is financed in the United States and finish with a discussion of one of the most significant expenses in college textbooks.

Why Are the Costs So High?

The reasons why college costs more than high school per student are both obvious and hidden. First, the obvious: On the average, college professors earn salaries that are almost twice those of elementary and secondary teachers.

FIGURE 34.1   College costs relative to CPI.

Source: Bureau of Labor Statistics, www.bls.gov/cpi/home.htm

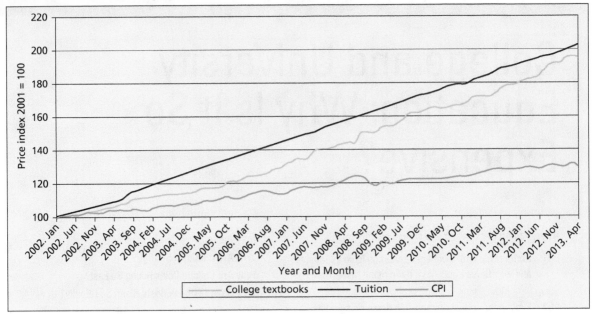

Colleges have libraries that dwarf what we might see in a high school, and librarians have no choice but to subscribe to wildly expensive journals, including many in the sciences that have five-figure subscription prices. If you have not already noticed, college professors teach far less than high school teachers do. A professor at a research-oriented university may teach only 3 to 6 hours a week, while a professor in a teaching-oriented community college may average 12 to 15 hours a week. High school teachers are in the classroom from around 8 a.m. to around 3 p.m., with some time off for lunch and preparation. They may teach five- or six-hour-long classes, five days a week. In net, a high school teacher is in class more in a single day than some professors are in a week.

Exploring reasons for the disparities between K–12 and college teachers gets us into some less obvious reasons why per-pupil college costs are so high. Educators at all levels must maintain a high level of expertise in their field. At the college level, it is accepted that professors need time for reading and studying. Professors who teach at the higher end of a discipline need particularly great amounts of time for scholarly study. Many professors are also judged by the degree to which they advance knowledge in their academic discipline. This research commands most of a professor's time at most

universities, whether or not they are regarded as prestigious. A sad fact of life in modern college education is that for a professor to advance within an institution, or to advance from a less prestigious school to a more prestigious school, research and other scholarly activity are more important than teaching.

That research is expensive. Research for an English professor requires a well-stocked library and a state-of-the-art computer. This is cheap compared to what it costs to set up a biologist to do advanced research. Not only do biologists require the well-stocked library; they require a fully stocked laboratory with equipment that can separate out DNA and that can magnify samples so that individual cells can be seen. The cost of some of this equipment is so high that if you used the money to equip high schools, you could equip all the high school labs of a medium-sized city for what it costs to fund the laboratory of a single professor at Harvard, MIT, or Stanford. On the other hand, research brings in a considerable amount of money to universities. At nearly $50 billion in 2011, the revenue associated with grants and contracts contributes almost as much money to higher education revenue as tuition does ($60 billion).

A final reason why college is so expensive relates to the subsidies. As shown in the previous chapter about

FIGURE 34.2   External benefits of a college education.

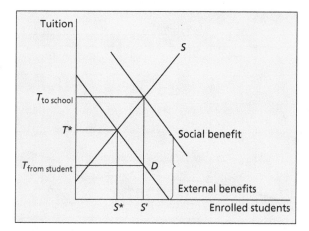

K–12 education, a college education provides private benefits to its students as well as external benefits to the public at large. The private benefits include the higher incomes college graduates earn as well as the fun college students have in and especially out of the classroom. The external benefits include the fact that the college educated pay far more in taxes over a lifetime than do those without such an education as well as the increased knowledge they bring to their voting and leadership activities. Thus, though perhaps not as significant as the external benefits of K–12 education, they are still high enough to justify having a considerable subsidy to that education.

Just as we used our supply and demand diagram in the previous chapter to illustrate the inefficiency of just having unsubsidized private K–12 education, we can apply the same models and principles here. Consider Figure 34.2 and what it suggests about the price of a college education. The price is the annual tuition and the quantity is the number of college students educated in a year. At low tuition rates, more will invest in a college education, so the resulting demand curve is downward sloping. However, if tuition is low, colleges and universities will be willing to educate fewer students.

The equilibrium tuition T* and the equilibrium number of enrolled students S* are what the unsubsidized market would yield. If there is an external benefit of the size shown, then the optimal number of students is much greater than the market amount. Unlike the K–12 case, the optimal number of students is likely not everyone and the optimal price is likely not zero. It does mean that students should not have to pay all of the costs and that taxpayers will have to pay a subsidy. Students should

pay $T_{from\ student}$, and taxpayers should pick up the rest so that the school gets the amount they need, $T_{to\ school}$, to teach S' students. Notice, though, what happens to the cost per student (not just to the student). It rises from the T* to $T_{to\ school}$. Subsidizing something contributes to its higher costs.

Why Are College Costs Rising So Fast?

As can be seen from Figure 34.3, though tuition has been rising fast, the rise in the revenues to universities has more to do with their other enterprises than it does with tuition. Total revenues to public universities increased by $200 billion over the period 1995 to 2011. Tuition increases only accounted for $37 billion of that increase. The staples of a public university's budget— especially a public university that is not the flagship of the state—are its tuition, its state (and to a lesser degree federal and local) appropriation, and its housing-based auxiliaries (shown in the figure as "aux-non-hospital").

There is little doubt, however, that the mix in revenues has changed dramatically throughout the years, even ignoring the largest part of the increase: that is, the increase in gift, investment, grant and contract, and affiliated hospital derived income.[1] Zeroing out those elements, the relative sizes of the wedges of the pie have changed markedly. Specifically, from 2007 to 2011, total federal, state, and local appropriations to public universities fell from nearly $80 billion to less than $75 billion. At that same time tuition revenue increased by 25 percent. Figure 34.4 shows that the share of revenues attributable to appropriations fell from 57 percent in 1995 to 47 percent in 2010, with almost the entirety of that difference being absorbed within tuition. Essentially, public universities are justifying their rapid increases in tuition on the relative decline in state appropriations.

Another reason for the increase in the cost of higher education is the degree to which student expectations of their environment have changed. The contrast between post–World War II student housing and modern student housing is remarkable. The floor of 40 two-to-a-room 10 × 15-foot prison cells with a common shower and bathroom facility has been replaced by suite-style housing with private or semiprivate showers and bathrooms.

---

[1]Some larger state universities operate hospitals as part of their medical schools, and the revenue from those hospitals significantly distorts the relative size of the revenue sources.

364   Chapter 34   *College and University Education: Why Is It So Expensive?*

FIGURE 34.3   Revenue to public degree-granting universities.

Source: National Center for Education Statistics, http://nces.ed.gov/programs/digest
*2001–2002 and 2002–2003 interpolated from available data.

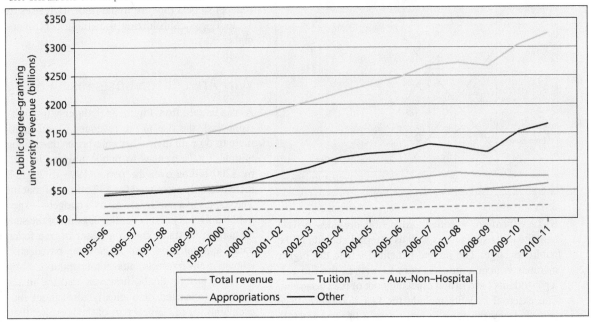

FIGURE 34.4   Share of university revenue: Appropriations, tuition, and non-hospital auxiliaries.

Source: National Center for Education Statistics, http://nces.ed.gov/programs/digest

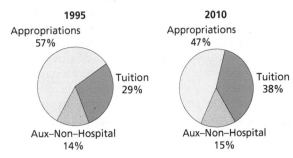

Building those newer facilities has led to a tenfold increase in debt for public universities in 10 years. Those costs have been passed on to students. Further, while not always directly demanding modern exercise facilities, students have chosen to enroll on campuses that have built them. The costs of constructing and equipping these recreation centers have been passed on to students either in the form of dedicated fees or in the form of higher tuition. Universities have built them largely for enrollment reasons. As public universities have come to increasingly depend on tuition revenue, they have become increasingly sensitive to student desires.

Why Have Textbook Costs Risen So Rapidly?

The market for college textbooks is a good example of a great many economic concepts: fixed and variable costs, the impact of patents and copyrights on the market for a good, the fuzziness of the line between oligopoly and monopolistic competition, and the degree to which increased technology increases supply. Before we get too deep into the analysis, you should understand how a textbook comes to market.

Either solicited or unsolicited, a faculty member will write a chapter or two to show a publisher why this new book would be better than those that exist. Very few of these prospective books make it past this step. Those sample chapters that meet with the publisher's expectations are sent out to faculty who, when the book is published, might consider using the book for their course. They are compensated for their feedback and, if the publisher senses from that feedback that the book will be successful, a contract is drawn up that specifies how the

FIGURE 34.5 Where the money goes.

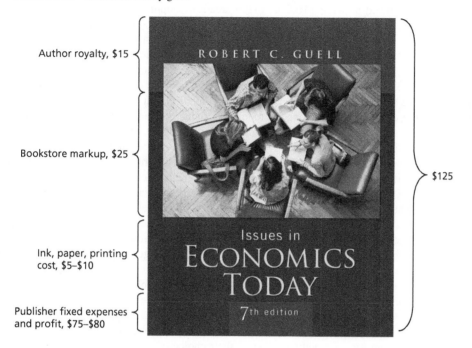

Author royalty, $15

Bookstore markup, $25

$125

Ink, paper, printing cost, $5–$10

Publisher fixed expenses and profit, $75–$80

author is to be paid. Typically the author will get a percentage of the sales (in the neighborhood of 15 percent) to bookstores (based on the wholesale price, net of returns). An **advance** is usually offered to the author against future **royalties**. The book takes at least a year to write, revise, edit, and publish. Often, a first edition takes much longer than subsequent editions because it is typically reviewed by a different collection of faculty around the country.

Once available for sale, the book is mailed, free of charge, to faculty all around the country that teach a course in which the book might be used. This could be thousands of books, as is the case when there is a rollout of a principles of economics book (that which is appropriate for business and economics majors) or a few hundred (when the book has a more limited audience). Faculty place their orders with their respective bookstores and the bookstores order them in the month leading up to the beginning of the semester.

advance
The amount of money paid to authors prior to a book's publication. This is typically counted against future royalties.

royalties
The amount of money paid to authors. Typically paid on a percentage basis.

To see where the money goes on the sale of a new book, consider the one you are reading. As shown in Figure 34.5, the previous edition of this book sold for $125 as a new book in my university's bookstore. The book was sold to the bookstore for $100 so its expenses and profit come out of the store's $25 markup. I get 15 percent of the amount that the publisher gets, or $15. The publisher keeps between $75 and $80. The publisher's costs include very high fixed costs for such things as supplements (recent textbooks have all needed to have expensively produced testbanks, instructor's manuals, website materials, study guides, PowerPoints, etc.) as well as costs associated with editorial staff and marketing. The variable costs also include the cost of the paper, ink, and printing of the book itself. In all, the marginal production cost of a textbook is less than $10, sometimes as little as $5. When all is said and done, the $75 to $80 margin that the publisher makes must cover all the fixed costs of production.

Here it gets tricky because the publisher, and by extension the author, makes money only when a new book is sold. You do not have to be in college very long to know that you can buy used textbooks for much less than new ones and that you can sell your books back to the bookstore at the end of the semester. Typically a book that sells new for \$125 will sell used for \$100. The bookstore will have purchased that used book from a previous student at the same university for around \$62.50.[2] The bookstore then stocks both new books and used books and makes a profit on either. There is some risk for the bookstore in overstocking a new book, since they have to pay a restocking fee to return new books to the publisher, but there is enormous risk in overstocking used books.

The bottom line for publishers is that they are in business to make money, and new sales increase profits and used book sales eat into profits. The break-even point on a book such as this one is around 5,000 units. The next 5,000 units can easily generate nearly a half million in profits for the publisher. This is why books are on relatively short production cycles. Calculus books, though the content hasn't changed since Newton figured it out, are revised regularly because publishers and authors make money only when the new edition sells for the first time.

A second significant cause behind the expense of textbooks is the market form. The book you are reading is the intellectual property of its owner. I gave that intellectual property to the publisher in exchange for the royalties they pay me for sales on the book. What the copyright does is to give McGraw-Hill Education the exclusive right to sell this material. It also prohibits you from walking down to FedEx-Kinko's and running off copies for your friends. Copyrights are necessary to bring intellectual property to market because without them producers of the books, songs, and inventions would have no financial motivation to produce them.

In some disciplines there is one standard textbook that everyone uses, while in others there are multiple texts that look very much the same. Though there are hundreds of textbooks on the market, most are not good substitutes for another. It does little good to bring your economics text to your poetry class. In the end, your professor probably had a relatively small number of books from which to choose. If you are using this book while taking a general education economics course for non-majors, your professor had to decide whether to cram a bunch of theory in or do an issues approach. Having chosen this book, your professor chose the issues approach. There are four books that really work in this niche. McGraw-Hill has a monopoly on this book but it

is a competitor in this niche. The market form best suited to this area is monopolistic competition.

The market for principles of economics texts is much greater and there are many more choices. There are four really big sellers and several scattered players. This is also an example of monopolistic competition. The differences between books is quite slight (mostly in presentation and emphasis), but the publishers still retain their monopoly rights. For an example of an area in which there are fewer sellers, consider the market for graduate-level textbooks in mathematical economics. For all intents and purposes, there are two. One is older than dirt and the other one is a few years old. This is an example of oligopoly. Some areas of economics are so narrow, with such a small market, that there is only one book.

A third reason why textbooks have increased rapidly in price is that, like prescription drugs, in most cases the consumer doesn't get to pick a cheaper alternative. Textbooks are chosen for you by faculty members who are often completely oblivious to the price that will be charged for the book because they get the book mailed to them free. When students go to the bookstore and get their books, they cannot choose which book to buy (beyond their choice of used versus new, buy versus rent, or print versus e-book). They have to decide to obtain the book or not. Thus the price of the book is irrelevant in the adoption decision. Under good circumstances, the adoption decision is typically made after a professor has looked at the choices in the area and selected the one that goes best with the course and the way the professor teaches. In the end, faculty often pick books that have the supplements they are looking for, have illustrations that simplify the subject, and that are pleasing to the eye. All of these add to the price of the book but the price often does not enter into the decision to adopt the book. The student is then made to choose between buying the book or not.

What a College Degree Is Worth

Now that we have seen a few reasons why college costs so much, we can ask whether it is worth the expense. To explore this question, we need again to understand and to use the concept of present value. If the interest-adjusted amount of money you spend on your education, the present value of the costs, is less than the interest-adjusted amount of the extra money you earn as a result of your education, the present value of the benefits, then your college education is worth the money you pay for it.

[2]There are several reasons why a student might get less than the full buyback price. Some include the existence of key codes for online content or custom content, or the fact that the book came in loose-leaf form.

AVOIDING HIGH TEXTBOOK PRICES

In recent years, there have been three significant changes to the textbook market that have jolted textbook companies. The first of these is the advent of a relatively old niche market for textbook rentals. Chegg and other Internet companies have revived this relatively small market in a significant way. These companies typically charge approximately half the retail price of the book but compel you to return the book to avoid being charged for the other half. To accomplish this, they will typically take a customer's credit card information for the sale and, if the book is not returned, charge it again. This amounts to the same issue as buying new books and selling them back, but the student doesn't take the risk that the book will be out of edition (and therefore worth much less).

Additionally, companies are beginning to see their e-book alternatives grow in popularity, in part thanks to the iPad. While some text-only books work well with e-readers such as Amazon's Kindle, graph and mathematics laden books with color are ill suited to the Kindle platform but are well suited to the iPad and PC platform. Again this is like renting a book but the book does not have to be returned; it simply becomes inaccessible after a semester (or year, depending on the seller's policies.)

Finally, an increasing number of faculty who have seen their students struggle with being able to afford their textbooks have chosen a path that is both interesting as an economist and troublesome as an author. It had been the case that when a new edition of a textbook came out, nearly every faculty member would adopt that new edition and the old editions would be of almost no value in the market. For instance, when the fifth edition of this book became available in the spring of 2010, it sold in bookstores for $125 and rented on Chegg for half that. At the same time, the fourth edition, which had sold in bookstores for $120 the semester before, was selling for less than $10 on the Internet's many used book outlets.

What seems to be occurring now is that some faculty order the old edition for everyone in their class so everyone in the class is in the same position. The faculty member has stayed with the author's book but there are no profits for the publisher or royalties for the author. The long-run impact of this strategy will, however, result in decreasing its viability as a strategy. As more faculty fail to "roll" to the new edition, the price of old editions will rise on the Internet as their easy availability shrinks. In addition, traditional bookstores will have an increasing difficulty finding and stocking the old editions in sufficient quantity to meet the demand. This new faculty strategy is both interesting and probably unsustainable.

Assume for a moment that your four years of college cost you $10,000 a year in out-of-pocket expenses and you give up another $12,000 a year in what you would have earned had you worked full time. The total cost of your education is then $22,000 a year, or a total of about $88,000. Since the expenses incurred in the second, third, and fourth years are in the future, you must discount them by the appropriate interest rate. Now assume that instead of making $12,000 a year without a degree, you will earn the degree and then make $30,000 a year. The benefit from going to college is the extra $18,000 you earn a year. We use $18,000 because this is roughly the difference in median income of households headed by people who have college degrees over that same figure for households headed by people with only a high school education. We must again discount these benefits, as they will happen in the future. If we assume that all of these dollar figures are inflation-adjusted and the real interest rate is 3 percent, then the present value of the costs is roughly $82,000 and the present value of 40 years of $18,000 extra a year is roughly $415,000. The net present value of a college degree is $333,000, making it so that dropping out of college is likely the most expensive noncriminal mistake you could ever make. Conversely, doing well in college may be the most lucrative thing you ever do.

How Do People Pay for College?

Many college students recognize the benefits of education but cannot see themselves paying for them. While we have just shown that it makes sense to complete college even if you have to borrow all of the money to do it, you know that merely racking up student loans does not mean you get a degree. This means that there is some risk involved. You have to weigh the risk of having the only thing you take away from college be debt against the benefit that you get the $333,000 in net present value. In addition, though it seems as if a college degree costs you a lot of money, consider the fact that at a public university you are getting a subsidy of nearly $1.50 for every $1 you spend. The subsidy of $1

FIGURE 34.6   College graduates as a percentage of the 24 and older population.

Source: United States Census Bureau, www.census.gov/hhes/socdemo/education/data/cps/index.html

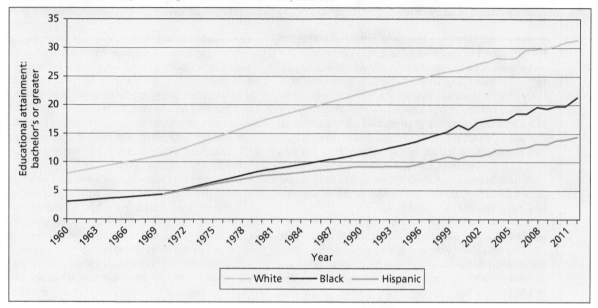

for every $1 at a private university is less, but it is still substantial. Subsidies to universities are computed from the value of interest-reduced loans and gifts to the universities. Whether you are a student at a public or private university, you are paying great sums of money, sums that would be even greater were it not for subsidies from national, state, and private sources.

One of the interesting changes over the last three decades has been the change in the way students pay for their portion of the costs of a higher education. In the 1940s, World War II veterans received the GI Bill, which allowed many former soldiers to go to college. Not only was their tuition paid, but they were also granted a stipend upon which to live. In the 1960s and 1970s, the federal government instituted programs such as the Pell Grant, which provided a similar benefit to children of poor families. In the 1980s, President Reagan shifted the focus to making student loans available at subsidized rates. In the 1990s, President Clinton reformulated the loan process by increasing federal government involvement and sponsored educational income tax deductions and credits. As a rarely discussed part of the Patient Protection and Affordable Care Act, President Obama's legislation reformed the student loan program to by-pass banks. The loans, instead, will be administered out of

the U.S. Department of Education. Taken together, these transformations have allowed more students to access some form of aid, but the aid is now more likely to come in the form of a subsidized loan.

Nationally, between 1992 and 2008, the percentage of students on some form of aid increased from 59 percent to 79.5 percent, and the percentage borrowing to pay for college increased from 31 percent to 53 percent, while the percentage receiving federally funded education grants has slowly increased to 33 percent.

Figure 34.6 shows that if we measure the success of higher education by looking at degrees granted, there is success. On the other hand, the United States is rapidly being caught (and surpassed) by other developed countries in the percentage of adults with a college education. The United States led OCED countries in 2008 with nearly a third of the adult population 25 to 64 having a college education. However, the U.S. rate for young adults (24–35) placed sixteenth on the list. The United States is not becoming less educated. It is that others are catching up. The college attainment rate for Americans has remained steady through the years, while the rate for other countries has increased rapidly. This could ultimately threaten the comparative advantage the United States had held in this particular area.

Summary

You now understand why a college education is an expensive thing to provide and why those costs have been rising faster than inflation over the years. You understand that a part of that rapidly rising set of costs is associated with the cost of textbooks. You understand that the principle of present value is useful in seeing why borrowing money to pay for a college education is a wise, if potentially risky, investment in future income potential and that the source of funds for students has increasingly moved from grants to loans. Finally, you understand that though higher educational attainment is higher in the United States than it is elsewhere, that advantage is evaporating as other countries' citizens are rapidly increasing their levels of educational attainment.

Key Terms

advance, 365

royalties, 365

Quiz Yourself

1. Which of the following has increased fastest?
   a. Overall prices.
   b. College textbook prices.
   c. College tuition.

2. What are the key reasons why college costs are higher than high school costs?
   a. The expenses of research.
   b. College faculty salaries are higher than K–12 faculty salaries.
   c. Subsidies to education cause increased demand for it.
   d. All of these.

3. The textbook production industry has a great deal in common with the pharmaceutical industry in that there are _____ fixed costs and _____ marginal costs.
   a. high; high
   b. high; low
   c. low; high
   d. low; low

4. Authors are typically paid for their work
   a. based on a percentage of the sales at college bookstores.
   b. based on a percentage of the sales from publishers to bookstores.
   c. a fixed amount regardless of sales.
   d. on a per-page basis.

5. The economic tool that proves the value of an expensive college education is
   a. production possibilities.
   b. the yield curve.
   c. supply and demand.
   d. present value.

6. The cost of educating a college student
   a. is less than the cost of educating a high school student because college classes are generally large.
   b. is equal to the cost of educating a high school student because, although college teachers make more money, their classes are generally larger.
   c. is less than it used to be.
   d. is much greater than the cost of educating a high school student because college professors make more money and teach fewer hours per week.

Think about This

Your education, from kindergarten through college, benefited you and it benefited society. The proportion of a typical college education paid by the student has risen in recent years. How much of your college education do you pay? (Consider the state appropriation to your school if it is public, the federal and state financial aid that you get, and the value of the guarantee on any of your student loans). Is this the right division of the burden?

Talk about This

How did cost figure into your choice of school? Did you have lots of options? If you could have gotten a "full ride," where would you have gone?

Behind the Numbers

Revenues, expenses, enrollments, sources of financing. Digest of Education Statistics—http://nces.ed.gov/programs/digest

Costs relative to other goods—www.bls.gov/cpi/home.htm

International comparisons—www.cgsnet.org/data-sources-international-comparisons-educational-attainment

Educational achievement—www.census.gov/hhes/socdemo/education/data/cps/index.html

CHAPTER THIRTY-SIX

Social Security

Learning Objectives

After reading this chapter you should be able to:

LO1 Describe what Social Security is and its basic tax and benefit structure.

LO2 Detail the history of changes to the program since its inception.

LO3 Explain the economic rationale for having such a system.

LO4 Enumerate the effects of the program on work and savings.

LO5 Show how economists use present value analysis to aid in determining for whom the program works and for whom it does not.

LO6 Explain the origin and purpose behind the Social Security Trust Fund.

LO7 Summarize present estimates of the future financial health of the Social Security system and evaluate the options for ensuring its long-run solvency.

Chapter Outline

When most people think about Social Security, they envision retirement checks for the elderly. Social Security has a much broader scope, including benefits for eligible widows and orphans in addition to medical and disability insurance. In this chapter we concentrate on retirement benefits.

We begin by reviewing the history of Social Security as a government pension program, and we include its tax, benefit, and structure. We then turn to why it is needed. We discuss the effects of Social Security on the economy in general and show that as a retirement program, it is better for retirees who are poor than for those who are rich and much better for those who retired before 1960 than after 1980. Last, we discuss why bankruptcy is likely without reform and what reform might look like.

The Basics

The Beginning

In 1935 the Social Security Act was passed and signed into law by President Franklin Roosevelt. The stock market crash of 1929 and the Great Depression of the 1930s had caused great upheavals in people's financial circumstances. Unemployment had reached a high of 25 percent. People who had been wealthy investors before the crash were lucky if they had a job that would allow them to at least live from paycheck to paycheck after the crash. Many banks closed when, as a result of the stock market crash, their investments were insufficient to pay their depositors. In this circumstance, even people who had saved diligently and invested prudently for their retirement found themselves without savings. Social Security guaranteed a safety net, come good times or bad, to generations who retired from the late 1930s on. At the time, it was not intended that Social Security be the only income on which a person lived. To nearly a third of recipients today it is just that.

Today, Social Security provides guaranteed retirement benefits averaging about $1,199 a month to 36 million American people over the age of 62. Social Security is a **pay-as-you-go pension** system where current workers' taxes are used to pay pensions to current retirees. This is unlike a traditional **fully funded pension** system where, for every benefit dollar it is required to pay in the future, there is an offsetting amount currently invested that is sufficient to pay off that dollar. It is the pay-as-you-go aspect that allowed money to go to the elderly right away (the first checks went out in 1936) but, as we will see, it is also this aspect that currently puts Social Security in the most jeopardy.

pay-as-you-go pension
A system where current workers' taxes are used to pay pensions to current retirees.

fully funded pension
A system that has an amount currently invested that is sufficient to pay every benefit dollar it is required to pay in the future.

Taxes

Social Security taxes (technically called FICA, or Federal Insurance Contribution Act taxes) are **payroll taxes**. That is, the amount workers pay is based on what workers earn from their work. This is different from an income tax in that interest, dividends, and other forms of unearned income are not subject to this tax. In addition, not all payroll is taxed; taxes are paid only up to a limited amount of income called the **maximum taxable earnings**. In 2013, this amount was $113,700 which means that workers did not have to pay the old-age portion of the Social Security tax for income they earned beyond that point. Both the employer and employee pay an equal amount of this tax so that if you have to pay $1,000 in tax, so does your employer. The self-employed pay both parts of the tax.

payroll taxes
Taxes owed on what workers earn from their work.

maximum taxable earnings
The maximum of taxable earnings subject to the payroll tax.

As part of a temporary stimulus agreement after the 2010 elections, the employee portion was reduced to 4.2 percent from 6.2 percent for the 2011 and 2012 tax years.

Benefits

On the benefit side, eligible retirees get benefit checks that are based on what they made during their working years. The **average index of monthly earnings (AIME)** is the monthly average of the 35 highest earnings years (capped by the maximum taxable earnings for each respective year) adjusted for wage inflation. The AIME is put into a formula that generates the **primary insurance amount (PIA)**.[1] Single people are paid the PIA and married couples get 1.5 times the highest of their PIAs, or the sum of their individual PIAs, whichever is higher. For full benefits workers cannot begin to collect until they reach the **retirement age**, though they can collect partial benefits at age 62.

average index of monthly earnings (AIME)
The monthly average of the 35 highest earnings years adjusted for wage inflation.

primary insurance amount (PIA)
The amount single retirees receive in a monthly check if they retire at their retirement age.

retirement age
The age at which retirees get full benefits.

Although the payroll tax structure is such that everyone with income under the maximum taxable earnings pays the same rate of tax, the benefit structure is such that, in net, Social Security redistributes income to the lower end of the income scale. To see this, consider the following example. Assume, inflation-adjusted, a person makes $5,000 per month for 35 years, so that person's AIME is $5,000. Inflation-adjusted, the employee and the employer each pay $382.50 (7.65% × $5,000) per month in taxes. That person would get a monthly Social Security check of $2,026. If someone else were in a similar situation with one-fifth the income, that person and his or her employer would combine to pay one-fifth the tax but the benefit would be $779 per month. Thus, this employee pays one-fifth the tax but receives one-third the benefit. This means that the person at the lower end of the income scale has a benefit dollar–to–tax dollar ratio that is twice that of the upper-income person. This is by design, and, as such, the program serves to redistribute money down the income line.

Changes over Time

Since its inception Social Security has added benefits. Payments to widows and orphans, called survivor

---

[1] The formula for 2013 was 90 percent of the first $791 plus 32 percent of the next $3,977 plus 15 percent of the remainder up to a maximum benefit that is computed using the maximum taxable earnings for each of the work years. This formula is adjusted yearly for inflation. For more information, see www.socialsecurity.gov

TABLE 36.1 History of Social Security's components at selected points in time.

Year	Maximum Taxable Earnings ($)	Old-Age and Disability Tax Rate (% of payroll)	Medicare Tax Rate (%)	Total Tax Rate That Both Employers and Employees Pay (%)	Retirement Age*		
					Year of Birth	Age	Benefits†
1937	$ 3,000	1.000%	0%	1.000%	1937	65	OA, S
1950	3,600	1.500	0	1.500	1950	66	OA, S
1955	4,200	2.000	0	2.000	1955	66 + 2 months	OA, S
1960	4,800	2.250	0	2.250	1960	67	OA, S, DI
1965	4,800	3.625	0	3.625	1965	67	OA, S, DI
1970	7,800	4.200	0.600	4.800	1970	67	OA, S, DI, HI
1975	14,100	4.950	0.900	5.850	1975	67	OA, S, DI, HI
1980	25,900	5.080	1.050	6.130	1980	67	OA, S, DI, HI
1985	39,600	5.700	1.300	7.000	1985	67	OA, S, DI, HI
1990	51,300	6.200	1.450	7.650	1990	67	OA, S, DI, HI
1995	61,200	6.200	1.450	7.650	1995	67	OA, S, DI, HI
2000	76,200	6.200	1.450	7.650	2000	67	OA, S, DI, HI
2013	113,700	6.200	1.450	7.650	2011	67	OA, S, D, HI

*Until 1983 the retirement age was 65. In 1983 the law was changed to increase it depending on year of birth. 1938, => 65 + 2 months; 1939, => 65 + 4 months; 1940, => 65 + 6 months; 1941, => 65 + 8 months; 1942, => 65 + 10 months; 1943−1954, => 66; 1955, => 66 + 2 months; 1956, => 66 + 4 months; 1957, => 66 + 6 months; 1958, => 66 + 8 months; 1959, => 66 + 10 months; 1960 on, 67.

†OA = old age; S = survivor; DI = disability; HI = health insurance (Medicare).

benefits, have been part of Social Security from its inception. Disability insurance, for workers who are unable to work for long periods of time, was added in 1956, and basic, highly subsidized health coverage (called Medicare) was added in 1966.

Table 36.1 shows how the tax rate, the maximum taxable earnings, and the retirement age have changed since the program began. This table shows how Social Security's components have been changed to ensure its survivability. As you can see, tax rates have risen, in part to pay for the other benefits described previously, but also to guarantee that retirement benefits would be there for each generation. The tax rate has risen from 1 percent to 7.65 percent while the maximum amount subject to tax has risen from $3,000 to $113,700. The retirement age has also risen. People born before 1938 can retire with full benefits at 65; those born after 1960 must wait until they are 67. A somewhat complicated transition formula determines the retirement age of those born between 1939 and 1959. In short, in contrast to the view that Social Security has been a monolithic and unalterable program, there have been many changes that have both broadened its scope and ensured its survivability.

Why Do We Need Social Security?

If you have worked through other issue chapters in this book by now, you know that it has been mentioned before that economists believe that government intervention in private enterprise must be justified on at least one of the following three grounds:

1. The need to control **externalities** that is, effects created by an unregulated market on people other than the buyer or seller, such as pollution, secondhand smoke, and drunk driving.

2. Concern about significant moral or ethical problems associated with the good being sold, for example, drugs, prostitution, and pornography.

3. Sellers or buyers are incapable of making rational decisions, because people either cannot be counted on to do the smart thing or have inadequate information upon which to base a decision.

externalities
Effects created by an unregulated market on people other than the buyer or seller.

It is a combination of the first and third reasons that makes some form of compulsory-saving/

retirement-benefit program necessary in the eyes of economists.

Ideally, rational and wise people will be able to save money for their own retirements based on their own preferences for consuming now versus consuming later. They will realize that money spent now has an opportunity cost, namely, money that cannot be spent later. Investment markets allow people to save or borrow as they please. If all the assumptions about well-functioning markets are valid in the investment market, then there is no reason for government to force people to save. They will save the right amount for themselves.

In opposition to the rationale put forth by economists is the contention that people may not be able to save the right amount for themselves. This is an argument that has little appeal among economists. Many economists maintain that if the government were not taxing workers for this purpose, workers could be saving the money on their own, and saving or not saving would therefore be their choice.

On the other hand, two arguments against a completely free market approach have some appeal among economists. First, our humanity prevents us from letting others starve. If people do not save for themselves, someone else will be forced to bail them out. Their decision not to save affects others. These "others" could be children, relatives, friends, or government. Social Security prevents people from not saving the right amount, and it protects others from having to bail them out.

Second, our rationality stems from our ability to learn from our mistakes. In most situations, and especially in most markets, we learn from our mistakes. For instance, if the first time you go grocery shopping for yourself you buy nothing but marshmallows and Red Bull, you will quickly learn that you need vegetables and fruits in your diet. If you do not save enough for retirement, you cannot just decide to live the first 65 years of your life over again. Government often prevents us from this sort of mistake. There are few guarantees that we will always do the right thing ourselves. There are other examples of this: (1) You cannot borrow money before age 18 without a cosignature; (2) you cannot drop out of school before you are 16; and (3) you cannot drink until you are 21. Society fears that you might suffer irreparable bankruptcy, poverty, or alcoholism, respectively; and it wants government to ensure that you will not make mistakes that cannot be undone. For these reasons, the question among economists is not whether some form of government-run retirement is needed but what form that system takes and how to fund it so that it is financially stable.

Social Security's Effect on the Economy

Effect on Work

Before Social Security was implemented, 51 percent of men over age 65 worked. Today, that number is 22 percent. While there is much dispute on the degree to which Social Security itself caused this to happen (in fact, this number has risen in recent years), Social Security has clearly made it easier for people to retire. This has good as well as bad aspects. Though the retired may be happier being retired, the economy is deprived of their labor and the fruit of their labor. On the other hand, as more people retire, positions are opened up throughout the labor scale as everyone moves up to fill vacated positions. Paradoxically, this is a circumstance in which the economy is hurt even though everyone in it is happier. (If this seems odd, revisit Chapter 6 and the section "Real Gross Domestic Product and Why It Is Not Synonymous with Social Welfare.")

Effect on Saving

Most economists believe that if people had to save for their own retirement, they would save more than they do now. Though these economists disagree on the magnitude of this effect, they have concluded that the existence of Social Security reduces the amount of money that is saved in the economy. This is primarily due to the **asset substitution effect**. If the government is taxing you on your earnings now and promising a pension payment later, the government is, in effect, saving for you. If the government is saving for you, you will save less for yourself.

asset substitution effect
Government is saving for you; thus you will save less for yourself.

induced retirement effect
People need to save more if they are going to retire earlier than they would have without Social Security.

Two counteracting effects to this are the **induced retirement effect** and the bequest effect. As mentioned, people are clearly retiring earlier than they did in the past. If Social Security did not exist, and people had no hope of ever retiring, they might not save anything. On the other hand, since Social Security makes retirement a possibility, people may save so as to retire. The induced retirement effect thus increases national savings because people need to save more if they are going to retire earlier than they would have without Social Security.

Another impact of Social Security is that it may increase national savings if the elderly are putting aside

TABLE 36.2 Present value analysis of Social Security.

Income ($)	Present Value of Social Security Taxes at 8% ($)	Present Value of Social Security Benefits at 8% ($)	Net Present Value of Social Security at 8% ($)	Real Rate of Return (%)
$ 15,000	$ 25,780	$ 11,434	−$ 14,346	2.6
20,000	34,374	13,836	−20,538	2.3
25,000	42,968	16,239	−26,729	2.1
30,000	51,561	18,446	−33,115	1.9
35,000	60,154	19,572	−40,582	1.7
40,000	68,748	20,698	−48,050	1.5

more money for bequests, that is, money that will go to younger family members when their elders die. It may be that Social Security provides a stable enough income for the elderly that they choose to save enough to pass on a larger inheritance than they would have if there had been no such program. The **bequest effect** thus increases national savings because people save more so as to give larger gifts to their descendants than they would have without Social Security.

bequest effect
People save more to give larger gifts to their descendants, thus increasing national savings.

Economists dispute the net effect of Social Security on savings. Martin Feldstein, in particular, was the first to estimate the effect of Social Security on savings. In 1974 he concluded that there was a dramatic reduction in savings. This was disputed by other economists, led by Alicia Munnell in 1977 and Dean Leimer and Selig Lesnoy in 1982, all of whom estimated that the net effect was zero. Not to be silenced, in 1996 Feldstein published revised estimates for 1992, when personal savings were actually $248 billion, indicating that it would have been $646 billion without Social Security. The upshot is that there is little agreement except for a middle ground that appears to indicate a small net negative impact of Social Security on savings.

Whom Is the Program Good For?

With a spreadsheet, a few assumptions, and some specialized terminology, you can compute whether Social Security is a good deal for you. To do this you will need to draw on the present value discussion of Chapter 7. We can then compare the taxes we pay today with the benefits we anticipate getting 40 or 50 years from now.

There is much literature on the present value of Social Security. C. Eugene Steuerle and Jon Bakija provide detailed present value estimates for different categories of people born in different generations. Though exact estimates vary by marital status, by earners, and by age, the results show unequivocally that the program was a net winner across the income scale for those retiring before 1980. However, because of the rapid increases in FICA taxes, this situation has steadily eroded, leaving only married couples, with only a single low-income earner, to benefit.

To get a flavor of what this kind of analysis entails, consider the following example. First, we need to make some basic assumptions. To estimate the present value of your Social Security taxes and benefits, we need to know your age, your marital status, the starting salary you can expect upon graduation, the rate at which your income will grow, an assumption of yearly inflation, your age at retirement, and, finally, your age at death. For Table 36.2 we will assume the following: You are 19; you will graduate at age 23; you will not get married; you will work until you are 67; you will die at 88; inflation will be 3 percent every year; your income will grow at 4 percent per year; and 8 percent is the appropriate interest rate. Though the old age and disability tax rate is 6.2 percent, the old age part is only 5.3 percent. This tax is on both the employer and employee, so we will assume that your old age Social Security contributions amount to 10.6 percent of your earnings (up to, of course, the maximum taxable earnings).[2]

Table 36.2 indicates that today's 19-year-olds would do better if their Social Security taxes were invested at 8 percent per year (inflation plus a 5 percent real rate of return) than they would do under Social Security. The first column shows the income assumed for the calculations, and the second indicates the present value, at 8 percent, of all taxes to be paid. The third column shows the present value, again at 8 percent, of all the benefits that

[2] We assume that employees bear the entire burden of the Social Security tax because empirical estimates of labor supply elasticity are nearly zero.

people will be entitled to from their retirements at age 67 until their deaths at 88. The last column indicates the appropriate real interest rate that equalizes the present value of taxes and benefits.

As can be seen from the first two columns, as people make more money, they also pay more taxes. Starting with people making minimum wage ($7.25/ hour × 2,080 hours in a year) and ending with people starting their working life with a $40,000 salary, the present value of their taxes increases from $25,780 to $68,748.[3] Also apparent from the table is that the present value of benefits for high-income people is greater than that for low-income people. This is because the more you make and contribute to the system, the bigger your benefit checks are at retirement. Note here that although the high earner makes much more than three times what the lower earner makes, the benefit check the high earner gets is a little more than twice that of the lower earner.

The fact that the net present value is negative means that Social Security will not pay as well as a private investment making 8 percent. As can be seen from the fourth column, everyone in your generation will do better if your money is privately invested. For those of you who are going to be high earners, this loss is significant. The last column shows that, as an investment, Social Security is a better deal, in terms of the real rate of return, for a low earner than for a high earner.

Two conclusions can be drawn from Table 36.2: (1) For no members of the current generation of college students is Social Security likely to beat their private alternatives; (2) the more money people are likely to make over their lifetimes, the worse the discrepancy between private investments and Social Security is likely to be.

There are a couple of logical questions that could be asked at this point so I'll ask them for you: (1) You assumed a 5 percent real interest rate. What would happen if you assumed something like 3 percent? In this case, the net present values would be near zero for the low earner and −$41,693 for the high earner. (2) What if I live until I'm 100? Can I beat the system? The power of compounding interest dwarfs your ability to live long enough to make the system work for you. Even though a high earner would get benefits in excess

of $100,000 a year, at age 90 the present value of this is around $2,000 a year.

If your parents, grandparents, and great-grandparents had run these numbers when they were your age, the outcomes would have been markedly different. For those retiring in 1960, the real rate of return averaged 15 percent while those retiring in 1980 saw an average 7 percent real rate of return. The basic reason for the difference in real rates of return between you and previous generations is that the Social Security tax rates they paid were much lower than the rates you can expect to pay. Those retiring in the 1960s faced tax rates of less than 3 percent for much of their working lives. Those who retired in the 1980s saw tax rates rise from 1 percent to 5 percent while they worked. You will face Social Security tax rates (old age) of at least 5.3 percent for your working life.

In part, Social Security has been viewed as a successful program because, until recently, it has been a good deal for everyone. For people alive when Social Security was introduced, it was an example of the great things that government can do. For people born between 1935 and the mid-1950s, Social Security provides a guaranteed retirement income that is about equal to, for married average wage earners, what they would have gotten in the stock market.[4] For those born after the mid-1950s, the real rate of return on Social Security is likely to be dwarfed by private investment opportunities. For those who are single people, for married dual-income earners, or for higher income earners, the year of birth for a breakeven status was as long ago as 35 years earlier. For such people, Social Security has returned to them much less than private investments would have.

The whole question of who benefits from Social Security is often seen as a loaded one. Simply asking it sometimes causes people to think that you favor its elimination. So given that this section may have struck you as a sales pitch for its elimination, remember that Social Security is part of what economists call "social insurance." It is not intended to be a good investment. It is intended to provide a secure source of income during retirement. As you will see when we discuss the reform question, that is where the debate centers. Those who favor some form of privatization judge the program using a yardstick, like rate of return, that others reject.

---

[3] The reason that the increase in taxes paid is less than proportional to the increase in income is that people with starting salaries of $40,000 and 4 percent growth per year will hit the maximum taxable earnings before they retire. So, whereas the taxes that a poor worker will pay will go up 4 percent every year, the taxes a richer person will pay will go up only 3 percent a year once they have hit that limit.

[4] Because the system has a built-in transfer from high-income earners to low-income earners, though the average earner would break even, the low-income earner would get more than the present value of taxes. A high-income earner would get less.

Will the System Be There for Me?

Why Social Security Is in Trouble

There has always been a concern about whether Social Security could survive. Tax rates have always risen faster than benefits have been added because the retired population has grown faster than the working population. In 1982 a significant concern was raised that the pay-as-you-go system could not handle the demographic bulge of the post–World War II baby boom. In the years following World War II, until around 1960, some 2.5 percent of all women gave birth each year. The advent of the birth control pill, the increased availability of abortion, and the social unrest of the 1960s and 1970s significantly altered America's birth rate. By 1976 only 1.5 percent of women gave birth each year.

As a result, the baby-boom generation, 50 to 68 years old in 2014, represents 22 percent of the current population. A comparable group before them, those between 70 and 85, are now only 7 percent of the population. Because of this, the number of taxpaying workers per benefit-receiving retiree will continue to fall precipitously. In 1950, there were more than 16 workers paying taxes for every retiree who was collecting benefits. Today, the number is 2.9, and current projections say it will drop to 2.2 by 2030 and to 1.9 by 2085. Figure 36.1 presents an overview of this situation.

The Social Security Trust Fund

To combat the demographic problem the **Social Security Trust Fund** was established in 1982 to collect more taxes than were needed to pay current benefits. In later years there would thus be money enough to pay benefits to baby-boom retirees. In 2012, there was approximately $2.7 trillion in U.S. government debt in this fund. As you may recall from Chapter 10, "Monetary Policy," or Chapter 12, "Federal Deficits, Surpluses, and the National Debt," the federal government owes itself $6.4 trillion.

Social Security Trust Fund
A fund established in 1982 to hold government debt which will be sold as necessary when tax revenues are less than benefits.

Whether this actually constitutes a true trust fund is debatable. It is a collection of debt that will either be issued for the first time or reissued to the public when there is less in Social Security tax revenues than benefits to pay. One way of looking at this issue is that the trust fund is money that was collected using the Social Security tax, rather than the income tax. This was begun in the 1980s and early 1990s to reduce what would otherwise have been a much larger deficit. If you look at it this way, the national debt that grew to $17 trillion by 2013 actually only grew to just $12 trillion (and just $10 trillion if you count Federal Reserve holdings of the national debt). As a result, should surpluses come in, we would be reducing the true national

FIGURE 36.1 Workers per retiree history and projections.

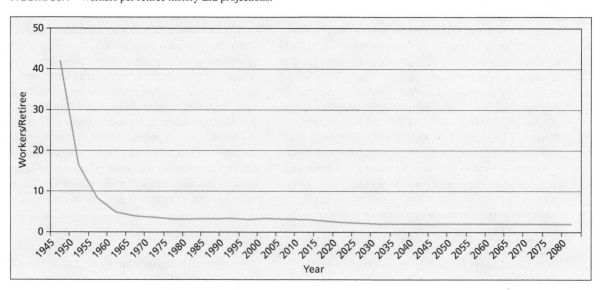

debt to allow ourselves the ability to borrow much more later. Either way it is essentially the same. Reissuing debt and borrowing money are functionally identical.

The Social Security trustees periodically issue reports that attempt to project how long this trust fund will suffice. They issue three different predictions based on three different sets of assumptions. The "optimistic" report is based on assumptions that economic growth will be higher than we have seen in the recent past, life spans will be shorter than current health trends are likely to yield, and interest rates will be lower than they are likely to be. The "pessimistic" report is based on assumptions of slow growth, long lives, and high interest rates.

The "intermediate" report is the most widely quoted, and it indicates that the Social Security system generally (except for 2010 through 2011 when revenues were down as a result of the recession) collects more in taxes than it pays in benefits and will likely do so through about 2025. Between 2025 and 2033 there will be less collected in taxes than paid in benefits, and the difference will come out of this fund. By 2033 the fund will run dry and the annual deficit could be as much as 23 percent of the benefits owed in 2033 and 26 percent of benefits owed in 2086. It is in 2033 that the system will have insufficient assets to pay off its obligations. This is what some would describe as bankruptcy, athough since the government could continue to pay the benefits with other revenues or borrowing, that term is not technically valid.

This intermediate view of whether Social Security will survive has to be balanced by the fact that much of it is based on assumptions that may or may not materialize. For instance, if the optimistic view holds, and the economy grows a single percentage point a year more than predicted, the problem is mostly solved. Changes, for example, in immigration policies that allow more workers to enter over the next 20 years, could help solve the remainder of the problem. Additionally, if inflation and interest rates are slightly less than predicted, Social Security bankruptcy is far from certain.

As a matter of fact, an increase in something as unrelated as the divorce rate would make the problem worse. Husbands and wives typically get less in benefits married than they do if they are divorced.

The long and the short of it is that economists cannot be sure that Social Security will be bankrupt. Significantly altering what many consider to be the nation's greatest social program on the basis of economic assumptions that may or may not come true strikes many as foolhardy. This is especially true, from the point of view of economist and Social Security expert Peter Diamond.

He notes that even if the trust fund is exhausted in 30, 40, or 50 years, the taxes paid will be sufficient to cover 75 percent of benefits. On the other hand, the possible solutions that we next describe also require several years to be effective if the goal is to make the program 100 percent solvent into the future.

Options for Fixing Social Security

The options for saving Social Security are plentiful, and they range from radical to timid. They all include a mixture of the following elements: raising payroll taxes, raising the retirement age further, cutting benefits to upper-income recipients, changing the target from indexing benefits using wage inflation to indexing using price inflation, investing the trust fund in corporate stocks and bonds, or carving out some of the payroll tax for privatized individual accounts.

Raising taxes is the option most preferred by those who like Social Security the way it is. This could be accomplished by raising the tax rate as well as raising or eliminating the maximum taxable earnings lid on what an individual has to pay. Estimates vary, but eliminating this provision so that the upper-income people would have to pay taxes on more than just the first of their earnings would solve about a third of the problem. Raising the overall payroll tax rate for the old age part from 5.3 percent to 6.3 percent would probably be sufficient to deal with the remainder.

Another alternative would be to raise the retirement age. Typically those who like this option argue that Social Security's original retirement age was pegged at life expectancy, which in 1935 was 65. If the retirement age is exactly life expectancy, then people who die at or before expectancy pay a lifetime of taxes and get no benefits. This ensures that there is enough money to pay for those who die after expectancy. Currently life expectancy is 78. For those who make it to 65, men can expect to live another 16 years, women 19 years. Though people are living much longer, the problem is that there is less Social Security retirement money to go around. Depending on how quickly we did it, raising the retirement age to 70 would also solve about a third of the problem. If the retirement age were not raised to age 70 until 2075, as some suggest, it would be of no help in resolving the problem scheduled to occur in 2033.

One of the great successes of Social Security is that it has brought the poverty rate among the elderly down greatly. On the other hand, many retirees have enjoyed financial success in their own right. Some have succeeded so well in this area that they are getting Social Security checks but have no need for them. The median net worth for a Social Security recipient is currently about twice that of a nonrecipient. One proposed solution to Social Security's problems is to subject its beneficiaries to a **means test**. Those with high incomes or great wealth would get less of their PIA than those who depend on the monthly check. Depending on how much a wealthy person's check is reduced, this could go a long way to staving off bankruptcy. Denying Social Security to anyone whose other income is greater than $50,000, for example, would eliminate the solvency issue altogether. Less radically, means testing could be introduced into the system by using a hybrid form of indexing espoused by economists Pozen, Schieber, and Shoven. They suggest indexing benefits for upper-income retirees using price inflation rather than wage inflation. Since the former is usually one percentage point lower than the latter, this would have the effect of slowly reducing the benefits paid to upper-income retirees. On the other hand, this could create problems. If benefits to the wealthy are reduced too much, this could seriously discourage savings among the upper- and upper-middle-income earners. Also, political support for the program might be seriously jeopardized, as it would resemble a welfare program more than a universal retirement program.

means test
Determination of the amount of one's government benefit on the basis of income or wealth.

Another way to save the system would be to invest the Social Security Trust Fund in corporate investments that yield higher rates of return. As mentioned above, the trust fund buys government debt and this debt "yields" between 2 percent and 3 percent. In this sense the government (the Treasury) owes the government (the trust fund) money and has to pay itself interest. Proponents of this solution contend that if the government invested the money in corporate stocks and bonds, the higher rates of return would generate enough to pay retirees' benefits.

There are problems with the approach. First, government would be in the business of picking stocks and might not do very well. Second, the process of picking

government investments might be unduly politicized. Given politicians' penchant for succumbing to special interests, it is not beyond the realm of possibilities that such investment would not be in the general interest. Third, though corporate securities do better in the long run than government bonds, they are also riskier.

The last option suggests that individuals be allowed to invest part of their taxes themselves. In the 2000 presidential election, candidate George W. Bush made this a cornerstone of his solution to the Social Security crisis. The precipitous declines in global stock markets that began in 2000 and did not abate until 2003 seriously undercut the political support such an option was beginning to build, but with his reelection in 2004, President Bush again pushed this option front and center. What he suggested was a system by which younger workers would have a portion of their taxes placed in an account under their control. Opponents of the president's plan focused on the fact that the guaranteed Social Security benefit would be significantly reduced while supporters countered that the proceeds of the accounts, if investments returned their normal historical rates, would more than make up the difference.

In late summer 2005, Hurricanes Katrina and Rita took over the headlines and the subsequent political damage to President Bush ended his ability to sell a major change to Social Security.

During his 2008 presidential campaign, Barack Obama rejected all forms of privatization and instead suggested that the 6.2 percent old-age portion of the Social Security tax be reimposed on incomes over $250,000. He did not specify whether the employer portion would also be reimposed or whether the $250,000 line would be based on the household's income or the specific person's income. Without other elements, this would push back the date when Social Security could not meet its full retirement obligations, but it would not fully eliminate the impending funding problem. Sadly, neither the president nor Governor Romney offered any serious proposals to address the issue during the 2012 campaign.

Summary

You now understand what Social Security is. You know its basic tax and benefit structure as well as the changes that have been made to the program since its inception. You understand the economic rationale for having the system to begin with, and you know the effects of the program on work and savings. You understand how economists use present value analysis to aid in determining for whom the program works and for whom it does not. You understand that, under present estimates, the system will be bankrupt by 2033, what the Social Security Trust Fund is, and what the options are for fixing the system so that it will not only be there for you but be good for you as well.

Key Terms

asset substitution effect, 385
average index of monthly earnings
   (AIME), 383
bequest effect, 386
externalities, 384

fully funded pension, 383
induced retirement effect, 385
maximum taxable earnings, 383
means test, 390
pay-as-you-go pension, 383

payroll taxes, 383
primary insurance amount
   (PIA), 383
retirement age, 383
Social Security Trust Fund, 388

Quiz Yourself

1. Social Security's revenue emanates from taxes on
   a. all income.
   b. payrolls.
   c. capital.
   d. estates.

2. One of the reasons a government-run annuity system such as Social Security may be better for society than simply relying on private savings is that
   a. no one would save for themselves.
   b. people, being overly risk averse, will save too much.
   c. people, being risk neutral, will save too much.
   d. people, having imperfect foresight, will save too little.

3. The average index of monthly earnings is indexed
   a. for wage inflation.
   b. for consumer price inflation.
   c. for producer price inflation.
   d. via a combination of wage and price inflation.

4. Since its inception, the portion of earnings that has been subject to the Social Security tax has
   a. remained roughly intact.
   b. increased substantially.
   c. decreased slightly.
   d. decreased substantially.

5. In 2013, a worker who earned $125,000 would have _____ in Social Security taxes taken out of his or her pay and _____ would also be paid by the employer.
   a. $17,396; $17,396 (both equal to $113,700*.153)
   b. $8,860.45; $8,860.45 (both equal to $113,700*.0765+.0145*$11,300)
   c. $8,470.65; $8,470.65 (both equal to $113,700*.0765)
   d. $9,562.50; $9,562.50 (both equal to $125,000*.0765)

6. The asset substitution effect implies that Social Security will _____ from where it would have been without it.
   a. increase savings
   b. increase work
   c. decrease work
   d. decrease savings

7. The question of whether Social Security increases or decreases savings depends mostly on whether the _____ effect outweighs the _____ effect or vice versa.
   a. bequest; asset substitution
   b. bequest; induced retirement
   c. asset substitution; induced retirement
   d. interest; asset substitution

8. When compared to people of your grandparents' generation, you can expect the net present value of Social Security to be
   a. much better.
   b. about the same.
   c. slightly worse.
   d. much worse.

Short Answer Questions

1. Why would comparing the benefit and tax structure of Social Security to what might be achieved in a private investment alternative be valid, and why might it not be valid?

2. How would a change in immigration policy affect the projected solvency of the Social Security system?

3. How much would an individual receive in benefits if she had a constant (wage-inflation adjusted) monthly income of $6,000, and how would that compare to someone who had an income one-third that size?

4. What economic concept do you use to compare benefits received in the distant future with taxes paid in the past, currently, and in the near future?

Think about This

How much risk is appropriate for a government-run annuity system? Is there an appropriate risk-return calculation to be made? Is Social Security risk free? What about political risk?

Talk about This

Defenders of the status quo in Social Security note the extremely low administrative costs of the system relative to those associated with private investment houses. Critics of the status quo note that the real rate of return to future recipients is so much less than the long-term historical average of stocks that paying the extra administrative costs would be worth it. Who's right? Given the methods of saving Social Security described in this chapter, which combination would you employ to save it?

For More Insight See

Aaron, Henry, "The Myths of Social Security Crisis: Behind the Privatization Push," *NTA Forum* 26 (Summer 1996).

Clark, Robert, "Social Security Financing: Facts, Fantasies, Foibles, and Follies," *American Economic Review* 94, no. 2.

Cogan, John F., and Olivia S. Mitchell, "Perspectives from the President's Commission on Social Security Reform," *Journal of Economic Perspectives* 17, no. 2.

Diamond, Peter, "Social Security," *American Economic Review* 94, no. 1.

Feldstein, Martin, "Social Security and Saving: New Time Series Evidence," *National Tax Journal* 49, no. 2 (June 1996), pp. 151–163.

Hyman, David, *Public Finance: A Contemporary Application of Theory to Policy,* 7th ed. (Fort Worth, TX: Harcourt College Publishers, 2001).

Journal of Economic Perspectives 10, no. 3 (Summer 1996). See articles by Edward M. Gramlich; and Peter A. Diamond, pp. 85–88.

Leimer, Dean, and Selig Lesnoy, "Social Security and Private Saving: New Time Series Evidence," *Journal of Political Economy* 90, no. 3 (June 1982), pp. 606–642.

Pozen, Robert, Sylvester J. Schieber, and John Shoven, "Improving Social Security's Progressivity and Solvency with Hybrid Indexing," *American Economic Review* 94, no. 2.

Rosen, Harvey S. and Ted Gayer, *Public Finance* (New York, NY: McGraw-Hill/Irwin, 2010).

Steuerle, C. Eugene, and Jon M. Bakija, *Retooling Social Security for the 21st Century: Right and Wrong Approaches to Reform* (Washington, DC: Urban Institute, 1994).

Behind the Numbers

Social Security information.

    Components, taxes, and bankruptcy.

      Social Security Administration—

      www.socialsecurity.gov

History and projections.

    Social Security Administration; 2012 Trustees Report—www.ssa.gov/oact/tr/2012/tr2012.pdf

CHAPTER THIRTY-FIVE

Poverty and Welfare

Learning Objectives

After reading this chapter you should be able to:

LO1 Describe how poverty is measured, summarize the demographics of poverty in the United States, and show how the percentage of the population that is poor has changed through the last 40 years.

LO2 Enumerate the significant problems associated with the federal government's official poverty rate.

LO3 List and describe the myriad programs that exist for the poor.

LO4 Explain why the government prefers programs that grant the recipient goods and services rather than money.

LO5 List the incentives and disincentives of welfare.

LO6 Summarize the welfare reform issues that we currently face.

Chapter Outline

Measuring Poverty

Programs for the Poor

Incentives, Disincentives, Myths, and Truths

Welfare Reform

Summary

Welfare and the reforming of welfare have been political issues from the time when the first "relief" bills were passed by Congress in the 1930s. In more recent times, President Bill Clinton vowed to "end welfare as we know it," and in 1996 a compromise was reached between his administration and the Republican majority in Congress. Shortly thereafter the welfare rolls were significantly cut and welfare programs in general were significantly changed. Even so, there are myriad programs that provide assistance to people in need, and we review them in this chapter. Some of these programs, such as TANF, and WIC, read like an alphabet soup; others have catchy names, like Head Start and Medicaid; still others have more straightforward names, like Food Stamps and the School Lunch and Breakfast program. Each program is designed to help poor people in specific ways. Some disburse cash; others provide goods or services at little or no cost.

After defining what constitutes a state of "poverty," we describe the people who meet the criteria. We present and discuss some of the modern history of poverty, and we discuss why the measure of poverty we outlined might not be adequate to the task of ascertaining who needs assistance and who does not. We then describe the programs that are available to the poor. We divide the programs into those that provide cash and those that provide goods and services. We discuss why we make such a division. Last, we discuss, in general terms, the incentives and disincentives endemic to welfare programs, and we show why it is so difficult to solve the problems of those who live in poverty.

Measuring Poverty

What does being "poor" really mean? Are you poor only if you are on the verge of starvation? This absolutist position would suggest that poverty in the United States is almost entirely gone. As we will see later in our discussion, one of the most significant health problems of America's poor is that they are obese rather than starving. On the other hand, there is the position that poverty is a relative concept. We note that someone who has the living standard of a median-income Somalian is in poverty in the United States but not in Somalia, and an American today with an average income has a living standard that 100 years from now will likely be considered unacceptably poor. To see this point, note that the poor of today live in larger homes than all but the very richest Americans did in 1900.

The Poverty Line

Surveys have established reasonably well that low-income families of four spend roughly a third of their income on food. Defining the poverty line as that level of annual income sufficient to provide a family with a minimally adequate standard of living, we created the first poverty line by multiplying the cost of a

poverty line
That level of income sufficient to provide a family with a minimally adequate standard of living.

minimally sufficient diet by 3, the reciprocal of one-third. In successive years, the amount has been raised by the amount of increase in the consumer price index. For other family sizes, a similar process takes place where the reciprocal of the fraction of income spent on food by low-income people of that family size is multiplied by the cost of the minimally sufficient diet. In 2012, these numbers were $11,484 for one person, $14,657 for two people, $17,916 for three people, and $23,021 for four people. The poverty rate is the percentage of people in households whose incomes are under the poverty line. In 2011, the poverty rate in the United States stood at 15.0 percent.

Another important measure of poverty is the poverty gap, a representation of the total amount of money that would have to be transferred to households below the poverty line in order for them to get out of poverty. The poverty gap in the United States was $91 billion as of 2011.

poverty rate
The percentage of people in households whose incomes are under the poverty line.

poverty gap
The total amount of money that would have to be transferred to households below the poverty line for them to get out of poverty.

Who's Poor?

Table 35.1 displays indicators of who is poor and compares that to their general portion of the population. Many

TABLE 35.1 Who's poor.

Source: U.S. Census Bureau: Current Population Survey, www.census.gov/hhes/www/poverty/data/index.html

Demographic	General Population (in millions)	Percentage of the General Population	Percentage of Those in Poverty	Poverty Rate (%)
White, non-Hispanic	195.0	63.2%	41.6	9.8
Hispanic	52.3	17.0	28.6	25.3
Black, non-Hispanic	39.6	12.8	23.6	27.6
Other race	21.6	7.0	6.3	13.4
Male	150.9	48.9	44.4	13.6
Female	157.6	51.1	55.6	16.3
Under 18	73.7	23.9	34.8	21.9
18–24	30.1	9.8	13.4	20.6
25–64	163.1	52.9	43.7	9.8
65 and over	41.5	13.5	7.8	8.7
Female-headed household, no husband present	48.1	15.6	35.7	34.2
High school dropout*	43.5	14.1	23.8	25.4
High school graduate (no college)*	70.6	22.9	22.7	14.9
College (without a degree)*	67.3	21.8	16.0	11.1
Bachelor's degree or greater*	66.2	21.5	7.4	5.1

There are different thresholds for different compositions of each group. These figures are for a single adult under 65, two adults, two adults and one child, and two adults and two children, respectively.

people think that most poor people are African American. While many academics are quick to dispel that myth, they often perpetuate another with a counterassertion that most poor people are white. Neither is true if you separate European Americans from Hispanic Americans. Table 35.1 shows disproportionate numbers of blacks and Hispanics are in poverty and that they, together with American Indians, Asians, and Pacific Islanders, comprise a majority of the Americans living below the poverty line. It is obvious that there is a significant degree of racial and ethnic distinction in U.S. rates of poverty.

The data indicate that women are more likely to be in poverty than men; and, if we define "families" as not including single adults, then of families in poverty, half are in female-headed households while half are families of married couples. Given that female-headed households with children make up only 15.6 percent of the general population, poverty is clearly a women's issue.

It is also true that children under 18 make up 34.8 percent of those who are poor, though they comprise only 23.9 percent of the general population. This is a poverty rate among children of 21.9 percent. Whether this indicates that the poor have more children or that raising children can itself lead families into poverty can be debated. Clearly, the picture of poverty is this: Minorities, women, and children are poor in numbers vastly out of proportion to their numbers in the general population.

Another key indicator of poverty is education or, more properly, the lack of it. Those with a bachelor's degree experience poverty at one-sixth the rate of high school dropouts. Simply completing high school cuts the chance of being in poverty by about half, and simply attending college reduces the chance of being in poverty from 14.9 percent to 11.1 percent. Completing college reduces the rate even further. Only 1 in 20 households headed by a college graduate is in poverty.

Poverty through History

Figure 35.1 indicates that although the number of people in poverty is roughly the same as it was in 1959, the poverty rate has fallen dramatically. As we will discuss later, the poverty rate shown fails to account for the many government benefits. This means that the reduction in the poverty rate since 1959 can be attributed to an economic strengthening for those whose incomes are at the bottom of the economic scale.

In considering the decline in the general trend in poverty, be aware of the following caveats. The poverty rate has remained largely unchanged since the middle 1960s when the "war on poverty" actually began. From that time to the present it has neither fallen below 11 percent nor, until the Great Recession, gone above 15 percent. The systemic reduction, as a matter of fact, occurred between 1959 and 1969, before the enactment of many of the antipoverty programs. Noting that the shaded bars in Figure 35.1 indicate recessions, we can see that the poverty rate has increased during recessions and lessened during periods of growth. Democratic presidents

FIGURE 35.1 Poverty since 1959.

Source: U.S. Census Bureau, www.census.gov/hhes/www/poverty.html

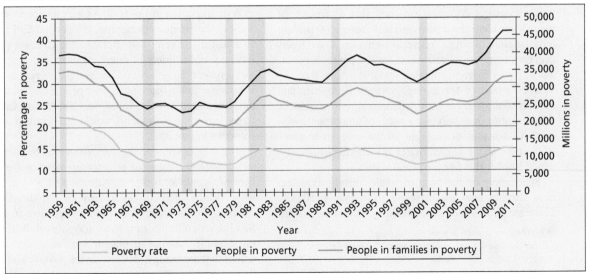

Kennedy and Johnson get much of the credit for the pre-1969 reduction in the poverty rate. However, this was a result more of a strong economy's providing excellent economic opportunities than anything these administrations did for the poor. The bulk of the pre-1969 decline took place prior to 1965 when these programs first began to become law. Since 1969 Democrats and Republicans have nearly identical records with respect to poverty. Generally speaking, the poverty rate is a reflection of the health of the overall economy.

Problems with Our Measure of Poverty

There is a host of reasons why using three times the cost of a minimally sufficient diet as a measure of poverty is inadequate to the task of measuring who is poor. First, it does not distinguish among families that are intact with one income earner and families that either are not intact or for other reasons have day-care costs. Since nearly 36 percent of families living in poverty are headed by single women with children under 18, this is potentially a significant problem. Since the one-third fraction that was used in the original poverty measure came from a survey conducted when there were fewer such female-headed households, the poverty line could be understated by all or part of the cost of day care. Since day-care costs can be between $4,500 and $14,000 per year per child under 12, this is a substantial area of mismeasurement.

Although this indicates that poverty is understated, there are problems with the measure that indicate that poverty may be overstated. Robert Rector of the conservative Heritage Foundation repeatedly updates statistics that purport to show that poverty is not a problem in the United States.[1] He uses government surveys and published statistical documents to show that 43 percent of households considered poor own their homes, 80 percent have air conditioning, 75 percent own a car, and 31 percent own two or more cars. He notes that the square footage of living space of America's poor is greater than the square footage of the average western European, and the diet of the average poor American equals or exceeds the recommended daily allowances of important nutrients. As a matter of fact, one of the singular features of the poor in the United States is their rate of obesity, which implies that few are actually starving.

Specifically on the point of wealth, nearly a million poor families own homes worth more than $150,000. There are hundreds of thousands of people in the United

[1] A recent version is available at www.heritage.org/Research/Reports/2007/08/How-Poor-Are-Americas-Poor-Examining-the-Plague-of-Poverty-in-America.

States who have little income but who are worth hundreds of thousands of dollars. Some are even millionaires. Admittedly, it is a small number of people like this who are rich, but called poor. However, it is important to note that the poverty line measures only people's income relative to a fixed standard that ignores measures of wealth.

Another shortcoming of the formula that is used to determine the poverty line is that it only includes income that is in cash. Thus programs that the poor take advantage of that are not cash-driven are incorrectly and absurdly omitted as if they have no value. For instance, the $200 in food stamps that a family might get a month is not counted and, if they found a subsidized rental apartment and free medical care, these also would not be counted. Depending on the study you believe, this failure to include income that is in forms other than cash overstates poverty by between two and four percentage points.

As we saw in Chapter 6, the consumer price index that is used to update the poverty line each year has many shortcomings. Best estimates are that it has overstated the cost of living by at least a full percentage point a year. Since the increase in the poverty line is generated using this flawed measure, it is likely that the poverty line has long been overstated relative to its real value in the 1960s. Figure 35.2 indicates that although the lower line, the adjusted version, tracks the upper line throughout the 1960s, the spread is significant enough that if you take the 1959 poverty line as the base on which to build the adjusted poverty line, you see that instead of being $23,021 in 2012 it should have been $13,531.

Besides the possible overstating of poverty that we have seen up to this point, there are additional problems with this measure that result in mislabeling some people as poor and others as not poor. As we mentioned specifically in the previous paragraph, the general CPI is used to adjust the poverty line. Because the CPI is a general indicator of the prices of many goods, it does not necessarily reflect the goods that are bought by people living in poverty. To the degree that poor people buy things that have increased in price more than the overall CPI, the "true" poverty line probably would fall between the two shown in Figure 35.2.

The way costs of living vary from area to area leads to yet another source of mismeasurement of the numbers of people who live in poverty, and it is a source about which there is uncertainty of the direction of the bias. Because it is much more expensive to live in San Francisco, California, than in Appleton, Wisconsin, for example, families of four in San Francisco with incomes that are a single dollar over the poverty line figure

FIGURE 35.2 Poverty line with and without CPI adjustment.

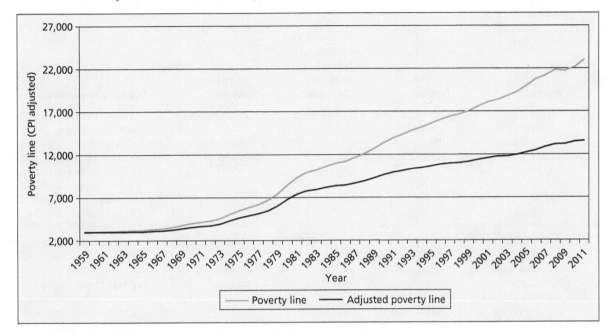

of $23,021 are significantly worse off than families of four in Appleton with incomes one dollar under the poverty line. In this way the poverty rate underestimates both urban poverty and poverty on the coasts. It overestimates the incidence of poverty in rural areas, small cities, in the South, and in the Midwest.

There is a final reason to doubt official poverty numbers, and that is a missing $2 trillion. In Chapter 6, when we talked about national income accounting, we briefly explained the sources of the numbers that make up the gross domestic product. It turns out that data used by the Census Bureau add up to substantially less, $2 trillion less, than the source numbers for personal income used in GDP calculations. While much of the missing $2 trillion is the in-kind transfers mentioned above, this certainly does not account for all of it. It is clearly true that most of that probably goes to the nonpoor. Some of it must also be in the hands of the poor, so there are clearly some who are labeled poor who are not.

Poverty in the United States versus Europe

As referred to in the opening, most countries have their own measures of poverty and they are not directly comparable. Timothy Smeeding, one of the foremost economists on the subject of poverty and income inequality, has attempted to create those comparable measures. He used

the U.S. poverty line, adjusted it for different currency values, and looked at the percentage of people in various European countries who would fall below this line. Using this measure, he noted that U.S. poverty rates were higher than eight of the nine countries examined. When he focused strictly on income inequality, measured by the percentage of people living on incomes below 40 percent of a country's median disposable income, he found that the United States had the most unequal income of any of the countries compared.

Programs for the Poor

In Kind versus In Cash

The programs available to the poor are many and complicated. They are better understood as varying from state to state rather than being one consistent program across the country. Further, these programs are best understood as being divided between cash payments and provisions of goods and services in forms other than cash. Economists refer to the latter types as **in-kind subsidies**. Table 35.2 describes the different programs, the functions, and the populations they serve, as well as the restrictions placed on eligibility to receive them.

in-kind subsidies Provisions of goods and services in forms other than cash.

TABLE 35.2 Programs for the poor and their characteristics, FY2014.

Sources: Data compiled by the author.

Program	Function	Cash or In-Kind and Annual Federal + State Cost ($ billions)	Population Served	Eligibility Requirements
Temporary Assistance to Needy Families (TANF); formerly called AFDC	Cash income to the poor (the welfare check)	Cash, $25	Poor parents and their children under 18	Though this varies from state to state, the following generalizations can be made: Recipients (1) have to have children; (2) cannot have much wealth (usually less than $5,000 net), including house and car; (3) can remain on the program for 24 consecutive months only
Women, Infants and Children (WIC)	Food, formula, and diapers	In-kind, $7.1	Pregnant women and new mothers	Low wealth and income; cutoffs depend on the state
Food Stamps (now called SNAP)	Vouchers that can be spent only on food	In-kind, $74	All poor	Low wealth and income; cutoffs depend on the state; recipients can remain on the program for only 24 consecutive months
Medicaid		In-kind, $408	All poor	Low wealth and income; cutoffs depend on the state
Section 8 or Housing Authority Apartment	Reduced rent or low-cost housing	In-kind, $35	All poor	Low wealth and income; cutoffs depend on the state
Head Start	Day care; preschool	In-kind, $9	Poor with children under 5	First come, first served for anyone below 1.25 poverty line
School Lunch	Lunch and breakfast	In-kind, $18	Poor with school-age children	Anyone below 1.25 poverty line
Supplemental Security Income (SSI)	Cash assistance to "deserving poor"	Cash, $53	Disabled and widow-(er)s and orphans Poor with school-age children	Someone (a parent, guardian, or spouse) must be disabled or must have died
Earned Income Tax Credit (EITC)	Negative tax; boost low-pay workers	Cash, $56	Working poor	Based on family size; phases in at incomes up to $12,549, then phases out for incomes between $16,450 and $40,362; family of four maximum now, $5,666

Why Spend $685 Billion on a $91 Billion Problem?

Given the preceding information on the extent of poverty and the dollar costs of poverty programs, the following should strike you: If the poverty gap is $91 billion, why do the various levels of government spend more than six times that on poverty programs? The answer is two-fold: (1) There are people above the poverty line in need whom we choose to help; and (2) poverty programs must be terribly inefficient if it genuinely takes $685 billion to cure a $91 billion problem.

Table 35.2 shows that billions more are spent on goods and services than are spent in cash benefits. Including some minor programs not mentioned in Table 35.2, cash benefits total around $134 billion, whereas in-kind benefits total $551 billion. Clearly the government spends far more money on programs that give it control over recipients' behavior. For instance, we think the poor do not have enough to eat, adequate medical services, adequate housing, and so on. Instead of providing them with enough money to pay for these things, the government provides them with what it thinks they need.

If there is a family whose members enjoy good health, it is conceivable they would rather have more money spent on food and less on medical care. They cannot make that substitution. People who live in poverty are denied the ability to make basic decisions when they are given specific goods and services rather than money. In many studies of the poor, it is clear that they value cash more than the goods they are provided. Some food stamp recipients show exactly how little they value food stamps and WIC vouchers by selling them on the black market for 50 cents on the dollar. Why haven't programs been designed so that people in need receive cash and are then encouraged to make their own decisions on how to spend it?

There are several reasons, but three are obvious. First, through their elected officials, voters have made it clear they do not trust the judgment of the people who receive government benefits concerning what goods they buy. Many believe that if the poor could make good decisions, they would not be poor to begin with.

Second, people are more concerned with the welfare of needy children than with the welfare of adults. If you look at the programs with this in mind, you will see that nearly all of them require the presence of a child for an adult to be eligible. If we want to guarantee services for children, it makes more sense to give the adult access to such services rather than cash. This minimizes the likelihood that the money will be diverted by adults away from the targeted children.

Third, some welfare benefits seem designed more to provide those who tender them with a feeling of magnanimity than to benefit the poor. If it is our own happiness we are maximizing and if our happiness is enhanced by the knowledge that we provided the poor with enough to survive, it may be even more important to us that we ensure that the poor are consuming what we think is good for them rather than what they want.

Is $685 Billion Even a Lot Compared to Other Countries?

Though the United States spends $685 billion on its antipoverty programs, the Smeeding analysis puts this in perspective by noting that European antipoverty programs are far more aggressive. He notes that after accounting for taxes and various welfare programs, the system in the United States reduces poverty (defined by him as the percentage of people living below 50 percent of median household disposable income) by only 26 percent, whereas the average European country's programs reduce their poverty by more than 60 percent.

Incentives, Disincentives, Myths, and Truths

While no one has ever intended this to be the case, many of the programs designed to help the poor are blamed for ensuring that people who live in poverty and who receive benefits have no incentive to become self-sufficient. The existence of welfare is accused of giving people a reason not to work. It is blamed for encouraging young women both to get pregnant and to carry the pregnancy to term. Welfare is indicted for encouraging recipients to have more children so that their WIC will be extended and their food stamps and TANF payments increased. The structure of TANF's predecessor, Aid to Families with Dependent Children (AFDC), was blamed for breaking up poor families by giving them the incentive to have the father leave. Together, these problems created the concern that welfare was becoming a way of life and that people were getting used to it.

From a theoretical perspective, each of the preceding arguments has merit, but the evidence from economic studies is not one-sided. First, there are several counterclaims. Birth rates among teenagers climbed steadily from the 1960s through the early 1990s and leveled off when the states and then the federal government

WELFARE'S BEST URBAN LEGEND

The world of welfare is replete with urban legends. My favorite goes something like this: "I was standing in line at the grocery store one day behind a nicely dressed woman who was buying beer, steak, shrimp, and a whole bunch of stuff I couldn't afford. She had them put the steak and shrimp on her food stamp card and used her cash to buy the beer. She packed up her groceries and went to her brand new SUV." In teaching this subject for years, I have heard this story in countless renditions from students who were either customers or grocery employees. The story is almost always the same. While the story may be about fraud, it is also quite likely about their misinterpreting the actions of a foster parent.

Most states give foster families Medicaid cards and an allotment on a food stamp card to pay for the food and medical expenses of the children in their care. That some of these families are wealthy enough to afford nice meals and nice vehicles does not diminish our obligation to pay them for the service they are providing us by caring for orphaned, discarded, or abused children or those children whose parents are in prison.

instituted welfare reforms designed to curb benefits. The truth is that the real dollar value of benefits per recipient is lower today than it was in the late 1960s. Thus, if poor teenagers were really considering the value of welfare in making decisions about having children, teen pregnancy rates would have fallen from the mid-1970s on as the real value of the benefits fell. It is more likely that the culture and teen sex drives had more to do with teen pregnancies than the prospect of receiving welfare checks.

Second, although it was and still is true that the more children you have, the more benefits you get, there is no systematic evidence that people on welfare had more children because they were on welfare. If welfare mothers were concerned only for themselves and the benefits they could get, it would make sense that they would have children so they would be eligible for more benefits. What had to have been evident to them, however, is that the increase in benefits does not cover any more than the increased cost of raising an additional child. Unless we want to claim that the poor do not care about their children, there is little likelihood that rational women would get pregnant and do the work of raising an additional child in order to keep a few extra dollars a month. They could make more money with less effort if they cleaned houses on the side.

Third, it is true that families on welfare are far more likely to have absent fathers, but it is hard to say whether the father's leaving was caused by the need to be welfare-eligible or the family became welfare-eligible because the father left. In order to accept the argument that welfare caused a rash of absent fathers, you must hold the cynical belief that a well-meaning father would abandon his children so they could receive benefits. Although this might have been the case prior to 1996, today, after welfare reform, the abandonment would have to be complete.

A mother now has to name and state the last known location of absent fathers to get benefits. Clearly, whether the need to apply for welfare leads to the breakup of families that would have stayed together is debatable. The reason that some welfare programs are contingent on a parent's being absent stems from the conviction that if there are two able-bodied adults in a household, one of them should be working. Either the problem of absent fathers is a coincidence or it is the price society is paying for building welfare requirements around a view that families with both parents present should not be eligible for assistance unless one is disabled.

Fourth, under AFDC, that is, prior to the welfare reforms of 1996, welfare dependency had been growing at an alarming rate. Some 26 percent of recipients had been receiving benefits from the program for 10 years or more at the same time that the percentage of families that had been on welfare for very short periods of time was falling. In addition, daughters of recipients were tending to become recipients themselves. These circumstances and others like them led Congress and the president to agree to change welfare programs to incorporate limits on the length of time people could receive benefits and to require that recipients become gainfully employed.

Welfare Reform

Is There a Solution?

To be successful, a social safety net must meet three goals:

1. The program that is designed cannot be so expensive that the taxpaying public will not sustain it.

2. The program must have an incentive built in that makes beneficiaries want to leave it.
3. The program must provide enough of a level of basic necessities that recipients have a socially acceptable standard of living.

The problem facing policy analysts in the United States has always been that these goals cannot be satisfied simultaneously.

Any program must have a phaseout level of income. If the phaseout is too quick, meaning that for every dollar you earn you lose significant welfare benefits, the disincentive to work will be too profound. The AFDC program reduced benefits by nearly a dollar for every dollar the recipient earned. This nearly 100 percent take-back rate meant that without a salary at least twice the minimum wage in a job, a single parent with two small children requiring day care would be far better off on welfare than working.

If the phaseout is too slow, then too many people will be getting welfare benefits and not enough will be paying taxes. Though this is possible, it violates the first goal, that of having a program that does not cost too much money. On the other hand, the phaseout could be slow and of low cost to taxpayers. The problem would then be that there would not be enough money for recipients to survive on.

The implicit choice made by policy makers prior to the reforms of welfare that were instituted in 1996 was to give up on providing incentives to leave the program. The increase in long-term dependency on the program can, at least in part, be blamed on this decision. The near 100 percent take-back rate on AFDC left people with no earned income better off than people making $10,000 a year. The result was that only those recipients who could invest in an education could ultimately afford to leave the program.

Welfare as We Now Know It

In the 1996 reforms, the problem of welfare dependency was tackled by simply ordering people to leave welfare. The institution of time limits was an acknowledgment of the concern that dependency was wrong and that monetary incentives for relinquishing benefits were too expensive. Instead of being offered incentives to leave the program, people are now told how long their benefits will keep coming. States are given block grants of money (TANF) that they are supposed to use to aid their poor. Instead of having to give it away in cash benefits, as they did under AFDC, they can now spend it on job training, child care, or tax breaks for businesses that are willing to hire welfare recipients. States must set time limits of 24 months or less and they must establish work requirements for some programs. Supplemental Security Income rules for disability have changed such that some people who were once eligible for full benefits are now eligible for only partial benefits.

By 1999, welfare caseloads had fallen to their lowest point in three decades. Though it is difficult to tell how much of this was due to the robust economy of the 1990s, it is clear that the reforms that were instituted have had some effect. Economist Rebecca Blank summarized the growing research that has been conducted on this issue by noting that through the reforms of providing assistance to work, monetary incentives to work, and requirements to work, the current array of programs is raising incomes and increasing employment in ways previous programs did not.

Is Poverty Necessarily Bad?

There are many economists who object to the implied premise of this entire chapter: namely, that poverty is a bad thing. Without a carrot—wealth, and a stick—poverty, these economists believe that people would have little incentive to "work hard and play by the rules."[2] If accepted as valid, this philosophy would suggest that there is a trade-off between rates of economic growth and rates of economic inequality. There is evidence from the 1980s through today that countries with low rates of economic inequality had low rates of economic growth, but there is much disagreement about whether the former caused the latter.

[2] This phrase was often used by President Clinton as a political mantra.

Summary

You now understand how poverty is measured, who is poor in the United States, and how the percentage of the population that is poor has changed through the last 40 years. You are able to describe some of the significant problems presented by the official poverty rate. You understand the myriad programs that exist for the poor, note that most of the programs grant the recipients goods and services rather than money, and understand why it is that government does this. Last, you are aware of the incentives and disincentives in the welfare state, and you know the welfare reform issues that we currently face.

Key Terms

in-kind subsidies, 375
poverty gap, 372

poverty line, 372

poverty rate, 372

Quiz Yourself

1. Poverty is a _____ concept in that a person with that income in the United States may be considered in poverty, while a person with that same income in Somalia may be in the upper quarter of income earners.
   a. relative
   b. absolute
   c. irrelevant
   d. ficticious

2. In a simple 300 million person world of all four-person families, if the poverty line is $12,500 and half of the 10 million families (with 40 million poor people) earn $10,000 and the other half earn $7,500, then the poverty gap is
   a. $125 billion (= 10 million * $12,500).
   b. $250 billion (= 20 million * $12,500).
   c. $150 billion (= 20 million * $2,500 + 20 million * $5,000).
   d. $37.5 billion (= 5 million * $2,500 + 5 million * $5,000).

3. In a simple 300 million person world of all four-person families, if the poverty line is $12,500 and half of the 10 million families (with 40 million poor people) earn $10,000 and the other half earn $7,500, then the poverty rate is
   a. 3.33% (10 million/300 million).
   b. 13.33% (40 million/300 million).
   c. 16.66% (50 million/300 million).
   d. 96.33% ((300 million − 10 million)/300 million).

4. Using a poverty line of $12,500, under the current system of calculating the poverty rate, which of the following people is not considered in poverty and probably ought to be?
   a. A rural family whose sole income earner is from a minimum wage ($10,300).
   b. A rural family whose combined income is $15,000.
   c. A New York City family whose combined income is $13,000.
   d. A retired couple whose multimillion dollar estate yields them no income.

5. Using a poverty line of $12,500, under the current system of calculating the poverty rate, which of the following people is considered in poverty and probably ought not to be?
   a. A rural family whose sole income is from a minimum wage ($10,300).
   b. A rural family whose combined income is $15,000.
   c. A New York City family whose combined income is $13,000.
   d. A retired couple whose multimillion dollar estate yields them no income.

6. The distribution of aid to the poor between in-kind and in-cash is
   a. roughly equal.
   b. weighted heavily toward in-cash benefits.
   c. weighted slightly toward in-kind benefits.
   d. weighted heavily toward in-kind benefits.

7. The most obvious pattern in poverty rates is the degree to which they are higher during
   a. Democratic administrations.
   b. wars.
   c. odd years.
   d. recessions.

8. The evidence is that welfare reform in 1996 resulted in _____ welfare rolls.
   a. a substantial increase in
   b. a slight increase in
   c. a substantial decrease in
   d. no impact on

Short Answer Questions

1. Compare the data on who is in poverty to whatever stereotype you may have had prior to reading this chapter.

2. What do the data suggest with regard to poverty and the age profile of those in poverty relative to the age profile generally?

3. What measure of poverty would give you the lowest possible estimate of the amount of money you would need to solve the nation's poverty problem? Why would only spending that amount not likely be a good solution to the problem?

4. If you were to construct a poverty measure, what would you put into the calculations to deal with the issues listed in the chapter?

Think about This

The wealth of one person, Bill Gates, is about equal to the annual poverty gap in the United States in one year, $91 billion. The United States has a more significantly unequal division of income than any other industrialized country. What are the consequences of that unequal distribution?

Talk about This

What other "urban legends" exist about the poor and welfare? What research could be conducted to dispel these legends or prove them to be factual?

For More Insight See

Blank, Rebecca M., "Evaluating Welfare Reform in the United States," *Journal of Economic Literature* XL (December 2002).

Journal of Economic Perspectives 11, no. 2 (Spring 1997). See articles by Peter Gottschalk; George Johnson; Robert Topel; and Nicole Fortin and Thomas Lemieux, pp. 21–96.

Journal of Economic Perspectives 12, no. 1 (Winter 1998). See articles by Dale Jorgenson; and Robert Triest, pp. 79–114.

Smeeding, Timothy, "Poor People in Rich Nations: The United States in Comparative Perspective," *Journal of Economic Perspectives* 20, no. 1 (Winter 2006).

Wolff, Edward, "Recent Trends in the Size Distribution of Household Wealth," *Journal of Economic Perspectives* 12, no. 3 (Summer 1998).

Behind the Numbers

Detailed Poverty Tabulations from the Current Population Survey—www.census.gov

Historical Poverty Tables, Current Population Survey—www.census.gov/hhes/www/poverty

Federal Spending on Programs for the Poor, Detailed Functional Tables—www.whitehouse.gov/omb/budget

Statistics of those in poverty.

The Heritage Foundation; paper by Robert Rector—www.heritage.org/Research/Reports/2007/08/How-Poor-Are-Americas-Poor-Examining-the-Plague-of-Poverty-in-America

CHAPTER TWENTY-FIVE

The Economics of Prescription Drugs

Learning Objectives

After reading this chapter you should be able to:

LO1 Apply the concepts of monopoly as well as consumer and producer surplus to the economics of prescription drugs.

LO2 Summarize why most health economists view prescription drugs as relatively inexpensive, even while most noneconomists view them as very expensive.

LO3 Explain why it is that most health economists do not favor price controls on prescription drugs.

LO4 Identify the consequences of an approval process that is too stringent or too lax.

Chapter Outline

Profiteers or Benevolent Scientists?

Monopoly Power Applied to Drugs

Important Questions

Summary

When people go to the doctor because they are sick or injured, they want the doctor to make them better. For certain injuries they may expect active treatments, like surgery. It is just part of the human psychological makeup to want to know that "everything is being done" to restore the patient's health. The same holds for the treatment of illnesses. Nothing is more frustrating to patients than to be told they have a "virus," because they accurately translate that to mean "go home and go to bed because there is nothing we can do for you." On the other hand, if patients go home having filled a prescription for a drug, they feel better simply because they think that taking medicine will make them well. In part they think this because the prescription drug industry has been so successful in treating everything from infections to impotence. When we have a virus and there is no prescription forthcoming, we lose hope for a quick end to our illness. In this sense we go to the doctor hoping for prescriptions because it is usually a drug the doctor prescribes, rather than something the doctor actually does, that makes us better.

It seems all the more strange to economists, then, that prescription drugs get as much criticism as they do when it comes to expense. The amount of money spent on prescription drugs is actually trivial relative to all health spending. In 2011, for example, all U.S. health spending amounted to more than $2.7 trillion dollars, and 10 percent of that was spent on prescription drugs.

This chapter has several purposes. We look at the degree to which prescription drug manufacturers are profiteers or good Samaritans. We use our monopoly model to discern why drugs are so costly, and we examine some of the new drugs and discuss whether they are expensive necessities or relatively inexpensive godsends. In doing this we will see the fundamental reasons why prescription drug companies are likely to remain unpopular even as they continue to provide important medicines. Last, we look at how other countries control prescription drug prices, and we offer a perspective on whether the United States should follow suit.

Profiteers or Benevolent Scientists?

Among the more interesting advertisements of the 1990s were the pharmaceutical industry's feel-good television spots that focused on a variety of hardworking scientists endeavoring to conquer a disease. These ads differed somewhat from the ads that commonly try to get us to go to the doctor to ask about problems like hair loss, seasonal allergies, or other afflictions. Just as McDonald's wants to sell burgers, so also the pharmaceutical ads are trying to sell us a particular drug. The feel-good ads are there, not to have us buy any particular product, but to persuade us to feel better about the industry in general.

Usually, the earlier ads discussed an emotional attachment the scientists had with curing the disease they were working on. A friend, spouse, relative, or parent had the disease and this, we were supposed to believe, motivated the scientist to spend long nights crouched over a microscope in search of a cure. With no attempt to criticize the scientists' sincerity, however, we know deep down that whether or not something altruistic motivates the scientist, what motivates the drug company is profit.

As with any invention, the fundamental economic problem is how to reward the inventor. Unless the inventor is given exclusive rights to his or her idea once the item has been invented, copycats can steal it. Knowing this, inventors will have little economic incentive to innovate. This is why we have laws that govern copyrights and **patents.** Within existing laws, a patent-holding inventor is the only person who can sell the invention for as long as the patent exists.

Monopoly power is particularly important in the so-called **orphan drug** industry, an industry that deals with diseases that afflict few people. Therapies that benefit small numbers of patients cannot hope to generate sufficient profits during normal patent lives for companies to justify research. For this reason drugs that are labeled orphan drugs are granted very long patent lives so that profits, though small, can be expected to last long into the future. Without this aspect of the patent law, research on such diseases would never be instituted by scientists working in the private sector.

In economic terms what this monopoly power does is give the inventor total control. As you recall from Chapter 5, monopoly means that there is one seller. It means, in turn, that there are no other companies producing the particular drug. When the drug is one-of-a-kind, as AZT was in the early 1990s, and it is the only hope a patient has, its monopoly power is dramatic. It is all the more dramatic when the disease it treats is fatal. Since most drugs cost very little to produce but may, as in the case of AIDS drugs, cost billions to discover and test, we are conflicted about high prices. We know that companies need to be rewarded for their investments, but we also find it troublesome that money has the power to determine whether a person gets a drug and lives or does not get a drug and dies.

On the other hand, when the drug is one of many, and it treats a non-life-threatening condition, as do the antiheartburn medications Nexium and Zantac, we are not at all conflicted. The problem is not life and death, and the power the companies have to charge high prices is limited only by competition and consumers' willingness to suffer through ailments that are merely annoying.

Whether we view drug companies as profiteers or benevolent scientists rests on whether they, in the end, do good and whether they charge what are perceived to be fair prices. Drug companies make a great deal of money, but they incur a great deal of risk. Much economic research has gone into studying whether their profits are out of line in comparison with those of similar industries. Although that research has not settled on a definitive answer, it does suggest that the rate of return to stockholders in the pharmaceutical industry is either at or slightly above that of similar industries. What is clear is that prescription drugs have both improved the quality of life for millions and made companies billions in profit.

Monopoly Power Applied to Drugs

As stated previously, the key economic attribute of the prescription drug industry is monopoly. While patents do run out and competition takes place in the form of generic drugs, monopoly reigns for several years at least. Figure 25.1 is the same graph that we saw in Chapter 5 for a monopolist's decision on price and production. As you know, a monopolist is the only seller of a good. This means that the demand curve that a monopolistic firm faces for its goods is the entire market demand curve. For such a firm, this has good and bad aspects. In contrast to perfect competition, the seller does not have to worry about other firms. On the downside, if the firm wants to

patent
A right granted by government to an inventor to be the exclusive seller of that invention for a limited period of time.

orphan drug
A drug that treats someone with a disease that afflicts few people.

FIGURE 25.1   The prescription drug monopolist.

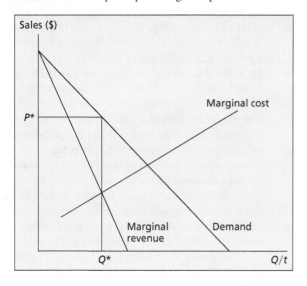

FIGURE 25.2   Comparing monopoly and perfect competition in prescription drugs.

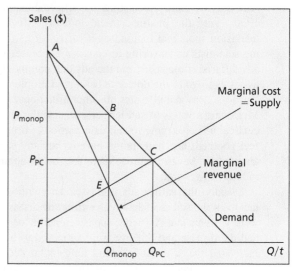

sell more goods, it not only has to lower the price to the people who will buy the extra goods; it has to lower the price to everyone else as well. This includes the people who would have purchased their goods at high prices, so the money gained from increasing sales is partially offset by the money that is lost from having to lower prices. The good news for the firm is that raising the price does not cause all customers to leave, as it does under perfect competition.

Figure 25.1 depicts a drug company that is the sole provider of a certain drug. It indicates that the marginal revenue curve, the curve that represents the additional revenue to the firm associated with the sale of one more unit of the good, is downward sloping rather than flat, as it would be under perfect competition.

Using the tools of consumer and producer surplus, we can show that with the price equal to P^* and the quantity equal to Q^*, relative to the societal optimum, the price is too high and the quantity too low. This can be seen by looking at Figure 25.2 and the assumptions that go along with it. For a moment suppose that the proper comparison to make with regard to the monopolistic production of prescription drugs is perfect competition.[1] As you saw in Chapter 5, the marginal cost curve for a perfect competitor—out of the minimum of average

variable cost—was the supply curve. If you adapt that notion here, the marginal cost curve for this monopolist in Figure 25.1 is also what the supply curve would be if the market were under perfect competition.

In Figure 25.2, monopoly is compared with perfect competition. The perfectly competitive market would produce Q_{PC} at a price of P_{PC}, because this is where supply crosses demand. The monopolistic producer charges much more, P_{monop}, and produces less, Q_{monop}, because this is where marginal cost equals marginal revenue. Our consumer and producer surplus analysis, then, allows us to show that companies profit not only at the expense of sick people, but also at the expense of society as a whole.

Figure 25.2 indicates that the consumer surplus (the area under the demand curve but above the price line) at the perfectly competitive price–quantity combination is $P_{PC}AC$, and the producer surplus (the area above the supply curve but under the price line) is $FP_{PC}C$. Under monopoly, the consumer surplus shrinks to $P_{monop}AB$, and the producer surplus rises to $FP_{monop}BE$. This means that producers are better off but not by as much as consumers are worse off.

deadweight loss
The loss in social welfare associated with production being too little or too great.

Stated differently, the **deadweight loss**, or loss to society of producing at the wrong price–quantity combination, can be shown as the difference between the sum of consumer and producer surplus between the perfect competition and monopoly situations. That area is depicted as *EBC* in Figure 25.2.

---

[1] Because of the large innovation costs, this is a poor assumption for the industry at all stages of production but a reasonable one after the drug has been invented and approved.

Important Questions

Expensive Necessities or Relatively Inexpensive Godsends?

In addition to the fact that we can show prices to be "high" in a theoretical sense, the data show they are also high in real life. In the United States in particular, drugs are often priced at 10 times their marginal production costs. In addition, drug prices are increasing far more rapidly than the overall inflation rate. As a matter of fact, from 1986 to 2013 drug prices went up more than 253 percent at a time when overall inflation increased general prices 111 percent. While some difference could have been expected, this difference is remarkable given that nonprescription drugs saw only a 61 percent price increase over the same period.

The reasons for increased prescription drug prices are many and varied, but they boil down to a few important issues: development costs, regulation, and litigation. There is also a problem with the mismeasurement of inflation in drug prices.

Development of new drugs costs a great deal of money, and drug companies need to recoup costs before they can make a profit. Since the "easy" diseases already have cures or treatments, we are left with some very difficult diseases to research. The training required to even understand how to start researching drug therapies takes several years after a researcher has earned a doctorate or a medical degree. People who get that kind of education for that long a period of time are going to command very high salaries once they start working. In addition to high labor costs, the equipment needed for this kind of work is specialized and expensive.

The capital and labor costs of drug research are extended even further by the years required to take a drug from successful trials to government approval. Typically, new drugs are first tested on small animals. They are then tested on primates. These tests are followed by small-scale human trials, designed primarily to gauge safety. Finally, a large-scale human trial requires that the drug be shown to work effectively while not causing unacceptable side effects. This lengthy process is expensive and it significantly extends the time before the company's revenue stream starts.

The concept of present value can shed light on how this contributes to the high costs of drugs. Let's use a numerical example to illustrate these issues. Assume a drug company sees that 1 million patients with a particular ailment are willing and able to pay for a treatment.

Suppose it costs $10 million a year for 10 years to invent a drug. Suppose it then takes another $10 million a year for another five years to test it and get it through the approval process. The law on how long a drug company has monopoly power over a drug is somewhat complicated, but we will assume that the company has that power for 10 years; after that, perfect competition takes hold and all economic profits disappear.[2] Add to this scenario the fact that few drugs make it from the scientist's lab to the pharmacy. Drug companies claim that the number of unsuccessful attempts is very high and that this is an additional reason for high costs.

Let's examine a hypothetical situation drug companies might face. Assume for every five drugs that reach the testing phase another five do not make it that far. Further, suppose that only one of every five that is tested is shown to be safe and effective. Thus for every 11 that incur invention costs, there are five that also incur testing costs. Only one produces revenue. Suppose at the very beginning of this process the manufacturer does not know which of these 11 plausible ideas will pay off, but it does know that one of them will. Also suppose that the manufacturer has a good idea that marginal production costs will amount to $10 per patient per year. Given all that, at a 10 percent real rate of return, the anticipated profit to the manufacturer from this one drug would have to be $520 million per year for the drug company to make back its initial investment. Thus, even if you ignore all of the markups that wholesalers and retailers charge from the manufacturer to the patient, the price per patient per year for our hypothetical example will have to be $530 dollars ($520 million dollars in profit/1 million patients +$10 in production costs).

In addition to all the preceding considerations, drug prices are made higher by our society's propensity for suing pharmaceutical companies. Americans sue each other more than any other group of people. Pharmaceutical firms have deep pockets. They produce products that do not work all the time and that sometimes do more harm than good. In the last 15 years, Vioxx and other Cox-2 inhibitors were approved and later had their safety called into question because they were shown to cause heart problems. Subsequent multimillion-dollar lawsuits were filed against their makers and, if upheld, they will completely wipe out the profit from the sale of these

---

[2]Manufacturers typically will make some economic profits on drugs after the expiration of the patent because of brand loyalty among physicians and patients. Drug company representatives encourage that loyalty with gifts. Sometimes these gifts are as innocuous as drug company pens while at other times they are expensive company-sponsored vacations.

drugs. With the fear of such judgments in mind, pharmaceutical firms will increase their prices so they have enough money on hand to account for such judgments and to have profit left over. In countries where lawsuits and judgments are limited, the prices of drugs tend to be commensurately lower.

Another phenomenon we must account for in analyzing the prices of drugs is that drug price indexes suffer from all of the problems that other price indexes suffer from. The consumer price index's lapses, discussed briefly in Chapter 6, are especially problematic with drugs. For an illustration of this, you need look no further than birth control pills. The pills your grandmother took in the early 1960s are nothing like those that are available now. The side effects of the early pills were much more severe than they are today. Part of the increase in the current price of birth control pills can be attributed to the improvement of quality rather than to the effects of inflation.

Taking all of the preceding into account, we are left with the fact that either drug prices are high or they seem to be high. The problem of the high expenses of drug therapies is shown very clearly in the cost of AIDS treatment. The drugs necessary to keep AIDS under control cost more than $12,000 a year. The "drug cocktail," a combination of AZT and protease inhibitors, can render AIDS a manageable disease in many. Instead of simply sedating patients as they die painfully, the only therapy in the middle 1980s, doctors can now offer many AIDS patients hope that they can manage the disease in a manner that is similar to the way patients with high blood pressure deal with their disease. That is to say, although the disease may eventually still kill them, the length and quality of their lives will be greatly enhanced. This is quite literally a life-saving cocktail of drugs, but it is one that forces many people into debt or requires that they quit work in order to qualify for Medicaid's health coverage. While bankruptcy is better than death, we can safely say that for AIDS patients this is an expensive necessity.

To counter some of the preceding negative characteristics, it must be said that the prescription drug industry can also lay claim to lowering health costs in some areas and to improving lives in nearly all areas. Drugs treat some diseases that either used to require surgery or, worse, that simply went untreated. There are drugs, also, that improve the quality of life and do so in a number of important areas. Some nonemergency heart conditions can now be treated with drug therapies rather than $30,000–$50,000 bypass or $10,000–$20,000 catheterization surgeries. Although the drugs are expensive and

cannot be used when a patient is suffering from near-complete arterial blockages, they can slowly open up the arteries, and they have been shown to have a success rate that is comparable to more invasive alternatives.

In other areas new drugs have simply improved life. From ailments as irritating as seasonal allergies to those as trivial as heartburn, to those as debilitating as asthma, new drugs have made the lives of people of all ages much better. While seasonal allergies and heartburn are never life-threatening, people's lives are changed when they are successfully treated.

Before the invention of nonsedating antihistamines such as Seldane[3] and Claritin, allergy sufferers like me were hard pressed to accomplish much out of doors in the spring and fall. These medications let allergy sufferers play golf, mow the lawn, and do many other enjoyable and productive things that used to only induce fits of sneezing. Claritin was also shown to be safe enough that the FDA allowed the drug to go "over the counter" (meaning no prescription is required) in 2003. Before antiheartburn medications such as Nexium,[4] spicy, high-acid, or rich dishes were simply off-limits for many middle-aged people. While it may seem trivial to the young, being unable to eat favorite foods affects people's quality of life. Being able to eat pizza, Cajun wings, or a piquant sauce does not rank high in the sphere of important medical issues, but being able to indulge once in a while does make life a little more enjoyable.

These latter cases are also not life-threatening, but they do represent serious quality-of-life issues. The drugs that treat these ailments may not be critical to life but they represent significant advances for people. Some would classify them as luxuries, but compared to not having the treatments available, others consider them to be inexpensive.

Why then do prescription drugs get such a bad rap? It is the reality that drug prices have increased significantly faster than inflation along with perceptions that economists claim are not well founded. Our perceptions tell us that the costs of prescription drugs are much higher than the actual 10 percent of medical spending for which they are responsible. For every dollar of expense incurred in hospital or doctor visits, less than 25 cents is paid by the patient in out-of-pocket expenses. On the other hand, more than 50 cents on the dollar is picked up by the patient for prescription drugs. This leaves the patient more

---

[3]This drug was pulled from the market because it was shown to interact in potentially fatal ways with heart medications.

[4]In extreme cases this drug has reduced the risk of esophageal cancer.

RESTLESS LEGS SYNDROME?

In 2006, a major pharmaceutical manufacturer, GlaxoSmithKline (yes, it is all one word) began producing and marketing Requip. The first thing it had to do was market the disease that Requip treated. So instead of describing the drug's ability to solve an obvious medical problem, like high blood pressure or heart disease, it had to tell people about "restless legs syndrome." This is what they say about this particular malady on their website (www.requip.com).

> Are your legs keeping you up at night?® Do you dread long business meetings, going to the movies, or traveling on an airplane because you know your restless legs won't let you sit still? You just know you'll have to get up to relieve the discomfort in your restless legs—disturbing your work colleagues, other moviegoers, and fellow passengers.

The drug has made millions for the company because they have effectively convinced people who can't stand to sit in confined areas that they have a curable ailment. They have also succeeded in marketing their product to people who can't get to sleep or stay asleep because they feel a compulsion to move. The cynical among us might suspect that this is an example of marketing a drug to a population who has money. Who has trouble on long flights? Who sits in long meetings? Who can't get to sleep or stay asleep? Middle-aged businesspeople with money and prescription drug coverage, that's who. Economically speaking, the purpose of advertising is to move the demand curve to the right. In this case, GlaxoSmithKline may have created it for themselves.

aware of and sensitive to increases in drug costs than increases in the costs of hospitals and doctors.

Price Controls: Are They the Answer?

Another of the facts that must be faced with regard to drug prices is that they are higher in the United States than anywhere else in the world. That is because in most other countries drug prices are regulated. Whether the drug prices themselves are controlled or the profits from their sales are controlled, people in other countries pay much less for drugs than we do. Go to El Paso, Texas, and price a drug, and you will find it at half price or less across the border in Mexico. You find the same thing in Detroit relative to Windsor, Canada. The drug is not safer in El Paso or Detroit; it is only more expensive. As a matter of fact, it is often in exactly the same package. Prices are lower in other parts of the world and one of the reasons is certainly price controls.

Would we be better off if the government controlled the price of drugs? Probably not. The world's drug inventors eye the profit that they get in the United States when they pour billions into their scientists and laboratories. If they could not make a profit in the United States, there would be no place to make one and they would not put the money into innovation. To mix metaphors, the United States is the drug industry's cash cow; by controlling prices, we would be killing the golden goose just as she is producing some very important life-improving and life-saving eggs.

The law with respect to prescription drugs is in flux. It has been against the law for companies to buy prescription drugs in a foreign country and resell them in the United States. Otherwise, a drug company could sell its products to a Canadian company at a low price determined by Canadian law. That Canadian company would then resell them to a U.S. retailer, thereby avoiding the high price in the United States. This would have the same effect as allowing Canada to control U.S. prices. This law has been under review for some time and with the election of President Obama is likely to be changed in favor of allowing reimportation.

FDA Approval: Too Stringent or Too Lax?

The approval for, and the regulation of, prescription drugs is performed by the Food and Drug Administration (FDA). In the early 1990s the FDA was under scrutiny for not allowing drugs to come to market quickly enough. The issue then was magnified by the excruciatingly slow process of getting AIDS drugs approved. As described earlier, the FDA's process is a multistage one where a drug is tested first for its safety and then for its effectiveness. A drug can be marketed only if both meet a high scientific standard.

While this sounds very good, the problem is that people will die of afflictions for which there are already existing drug therapies. For example, in the early 1990s the AIDS-combating protease inhibitors had been shown to be safe but scientists had not yet had the time to show their effectiveness. Reasoning that unforeseen drug interactions were the least of their worries, dying AIDS patients wanted the drugs immediately. The problem of overly stringent FDA regulation is that people die when they could be saved with a less stringent process.

During the middle 1990s the FDA began to experiment with a fast-track approval process. Here, drugs that are shown to be safe get an expedited review for effectiveness. The problem is that the initial safety review is conducted using a relatively small sample of people, while the effectiveness review is conducted using a much larger one. Adverse drug interactions and relatively rare and unforeseen safety issues come to light during this effectiveness testing. Expediting the effectiveness testing causes some safety issues to be missed, and as a result the FDA sometimes has to subsequently pull drugs off the shelves. This was Fen-Phen's fate and it may end up being the fate of all Cox-2 inhibitors.

This is a prime example of how the marginal analysis of economics can be used to aid in decision making. The marginal benefit of increasing FDA stringency is the decrease in the health problems accruing to those who take approved drugs that later are found to be unsafe. The marginal cost

of increasing FDA stringency is the forgone increase in the health of people who could have been treated but were not. The optimal degree of FDA stringency is where the marginal cost equals the marginal benefit.

Whether a particular drug goes over the counter is also a matter for FDA approval. When a new drug shows that it is sufficiently safe that it can be used by consumers with little or no consultation with a doctor, the FDA will approve it for use over the counter. When that occurs, the price of the drugs falls precipitously because it can be more easily mass-marketed. Whether that translates into consumers saving money is another story. It is ironic that when Claritin went over the counter in 2003, consumers without prescription drug coverage on their health insurance saw the price fall from more than $100 per month to around $35 per month, while those with insurance saw the cost to them rise because no insurance companies cover over-the-counter drugs. Former Claritin users with insurance were then motivated to seek more expensive prescription solutions such as Allegra. Insurance companies have since responded to this trend by requiring over-the-counter options to be tried before prescription options are tried.

Summary

You are now able to apply the concept of monopoly as well as consumer and producer surplus to the analysis of the costs of prescription drugs. You are able to apply those concepts to see the reasons most health economists view prescription drugs as relatively inexpensive even while most noneconomists view them as very expensive. You also understand why it is that most health economists do not favor price controls on prescription drugs. Last, you understand how economists see the issue of FDA approval and the appropriate degree of stringency.

Key Terms

deadweight loss, 284   orphan drug, 283   patent, 283

Quiz Yourself

1. The prescription drug industry is characterized by products that have
   a. low fixed costs and low marginal costs.
   b. low fixed costs and high marginal costs.
   c. high fixed costs and low marginal costs.
   d. high fixed costs and high marginal costs.

2. A patent is necessary to motivate innovation in areas where the innovation is
   a. costly to figure out and easily copied.
   b. cheap to figure out and difficult to copy.
   c. costly to figure out and difficult to copy.
   d. cheap to figure out and cheap to copy.

3. The reason orphan drug laws were created was that the motivation to invent drugs for these diseases was
   a. much greater than normal because prices could be high.
   b. much less than normal because prices would be too low.
   c. much less than normal because firms anticipated few sales.
   d. much greater than normal because firms anticipated high sales.

4. The market form for a new drug in an area where there are no competitors is
   a. perfect competition.
   b. monopolistc competition.
   c. oligopoly.
   d. monopoly.

5. The market form for a new drug in an area that has one other drug is
   a. perfect competition.
   b. monopolistc competition.
   c. oligopoly.
   d. monopoly.

6. The approval process for new drugs, if governed by economic thinking, should set stringency standards so that the _____ equals the _____.
   a. total cost; total benefit
   b. average cost; average benefit
   c. marginal cost; marginal benefit
   d. cost of production; revenue from sales

7. When an existing prescription drug goes over the counter
   a. everyone wins.
   b. drug companies win but consumers lose.
   c. drug companies lose but consumers win.
   d. drug companies likely win because of the increase in sales, and consumers may win depending on whether prescriptions are covered by insurance.

Short Answer Questions

1. What reasons are there for not limiting the price, or at least the increase in the price, of prescription drugs that have already been invented?

2. What are the reasons why, even if it is in the best interests of every other country to limit prescription drug prices, it might not be in the best interests of the United States to limit those prices?

3. Why might legalizing drug re-importation be equivalent to limiting drug prices?

4. What is lost in terms of societal welfare if, in the cause of safety, a drug or medical device has its approval delayed by a year or two?

Think about This

Vioxx and other Cox-2 inhibitors were invented because the existing pain medications (when taken for persistent pain) did damage to the lining of the stomach. After years of clinical trials, they were determined to be safe. It was only after use by millions of people that we became aware of the fact that they affected the heart. Under what conditions should their makers be legally liable for these side effects?

Talk about This

When a disease has no cure, people with the disease have no options. Suppose a prescription drug is invented but is so expensive that some patients cannot afford it. Are we better off with a drug being available, but only to those with insurance? What are the social consequences of this?

For More Insight See

Scherer, F. M., "Pricing, Profits, and Technological Progress in the Pharmaceutical Industry," *Journal of Economic Perspectives* 7, no. 3 (Summer 1993), pp. 97–115.

Behind the Numbers

Health, United States—www.cdc.gov/nchs
Overall and prescription drug prices—www.bls.gov/cpi/home.htm

CHAPTER TWENTY-FOUR

Government-Provided Health Insurance: Medicaid, Medicare, and the Child Health Insurance Program

Learning Objectives

After reading this chapter you should be able to:

LO1   Describe Medicaid as a program that covers medical expenses for many of this nation's poor.

LO2   Describe Medicare as a public insurance program for the elderly.

LO3   Distinguish Medicaid from Medicare and understand their relationship.

LO4   Describe the Child Health Insurance Program as one that serves the children of the working poor.

Chapter Outline

Since the early 1900s, the United States has been subsidizing medical care for citizens whose incomes are extremely low. The number of people who were covered by some form of federal medical care increased until 1967, when the Medicaid program came into full fruition. From that point on, millions of Americans have benefited from free medical care. Today, 39 million children and another 30 million adults have nearly all of their medical expenses paid for by Medicaid and its companion program, State Child Health Insurance Programs.

In this chapter we describe the Medicaid program in full, and we provide information about the people who are eligible for its benefits and what coverage they receive. We also discuss the groups that draw most heavily on Medicaid benefits. We describe the relationship

between the federal government and the states in funding and administering the Medicaid program. We outline how doctors and hospitals are reimbursed when they work with patients whose costs are paid through Medicaid. We move on to use our supply and demand model to explain why Medicaid costs so much, and we focus attention on Medicaid's treatment of two very different populations: the very old and the very young. Then we consider provisions in Medicaid that are intended to keep costs down.

Medicare and Social Security are the centerpieces of the United States' policy toward its elderly. Social Security ensures an income for the retired, and Medicare guarantees heavily subsidized health insurance for everyone over 65, retired or not. Social Security began in the New Deal 1930s; Medicare in the second great wave of social programs during the Johnson administration's Great Society of the 1960s. In its first full year in operation, 1967, the cost of its benefits totaled $2.7 billion; by 2011 it cost $554 billion.

Medicare comprises two programs: Medicare Part A, a mandatory program that covers expenses derived from hospital stays; and Medicare Part B, a voluntary program that covers doctor visits. This section begins by laying out why a government health insurance program for the elderly makes economic sense, and reviews the problems that such health insurance programs inevitably face. After discussing how each part of Medicare works, we focus on ways that each part has attempted to control costs. We then look at the Medicare Trust Fund and its projected problems in staying solvent, and we suggest ways Medicare can stave off bankruptcy. As part of that discussion, we talk about the relationship between Medicaid and Medicare, the program for Americans 65 or older.

Finally we take up the relatively new Child Health Insurance Program and its function of providing health insurance to the children of working families where the parents have no employer-provided health insurance.

Medicaid: What, Who, and How Much

Medicaid was established in 1964 to consolidate and expand existing programs that had been charged with providing health care to those who could not otherwise afford it. In 2011 the program cost the federal and state governments $408 billion. We begin our discussion of the Medicaid system by describing who is eligible, what is covered, who is enrolled, which groups cost the most, what relationship the federal government has to the states, and how doctors and hospitals are reimbursed.

People who are eligible for Medicaid must meet one of many criteria. In general, anyone who is in a family that is eligible for cash assistance under Temporary Assistance to Needy Families (TANF) or Supplemental Security Income (SSI) is automatically eligible for Medicaid. Eligibility standards were altered by the Patient Protection and Affordable Care Act (PPAPA) such that in 2014 many more adults were to have been covered by Medicaid. Prior to that act's passage, any children under 19 whose parents' income was less than 133 percent of the appropriate poverty line for their family size or pregnant women and children under a year old whose family income was less than 185 percent of that poverty line were also eligible, as were relatively few others who were affected by a variety

of other rules. Under the rules prior to 2014, adults who did not have children under the age of 19 could have very little income and not be covered by Medicaid because their wealth made them ineligible for TANF or SSI.

The PPACA, as originally passed, required states to expand Medicaid eligibility to include anyone in the household if the household income was less than 133 percent of the poverty line unless the states were willing to forgo all federal money for Medicaid. The Supreme Court decision that validated many parts of the act invalidated this provision. This meant that states could decide whether or not to participate. This also meant that although Medicaid enrolled more than 61 million, and SCHIP enrolled another 7.9 million, only half of those whose incomes were below 150 percent of the poverty line received its benefits. Approximately half of states had formally declined the Medicaid expansion or were leaning that way in 2013, despite the provision that the federal government would pick up the vast majority of the extra costs. Whether this was rationally or politically motivated, the impact on Medicaid eligibility remained cloudy through 2013.

Medicaid pays for nearly everything that is considered necessary from a medical standpoint, and it pays for some things that can be questioned. Doctor visits, emergency room visits, surgery, outpatient procedures, medicines, birth control pills, permanent and semipermanent birth control procedures and devices, eye care, long-term care—you name it, Medicaid probably pays for it. Literally, the only things that are not covered are most abortions, cosmetic surgeries, and drugs for weight loss and hair growth. Abortions are paid for by Medicaid in only a few states, and in those states the state must pay the whole fee. Whenever a pregnancy is the result of rape or incest, or threatens the life of the mother, Medicaid pays as it would for any other procedure.

Far more women and young people are served by Medicaid than their proportion in the general population. Whereas 51 percent of the population is female, nearly 59 percent of the Medicaid population is. Only 25 percent of the population is under 18, yet 50 percent of the Medicaid population is under 18. If you look simply at the adults on Medicaid, 70 percent are female. Additionally, though the population of Medicaid recipients is disproportionately young, we will show that the dollars spent are disproportionately allocated to care for the elderly.

In racial makeup, Medicaid recipients mirror the population of those who live in poverty nearly perfectly: 37 percent white, 21 percent black, and 19 percent Hispanic.

Medicaid is a cooperative effort of federal and state governments. The federal government mandates that the states enroll all people who are eligible, and it gives them guidelines to use if they wish to enroll others. States have the option of covering or denying coverage of certain specified expenses (like the previously mentioned abortions), as they wish.

The federal mandates are partially covered by federal matching money, and states are reimbursed according to their relative GDPs. Poorer states are given greater reimbursement rates, and richer states are given smaller ones. Fourteen states get the minimum 50 percent matching percentage from the federal government, while 6 other states and the District of Columbia get at least a 70 percent match. To motivate state participation in Medicaid's eligibility standards, the Patient Protection and Affordable Care Act temporarily raised these rates 7.6 to 15 percentage points to assist states' transition. The differential rates make Medicaid less of a burden for poorer states to fund.

Whether or not they participate in the expanded Medicaid provisions, some states make it easier to get on Medicaid than others. States have different income and wealth standards for TANF, and people who are eligible for Medicaid in New York and Wisconsin, for example, would not be eligible in states like Texas and Arkansas. This difference is effective only for adults, since children under one year of age are eligible, regardless of the state they live in, under a federal standard that makes them eligible if their family's income is less than 185 percent of the poverty line. All other children are similarly eligible as long as their family income is less than 133 percent of the poverty line.

When they treat patients whose bills are paid by Medicaid, doctors and hospitals are reimbursed at widely varying rates. States pay different amounts for the same procedures. These variations come about because Medicaid payments start at the state level with the federal government matching the state's payments. States must set reimbursement rates high enough that there are enough physicians and hospitals in all areas to treat Medicaid patients adequately. When many physicians are in competition with one another, rates can be lower; when there are few, rates must be higher.

For doctors and hospitals, Medicaid is an all-or-nothing proposition. When doctors and hospitals agree to take Medicaid patients, they agree to accept the state reimbursement rate as payment in full. They also agree to take any and all Medicaid patients who show up for treatment. They cannot limit their practice to a certain percentage, and they cannot accept patients with one disease and not another. Finding these restrictions to be unreasonable and reimbursement rates too low, many private hospitals and prestigious doctors do not take Medicaid patients.

Why Medicaid Costs So Much

Medicaid is an expensive program. To examine why it costs as much as it does, it will be helpful to put it into our supply and demand context. In 2011, the federal and state governments spent $420 billion to provide health care for 69 million Americans of Medicaid and Medicaid's companion program, State Child Health Insurance Programs (SHCIPs). Netting out the SCHIPs enrollment and costs, that amount translates to just under $7,000 per recipient. People not on Medicaid spend about the same as that. As a matter of fact, until quite recently those on Medicaid accounted for substantially greater per capita expenditures than those not on Medicaid. Why is it that the expenses of people who pay for their own health care are almost identical to the expenses of people whose health care is paid through Medicaid?

Let's turn to our supply and demand model for an explanation. As it is with any other good, the demand for health care is downward sloping. This is because when the price is high, people forgo care for ailments that are not all that troubling. Although price is always a concern, there are ailments that people will have treated pretty much regardless of cost. Keeping our upward-sloping supply curve makes sense because it takes more money to get doctors and hospitals to provide the greater quantities of care we desire and the higher quality of care that we also desire.

Figure 24.1 differs from every other supply and demand diagram you have seen, though, in that we have

FIGURE 24.1   The supply and demand for health care without Medicaid.

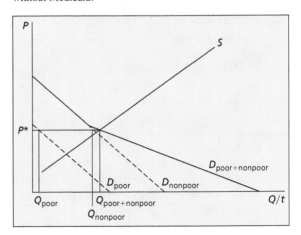

separated the demand by people in poverty from the demand by the people whose incomes are above the poverty line. The demand curve $D_{nonpoor}$ for the nonpoor is further to the right than the demand curve D_{poor} for the poor. To get the market demand curve $D_{poor + nonpoor}$, we must add the quantities of care that both the nonpoor and poor want at each price. At some prices the poor cannot afford any health care, and they therefore do not demand any health care. As prices fall, the poor begin to demand health care, and the nonpoor begin to demand more health care. To find where the market demand curve cuts the horizontal axis, you add the quantity of health care that each would want if it were provided free of charge. This horizontal adding of demand curves gives us the market demand curve.

Where the market demand curve $D_{poor + nonpoor}$ crosses the market supply curve S, we get the equilibrium price P^* and quantity $Q_{poor + nonpoor}$. When we take that price over to the nonpoor person's demand curve, we can read off the quantity of health care the nonpoor person will get as $Q_{nonpoor}$. Taking it further, to the poor person's demand curve, we can read off what the poor person wants as Q_{poor}. If the health care system is such that the poor cannot get access to care at affordable prices, there will be a disparity between the health care received by the nonpoor and that received by the poor that some people will consider to be unacceptable.

If the poor are provided health care free of charge, as they are with Medicaid, a different problem arises. The market demand curve does not stay as it was in Figure 24.1 but moves to its position in Figure 24.2. This new demand curve is made up by adding the quantity Q_{poor} of care poor people will want if it is free

FIGURE 24.2 The supply and demand for health care with Medicaid.

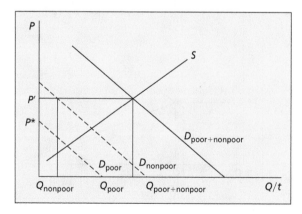

to the demand curve $D_{nonpoor}$ for the nonpoor. At the intersection of market supply and market demand, the price rises to P', which is substantially above its old price at P^*. It also results in greater access for the poor and less access for the nonpoor. Figure 24.2 exaggerates this effect, but in the real world Medicaid recipients consume slightly more health care than those who have private insurance.

Why Spending Is Greater on the Elderly

In terms of expenses, Medicaid dollars are spent disproportionately on the elderly. This stands to reason in that older people need care that tends to be more expensive, and they need it more often than do those who are younger. The average Medicaid recipient utilized more than $8,000 in medical care in 2011. In 2009, the average child who was covered by Medicaid cost the government only $2,848, while the average covered person over 65 cost $15,678. Thus, though children make up slightly less than half of Medicaid's population, they account for only 20 percent of the bills, and although those over 65 (and not disabled) make up less than 10 percent of its population, they account for 22 percent of the bills. This is in addition to the $554 billion that they account for in Medicare bills.

As mentioned previously, the central reason for Medicaid's spending more on the elderly than it does on the young is that older people tend to get illnesses that cost more than those of younger people. However, there is a reason that comes in a close second: nursing home care. Nursing home care is not part of either Medicare Part A or Part B. People who are elderly must therefore pay for this care themselves, unless, of course, they cannot. When elderly people's incomes are low enough that they qualify for assistance, Medicaid will pick up the tab for nursing home care. This can cost anywhere between $30,000 and $70,000 a year, constituting a substantial outlay for Medicaid. In the final analysis, Medicaid spends 35 percent of its total budget on long-term care, of which about three-quarters is on care for the aged.

The problem that this generates for elderly Americans is that they have to qualify for Medicaid before Medicaid will start paying. For widows and widowers this is not that difficult; they simply pay all their medical and nursing home expenses until their money is gone. Then Medicaid starts paying. Oftentimes, adult children with power of attorney try to hasten the point at which Medicaid pays their parents' medical expenses by draining the wealth of their parents by making gifts of it to themselves and their own children. It is legal to do this but only up to a point. Any money that is given to children and grandchildren in the name of the elderly relatives in the two-year period leading up to their enrollment in Medicaid is treated as a semifraudulent way of avoiding paying for nursing home care. The government monitors this and takes back any money that was given away within that period.

Giving away an elderly person's assets does not solve the nursing home problem entirely, in any case, because many times an elderly married couple has one partner who needs care and another who does not. This is especially true when an otherwise healthy person gets Alzheimer's disease. Medicaid used to require that the entire household's wealth be spent down before it would pay anything to a nursing home. This left many healthy spouses destitute because of the need to finance health care for their partner. At the time, the only alternative for the couple was to file for divorce the minute one of them was placed in a nursing home. That way, the assets were divided in half so that only half would be spent down, and the other half would be available for the healthy spouse. The needless emotional trauma of divorcing a long-time spouse is now avoided because the law now allows the assets of the couple's household to be divided equally between what will be spent down and what will be left untouched when one member of the married couple is admitted to a nursing home.

Cost-Saving Measures in Medicaid

During the early 1990s Medicaid costs were rising by more than 10 percent a year. This trend, coupled with other welfare concerns, motivated many of the welfare reform measures of the middle part of that decade. During that time states began to shift their Medicaid systems from individual doctors reimbursed for expenses to health maintenance organizations (HMOs). From 1990 to 2004, doctors in HMOs went from treating fewer than 5 percent of Medicaid patients to treating 60 percent of them.

When HMOs are in place, people are denied coverage unless it is authorized by the doctors who have been designated as their primary care physicians. Under HMOs, primary care physicians are charged with providing basic care, and they are the only people who can refer patients to specialists. The use of HMOs has stemmed the unfortunate practice of Medicaid patients' use of emergency room treatments for basic care. Nonemergency Medicaid patients are now counseled that if they show up at an emergency room for treatment of nonserious matters, they may be turned away. They are also counseled about the benefits of having a physician who follows their particular health needs. In this way HMOs are saving the state and federal governments money and, at the same time, are helping to improve the health of the people they are serving.

One other way in which states began cutting their Medicaid budgets in 2011 was to drop many optional coverages. Specifically, states that covered eyeglasses began to consider dropping such coverage for Medicaid recipients.

Medicare: Public Insurance and the Elderly

Why Private Insurance May Not Work

There are two main arguments for government provision of health insurance for the elderly: equity and efficiency. While it was appropriate in earlier times to argue that it was only fair to provide for the elderly in that the elderly were poorer than younger people, such arguments are less appropriate today. Today's elderly are among the least likely of our citizens to be in poverty, due in some measure to these programs. What remains are arguments that the market cannot provide health insurance efficiently to people who are not in groups.

The problem with health insurance, in general, is that people who really need it, those who are sick, are more than willing to pay very high prices for it; and those who are healthy are only willing to pay low prices. Most people have in mind two kinds of health expenses when they are thinking about buying insurance, the expenses they are rather sure they will incur and expenses of which they are not as certain. They will buy insurance readily if the expenses they expect are greater than the premiums they have to pay. People will pay for insurance that covers them in areas they are not certain they will need, but if premiums are too high, only the sickest will want to buy insurance. If this group were to become the only one that buys insurance, the expenses to the insurance company would be greater than the premiums received and premiums would have to rise. This would make the problem worse, as only the sickest of the sick would buy the insurance. This problem is referred to by economists as adverse selection.

This vicious cycle would go on and on until there was no insurance at all. Fortunately, this is not much of a problem in the United States because most private health insurance is group insurance that employers buy for their employees. In each group there are undoubtedly some people who are sick, some who are healthy, and many who are somewhere in between. The healthy subsidize the sick. Because being part of a group affords such important benefits both to the insurance companies and to members of the group, people who buy health insurance as individuals always run into problems not encountered by people who buy into group health insurance.

This would not be a problem if the elderly were still with their employers. They are not; they are retired, and many employers do not offer membership in company health groups to retirees. With the efficacy of offering health plans to people in groups, and with millions of individual retirees needing health insurance, it has made sense for the government to offer such insurance, and it does so through Medicare.

What remains debatable about Medicare is who pays for it—its beneficiaries (as with normal health insurance), or all taxpayers, or a combination of these groups. At the outset it was intended that the cost split would be about 50–50, proportions that offered the elderly a substantial subsidy. Today the subsidy is such that about three-quarters of the total expenses are paid out of tax dollars and only about a quarter by its beneficiaries.

Why Medicare's Costs Are High

All government health insurance programs suffer from problems of cost control, problems that are compounded in an era of rapid advances in medical technology that vastly improve health care but increase costs as well.

Anytime the consumption of a good is subsidized via insurance, several basic problems ensue. The first problem is that you risk increasing its consumption to an inefficient level. The second problem, referred to by economists as the third-party payer problem, is that by insuring consumers and thereby insulating them from costs, neither consumers nor producers have incentives for holding down costs. These and other insurance problems were explained in detail in Chapter 23 on health care.

As with all other government health insurance programs, then, the costs of Medicare have escalated dramatically. Figure 24.3 shows the increase in the costs of Medicare since its inception in 1967.

For most programs, spending can rise only because prices rise or beneficiaries become more numerous. Medicare spending has risen for these reasons and one other: increases in numbers of available medical services. Medicare beneficiaries are not limited to the medical procedures that existed in 1967. They can avail themselves of the best that medical science has to offer in the 2000s. This means that some patients who would have died 20 years ago, and who therefore would no longer be drawing on Medicare's resources, are now given medicines and procedures that are allowing them to live much longer.

It would be unconscionable to deny medical treatment to Medicare patients, even if it would be expensive, to improve their life or their life span. Moreover, it would be unrealistic to assume that they would deny themselves expensive treatments in the name of cost savings. Thus,

FIGURE 24.3   Medicare spending in billions of 2005 dollars.

Source: Refer to Table 8.6: www.whitehouse.gov/omb/budget/Historicals

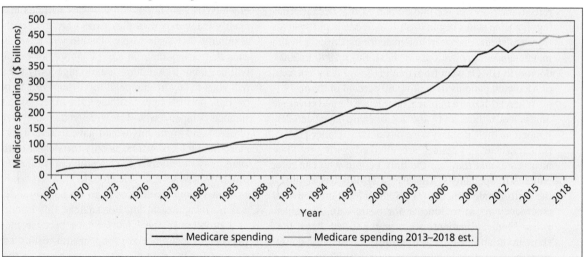

as treatments for health problems continue to become more effective and life expectancies increase, we will see a continued escalation of Medicare spending. As you will see in our section on the Medicare Trust Fund, it is this quickly increasing expense that has put Medicare on a course that is likely to lead it to bankruptcy.

One of the ways to deal with this kind of problem is to transfer the incentive to save money from the consumer to the producer. While it is usually consumers who want to limit the amount of money they pay, with insurance this incentive is either drastically reduced or even eliminated. As discussed above, if no one has an incentive to keep expenses down, no one will keep expenses down. It is possible, though, to make producers the cost-conscious parties by paying them prospectively rather than retrospectively.

Retrospective payment is what people are used to when they buy services. When a person has a car repaired, a garage worker finds the problem, asks whether the customer wants it fixed, tells what it will cost, and fixes it. At that point the retrospective payment is made. Under normal circumstances, this is not a problem because the customer still has the incentive to keep costs down. Problems arise when retrospective payments are used with insurance. When you have an accident that is someone else's fault, it is the other person's insurance that is paying the bill. Here you want everything fixed perfectly, with original parts, and the repair shop is only too happy to oblige because the mechanic can rack up the charges. If you had to pay for the repair, you would be more likely to be satisfied with "good enough" and to accept substitute parts. That is why either you are required to get two or three estimates before the work starts, or the single estimate and the repairs must be preapproved by an insurance adjuster. Both multiple estimates and insurance adjusters' oversight serve to keep repair shops competing with one another and prevent or lessen overbilling.

In health care it is unusual for an insurance company to have you go to several doctors to get estimates, though some may require second opinions. This is why some insurance companies and Medicare have gone to a system of prospective payments. Prospective payments are made prior to the service being performed. The hospital gets paid up front to treat its patients, and it then has an incentive to keep costs below what it has been paid. In the private arena, health maintenance organizations (HMOs) are designed to take advantage of such payments. Gatekeeper doctors, who are usually family practice physicians, pediatricians, or obstetrician/gynecologists, are paid specified sums per patient under their care, and they are paid

the sums whether the patients require a great deal of care or no care at all. Medicare HMOs work this way as well, and, as we will see, so does Medicare Part A.

Medicare's Nuts and Bolts

As we discussed before, Medicare is divided into two categories. Medicare Part A is mandatory for people over age 65, and it covers hospital care. Medicare Part B is voluntary, and it covers doctor visits. No part of Medicare covers common out-of-the-hospital prescription drugs or long-term nursing home care.

Provider Types

The first choice a Medicare recipient has to make is whether to choose traditional Medicare or a Medicare HMO. Medicare HMOs are approved by the government, and doctors who participate in them are paid per patient under their charge. The government pays less per HMO patient than per non-HMO patient on average, probably because healthy elderly people are more likely to enroll in an HMO. The cost controls that HMOs offer are usually enough that HMO premiums are significantly lower than normal Medicare premiums. People who opt for traditional Medicare are automatically enrolled in Part A; they may choose to enroll in Part B.

Part A

For people who work 10 years before reaching 65, Medicare Part A has no premium. For everyone else, the premium charged for Medicare Part A differs, depending on how long they worked. In 2013 the deductible was a relatively high $1,184 for the first day in the hospital. The costs for the next 60 days were paid by Medicare. After 60 days in the hospital, patients paid $296 per day, Medicare paid the rest, and after 90 days patients paid $592 per day. From day 91 on, patients have a 60-day reserve of days upon which to draw. When that reserve is gone, patients must pay the rest themselves.

From the hospital's position, Medicare is paying amounts that it has settled on for specific diagnoses. These payments, and they are prospective payments, are determined by where the patients' ailments put them on a list of more than 500 diagnosis-related groups (DRGs). All Medicare patients who enter the hospital are placed in a DRG, and rather than paying for specific expenses that are incurred, Medicare pays the hospital a predetermined amount that is considered appropriate for that DRG. This motivates the hospital to keep costs down.

Medicare had paid for every bandage, meal, and service until the mid-1980s, when it found that hospitals were racking up costs of questionable medical value just to increase their profit margins. Under fixed payments for DRGs, Medicare has kept much better control of cost increases. This policy has also led to a significant shortening of average hospital stays for specific problems. The current system also provides an incentive for hospitals to discharge patients as soon as possible.

This system for reimbursement is not without its critics. Specifically, President Obama derogatorily labels this prospective payment system as paying hospitals based on what the patients have when they walk in the door not for what the hospitals do to make the patients better, or even by what services they perform. This criticism is not new, but the balance that was struck when the DRG-based prospective reimbursement was instituted was that paying hospitals on performance (how much patients improve from when they were admitted) will cause hospitals to specialize in low-mortality, low-risk treatments, and that paying hospitals based on the services they provide will motivate hospitals to over-treat patients, thereby running up the costs. Though not without its critics, the current system is favored by most health economists as being one that keeps costs down, and with Medicare costs rising rapidly in the near future due to the aging of the baby boom generation, this is of primary concern.

Part B

Medicare Part B, the voluntary insurance program that pays for visits to doctors, has a monthly premium and an annual deductible. In 2013, the premium depended on your income. For those with incomes under $85,000 ($170,000 for married couples filing joint tax returns), the premium was $104.90 and the deductible was $147. Because neither the premium nor the deductible has increased at the rate of medical inflation, this part of the program is now being subsidized at a rate approaching 75 percent. What this means is that for every dollar a patient pays, Medicare Part B pays $3 out of tax revenues. Accordingly, there is virtually no reason for an elderly person not to enroll in Part B. For those who cannot afford the premium, Medicaid, the parallel program that provides health insurance for the poor, typically steps in. For everyone else, that $104.90 premium is a small enough amount that nearly 100 percent of the non-Medicaid eligible elderly are enrolled.

From a doctor's perspective, Medicare Part B pays a regional standard for each treatment. Unlike Part A,

Part B is billed expense by expense with retrospective payment. Medicaid pays a fixed amount for each service, but each service is billed individually rather than being grouped in a DRG.

The reason that prospective payments do not work for non-HMO Medicare Part B is that, with a huge range of possible ailments, there are many potential doctors a patient may want to see. In a Medicare HMO, a gatekeeper is in charge of referrals to specialists, but non-HMO patients can go at any time to the doctors of their choice. It would be impossible to predict such choices in advance, and since no single doctor, HMO, or hospital is in total charge of their care under Part B, prospective payments cannot be made to work.

Prescription Drug Coverage (Part D)

As part of the 2003 reauthorization of Medicare, the costs of prescription drugs are now covered. Prior to this change, health care economists were of two minds. First, they saw a distortion of the market when surgery was covered but medicines were not. Second, they noted Medicare's precarious financial state and worried that the additional benefit would make it that much worse.

As expensive as most drugs are, drug-based treatments are less expensive than their surgical alternatives. Because Medicare did not cover prescription drugs and it did cover surgery, patients may have elected surgery even though it may have been more expensive.

On the other side of the debate were the concerns over the cost of any prescription drug program. Initial estimates in the 2003 Medicare reauthorization placed the cost of such a program at $400 billion over 10 years. Those estimates were quickly revised. Currently the program is anticipated to cost at least $1 trillion over 10 years. What must be understood about any such estimates is that they are highly sensitive to assumptions about price elasticity for drugs. If the estimator uses data on the number of prescriptions filled and multiplies that number by the cost per prescription covered by the government (assuming perfectly inelastic demand), this would seriously underestimate costs. There are people who will benefit from prescriptions who did not go to the doctor because they knew they would get a prescription slip they could not afford to fill. Additionally, there were elderly who used to get multiple prescriptions and fill only a fraction of them because they could not afford to fill them all. Taking this into account, cost estimates are likely to be exceeded and higher deficits will ensue.

The 2003 reauthorization also introduced means testing to Medicare. The Republican-authored bill made premiums and coverage dependent on income and required most seniors to pay as much as $3,600 out of pocket. Medicare Part D is not really a national plan but was intended to foster many private alternatives with substantial government subsidies. Premiums, deductibles, and co-pays are features of each plan and are highly localized, and as a result much more confusing to beneficiaries than Medicare Part A or B. Democrats, who had sought a government-run program akin to the other parts of Medicare, generally opposed the plan. Republican defenders sought to introduce private market incentives to keep costs under control. Neither seems to have the upper hand on this issue as the system was initially very confusing, but the most recent estimates suggest that it will cost the government 30 percent less than it was originally projected to cost. A particularly troubling part of the original law was the existence of a "donut hole" where coverage began at one level of individual spending, then stopped until another higher level of spending was arrived at, and then began again. The donut hole is slated to be reduced under the Patient Protection and Affordable Care Act.

Cost Control Provisions in Medicare

Medicare has been attempting to keep costs under control since its inception, but, unfortunately, it has enjoyed little success. Ultimately the reasons for this lack of success boil down to two:

1. Medical care is increasingly sophisticated, with continually improving success rates, and it is therefore more costly.
2. There is no economic incentive for either patient or doctor to control costs.

While the aforementioned DRGs have helped control costs in Part A, and Medicare HMOs have helped control costs in Part B, neither has been foolproof. The DRGs, however, have succeeded in doing a couple of important things with regard to costs. First, basing the payments on DRGs has given hospitals the incentive to take many procedures that used to require one night in the hospital and turn them into outpatient procedures. Second, hospitals have put pressure on doctors and patients to shorten the average length of stay of many multiday procedures.

Given that DRGs pay a fixed amount for a procedure, hospitals have the incentive to cut costs. Since one of a hospital's greatest costs is keeping someone in a bed

overnight, converting a procedure that formerly involved a hospital stay to one that is done on an outpatient basis helps to raise profits. Heart bypass surgery is not likely to be an outpatient procedure anytime soon, but many other procedures are candidates. While many people are concerned about the health consequences of turning out patients who would have stayed a night, there has been little medical evidence that sending people home right away has had adverse effects.

A second area where costs have come down is the shortening of the length of stay for many multiday procedures. Surgeries that used to require a three- or four-day stay in the hospital to recuperate now require only two or three. In part this is because surgeons are better at limiting the trauma to the body from surgery, and in part it is because postsurgical rehabilitation has improved.[1]

The Medicare Trust Fund

One of the greatest concerns today is the fiscal health of the Medicare program that provides for our elderly's physical health. The Medicare Trust Fund enjoyed assets of $325 billion in 2011. This trust fund was set up to handle the anticipated medical expenses of the baby boom generation. Like the Social Security Trust Fund, it deliberately collected more in taxes than was necessary in order to build savings for the period between 2015 and 2035, when it was anticipated that the high numbers of the baby boom generation were likely to strain the system. Like the Social Security Trust Fund, the Medicare Trust Fund is invested only in U.S. government debt. In 1997, however, the trustees of the Medicare Trust Fund issued an alarming report. They estimated that long before the serious crisis hit, the trust fund would be bankrupt. While later trustees' reports have been somewhat more optimistic about the fiscal health of the program, eventual bankruptcy remains its conclusion. In fact, in 2008 the balance of the trust fund began to shrink for the first time in its history.

The annual reports of the trustees have been based on three different projections of the future: one very optimistic, the second very pessimistic, and the third on

[1] While the data on length of stay have not shown a decline, this is misleading because of the aforementioned outpatient substitution. Since the length-of-stay data are based on the number of days a patient stays in a hospital, the procedures that are now outpatient do not count at all. If length of stay for the other procedures had remained the same as it was before the outpatient substitution, then the overall average would have risen substantially since whenever you remove short stays and leave only the longer stays, the average rises. Since the overall average has remained constant, we know the length of stay for longer-stay procedures has fallen.

FIGURE 24.4   The Medicare Trust Fund under alternative assumptions.

Source: Medicare Trustees Report.

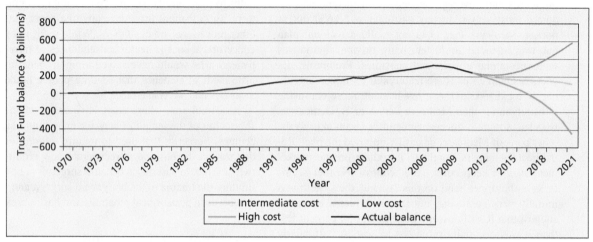

what the trustees judged to be the most realistic assumptions. Assumptions have been made about two economic variables and two demographic variables. The economic considerations have been the growth in inflation-adjusted wages and the real interest rate. The demographic variables have been the fertility rate and life expectancy. The higher the projected growth rate in wages, the more projected tax revenues would be; the higher the projected real interest rate, the better return on the trust fund would be; and because it is held that greater numbers of children will produce more tax revenue, the higher the projected fertility rate, the greater the projected tax revenues. Last, longer projected life expectancy would be anticipated to create greater Medicare expenses.

Figure 24.4 shows the actual balance of the Medicare Trust Fund from 1970 to 2011 and the projected balance of the trust fund until 2021 under the alternative assumptions just outlined. The estimates of low costs are based on the following assumptions: Real wages will grow quickly, at a rate of 1.6 percent; real interest rates will be a high rate of 3.7 percent; and fertility will be high, at 2.2 children per woman. The figures that reflect the estimate of high costs are just the opposite: Real wages will grow at 0.6 percent; real interest rates will be 2.2 percent; and fertility will be 1.7 children per woman. The intermediate cost projections are that real wages will rise at 1.1 percent; real interest rates will be at 3.0 percent; and the average woman will have 1.95 children.

If the assumptions leading to high costs are correct, Medicare is genuinely on the verge of bankruptcy. If the costs turn out to be low, the year of bankruptcy is beyond

the immediate projections of the report, but it still happens in the middle of the 21st century. The 1997 report used the intermediate assumptions and projected bankruptcy in 2008. The 1999 update of the report projected that the system would be bankrupt in 2015. The 2000 through 2008 versions have produced a relatively stable projection for around the 2020s.

The 2009 report was significantly less optimistic, while the 2010 report returned to projections of difficulties in the 2020s. These estimates have become somewhat political in that they were used to justify the need for the Patient Protection and Affordable Care Act, and assumptions were made in them that most political observers understood would never actually take place. Specifically, the rate at which Medicare reimburses hospitals and doctors was, by previous statute supposed to decline 20 percent as a result of cost estimates exceeding previously established benchmarks. Every year since the benchmarks were surpassed, Congress has acted to waive those rate reductions. As unrealistic as it is, the trustees are required to assume that Congress will not change the law, which means that they are supposed to assume that the last time Congress waived the rate reductions will be the last time they ever do.

To forestall the projected bankruptcy, it seems reasonable to consider simply raising taxes along the way in a pay-as-you-go format. This would presuppose that nothing is done to alter the current program. If we go to a pay-as-you-go system where taxes have to increase each year to meet the health care needs of the elderly, tax rates may rise substantially.

Under current law, the payroll tax that funds Part A of Medicare is 2.9 percent. That is, you and your employer each contribute 1.45 percent of everything you make on the job. (The self-employed contribute the full 2.9 percent.) Under the most likely scenario, the rate would more than double to 3.3 percent each.

If raising taxes to the necessary levels is unacceptable, other solutions may be explored. The age at which people become eligible could be raised, premiums and deductibles could be raised to their inflation-adjusted 1970 level or beyond, all beneficiaries could be required to have gatekeeper physicians (as in HMOs), and it could be mandated that at certain income or wealth levels the elderly would get reduced subsidies. Many people are dissatisfied with these alternatives, and none meet with the approval of the main lobbying organization for the elderly, the American Association of Retired Persons.

The Relationship between Medicaid and Medicare

Besides beginning with the same act of Congress and besides sharing the first six letters of their eight-letter titles, Medicare and Medicaid share other features. The most significant is a commingling of tasks when people are both old and poor. Medicare was set up to deal with only the aged and Medicaid was set up to deal with only the poor. When someone is both old and poor, both programs come into play.

When a person is of an age to be eligible for Medicare and is also poor and qualifies on that ground for Medicaid, the first to pay is Medicare. Medicaid is the payer of last resort. Since Medicare has two parts and since Medicaid's costs are shared by both the federal and state governments, the story gets even more complicated.

All elderly are required to participate in Medicare Part A, which covers hospital expenses, and they can elect to participate in Medicare Part B, coverage for doctors' visits. When people are poor as well and qualify for Medicaid, the Medicare premiums and deductibles for Part A are paid by Medicaid and the remainder are paid by Medicare. For Part B, the state can then elect to pay the Medicare Part B premiums and deductibles and have Medicare Part B pick up the bulk of the expenses. In any event, when elderly people are eligible for Medicaid, there is significant overlap between Medicare and Medicaid.

Child Health Insurance Program

In 1997 the Child Health Insurance Program was created to help the children of the working poor. It allowed states either to expand Medicaid coverage to those making less than 200 percent of the poverty line or to create a separate program to serve that population. The states have chosen a variety of strategies to implement their programs. In general, though, when a child's low-income parents have no insurance through their employer, they can purchase highly subsidized health insurance. The premiums are held below $20 per family per month, a tiny fraction of what they would be for private insurance. Similarly, the deductibles and co-payments are low as well. An interesting feature is that well-baby visits and immunizations are required to be free for children in the program.

The program is structured very much like Medicaid in that there is a matching rate for states depending on their per capita income and minimum coverage expectations to ensure that all covered children are given adequate care regardless of where they live. The matching rates are closely tied to the regular Medicaid matching rates but are, on average, 12 percentage points higher. The program now serves more than 7.9 million children at a cost of more than $11 billion per year.

Summary

At this point you understand that Medicaid is a program that covers medical expenses for a subset of this nation's poor. You understand that eligibility for Medicaid benefits is tied to family income and the age of dependent children, and, as a result, there are many people who are in poverty and not covered by the program. You understand that the beneficiaries are disproportionately women but that in other demographic dimensions they mirror those who are in poverty. You understand how much the program costs, and you know why those costs are high relative to the costs of those who are covered by private insurance. You know that a disproportionate amount of money is spent on the elderly, and you are able to articulate why that is the case. You understand the relationship between Medicaid and the companion program for the elderly, Medicare. Last, you are aware of the cost-saving measures that have been put in place for Medicaid.

Quiz Yourself

1. In 2011, a five-year-old child from a family making more than 133 percent but less than 200 percent of the poverty line is
   a. ineligible for any health care assistance.
   b. eligible for Medicare's prescription drug plan only.
   c. eligible for all of Medicare.
   d. eligible for Medicaid.

2. When a 65-year-old goes to the hospital, the part of Medicare that pays for the hospital bill is
   a. Part A.
   b. Part B.
   c. Part C.
   d. Part D.

3. When a program like Medicaid is introduced, the market demand curve for health care will
   a. increase and flatten.
   b. increase and become more steep.
   c. decrease and flatten.
   d. decrease and become more steep.

4. Medicaid spending per recipient is
   a. twice that of the average citizen's use of health care.
   b. somewhat less than the average citizen's use of health care.
   c. somewhat greater than the average citizen's use of health care.
   d. half that of the average citizen's use of health care.

5. The DRG system controls Medicare expenses by
   a. preventing doctors from using particular procedures.
   b. paying hospitals after they submit bills.
   c. paying hospitals on the basis of a disease or injury rather than expenses.
   d. paying the patient who then pays the hospital.

6. The Medicare Trust Fund is necessary because
   a. current expenses are greater than current revenues.
   b. current expenses are less than current revenues.
   c. future expenses will be greater than future revenues.
   d. future expenses will be less than future revenues.

7. Medicare's prescription drug coverage will likely
   a. cost substantially more than it was estimated to cost in 2003.
   b. cost substantially less than it was estimated to cost in 2003.
   c. cost slightly less than it was estimated to cost in 2003.
   d. cost about what it was estimated to cost in 2003.

Short Answer Questions

1. How might the elasticity of demand for a health care service be used to estimate the demand created for a health care service when there is a new program for government coverage?

2. Why is the Medicare Trust Fund estimated date of fund exhaustion so dependent on the assumption made with regard to economic growth, interest rates, and political changes?

3. What are the benefits and costs associated with reimbursing hospitals based on their actual services performed rather than based on the problems the patients have when they come to the hospital?

Think about This

One of the suggestions for providing the working poor with health insurance has been to require employers to provide health insurance benefits for all workers by having employers "buy them into Medicaid." Requiring this would raise the cost to employers of hiring new workers. Under what circumstances would this be good for workers? Under what circumstances would it not be good?

Talk about This

When public provision of health care is discussed in most political arenas, providing more coverage (e.g., prescriptions and long-term care) for the elderly typically garners more attention than expanding coverage to the working poor. Why is that? Is this the right priority in your mind?

For More Insight See

Garrett, Major, "Medicare: Healthier for Now," *U.S. News & World Report,* April 12, 1999, p. 29.

Lee, Ronald, and Jonathan Skinner, "Will Aging Baby Boomers Bust the Federal Budget?" *Journal of Economic Perspectives* 13 (Winter 1999), pp. 117–140.

Miller, Matthew, "Premium Idea," *The New Republic,* April 12, 1999, pp. 24–27.

Newhouse, Joseph, "Policy Watch: Medicare," *Journal of Economic Perspectives* 10 (Summer 1996), pp. 159–168.

Phelps, Charles, *Health Economics* (Reading, MA: Addison-Wesley, 1997), esp. Chapter 13.

"Survey: Health Care," *The Economist,* July 6, 1991.

2000 Annual Report of the Board of Trustees of the Federal Hospital Insurance Trust Fund.

Behind the Numbers

Historical data.

Federal Medicare spending.

Budget of the United States Government; historical tables—

www.whitehouse.gov/omb/budget/Historicals

Matching rates to the states—

http://aspe.hhs.gov/health/fmap11.pdf

Historical and projected Medicare Trust Fund assets, 1970–2019.

Centers for Medicare and Medicaid Services; Trustees Report—

www.cms.gov/Research-Statistics-Data-and-Systems/Statistics-Trends-and-Reports/Reports TrustFunds/downloads/tr2012.pdf

Medicaid spending and population characteristics, Medicaid and Medicare recipients, eligibility, and costs; Centers for Medicare and Medicaid Services—

www.cms.hhs.gov

www.cms.gov/ActuarialStudies/downloads/Medicaid Report2010.pdf

www.cms.gov/MedicaidDataSourcesGenInfo

Health, United States, 2010, with chartbook on trends in the health of Americans, National Center for Health Statistics—www.cdc.gov/nchs/data/hus/hus10.pdf

CHAPTER TWENTY-THREE

Health Care

Learning Objectives

After reading this chapter you should be able to:

LO1 Summarize how the system of health care finance seriously alters the market for health care services.

LO2 Conclude that in the United States 52 percent of the health care tab is picked up by the taxpayer with the remainder being paid either directly by patients or by their insurance companies.

LO3 Analyze the health care industry using the supply and demand model and discuss the limitations of the model when applied to this industry.

LO4 Demonstrate that both private insurance and taxpayer-financed health care systems increase the overall price of health care.

LO5 Compare and contrast privately financed and single-payer, taxpayer-financed health care systems by noting their respective advantages and disadvantages.

Chapter Outline

Where the Money Goes and Where It Comes From

Insurance in the United States

Economic Models of Health Care

Comparing the United States with the Rest of the World

Summary

Health care in the United States has two characteristics that seem to be fundamentally inconsistent. No other country on earth can match the United States in terms of the quality of care that is available, but no developed country has our infant mortality rate. Additionally, in no other country are doctors as skilled, and in no other country are doctors as highly paid. In no other country is the quality of care as high, but in no other developed country is care denied so often because patients are unable to pay for it. At its root, the problem of having high-quality care that is not available to everyone who needs it is attributed only to the way we finance health care.

In this chapter we explain health care in the United States by first detailing the money spent and by whom it is spent. We discuss how private and public insurance work in the United States and discuss the problems associated with each. We then turn to why the economics of health care differs so much from the economics of any other good. Along the way we compare our health care financing system with the model used in most other developed countries and hit the high points of the Patient Protection and Affordable Care Act, (PPACA).

Where the Money Goes and Where It Comes From

In defeating the health care plan that the Clinton administration attempted to implement, Republicans claimed that Democrats were trying to take over one-sixth of the economy. Indeed, while in 2011 one-sixth of the gross domestic product (2.7 trillion of 15.1 trillion) was spent on health-related goods and services, the government's portion was already half (51.8 percent, or 1.4 trillion) of health care expenditures. President Clinton and his

Democratic supporters were merely attempting to federalize the private portion of health care expenditure.

Of the $1.4 trillion that government spent on health care in the United States in 2011, some $554 billion was spent on Medicare (the government health insurance program for the elderly) and $408 billion was spent on Medicaid (the government health insurance program for the poor). The remainder was spent by all levels of government on local, state, and veterans' hospitals and in support of medical research.

Medicare
Public health insurance in the United States which covers those over age 65.

Medicaid
Public health insurance in the United States that covers the poor.

Of the $1.3 trillion that was spent on health care in the private sector in 2011, some $896 billion came from premiums paid to insurance companies and by the money that insurance companies realized from their investments. People paid an additional $308 billion in out-of-pocket expenditures, and the remainder was spent by private medical research companies.

In general, of the $2.7 trillion spent on health care in the United States in 2011, $851 billion went to hospitals and $541 billion went to doctors. Drugs accounted for $263 billion and medical research spending accounted for $50 billion.

Insurance in the United States

Most people in the United States are covered by some form of health insurance for at least part of the year. In 2011, for example, 76 percent of the 308 million people in the United States had coverage all year, another 8 percent had coverage for part of the year, and 16 percent had no coverage at all. The coverage during that year came from a variety of sources. The largest group, 170 million people, was covered by group insurance policies, 30 million had individual policies, 48 million were on Medicare, 51 million were on Medicaid,[1] and of those 9 million were on both.

How Insurance Works

Whether we are discussing health insurance, life insurance, or auto insurance, private insurance of any kind works like this. There is a small chance that something bad will happen to you, and there is a large chance that nothing

bad will happen to you. You spend a little money on insurance that will cushion the effects of the bad prospect, should it occur. In other words, you pay a premium so that if the bad thing happens, the insurance provider (whether it be the government or an insurance company) will pay to make things better. In the case of health insurance, people pay premiums so that when they get sick their provider pays most of the expense of dealing with their illnesses.

It is perfectly rational to buy insurance even when the average expense you would face is less than the cost of the insurance. The reason is that most people are risk averse: They prefer to be guaranteed a particular outcome, even when the odds are that for the average person, over an average lifetime, insurance is more expensive than the problem they are insuring themselves against. As an example, suppose there is a 1 percent chance that you will have a major health-related expense of $100,000 and a 99 percent chance that you will have only $1,000 of typical health expenses. A risk-neutral person would look at the expected expense, $1,990,[2] and not be willing to pay any more than that for full insurance coverage. People who are risk averse, on the other hand, would be willing to pay more than that to guarantee themselves that they would not have to pay any more.

risk averse
A characteristic of a person who would pay extra to guarantee the expected outcome.

risk neutral
A characteristic of a person who would not pay extra to guarantee the expected outcome.

Nearly all private health insurance plans have a number of characteristics in common. You owe a premium that, for most Americans, is paid partly by you and partly by your employer.[3] Insurance companies use premiums for three things: (1) to pay doctor and hospital bills of their patients, (2) to cover administrative expenses, and (3) to provide profit for the owners (usually shareholders) of the insurance company.

If you get sick and have a health expense, it is usually the case that both you and your insurance company will pay part of the bill. There are four key pieces of vocabulary that determine who pays how much. The deductible is the amount of health spending a year that you have to pay before the insurance

deductible
The amount of health spending a year that you have to pay before the insurance company pays anything.

---

[2] $.99 \times 1,000 + .01 \times 100,000 = 1,990$.

[3] This aspect is actually an artifact of World War II. Because of inflation fears during that time, it was against the law to raise wages to attract workers. Instead, companies increased benefits in the form of group insurance subsidies, and the practice survived the war.

---

[1] Because Medicaid's enrollment is fluid, as many as 70 million have Medicaid at some point during the year.

company pays anything. This very much depends on the type of plan you have but can be as low as nothing and as high as several thousand dollars. Typically, the deductible for a plan is between $200 and $300 per person and between $600 and $1,000 per family per year. For instance, if you have an insurance plan with a $200 deductible and you have a covered medical expense that totals $500, you will have to pay $200 before your insurance company pays anything.

co-payment
Either a set amount or the percentage of the bill after the deductible has been taken out that you have to pay.

maximum out of pocket
The most that a person or family will have to pay over a year for all covered health expenses.

mini-med
Low premium health insurance with a low annual maximum.

The **co-payment** is either a set amount or the percentage of the bill, after the deductible has been taken out, that you have to pay. This also has a wide range. Some plans have no copayment; others as much as 30 percent. The **maximum out of pocket** is the most that a person or family will have to pay over a year for all covered health expenses. This means that a $500,000 health expense will not bankrupt the typical person because the maximum out of pocket is usually between $2,000 and $6,000 a year.

Some companies offer what are called **mini-meds**. Mini-med insurance policies are usually only offered to young people, have fairly low premiums and, as one of the features, have low (usually no more than $10,000) annual maximum amounts that the insurance company will pay. These limits are illegal, in general, but these policies serve a niche market that the Obama administration did not want to harm when they banned the general practice of capping health insurance company liability. The fear was that by outlawing all mini-meds, they would reduce health insurance coverage for many young people in their first jobs.

Varieties of Private Insurance

There are several types of private insurance plans out there, but they boil down to three large groups: (1) fee for service, (2) health maintenance, and (3) preferred provider. A fee-for-service provider allows sick people to go to any doctor they want, wherever they want, for whatever ails them. The doctor then bills the insurance company, the insurance company pays its share, and the doctor bills the patient for the remainder. Because there are few controls on spending in a system like this, it is very costly. Patients and doctors, however, have few complaints.

A health maintenance organization (HMO) requires that people see specific doctors at the beginning of any problem. These doctors are referred to as **primary care physicians (PCP)** or, familiarly, as *gatekeepers*. Patients can see specialists only after their primary care physician makes a referral, and the PCP, or gatekeeper, has the job of making sure that his or her patients get the appropriate care as inexpensively as possible. Usually HMO PCPs receive a fixed fee for every patient assigned, and specialists are either salaried or also have fixed fees for every referral. Patients and doctors complain about the controls on spending in HMOs, but these serve to keep costs down.

primary care physician (PCP)
Physician in managed care operations charged with making the initial diagnosis and making referrals. Also called a *gatekeeper*.

A preferred provider organization (PPO) is somewhat of a hybrid. People can choose the doctor they want from a list of doctors. The doctors agree to charge a specific amount per procedure or disease, and they take a lower fee than usual in order to be guaranteed a large number of potential patients.

Table 23.1 outlines the advantages and disadvantages of each of these private insurance options from the patient's standpoint.

Public Insurance

Public insurance, provided by the government, is divided into three main programs: Medicare, Medicaid, and the Children's Health Insurance Program. Medicare is available to eligible citizens who are 65 years old and older. It works very much like a generous fee-for-service health insurance plan, except that the burden for high premiums is placed on the taxpayer rather than the patient or the patient's employer. The tax that funds Medicare appears on your paycheck in the same place your Social Security tax does; they are both under FICA (Federal Insurance Contributions Act). The portion that is used for Medicare is 1.45 percent of your salary, wages, and tips; you and your employer each pay that rate. For part of Medicare, money is also taken from the general tax revenues of the government.

Medicare is generous in the following sense: By private health care standards its premiums are very low, and the co-payments and the deductibles are also low. In truth Medicare is really two programs, a compulsory program that covers hospital-related expenses and a voluntary program that covers doctors' charges. In 2013, those who were eligible for the compulsory version,

TABLE 23.1   Advantages and disadvantages to patients of different forms of private insurance.

Source: Medicare, www.medicare.gov

Insurance Type	Advantages	Disadvantages
Fee for service	Maximum physician choice Little insurance company meddling in doctors' decisions	Highest premiums, deductibles, and co-payment rates because of little control over expensive and unnecessary procedures
HMO	Maximum control over expensive and unnecessary procedures so premiums, deductibles, and co-payment rates are low	Minimal physician choice Significant meddling in physician decisions, especially when differing procedures have significant cost differences
PPO	Some physician choice Moderate premiums, deductibles, and co-payment rates Some control over expensive procedures Minor meddling in physician decisions	

Medicare Part A, and worked between 30 and 39 quarters paid a $243 monthly premium. Those who worked less than 30 quarters paid $441 per month, and for those who worked more than 40 quarters, it was free. The voluntary version, Medicare Part B, cost beneficiaries between $104.90 and $335.70 per month depending on their 2011 income, and covered doctor-related expenses. Elderly people who are eligible for the primary welfare program for the old and poor, Supplemental Security Income, have Medicaid pick up the Part A premium and often the Part B premium as well.

In contrast with Medicare, Medicaid is a no-premium, no-deductible, very low or no co-payment health plan for the poor.[4] Under Medicaid, doctors are reimbursed at rates that are low relative to what Medicare pays and extremely low relative to what private insurance pays. Hospitals and doctors can and do refuse to treat Medicaid patients when they judge the reimbursement rates to be too low.

In 2011 there were 49 million Americans who survived, at least part of the year, without any health insurance at all. Many of these are people who move from one job to another and whose insurance runs out while they are unemployed.[5] On the other hand, a 1994 study by Katherine Swartz indicated that 21 million Americans were without any health insurance for more than a year. Of the uninsured, 18 million are between the ages of 18 and 34. Their lack of insurance may be voluntary in the sense that they may be able to afford insurance but are healthy and therefore choose not to purchase it. A recently emerging group of people without health insurance is those who retire early and are waiting for Medicare to kick in when they turn 65.

Among the uninsured for at least some portion of the year are the nearly 12 million who are under 18. It was in reaction to more than 16 million children living without health insurance that the Children's Health Insurance Program was created in the 1990s. Its function is like that of Medicaid, but it is focused, as the name suggests, on children who live in families where the breadwinners do not have insurance through their employer and do not make enough to purchase it themselves.

Economic Models of Health Care

We can use our supply and demand model to look at what happens when the good in question is not something tangible, like an apple, but intangible, like health care. Additionally, in the context of this model, we can explore how the health care finance system alters people's behavior.

Why Health Care Is Not Just Another Good

Health care is not like any other good. You can look at an apple grown in 1998 and say that it is comparable to an apple grown in 1995 or 1885. An apple is pretty much the

[4]States may impose small co-payments to discourage abusive overuse.
[5]Workers have the right to continue their employer-sponsored health insurance even after they quit or are fired. The problem is that most employers do not continue subsidizing the premiums, which means people are not likely to be able to afford to exercise this right.

PPACA PROVISIONS TO EXPAND COVERAGE

There are three significant provisions of the PPACA that serve to expand coverage to those who have been without it. First, beginning in 2014, employers of more than 50 full-time employees will be required to provide their employees with at least a minimal insurance plan or else pay a tax. Second, Medicaid will be expanded to cover everyone in families earning under 133 percent of the poverty line in those states that agree to pay a small portion of the added expense. Third, subsidies will be paid to those earning under 400 percent of the poverty line when they purchase health insurance through an approved exchange.

These provisions are not without controversy. The first provision forces employers that do not provide at least minimal health insurance to pay a fine if even one of their employees is given a subsidy to buy insurance. This provision has some economists worried that the PPACA lessens the incentive that firms have to employ new workers by raising the cost of that worker. The Medicaid expansion worries governors and legislatures regarding its impact on state budgets so much that (at this spring 2014 writing) fewer than 20 states have agreed to the expansion. Finally, because the PPACA was such a charged political issue for so long, fewer than 20 states have agreed to create the exchanges and it is unclear whether they will ever materialize.

same through time. On the other hand, health care tends to be changeable. The medical CPI has risen at or above the overall rate of inflation for several years. However, we cannot be sure how much of this increase is an increase in prices, how much is an increase in quality, and how much is the availability of new procedures or treatments.

To illustrate, let's discuss the treatment of acquired immunodeficiency syndrome (AIDS). In 1985 there was no standard treatment for AIDS. Morphine was sometimes given to ease pain—a terribly ineffective but "cheap" treatment compared to today. In 2001 the treatment became a "drug cocktail" of zidovudine (AZT) and a group of protease inhibitors. Newer drug cocktails cost more than $30,000 per patient per year, but they can sustain a good quality of life for several years. Which "treatment" costs more? You do not have to answer the question because you know that you are not pricing the same thing. The quality of the treatment has improved so greatly that to say that the price of the treatment has increased is simply wrong. The quality of the treatment has improved, and because there was no effective treatment to compare the current one to, the "price" has fallen from infinity.

Many of the complaints about the increase in the cost of health care over the past few years are misdirected. The cost of things that do not change in quality (syringes, bandages, etc.) has surely gone up. But, just as surely, we cannot measure the price of things whose quality is constantly changing. A night in a hospital, for instance, is not the same in 2011 as it was in 1985. Though some definitions are the same (semiprivate has meant and still means two beds in a room, for example), other aspects of the night's stay are different. Today television sets and other creature comforts and sophisticated medical equipment, including beds that monitor vital signs, are standard. Not long ago these were either optional or simply unavailable.

Another key problem with using a supply and demand model for health care services is that one of the assumptions that we made for such a model to work was perfect knowledge. One of the reasons we go to the doctor in the first place is that we do not know what is wrong with us. We go not only to stop the pain but also to find out why the pain exists. This is distinctly different from buying an apple. We know what an apple is, we know why we want it, and we know what it costs to get one. In health care we have to trust the seller (the doctor) to tell us what we need and how much it will cost.

Implications of Public Insurance

Though considerations such as these are important, we can still examine the effect of our financing system on the supply and demand model for health care services. As you can see in Figure 23.1, if there were no program to provide health care services to the poor, the nonpoor would get many services and the poor few. If D_{poor} is the demand for health care by the poor and $D_{nonpoor}$ is the demand for health care by the nonpoor, then $D_{poor\ 1\ nonpoor}$ is the market demand for health care services. This is arrived at by adding the two demand curves together horizontally. Specifically, at each price, the quantity demanded of the poor is added to the quantity demanded of the nonpoor. If the supply curve is as shown, then the price is P^* and the poor consume Q_{poor}, much less than the nonpoor $Q_{nonpoor}$.

FIGURE 23.1   Health care: who gets it without subsidies.

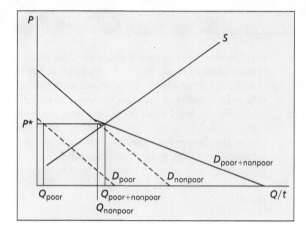

FIGURE 23.2   Health care: who gets it with subsidies.

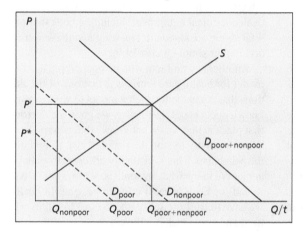

On the other hand, if the poor were to get the services at no cost, then the situation might be quite different. Figure 23.2 shows that in this case, the market demand is the amount that the poor would consume if it were free to them, Q_{poor}, plus the demand by the nonpoor. As you can see, the poor would consume much more, Q_{poor}, while the nonpoor would consume less. Prices would also be higher.

Efficiency Problems with Private Insurance

What private insurance does to the market for health care is as disruptive as public insurance. Recall the idea of co-payments: After the deductible is met, for every dollar of covered medical expense, a low percentage (usually 20 percent) is paid by the patient and the remainder is paid by the insurance company. How does that affect the demand for health care? For simplicity's sake, assume the deductible has either been met or is zero.

FIGURE 23.3   The effect of co-payments on the market for health care.

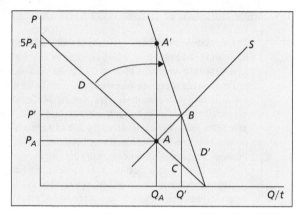

Figure 23.3 shows that the demand curve will rotate out to the right and that this will cause a greater consumption of health care services and higher prices. Let's look at why the curve rotates out to the right. Take the equilibrium point prior to any insurance; call that point A. A person is willing to pay P_A and consumes Q_A medical services prior to insurance. Suppose that person now has insurance with a 20 percent co-payment rate. If that is the case, that person would be willing to consume Q_A medical services even if the price were five times that of P_A. This is because the effective price to the insured person is 20 percent of $5P_A$, or just P_A. The reason it rotates out of the horizontal intercept of the demand curve is that if health care services were free, the effect of co-payments would not matter. Twenty percent of nothing would be nothing and five times of nothing would still be nothing.

Whenever there is a situation where someone other than the consumer is paying the bill, economists call this other entity a **third-party payer**.

third-party payer
An entity other than the consumer who pays part of the costs.

When this happens, the usual role of keeping costs down is taken out of the hands of the consumer.

Since our demand curve rotates out, we buy more health care services and pay more for them. The good news here is that this effect is lessened if the underlying demand curve D is itself inelastic. It can certainly be argued that the demand for health care services is relatively inelastic, and the evidence from an extensive study started in the late 1970s and published in 1987 suggests just that. This is because we would not have an unnecessary operation even if it got less expensive, and most people will have a necessary operation even if the price is high. This study suggests that patient sensitivity to price is greater for visits to doctors than for hospitalizations. Overall health elasticity estimates from this study indicate that a 10 percent increase in the out-of-pocket expenses of the patient is associated with a 1 percent to 3 percent reduction in health care utilization.

The increase in health care utilization also has an efficiency implication. Recall from the Chapter 3 discussion of consumer and producer surplus that the deadweight loss is the yardstick by which economists measure inefficiency. Here the triangle *ABC* is the amount of the inefficiency.

Another area of inefficiency with health care insurance in particular comes in the form of moral hazard.

moral hazard
Having insurance increases the demand for the insured good.

People who have insurance consume more health care. This is a problem with all forms of insurance, and the clearest example is in automobile insurance. If you drive more recklessly when you have insurance than when you do not, having insurance makes you more likely to need insurance. In the field of health care, if having insurance makes you more likely to get tested for certain diseases, or even worse, fail to exercise or eat right, then moral hazard is a problem.

A final area of inefficiency in the health insurance market is the greatest threat to its existence and that is adverse selection. Adverse se-

adverse selection
Those in most need of insurance are the most willing to pay for insurance and drive up the price of insurance with their illnesses to such a degree that those people who are not as sick leave the market altogether.

lection arises when, instead of a true cross-section of the population buying insurance, those in most need of insurance are the most willing to pay for insurance and drive up the price of insurance with their illnesses to such a degree that those people who are not as sick leave the market altogether.

To understand the problem, suppose there are three types of people who initially do not know their own health status and their own need for health insurance. Unbeknownst to them, they are the "healthy," "somewhat healthy," or "unhealthy." Suppose the healthiest category of people have no serious illnesses in the offing and face few risks other than accidents that are equally likely to occur throughout the population. Suppose the unhealthiest category of people face many risks associated with expensive treatments as well as those same injury risks. Now suppose there are two periods: now and later. If no one knows his or her health status "now" and everyone is risk averse, everyone will likely buy insurance "now." They will pay the costs

of that insurance (through premiums), which will equal the average cost of care plus the administrative costs plus the profit for the insurance company. In that sense, when no one knows anything, insurance works fine. Once they know their health status, they will be able to compare the premiums to their expected costs by going it alone. If the difference is dramatic, the healthiest group may drop out. Doing so will raise the average costs to everyone else left in the insurance pool. It may raise it so much that the somewhat healthy people drop their insurance. This has been labeled by some as the "insurance death spiral."

You can solve this particular problem of adverse selection in one of three ways: charging unhealthy people more than healthy people (which is what we do with car insurance in that bad drivers pay more), having a system in which everyone gets insurance through some means other than individual choice (which could be through their employer or through the government), or we can mandate that people buy health insurance. The first method is considered, by many, unethical because lack of coverage is frequently translated as lack of care and lack of care for the sick is considered immoral.

The second method, which is what most of those in group insurance live with, is the system that existed in the United States prior to health care reform in 2010. Prior to that time most Americans either got insurance through the government or through their employer, while some purchased it as individuals; and some of those in the individual market who were sick were denied coverage by insurers. The PPACA changed that. Insurance companies were required to cover them without considering their health status. Closing that option off for insurance companies, though, left the companies vulnerable to adverse selection.

The resolution to this problem and the final method of dealing with adverse selection is mandation. Mandation is the requirement that everyone buy insurance. By requiring the healthy to buy insurance (forcing them to

mandation
The requirement to purchase insurance.

pay a tax or fine if they do not), the problem of adverse selection disappears.

Major Changes to Insurance Resulting from PPACA

Several provisions of the bill change how the health insurance industry operates. Under laws existing prior to the enactment of PPACA, health insurers could cut off dependent children from coverage under their parents' health insurance the first year after their children reached

23 and were free to consider, charge more for, and deny coverage for any medical condition a prospective client had prior to purchasing insurance through the company.

They were free to set annual and lifetime limits on how much they would cover. They were free to set prior conditions by which they could rescind coverage, and they were free to raise the rates of those who became ill (and therefore expensive to the company). They were free to charge rates that were different for men and women. They were free from most government intervention when it came to premiums, profit, and the proportion of premiums taken up with administrative costs. Much of this ended or was scheduled to end with the passage of PPACA.

The law as it stands (or in some cases as it will soon stand) will require that health insurers allow dependent children to stay on their parents' health insurance through age 26, that the insurers accept everyone without regard to health status, charge the same to healthy and the unhealthy alike, and charge the same for men and women. They can no longer set lifetime limits, and after 2014, they can no longer set annual limits. They can no longer rescind coverage or raise rates on the sick.

To the untrained eye and ear, each of these provisions might be considered unambiguously good, but consider the fact that each one of them will come with a cost that will, in all likelihood, be passed on to the people who pay the premiums for health insurance, the people who work for companies who provide them with health insurance, and the people who buy goods and services from those companies. Take the most simple of these provisions, the extension of dependent coverage to children through age 26. This provision means that you (because the majority of those reading this book are college students under age 26) will be able to go to graduate school and/or have some time to find that first good job. However, your parents' employer will face extra costs associated with having you on their health insurance plan. How will they react? Depending on the elasticity of demand and supply for labor, the elasticity of demand for the good or service your parents' employer produces, and some other factors, that means your parents' paychecks will be smaller than they would otherwise be, your parents' employer may employ fewer workers than they might have and will have smaller profits than they might have had, the people who buy the goods or services your parents produce will have to pay more, or some combination of these. The cost of providing you with health insurance, or the cost of paying whatever health-related bills you face as a 24-, 25-, or 26-year-old will go from being

your problem (perhaps with your parents' help) to being someone else's problem. While that is good for you, it is not necessarily good for society.

All of these other provisions have a similar problem associated with them. Again the benefits to those not cut off, or not charged more, or not denied coverage will be greater. However, those costs and burdens will go somewhere. They will not disappear. Take another example. Women, on average, are more costly than men throughout the health care life cycle because they face cancer risks—specifically, ovarian, breast, and uterine cancer—that men either do not face or, in the case of breast cancer, with much less frequency. Just as in the auto insurance industry teenage boys pay more for car insurance than teenage girls because boys get in more serious accidents than do girls, women used to have to pay more for individual health insurance, and groups that were disproportionately women paid more than groups of the same size that were disproportionately men. What does that mean with regard to this provision? Men will pay more because women are paying less.

The aforementioned provisions affecting insurance that present the greatest challenge to the health insurance industry itself are the provisions that prevent insurance companies from denying coverage to the people based on pre-existing conditions. This, by itself, could (were it not accompanied with another provision requiring that everyone buy health insurance or have it provided to them) lead to the end of all private health insurance, through the aforementioned death spiral.

The resolution to the death spiral imagined by the PPACA is through a combination of provisions that expand coverage. Through a large expansion of Medicaid through state-run insurance exchanges, and through an employer requirement (all explained later in this chapter), coverage will likely be extended to three-quarters of those who are currently uninsured. Still, those provisions alone would likely not be enough to forestall the death spiral. It is mandation that does this. Mandation is the requirement that everyone buy insurance if insurance is not provided to them. Requiring the healthy to buy insurance (forcing them to pay a tax or fine if they do not) makes the problem of adverse selection disappear.

In the individual health insurance market, insurance companies will have significantly less freedom to charge differential prices to buyers. They will be allowed to charge older customers no more than three times what they charge younger ones (though younger ones typically cost one-fifth or less than what older ones cost), and only be able to charge 50 percent more to tobacco users.

They may set up broad geographic price differences and may charge more for larger families than smaller ones. This all is opposed to few, if any, federal limits that had been in place with regard to market segmentation. Remember that, under normal circumstances, insurers maximize profits by charging premiums based on actual experience.

There is one other, in the grand scheme of things, relatively minor provision change that is potentially important to young people; that is the provision that requires that administrative costs and profits make up not more than 15 percent of premiums (in large groups and 20 percent for small groups). It is this provision that affects those in the relatively low-wage restaurant and retail industries. Full-time employees are frequently offered the ability to buy mini-med policies that provide, for a low premium, some minimalist benefits. These policies tend to be very expensive to administer.

The Blood and Organ Problem

One problem associated with our current system is the scarcity of blood and organs. To an economist, the shortage of blood and organs is directly and unambiguously determined by the fact that it is illegal for people to sell these items for medical use. The ban on the sale of blood and organs for medical use is almost entirely justified on moral grounds. For instance, it is not illegal to sell your blood for use in cosmetics.

If a price can be forced to be zero, the quantity supplied will be reduced and the quantity demanded enhanced. This offers another moral dilemma. If a market were allowed, there would be people who would not be able to pay the price for a needed organ, and, as a result, they would die while someone else who could afford that organ would live. On the other side of that moral debate, though, is the fact that if there were a legal market, more organs would become available and more people would live.

Note that although both the supply and demand for organs are inelastic, neither is perfectly inelastic.[6] There are people who would choose not to pay an exorbitant price to live, and there are people who would be more likely to sign their donor cards if there were a high reward that they could bestow on their heirs by doing so.

The downside of such a market is similar to the downside of the market for tobacco. Poor information can cause people to make life-altering mistakes. For instance,

you can live on one kidney, and therefore you could sell the other if the price were right. However, you might underestimate the likelihood that you will ultimately need that other kidney. The sale of organs may be a poor idea, but selling blood may not. There is little economic reason to ban the sale of blood for medical purposes because, unlike organs, blood is self-replenishing.

Comparing the United States with the Rest of the World

Every industrialized nation on earth has a distinct health care system. The one thing that is common throughout the rest of the developed world, though, is that government is the health care provider, insurer, or insurer of last resort. There are distinct advantages to the way the rest of the world does this, but there are disadvantages as well. Having a **single-payer system**, where the government collects significantly high taxes to pay for everyone's health care, benefits those who could not afford health care any other way. It creates serious shortages as well.

single-payer system
The government collects (usually very high) taxes to pay for everyone's health care.

In Canada, England, and much of Europe, being a citizen of the country grants you unlimited rights to necessary health care that is either free or close to it. While the financial arrangements (shown in Table 23.2) in these countries differ, the citizenry need not worry about access to basic health care regardless of their ability to pay. This helps explain the very low occurrences of infant mortality and relatively long life spans in these countries, as seen in Table 23.3. The unemployed and the employed, the working and the retired, the young and the old, the rich and the poor are treated with a degree of equality that cannot be claimed in the United States. In addition, because the doctors are paid salaries by the government instead of fees for seeing patients, they do not have an incentive to order expensive tests and perform costly surgeries. Further, as government employees, they are usually protected from lawsuits. Thus universal access is accomplished at lower overall costs than in the United States.

This, however, comes at a cost. These countries have severe doctor shortages because, in an effort to keep costs down, physicians are paid much less than they are paid in the United States. One principal reason why you see many foreign-born physicians in the United States is that they can make a great deal more money here than in their own countries. Additionally, there is no monetary

---

[6]If both were perfectly inelastic at different quantities, there would be no market-clearing price.

TABLE 23.2 International health care finance schemes.

Source: OECD Health Data, www.oecd.org

Country	Public Expenditures as a Percent of Total, 2009–2011	Hospitals	Physicians	Function of Private Insurance
Australia	68.5	Mostly public	A	a
Canada	70.4	Mostly private	A, B	a
France	77.0	Mostly public	A	b
Germany	76.8	Mix of public and private	A	a
Japan	80.5	Mostly private	A, B	None
United Kingdom	83.2	Mostly public trusts	C	a
United States	48.2	Mostly private	A	c

A—mostly private fee for service.
B—government-imposed fee schedule.
C—public employees.
a—option to purchase private insurance for all expenses.
b—option to purchase private insurance for noncovered expenses.
c—all non-Medicare, non-Medicaid.

TABLE 23.3 International comparisons of health expenditures, infant mortality, and life expectancy.

Source: U.S. Census Bureau, www.census.gov/compendia/statab/cats/international_statistics/vital_statistics_health_elections_education.html; OECD Health Data, www.oecd.org

Country	Health Expenditures/ GDP, 2010	Infant Mortality Rate per 1,000 Births, 2010	Life Expectancy, 2010	Five-Year Survival Rates	
				Prostate Cancer	Breast Cancer
United States	17.6	6.1	78.7	98.6	88.7
United Kingdom	9.6	4.2	80.6	71.0	81.0
France	11.6	3.6	81.4	61.7	80.3
Germany	11.6	3.4	80.5	67.6	71.7
Japan	9.5	2.3	83.0		

incentive to become a doctor when you cannot get rich by being one. The effect of having doctors on salary also is seen when these doctors are reluctant to put in long hours. Physicians are among the hardest-working people in the United States. You can also see the effect of this public health provision in the five-year survival rates of breast and prostate cancers. The United States enjoys the highest survival rates among these countries. Another factor weighing in favor of the U.S. system is immediate access to procedures that require long waiting periods elsewhere.

In the United States a 50-year-old man with blocked arteries is hospitalized and operated on within hours of being admitted, whereas the waiting period for bypass surgery in Canada has been as high as six months. Though some waiting periods have shortened, this is in part due to the recognition by physicians that expensive procedures must be rationed. In the United States the elderly with kidney disease will be given dialysis as long as they are physically able to stand it (lengthening life by

a year or more). A similar English patient cannot schedule routine dialysis treatments under the British government-run system.

Another important area that would be lost if the United States were to go to a single-payer system would be innovation. Prescription drug, medical device, and medical procedure innovation has been highly concentrated in the United States, largely because the innovator makes money that cannot be made in the single-payer countries. Furthermore, the innovation that takes place abroad is likely motivated by profits that can be made in the United States. As a result, very few health care economists believe that turning the United States into a single-payer environment would be good for health care innovation.

Last, because doctors are typically immune from lawsuits in countries with single-payer systems, accountability for mistakes is left to professional standards boards. While these mechanisms can work, very often they end up being a system for physicians to protect their own.

Summary

You should now understand how the system of health care finance seriously alters the market for health care services. You also understand that in the United States 52 percent of the health care tab is picked up by the taxpayer, with the remainder being picked up either by patients directly or through their insurance companies. You understand why health care is not like most other goods that economists study but that we can look at it using the same supply and demand tools discussed earlier. You understand that both taxpayer-financed health care and private insurance–financed health care increase the overall price of health care. Last, you understand why a single-payer, taxpayer-financed health care system would have both advantages and disadvantages.

Key Terms

adverse selection, 263
co-payment, 259
deductible, 258
mandation, 263
maximum out of pocket, 259

Medicaid, 258
Medicare, 258
mini-med, 259
moral hazard, 263
primary care physician (PCP), 259

risk averse, 258
risk neutral, 258
single-payer system, 265
third-party payer, 262

Quiz Yourself

1. The primary motivation for the purchase of any insurance lies in the fact that most people are
   a. risk lovers.
   b. risk averse.
   c. risk neutral.
   d. risk tolerant.

2. The risk-averse person will buy health insurance
   a. only if the expected health costs equal the insurance premium.
   b. only if the expected health costs are greater than the insurance premium.
   c. even if the expected health costs are less than the insurance premium.
   d. under no circumstances.

3. The government, in the form of Medicare, Medicaid, and the Children's Health Insurance Program, pays for _____ of health care costs.
   a. less than 10 percent
   b. slightly less than half
   c. about 75 percent
   d. all

4. If you have a $2,000 covered health expense, a deductible of $500, and a 20 percent co-pay, then you pay _____ and the insurance company pays _____.
   a. $1,500, $500
   b. $1,000, $1,000
   c. $800, $1200
   d. $700, $800

5. Which of the following forms of private insurance is likely to have the lowest premiums and least doctor choice flexibility?
   a. Medicare.
   b. An HMO.
   c. A PPO.
   d. A fee-for-service plan.

6. Medical care inflation is likely to be easily overstated (if you look simply at the increase in the cost of a hospital stay) because that calculation ignores
   a. the original costs.
   b. the new costs.
   c. quality increases.
   d. quality decreases.

7. The problem of the "third-party payer" arises in health care in the form of
   a. doctors having to pay part of their own expenses.
   b. government and/or private insurance paying a significant part of the costs.
   c. patients having to pay a significant part of the costs.
   d. hospitals not being able to collect from many patients.

8. One significant feature of a "single-payer" system lacking in the U.S. system is
   a. government involvement in health care.
   b. coverage for the elderly.
   c. coverage for the poor.
   d. universal coverage.

Short Answer Questions

1. Why would eliminating the ability to deny coverage to those with pre-existing conditions require mandation to accompany it?
2. Why would risk-averse people be more likely to buy insurance?
3. For who would a mini-med health insurance policy be a good policy to have relative to the alternative and why?
4. Why is it more likely that health expenses will rise faster in the United States than in Canada or the United Kingdom?
5. How might you apply the notion of "moral hazard" to decisions you make about exercise?

Think about This

List the pros and cons associated with the U.S. system of financing health care relative to the U.K. system. Do the same relative to the Canadian system. Use your understanding of opportunity cost to think about why we can't have "the best of both worlds."

Talk about This

In the United States a terminally ill patient can decide to decline extraordinary medical treatment, but in all cases the patient, or the spouse, is the one who makes that decision (either with prior instructions or by making his or her wishes known to the health care provider). In the United Kingdom, the government can, and does, limit the availability of extraordinary medical treatment. Thus, though care is free (or nearly free) to the patient, it can be limited against their will. The U.K. government's contention is that health care resources are scarce and they would be wasted extending the life of a terminally ill patient by a few days. Which is worse, the aspect of the U.S. system where people are denied care when they are unable to pay, or the U.K. system where they are denied care because their treatment would not lead to a significant increase in the quality of life?

For More Insight See

Health Care Finance Association statistical tables—www.hcfa.gov

Phelps, Charles E., *Health Economics* (Reading, MA: Addison-Wesley, 2009).

www.census.gov/prod/2004pubs/04statab/health.pdf

International Comparisons of Types of Health Care Finance Systems—www.nao.org.uk/publications

Behind the Numbers

International comparisons of vital statistics and health care expenditures.

Statistical Abstract of the United States; comparative international statistics—www.census.gov/compendia/statab

Health care expenditures.

Centers for Medicare and Medicaid Services; historical tables—www.cms.gov/NationalHealth ExpendData

Health insurance coverage.

Coverage type—

www.census.gov/hhes/www/hlthins/hlthins.html

Lack of coverage.

Centers for Disease Control and Prevention—www.cdc.gov/nchs/nhis.htm

Medicare premiums.

Centers for Medicare and Medicaid Services—www.cms.hhs.gov

European Debt Crisis

Learning Objectives

After reading this chapter you should be able to:

LO1 Understand that the creation of the euro integrated monetary policy across member nations without effective integrating fiscal policies.

LO2 Understand that the integration of the monetary systems in the European Union allowed for the influx of relatively cheap capital into poorer European nations.

LO3 Understand that the causes of the Irish and Spanish crises differed markedly from the Italian and Greek crises.

LO4 Understand that the policies that the United States used to mitigate the Great Recession were largely unavailable to those European nations faced with crises.

LO5 Understand that the exit of individual countries from the euro could have set off a Europe-wide banking crisis had it occurred during the crisis.

Chapter Outline

Introduction
In the Beginning There Were 17 Currencies in 17 Countries
The Effect of the Euro
Why Couldn't They Pull Themselves Out? The United States Did
Is It Too Late to Leave the Euro?
Where Should Europe Go from Here?
Summary

Introduction

From late 2008 through all of 2012 (and perhaps beyond), the world economy was either in free fall or recovering at a painfully slow rate. The United States experienced the Great Recession (the subject of Chapters 13 and 14), while China's growth slowed and Europe stumbled from one crisis to the next. In the process, there was a constant threat that Europe's troubles would/could drag the world into another, perhaps even deeper, global recession. This chapter explores the causes of Europe's problems during this period by going back to the scene of the crime—the creation of the euro. The chapter continues with an analysis of the impact of the euro's creation on housing markets in Ireland and Spain and on the borrowing habits of Italy and Greece. The chapter then describes why the

existence of the euro made it very difficult for governments in the most hard-hit countries to recover and why there is so much disagreement over the austerity policies many countries were compelled to employ to secure the help of healthier European economies. The chapter concludes by recognizing that some countries may be better off in the future if they leave the euro, and those countries that remain with that currency may be better off if the weaker ones do leave.

In the Beginning There Were 17 Currencies in 17 Countries

After World War II when country borders were redrawn by the allied powers, each of the countries of Europe reestablished their individual currencies. Germany had the mark; France had the franc; Italy had the lira; Greece had the drachma; and so on. Very quickly it became clear to the various governments that the European economies would recover more quickly with a free-trade union allowing freight to travel between the countries without having to stop at each border crossing. In 1958 the European Union's predecessor, the European Economic Community, was created to establish travel and trade rules throughout the member nations.[1] Through the years, the movement for European integration intensified, culminating in a series of referendum votes in the 1990s approving the Maastricht Treaty that created a common currency for 16 countries.[2] The currency was in use in financial markets only from 1999 to 2001 and has circulated as the currency of the member states since.

By joining the euro, countries gave up a major symbol of their sovereignty, their currency. They also gave up the ability to use monetary policy (described in Chapter 10) as individual countries because they had to cede that authority to the European Central Bank (the counterpart to the United States' Federal Reserve). It was for these reasons that some European Union nations, most notably the United Kingdom, refused to join. The transition process was remarkably smooth. Bank balances were converted from home currencies to euro-denominated balances at specified rates, and actual paper and coin currency was recalled and exchanged. This typically occurred when businesses would deposit their local currency at local banks. At that time they would receive credit for those deposits in euros.

Several other provisions of the Treaty on the Functioning of the European Union were put in place to avoid the kind of economic catastrophe that we have seen in Greece and Spain. One such provision, Article 126, was that countries were required to maintain a deficit to GDP ratio of less than 3 percent and work to a debt to GDP ratio of less than 60 percent. Another, Article 123, stated

that the European Central Bank could not purchase member nation debt. A third, Article 125, prohibited bailouts of one country by the union or by any member state unless it was viewed as necessary to avoid a systemic financial collapse of the entire union.

The Effect of the Euro

The effect of the creation of the euro and these provisions was that the poorer members, some southern European countries, in particular, saw relatively rapid growth. As can be seen in Figure 19.1, growth in Ireland, Spain, and Greece exceeded that of the euro area and the United States from 2001 through 2007.

As can be seen in Figure 19.2, there was and is a considerable discrepancy between the per capita GDP of these countries. With the European Union-27 member nations indexed as 100, the interpretation of the data below is that in 2001 Greece had a per capita GDP 50 percent lower than the Netherlands and Germany. Spain was 15 percent poorer than Germany.

That these countries were growing faster than the richer countries promoted considerable lending to poorer member countries largely because interest rates to poorer member countries converged to the already low rates of the richer member countries. This was because investors believed that a loan to a euro-member country or a financial institution in a euro-member country was largely the same regardless of whether that nation was relatively rich or poor. As can be seen in Figure 19.3, the interest rates on 10-year government debt were, during the period from 2001 to 2007, largely identical across Europe's largest governments.

These low interest rates and the relatively attractive weather of Ireland and Spain generated housing bubbles in those two countries that were even more inflated than those in the United States. Figure 19.4 shows that, between 2000 and 2009 and relative to first quarter 2000, housing prices doubled in the United States, but increased by 125 percent in Spain and by 150 percent in Ireland. The sources of those mortgage loans, however, differed. In the United, Fannie Mae and Freddie Mac bought and securitized mortgages as mortgage-backed securities (MBS). In Europe, the instrument was the "covered bond." In that method, the loans remained with the originating banks (unlike in the United States where the originating bank sold the mortgages within days) and then sold bonds that were backed by those mortgages. As a result, a bank in the

[1] Current members: Austria, **Belgium,** Bulgaria, Cyprus, the Czech Republic, Denmark, Estonia, Finland, **France, Germany**, Greece, Hungary, Ireland, **Italy,** Latvia, Lithuania, **Luxembourg,** Malta, the **Netherlands,** Poland, Portugal, Romania, Slovakia, Slovenia, Spain, Sweden, and the United Kingdom. **Bold = original members**

[2] There are now 17 countries that are part of the currency union. They are Austria, Belgium, Cyprus, Estonia, Finland, France, Germany, Greece, Ireland, Italy, Luxembourg, Malta, the Netherlands, Portugal, Slovakia, Slovenia, and Spain. Estonia joined in 2010 and was not part of the original 16. Further, millions more live in countries with currencies whose value is pegged to the euro.

220   Chapter 19   *European Debt Crisis*

FIGURE 19.1   GDP growth in euro countries and the United States.

Source: European Central Bank, www.ecb.int/stats/html/index.en.html

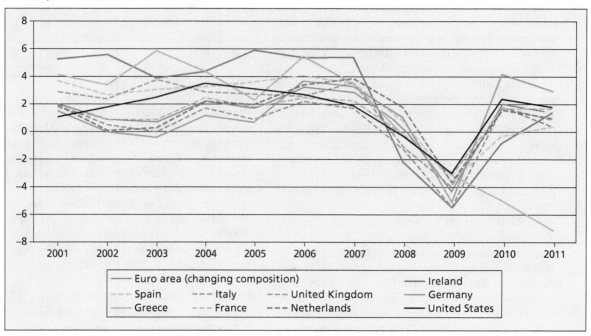

FIGURE 19.2   Per capita GDP across Europe and the United States relative to EU-27.

Source: Eurostat, http://epp.eurostat.ec.europa.eu/portal/page/portal/eurostat/home

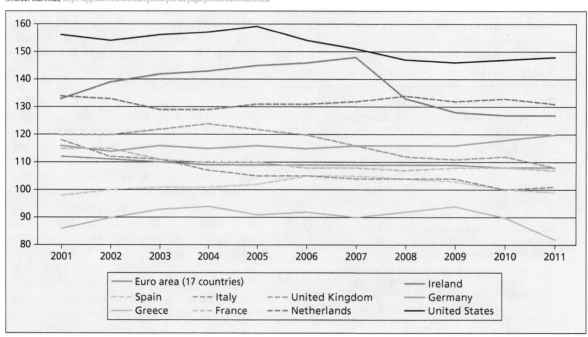

FIGURE 19.3   Long-term interest rates.

Source: European Central Bank, http://sdw.ecb.europa.eu

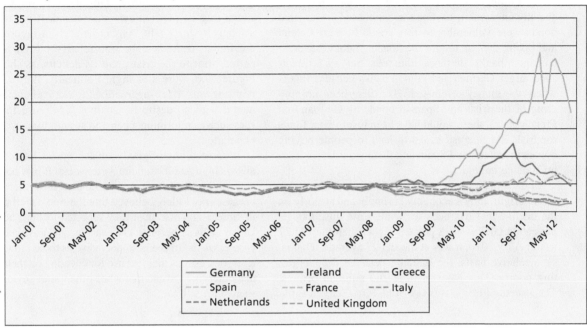

FIGURE 19.4   Housing prices in Spain, Ireland, and the United States.

Source: www.statcentral.ie; www.standardandpoors.com

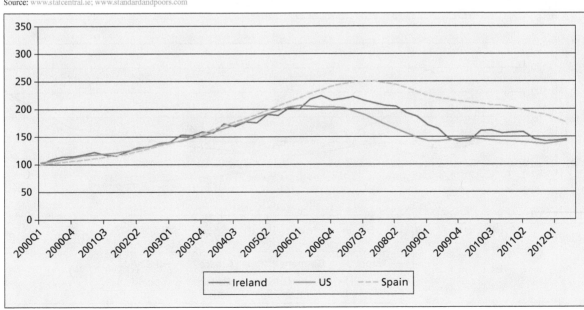

222   Chapter 19   *European Debt Crisis*

United States that did not purchase MBS for its own portfolio could have largely escaped the housing crisis. In Europe, however, any bank that made the loans and any financial institution that purchased the covered bonds were vulnerable to this crisis. In both Ireland and Spain, the bursting of the housing bubble severely damaged banks in those countries but also threatened larger German and French banks because this is where the money originated. Had there been no covering of the Irish and Spanish bonds by German and French banks, there would have been insufficient funds for Irish and Spanish banks to lend to people buying homes in Ireland and Spain and there would have been no housing bubble.

In Italy, the recession and fiscal crisis had a very different origin. Italy's economy is simply and steadily on the decline and has been for some time. In 2000, its per capita GDP was 18 percent higher than the EU-27 average. By 2010, it was at the EU-27 average. That is, on a relative basis, the Italians spent the decade getting poorer. This has structural and political origins. The structural origin was two-fold. First, Italy is aging

more rapidly than any other major European economy because the birth rate has plummeted for the better part of 40 years. Fewer births translate to fewer workers supporting its pension system. Second, it began with a relatively high debt. As can be seen in Figure 19.5, the Italian national debt was relatively high for the period prior to the crisis, and its deficits, as shown in Figure 19.6, were also high. Politically, Italy's prime minister was a self-aggrandizing, womanizing media mogul with no desire to tackle difficult structural issues such as reforming a pension system for a declining population.

In Greece, the origins were far worse. Its debt was always high and its deficits were worse. If it is possible, they were actually worse than the data show them to be because it is widely believed that the true deficit picture in Greece is worse than they reported to the European Union. This is because tax evasion by individuals and businesses in Greece is so pervasive as to be intractable. Everyone uses as their excuse for cheating on their taxes that others are too and that when others start paying their share, they will too.

FIGURE 19.5   Debt to GDP.

Source: Eurostat, http://epp.eurostat.ec.europa.eu/portal/page/portal/eurostat/home

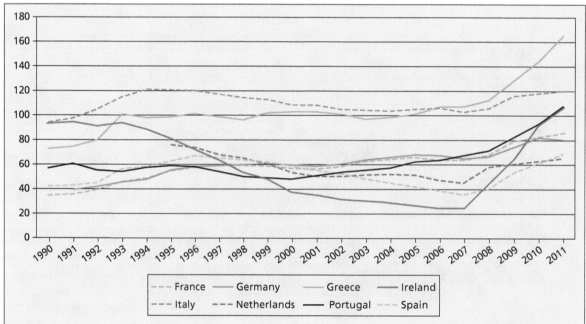

FIGURE 19.6   Deficits to GDP.

Source: Eurostat, http://epp.eurostat.ec.europa.eu/portal/page/portal/eurostat/home

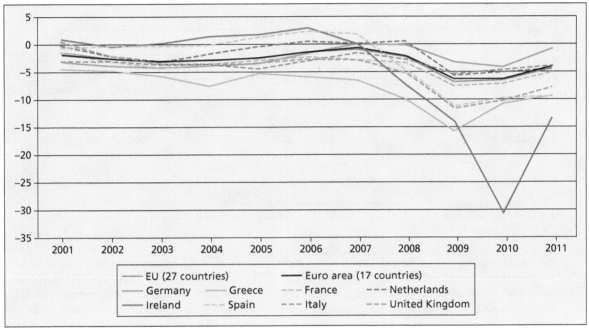

Why Couldn't They Pull Themselves Out? The United States Did

Though the start of the decline in economic activity among powers began in the United Kingdom, it got its first major push in the United States with the collapse of the American housing bubble in late 2008. The United States did three big things to counter the impact of the Great Recession: (1) TARP (the bank bailout), (2) acts of monetary policy on an unprecedented scale, and (3) fiscal policy–induced explosions in deficits in the form of Bush and Obama stimulus packages. The United Kingdom and France did the latter; Germany did not. The deficits in Germany in 2009 and 2010 were on the scale of their 2001–2005 deficits, whereas the deficits in the United States and France were two to three times those levels.

As for monetary policy, as Chapters 10, 13, and 14 noted, the Federal Reserve of the United States created and exercised authority in the area of monetary policy well beyond what any previous Federal Reserve chairperson would recognize. As a result of those actions, interest rates throughout the United States were at or near all-time lows. The Treasury was borrowing money on the short-term market for nearly zero interest. In the long-term market, interest rates were so low that 15-year mortgages were being offered for less than half of previous 1960s era records. These were directly the result of the Federal Reserve's purchasing U.S. debt at record rates.

Why did European nations not do the same thing? Simply put, they couldn't. They couldn't do so individually because interest rates were too high, and they couldn't do so collectively because of the Article 123 provision that prohibited the purchase of member-nation debt by the European Central Bank. Italy, Ireland, Greece, and Spain did not have any tools of monetary policy, let alone the expanded ones because, just like the state of Maryland doesn't have its own central bank, neither do individual EU countries.

Further, at its creation, the European Central Bank had one and only one mission—inflation control—and it is governed by the Germans, the Dutch, the French, and the Belgians, who have little interest in generating a threat of inflation for themselves by engaging in monetary policy

FIGURE 19.7 Unemployment rates in Europe.

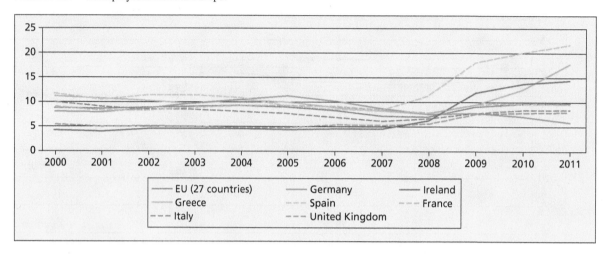

that would help the Greeks, Spanish, Italians, and Irish. To make things worse, the individual country's governments had limited ability at best to engage in their own version of TARP, though the Irish tried. They would have had to borrow the money to do so and, as can be seen by Figure 19.3, the interest rates they faced on borrowing was prohibitive. Further, and for the same reason, they could not engage in fiscal policy to stimulate their economies on their own because, again, they would have to borrow the money to do it. The bottom line is that everything the United States did to minimize the impact of the Great Recession was unavailable to the weaker economies of Europe, largely because they had no control over the value of their currency and had no ability to borrow at reasonable interest rates.

Because there was a growing recognition among the Germans and French that their economies were threatened by the instability of weaker ones, there was a willingness among the Germans and French to help the Greeks, Spaniards, Irish, and Italians. This formal recognition of the threat to the EU, generally, allowed for the cross-national bailouts because the systemic risk clauses of Articles 123 and 125 were invoked. For political and economic purposes, though, the Germans and French insisted that the weaker economies reform their budgets before they received the assistance. In each case the demand was for spending cuts and tax increases. These austerity policies had consequences. Figure 19.7 shows that unemployment rose everywhere but rose more dramatically in these weaker economies. Governments laid off employees, cut pensions, and increased taxes.

From a Keynesian economist's point of view, this is a predictable result of austerity. As can be seen from Figure 19.8, a decrease in government spending and an increase in taxes will result in a decrease in aggregate demand. That will result in a decrease in economic activity and that will result in an increase in unemployment. Austerity could even be self-defeating. The loss of jobs would increase demands on the social safety net and decrease tax revenues. Austerity can ultimately lead to a larger deficit if the austere actions of budget cuts and tax increases plunge the economy into such a poor state that the impacts on the economy generate larger revenue losses than the deficit reductions resulting from the budget cuts and tax increases.

FIGURE 19.8 Result of austerity.

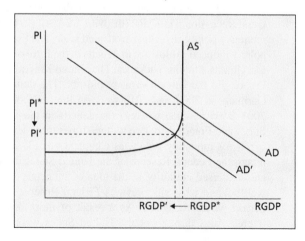

Is It Too Late to Leave the Euro?

For much of 2011 and 2012, speculation was rampant that Greece would leave the euro. The reasons why Greece would want to leave the euro should now be obvious. If you want to regain the ability to print your own currency and engage in monetary policy, you have to have your own currency to do it. Creating their own currency would not be difficult. Getting people to accept it would be difficult. However, if the Greek government were to order all Greek banks to convert euro-denominated accounts into drachma-denominated accounts, the effect would be quick. Though the Greek government could easily issue this order, they would have little power to maintain the value of the drachma, and its value would almost certainly plummet. The inflation in Greece would be dramatic. From some perspectives, that would be a good thing. That's because it would operate as an across-the-board tax on everyone. Your 1,000 euro account would have 1,000 drachmas in it, and then the drachma would lose half its value. You would be able to buy about half as much from the rest of Europe as you had been able to buy, and you would look to Greek providers of the goods or services because their drachma-denominated prices would look relatively more attractive. The attractive aspect of the idea of the "Grexit" (Greek exit from the euro) is that it would fairly quickly stabilize the Greek situation by taxing each Greek by half their wealth as inflation of 100% cuts the buying power of wealth in half.

But, alas, it isn't that easy. Smart Greeks had already anticipated the change. They became convinced that it would eventually happen just this way, so they closed their euro-denominated banks accounts in Greece and took those accounts to other countries. They converted their euros into assets out of the reach of the Greek government. As a result, the only people with any euro-denominated accounts in Greece were those who were either poor (and therefore couldn't afford to do their banking with a foreign bank) or unaware (and therefore vulnerable).

This bankrupted Greek banks because they simply did not have the euros to pay off their depositors. Understand that no American bank could withstand a demand by a large number of its depositors for a cash withdrawal either. Thus the threat of a Greek exit both increased the likelihood of a Greek exit and diminished the viability and desirability of a Greek exit. It also made it harder for the rest of Europe to keep them in. The problem was made worse because if the Greeks left, it would be difficult to contain the concerns of Spaniards that their country would be next. That would jeopardize Spanish banks. Spain would topple Italy and, if Italy was toppled, the euro would be a memory. As a result, as difficult as it was to achieve, the Germans and French felt compelled to keep Greece in the euro. It was a mess that only got better very slowly. It could still collapse, though, at this writing in the spring of 2013, it has not.

Where Should Europe Go from Here?

The irony of the situation is that Greece needed to leave the euro at a time that it could not, and Germany and France needed Greece to be out of the euro but could not allow it to happen out of fear of what the consequences might be. Once stability and growth are achieved, what is possible economically may be even more difficult politically, because those opposed to Greece's exiting the euro will ask why the suffering had to occur to keep them in if the only result was going to be that they would ultimately be out. Perhaps the only likely scenario is that new rules for the EU banking, monetary, and fiscal systems will be put in place to decrease the likelihood of another bubble-created or government-debt fostered threat to the system.

Summary

From late 2008 through all of 2012, the United States experienced and made its way through the Great Recession while Europe stumbled from one economic crisis to the next. The origin of European difficulties was in that they created a currency, the euro, thereby unifying their monetary systems without unifying their fiscal systems. As a result, whether it was Ireland and Spain with housing-bubble-related crises or Italy and Greece with fiscal crises, the challenge for stronger EU countries was how to save the euro without the tools the United States used to weather the Great Recession.

Quiz Yourself

1. The cause of the European financial crisis had its origins in
   a. the creation of the euro.
   b. vast overspending in Germany.
   c. uncompetitive tax collections in Greece.
   d. speculative home buying in Belgium.

2. The proximate cause of the Spanish problem was
   a. vast overspending during the previous decade.
   b. lax tax collections during the previous decade.
   c. a burst housing bubble.
   d. both a and b.

3. The proximate cause of the Greek problem was
   a. vast overspending during the previous decade.
   b. lax tax collections during the previous decade.
   c. a burst housing bubble.
   d. both a and b.

4. The reason the Greeks didn't use a plan similar to TARP to save their banks was that
   a. the Greek Central Bank had no funds.
   b. the interest rates Greece would have had to pay on the loans would have been unaffordable.
   c. banks weren't a problem in Greece.
   d. there was no political will in Greece to borrow that kind of money.

5. The reason the European Central Bank (ECB) didn't engage in the kind of expansionary monetary policy that the Federal Reserve did for the United States was that
   a. the ECB didn't view the problem as serious.
   b. the ECB could not raise the capital.
   c. the provisions of the treaty that created the ECB did not allow for it to buy the debt of member nations unless there was systemic risk.
   d. there was no debt for the ECB to buy.

6. The reason the ECB did not want the Greeks to exit the euro was that
   a. Greece was viewed as a valuable member in temporary distress.
   b. Greece was viewed as so unimportant that it did not want the perception that countries were leaving for any reason.
   c. Greece was a founding member and political friendships were important to the ECB leaders.
   d. Greece was viewed as the first domino in a series of dominos that, if Greece left, it would jeopardize the whole euro system.

Short Answer Questions

1. What should the Maastrict Treaty have included to allow for an adequate response to the various European economic crises?

2. When would be the right time and what would be the correct mechanism for getting a country out of the euro?

3. What would the problems associated with the ECB being allowed to purchase the debt of member nations?

Think about This

For full integration of the European Union, some argue that the nations should be like states of the United States with the central government having limited and enumerated powers. What would those powers be?

If Greece is analogous to Mississippi (relatively poor) and Germany is analogous to New York (relatively rich), what is present in the United States that makes it relatively easy for Mississippi to be in the same country as New York that is absent that makes it relatively hard for Greece and Germany to imagine themselves in the same country.

Talk about This

The bursting of the housing bubble hit Phoenix and Miami much harder than Dallas/Ft.Worth. Why should the taxpayers of Texas have consented to programs that helped only citizens of Phoenix and Miami? Why, then, should Germans care if the Irish housing bubble caused problems in Ireland?

Behind the Numbers

European economic data—http://epp.eurostat.ec.europa.eu/portal/page/portal/eurostat/home

European interest rates—http://sdw.ecb.europa.eu

CHAPTER 19

Current Issues in Macro Theory and Policy

Learning Objectives

LO19.1 Describe alternative perspectives on the causes of macroeconomic instability, including the views of mainstream economists, monetarists, real-business-cycle advocates, and proponents of coordination failures.

LO19.2 Discuss why new classical economists believe the economy will "self-correct" from aggregate demand and aggregate supply shocks.

LO19.3 Identify and describe the variations of the debate over "rules" versus "discretion" in conducting stabilization policy.

LO19.4 Summarize the fundamental ideas and policy implications of mainstream macroeconomics, monetarism, and rational expectations theory.

As any academic discipline evolves, it naturally evokes a number of internal disagreements. Economics is no exception. In this chapter we examine a few alternative perspectives on macro theory and policy. We focus on the disagreements that various economists have about the answers to three interrelated questions: (1) What causes instability in the economy? (2) Is the economy self-correcting? (3) Should government adhere to *rules* or use *discretion* in setting economic policy?

What Causes Macro Instability?

LO19.1 Describe alternative perspectives on the causes of macroeconomic instability, including the views of mainstream economists, monetarists, real-business-cycle advocates, and proponents of coordination failures.

As earlier chapters have indicated, capitalist economies experienced considerable instability during the twentieth century. The United States, for example, experienced the Great Depression, numerous recessions, and periods of inflation. This instability greatly moderated between the early 1980s and 2007, but then the deep recession of 2007–2009 occurred. Economists have different perspectives about why instability like this happens.

Mainstream View

For simplicity, we will use the term "mainstream view" to characterize the prevailing macroeconomic perspective of the majority of economists. According to that view, instability in the economy arises from two sources: (1) price stickiness and (2) unexpected shocks to either aggregate demand or aggregate supply.

As we explained in detail in Chapter 18, in the long run, when both input and output prices are fully flexible and have time to adjust to any changes in aggregate demand or short-run aggregate supply, the economy will always return to producing at potential output. In the shorter run, however, stickiness in either input or output prices will mean that any shock to either aggregate demand or aggregate supply will result in changes in output and employment. Although they are not new to you, let's quickly review shocks to aggregate demand and aggregate supply.

Changes in Aggregate Demand Mainstream macroeconomics focuses on aggregate spending and its components. Recall that the basic equation underlying aggregate expenditures is

$$C_a + I_g + X_n + G = \text{GDP}$$

That is, the aggregate amount of after-tax consumption, gross investment, net exports, and government spending determines the total amount of goods and services produced and sold. In equilibrium, $C_a + I_g + X_n + G$ (aggregate expenditures) is equal to GDP (real output). A decrease in the price level increases equilibrium GDP and thus allows us to trace out a downsloping aggregate demand curve for the economy (see the appendix to Chapter 12). Any change in one of the spending components in the aggregate expenditures equation shifts the aggregate demand curve. This, in turn, changes equilibrium real output, the price level, or both.

Investment spending in particular is subject to wide "booms" and "busts." Significant increases in investment spending are multiplied into even greater increases in aggregate demand and thus can produce demand-pull inflation. In contrast, significant declines in investment spending are multiplied into even greater decreases in aggregate demand and thus can cause recessions.

Adverse Aggregate Supply Shocks In the mainstream view, the second source of macroeconomic instability arises on the supply side. Occasionally, such external events as wars or an artificial supply restriction of a key resource can boost resource prices and significantly raise per-unit production costs. The result is a sizable decline in a nation's aggregate supply, which destabilizes the economy by simultaneously causing cost-push inflation and recession.

Monetarist View

Monetarism (1) focuses on the money supply, (2) holds that markets are highly competitive, and (3) says that a competitive market system gives the economy a high degree of macroeconomic stability.

Monetarists argue that the price and wage flexibility provided by competitive markets should cause fluctuations in aggregate demand to alter product and resource prices rather than output and employment.

ORIGIN OF THE IDEA

O19.1
Monetarism

Thus, the market system would provide substantial macroeconomic stability *were it not for government interference in the economy.*

The problem, as monetarists see it, is that government has promoted downward wage inflexibility through the minimum-wage law, pro-union legislation, guaranteed prices for certain farm products, pro-business monopoly legislation, and so forth. The free-market system is capable of providing macroeconomic stability, but, despite good intentions, government interference has undermined that capability. Moreover, monetarists say that government has contributed to the economy's business cycles through its clumsy and mistaken attempts to achieve greater stability through its monetary policies.

Equation of Exchange The fundamental equation of monetarism is the **equation of exchange**:

$$MV = PQ$$

where M is the supply of money; V is the **velocity** of money, that is, the average number of times per year a dollar is

ORIGIN OF THE IDEA

O19.2
Equation of exchange

spent on final goods and services; P is the price level or, more specifically, the average price at which each unit of physical output is sold; and Q is the physical volume of all goods and services produced.

The left side of the equation of exchange, MV, represents the total amount spent by purchasers of output, while the right side, PQ, represents the total amount received by sellers of that output. The nation's money supply (M) multiplied by the number of times it is spent each year (V) must equal the nation's nominal GDP ($= P \times Q$). The dollar value of total spending has to equal the dollar value of total output.

Stable Velocity Monetarists say that velocity, V, in the equation of exchange is relatively stable. To them, "stable" is not synonymous with "constant," however. Monetarists are aware that velocity has generally trended upward over the last several decades. Shorter pay periods, widespread use of credit cards, and faster means of making payments enable people to hold less money and to turn it over more rapidly than was possible in earlier times. These factors have enabled people to reduce their holdings of cash and checkbook money relative to the size of the nation's nominal GDP.

When monetarists say that velocity is stable, they mean that the factors altering velocity change gradually and predictably and that changes in velocity from one year to the next can be readily anticipated. Moreover, they hold that velocity does not change in response to changes in the money supply itself. Instead, people have a stable desire to hold money relative to holding other financial assets, holding real assets, and buying current output. The factors that determine the amount of money the public wants to hold depend mainly on the level of nominal GDP.

Example: Assume that when the level of nominal GDP is $400 billion, the public desires $100 billion of money to purchase that output. That means that V is 4 (= $400 billion of nominal GDP/$100 billion of money). If we further assume that the actual supply of money is $100 billion, the economy is in equilibrium with respect to money; the actual amount of money supplied equals the amount the public wants to hold.

If velocity is stable, the equation of exchange suggests that there is a predictable relationship between the money supply and nominal GDP (= PQ). An increase in the money supply of, say, $10 billion would upset equilibrium in our example since the public would find itself holding

more money or liquidity than it wants. That is, the actual amount of money held ($110 billion) would exceed the amount of holdings desired ($100 billion). In that case, the reaction of the public (households and businesses) is to restore its desired balance of money relative to other items, such as stocks and bonds, factories and equipment, houses and automobiles, and clothing and toys. But the spending of money by individual households and businesses would leave more cash in the checkable deposits or billfolds of other households and firms. And they too would try to "spend down" their excess cash balances. But, overall, the $110 billion supply of money cannot be spent down because a dollar spent is a dollar received.

Instead, the collective attempt to reduce cash balances increases aggregate demand, thereby boosting nominal GDP. Because velocity in our example is 4—that is, the dollar is spent, on average, four times per year—nominal GDP rises from $400 billion to $440 billion. At that higher nominal GDP, the money supply of $110 billion equals the amount of money desired ($440 billion/4 = $110 billion), and equilibrium is reestablished.

The $10 billion increase in the money supply thus eventually increases nominal GDP by $40 billion. Spending on goods, services, and assets expands until nominal GDP has gone up enough to restore the original 4-to-1 equilibrium relationship between nominal GDP and the money supply.

Note that the relationship GDP/M defines V. A stable relationship between nominal GDP and M means a stable V. And a change in M causes a proportionate change in nominal GDP. Thus, monetarists say that changes in the money supply have a predictable effect on nominal GDP (= $P \times Q$). An increase in M increases P or Q, or some combination of both; a decrease in M reduces P or Q, or some combination of both.

WORKED PROBLEMS

W19.1
Equation of exchange

Monetary Causes of Instability Monetarists say that inappropriate monetary policy is the single most important cause of macroeconomic instability. An increase in the money supply directly increases aggregate demand. Under conditions of full employment, that rise in aggregate demand raises the price level. For a time, higher prices cause firms to increase their real output, and the rate of unemployment falls below its natural rate. But once nominal wages rise to reflect the higher prices and thus to restore real wages, real output moves back to its full-employment level and the unemployment rate returns to its natural rate. The inappropriate increase in the money supply leads to inflation, together with instability of real output and employment.

Conversely, a decrease in the money supply reduces aggregate demand. Real output temporarily falls, and the unemployment rate rises above its natural rate. Eventually, nominal wages fall and real output returns to its full-employment level. The inappropriate decline in the money supply leads to deflation, together with instability of real GDP and employment.

The contrast between mainstream macroeconomics and monetarism on the causes of instability thus comes into sharp focus. Mainstream economists view the instability of investment as the main cause of the economy's instability. They see monetary policy as a stabilizing factor. Changes in the money supply raise or lower interest rates as needed, smooth out swings in investment, and thus reduce macroeconomic instability. In contrast, monetarists view changes in the money supply as the main cause of instability in the economy. For example, they say that the Great Depression occurred largely because the Fed allowed the money supply to fall by roughly one-third during that period. According to Milton Friedman, a prominent monetarist,

> And [the money supply] fell not because there were no willing borrowers—not because the horse would not drink. It fell because the Federal Reserve System forced or permitted a sharp reduction in the [money supply], because it failed to exercise the responsibilities assigned to it in the Federal Reserve Act to provide liquidity to the banking system. The Great Contraction is tragic testimony to the power of monetary policy—not, as Keynes and so many of his contemporaries believed, evidence of its impotence.[1]

Real-Business-Cycle View

A third modern view of the cause of macroeconomic instability is that business cycles are caused by real factors that affect aggregate supply rather than by monetary, or spending, factors that cause fluctuations in aggregate demand. In the **real-business-cycle theory,** business fluctuations result from significant changes in technology and resource availability. Those changes affect productivity and thus the long-run growth trend of aggregate supply.

An example focusing on recession will clarify this thinking. Suppose productivity (output per worker) declines sharply because of a large increase in oil prices, which makes it prohibitively expensive to operate certain

---

[1]Milton Friedman, *The Optimum Quantity of Money and Other Essays* (Chicago: Aldine, 1969), p. 97.

FIGURE 19.1 The real-business-cycle theory. In the real-business-cycle theory, a decline in resource availability shifts the nation's long-run aggregate supply curve to the left from AS_{LR1} to AS_{LR2}. The decline in real output from Q_1 to Q_2, in turn, reduces money demand (less is needed) and money supply (fewer loans are taken out) such that aggregate demand shifts leftward from AD_1 to AD_2. The result is a recession in which the price level remains constant.

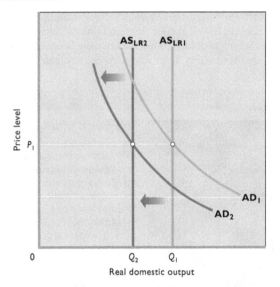

types of machinery. That decline in productivity implies a reduction in the economy's ability to produce real output. The result would be a decrease in the economy's long-run aggregate supply curve, as represented by the leftward shift from AS_{LR1} to AS_{LR2} in Figure 19.1.

As real output falls from Q_1 to Q_2, the public needs less money to buy the reduced volume of goods and services. So the demand for money falls. Moreover, the slowdown in business activity means that businesses need to borrow less from banks, reducing the part of the money supply created by banks through their lending. Thus, the supply of money also falls. In this controversial scenario, changes in the supply of money respond to changes in the demand for money. The decline in the money supply then reduces aggregate demand, as from AD_1 to AD_2 in Figure 19.1. The outcome is a decline in real output from Q_1 to Q_2, with no change in the price level.

Conversely, a large increase in aggregate supply (not shown) caused by, say, major innovations in the production process would shift the long-run aggregate supply curve rightward. Real output would increase, and money demand and money supply would both increase. Aggregate demand would shift rightward by an amount equal to the rightward shift of long-run aggregate supply. Real output would increase, without driving up the price level.

Conclusion: In the real-business-cycle theory, macro instability arises on the aggregate supply side of the economy, not on the aggregate demand side as mainstream economists and monetarists usually claim.

Coordination Failures

A fourth and final modern view of macroeconomic instability relates to so-called **coordination failures.** Such failures occur when people fail to reach a mutually beneficial equilibrium because they lack a way to coordinate their actions.

CONSIDER THIS . . .

Too Much Money?

The severe recession of 2007–2009 fits the mainstream view that recessions are caused by AD shocks rather than the real-business-cycle view that they are caused by AS shocks. Recall that the recession began with a financial crisis that caused significant reductions in investment spending and consumption spending and therefore reduced aggregate demand. As inventories increased, businesses further curtailed their investment spending, and aggregate demand, output, and income dropped even more.

Economists with monetarist leanings, however, cite monetary factors as the main cause of the financial crisis that led to the initial declines in aggregate demand. They argue that the Federal Reserve flooded the economy with too much money and held interest rates too low for too long in promoting recovery from the 2001 recession. In this line of reasoning, the excess money and low interest rates contributed to the bubble in the housing market. When that bubble burst, the resulting loan defaults set in motion the forces that produced the declines in AD and therefore the recession.

All economists agree that the bursting of the housing bubble led to the recession. And too-loose monetary policy may have contributed to the bubble. But economists also cite the role of the very large international flows of foreign savings into the United States during this period. These inflows drove down interest rates and helped to fuel the housing bubble. Other factors such as "pass-the-risk" lending practices, government policies promoting home ownership, and poorly designed and enforced financial regulations certainly came into play. The mainstream view is that causes of the financial crisis and recession are numerous and complex.

Noneconomic Example Consider first a noneconomic example. Suppose you hear that some people might be getting together at the last minute for an informal party at a nearby beach. But because of a chance of rain, there is some doubt about whether people will actually come out. You make a cell phone call or two to try to get a read on what others are thinking, and then base your decision on that limited information. If you expect others to be there, you will decide to go. If you expect that no one will go, you will decide to stay home. There are several possible equilibrium outcomes, depending on the mix of people's expectations. Let's consider just two. If each person assumes that all the others will go to the party, all will go. The party will occur and presumably everyone will have a good time. But if each person assumes that everyone else will stay home, all will stay home and there will be no party. When the party does not take place, even though all would be better off if it did take place, a coordination failure has occurred.

Macroeconomic Example Now let's apply this example to macroeconomic instability, specifically recession. Suppose that individual firms and households expect other firms and consumers to cut back their investment and consumption spending. As a result, each firm and household will anticipate a reduction of aggregate demand. Firms therefore will reduce their own investment spending since they will anticipate that their future production capacity will be excessive. Households will also reduce their own spending (increase their saving) because they anticipate that they will experience reduced work hours, possible layoffs, and falling incomes in the future.

Aggregate demand will indeed decline and the economy will indeed experience a recession in response to what amounts to a self-fulfilling prophecy. Moreover, the economy will stay at a below-full-employment level of output because, once there, producers and households have no individual incentive to increase spending. If all producers and households would agree to increase their investment and consumption spending simultaneously, then aggregate demand would rise, and real output and real income would increase. Each producer and each consumer would be better off. However, this outcome does not occur because there is no mechanism for firms and households to agree on such a joint spending increase.

In this case, the economy is stuck in an *unemployment equilibrium* because of a coordination failure. With a different set of expectations, a coordination failure might leave the economy in an *inflation equilibrium*. In this view, the economy has a number of such potential equilibrium positions, some good and some bad, depending on people's mix of expectations. Macroeconomic instability, then, reflects the movement of the economy from one such equilibrium position to another as expectations change.

QUICK REVIEW 19.1

- Mainstream economists say that macroeconomic instability usually stems from swings in investment spending and, occasionally, from adverse aggregate supply shocks.
- Monetarists view the economy through the equation of exchange ($MV = PQ$). If velocity V is stable, changes in the money supply M lead directly to changes in nominal GDP ($P \times Q$). For monetarists, changes in M caused by inappropriate monetary policy are the single most important cause of macroeconomic instability.
- In the real-business-cycle theory, significant changes in "real" factors such as technology, resource availability, and productivity change the economy's long-run aggregate supply, causing macroeconomic instability.
- Macroeconomic instability can result from coordination failures—less-than-optimal equilibrium positions that occur because businesses and households lack a way to coordinate their actions.

Does the Economy "Self-Correct"?

LO19.2 Discuss why new classical economists believe the economy will "self-correct" from aggregate demand and aggregate supply shocks.

Just as there are disputes over the causes of macroeconomic instability, there are disputes over whether or not the economy will correct itself when instability does occur. And economists also disagree on how long it will take for any such self-correction to take place.

New Classical View of Self-Correction

New classical economists tend to be either monetarists or adherents of **rational expectations theory:** the idea that businesses, consumers, and workers expect changes in policies or circumstances to have certain effects on the economy and, in pursuing their own self-interest, take actions to make sure those changes affect them as little as possible. The **new classical economics** holds that when the economy occasionally diverges from its full-employment output, internal mechanisms within the economy will automatically move it back to that output. Policymakers should stand back and let the automatic correction occur, rather than engage in active fiscal and monetary policy. This perspective is often associated with the vertical long-run Phillips Curve, which we discussed in Chapter 18. But we will analyze it here using the extended AD-AS model that was also developed in Chapter 18.

ORIGIN OF THE IDEA

019.3
Rational expectations theory

Graphical Analysis Figure 19.2a relates the new classical analysis to the question of self-correction. Specifically, an increase in aggregate demand, say, from AD_1 to AD_2, moves

FIGURE 19.2 New classical view of self-correction. (a) An unanticipated increase in aggregate demand from AD_1 to AD_2 first moves the economy from a to b. The economy then self-corrects to c. An anticipated increase in aggregate demand moves the economy directly from a to c. (b) An unanticipated decrease in aggregate demand from AD_1 to AD_3 moves the economy from a to d. The economy then self-corrects to e. An anticipated decrease in aggregate demand moves the economy directly from a to e. (Mainstream economists, however, say that if the price level remains at P_1, the economy will move from a to f, and even if the price level falls to P_4, the economy may remain at d because of downward wage inflexibility.)

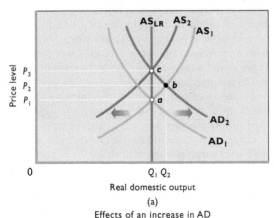

(a)
Effects of an increase in AD

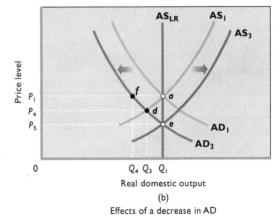

(b)
Effects of a decrease in AD

the economy upward along its short-run aggregate supply curve AS_1 from a to b. The price level rises and real output increases. With the economy producing beyond potential output, high resource demand drives up the prices of labor and other productive inputs. Per-unit production costs increase and the short-run aggregate supply curve shifts leftward, eventually from AS_1 to AS_2. The economy moves from b to c, and real output returns to its full-employment level, Q_1. This level of output is dictated by the economy's vertical long-run aggregate supply curve, AS_{LR}.

Conversely, a decrease in aggregate demand from AD_1 to AD_3 in Figure 19.2b first moves the economy downward along its short-run aggregate supply curve AS_1 from point a to d. The price level declines, as does the level of real output. With the economy producing below potential output, low resource demand drives down the prices of labor and other productive inputs. When that happens, per-unit production costs decline and the short-run aggregate supply curve shifts to the right, eventually from AS_1 to AS_3. The economy moves to e, where it again achieves its full-employment level, Q_1. As in Figure 19.2a, the economy in Figure 19.2b has automatically self-corrected to its full-employment output and its natural rate of unemployment.

Speed of Adjustment

There is some disagreement among new classical economists on how long it will take for self-correction to occur. Monetarists usually hold the *adaptive expectations* view that people form their expectations on the basis of present realities and only gradually change their expectations as experience unfolds. This means that the shifts in the short-run aggregate supply curves shown in Figure 19.2 may not occur for 2 or 3 years or even longer. Other new classical economists, however, accept the rational expectations assumption that workers anticipate some future outcomes before they occur. When price-level changes are fully anticipated, adjustments of nominal wages are very quick or even instantaneous. Let's see why.

Although several new theories incorporate rational expectations, our interest here is the new classical version of the rational expectations theory (hereafter, RET). RET is based on two assumptions:

- People behave rationally, gathering and intelligently processing information to form expectations about things that are economically important to them. They adjust those expectations quickly as new developments affecting future economic outcomes occur. Where there is adequate information, people's beliefs about future economic outcomes accurately reflect the likelihood that those outcomes will occur. For example, if it is clear that a certain policy will cause inflation, people will recognize that fact and adjust their economic behavior in anticipation of inflation.

- RET economists assume that all product and resource markets are highly competitive and that prices and wages are flexible both upward and downward. But the RET economists go further, assuming that new information is quickly (in some cases, instantaneously) taken into account in the demand and supply curves of such markets. The upshot is that equilibrium prices and quantities adjust rapidly to unforeseen events—say, technological change or aggregate supply shocks. They adjust instantaneously to events that have known outcomes—for example, changes in fiscal or monetary policy.

Unanticipated Price-Level Changes The implication of RET is not only that the economy is self-correcting but that self-correction occurs quickly. In this thinking, unanticipated changes in the price level—so-called **price-level surprises**—*do* cause temporary changes in real output. Suppose, for example, that an unanticipated increase in foreign demand for U.S. goods increases U.S. aggregate demand from AD_1 to AD_2 in Figure 19.2a. The immediate result is an unexpected increase in the price level from P_1 to P_2.

But now an interesting question arises. If wages and prices are flexible, as assumed in RET, why doesn't the higher price level immediately cause wages and other input prices to rise, such that there is no increase in real output at all? Why does the economy temporarily move from point a to b along AS_1? In RET, firms increase output from Q_1 to Q_2 because of misperceptions about rising prices of their own products relative to the prices of other products (and to the prices of labor). They mistakenly think the higher prices of their own products have resulted from increased demand for those products relative to the demands for other products. Expecting higher profits, they increase their own production. But in fact *all* prices, including the price of labor (nominal wages), are rising because of the general increase in aggregate demand. Once firms see that *all* prices and wages are rising, they decrease their production to previous levels.

In terms of Figure 19.2a, the increase in nominal wages shifts the short-run aggregate supply curve leftward, ultimately from AS_1 to AS_2, and the economy moves from b to c. Thus, the increase in real output caused by the price-level surprise corrects itself.

The same analysis in reverse applies to an unanticipated price-level decrease. In the economy represented by Figure 19.2b, firms misperceive that the prices of their own products are falling due to decreases in the demand for those products relative to other products. They incorrectly anticipate declines in profit and cut production. As a result of their collective actions, real output in the economy falls. Once firms see what is really happening—that *all* prices and wages are dropping—they increase their output to prior levels. The short-run aggregate supply curve in Figure 19.2b shifts rightward from AS_1 to AS_3, and the economy "self-corrects" by moving from *d* to *e*.

Fully Anticipated Price-Level Changes In RET, fully *anticipated* price-level changes do not change real output, even for short periods. In Figure 19.2a, again consider the increase in aggregate demand from AD_1 to AD_2. Businesses immediately recognize that the higher prices being paid for their products are part of the inflation they had anticipated. They understand that the same forces that are causing the inflation result in higher nominal wages, leaving their profits unchanged. The economy therefore moves directly from *a* to *c*. The price level rises as expected, and output remains at its full-employment level Q_1.

Similarly, a fully *anticipated* price-level decrease will leave real output unchanged. Firms conclude that nominal wages are declining by the same percentage amount as the declining price level, leaving profits unchanged. The economy represented by Figure 19.2b therefore moves directly from *a* to *e*. Deflation occurs, but the economy continues to produce its full-employment output Q_1. The anticipated decline in aggregate demand causes no change in real output.

Mainstream View of Self-Correction

Almost all economists acknowledge that the new classical economists have made significant contributions to the theory of aggregate supply. In fact, mainstream economists have incorporated some aspects of RET into their own models. However, most economists strongly disagree with RET on the question of downward price and wage flexibility. While the stock market, foreign exchange market, and certain commodity markets experience day-to-day or minute-to-minute price changes, including price declines, that is not true of many product markets and most labor markets. There is ample evidence, say mainstream economists, that many prices and wages are inflexible downward for long periods. As a result, it may take years for the economy to move from recession back to full-employment output, unless it gets help from fiscal and monetary policy.

Graphical Analysis To understand this mainstream view, again examine Figure 19.2b. Suppose aggregate demand declines from AD_1 to AD_3 because of a significant decline in investment spending. If prices are sticky downward for a

while and therefore the price level is temporarily stuck at P_1, the economy will not move from *a* to *d* to *e*, as suggested by RET. Instead, the economy will move from *a* to *f*, as if it were moving along the white horizontal P_1 price line between those two points. Real output will decline from its full-employment level, Q_1, to the recessionary level, Q_4.

But let's assume that large amounts of unsold inventories eventually cause the price level to fall to P_4. Will this lead to the decline in nominal wages needed to shift aggregate supply from AS_1 to AS_3, as suggested by the new classical economists? "Highly unlikely" say mainstream economists. Even more so than prices, nominal wages tend to be inflexible downward. If nominal wages do not decline in response to the decline in the price level, then the short-run aggregate supply curve will not shift rightward. The self-correction mechanism assumed by RET and new classical economists will break down. Instead, the economy will remain at *d*, experiencing less-than-full-employment output and a high rate of unemployment.

Downward Wage Inflexibility In Chapter 12 we discussed several reasons why firms may not be able to, or may not want to, lower nominal wages. Firms may not be able to cut wages because of wage contracts and the legal minimum wage. And firms may not want to lower wages if they fear potential problems with morale, effort, and efficiency.

While contracts are thought to be the main cause of wage rigidity, so-called efficiency wages and insider-outsider relationships also may play a role. Let's explore both.

Efficiency Wage Theory Recall from Chapter 12 that an **efficiency wage** is a wage that minimizes the firm's labor cost per unit of output. Normally, we would think that the market wage is the efficiency wage since it is the lowest wage at which a firm can obtain a particular type of labor. But where the cost of supervising workers is high or where worker turnover is great, firms may discover that paying a wage that is higher than the market wage will lower their wage cost per unit of output.

Example: Suppose a firm's workers, on average, produce 8 units of output at a $9 market wage but 10 units of output at a $10 above-market wage. The efficiency wage is $10, not the $9 market wage. At the $10 wage, the labor cost per unit of output is only $1 (= $10 wage/10 units of output), compared with $1.12 (= $9 wage/8 units of output) at the $9 wage.

How can a higher wage result in greater efficiency?

• *Greater work effort* The above-market wage, in effect, raises the cost to workers of losing their jobs as a result of poor performance. Because workers have a strong incentive to retain their relatively high-paying jobs, they are more likely to provide greater work effort. Looked at differently, workers are more reluctant to shirk (neglect or avoid work) because the higher wage makes job loss more costly to them. Consequently, the above-market wage can be the efficient wage; it can enhance worker productivity so much that the higher wage more than pays for itself.

- *Lower supervision costs* With less incentive among workers to shirk, the firm needs fewer supervisory personnel to monitor work performance. This, too, can lower the firm's overall wage cost per unit of output.

- *Reduced job turnover* The above-market pay discourages workers from voluntarily leaving their jobs. The lower turnover rate reduces the firm's cost of hiring and training workers. It also gives the firm a more experienced, more productive workforce.

The key implication for macroeconomic instability is that efficiency wages add to the downward inflexibility of wages. Firms that pay efficiency wages will be reluctant to cut wages when aggregate demand declines, since such cuts may encourage shirking, require more supervisory personnel, and increase turnover. In other words, wage cuts that reduce productivity and raise per-unit labor costs are self-defeating.

ORIGIN OF THE IDEA

O19.4 Efficiency wages

Insider-Outsider Relationships Other economists theorize that downward wage inflexibility may relate to relationships between "insiders" and "outsiders." Insiders are workers who retain employment even during recession. Outsiders are workers who have been laid off from a firm and unemployed workers who would like to work at that firm.

When recession produces layoffs and widespread unemployment, we might expect outsiders to offer to work for less than the current wage rate, in effect, bidding down wage rates. We also might expect firms to hire such workers to reduce their costs. But, according to the **insider-outsider theory**, outsiders may not be able to underbid existing wages because employers may view the nonwage cost of hiring them to be prohibitive. Employers might fear that insiders would view acceptance of such underbidding as undermining years of effort to increase wages or, worse, as "stealing" jobs. So insiders may refuse to cooperate with new workers who have undercut their pay.

Where teamwork is critical for production, such lack of cooperation will reduce overall productivity and thereby lower the firms' profits.

Even if firms are willing to employ outsiders at less than the current wage, those workers might refuse to work for less than the existing wage. To do so might invite harassment from the insiders whose pay they have undercut. Thus, outsiders may remain unemployed, relying on past saving, unemployment compensation, and other social programs to make ends meet.

As in the efficiency wage theory, the insider-outsider theory implies that wages will be inflexible downward when aggregate demand declines. Self-correction may eventually occur but not nearly as rapidly as the new classical economists contend.

QUICK REVIEW 19.2

- New classical economists believe that the economy "self-corrects" when unanticipated events divert it from its full-employment level of real output.
- In RET, unanticipated price-level changes cause changes in real output in the short run but not in the long run.
- According to RET, market participants immediately change their actions in response to anticipated price-level changes such that no change in real output occurs.
- Mainstream economists say that the economy can get mired in recession for several months or more because of downward price and wage inflexibility.
- Sources of downward wage inflexibility include contracts, efficiency wages, and insider-outsider relationships.

Rules or Discretion?

LO19.3 Identify and describe the variations of the debate over "rules" versus "discretion" in conducting stabilization policy.

These different views on the causes of instability and on the speed of self-correction have led to vigorous debate on macro policy. Should the government adhere to policy rules that prohibit it from causing instability in an economy that is otherwise stable? Or should it use discretionary fiscal and monetary policy, when needed, to stabilize a sometimes-unstable economy?

In Support of Policy Rules

Monetarists and other new classical economists believe policy rules would reduce instability in the economy. They believe that such rules would prevent government from trying

CONSIDER THIS . . .

On the Road Again

Economist Abba Lerner (1903–1982) likened the economy to an automobile traveling down a road that had traffic barriers on each side. The problem was that the car had no steering wheel. It would hit one barrier, causing the car to veer to the opposite side of the road. There it would hit the other barrier, which in turn would send it careening to the opposite side. To avoid such careening in the form of business cycles, said Lerner, society must equip the economy with a steering wheel. Discretionary fiscal and monetary policy would enable government to steer the economy safely between the problems of recession and demand-pull inflation.

Economist Milton Friedman (1912–2006) modified Lerner's analogy, giving it a different meaning. He said that the economic vehicle does not need a skillful driver who is continuously turning the wheel to adjust to the unexpected irregularities of the route. Instead, the economy needs a way to prohibit the monetary passenger in the back seat from occasionally leaning over and giving the steering wheel a jerk that sends the car off the road. According to Friedman, the car will travel down the road just fine unless the Federal Reserve destabilizes it.

Lerner's analogy implied an internally unstable economy that needs steering through discretionary government stabilization policy. Friedman's modification of the analogy implied a generally stable economy that is destabilized by inappropriate monetary policy by the Federal Reserve. For Lerner, stability required active use of fiscal and monetary policy. For Friedman, macroeconomic stability required a monetary rule forcing the Federal Reserve to increase the money supply at a set, steady annual rate.*

---

*In his later years, Friedman softened his call for a monetary rule, acknowledging that the Fed had become much more skillful at keeping the rate of inflation in check through prudent monetary policy.

to "manage" aggregate demand. That would be a desirable trend because, in their view, such management is misguided and thus is likely to *cause* more instability than it cures.

Monetary Rule Since inappropriate monetary policy is the major source of macroeconomic instability, say monetarists, the enactment of a **monetary rule** would make sense.

FIGURE 19.3 Rationale for a monetary rule. A monetary rule that required the Fed to increase the money supply at an annual rate linked to the long-run increase in potential GDP would shift aggregate demand rightward, as from AD_1 to AD_2, at the same pace as the shift in long-run aggregate supply, here, AS_{LR1} to AS_{LR2}. Thus the economy would experience growth without inflation or deflation.

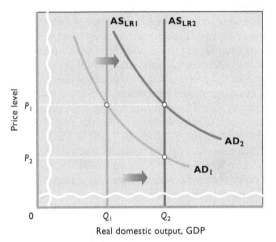

One such rule would be a requirement that the Fed expand the money supply each year at the same annual rate as the typical growth of the economy's production capacity. That fixed-rate expansion of the money supply would occur whatever the state of the economy. The Fed's sole monetary role would be to use its tools (open-market operations, the discount rate, interest on reserves, and reserve requirements) to ensure that the nation's money supply grew steadily by, say, 3 to 5 percent a year. According to Milton Friedman,

> Such a rule . . . would eliminate . . . the major cause of instability in the economy—the capricious and unpredictable impact of countercyclical monetary policy. As long as the money supply grows at a constant rate each year, be it 3, 4, or 5 percent, any decline into recession will be temporary. The liquidity provided by a constantly growing money supply will cause aggregate demand to expand. Similarly, if the supply of money does not rise at a more than average rate, any inflationary increase in spending will burn itself out for lack of fuel.[2]

Figure 19.3 illustrates the rationale for a monetary rule. Suppose the economy represented there is operating at its full-employment real output, Q_1. Also suppose the nation's long-run aggregate supply curve shifts rightward, as from AS_{LR1} to AS_{LR2}, each year, signifying the average annual increase in potential real output. As you saw in earlier chapters, such annual increases in "potential GDP"

---

[2]As quoted in Lawrence S. Ritter and William L. Silber, *Money*, 5th ed. (New York: Basic Books, 1984), pp. 141–142.

result from added resources, improved resources, and improved technology.

Monetarists argue that a monetary rule would tie increases in the money supply to the typical rightward shift of long-run aggregate supply. In view of the direct link between changes in the money supply and aggregate demand, this would ensure that the AD curve would shift rightward, as from AD_1 to AD_2, each year. As a result, while GDP increases from Q_1 to Q_2, the price level would remain constant at P_1. A monetary rule, then, would promote steady growth of real output along with price stability.

Generally, rational expectations economists also support a monetary rule. They conclude that an expansionary or restrictive monetary policy would alter the rate of inflation but not real output. Suppose, for example, the Fed implements an easy money policy to reduce interest rates, expand investment spending, and boost real GDP. On the basis of past experience and economic knowledge, the public would anticipate that this policy is inflationary and would take protective actions. Workers would press for higher nominal wages; firms would raise their product prices; and lenders would lift their nominal interest rates on loans.

All these responses are designed to prevent inflation from having adverse effects on the real income of workers, businesses, and lenders. But collectively they would immediately raise wage and price levels. So the increase in aggregate demand brought about by the expansionary monetary policy would be completely dissipated in higher prices and wages. Real output and employment would not be increased by the easy money policy.

In this view, the combination of rational expectations and instantaneous market adjustments dooms discretionary monetary policy to ineffectiveness. If discretionary monetary policy produces only inflation (or deflation), say the RET economists, then it makes sense to limit the Fed's discretion and to require that Congress enact a monetary rule consistent with price stability at all times.

In recent decades, the call for a Friedman-type monetary rule has faded. Some economists who tend to favor monetary rules have advocated **inflation targeting,** under which the Fed would be required to announce a targeted band of inflation rates, say, 1 to 2 percent, for some future period such as the following 2 years. It would then be expected to use its monetary policy tools to keep inflation rates within that range. If it did not hit the inflation target, it would have to explain why it failed.

Strictly interpreted, inflation targeting would focus the Fed's attention nearly exclusively on controlling inflation and deflation, rather than on counteracting business fluctuations. Proponents of inflation targeting generally believe the economy will have fewer, shorter, and less severe business cycles if the Fed adheres to the rule "Set a known inflation goal and achieve it."

We discussed another modern monetary rule—the Taylor rule—in Chapter 16 on monetary policy. This rule specifies how the Fed should alter the federal funds rate under differing economic circumstances. We discuss this rule in more depth in this chapter's Last Word.

Balanced Budget   Monetarists and new classical economists question the effectiveness of fiscal policy. At the extreme, a few of them favor a constitutional amendment requiring that the federal government balance its budget annually. Others simply suggest that government be "passive" in its fiscal policy, not intentionally creating budget deficits or surpluses. They believe that deficits and surpluses caused by recession or inflationary expansion will eventually correct themselves as the economy self-corrects to its full-employment output.

Monetarists are particularly strong in their opposition to expansionary fiscal policy. They believe that the deficit spending accompanying such a policy has a strong tendency to "crowd out" private investment. Suppose government runs a budget deficit by printing and selling U.S. securities—that is, by borrowing from the public. By engaging in such borrowing, the government is competing with private businesses for funds. The borrowing increases the demand for money, which then raises the interest rate and crowds out a substantial amount of private investment that would otherwise have been profitable. The net effect of a budget deficit on aggregate demand therefore is unpredictable and, at best, modest.

RET economists reject discretionary fiscal policy for the same reason they reject active monetary policy: They don't think it works. Business and labor will immediately adjust their behavior in anticipation of the price-level effects of a change in fiscal policy. The economy will move directly to the anticipated new price level. Like monetary policy, say the RET theorists, fiscal policy can move the economy along its vertical long-run aggregate supply curve. But because its effects on inflation are fully anticipated, fiscal policy cannot alter real GDP even in the short run. The best course of action for government is to balance its budget.

In Defense of Discretionary Stabilization Policy

Mainstream economists oppose both a strict monetary rule and a balanced-budget requirement. They believe that monetary policy and fiscal policy are important tools for achieving and maintaining full employment, price stability, and economic growth.

Discretionary Monetary Policy In supporting discretionary monetary policy, mainstream economists argue that the rationale for the Friedman monetary rule is flawed. While there is indeed a close relationship between the money supply and nominal GDP over long periods, in shorter periods this relationship breaks down. The reason is that the velocity of money has proved to be more variable and unpredictable than monetarists contend. Arguing that velocity is variable both cyclically and over time, mainstream economists contend that a constant annual rate of increase in the money supply might not eliminate fluctuations in aggregate demand. In terms of the equation of exchange, a steady rise of M does not guarantee a steady expansion of aggregate demand because V—the rate at which money is spent—can change.

Look again at Figure 19.3, in which we demonstrated the monetary rule: Expand the money supply annually by a fixed percentage, regardless of the state of the economy. During the period in question, optimistic business expectations might create a boom in investment spending and thus shift the aggregate demand curve to some location to the right of AD_2. (You may want to pencil in a new AD curve, labeling it AD_3.) The price level would then rise above P_1; that is, demand-pull inflation would occur. In this case, the monetary rule will not accomplish its goal of maintaining price stability. Mainstream economists say that the Fed can use a restrictive monetary policy to reduce the excessive investment spending and thereby hold the rightward shift of aggregate demand to AD_2, thus avoiding inflation.

Similarly, suppose instead that investment declines because of pessimistic business expectations. Aggregate demand will then increase by some amount less than the increase from AD_1 to AD_2 in Figure 19.3. Again, the monetary rule fails the stability test: The price level sinks below P_1 (deflation occurs). Or if the price level is inflexible downward at P_1, the economy will not achieve its full-employment output (unemployment rises). An expansionary monetary policy can help avoid each outcome.

Mainstream economists quip that the trouble with the monetary rule is that it tells the policymaker, "Don't do something; just stand there."

Discretionary Fiscal Policy Mainstream economists support the use of fiscal policy to keep recessions from deepening or to keep mild inflation from becoming severe inflation. They recognize the possibility of crowding out but do not think it is a serious problem when business borrowing is depressed, as is usually the case in recession. Because politicians can abuse fiscal policy, most economists feel that it should be held in reserve for situations where monetary policy appears to be ineffective or working too slowly.

As indicated earlier, mainstream economists oppose requirements to balance the budget annually. Tax revenues fall sharply during recessions and rise briskly during periods of demand-pull inflation. Therefore, a law or a constitutional amendment mandating an annually balanced budget would require that the government increase tax rates and reduce government spending during recession and reduce tax rates and increase government spending during economic booms. The first set of actions would worsen recession, and the second set would fuel inflation.

Policy Successes

Finally, mainstream economists point out several specific policy successes in the past four decades:

- A tight money policy dropped inflation from 13.5 percent in 1980 to 3.2 percent in 1983.
- An expansionary fiscal policy reduced the unemployment rate from 9.7 percent in 1982 to 5.5 percent in 1988.
- An easy money policy helped the economy recover from the 1990–1991 recession.
- Judicious tightening of monetary policy in the mid-1990s, and then again in the late 1990s, helped the economy remain on a noninflationary, full-employment growth path.
- In late 2001 and 2002, expansionary fiscal and monetary policy helped the economy recover from a series of economic blows, including the collapse of numerous Internet start-up firms; a severe decline in investment spending; the impacts of the terrorist attacks of September 11, 2001; and a precipitous decline in stock values.
- In 2004 and 2005 the Fed tempered continued expansionary fiscal policy by increasing the federal funds rate in $\frac{1}{4}$ percentage-point increments from 1 percent to 4.25 percent. The economy expanded briskly in those years, while inflation stayed in check. The mild inflation was particularly impressive because the average price of a barrel of crude oil rose from $24 in 2002 to $55 in 2005. The Fed's further increases in interest rates to 5.25 percent in 2006 also kept inflation mild that year and the next despite continued strong growth and oil reaching $99 per barrel in late 2007.
- In 2007 the Fed vigorously responded to a crisis in the mortgage market by ensuring monetary liquidity

LAST WORD

The Taylor Rule: Could a Robot Replace Ben Bernanke?

Macroeconomist John Taylor of Stanford University Calls for a New Monetary Rule That Would Institutionalize Appropriate Fed Policy Responses to Changes in Real Output and Inflation.

In our discussion of rules versus discretion, "rules" were associated with a *passive* monetary policy—one in which the monetary rule required that the Fed expand the money supply at a fixed annual rate regardless of the state of the economy. "Discretion," on the other hand, was associated with an *active* monetary policy in which the Fed changed interest rates in response to actual or anticipated changes in the economy.

Economist John Taylor has put a new twist on the rules-versus-discretion debate by suggesting a hybrid policy rule that dictates the precise active monetary actions the Fed should take when changes in the economy occur. You first encountered this Taylor rule in our discussion of monetary policy in Chapter 16. The **Taylor rule** combines traditional monetarism, with its emphasis on a monetary rule, and the more mainstream view that active monetary policy is a useful tool for taming inflation and limiting recession. Unlike the Friedman monetary rule, the Taylor rule holds, for example, that monetary policy should respond to changes in both real GDP and inflation, not simply inflation. The key adjustment instrument is the interest rate, not the money supply.

The Taylor rule builds on the belief held by many economists that central banks are willing to tolerate a small positive rate of inflation if doing so will help the economy to produce at potential output. The Taylor rule assumes that the Fed has a 2 percent "target rate of inflation" that it is willing to tolerate and that the Fed follows three rules when setting its target for the federal funds rate (the rate of interest that commercial banks with excess reserves charge on overnight loans to banks that wish to borrow reserves in order to meet their reserve requirements). The three rules are:

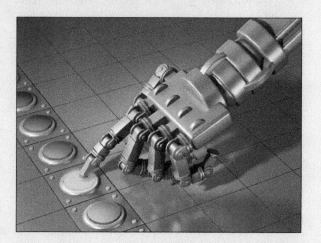

- When real GDP equals potential GDP and inflation is at its target rate of 2 percent, the federal funds target rate should be 4 percent, implying a *real* federal funds rate of 2 percent (= 4 percent nominal federal funds rate *minus* 2 percent inflation rate).

- For each 1 percent increase of real GDP above potential GDP, the Fed should raise the *real* federal funds rate by $\frac{1}{2}$ percentage point.

- For each 1 percent increase in the inflation rate above its 2 percent target rate, the Fed should raise the *real* federal funds rate by $\frac{1}{2}$ percentage point.*

*John Taylor, *Inflation, Unemployment, and Monetary Policy* (Cambridge, Mass.: MIT Press, 1998), pp. 44–47.

Taylor has neither suggested nor implied that a robot, programmed with the Taylor rule, should replace Ben Bernanke, chairman of the Federal Reserve System. The Fed's discretion to override the rule (or "contingency plan for policy") would be retained, but the Fed would have to explain why its policies diverged from the rule. So the rule would remove the "mystery" associated with monetary policy and increase the Fed's accountability. Also, says Taylor, if used consistently, the rule would enable market participants to predict Fed behavior, and this would increase Fed credibility and reduce uncertainty.

Critics of the Taylor rule acknowledge that it is closer in tune with actual Fed countercyclical policy than is the Friedman monetary rule. They also acknowledge that adherence to the Taylor rule would have raised interest rates more rapidly during the two years prior to the mortgage debt crisis of 2007. Those higher interest rates might have reduced the excessive mortgage borrowing that eventually led to the crisis. But critics of the Taylor rule say that it is unwise to limit the Fed's future discretion in adjusting interest rates as it deems necessary. They note that the Fed has successfully kept inflation in check over the past two decades and has used monetary policy creatively and decisively when necessary during financial and economic emergencies. In view of the overall success, critics conclude that a mechanical monetary rule is certainly unnecessary and might even be detrimental.

in the banking system. Besides aggressively lowering the federal funds rate from 5.25 percent in the summer of 2007 to just 2 percent in April 2008, the Fed greatly increased the reserves of the banking system by creating and using its term auction facility. It also undertook other lender-of-last-resort actions to unfreeze credit and prevent a possible collapse of the entire financial system. During the severe recession of 2007–2009, the Fed lowered the federal funds rate further, holding it in the 0 to 0.25 percent range to break the downward slide of the economy and help promote economic recovery.

QUICK REVIEW 19.3

- Mainstream economists disagree with monetarist and rational expectations economists as to whether the Fed should use rules or utilize discretion.

- Monetarist and rational expectations economists oppose discretion because they believe that discretion adds more instability to the business cycle than it cures.

- Mainstream economists oppose strict monetary rules and defend both monetary and fiscal policy discretion because they believe that both theory and evidence suggest that discretionary policies are helpful in achieving full employment, price stability, and economic growth.

Summary of Alternative Views

LO19.4 Summarize the fundamental ideas and policy implications of mainstream macroeconomics, monetarism, and rational expectations theory.

In Table 19.1 we summarize the fundamental ideas and policy implications of three macroeconomic theories: mainstream macroeconomics, monetarism, and rational expectations theory. Note that we have broadly defined new classical economics to include both monetarism and the rational expectations theory since both adhere to the view that the economy tends automatically to achieve equilibrium at its full-employment output.

These different perspectives have obliged mainstream economists to rethink some of their fundamental principles and to revise many of their positions. Although considerable disagreement remains, mainstream macroeconomists agree with monetarists that "money matters" and that excessive growth of the money supply is the major cause of long-lasting, rapid inflation. They also agree with RET proponents and theorists of coordination failures that expectations matter. If government can create expectations of price stability, full employment, and economic growth, households and firms will tend to act in ways to make them happen. In short, thanks to ongoing challenges to conventional wisdom, macroeconomics continues to evolve.

TABLE 19.1 Summary of Alternative Macroeconomic Views

		New Classical Economics	
Issue	**Mainstream Macroeconomics**	**Monetarism**	**Rational Expectations**
View of the private economy	Potentially unstable	Stable in long run at natural rate of unemployment	Stable in long run at natural rate of unemployment
Cause of the observed instability of the private economy	Investment plans unequal to saving plans (changes in AD); AS shocks	Inappropriate monetary policy	Unanticipated AD and AS shocks in the short run
Assumptions about short-run price and wage stickiness	Both prices and wages stuck in the immediate short run; in the short run, wages sticky while prices inflexible downward but flexible upward	Prices flexible upward and downward in the short run; wages sticky in the short run	Prices and wages flexible both upward and downward in the short run
Appropriate macro policies	Active fiscal and monetary policy	Monetary rule	Monetary rule
How changes in the money supply affect the economy	By changing the interest rate, which changes investment and real GDP	By directly changing AD, which changes GDP	No effect on output because price-level changes are anticipated
View of the velocity of money	Unstable	Stable	No consensus
How fiscal policy affects the economy	Changes AD and GDP via the multiplier process	No effect unless money supply changes	No effect because price-level changes are anticipated
View of cost-push inflation	Possible (AS shock)	Impossible in the long run in the absence of excessive money supply growth	Impossible in the long run in the absence of excessive money supply growth

SUMMARY

LO19.1 Describe alternative perspectives on the causes of macroeconomic instability, including the views of mainstream economists, monetarists, real-business-cycle advocates, and proponents of coordination failures.

The mainstream view is that macro instability is caused by a combination of price stickiness and shocks to aggregate demand or aggregate supply. With prices inflexible in the shorter run, changes in aggregate demand or short-run aggregate supply result in changes in output and employment. In the long run when both input and output prices are fully flexible, the economy will produce at potential output.

Monetarism focuses on the equation of exchange: $MV = PQ$. Because velocity is thought to be stable, changes in M create changes in nominal GDP ($= PQ$). Monetarists believe that the most significant cause of macroeconomic instability has been inappropriate monetary policy. Rapid increases in M cause inflation; insufficient growth of M causes recession. In this view, a major cause of the Great Depression was inappropriate monetary policy, which allowed the money supply to decline by roughly one-third.

Real-business-cycle theory views changes in resource availability and technology (real factors), which alter productivity, as the main causes of macroeconomic instability. In this theory, shifts of the economy's long-run aggregate supply curve change real output. In turn, money demand and money supply change, shifting the aggregate demand curve in the same direction as the initial change in long-run aggregate supply. Real output thus can change without a change in the price level.

A coordination failure is said to occur when people lack a way to coordinate their actions in order to achieve a mutually beneficial equilibrium. Depending on people's expectations, the economy can come to rest at either a good equilibrium (noninflationary full-employment output) or a bad equilibrium (less-than-full-employment output or demand-pull inflation). A bad equilibrium is a result of a coordination failure.

The rational expectations theory rests on two assumptions: (1) With sufficient information, people's beliefs about future economic outcomes accurately reflect the likelihood that those outcomes will occur; and (2) markets are highly competitive, and prices and wages are flexible both upward and downward.

LO19.2 Discuss why new classical economists believe the economy will "self-correct" from aggregate demand and aggregate supply shocks.

New classical economists (monetarists and rational expectations theorists) see the economy as automatically correcting itself when disturbed from its full-employment level of real output. In RET, unanticipated changes in aggregate demand change the price level, and in the short run this leads firms to change output. But once the firms realize that all prices are changing (including nominal wages) as part of general inflation or deflation, they restore their output to the previous level. Anticipated changes in aggregate demand produce only changes in the price level, not changes in real output.

Mainstream economists reject the new classical view that all prices and wages are flexible downward. They contend that nominal wages, in particular, are inflexible downward because of several factors, including labor contracts, efficiency wages, and insider-outsider relationships. This means that declines in aggregate demand lower real output, not only wages and prices.

LO19.3 Identify and describe the variations of the debate over "rules" versus "discretion" in conducting stabilization policy.

Monetarist and rational expectations economists say the Fed should adhere to some form of policy rule, rather than rely exclusively on discretion. The Friedman rule would direct the Fed to increase the money supply at a fixed annual rate equal to the long-run growth of potential GDP. An alternative approach—inflation targeting—would direct the Fed to establish a targeted range of inflation rates, say, 1 to 2 percent, and focus monetary policy on meeting that goal. They also support maintaining a "neutral" fiscal policy, as opposed to using discretionary fiscal policy to create budget deficits or budget surpluses. A few monetarists and rational expectations economists favor a constitutional amendment requiring that the federal government balance its budget annually.

Mainstream economists oppose strict monetary rules and a balanced-budget requirement, and defend discretionary monetary and fiscal policies. They say that both theory and evidence suggest that such policies are helpful in achieving full employment, price stability, and economic growth.

LO19.4 Summarize the fundamental ideas and policy implications of mainstream macroeconomics, monetarism, and rational expectations theory.

Macroeconomics continues to evolve because of the debate among the three main schools of economic thought: the mainstream, monetarism, and rational expectations.

Mainstream economics believes the economy to be potentially unstable and prone to business cycles due to sticky prices and wages interacting with economic shocks. The mainstream believes in active monetary and fiscal policy that can change AD through the multiplier process and that changes in the money supply affect the economy by changing the interest rate and investment. The mainstream believes the velocity of money to be unstable and holds that cost-push inflation exists and is caused by AS shocks.

Monetarism believes the economy to be fundamentally stable unless inappropriate monetary policies are applied. It believes wages and prices are fully flexible at all time horizons, allowing the economy to adjust on its own back to equilibrium. It argues that business cycles will only occur if monetary policy is either overly tight or overly loose. To prevent either, monetarists support the application of a *monetary rule* to guide monetary policy. Monetarism views the velocity of money as stable and believes cost-push inflation to be impossible in the long run in the absence of excessive money supply growth. Monetarists believe that fiscal policy cannot affect AD or GDP unless there are accompanying changes in monetary policy. On the other hand, monetary policy can shift AD and thereby affect GDP.

The rational expectations camp believes the economy to be stable in the long run at the natural rate of unemployment due to its assumption that prices are flexible at all time horizons. But over shorter time horizons, recessions and booms can happen due to unexpected AD or AS shocks. Rational expectations proponents support a monetary rule in order to guide expectations, so that monetary policy changes will never be a surprise that could shift the economy away from its equilibrium. They also agree with monetarists in the belief that cost-push inflation should be impossible without excessive money supply growth. Finally, rational expectations economists believe that anticipated fiscal and monetary policy changes will have no effect on GDP because they will lead only to price-level changes. For either to be effective in shifting GDP in the short run, they must come as a surprise.

TERMS AND CONCEPTS

monetarism	rational expectations theory	monetary rule
equation of exchange	new classical economics	inflation targeting
velocity	price-level surprises	Taylor rule
real-business-cycle theory	efficiency wage	
coordination failures	insider-outsider theory	

The following and additional problems can be found in **connect**
ECONOMICS

DISCUSSION QUESTIONS

1. According to mainstream economists, what is the usual cause of macroeconomic instability? What role does the spending-income multiplier play in creating instability? How might adverse aggregate supply factors cause instability, according to mainstream economists? **LO19.1**

2. What is an efficiency wage? How might payment of an above-market wage reduce shirking by employees and reduce worker turnover? How might efficiency wages contribute to downward wage inflexibility, at least for a time, when aggregate demand declines? **LO19.1**

3. How might relationships between so-called insiders and outsiders contribute to downward wage inflexibility? **LO19.1**

4. Briefly describe the difference between a so-called real business cycle and a more traditional "spending" business cycle. **LO19.1**

5. Craig and Kris were walking directly toward each other in a congested store aisle. Craig moved to his left to avoid Kris, and at the same time Kris moved to his right to avoid Craig. They bumped into each other. What concept does this example illustrate? How does this idea relate to macroeconomic instability? **LO19.1**

6. State and explain the basic equation of monetarism. What is the major cause of macroeconomic instability, as viewed by monetarists? **LO19.1**

7. Use the equation of exchange to explain the rationale for a monetary rule. Why will such a rule run into trouble if V unexpectedly falls because of, say, a drop in investment spending by businesses? **LO19.1**

8. Explain the difference between "active" discretionary fiscal policy advocated by mainstream economists and "passive" fiscal policy advocated by new classical economists. Explain: "The problem with a balanced-budget amendment is that it would, in a sense, require active fiscal policy—but in the wrong direction—as the economy slides into recession." **LO19.3**

9. You have just been elected president of the United States, and the present chairperson of the Federal Reserve Board has resigned. You need to appoint a new person to this position, as well as a person to chair your Council of Economic Advisers. Using Table 19.1 and your knowledge of macroeconomics, identify the views on macro theory and policy you would want your appointees to hold. Remember, the economic health of the entire nation—and your chances for reelection—may depend on your selection. **LO19.1**

10. **LAST WORD** Compare and contrast the Taylor rule for monetary policy with the older, simpler monetary rule advocated by Milton Friedman.

REVIEW QUESTIONS

1. If prices are sticky and the number of dollars of gross investment unexpectedly increases, the _____ curve will shift _____. **LO19.1**
   a. AD; right.
   b. AD; left.
   c. AS; right.
   d. AS; left.

2. First, imagine that both input and output prices are fixed in the economy. What does the aggregate supply curve look like? If AD decreases in this situation, what will happen to equilibrium output and the price level? Next, imagine that input prices are fixed, but output prices are flexible. What does the aggregate supply curve look like? In this case, if AD decreases, what will happen to equilibrium output and the price level? Finally, if both input and output prices are fully flexible, what does the aggregate supply curve look like? In this case, if AD decreases, what will happen to equilibrium output and the price level? (To check your answers, review Figures 12.3, 12.4, and 12.5 in Chapter 12). **LO19.1**

3. Suppose that the money supply is $1 trillion and money velocity is 4. Then the equation of exchange would predict nominal GDP to be: **LO19.1**
   a. $1 trillion.
   b. $4 trillion.
   c. $5 trillion.
   d. $8 trillion.

4. If the money supply fell by 10 percent, a monetarist would expect nominal GDP to _____. **LO19.1**
   a. Rise.
   b. Fall.
   c. Stay the same.

5. An economy is producing at full employment when AD unexpectedly shifts to the left. A new classical economist would assume that as the economy adjusted back to producing at full employment, the price level would _____. **LO19.2**
   a. Increase.
   b. Decrease.
   c. Stay the same.

6. Use an AD-AS graph to demonstrate and explain the price-level and real-output outcome of an anticipated decline in aggregate demand, as viewed by RET economists. (Assume that the economy initially is operating at its full-employment level of output.) Then demonstrate and explain on the same graph the outcome as viewed by mainstream economists. **LO19.2**

7. Place "MON," "RET," or "MAIN" beside the statements that most closely reflect monetarist, rational expectations, or mainstream views, respectively: **LO19.4**
   a. Anticipated changes in aggregate demand affect only the price level; they have no effect on real output.
   b. Downward wage inflexibility means that declines in aggregate demand can cause long-lasting recession.
   c. Changes in the money supply M increase PQ; at first only Q rises, because nominal wages are fixed, but once workers adapt their expectations to new realities, P rises and Q returns to its former level.
   d. Fiscal and monetary policies smooth out the business cycle.
   e. The Fed should increase the money supply at a fixed annual rate.

PROBLEMS

1. Suppose that the money supply and the nominal GDP for a hypothetical economy are $96 billion and $336 billion, respectively. What is the velocity of money? How will households and businesses react if the central bank reduces the money supply by $20 billion? By how much will nominal GDP have to fall to restore equilibrium, according to the monetarist perspective? **LO19.1**

2. Assume the following information for a hypothetical economy in year 1: money supply = $400 billion; long-term annual growth of potential GDP = 3 percent; velocity = 4.

Assume that the banking system initially has no excess reserves and that the reserve requirement is 10 percent. Also suppose that velocity is constant and that the economy initially is operating at its full-employment real output. **LO19.1**
   a. What is the level of nominal GDP in year 1?
   b. Suppose the Fed adheres to a monetary rule through open-market operations. What amount of U.S. securities will it have to sell to, or buy from, banks or the public between years 1 and 2 to meet its monetary rule?

FURTHER TEST YOUR KNOWLEDGE AT www.mcconnell20e.com

Practice quizzes, student PowerPoints, worked problems, Web-based questions, and additional materials are available at the text's Online Learning Center (OLC), **www.mcconnell20e.com**, or scan here. Need a barcode reader? Try ScanLife, available in your app store.

CHAPTER 5

Government's Role and Government Failure

Learning Objectives

LO5.1 Describe how government's power to coerce can be economically beneficial and list some of the difficulties associated with managing and directing the government.

LO5.2 Discuss "government failure" and explain why it happens.

LO5.3 (Appendix) Explain the difficulties of conveying economic preferences through majority voting.

Governments in market economies perform several economic tasks. As discussed in various places in the book, these include promoting production and trade by defining property rights, enforcing contracts, and settling disputes; enforcing laws designed to maintain competition; redistributing income via taxes and transfers; reallocating resources by producing public goods and intervening to correct negative and positive externalities; and promoting economic growth and full employment.

In this chapter, we deepen our understanding of government's role in the market economy by examining some of the difficulties that democratic governments face when making specific laws related to the economy. We will find that governments sometimes pursue policies for which costs outweigh benefits. These inefficient outcomes happen often enough that we need to be just as vigilant in looking for instances of *government failure* as we are in looking for instances of *market failure*.

Government's Economic Role

LO5.1 Describe how government's power to coerce can be economically beneficial and list some of the difficulties associated with managing and directing the government.

As discussed in Chapter 2, the U.S. economy is a *market system* that uses mostly markets and prices to coordinate and direct economic activity. But the government also has a prominent role in how the economy functions. Among other things, the government sets the laws governing economic activity, provides goods and services that would otherwise be underproduced by private firms, and modifies the distribution of income. The government also promotes both economic stability and economic growth.

Government's Right to Coerce

One key difference between the economic activities of government and those of private firms and individuals is that government possesses the legal right to force people to do things. Whereas private-sector economic activities consist primarily of voluntary transactions, government has the legal right to enforce involuntary transactions. Among other things, the government can put you in jail if you do not pay your taxes, fine you if you violate pollution laws, jail you if you commit fraud, and remove your business license if you violate health and safety regulations.

Force and Economic Efficiency From an economic perspective, the government's ability to force people to do things can be quite beneficial because it can be used to increase economic efficiency.

Correcting for Market Failures Consider public goods and externalities. As discussed in Chapter 4, these market failures cause resource misallocations. When it comes to both public goods and products offering positive externalities, private producers fail to produce enough output because it is impossible to charge many of the beneficiaries for the benefits that they receive from the producers' products. In such cases, the government can improve economic efficiency by using involuntarily collected tax money to subsidize production.

By contrast, products that generate negative externalities are overproduced by the private sector because many of their costs are borne by third parties rather than by their producers. The government can reduce that overproduction and improve economic efficiency by using involuntary policies such as direct controls, pollution

taxes, and cap-and-trade schemes to force producers to bear higher costs.

Reducing Private-Sector Economic Risks Government's ability to force people to do things is also crucial in reducing private-sector economic risks. To begin with, the government helps to ensure that only mutually agreeable transactions take place by making blackmail, extortion, and other forms of private coercion illegal. The government also uses its legal powers to outlaw various forms of theft, deception, and discrimination as well as restraints on trade, price-fixing, and refusal to honor a contract.

These limitations encourage economic activity by giving greater security to both individuals and firms. Because they know that the government will use its massive resources to arrest and punish those who break the law, they know that other individuals and firms are less likely to try to take advantage of them. That reduction in risk encourages higher levels of investment, the formation of more new businesses, and the introduction of more new goods and services. In economic terminology, both allocative and productive efficiency increase.

The Problem of Directing and Managing Government

As just discussed, the government can substantially improve allocative and productive efficiency if it directs its awesome coercive powers toward rectifying market failures and providing a low-risk economic environment for the private sector. However, it has only been in recent centuries that democratic political institutions have been able to tame government and direct it toward those goals. Until that happened, most governments were tyrannical, with their powers almost always directed toward enriching the small minority that controlled each government.

Because modern democratic governments serve much broader constituencies, they are much more likely to pursue economic policies with widespread social benefits. Their ability to deliver economically optimal outcomes is hindered, however, by the wide variety of government failures that this chapter will discuss in detail.

But before discussing them, it will be useful to first point out that governing a nation is not easy. In particular, governments face the daunting challenge of organizing millions of employees to carry out thousands of tasks—everything from cleaning sewers to researching cures for cancer to delivering the mail. An understanding

CONSIDER THIS . . .

Does Big Government Equal Bad Government?

You will sometimes hear politicians (and maybe your grumpy uncle) complaining about Big Government. Their implication is that large government initiatives are inherently inefficient or incompetent.

Since economics is focused on efficiency, you might wonder where economists stand on the subject.

The answer is that economists focus not on bigness or smallness *per se*, but on marginal benefit (MB) and marginal cost (MC). Spending should be increased up to the point where MB = MC. For some programs, that will be a small dollar amount. For other programs, that will be a large dollar amount.

Thus, economists don't see much point in having an abstract debate over "big government" versus "small government." What matters is allocative and productive efficiency and directing government's limited resources toward the programs that generate the largest net benefits for society.

From that vantage point, we should not condemn large government programs just for being large. We must first compare MB with MC. Only if MB < MC should large programs be reduced or eliminated.

of those challenges and complexities will give you a better sense of how well most governments manage to do *despite* all of the problems associated with government failure.

No Invisible Hand Government economic polices are not self-correcting. Unlike the private sector—where competitive forces and Adam Smith's "invisible hand" help to automatically direct resources to their best uses—poorly designed government policies can misallocate resources indefinitely unless active steps are taken by legislators or administrators.

Massive Size and Scope Identifying and correcting inefficient government policies is hampered by government's massive size and scope. Consider the U.S. federal government. In 2010, it had 4.4 million employees spread over 500 agencies that were collectively charged with enforcing hundreds of thousands of pages

of laws and regulations while attempting to wisely spend $3.4 trillion.

The Need for Bureaucracy By law, those 4.4 million federal employees are ultimately supervised and directed by just 536 elected officials: one president, 435 representatives, and 100 senators. Since 536 elected officials could never hope to directly supervise 4.4 million people, governments rely on many layers of supervisors and supervisors-of-supervisors to manage the government's affairs. They collectively form a massive, hierarchical, many-layered bureaucracy.

The Need for Paperwork and Inflexibility To make sure that laws are uniformly enforced and do not vary at the whim of individual bureaucrats, the bureaucracy is regulated by detailed rules and regulations governing nearly every possible action that any individual bureaucrat might be called upon to make. These rules and regulations ensure that laws and regulations are uniformly applied. But they do so at the cost of massive amounts of paperwork and an inability to expeditiously process non-routine situations and requests.

The Information Aggregation Problem Because of their massive size and scope, bureaucracies have difficulty with effectively aggregating and conveying information from their bottom layers to their top layers. As a result, top officials will tend to make many inefficient choices because they do not have enough information to sensibly compare the marginal benefits and marginal costs of individual programs and because they are unable to comprehensively assess opportunity costs and where to best spend funds across the wide variety of programs run by the government.

Lack of Accountability Governments also struggle with accountability. Democratic elections do take place for the elected officials at the top, but because the government undertakes so many activities simultaneously, it is difficult for the electorate to know the details of even a small fraction of what the government is up to at any particular time. As a result, hundreds or even thousands of individual programs may be poorly run without affecting the reelection chances of the incumbent politicians who are supposed to be supervising everything.

Within the bureaucracy itself, individual accountability is also hard to enforce because most bureaucrats have civil service protections that effectively guarantee them a job for life. Those protections reduce corruption by shielding bureaucrats from political pressures. But they also severely constrain the ability of elected officials to hold individual bureaucrats personally responsible for bad decisions.

QUICK REVIEW 5.1

- Government's ability to enforce nonvoluntary transactions can improve economic outcomes by compensating for resource misallocations and by providing a low-risk economic environment for individuals and firms.
- Government economic actions are not automatically self-correcting (as with the "invisible hand" in competitive markets.)
- Democratic governments face several challenges in directing and supervising government's actions, including inflexibility, information aggregation, comparing marginal costs with marginal benefits, assessment of opportunity costs, and accountability.

Government Failure

LO5.2 Discuss "government failure" and explain why it happens.

The term **government failure** refers to economically inefficient outcomes caused by shortcomings in the public sector. One cause of government failure is the voting problems that we discuss at length in this chapter's appendix. But government failures caused by voting problems are somewhat unique in that they are driven by a lack of information about voter preferences. By contrast, most instances of government failure happen *despite* government officials knowing what voters prefer.

In these situations, government failures occur because the incentive structures facing government officials lead them to either put their own interests ahead of voter interests or to put the interests of a minority of voters ahead of those of the majority of voters. Let's examine what economic theory has to say about these situations.

Representative Democracy and the Principal-Agent Problem

Our system of representative democracy has the advantage of allowing us to elect full-time representatives who can specialize in understanding the pros and cons of different potential laws and who have more time to digest their details than the average citizen. But the system also suffers from principal-agent problems.

Principal-agent problems are conflicts that arise when tasks are delegated by one group of people (principals) to another group of people (agents). The conflicts arise because the interests of the agents may not be the same as the interests of the principals, so that the agents may end up taking actions that are opposed by the principals whom they are supposed to be representing.

In the business world, principal-agent problems often arise when the company's managers (the agents) take actions that are not in the best interests of the company's shareholders (the principals). Examples include the managers spending huge amounts of company money on executive jets and lavish offices or holding meetings at expensive resorts. These luxuries are obviously enjoyable to managers but are, of course, not in the best interest of shareholders because the money spent on them could either be reinvested back into the firm to increase future profits or paid out to shareholders immediately as dividends. But to the extent that managers are free to follow their own interests rather than those of their shareholders, they may indeed take these and other actions that are not in the better interests of their shareholders. Hence the conflicts.

In a representative democracy, principal-agent problems often arise because politicians have goals such as reelection that may be inconsistent with pursuing the best interests of their constituents. Indeed, casual reflection suggests that "sound economics" and "good politics" often differ. Sound economics calls for the public sector to pursue various programs as long as marginal benefits exceed marginal costs. Good politics, however, suggests that politicians support programs and policies that will maximize their chances of getting reelected. The result may be that the government will promote the goals of groups of voters that have special interests to the detriment of the larger public. Economic inefficiency is the likely outcome.

Special-Interest Effect   Efficient public decision making is often impaired by the **special-interest effect.** This is any outcome of the political process whereby a small number of people obtain a government program or policy that gives them large gains at the expense of a much greater number of persons who individually suffer small losses.

The small group of potential beneficiaries is well informed and highly vocal on the issue in question, and they press politicians for approval. The large number of people facing the very small individual losses, however, are generally uninformed on the issue. Politicians feel they will lose the campaign contributions and votes of the small special-interest group that backs the issue if they legislate against it but will lose very little support from the large group of

CONSIDER THIS . . .

Mohair and the Collective-Action Problem

Smaller groups can sometimes achieve political victories against larger groups by taking advantage of the **collective-action problem**—the fact that larger groups are more difficult to organize and motivate than smaller groups.

Larger groups are harder to organize and motivate for two main reasons. First, the larger the group, the smaller each member's share of the benefits if the group gets its way. Second, the larger the group, the higher its organizing costs, as it will have to contact and recruit large numbers of strangers via e-mails, telephone calls, and mass mailings.

Smaller groups can take advantage of these difficulties and generally get their way against larger groups as long as they are pressing for policies that only cause small amounts of harm to the members of the larger groups.

Consider the infamous subsidy for mohair, the wool produced by Angora goats. Each year the federal government provides millions of dollars in subsidized loans to Angora goat farmers in Texas, Arizona, and New Mexico. The federal government began the subsidy in the late 1940s to ensure a large supply of insulation for the jackets needed to keep pilots and other crew members warm in the unheated airplanes used during that period.

The mohair subsidy should have ended in the 1950s when heated cabins were developed, but it survives because it costs taxpayers only a few cents each. This means that it would cost them more to organize and defeat the mohair subsidy than they would save by having the subsidy terminated.

More generally, the collective-action problem explains why nearly every example of the special-interest effect is characterized by "concentrated benefits and diffuse costs." Concentrated benefits make proponents easy to organize, while diffuse costs make opponents difficult to organize.

uninformed voters, who are likely to evaluate the politicians on other issues of greater importance to them.

The special-interest effect is also evident in so-called *pork-barrel politics*, a means of securing a government project that yields benefits mainly to a single political district and its political representative. In this case, the special-interest group comprises local constituents, while the larger group consists of relatively uninformed taxpayers scattered across a much larger geographic area. Politicians clearly have a strong incentive to secure government projects ("pork") for their local constituents. Such projects

win political favor because they are highly valued by constituents and the costs are borne mainly by taxpayers located elsewhere.

At the federal level, pork-barrel politics often consist of congressional members inserting specific provisions that authorize spending for local projects (that will benefit only local constituents) into comprehensive legislation (that is supposed to be about making laws for the entire country). Such narrow, specifically designated authorizations of expenditure are called **earmarks**. In 2012, legislation contained 152 such earmarks, totaling $3.3 billion. These earmarks enable senators and representatives to provide benefits to in-state firms and organizations without subjecting the proposals to the usual evaluation and competitive bidding. Although some of the earmarked projects deliver benefits that exceed costs, many others are questionable, at best. These latter expenditures very likely reallocate some of society's scarce resources from higher-valued uses to lower-valued uses. Moreover, logrolling, discussed in the chapter appendix, typically enters the picture. "Vote for my special local project and I will vote for yours" becomes part of the overall strategy for securing "pork" and remaining elected.

Finally, a politician's inclination to support the smaller group of special beneficiaries is enhanced because special-interest groups are often quite willing to help finance the campaigns of "right-minded" politicians and politicians who "bring home the pork." The result is that politicians may support special-interest programs and projects that cannot be justified on economic grounds.

Rent-Seeking Behavior The appeal to government for special benefits at taxpayers' or someone else's expense is called **rent seeking**. The term "rent" in "rent seeking" is used loosely to refer to any payment in excess of the minimum amount that would be needed to keep a resource employed in its current use. Those engaged in "rent seeking" are attempting to use government influence to get themselves into a situation in which they will get paid more for providing a good or service than the minimum amount you would actually have to pay them to provide that good or service. (These excess, or surplus, payments are akin to *land rent*, which is also a surplus payment.)

Rent seeking goes beyond the usual profit seeking through which firms try to increase their profits by adjusting their output levels, improving their products, and incorporating cost-saving technologies. Rent seeking looks to obtain extra profit or income by influencing government policies. Corporations, trade associations, labor unions, and professional organizations employ vast resources to secure favorable government policies that result in rent— higher profit or income than would otherwise occur. The government is able to dispense such rent directly or indirectly through laws, rules, hiring, and purchases. Elected officials are willing to provide such rent because they want to be responsive to the key constituents who can help them remain in office.

Here are some examples of "rent-providing" legislation or policies: tariffs on foreign products that limit competition and raise prices to consumers; tax breaks that benefit specific corporations; government construction projects that create union jobs but cost more than the benefits they yield; occupational licensing that goes beyond what is needed to protect consumers; and large subsidies to farmers by taxpayers. None of these is justified by economic efficiency.

Clear Benefits, Hidden Costs

Some critics say that vote-seeking politicians will ignore economic rationality by failing to objectively weigh costs and benefits when deciding which programs to support. Because political officeholders must seek voter support every few years, they favor programs that have immediate and clear-cut benefits and vague or deferred costs. Conversely, politicians will reject programs with immediate and easily identifiable costs but with less measurable but very high long-term benefits.

Such biases may lead politicians to reject economically justifiable programs and to accept programs that are economically irrational. Example: A proposal to construct or expand mass-transit systems in large metropolitan areas may be economically rational on the basis of cost-benefit analysis. But if (1) the program is to be financed by immediate increases in highly visible income or sales taxes and (2) benefits will occur only years from now when the project is completed, then the vote-seeking politician may oppose the program.

Assume, on the other hand, that a program of federal aid to municipal police forces is not justifiable on the basis of cost-benefit analysis. But if the cost is paid for from budget surpluses, the program's modest benefits may seem so large that it will gain approval.

Unfunded Liabilities

The political tendency to favor spending priorities that have immediate payouts but deferred costs also leads to many government programs having unfunded liabilities. A government creates an **unfunded liability** when it commits to making a series of future expenditures without simultaneously committing to collect enough tax revenues to pay for those expenditures.

The most famous example of an unfunded liability belongs to the Social Security program, under which the U.S. federal government supplements the incomes of the elderly and the disabled. The government does collect Social Security taxes to help defray the expected future costs of the program, but the current tax rates will not generate nearly enough revenue to pay for all of the expected outlays. In fact, it is estimated that Social Security has an unfunded liability (= total value of spending commitments minus expected value of tax revenues) of $20.5 trillion.

Social Security is not the only major unfunded government liability. Medicare, which provides healthcare to the elderly and disabled in the United States, has an unfunded liability of $4.8 trillion, while state and local governments are estimated to have $4.6 trillion in unfunded retirement and healthcare commitments.

Chronic Budget Deficits

A government runs an annual **budget deficit** whenever its tax revenues are less than its spending during a particular year. To make up for the shortfall, the government must borrow money, usually by issuing bonds. Whatever it borrows in a given year gets added to its overall pile of debt, which is the accumulation of all past budget deficits and budget surpluses.

Many governments run budget deficits year after year. These chronic deficits can be attributed to a pair of conflicting incentives that confront politicians. On the one hand, many government programs are highly popular with voters, so that there is almost always political pressure to either maintain or increase spending. On the other hand, hardly anyone likes paying taxes, so there is almost always political pressure to reduce taxes. Faced with those two conflicting pressures, politicians tend to opt for spending levels that exceed tax revenues.

That may be problematic because chronic deficits can pose several economic challenges, including

- *Economic Inefficiency* Deficits may allow the government to control and direct an inefficiently large fraction of the economy's resources. To the extent that deficit spending facilitates an underallocation of resources to the private sector and an overallocation of resources to the government sector, there will be a tendency to underproduce private goods and overproduce public goods. If that occurs, the economy will experience a decrease in both allocative and productive efficiency.

- *Debt Crises* A government's accumulated debt level may rise so high that investors lose faith in the government's ability or willingness to repay its debts.

If that happens, the government will find itself in the middle of a **debt crisis,** unable to borrow any more money. Cut off from borrowing, the government will be forced to undertake some combination of drastic spending cuts or massive tax increases. Either of those actions will tend to plunge the economy into a recessionary period in which unemployment rises and output falls.

To prevent politicians from succumbing to voter preferences for deficits, many state and local governments have balanced-budget laws that make deficits illegal. No such law exists at the national level, however. As a result, federal politicians were able to run budget deficits in 47 of the 52 years between 1960 and 2012.

Misdirection of Stabilization Policy

Economies go through alternating periods of expansion and recession. Multiyear periods during which output expands, employment increases, and living standards rise alternate with periods during which output contracts, employment decreases, and living standards fall.

Governments often attempt to smooth out these so-called *business cycles* by using two types of macroeconomic stabilization policy:

- **Fiscal policy** attempts to use changes in tax rates and spending levels to offset the business cycle. For example, if the economy is going into a recessionary period with falling output and rising unemployment, the government may attempt to stimulate the economy by lowering tax rates or increasing government spending. Either action should increase spending on goods and services and consequently induce business to produce more output and hire more workers.

- **Monetary policy** attempts to use changes in interest rates to regulate the economy. In particular, the government can use its control over the money supply to lower interest rates during a recession. The lower interest rates stimulate spending by making it cheaper for individuals and businesses to borrow money to pay for capital goods such as houses, cars, and machinery. As spending on those items increases, firms are induced to produce more output and hire more workers.

Politicization of Fiscal and Monetary Policy   Fiscal and monetary policy are both subject to politicization. In the case of fiscal policy, if the economy goes into recession

and there are calls to stimulate the economy through lower taxes or increased spending, politicians often spend more time attempting to target any tax cuts or spending increases toward special interests than they do making sure that their fiscal policy actions will actually stimulate the overall economy. The recession also provides political cover for increasing the size of the deficit.

Monetary policy can be similarly politicized, with the biggest problem being that incumbent politicians will want to cut interest rates to boost the economy right before they are up for reelection. That is problematic because monetary stimulus is only helpful if the economy is in recession. If the economy is doing well, monetary stimulus can actually make things worse because it can raise the rate of inflation and drive up prices all over the economy.

To prevent that, most countries have put politically independent central banks in charge of monetary policy. In the United States, the Federal Reserve serves this function. Other top central banks include the Bank of Japan, the Bank of England, and the European Central Bank. Each is run by professional economists who are insulated from political pressures so that they may use their independent expertise and judgment to decide if and when monetary stimulus should be used.

QUICK REVIEW 5.2

- Principal-agent problems are conflicts that occur when the agents who are supposed to be acting in the best interests of their principals instead take actions that help themselves but hurt their principals.
- Because larger groups are more difficult to organize and motivate than smaller groups, special interests can often obtain what they want politically even when what they want is opposed by a majority of voters.
- Rent seeking involves influencing government policies so that one can get paid more for providing a good or service than it costs to produce.
- Political pressures cause politicians to favor policies such as unfunded liabilities and budget deficits that have immediate benefits and delayed costs.

Limited and Bundled Choice

Economic theory points out that the political process forces citizens and their elected representatives to be less selective in choosing public goods and services than they are in choosing private goods and services.

In the marketplace, the citizen as a consumer can exactly satisfy personal preferences by buying certain goods and not buying others. However, in the public sector the citizen as a voter is confronted with, say, only two or three candidates for an office, each representing a different "bundle" of programs (public goods and services). None of these bundles of public goods is likely to fit exactly the preferences of any particular voter. Yet the voter must choose one of them. The candidate who comes closest to voter Smith's preference may endorse national health insurance, increases in Social Security benefits, subsidies to tobacco farmers, and tariffs on imported goods. Smith is likely to vote for that candidate even though Smith strongly opposes tobacco subsidies.

In other words, the voter must take the bad with the good. In the public sector, people are forced to "buy" goods and services they do not want. It is as if, in going to a sporting-goods store, you were forced to buy an unwanted pool cue to get a wanted pair of running shoes. This is a situation where resources are not being used efficiently to satisfy consumer wants. In this sense, the provision of public goods and services is inherently inefficient.

Congress is confronted with a similar limited-choice, bundled-goods problem. Appropriations legislation combines hundreds, even thousands, of spending items into a single bill. Many of these spending items may be completely unrelated to the main purpose of the legislation. Yet congressional representatives must vote on the entire package—yea or nay. Unlike consumers in the marketplace, they cannot be selective.

Bureaucracy and Inefficiency

Some economists contend that public agencies are generally less efficient than private businesses. The reason is not that lazy and incompetent workers somehow end up in the public sector while ambitious and capable people gravitate to the private sector. Rather, it is that the market system creates incentives for internal efficiency that are absent from the public sector. Private enterprises have a clear goal—profit. Whether a private firm is in a competitive or monopolistic market, efficient management means lower costs and higher profit. The higher profit not only benefits the firm's owners but enhances the promotion prospects of the firm's managers. Moreover, part of the managers' pay may be tied to profit via profit-sharing plans, bonuses, and stock options. There is no similar gain to government agencies and their managers—no counterpart to profit—to create a strong incentive to achieve efficiency.

CONSIDER THIS . . .

Unintended Consequences

As explained in Chapters 2 and 4, the "invisible hand" of a properly functioning market will allocate resources to their best uses without anyone being in charge or intentionally aiming for efficiency. By contrast, governments are willful and intentional. They deliberately create and enforce laws to try to make improvements in society. In some cases, however, government actions can have **unintended consequences** that offset some or all of the intended benefits.

- Government fuel-efficiency requirements for automobiles have forced automakers to produce smaller, lighter vehicles. But when smaller, lighter vehicles get into accidents, their occupants are more likely to be killed or severely injured. Some estimates put the death toll at over 120,000 additional deaths in the United States since 1970.

- San Francisco banned plastic grocery bags in 2007. This led to about 5 additional deaths per year from food-borne illnesses because reusable grocery bags almost never get washed out. Drippings from one trip often fester and contaminate whatever they touch on subsequent trips.

- The main point of the 2010 healthcare reform law (commonly known as Obamacare) was to get health insurance coverage for all Americans. To that end, the law required larger companies to either pay for extremely costly health insurance policies for their full-time workers or face massive fines. But since that requirement only applied to full-time workers, many firms responded by cutting a lot of their employees' work hours down from full time to part time. Thus, millions of workers went from lacking health insurance but having a full-time job to still lacking health insurance but only having a part-time job.

The market system imposes a very obvious test of performance on private firms: the test of profit and loss. An efficient firm is profitable and therefore successful; it survives, prospers, and grows. An inefficient firm is unprofitable and unsuccessful; it declines and in time goes out of business. But there is no similar, clear-cut test with which to assess the efficiency or inefficiency of public agencies. How can anyone determine whether a public hydroelectricity provider, a state university, a local fire department, the Department of Agriculture, or the Bureau of Indian Affairs is operating efficiently?

Cynics even argue that a public agency that inefficiently uses its resources is likely to survive and grow! In the private sector, inefficiency and monetary loss lead to the abandonment of certain activities or products or even firms. But the government, they say, does not like to abandon activities in which it has failed. Some suggest that the typical response of the government to a program's failure is to increase its budget and staff. This means that public sector inefficiency just continues on a larger scale.

Furthermore, economists assert that government employees, together with the special-interest groups they serve, often gain sufficient political clout to block attempts to pare down or eliminate their agencies. Politicians who attempt to reduce the size of huge federal bureaucracies such as those relating to agriculture, education, health and welfare, and national defense incur sizable political risk because bureaucrats and special-interest groups will team up to defeat them.

Finally, critics point out that government bureaucrats tend to justify their continued employment by looking for and eventually finding new problems to solve. It is not surprising that social "problems," as defined by government, persist or even expand.

The Last Word at the end of this chapter highlights several recent media-reported examples of the special-interest effect (including earmarks), the problem of limited and bundled choices, and problems of government bureaucracy.

Inefficient Regulation and Intervention

Governments regulate many aspects of the market economy. Examples include health and safety regulations, environmental laws, banking supervision, restrictions on monopoly power, and the imposition of wage and price controls.

These interventions are designed to improve economic outcomes, but several forms of regulation and intervention have been known to generate outcomes that are less beneficial than intended.

Regulatory Capture A government agency that is supposed to supervise a particular industry is said to have suffered from **regulatory capture** if its regulations and enforcement activities come to be heavily influenced by the industry that it is supposed to be regulating.

Regulatory capture is often facilitated by the fact that nearly everyone who knows anything about the details of a regulated industry works in the industry. So when it comes time for the regulatory agency to find qualified people to help write intelligent regulations, it ends up hiring a lot of people from regulated firms. Those individuals bring their old opinions and sympathies with them when they become bureaucrats. As a result, many regulations end up favoring the interests of the regulated firms.

Regulatory Capture in the Railroad Industry The classic example of regulatory capture is that of railroad regulation during the nineteenth and twentieth centuries. In response to public complaints that the nation's railroads were often charging exorbitant rates, the federal government established the Interstate Commerce Commission (ICC) in 1887 as the government agency charged with regulating competition and prices within the railroad industry.

Within a generation, railroad executives had achieved regulatory capture by manipulating the ICC into a policy that simultaneously fixed rates at profitable levels while also eliminating competition between different railroad companies. The public justification for these policies was that competition had to be restricted in order to prevent larger railroads from bankrupting smaller railroads and thereby becoming monopolies that could easily exploit the public. But the railroad industry's true motive was to establish a regulatory regime in which both larger and small railroads were guaranteed steady, competition-free profits.

These days, activists often complain that various government bureaucracies are subject to regulatory capture. At the federal level, complaints are voiced about the Food and Drug Administration's supervision of the pharmaceutical industry, the Securities and Exchange Commission's supervision of Wall Street financial firms, and the Bureau of Land Management's policies with respect to leasing federal lands for oil drilling, mining, and forestry.

Deregulation as an Alternative Economists are divided about the intensity and inefficiency of regulatory capture as well as what to do about it. One potential solution is for the government to engage in **deregulation** and intentionally remove most or even all of the regulations governing an industry.

Deregulation solves the problem of regulatory capture because there is no regulatory agency left to capture. But it only works well in terms of economic efficiency if the deregulated industry becomes competitive and is automatically guided toward allocative and productive efficiency by competitive forces and the invisible hand. If the deregulated industry instead tends toward monopoly or ends up generating substantial negative externalities, continued regulation might be the better option.

Proponents of deregulation often cite the deregulation of interstate trucking, railroads, and airlines in the 1970s and 1980s as examples of competition successfully replacing regulation. They do so because after regulation was removed, robust competition led to lower prices, increased output, and higher levels of productivity and efficiency.

But for government agencies tasked with environmental protection, human safety, and financial regulation, there is less confidence as to whether competitive pressures might be able to replace regulation. For those industries, regulation may always be necessary. If so, then some amount of regulatory capture may always be likely due to the fact that regulated firms will always want to capture their regulators.

Government's Poor Investment Track Record

Governments are often asked to use taxpayer money to directly invest in private businesses that have been unable to secure funding from private sources such as banks. Unfortunately, researchers have found that low and negative rates of return are the norm for government investments. In addition, government funding often allows inefficient firms to persist in operation long after competitive forces would have put them out of operation and freed up their resources for higher-valued projects elsewhere in the economy.

Critics also note that many government investments look like prime examples of rent seeking and the special-interest effect, especially when the firms receiving government investments are found to have made substantial financial contributions to influential politicians. In too many cases, the government's investment decisions appear to be based on political connections rather than on whether specific investments can produce substantial net benefits for society.

Loan Guarantees

Loan Guarantees The government also tends to earn low or negative returns when it subsidizes private-sector investments with **loan guarantees.** The startup company named Solyndra provides a good example of what can go wrong.

The Solyndra Subsidy In 2009, Solyndra was unable to convince private investors to lend it enough money to start producing solar panels with its new technology. The private investors sensibly feared that the company's new technology was too expensive and that its solar panels would not be able to compete with those made by the industry's more established firms.

At that point, Solyndra turned to a federal loan-guarantee program under which the Department of Energy told potential investors that it would cosign any loan taken out by Solyndra and thereby guarantee that if Solyndra went bankrupt, the federal government would use taxpayer money to repay the loan.

With that loan guarantee in place, the otherwise-reluctant private investors were willing to put in $535 million. After all, they had nothing to lose and everything to gain. If Solyndra went bankrupt, they would get their money back from the government. But if Solyndra somehow did well, they would collect substantial returns.

Unfortunately, the investors' original doubts proved to be well founded. Solyndra was unable to compete effectively with incumbent firms and went bankrupt in 2011, leaving taxpayers on the hook for the full $535 million.

Socializing Losses, Privatizing Gains Government loan guarantees can be socially beneficial if they help to increase the production of beneficial products that are being underproduced by the private sector—as would be the case for products that generated positive externalities. But the loan guarantees also provide an inducement toward reckless investing because they remove from private investors any consideration of losses. Indeed, loan guarantees are often criticized for "socializing losses and privatizing gains" because if things go wrong, any losses go to the taxpayer, while if things go well, any profits go to private investors.

In addition, the process by which loan guarantees are awarded is often criticized for being highly politicized and likely to award loan guarantees not to the firms whose projects are the most likely to increase economic efficiency but to those with the best political connections.

On the other hand, there may be legitimate cases where a new technology that would generate net benefits cannot be developed without government loan guarantees, so proponents of loan-guarantee programs argue that the programs should remain in place, but with tight controls against rent seeking and the special-interest effect.

Corruption

Political corruption is the unlawful misdirection of governmental resources or actions that occurs when government officials abuse their entrusted powers for personal gain. For instance, a police supervisor engages in political corruption if she accepts a bribe in exchange for illegally freeing a thief who had been lawfully arrested by another

GLOBAL PERSPECTIVE 5.1

Percentage of Households Paying a Bribe in the Past Year

The Global Corruption Barometer is an international survey that asks individuals about their personal experiences with government corruption. The 2010–2011 survey of 105,507 people in 100 countries included a question that asked participants whether they or anyone in their respective households had paid a bribe in any form during the previous 12 months. Here are the results for 10 selected countries.

Percent of Households Paying a Bribe in the Past Year

Source: Adapted from *Global Corruption Barometer.* Copyright 2011 Transparency International: the global coalition against corruption. Used with permission. For more information, visit **www.transparency.org**.

officer. Similarly, a government bureaucrat engages in political corruption if he refuses to issue a building permit to a homebuilder who is in full compliance with the law unless the homebuilder makes a "voluntary contribution" to the bureaucrat's favorite charity.

While relatively uncommon in the United States, political corruption is a daily reality in many parts of the world, as can be seen in Global Perspective 5.1, which gives the percentages of survey respondents in 15 countries who reported that they or someone else in their respective households paid a bribe during the previous 12 months.

Political corruption comes in two basic forms. In the first, a government official must be bribed to do what he should be doing as part of his job—as with the bureaucrat in our earlier example who demands a bribe to issue a permit to a homebuilder who is in full compliance with the law. In the second, a government official demands a bribe to do something that she is not legally entitled to do—as

with the police supervisor in our earlier example who illegally freed a thief.

If a candidate accepts campaign contributions from a special-interest group and then shows subsequent support for that group's legislative goals, has a subtle form of political corruption taken place? While there are strong opinions on both sides of the issue, it is often hard to tell in any particular case whether a special interest's campaign contribution amounts to a bribe. On the one hand, the special interest may indeed be trying to influence the politician's vote. On the other hand, the special interest may simply be trying to support and get elected a person who already sees things their way and who would vote the way they wanted no matter what.

That being said, the impression of impropriety lingers, and so laws have been passed in the United States limiting the amount of money that individuals can donate to specific candidates and making it illegal for certain groups such as companies to donate money directly to individual politicians (as distinct from directing funds toward supporting specific issues or advocacy groups—which is both legal and unrestricted). Proponents of these laws hope that the limitations strike a good balance—allowing contributions to be large enough that individuals and groups can meaningfully support candidates they agree with but keeping contributions small enough that no one individual or group can singlehandedly donate enough money to sway a politician's vote.

Imperfect Institutions

It is possible to argue that the wide variety of criticisms of public sector inefficiency that we have discussed in this chapter are exaggerated and cynical. Perhaps they are. Nevertheless, they do tend to shatter the concept of a benevolent government that responds with precision and efficiency to the wants of its citizens. The market system of the private sector is far from perfectly efficient, and government's economic function is mainly to correct that system's shortcomings. But the public sector is also subject to deficiencies in fulfilling its economic function. "The relevant comparison is not between perfect markets and imperfect governments, nor between faulty markets and all-knowing, rational, benevolent governments, but between inevitably imperfect institutions."[1]

Because markets and governments are both imperfect, it is sometimes difficult to determine whether a particular activity can be performed with greater success in the private

---

[1]Otto Eckstein, *Public Finance*, 3d ed. (Englewood Cliffs, N.J.: Prentice-Hall, 1973), p. 17.

LAST WORD

"Government Failure" in the News

The Media Continually Report Government Actions That Illustrate Pork-Barrel Politics, Limited and Bundled Choices, or Bureaucratic Inefficiency.

Examples:

- A 2004 spending bill set aside $1 million for the Norwegian American Foundation; $443,000 to develop salmon-fortified baby food; $350,000 for music education programs at the Rock and Roll Hall of Fame in Cleveland; and $250,000 for sidewalks, street furniture, and façade improvements in Boca Raton, Florida. (Associated Press)

- The corporate tax relief bill of 2004 contained 633 pages, with 276 special provisions. Included were provisions that benefited "restaurant owners and Hollywood producers; makers of bows, arrows, tackle boxes, and sonar fish finders; NASCAR track owners; native Alaska whalers; and even importers of Chinese fans." (*The Washington Post*)

- Government investigations determined that millions of dollars of disaster relief for victims of Hurricane Katrina were squandered. For example, investigators discovered that the Federal Emergency Management Agency (FEMA) made payouts on as many as 900,000 claims for disaster relief that contained invalid Social Security numbers or false names and addresses. (*The Seattle Times*)

- The $878 billion American Recovery and Reinvestment Act of 2009 was laden with many dubious spending projects, including $10 million to renovate a train station in Elizabethtown, Pennsylvania, that hadn't been used in 30 years; $1.15 million to build a guardrail for an artificial lake in Woodward, Oklahoma, that had never been filled with water; and an unrequested $587,661 grant that was given to the upscale town of Union, New York, to fight a homeless problem that it didn't have. (*Lancaster Newspapers*, **newson6.com**, *Binghamton Press & Sun Union*)

- The year 2009 also saw Congress approve a $2.5 billion earmark to purchase ten C-17 aircraft despite the Department of Defense adamantly stating that its existing fleet of 205 C-17s was "sufficient to meet the Department's future airlift needs—even under the most stressing situations." (**investinganswers.com**)

- In 2011, Congress funded a sanctuary for white squirrels, an antique bicycle museum, and a giant roadside coffee pot as part of 2011 federal highway spending. It also spent $765,828 to subsidize the construction of an IHOP restaurant and $113,277 to aid in the historical preservation of video games. (*Human Events, Washington Examiner, Gamasutra*)

- A 2011 audit revealed that the federal government had paid $600 million in retirement benefits to deceased federal retirees over the previous five years. Checks had been illegally cashed by living relatives. One son received cumulative payments of $515,000 over the 37 years after his father died in 1971. The fraud was only discovered after the son died in 2008. (Associated Press)

sector or in the public sector. It is easy to reach agreement on opposite extremes: National defense must lie with the public sector, while automobile production can best be accomplished by the private sector. But what about health insurance? Parks and recreation areas? Fire protection? Garbage collection? Housing? Education? It is hard to assess every good or service and to say absolutely that it should be assigned to either the public sector or the private sector. Evidence: All the goods and services just mentioned are provided in part by *both* private enterprises and public agencies.

QUICK REVIEW 5.3

- Unlike the private sector—where the profit motive helps to ensure efficiency and variety—government lacks a strong incentive to be efficient and typically offers only limited and bundled choices.

- Regulatory capture occurs when a regulated industry can control its government regulator and get it to implement policies that favor the industry.

- Political corruption occurs when government officials abuse their powers for personal gain.

SUMMARY

LO5.1 Describe how government's power to coerce can be economically beneficial and list some of the difficulties associated with managing and directing the government.

Government's legal right to use coercion and force can help to improve economic efficiency by correcting for market failures and by enforcing laws and regulations that reduce the risk that individuals and firms will be taken advantage of.

LO5.2 Discuss "government failure" and explain why it happens.

Special interests can succeed in perpetuating policies that are opposed by the majority of voters because the costs of organizing and motivating groups to take political action increase with group size. This collective-action problem implies that special interests can perpetuate unpopular policies as long as the costs of organizing an opposition exceed the costs that the general public is currently suffering as a result of those policies.

There are powerful incentives for politicians to accommodate rent seeking and support special-interest legislation.

Because voters like receiving the benefits of government programs but do not like having to pay the taxes necessary to finance them, politicians tend to favor programs that offer easily identified immediate benefits but vague or deferred costs. This tendency helps to explain the unfunded liabilities of programs including Social Security as well as the federal government's tendency to run budget deficits.

When the economy goes into recession, politicians often use the need for fiscal policy stimulus as political cover to direct lower taxes or increased spending toward politically powerful special-interest groups. To prevent politicians from using lower interest rates and monetary stimulus as a way of increasing their reelection chances, most governments have put politically independent central banks in charge of monetary policy.

Economic theorists cite several reasons why government might be inefficient in providing public goods. (a) Citizens as voters and congressional representatives face limited and bundled choices as to public goods, whereas consumers in the private sector can be highly selective in their choices. (b) Government bureaucracies have less incentive to operate efficiently than do private businesses. (c) Regulated industries may sometimes capture their government regulatory agencies and mold government polices toward their own best interests.

Government's track record as an investor in private-sector firms is very poor, with most government investments into private sector businesses generating low or negative returns for taxpayers.

Government attempts to increase private investment by offering loan guarantees often cause resources to be misdirected toward high-risk projects that have an extremely low likelihood of success. These arrangements "socialize losses and privatize gains" because if the businesses go bankrupt, the government bears the losses, but if they do well, private individuals receive the profits.

Political corruption may cause governmental resources or actions to be misdirected.

Neither governments nor markets are perfect economic institutions. Each has its own set of shortcomings and citizens should be aware of where each is likely to fail and where each is likely to succeed.

TERMS AND CONCEPTS

government failure

principal-agent problems

collective-action problem

special-interest effect

earmarks

rent seeking

unfunded liability

budget deficit

debt crisis

fiscal policy

monetary policy

unintended consequences

regulatory capture

deregulation

loan guarantees

political corruption

The following and additional problems can be found in **connect**

DISCUSSION QUESTIONS

1. Why might citizens interested in maximizing economic efficiency be happy to invest their government with the right to coerce them in at least some situations? **LO5.1**

2. Jean-Baptiste Colbert was the Minister of Finance under King Louis XIV of France. He famously observed, "The art of taxation consists in so plucking the goose as to obtain the

largest possible amount of feathers with the smallest possible amount of hissing." How does his comment relate to special interests and the collective-action problem? **LO5.2**

3. What is rent seeking and how does it differ from the kinds of profit maximization and profit seeking that we discussed in previous chapters? Provide an actual or hypothetical example of rent seeking by firms in an industry. By a union. By a professional association (for example, physicians, school teachers, or lawyers). Why do elected officials often accommodate rent-seeking behavior, particularly by firms, unions, and professional groups located in their home states? **LO5.2**

4. How does the problem of limited and bundled choice in the public sector relate to economic efficiency? Why are

public bureaucracies possibly less efficient than business firms? **LO5.2**

5. Discuss the political incentives that helped motivate federal politicians to approve budget deficits in all but four years between 1960 and 2012. **LO5.2**

6. Explain: "Politicians would make more rational economic decisions if they weren't running for reelection every few years." **LO5.2**

7. Critique: "Thank goodness we have so many government regulatory agencies. They keep Big Business in check." **LO5.2**

8. **LAST WORD** How do the concepts of pork-barrel politics and the special-interest effect relate to the items listed in the Last Word?

REVIEW QUESTIONS

1. Select all of the following that are true. To an economist, a coercive government can be useful in order to: **LO5.1**
   a. Reallocate resources in order to improve efficiency.
   b. Fight negative externalities.
   c. Ensure low gasoline prices.
   d. Provide a low-risk economic environment for individuals and firms.

2. To an economist, a government program is too big if an analysis of that program finds that MB _____ MC. **LO5.1**
   a. Is greater than.
   b. Is less than.
   c. Is equal to.
   d. Is less than twice as large as.
   e. Is more than twice as large as.

3. Tammy Hall is the mayor of a large U.S. city. She has just established the Office of Window Safety. Because windows sometimes break and spray glass shards, every window in the city will now have to pass an annual safety inspection. Property owners must pay the $5-per-window cost—and by the way, Tammy has made her nephew the new head of the Office of Window Safety. This new policy is an example of: **LO5.2**
   a. Political corruption.
   b. Earmarks.
   c. Rent seeking.
   d. Adverse selection.

4. A few hundred U.S. sugar makers lobby the U.S. government each year to make sure that the government taxes imported sugar at a high rate. They do so because the policy drives up the domestic price of sugar and increases their profits. It is estimated that the policy benefits U.S. sugar producers by about $1 billion per year while costing U.S. consumers upwards of $2 billion per year. Which of the following concepts apply to the U.S. sugar tax? **LO5.2**
   Select one or more of the choices shown.
   a. Political corruption.
   b. Rent-seeking behavior.
   c. The collective-action problem.
   d. The special-interest effect.

5. _____ occur when politicians commit to making a series of future expenditures without simultaneously committing to collect enough tax revenues to pay for those expenditures. **LO5.2**
   a. Budget deficits.
   b. Debt crises.
   c. Loan guarantees.
   d. Unfunded liabilities.

PROBLEMS

1. Suppose that there are 1 million federal workers at the lowest level of the federal bureaucracy and that above them there are multiple layers of supervisors and supervisors-of-supervisors. Assume that each higher level is one-tenth the size of the one below it because the government is using a 10:1 ratio of supervisees to supervisors. That is, for every 10 workers at the bottom, there is 1 supervisor; for every 10 of those supervisors, there is 1 supervisor-of-supervisors; for every one of those supervisors-of-supervisors, there is a

supervisor-of-supervisors-of-supervisors; and so on, all the way up the bureaucratic pyramid to the president. **LO5.1**
   a. How many supervisors will there be in each supervisory layer of the federal bureaucracy? Start with the layer of supervisors directly above the 1 million workers at the bottom.
   b. How many supervisors are there in total at all levels of the federal bureaucratic pyramid, including the president?

c. If you count the 1 million workers at the bottom as the first layer of the federal bureaucracy, how many total layers are there, including the president?

d. How many federal employees are there in total at all layers, including the president?

e. What fraction of all federal employees are supervisory, including the president?

2. Consider a specific example of the special-interest effect and the collective-action problem. In 2009, it was estimated that the total value of all corn production subsidies in the United States was about $4 billion. The population of the United States was approximately 300 million people that year. **LO5.2**

a. On average, how much did corn subsidies cost per person in the United States in 2009? (Hint: A billion is a 1 followed by nine zeros. A million is a 1 followed by six zeros.)

b. If each person in the United States is only willing to spend $0.50 to support efforts to overturn the corn subsidy, and if antisubsidy advocates can only raise funds from 10 percent of the population, how much money will they be able to raise for their lobbying efforts?

c. If the recipients of corn subsidies donate just one percent of the total amount that they receive in subsidies, how much could they raise to support lobbying efforts to continue the corn subsidy?

d. By how many dollars does the amount raised by the recipients of the corn subsidy exceed the amount raised by the opponents of the corn subsidy?

3. Consider a corrupt provincial government in which each housing inspector examines two newly built structures each week. All the builders in the province are unethical and want to increase their profits by using substandard construction materials, but they can't do that unless they can bribe a housing inspector into approving a substandard building. **LO5.2**

a. If bribes cost $1,000 each, how much will a housing inspector make each year in bribes? (Assume that each

inspector works 52 weeks a year and gets bribed for every house he inspects.)

b. There is a provincial construction supervisor who gets to hire all of the housing inspectors. He himself is corrupt and expects his housing inspectors to share their bribes with him. Suppose that 20 inspectors work for him and that each passes along half the bribes collected from builders. How much will the construction supervisor collect each year?

c. Corrupt officials may have an incentive to reduce the provision of government services to help line their own pockets. Suppose that the provincial construction supervisor decides to cut the total number of housing inspectors from 20 to 10 in order to decrease the supply of new housing permits. This decrease in the supply of permits raises the equilibrium bribe from $1,000 to $2,500. How much per year will the construction supervisor now receive if he is still getting half of all the bribes collected by the 10 inspectors? How much more is the construction supervisor getting now than when he had 20 inspectors working in part *b*? Will he personally be happy with the reduction in government services?

d. What if reducing the number of inspectors from 20 to 10 only increased the equilibrium bribe from $1,000 to $1,500? In this case, how much per year would the construction supervisor collect from his 10 inspectors? How much *less* is the construction supervisor getting than when he had 20 inspectors working in part *b*? In this case, will the construction supervisor be happy with the reduction in government services? Will he want to go back to using 20 inspectors?

Public Choice Theory and Voting Paradoxes

LO5.3 Explain the difficulties of conveying economic preferences through majority voting.

Public Choice Theory

Market failures, such as public goods and externalities, impede economic efficiency and justify government intervention in the economy.

But the government's response to market failures is not without its own problems and pitfalls. In fact, government can sometimes fail as badly or even worse than markets in terms of delivering economic efficiency and directing resources to the uses where they will bring the largest net benefits.

That is why it is important to study **public choice theory**—the economic analysis of government decision making, politics, and elections. Just as the study of *market failure* helps us to understand how regulating markets may help to improve the allocation of resources, the study of *government failure* can help us to understand how changes in the way government functions might help it to operate more efficiently.

ORIGIN OF THE IDEA

O5.1

Public choice theory

As we will discuss shortly, many instances of government failure can be traced to incentive structures that lead political representatives to pursue policies that go against the preferences of the people that they are representing. But an even more fundamental problem exists. The majority voting systems that we rely upon may make it difficult or even impossible to correctly discern voter preferences. In such cases, it is not surprising that government fails to deliver what the voters actually want.

Revealing Preferences through Majority Voting

Through some process, society must decide which public goods it wants and in what amounts. It also must determine the extent to which it wants government to intervene in private markets to correct externalities. Decisions need to be made about the extent and type of regulation of business that is necessary, the amount of income redistribution that is desirable, what policies the government might enact to mitigate asymmetric information problems, and other such choices. Furthermore, society must determine the set of taxes it thinks is best for financing government. How should government apportion (divide) the total tax burden among the public?

Decisions such as these are made collectively in the United States through a democratic process that relies heavily on majority voting. Candidates for office offer alternative policy packages, and citizens elect people who they think will make the best decisions on their collective behalf. Voters "retire" officials who do not adequately represent their collective wishes and elect persons they think do. Also, citizens periodically have opportunities at the state and local levels to vote directly on public expenditures or new legislation.

Although the democratic process does a reasonably good job of revealing society's preferences, it is imperfect. Public choice theory demonstrates that majority voting can produce inefficiencies and inconsistencies.

Inefficient Voting Outcomes

Society's well-being is enhanced when government provides a public good whose total benefit exceeds its total cost. Unfortunately, majority voting does not always deliver that outcome.

Illustration: Inefficient "No" Vote Assume that the government can provide a public good, say, national defense, at a total expense of $900. Also assume that there are only three individuals—Adams, Benson, and Conrad—in the society and that they will share the $900 tax expense equally, each being taxed $300 if the proposed public good is provided. And assume, as Figure 1a illustrates, that Adams would receive $700 worth of benefits from having this public good; Benson, $250; and Conrad, $200.

What will be the result if a majority vote determines whether or not this public good is provided? Although people do not always vote strictly according to their own economic interest, it is likely Benson and Conrad will vote "no"

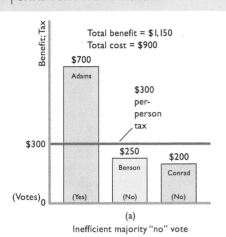

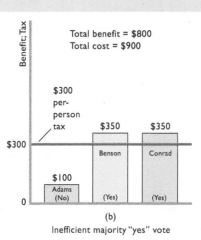

FIGURE 1 **Inefficient voting outcomes.** Majority voting can produce inefficient decisions. (a) Majority voting leads to rejection of a public good that would entail a greater total benefit than total cost. (b) Majority voting results in acceptance of a public good that has a higher total cost than total benefit.

(a) Inefficient majority "no" vote

(b) Inefficient majority "yes" vote

because they will incur tax costs of $300 each while gaining benefits of only $250 and $200, respectively. Adams will vote "yes." So the majority vote will defeat the proposal even though the total benefit of $1,150 (= $700 for Adams + $250 for Benson + $200 for Conrad) exceeds the total cost of $900. Resources should be devoted to this good, but they will not be. Too little of this public good will be produced.

Illustration: Inefficient "Yes" Vote Now consider a situation in which the majority favors a public good even though its total cost exceeds its total benefit. Figure 1b shows the details. Again, Adams, Benson, and Conrad will equally share the $900 cost of the public good; each will be taxed $300. But since Adams' benefit now is only $100 from the public good, she will vote against it. Meanwhile, Benson and Conrad will benefit by $350 each. They will vote for the public good because that benefit ($350) exceeds their tax payments ($300). The majority vote will provide a public good costing $900 that produces total benefits of only $800 (= $100 for Adams + $350 for Benson + $350 for Conrad). Society's resources will be inefficiently allocated to this public good. Too much of it will be produced.

Implications The point is that an inefficient outcome may occur as either an overproduction or an underproduction of a specific public good, and therefore as an overallocation or underallocation of resources for that particular use. In Chapter 4 we saw that government can improve economic efficiency by providing public goods that the market system will not make available. Now we have extended that analysis to reveal that government may not provide some of those public goods or may provide them in the wrong amounts. In other cases, it may provide public goods that are not economically warranted.

In our examples, each person has only a single vote, no matter how much he or she might gain or lose from a public good. In the first example (inefficient "no" vote), Adams

would be willing to purchase a vote from either Benson or Conrad if buying votes were legal. That way Adams could be assured of obtaining the national defense she so highly values. But since buying votes is illegal, many people with strong preferences for certain public goods may have to go without them.

When individual consumers have a strong preference for a specific *private good*, they usually can find that good in the marketplace even though it may be unpopular with the majority of consumers. A consumer can buy beef tongue, liver, and squid in some supermarkets, although it is doubtful that any of these products would be available if majority voting stocked the shelves. But a person cannot easily "buy" a *public good* such as national defense once the majority has decided against it.

Conversely, a consumer in the marketplace can decide against buying a particular product, even a popular one. But although you may not want national defense, you must "buy" it through your tax payments when the majority have decided they want it.

Conclusion: Because majority voting fails to incorporate the *strength* of the preferences of the individual voter, it may produce economically inefficient outcomes.

Interest Groups and Logrolling Some, but not all, of the inefficiencies of majority voting get resolved through the political process. Two examples follow.

Interest Groups People who share strong preferences for a public good may band together into interest groups and use advertisements, mailings, and direct persuasion to convince others of the merits of that public good. Adams might try to persuade Benson and Conrad that it is in their best interest to vote for national defense—that national defense is much more valuable to them than their $250 and $200 valuations. Such appeals are common in democratic politics. Sometimes they are successful; sometimes they are not.

Political Logrolling Perhaps surprisingly, **logrolling**—the trading of votes to secure desired outcomes—can also turn an inefficient outcome into an efficient one. In our first example (Figure 1a), suppose that Benson has a strong preference for a different public good, for example, a new road, which Adams and Conrad do not think is worth the tax expense. That would provide an opportunity for Adams and Benson to trade votes to ensure provision of both national defense and the new road. That is, Adams and Benson would each vote "yes" on both measures. Adams would get the national defense and Benson would get the road. Without the logrolling, both public goods would have been rejected. This logrolling will add to society's well-being if, as was true for national defense, the road creates a greater overall benefit than cost.

But logrolling need not increase economic efficiency. Even if national defense and the road each cost more than the total benefit each produces, both might still be provided if there is vote trading. Adams and Benson might still engage in logrolling if each expects to secure a sufficient net gain from her or his favored public good, even though the gains would come at the clear expense of Conrad.

Logrolling is very common in state legislatures and Congress. It can either increase or diminish economic efficiency, depending on the circumstances.

Paradox of Voting

ORIGIN OF THE IDEA

05.2
Paradox of voting

Another difficulty with majority voting is the **paradox of voting,** a situation in which society may not be able to rank its preferences consistently through paired-choice majority voting.

Preferences Consider Table 1, in which we again assume a community of three voters: Adams, Benson, and Conrad. Suppose the community has three alternative public goods from which to choose: national defense, a road, and a weather warning system. We expect that each member of the community prefers the three alternatives in a certain order. For example, one person might prefer national defense to a road and a road to a weather warning system. We can attempt to determine the preferences of the community through paired-choice majority voting. Specifically, a vote can be held between any two of the public goods, and the winner of that vote can then be matched against the third public good in another vote.

The three goods and the assumed individual preferences of the three voters are listed in the top part of Table 1.

TABLE 1 Paradox of Voting

Public Good	Preferences		
	Adams	**Benson**	**Conrad**
National defense	1st choice	3d choice	2d choice
Road	2d choice	1st choice	3d choice
Weather warning system	3d choice	2d choice	1st choice

Election	Voting Outcomes: Winner
1. National defense vs. road	National defense (preferred by Adams and Conrad)
2. Road vs. weather warning system	Road (preferred by Adams and Benson)
3. National defense vs. weather warning system	Weather warning system (preferred by Benson and Conrad)

The data indicate that Adams prefers national defense to the road and the road to the weather warning system. This implies also that Adams prefers national defense to the weather warning system. Benson values the road more than the weather warning system and the warning system more than national defense. Conrad's order of preference is weather warning system, national defense, and road.

Voting Outcomes The lower part of Table 1 shows the outcomes of three hypothetical elections decided through majority vote. In the first, national defense wins against the road because a majority of voters (Adams and Conrad) prefer national defense to the road. In the second election, to see whether this community wants a road or a weather warning system, a majority of voters (Adams and Benson) prefer the road.

We have determined that the majority of people in this community prefer national defense to a road and prefer a road to a weather warning system. It seems logical to conclude that the community prefers national defense to a weather warning system. But it does not!

To demonstrate this conclusion, we hold a direct election between national defense and the weather warning system. Row 3 shows that a majority of voters (Benson and Conrad) prefer the weather warning system to national defense. As listed in Table 1, then, the three paired-choice majority votes imply that this community is irrational: It seems to prefer national defense to a road and a road to a weather warning system, but would rather have a weather warning system than national defense.

The problem is not irrational community preferences but rather a flawed procedure for determining those preferences. We see that the outcome from paired-choice majority voting may depend on the order in which the votes are taken. Different sequences of majority votes can lead to different outcomes, many of which may fail to reflect the electorate's underlying preferences. As a consequence, government may find it difficult to provide the "correct" public goods by acting in accordance with majority voting. Important note: This critique is not meant to suggest that some better procedure exists. Majority voting is much more likely to reflect community preferences than decisions by, say, a dictator or a group of self-appointed leaders.

Median-Voter Model

One other aspect of majority voting reveals further insights into real-world phenomena. The **median-voter model** suggests that, under majority rule and consistent voting preferences, the median voter will in a sense determine the outcomes of elections. The median voter is the person holding the middle position on an issue: Half the other voters have stronger preferences for a public good,

---

CONSIDER THIS . . .

Voter Failure

Inefficient voting outcomes and the paradox of voting imply that governments may sometimes fail to deliver the best combination of public goods because it may be very difficult for politicians to discern what voters actually want. In other cases, though, economists worry that governments may end up failing to deliver allocative and productive efficiency not because politicians can't tell what people want—but because they *can*.

The problem is that voters sometimes support policies that reduce rather than enhance allocative and productive efficiency. Examples include several types of wage and price controls, punitive tariffs on foreign products, and various industrial and agricultural subsidies.

These policies almost always reduce economic efficiency, but they are also extremely popular with voters in many countries. Faced with that reality, a politician may well end up supporting such policies even if he personally understands that they will create more economic harm than benefit.

That behavior makes some observers wish for braver politicians who might be willing to oppose these instances of "voter failure." But others argue that it is too much to hope for braver politicians. Instead, efforts should be directed toward educating the public and convincing them to support government policies that are economically efficient.

---

amount of taxation, or degree of government regulation, while half have weaker or negative preferences. The extreme voters on each side of an issue prefer the median choice rather than the other extreme position, so the median voter's choice predominates.

Example Suppose a society composed of Adams, Benson, and Conrad has reached agreement that as a society it needs a weather warning system. Each person independently is to submit a total dollar amount he or she thinks should be spent on the warning system, assuming each will be taxed one-third of that amount. An election will determine the size of the system. Because each person can be expected to vote for his or her own proposal, no majority will occur if all the proposals are placed on the ballot at the same time. Thus, the group decides on a paired-choice vote: They will first vote between two of the proposals and then match the winner of that vote against the remaining proposal.

The three proposals are as follows: Adams desires a $400 system; Benson wants an $800 system; Conrad opts for a $300 system. Which proposal will win? The median-voter model suggests it will be the $400 proposal submitted by the median voter, Adams. Half the other voters favor a more costly system; half favor a less costly system. To understand why the $400 system will be the outcome, let's conduct the two elections.

First, suppose that the $400 proposal is matched against the $800 proposal. Adams naturally votes for her $400 proposal, and Benson votes for his own $800 proposal. Conrad, who proposed the $300 expenditure for the warning system, votes for the $400 proposal because it is closer to his own. So Adams' $400 proposal is selected by a 2-to-1 majority vote.

Next, we match the $400 proposal against the $300 proposal. Again the $400 proposal wins. It gets a vote from Adams and one from Benson, who proposed the $800 expenditure and for that reason prefers a $400 expenditure to a $300 one. Adams, the median voter in this case, is in a sense the person who has decided the level of expenditure on a weather warning system for this society.

Real-World Applicability Although our illustration is simple, it explains a great deal. We do note a tendency for public choices to match most closely the median view. Political candidates, for example, take one set of positions to win the nomination of their political parties; in so doing, they tend to appeal to the median voter within the party to get the nomination. They then shift their views more closely to the political center when they square off against opponents from the opposite political party. In effect, they redirect their appeal toward the median voter within the total population. They also try to label their opponents as being too liberal, or too conservative, and out of touch with "mainstream America." And they conduct polls and adjust their positions on issues accordingly.

Implications The median-voter model has two important implications:

- At any point in time, many people will be dissatisfied by the extent of government involvement in the economy. The size of government will largely be determined by the median preference, leaving many people desiring a much larger, or a much smaller, public sector. In the marketplace you can buy no zucchinis, 2 zucchinis, or 200 zucchinis, depending on how much you enjoy them. In the public sector you will tend to get the number of Stealth bombers

and new highway projects that the median voter prefers.

- Some people may "vote with their feet" by moving into political jurisdictions where the median voter's preferences are closer to their own. They may move from the city to a suburb where the level of government services, and therefore taxes, is lower. Or they may move into an area known for its excellent, but expensive, school system. Some may move to other states; a few may even move to other countries.

For these reasons, and because our personal preferences for publicly provided goods and services are not static, the median preference shifts over time. Moreover, information about people's preferences is imperfect, leaving much room for politicians to misjudge the true median position. When they do, they may have a difficult time getting elected or reelected.

APPENDIX SUMMARY

LO5.3 Explain the difficulties of conveying economic preferences through majority voting.

Public choice theory suggests that governments may sometimes suffer from government failures because majority voting fails to correctly indicate voter preferences.

Majority voting creates the possibility of (a) underallocations or overallocations of resources to particular public goods

and (b) inconsistent voting outcomes that make it impossible for a democratic political system to definitively determine the will of the people.

The median-voter model predicts that, under majority rule, the person holding the middle position on an issue will determine the outcome of an election involving that issue.

APPENDIX TERMS AND CONCEPTS

public choice theory

logrolling

paradox of voting

median-voter model

The following and additional problems can be found in **connect**
ECONOMICS

APPENDIX DISCUSSION QUESTIONS

1. Explain how affirmative and negative majority votes can sometimes lead to inefficient allocations of resources to public goods. Is this problem likely to be greater under a benefits-received or an ability-to-pay tax system? Use the information in Figures 1a and 1b to show how society might be better off if Adams were allowed to buy votes. **LO5.3**

2. "Majority voting ensures that government will produce only those public goods for which benefits exceed costs." Discuss. **LO5.3**

3. "The problem with our democratic institutions is that they don't correctly reflect the will of the people! If the people—rather than self-interested politicians or lobbyists—had control, we wouldn't have to worry about government taking actions that don't maximize allocative and productive efficiency." Critique. **LO5.3**

132 | **CHAPTER FIVE APPENDIX**

APPENDIX REVIEW QUESTIONS

1. Explain the paradox of voting through reference to the accompanying table, which shows the ranking of three public goods by voters Jay, Dave, and Conan: LO5.3

Public Good	Rankings		
	Jay	Dave	Conan
Courthouse	2nd choice	1st choice	3d choice
School	3d choice	2d choice	1st choice
Park	1st choice	3d choice	2d choice

2. We can apply voting paradoxes to the highway construction example of Chapter 4. Suppose there are only five people in a society and each favors one of the five highway construction options listed in Table 4.4 ("No new construction" is one of the five options). Explain which of these highway options will be selected using a majority paired-choice vote. Will this option be the optimal size of the project from an economic perspective? LO5.3

3. True or False: The median-voter model explains why politicians so often stake out fringe positions that appeal only to a small segment of the electorate. LO5.3

APPENDIX PROBLEMS

1. Look back at Figures 1a and 1b, which show the costs and benefits to voters Adams, Benson, and Conrad of two different public goods that the government will produce if a majority of Adams, Benson, and Conrad support them. Suppose that Adams, Benson, and Conrad have decided to have one single vote at which the funding for both of those public goods will be decided simultaneously. LO5.3

   a. Given the $300 cost per person of each public good, what are Adams' net benefits for each public good individually and for the two combined? Will he want to vote yes or no on the proposal to fund both projects simultaneously?

   b. What are Conrad's net benefits for each public good individually and for the two combined? Will he want to vote yes or no on the proposal to fund both projects simultaneously?

   c. What are Benson's net benefits for each public good individually and for the two combined? Will he want to vote yes or no on the proposal to fund both projects simultaneously—or will he be indifferent?

   d. Who is the median voter here? Who will the two other voters be attempting to persuade?

2. Political advertising is often directed at winning over so-called swing voters, whose votes might go either way. Suppose that two political parties—the Freedom Party and the Liberty Party—disagree on whether to build a new road. Polling shows that of 1,000 total voters, 450 are firmly for the new road and 450 are firmly against the new road. Thus, each party will try to win over a majority of the 100 remaining swing voters. LO5.3

   a. Suppose that each party spends $5,000 on untargeted TV, radio, and newspaper ads that are equally likely to reach any and all voters. How much per voter will be spent by both parties combined?

   b. Suppose that, instead, each party could direct all of its spending toward just the swing voters by using targeted ads that exploit Internet social media. If all of the two parties' combined spending was targeted at just swing voters, how much would be spent per swing voter?

   c. Suppose that only the Freedom Party knows how to target voters using social media. How much per swing voter will it be spending? If at the same time the Liberty Party is still using only untargeted TV, radio, and newspaper ads, what portion of its total spending is likely to be reaching the 100 swing voters? How much per swing voter does that portion amount to?

   d. Looking at your answers to part c, how much more per swing voter will the Freedom Party be spending than the Liberty Party? If spending per swing voter influences elections, which party is more likely to win?

Online Supplements

Connect Economics with LearnSmart One-Semester Online Access for Macroeconomics, 20th Edition

McGraw-Hill Connect is a digital teaching and learning environment that improves performance over a variety of critical outcomes. With Connect, instructors can deliver assignments, quizzes and tests easily online. Students can practice important skills at their own pace and on their own schedule.

HOW TO REGISTER

Using a <u>Print Book</u>?
To register and activate your Connect account, simply follow these easy steps:
1. **Go to the Connect course web address provided by your instructor or visit the Connect link set up on your instructor's course within your campus learning management system.**
2. **Click on the link to register.**
3. **When prompted, enter the Connect code found on the inside back cover of your book and click Submit. Complete the brief registration form that follows to begin using Connect.**

Using an <u>eBook</u>?
To register and activate your Connect account, simply follow these easy steps:
1. **Upon purchase of your eBook, you will be granted automatic access to Connect.**
2. **Go to the Connect course web address provided by your instructor or visit the Connect link set up on your instructor's course within your campus learning management system.**
3. **Sign in using the same email address and password you used to register on the eBookstore. Complete your registration and begin using Connect.**

Note: Access Code is for one use only. If you did not purchase this book new, the access code included in this book is no longer valid.

Need help? Visit mhhe.com/support